# A Great Civil War

# A GREAT CIVIL

# RUSSELL F. WEIGLEY

# WAR

## A MILITARY AND POLITICAL HISTORY, 1861–1865

*Indiana University Press*

BLOOMINGTON AND INDIANAPOLIS

This book is a publication of
*Indiana University Press*
601 North Morton Street
Bloomington, Indiana 47404-3797 USA

www.indiana.edu/~iupress

*Telephone orders* 800-842-6796
*Fax orders* 812-855-7931
*Orders by e-mail* iuporder@indiana.edu

The paper used in this publication meets the minimum requirements of American National Standard for Information Sciences — Permanence of Paper for Printed Library Materials, ANSI Z39.48-1984.

Manufactured in the United States of America

**Library of Congress Cataloging-in-Publication Data**

Weigley, Russell Frank.
    A great Civil War : a military and political history, 1861–1865 / Russell F. Weigley.
        p.   cm.
    Includes bibliographical references (p.   ) and index.
    ISBN 0-253-33738-0 (alk. paper)
    1. United States — History — Civil War, 1861–1865. 2. United States — History — Civil War, 1861–1865 — Campaigns. 3. United States — Politics and government — 1861–1865.   I. Title.

E468 . W425 2000
973.7 — dc21

                                                        99-089885

1   2   3   4   5      05   04   03   02   01   00

## DEDICATION

*To the members of my paternal and maternal families,*
*the Weigleys and the Rohrbachs,*
*who were touched by the war.*

# Contents

# Maps

## MAP SYMBOLS USED

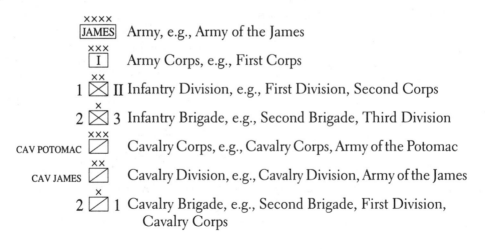

The maps were prepared by Gerry Krieg, cartographer, of Philadelphia, in association with the Temple University Cartographic Laboratory, Mark T. Mattson, director, and particularly Noel Lojeski.

# Note on Style

In the Confederate Army, brigades, divisions, and often corps habitually received their official designation from the name of their formal commanding officer (generally retaining that designation when another officer was in temporary command). Therefore the words brigade, division, or corps are capitalized herein when they refer to Confederate organizations and follow the formal commander's name, such as Kershaw's Brigade, McLaw's Division, Longstreet's Corps. In the Union Army, however, such units were for the most part officially designated numerically, such as First Brigade, First Division, First Corps. Consequently, Meredith's brigade was an unofficial designation for that unit, and the words brigade, division, and corps are in such instances not capitalized.

Numerically designated army corps of the Civil War were not at the time customarily indicated by Roman numerals, as corps usually are in the twentieth century. Therefore this work will employ the style First Army Corps, or First Corps, rather than I Corps.

# Introduction

## To the Gettysburg Address

Every year but one through my boyhood and early adolescence — World War II gasoline rationing once got in the way — my parents and I traveled to the battlefield of Gettysburg from our home ninety miles away in Reading. This ritual repeated a journey to Gettysburg slightly shorter in distance, but otherwise obviously more laborious, that my paternal great-great-grandfather's family undertook by horse and presumably farm wagon from the village of Millbach in Lebanon County, Pennsylvania in July 1863 as soon as they had the news of the outcome of the battle. My great-grandfather Jacob Weigley, seventeen at the time, soon received due admonition from his twenty-year-old brother, Francis Adam Weigley, off in the West with Company A of the 7th Pennsylvania Volunteer Cavalry Regiment in the Army of the Cumberland, that viewing the field of battle even a few days after the carnage was by no means equivalent to seeing what he, the soldier, had witnessed in action across other bloodied hills and valleys.[1] But there remained much to sear the mind, the memory, and especially the nostrils around Gettysburg in mid-July of 1863. The dead soldiers had been buried after a fashion, but many lay in shallow graves where foraging pigs might uproot them, while numerous fallen horses still lay bloated and unburied, and the wounded groaned in crowded public places and private houses all through the town, while the consolidated tent hospital called Camp Letterman was only beginning to take shape on the northeastern outskirts.[2] The seventy-mile journey from Millbach still led to a horrible place.

Nearly a century later, the family expeditions to Gettysburg were glorified picnics and summer outings. But a visit to the battlefield can never be only that. As recently as the 1940s, the motels, fast-food restaurants, and commercialized museums that were to proliferate on the fringes of Gettysburg National Military Park during and after the 1960s centennial were part of an unimagined future. The field generally lay quiet. Especially in those parts of it relatively remote from the borough of Gettysburg and the High Water Mark of Pickett's Charge, the visitor could often be almost alone. The only companions might be the ghosts, readily conjured up in the ambiance of a place where, as the historian Kenneth P. Williams observed, "even the names were rugged or had an alarming sound: Cemetery Hill, Culp's Hill, Rock Creek, Spangler's Spring, Little Round Top, Round Top, Ziegler's Grove, the Devil's Den, the Codori house, the Trostle house."[3]

The late-Victorian battle monuments in their profusion could, when met at the right moments, invoke well enough their grim reasons for being. As the 1940 Works Projects Administration *Pennsylvania* volume in the *American Guide Series* expressed it: "In some places lifelike bronze figures stand erect; others, lying prone, startle the beholder when encountered at dusk."[4] "The Gettysburg battlefield," Kent Gramm writes of the more crowded and cluttered scene in the 1990s, "is not only one of the most beautiful places on earth, it can be one of the most frightening. Its woods and hollows, its strange 'Dutch' barns and undulating fields, its weird boulders, its sudden statues, its silent cannons, all lovely under a sunny springtime sky — cumulus white puffed here and there in the bright, clear blue — are all unearthly features of one vast graveyard."[5] The battleground of Gettysburg offers the bright face of a vacation destination at warm noontime, but there is always a chill in the air nevertheless, and at dawn or dusk the emanations from too much violence, suffering, and killing become palpable. I have been surprised alone by an abrupt November nightfall at the Devil's Den; I know the ghosts.

Those emanations of violence form a large part of what it is that binds not only Gettysburg but the whole era of the Civil War so closely to the national myths that symbolize to the American people the meaning of our past and of ourselves. Only the frontier experience rivals the Civil War as a source of defining mythology from which we Americans draw our understanding of our national character. Our national mythology — our agreed-upon system of beliefs about what our historical experience has comprised and what it signifies — emphasizes that violence has played an uncommonly conspicuous part in shaping us and our society.[6]

The frontier experience molded America, and the frontier experience meant that at one time or another every part of the United States has stood on the cutting edge of the advance of one kind of social order into the domains of another, a cutting edge that frequently entailed the literal cutting down of American Indians by invading Europeans and Africans. Because the frontier experience in turn set Americans apart from the peoples of the Old World in values and ambitions, the experience implied frequent conflict to the east as well as to the west. While the advancing line of settlers fought Indians to the west, they also had to struggle to free themselves from the too effetely civilized societies back on the other side of the Atlantic, those that had not been altered and toughened by the frontier experience, and whose restraints the Americans discovered it necessary to break in the War of the Revolution and the War of 1812.

Moreover, the violence of the Civil War has seemed closely bound to the frontier experience both in origins and in significance. The flux and tumult of the frontier did much to make possible the rise of slavery in America among peoples who had not known slavery for centuries before. Slavery in turn undermined from the beginning the frontier's promise of a new egalitarianism that would destroy Old World privileges and distinctions of social and economic class. With it becoming a national conviction that violence was peculiarly pervasive in America and that it contributed in some special way to forming the American character, finally the violence of the Civil War could well seem foreordained as the means by which the curse of slavery was at last purged from the United States and probably doomed elsewhere in the New World, and the frontier's promises of equality eventually restored. In America, only the shattering violence of a great Civil War, its more than 600,000 dead and at least 470,000 wounded,[7] could fittingly redeem in blood drawn by the sword the blood drawn by the lash of slavery.

Notwithstanding the centrality of violence in Americans' self-defining national mythology, the United States has by no means been in fact the most violent of nations. Harsh as were slavery and the whites' invasions of the homelands of the North American Indians, to find deliberately genocidal policies we must look beyond this continent to Germany's infliction of the Holocaust upon the Jews; to the hecatombs visited by the Khmer Rouge upon Cambodia; and recently to the civil wars of Bosnia, the Sudan, and Rwanda. American violence has on the whole been more individualistically entrepreneurial, as practiced for example by cowboy gunfighters or big-city gangsters, and its targets more circumscribed than those of the true monsters of history.

Nevertheless, within the boundaries of modern "civilized" war fought according to the constraints of the international war convention with its principle of noncombatant immunity — and sometimes straining those boundaries — the American Civil War became a conflict of peculiarly intense destructiveness, of peculiarly unrestrained military means deployed in pursuit of notably absolute objectives. The government of the Federal Union chose as its first war aim the complete and unconditional surrender by the Southern states of all their pretensions to sovereignty. To that end, President Abraham Lincoln's government eventually resorted to a military strategy aiming at the virtual annihilation of the Confederate States Army, so that a militarily helpless South would become altogether malleable in Union hands. Lincoln's government also inflicted social and economic revolution upon the

South in the form of confiscation of property in slaves, and it sponsored the campaigns of Major-Generals William Tecumseh Sherman in Georgia and the Carolinas and Philip H. Sheridan in the Shenandoah and Loudoun Valleys of Virginia to destroy a good deal of additional private property that might otherwise aid the Confederate war effort, and at the same time deliberately to strike terror into the hearts of the Confederacy's citizens.

In response, the Southern Confederacy, fighting to defend the entire Southern way of life, committed itself so fully to the battle that it made nearly every one of its potential soldiers an actual soldier, by putting almost its entire white male citizenry of military age under arms.[8] The Civil War became a clash of a nearly totally mobilized Southern population against a not much less fully mobilized North. It was the first occasion in the modern history of Western civilization when not only officers drawn largely from the upper social classes and rank-and-file soldiers crimped from the lowest rungs of the socioeconomic ladder went to war, but also in many thousands the sons of the middle classes. That would not happen in Europe until World War I. And sending their sons and husbands to war from all kinds of homes, both sides in the American Civil War also accepted casualty rates that would have seemed intolerable to Americans of World War II, to say nothing of the post-Vietnam era, in order to impose still higher casualties upon the enemy and indeed to destroy the enemy's armies.

This intensity of its destructive violence made the Civil War a landmark in world military history, the harbinger of the mass slaughter in the World Wars of the twentieth century and also of our own century's increasingly callous disregard, at least until its final years, of the historic war-convention principle of noncombatant immunity. In this disregard we have sunk from the unrestricted submarine warfare of World War I, on through promiscuous aerial bombing of civilians in World War II, to the widespread plague of indiscriminate terrorist murder in the second half of the century. In the Civil War, however, Sherman and Sheridan waged war against civilians not by killing them — their soldiers displayed remarkable restraint from doing physical violence to the persons of noncombatants — but by destroying or commandeering any of their property that might assist the Confederate war effort. Still, to shift the objectives of war from soldiers to civilians was to plant the seed of the later, more brutal attacks upon noncombatants, all the more because instilling fear was a deliberate intent, and because to wreck a family's property in a middle-class, property-oriented society went a tragically long way toward crushing what made life seem worthwhile.

Pivotal as the American Civil War became in the general history of warfare, nevertheless, it remains also in Americans' minds an event distinctively belonging to their own national past and national character. It was the most epochal single embodiment of the centrality of violence in the myths defining that past and character. By assuring the unity of the arena in which the defining of the national character would further work itself out, the war has represented to many Americans a fulfillment of destiny. Even the individual persons who played the principal leadership roles in the war have appeared as quintessentially American, as living expressions of salient elements in the national character: Abraham Lincoln, symbol of the frontier ethos, and Robert E. Lee, the heir to the George Washington legend and thus to the legacy of the first American Revolution. Each in the manner appropriate to his own section and social class, Lincoln and Lee brooded over the meaning and pain that they themselves felt compelled to inflict upon the country.

Lincoln carried on with the burdens of the war in order to redefine the nation. Most Northerners perceived to some degree that they were accomplishing such a redefinition. Lincoln saw it more clearly than most. Because he did, in his Gettysburg Address of November 19, 1863 he was able to present a statement of fundamental meanings for the redefined nation just as Thomas Jefferson's Declaration of Independence of July 4, 1776 had first stated the fundamental principles of the original American Union. Indeed, the ultimate national significance of the Civil War is that with it, the Gettysburg Address superseded the Declaration of Independence as the most basic assertion of the principles embodied by the United States of America.

Referring to the American Union created by Jefferson's Declaration and the Revolution of 1776, Lincoln said: "Now we are engaged in a great civil war, testing whether that nation, or any nation so conceived and so dedicated, can long endure."[9] The address signifies, however, that more than the enduring of the old nation was at stake in the great Civil War. New principles were at hand. To begin with, Jefferson's Declaration was ahistorical. It appealed to no past. Instead it rested its assertion of the rightness of the independence of the United States upon timeless principles of natural law.[10] From its first words, in contrast, "Four score and seven years ago," Lincoln's Address appeals to history. Unlike the Declaration, it is a statement of the obligations that the present owes to the past.

It is the historical foundation of the Gettysburg Address that establishes the principle most dramatically setting it apart from the Declaration of Independence. The Declaration is a ringing manifesto for the right of revolution. The Address, reinforced by all the rest of Lincoln's conduct of the Civil War and his explanations of that conduct, is a rejection of any right of revolution within the United States. Because the Address differs from the Declaration in appealing not to abstractions but to American history, Lincoln could argue that we have too deep an obligation to the generations that had created and nourished "a new nation, conceived in Liberty," to permit us to undo their work. Our bonds and responsibilities to the past dictate that within the United States there is no longer a right of revolution. We owe too much to those who have gone before us, and to "[t]he brave men, living and dead," who have already struggled to preserve the nation created in 1776, to undo it now.

Nor need we. Lincoln's further implication is that "government of the people, by the people, and for the people" does not require a right of revolution. It contains within itself all necessary capacity for improvement and for change.[11]

The great Civil War demonstrated that capacity for change. It carried the United States over long strides toward integrated, even centralized nationhood. Even if there remained a far distance to go before the twentieth-century centralizing movements of Theodore Roosevelt's New Nationalism and Franklin D. Roosevelt's New Deal, a changed direction was set. National systems of organization, not least those emanating from the Federal government, but private as well, would increasingly predominate over the looser Jeffersonian bonds of unity that had preceded the great Civil War.

It is easy to feel nostalgia for the idea of a Jeffersonian right of revolution. In the final years of the twentieth century, however, the appropriation of the idea by extremists of right and left of the sort who resist taxes from isolated areas of the West and proclaim their own republics reminds us that following a too literally Jeffersonian path breeds chaos.

The great Civil War gave birth to a new and different American Republic, whose nature is to be discerned less in the Declaration of Independence than in the Address Delivered at the Dedication of the Cemetery at Gettysburg. The powerful new Republic shaped by the bayonets of the Union Army of the Civil War wears a less benign aspect than the older, original American Republic. But it also carries larger potential to do good for "the proposition that all men are created equal" both at home and around the world.[12]

## NINETEENTH-CENTURY AMERICANS AT WAR

To introduce a largely military history of the Civil War, several observations need to be made on the nature of war in the middle of the nineteenth century. The horrendous casualty rates of the Civil War sprang partly from the conflict's expression of a historic American propensity toward violence exacerbated by the intensity of the issues and emotions involved, but beyond that they reflected particular circumstances of armed conflict in the war's time and place.

Difficulties of command, communications, and control of armies in battle in the 1860s required that they fight generally in massed formations, with the men marching shoulder to shoulder in long lines several ranks deep into the mouths of the enemy's muskets and cannon. Unless the soldiers thus fought en masse, the smoke clouds generated by black powder that almost completely obscured visibility on the battlefield, along with the deafening noise of musketry and artillery fire, assured that officers would mainly lose control of their men as soon as combat began.

The introduction of rifled muskets and cannon as standard weapons during the Civil War enhanced the accurate range of firearms enough that they almost certainly aggravated the deadliness already implicit in combat between tightly massed formations. Since the Civil War, a variety of tactical and technological developments, particularly including improved means of battlefield communication, have created the modern phenomenon of the empty battlefield: the enemy is present, but he and in fact one's own comrades can scarcely be seen. As opposing soldiers have become less visible to each other, the lethality of the battlefield has apparently declined in spite of further improvements in the accuracy of weapons and increases in the volume of firepower.[13] The Civil War, in contrast, occurred when circumstances made the battlefield a killing ground par excellence. (It is possible that in the future, continuing advances in precision-guided munitions may restore battlefields to the lethality of the 1860s).

Yet another and perhaps equally important source of the large casualties and intense violence of the Civil War may well have resided in the ramshackle and chaotic manner in which Americans of the 1860s could not help but conduct war. The Civil War may have been devastatingly violent largely because Americans lacked the political and social means of discipline to rein in its sprawling, shambling destructiveness. The advance of centralized power in both the Union and Confederate governments notwithstanding — in the Union often as a conscious purpose — the Civil War was so vast in numbers of people and quantities of matériel involved and in multiplicity of battlefronts that neither side could effectively shape it. Sufficient governmental authority and social discipline were not yet in existence. Not until World War II, with yet another difficult learning experience in the form of World War I behind it, and building upon the growth of Federal power necessitated by the Great Depression, was the United States able to wield large military resources with rational, consistent strategic purpose throughout multiple theaters of conflict.

During the Civil War, moreover, part of the problem of inadequate direction sprang from the simple lack of a serviceable conception of what it is that military strategy in wartime signifies and entails. Defining and categorizing the various activities of war can lead to an excessively rigid and inflexible conduct of war; but it is nevertheless useful for military commanders and their civilian superiors to possess a modicum of clear understanding of such concepts as strategy, operations, and tactics, as guides toward perceiving the most effective means of waging war. In the America of the 1860s, such understanding was wanting.

The standard American military textbook of the period was Henry Wager Halleck's *Elements of Military Art and Science*. It stated: "*Strategy* is defined to be the art of directing masses on decisive points, or the hostile movements of armies beyond the range of each other's cannon." Halleck also said: "*Strategy* regards the theatre of war, rather than the field of battle." "*Tactics*," he said, "is the art of bringing troops into action, or of moving them in the presence of an enemy, that is, within his view, and within the reach of his artillery."[14]

These definitions failed to provide satisfactory conceptual guidance to the conduct of war. The prevailing idea of strategy blurred the line between it and the concept of operations as a military activity intermediate between strategy and tactics. We now regard military strategy in wartime as meaning the use of all the resources of a nation, particularly its military resources, to attain the objects of the war. By identifying strategy with the theater of war, Halleck created ambiguity between the entire war and a particular theater of campaign, in the Civil War, for example, the area between Washington and Richmond, or the Mississippi River Valley. In emphasizing "hostile movements of armies beyond the range of each other's cannon," he still more tended to constrict strategic vision within an excessively limited horizon, not likely to encompass the entire war effort. The 1860s definitions failed to provide commanders at the highest level enough stimulus to explore systematically the question of how to apportion their resources most effectively to win the whole war. The definitions tempted commanders to focus too narrowly on one theater at a time.

To make the conceptual problem worse, the definitions mixed up strategy with operations, which in modern conceptualization means the use of military resources not for the overall winning of the war but for the achievement of the objectives of a campaign, with the campaign perceived as an endeavor beyond the particular battle, and especially though not necessarily entailing the use of several autonomous, independently maneuvering formations. Because military thought lacked a focus on theaters of war disentangled from the entire war, and on activities intermediate between the whole war and the individual battle, not only was the designing of a comprehensive, war-winning strategy compromised; so was the ability of military commanders to think beyond a particular battle. Disturbingly often, the study of battles of the Civil War — Fredericksburg and Chancellorsville especially come to mind — gives the impression that even had the defeated general won the battle instead of losing it, he would not have known what to do with his battlefield victory, because he had not thought operationally — he had not thought beyond the battle to the campaign.

The deficiencies in strategic thinking, and the conceptual problems caused by wrapping together the entire war and the particular theater and campaign within the idea of strategy, revealed themselves in the inability of both sides to sort out a system of priorities to be accorded to specific theaters and campaigns, in order most effectively to piece together a strategy for the war. The Confederate General Robert E. Lee seemed to many citizens and soldiers of the Western Confederacy, and perhaps to President Jefferson Davis himself, to be excessively preoccupied with the Washington-Richmond theater wherein he commanded the Army of Northern Virginia through most of the war, not fully acknowledging the importance of other theaters or showing sufficient willingness to share resources with them. In fact, however, a systematic evaluation of theater priorities such as a clearer conception of strategy would have encouraged would have pointed to Lee's theater as the one deserving not only the emphasis he gave it but still more.

Lee rightly believed that the longer the war, the smaller the Confederacy's chances of winning it, because of the relative scarcity of Confederate resources. The South's best hope of keeping the war short lay in the Washington-Richmond theater. Considering that the Confederacy consistently lost both battles and campaigns in the West anyway, and that various kinds of inferiority to Lee's Army of Northern Virginia plagued the Western Confederate armies so that a remedy for consistent losing is not readily imaginable, it would have made sense to relegate the West more candidly to mere delaying operations, thereby making it possible to reinforce Lee enough that he could win his battles and campaigns by more decisive margins than he did, and that he could seriously threaten if not capture Washington. For it was only by winning a Second Manassas or Chancellorsville style of victory on Northern soil, and thereby imperiling if not taking Washington, that the Confederacy could hope to force peace negotiations under conditions that might award it the short war it needed. But the Confederacy possessed neither the general staff for comprehensive strategic planning nor the very conception of strategy to permit so rational a clarification of priorities; and the perceptive General Lee, merely a theater commander until too late, did not get his way.[15]

It might be responded that if the Confederacy had so concentrated its forces in the Virginia theater, the North would have followed suit, and with larger forces to concentrate. Perhaps so — although the political calculations that admittedly militated against any strategy so rational as suggested here probably exerted a greater pressure in the direction of the Western states in the North than toward the Western states of the South, given that under Lee's powerful influence the Confederacy already imbalanced its strategy and resources eastward to a greater extent than did the Union. Be that as it may, for the Union to have effected a greater concentration upon the East could also have represented a more rational allocation of priorities than actually occurred.

Sentimentally, it is easy to make much of the idea that the Union needed the Great West and a united valley of democracy along the entire length of the Mississippi to win the war. In more exacting military terms, winning the war in the West by occupying the whole Mississippi Valley was bound to take a long time, as it did; while for the Union as well as for the Confederacy the Washington-Richmond theater offered the most promising opportunity for a short war and thereby the limitation of costs and destructive violence. To capture Richmond might not only have delivered a potentially fatal moral blow because Richmond was the political capital of the Confederacy. The South also could not afford to lose Richmond's heavy industry, particularly the Tredegar Iron Works. Furthermore, capturing Richmond by concentrating superior resources against it could well have involved also the crushing defeat of the Confederacy's best army and its best generals, and the North had no surer way of speeding victory than that.

A strategic concentration on the Washington-Richmond theater by either side would have been more likely to succeed if either side had also possessed an adequate conception of the military operational art, of thinking in terms of campaigns to link individual battles to the entire war effort. The Prussian and German Armies in the late nineteenth and early twentieth centuries led the military forces of the world in developing the idea of the operational art, with the American Army lagging well behind and not thinking systematically about operations as late as World War II. To the Germans, thinking beyond particular battles toward the most effective methods of conducting whole campaigns came to suggest especially the idea touched on at the beginning of this discussion of operations, that of deploying multiple autonomous forces in a single theater of campaign.

By that means the Germans could better pursue the traditional military

goal of destroying the enemy army as an effective force. The German understanding of the operational art pointed to the employment of one or more of
the autonomous maneuver formations in the theater to fix the enemy army
in position, while the remaining autonomous forces completed an envelopment maneuver to trap him and assure his destruction. Such a scheme underlay the German design for the invasion of France and the destruction of
the French Army in 1914, when to be sure it did not work after all — because
in that instance operational soundness was undercut by logistical over-
stretch. But essentially the same design succeeded devastatingly against Po-
land in 1939, against France in 1940, and against the Soviet Union in the
first stages of the 1941 invasion. It does not make German operational conceptions any less sound in themselves to remark that again in 1941 as in 1914
the Germans' reach exceeded their logistical grasp.

In the idea of the operational art as emphasizing the deployment of
autonomous formations in a single theater for the sake of pinning the enemy
in place while also enveloping him there surely lies an echo of Napoleon.
Nevertheless, in spite of the prevalent admiration and study of the Emperor
of the French among American soldiers of the Civil War, the absence of a
concept of the operational art helped impede Civil War generals from reaching beyond victory in battle to larger victories in campaigns. Not even Lee,
the most Napoleonic battlefield general since Napoleon himself, sufficiently
assimilated operational thinking into his conduct of war. Early in the conflict, while he was military adviser to President Jefferson Davis, he briefly
offered a superb display of the coordination of autonomous formations in
a single theater, when he helped orchestrate Major-General Thomas J.
"Stonewall" Jackson's Valley Campaign of 1862 in western Virginia to assist
in the defense of Richmond in eastern Virginia. To a degree, Lee's Second
Manassas campaign later in the year saw him similarly maneuvering Jackson's and Major-General James Longstreet's wings of the Army of Northern
Virginia in operational fashion to come close to destroying the Federal Army
of Virginia. Through most of the war, however, Lee employed the Army of
Northern Virginia in a unitary manner and focused on the battle rather than
the campaign, Lieutenant-General Jubal A. Early's Shenandoah Valley
Campaign of 1864 representing a late — too late — exception. Of course, if
Lee had received the larger resources he desired, he might have been encouraged to establish autonomous maneuver formations, and might have
done better.

On the Union side the display of limited operational thinking was much
the same. Early in the war, upon the launching of his Peninsula Campaign,
Major-General George B. McClellan utilized his main Army of the Potomac

in coordination with other Union forces in the Fredericksburg area and in the Shenandoah Valley in a tentative approach to maneuvering multiple autonomous formations within the theater. But Lee's and Jackson's more assured and aggressive execution of the idea in the latter's Valley Campaign quickly put a stop to any such bold generalship by McClellan. Thereafter the Union war effort in the East entered its long confinement to generals unable to think beyond the next battle even if they had been able to win the battle. Even Lieutenant-General Ulysses S. Grant in his Virginia campaign of 1864–1865, though he employed two armies in the theater, the Army of the James in addition to the Army of the Potomac, and sometimes more, neglected to exploit their potential for coordinated though autonomous activities until almost the last, in the campaign from Petersburg and Richmond to Appomattox Courthouse. Similarly, in the final campaigns in the West, and especially in the 1864 campaign from Chattanooga to Atlanta, Sherman commanded multiple field armies in what today would be called an army group, but habitually he maneuvered them only on a tactical scale.

The politics of the Civil War could have posed impediments to many of these strategic and operational suggestions, though not necessarily crippling ones. The military leaders, however, never got as far as attempting to overcome political obstacles to coherent and articulated strategic priorities, because they never fully developed such priorities. To be sure, the strategic and operational possibilities advanced here would also have revealed flaws of their own had they been tested. That always happens in the real world. Still, having a coherent strategy, even the wrong strategy, is preferable to having no strategy at all; and the failure of North and South to choose strategic priorities approached having no strategy.

The United States and the Confederacy remained too inchoate as political, military, and social entities to prevent war from becoming inchoate as well. Therefore the strong tendencies toward unrestrained violence derived from American tradition and from tactical circumstances could only partially and very imperfectly be curbed by the rival governments. Limited governmental power encouraged unlimited war. Lincoln discerned that fact clearly enough to try to point the great Civil War in a different direction through the Gettysburg Address.

## WHY DID THEY FIGHT?

Why did men enlist as soldiers for what proved to be so terrible a war, and beyond that, why did they persevere when the terrors of the war became evident?

The early enlistments of course swelled upward on a tide of patriotic enthusiasm, in the North because the Stars and Stripes had suffered insult when the Confederates fired on and compelled the lowering of the old flag at Fort Sumter, in the South because the North's mobilization of armies of invasion threatened the end of self-government and, even while the Union denied such intentions, the arrival of legions of John Browns to ignite a racial war. The flag-waving enthusiasms expanded also under social pressures, as community rallies cheered those who volunteered to fight but presumed cowardice in those who did not. Rallies aside, the young man reluctant to become a soldier often met hostile stares as he walked the streets and byways. Girl friends, fiancées, even wives might be willing to bear the pain of parting with their men — initially most thought it would be only for a short time anyway — and therefore to urge enlisting, lest they themselves be perceived as tied to cowards. Meanwhile, the alarms of war precipitated some months of economic slowdown in many areas, to add economic to social pressures to volunteer. In the early days, also, there was the prospect of high adventure, to exchange dull civilian routine for the glories of following the trumpet and the drum.

In the era of the Second World War, Bell Irvin Wiley wrote the first comprehensive social histories of the experiences of Confederate and Union soldiers, *The Life of Johnny Reb: The Common Soldier of the Confederacy* and *The Life of Billy Yank: The Common Soldier of the Union.* The Second World War was a conflict in which American soldiers and sailors generally disdained florid patriotic enthusiasms such as the nation believed had marked its participation in World War I but had helped open the way to disillusionment after that war. Soldiers of the Second World War apparently fought not so much for God and country as to get the trouble over with and go home quickly. They were in the armed forces mostly because they were drafted or had decided to preempt the draft. Once they were in combat, they fought not for grand ideals but in order not to let their buddies down. They were mainly good soldiers, but they were not enthusiasts or ideologues. Wiley applied such World War II attitudes to the Civil War. He saw in Civil War soldiers' letters and diaries the same sort of emotional detachment that he observed in World War II. His Civil War soldiers joined up under social and economic pressures, and then they served out their enlistments, or even reenlisted when their first terms expired, for the sake of their buddies.[16]

All that seemed convincing to the generation that like Wiley experienced the Second World War but may well have failed to take adequately into account the cultural differences between nineteenth- and twentieth-century Americans. Displays of emotion and the inner cultivation of it were more in the style of the older century than the newer. Patriotic and religious sentiments could not only be expressed more openly without provoking derision but probably resided deeper in individual and community character and belief. More recent historians have looked anew at the same kinds of documentation that Wiley examined, personal letters and diaries of Civil War soldiers and their families, and found in them evidence of different kinds of motivation.

James M. McPherson in particular has discovered among the motives for volunteering a commitment to ideology largely alien to the World War II generation. To the recent historians of Civil War soldiers' motivation, Northern volunteers, nurtured by the common schools and other social institutions in the civic religion of United States nationalism — a civic religion enveloped, furthermore, in varieties of Christianity that claimed to validate the principles of democracy and individualism of the American secular world — enlisted often in behalf of an ideological imperative, to preserve the ideals embodied by the United States, to reaffirm the victory for those ideals won in the American Revolution. Southern volunteers enlisted to preserve differing aspects of the same ideals, perceived differently through the prism of the particular institutions of the South, especially but not only slavery. They volunteered to protect the American Revolution's legacy of self-government.[17]

On both sides, the slavery issue entered into the ideological commitment. Southern soldiers enlisted candidly to protect slavery. Northern soldiers often took longer to add the elimination of slavery to their ideological purposes, just as Lincoln's government did, but like their government they largely came to embrace a wider freedom, freedom for black people as well as white, as part of their cause — more and more firmly as the war went on, and as more and more Union soldiers witnessed the realities of slavery.[18]

McPherson especially has gone beyond examining why soldiers enlisted to study why they continued to fight in spite of the hardships and horrors surpassing anything imagined by most of them when they signed up. He finds faithfulness to ideological principles reinforced by two conceptions pervasive in Victorian America: duty and honor. Both duty and honor demanded upholding ideological belief through deeds in addition to words; both demanded that there be no abandonment of ideological commitment. Devotion to duty represented a moral obligation in both North and South. The North emphasized duty somewhat more than honor; the South accorded somewhat greater emphasis to honor, a more masculine concept that resonated with the Southern idea that the contest was a defense of a courtly, chivalric society. Whatever the emphasis, the results were the same. Duty and honor alike required fighting faithfully as long as fighting was possible.

The Civil War armies therefore were ideological armies, waging war out of commitment to the beliefs and values of their respective societies in a way that American armies at least from World War II apparently have not done. The later armies contended for the survival of national interests conceived in less grandiose terms. In one important respect, however, the soldiers of the Civil War and of more recent wars fought for similar reasons. Whatever his other motives, the soldier's bonding with his comrades, his buddies, was a major part of what kept him enduring war. He must go on earning the respect of his fellow soldiers, and he did not dare to betray their respect. The Civil War soldier felt bound by duty and honor to persevere in the war, but he fought for his comrades, too. Moreover, because the comrades showed commitment to the cause, obligations to ideology and to comradeship reinforced each other.[19]

Such doubly binding, mutually reinforcing commitments no doubt go far toward explaining why both the Civil War soldiers themselves and the people back home tolerated casualty rates that would have seemed unacceptable even in World War II, let alone at the close of the twentieth century when the prospect of almost any loss of life tends to make military actions politically forbidden in the United States.

Yet a caution must also be expressed. The commitment of the Southern soldiers and the Southern people to their cause was less profound than wartime rhetoric, even the rhetoric of personal letters, made it seem. Duty and even the Southern dedication to honor could not quite overcome a certain ambivalence within the purposes and even the psyche of the South. The beliefs for which the South and its soldiers fought were indeed too closely akin to the values of the North for the good of the Confederacy. Southerners as well as Northerners had been nurtured from birth in the civic religion of United States nationalism, endorsed by American varieties of Christianity. Southerners could not shake off their nurturing so abruptly as secession and the creation of the Confederacy demanded. The patriotic symbols of the old Union lingered in the flags, public rhetoric, stamps and coins, and other icons of the new Confederacy, signifying an ambivalent commitment. Could Southerners who had been United States patriots fully believe that the Union of the American Revolution deserved to be destroyed, and that they should participate in its undoing? Always there was a psychological rift deep inside Southern purposes.

Though the Confederate soldiers fought stubbornly, often heroically, in the end they did not fight hard enough to save the Confederacy. They and other Southerners did not display the devotion to Confederate independence that in many other independence movements of modern history has kept the cause alive after conventional military defeat, if necessary in the form of guerrilla war. Partly no doubt because of the difficulties that the South's African Americans would have caused for white guerrillas, but almost certainly for larger if less tangible reasons, the Confederacy subsided quickly when its armies surrendered. To say that is to draw a stark contrast between it and many other national independence movements, making it remarkable not that the Civil War was so long and costly, but that it ended relatively so soon.

The combat motivation of the Northern soldier did not suffer such self-inflicted impediments. Instead, encouraged by Abraham Lincoln and eventually in particular by his Gettysburg Address, the Union volunteer could commit his duty and his honor not only to upholding the ideals of his country as molded by the American Revolution, but to the advancing ideals of an ever more perfect Union, with freedom for all its inhabitants.

# A Great Civil War

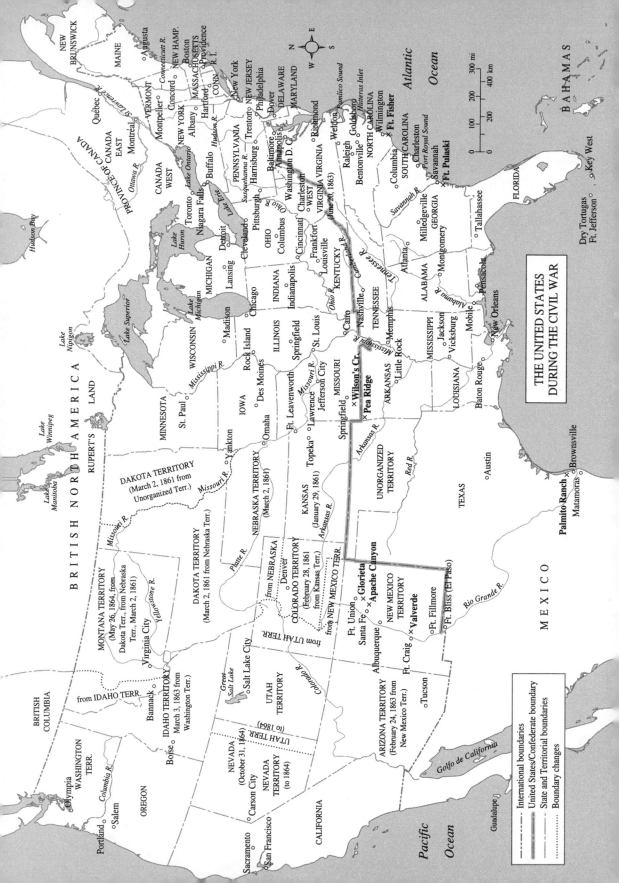

# ONE

# From Secession to War

## THE FORTS AT CHARLESTON

If the secession of seven Southern states from the Union meant war, the tinder with which to ignite the flame lay immediately at hand in Charleston harbor, South Carolina, in the state where secession fever ran hottest. On the Battery, Charleston's most desirable galleried mansions surveyed the meeting of the Ashley and Cooper Rivers and looked toward three United States forts: Castle Pinckney close at hand on a small island at the mouth of the Cooper River, Fort Sumter on an artificial island some three miles down the harbor, and Fort Moultrie, barely visible on the horizon on Sullivan's Island at the harbor entrance.

The forts were part of an elaborate system planned after the War of 1812 to guard all the principal seaports of the United States. Like most of the system, they had never been finished.[1] Typically, of the 135 guns planned for Fort Sumter, only fifteen were mounted. The forts were lightly garrisoned as well as incomplete, because the U.S. Army had to commit most of its small peacetime strength to the Indian frontier, and national policy had always anticipated that against foreign attack the garrisons would be recruited to full strength from the local militia. Weak as the forts were, however, and although their purpose had been to turn back foreign assailants from Charleston, they and their guns, especially if reinforced, might now close to world commerce the principal port of an independent South Carolina. Even if the forts were not reinforced, South Carolina was unlikely to convince the world of its independence as long as these outposts of the United States watched over its doorstep.

The Charleston forts consequently became a source of tension even before South Carolina adopted its ordinance of secession. Anticipating secession, the commander of the forts, Lieutenant-Colonel (Brevet Colonel) John L. Gardner, 1st United States Artillery Regiment, attempted on November 7, 1860 to transfer ammunition stored in the city of Charleston to Fort Moultrie. This was the day after Abraham Lincoln's election by popular vote to the Presidency. A crowd thwarted Gardner. President James Buchanan, intent on a conciliatory policy to prevent both disunion and war, thereupon relieved Gardner, a Bostonian; Buchanan sent him to Texas lest at Charleston he function as an irritant. The replacement was Major Robert Anderson, 1st Artillery, a Kentuckian of Virginia ancestry married to Elizabeth Clinch of Georgia. Anderson was thus thought likely to assist conciliation.

While sympathetic toward the South, however, Major Anderson believed that his oath to the United States commanded his first loyalty. When he appraised the excited atmosphere of Charleston as the city hurried into secession and surveyed the weakness of his garrisons, Anderson appealed to Washington for reinforcements to hold the forts against a possible Carolinian coup. He had eight officers in addition to himself and sixty-eight noncommissioned officers and private soldiers, comprising the skeletonized Companies E and H of the 1st Artillery, plus eight musicians of the regimental band and forty-three noncombatants.[2] At Castle Pinckney, there were only a caretaker and his family. At Fort Sumter, several of the officers supervised workmen continuing the slow completion of the fort. Most of Anderson's command was at Fort Moultrie, where it was vulnerable to attack from sand hills that overlooked the landward side of the fort and were easily accessible from the mainland.

Anderson's request much disturbed the already harried President Buchanan. The Southern members of Buchanan's Cabinet, Secretary of the Treasury Howell Cobb of Georgia, Secretary of War John B. Floyd of Virginia, and Secretary of the Interior Jacob Thompson of Mississippi, urged against reinforcement. Secretary of State Lewis Cass of Michigan and Attorney General Jeremiah Black of Pennsylvania argued that the United States must defend its property and that reinforcements must be sent. Secretary of the Navy Isaac Toucey of Connecticut shared Buchanan's own outlook, which was one of indecision.[3]

During the last week of November 1860, Buchanan veered toward reinforcement, but then he allowed Secretary Floyd to delay action while the Southern coterie in Washington secured a pledge from Governor William H. Gist of South Carolina that the national property would be safe. Meanwhile, one of the strong men of the President's party in Congress, Democratic Senator Jefferson Davis of Mississippi, arrived in the capital in advance of the December Congressional session, having been invited by Buchanan to help compose the President's annual message to Congress. Davis added his considerable influence to that of Cobb, Floyd, Thompson, and other Southerners against reinforcement, suggesting that if every Federal fort in the South simply remained in custody of a caretaker, the states would all respect Federal property rights. Buchanan felt confirmed in the wisdom of doing nothing, though on December 10 Secretary Cass tried to redeem a long career as a pro-Southern "doughface" by resigning from the Cabinet in protest against the weakness of the Charleston forts.

In his address to Congress on December 3, the President deplored secession but held that he had no legal powers to combat it,[4] rejecting Jeremiah Black's plea that he should at least assert the right to defend Federal property. By the time a South Carolina convention carried through with the state's threats to leave the Union by adopting an ordinance of secession on December 20, Buchanan thus had done nothing to discourage the new governor of the state, Francis W. Pickens, from further raising the temperature in Charleston harbor. Pickens did so by sending a letter to the President suggesting that a South Carolina garrison be allowed to occupy Fort Sumter immediately.[5] South Carolina also dispatched Robert W. Barnwell, James H. Adams, and James L. Orr as commissioners to Washington to negotiate formally for the transfer of Federal property to the newly independent state.

The Southern circle around Buchanan recognized that Governor Pickens had overreached in asking for the surrender of Sumter, because Northerners were already beginning to talk about impeachment of a President who did so little to resist disunion. Black, promoted on December 17 to the Department of State in succession to Cass,[6] would not allow Buchanan to forget that personal danger. The Southerners in Washington settled for a pledge from Secretary Floyd that the War Department would take no action to injure South Carolina or to give cause for alarm.

Floyd thought he could safely offer the pledge because, after the earlier understanding with Governor Gist, Brevet Major and Assistant Adjutant General Don Carlos Buell (First Lieutenant, 3rd Infantry), had gone from the War Department to South Carolina to repeat both orally and in writing presidential instructions to Major Anderson to take no step that might provoke an attack.[7] Floyd nevertheless was mistaken about what Anderson would do. The garrison commander sensed all too acutely the excitement in Charleston that Governor Pickens was trying to use to blackmail Buchanan, and the state authorities' encouragement of it. He was sure that Sumter would soon be seized unless he did something to prevent it, depriving him of a sea-girt fortress with masonry walls five feet thick and leaving him exposed to land attack at Fort Moultrie. Despite the President's extreme caution, the instructions delivered by Buell authorized Anderson to put his command into any of the forts "which you may deem most proper to increase its power of resistance," if he should be attacked or had "tangible evidence of a design to proceed to a hostile act."[8] On the night of December 26–27, after careful and skillful preparations and the spiking of the guns he left behind, Anderson quietly transferred his troops and their women and children to Fort Sumter in the harbor.

South Carolinians predictably expressed outrage at the presumption of a U.S. officer who would seek to defend himself and his flag against them, and their government interpreted Anderson's move as a breach of the Buchanan administration's pledges. An angry Charleston crowd gathered at the Battery. Governor Pickens took possession of the Federal arsenal in Charleston, the customs house, the post office, and a branch of the U.S. Treasury, while state troops occupied Castle Pinckney and Fort Moultrie. In Washington, Jefferson Davis and other Southerners quickly carried the news of Anderson's move to President Buchanan, who was characteristically apologetic and unnerved. Secretary Floyd sent Major Anderson an impatient telegram demanding that he explain the meaning of the report that he had shifted his garrison to Sumter.[9]

Buchanan possessed at least the presence of mind to postpone until the next day, December 28, a meeting he had scheduled with the South Carolina commissioners to discuss the transfer of property. In the interval the President met with his Cabinet. Cobb had resigned on December 8 to return to Georgia,[10] but Floyd and Thompson were left to rage against Anderson's effrontery. Cobb's successor, Philip F. Thomas of Maryland, sympathized with them but carried little influence. Black and the new Attorney General, another Pennsylvanian named Edwin M. Stanton, appointed December 17,[11] called attention, in contrast, to Anderson's instructions regarding what he was authorized to do if he received evidence of an intended attack.

Floyd proposed to order Anderson's garrison to withdraw completely from Charleston harbor, but under contrary pressure from Black and Stanton the President reverted from a capitulatory mood to his customary mere indecisiveness. When the South Carolina commissioners, received by Buchanan only in their capacities as private gentlemen, took up the call for abandoning all the forts next day, the President told them they were pushing him too hard. When Floyd failed to get his way at another Cabinet meeting that evening, the Virginian took this opportunity to resign from the War Department.[12] He thus staged his exit just ahead of the full development of another problem that was coincidentally enveloping him, a scandal over missing department funds and his relationship with certain venal contractors.

With Floyd departed, Black and Stanton unquestionably dominated the Cabinet. By threatening to resign also and thereby to leave the executive branch in still more chaos than even Buchanan could tolerate, they drove the President into a rejection of all South Carolina's requests and demands. On December 30, Buchanan told the South Carolina commissioners that his first impulse after hearing of Anderson's move to Sumter had indeed been to order him back to Moultrie, but that South Carolina itself had changed the situation by occupying Pinckney and Moultrie. He was now asked to surrender Sumter as well and thus all Federal property in Charleston, but "This I cannot do; this I will not do."[13]

The disappointed South Carolina commissioners responded with a complaint that by transferring his garrison Major Anderson was already waging war against their state. Against so curious a description of war, Buchanan clung to his new firmness. He was being prodded by now not only by Black and Stanton but also by Major-General and Brevet Lieutenant-General Winfield Scott, the Commanding General of the Army, who had just come to Washington from his usual headquarters in New York. Particularly under Scott's urging, the President decided to reinforce Sumter with arms, supplies, and "two hundred well instructed men."[14]

At first Scott intended to send the reinforcement on the U.S. Navy sloop-of-war *Brooklyn*, but because South Carolina had sunk vessels to block the channel into Charleston harbor, he substituted the light-draft merchant steamer *Star of the West*. This ship steamed out of New York on January 5, quietly but with Southerners including Secretary Thompson promptly dispatching word to South Carolina. By this time the South Carolinians were constructing a battery on Morris Island as well as repairing guns at Fort Moultrie, from both of which places they could fire on ships attempting to enter the harbor. When the *Star of the West* arrived at dawn on January 9, flying the United States flag, and sailed close to Morris Island toward the harbor, the South Carolina batteries opened fire. The ship then hoisted a full-sized U.S. garrison flag to her fore, but the hostile firing persisted and began to score hits.

Anderson's guns at Fort Sumter might well have been able to overpower the lightly protected batteries that were attacking the *Star of the West*, but Anderson had received no indication from the War Department regarding the conduct expected of him more recent than Secretary Floyd's rebuke for his simply moving his troops. On January 5, Lieutenant-Colonel Lorenzo Thomas, Assistant Adjutant General, had drafted a letter of instruction to Anderson from General Scott, authorizing him to silence the fire of any battery in the harbor that might open against a vessel bringing reinforcements or supplies, but Anderson had not yet received it. Nor had he received Thomas's assurance that Scott commended his conduct to this point.[15] Nor had the newly appointed Secretary of War, Joseph Holt, a stout Kentucky Unionist,[16] yet found the opportunity to add his commendation of Anderson's previous conduct. Knowing so little and having as far as he was aware met disapproval for doing much less than shooting, Anderson believed he dared not fire on the South Carolina batteries. When ships emerged from around Fort Moultrie apparently intending to cut her off, the *Star of the West* turned away.

Although the South Carolina guns continued to fire on her as long as she was within range, neither the North nor the South was yet ready to accept the attack on the *Star of the West* as an irrevocable commitment to war. Nevertheless, the South Carolinians now so hastened the strengthening of their batteries guarding the approaches to the harbor that there would be no more opportunity to reinforce or supply Fort Sumter against South Carolina resistance except by a major expedition of armed ships. The possibility of avoiding further warlike confrontation had dangerously narrowed.

Other possibilities and opportunities had perhaps also been lost. Even the Buchanan administration, for all its vacillations, could not in the end surrender the last Federal fort at Charleston with no resistance at all. If Buchanan had made this fact clear from the beginning, that there could be no removal of all United States authority from the Southern states without a fight, he might just possibly have added decisively to the resistance against secession in those Southern states that were less unanimous than South Carolina, and slowed the Southern march toward formation of an independent Southern Confederacy. But he did nothing of the sort.

## THE ANOMALOUS SOUTHERN NATION

The secessionist fervor that threatened Major Anderson and that radiated from South Carolina throughout the South with only slightly diminished intensity sprang from the Southern conviction that parting from the North had become essential to preserving nothing less than the South's entire way of life, all its values and its existence as a civilized society. Everything worth preserving in the South, many leaders of the section had convinced themselves and their followers, depended on perpetuating slavery. If slavery fell, law and order in a biracial society would give way to chaos and barbarism. And the election of the antislavery Republican Abraham Lincoln to the United States Presidency, such Southerners believed, signified that slavery could be perpetuated only outside the old Union. This identification of slavery with Southern civilization goes far, obviously, toward accounting for the zeal behind secession and the intensity with which the seceded states were about to engage in war.

Like most expressions of emotional zeal, however, the secessionist movement flew squarely in the face of rational self-interest. The Republicans' determination to forbid the expansion of slavery into the Western territories triggered secession, but by seceding the Southern states abandoned their ability to fight for the West in Congress and the Supreme Court — which they still controlled — and practically gave away most of their claims upon the West. Southerners might dream of new filibustering expeditions to expand slavery and their own influence in Latin America, but such dreams were bound to be still more ephemeral than their hopes of planting slavery in the valleys of the Colorado or the Sacramento. Furthermore, by seceding the South also abandoned hope for enforcement of the Fugitive Slave Law to prevent slave escapes into the North, along with most other kinds of effective help from Northern sympathizers. Secession threw away the considerable ability of the South, assisted by a largely friendly Democratic Party, to resist the antislavery movement on its own political ground.

Upon seceding, moreover, the Southern states found themselves in a perilous situation. They professed to be independent republics, but they did not possess the complete appurtenances of sovereignty. In particular, while they had their militia systems, they did not separately have the ability to protect themselves from the potential military power of the Union. They must form a new union of Southern states, and quickly, to shield themselves against the Northern threat — but also because secession sprang at least as much from the idea of a Southern civilization to be upheld by Southern nationhood as from states' rights.

On the day South Carolina seceded, Robert W. Barnwell, a political protégé of John C. Calhoun, introduced into the secession convention a resolution calling upon the Southern states to send delegates to a convention to form a national government, with Montgomery, the capital of Alabama, as the suggested site. The resolution having passed, the Alabama secession

convention issued the appropriate invitation — it was important that the seceding states should find a broader base for leadership of combined action
than that provided by hotheaded South Carolina — and delegates from the
six seceded states of South Carolina, Mississippi, Florida, Alabama, Georgia,
and Louisiana assembled at Montgomery on February 4, 1861. Texas, whose
convention passed an ordinance of secession on February 1, sent delegates
who arrived later.[17]

The members of the Montgomery convention proved to be mostly politicians experienced in officeholding under the old Federal government. Indeed, there are hints in all that we know of their farewells from Washington
as well as what they said and did at Montgomery that many among them still
envisaged themselves less as creators of a new nation than as reformers of
the old one, applying in unprecedentedly drastic form — by going to the
length of acting out the threats — the warnings of disunion that so often in
the past had served to render the North conciliatory. Often mere talk of secession had bullied the North into caving in to Southern demands; now the
South was actually going through the forms of seceding — but once again
perhaps mainly to twist Northern politicians' arms. Such a method of political blackmail to wring from the North new concessions to slavery offered,
after all, a much more rational means of defending Southern interests than
going through with secession and separate nationhood. Not every Southern
politician was zealously emotional. This ambiguous element in the formation of the new Southern union was destined to affect the coming war in a
manner contradictory to the forces unleashed by the emotional defense of
slavery. Be that as it may, the Union's President-elect refused to rise to the
bait, no concessions on the vital issue of slavery in the territories were forthcoming from him, and the Montgomery convention found itself with no
choice but to proceed with its ostensible business of creating a new confederacy.

Significantly in light of the reforming as distinguished from the revolutionary impulse behind the Montgomery convention, the delegates chose as
president of the gathering Howell Cobb, recently Secretary of the Treasury,
who was conspicuous for his veneration of the Constitution of the United
States. Cobb's elevation to leadership and then his personal influence
helped assure the participation in the convention's labors of a still more dedicated worshipper of the old Constitution, his fellow Georgian Alexander
H. Stephens.

Cobb also proved to be a most efficient parliamentarian. He lost no
time in appointing and hurrying on the work of a committee to prepare a
provisional constitution, chaired by Christopher G. Memminger, an experi-

enced South Carolina legislator, so that some form of united government might begin functioning at once. Memminger's committee reported and the convention accepted its handiwork as early as February 8. Under the Provisional Constitution, the convention became the unicameral Congress of the Provisional Confederate States of North America, acting in that capacity by day while continuing as a constitutional convention to write a permanent constitution at night. In the Provisional Congress, each state would have one vote, while usually being represented by as many delegates as it had had members in the old Federal Congress. The Provisional Constitution was to endure for one year after the inauguration of a Provisional President, or until a permanent constitution could be put into effect.[18]

Obliged by the absence of any Northern rush to conciliate to proceed with their avowed purpose, but guided by such men as Cobb and Stephens, the Montgomery delegates wrote for the Confederate States of America a permanent Constitution that was almost a recapitulation of the old Constitution. The most important departures from the latter all had as their intent the buttressing of a conservative, agrarian, slaveholding society.[19]

Alexander Stephens caused a certain embarrassment when in a speech at Savannah on March 21 he said of the new Confederate States government that *"its foundations are laid, its cornerstone rests, upon the great truth that the negro is not equal to the white man; that slavery, subordination to the superior race, is his natural and moral condition."*[20] The embarrassment was simply such as is usually prompted by unvarnished plain-spoken truth. The writers of the Confederate States Constitution were not so embarrassed that they declined to mention slaves and slavery by name; they eschewed the circumlocution of the old Constitution. There was to be no Confederate States law "denying or impairing the right of property in negro slaves." In Confederate States territories "the institution of negro slavery, as it now exists in the Confederate States, shall be recognized and protected by Congress and the Territorial government; and the inhabitants of the several Confederate States and Territories shall have the right to take to such Territory any slaves lawfully held by them in any of the States or Territories of the Confederate States." Although a state of the Confederacy might conceivably abolish slavery, given the principle of states' rights, nevertheless slaveowners "shall have the right of transit and sojourn in any State of this Confederacy, with their slaves and other property; and the right of property in said slaves shall not be thereby impaired." The assertion of the rights of slavery did not extend, however, to the reopening of the overseas slave trade. Importation of slaves was forbidden, except from the United States, and Congress might prohibit the latter trade as well.[21]

Altogether, the departures of the Confederate States from the U.S. Constitution were so few, the old Constitution was copied so literally, except for the efforts to safeguard slavery, that textual comparison of the two constitutions suggests not only conservatism among the Montgomery statesmen, but another deep-seated attitude as well, the one that collided against the defense of slavery: an inability to wrench free from old loyalties to the United States. At sunrise on March 4 Letitia Christian Tyler, daughter of Robert Tyler and granddaughter of John Tyler, the only former President of the United States to embrace the Confederacy, unfurled the newly designed Confederate States flag for the first time publicly, over the white dome of the Capitol at Montgomery.[22] Having copied the Constitution of the United States, the Confederacy had plagiarized the old flag and now sanctioned it by means of association with the Presidency of the United States. For as the heir apparent to the French throne and soon-to-be war historian, Louis Philippe Albert d'Orléans, comte de Paris, said of the Confederate Stars and Bars: "They selected for their new flag that which most resembled the banner of 1776" (or, to quibble with this foreign observer, the banner of 1777).[23] All of which was curious conduct for rebels.

Did not the founders of the Confederacy display a remarkable propensity to gaze backward not only toward an old-fashioned social order but toward old loyalties as well? Professor Charles P. Roland in his history of *The Confederacy* writes of "the fatal rift in the psyche of the South": the incompleteness of the psychological break with the old Union.[24] This fatal rift was nowhere more evident than in the most basic foundations of the Confederate claim to nationhood. It may well have had much to do with ultimate Southern defeat in the coming war.

## THE SOUTH BEGINS TO MOBILIZE

But the defiant act of secession had been committed, and the pose of defiance had to be maintained. Though many Southerners, including many in the Montgomery convention, affected to believe that the North would allow secession to proceed in peace, there hung over every moment of the convention the threat that the United States might invoke force to try to save itself from disruption, and that the new Confederacy might shortly face war.

It was therefore imperative that the convention not simply deliberate in leisurely fashion over a new constitution, but that a functioning government be put in motion immediately. The Provisional Constitution provided for a Provisional President, a Provisional Vice President, and executive departments as well as the Provisional Congress.[25] The need for executive action to protect the Confederate States against possible United States repression was so urgent that the convention nearly acted to choose a President on the very day it adopted the Provisional Constitution. At least one night's postponement seemed desirable, however, if not for reflection on the possible candidates, then at least for canvassing the delegates and trading off support, so there was a deferment to February 9.

Again significantly, secessionist fire-eaters such as William Lowndes Yancey of Alabama and Robert Barnwell Rhett of South Carolina were never seriously in the running for the Presidency. The very vehemence of their calls for disunion had suggested that the fire-eaters were not securely members of the Southern establishment; they protested too much. Their character as outsiders in relation to the establishment combined with doubts about their stability and capacity for constructive action to exclude them from the highest offices.

Among more moderate statesmen, the populous, centrally located, and therefore strategically important State of Georgia had two major contenders for the Confederate Presidency, Howell Cobb and former U.S. Senator Robert A. Toombs. But Cobb lacked the personal magnetism desirable in a President who might have to be a rallying point, while Toombs was so overbearing a personality that he repelled as much and as strongly as he attracted. Furthermore, the two Georgia candidates divided their own state's delegation and thus tended to cancel each other out. The choice for Provisional President therefore came around to ex-Senator Jefferson Davis of Mississippi.[26] Ten years earlier Davis had been among the most radical Southern Congressional leaders, but his opinions had moderated until in the crisis of 1860–1861 he had proved a reluctant secessionist. Meanwhile his service as Franklin Pierce's Secretary of War had earned him a reputation as an able, farseeing administrator; he was the best Secretary of War since John C. Calhoun had held the post in 1817–1825. The War Department experience also suggested knowledge and skill in an area likely to be especially pertinent to the Confederacy, as did the fact that Davis was a United States Military Academy graduate, class of 1828, and had led the Regiment of Mississippi Rifles with distinction during the Mexican War. Davis was tall, thin, imposing, austere, an effective public speaker if not usually an eloquent one, and in general a man fitting the Presidential image.

Georgia received the consolation prize of the Vice Presidency, which went to "Little Elleck" Stephens — short, wizened, sickly, seemingly always on the brink of the grave but nevertheless intensely ambitious. He had opposed his state's secession virtually until the moment when it was an accomplished fact. This outlook and his reverence for the U.S. Constitution made his selection still another expression of the Montgomery convention's and the Confederacy's divided psyche. On the level of conscious thought, however, the Montgomery delegates saw their choice of Stephens as another endorsement of the constructive and positive variety of statesmanship, as distinguished from fire-eating. Stephens was also a former Whig to balance Davis's previous adherence to the Democracy. The delegates neglected the possibility that old partisan differences, conflicting ambitions, and Stephens's deep misgivings about the secession experiment might make the President and Vice President an ill-matched team.[27]

Davis received notice of his election while he was tending his roses at Brierfield, his Mississippi plantation. He was even more impressed by his West Point credentials than were those who had elected him, and he believed that these credentials indicated he should continue in his current post as major-general commanding the Mississippi State Militia and then, if war came, he should go on to other military activities and glory.[28] Therefore he accepted the Presidency without enthusiasm. But he was a worshipper of duty, so accept he did, and he set off for Montgomery on a roundabout train journey through Chattanooga and Atlanta (which reflected one of the military and economic liabilities of the Confederate States, in that there was no direct line).

He reached Montgomery on February 15. The Provisional Congress had wanted to betray no divisions or dissensions to the outside world, and so Davis's choice had been engineered to be unanimous; but the choice having been made, Southerners promptly reflected that no other man among them was so patently fitted to be the Confederate President as Jefferson Davis. On February 18 Davis took the oath of office under auspiciously bright sunshine and offered the world beyond the Confederacy's borders both friendship and a firm resolution to preserve Confederate independence.[29]

With an appropriate bow to the states'-rights creed, Davis saw to it that all the states of the Confederacy except his own Mississippi were represented in his Cabinet. Toombs of Georgia as a senior statesman and Presidential aspirant became Secretary of State. The diligent chairman of the committee that had drafted the Provisional Constitution, Memminger of South Carolina, received the Treasury portfolio, which was sure to demand diligence because the South had few strong financial institutions and the Confederacy little available specie. Davis expected to be essentially his own Secretary of War, so he gave the War Department to an unassertive and little-known Alabamian, Leroy Pope Walker. The Navy Department went to one of his best choices, one of the two men who would serve out the Davis administration while remaining in his initial post, Stephen R. Mallory of Florida. Mallory not only possessed suitable maritime interests, having been chairman of the U.S. Senate Committee on Naval Affairs, but he proved to have an innovative flair that permitted him to make the most of extremely modest resources. He presided over the Confederacy's spectacular program of commerce raiding. More than that, he pressed for the construction of powerful, advanced-design ironclads, and although his success was limited, he secured ships more powerful than the technologically straitened Confederacy would have produced under any but the most driving leadership. Judah P. Benjamin of Louisiana, the Attorney General, was one of the austere Davis's few personal confidants. John H. Reagan of Texas consented to become Postmaster General only with much reluctance, because he foresaw many of the difficulties that were to plague his department under the Confederacy's disadvantages in rail and water transport; but he worked hard and became the other Cabinet member to stay in one post during the whole history of the administration.[30]

Because it was so conservative and orderly a revolutionary enterprise, the Confederacy inherited from the United States a governmental machinery already functioning in many ways. By and large, the Confederate courts and the executive departments simply adopted the available personnel and the procedures of the old Federal government. For a time, where ports were open the Confederacy continued to collect the U.S. customs duties. The Post Office Department in the seceded states went about its business practically without change, until during the night of May 31–June 1, 1861, the postmasters, clerks, and carriers were transformed from United States into Confederate States functionaries. The Provisional Congress asserted the principle that all U.S. statutes as of November 1860 were still in effect, provided they were compatible with the Confederate Constitution and not specifically repealed by the Confederate Congress. On March 12, the Provisional Congress appointed a committee to review the laws of the United States and report on their applicability to the Confederacy.[31]

Similarly, on March 4 the Provisional Congress adopted with few changes the Rules and Articles of War of the United States for the governance of an army.[32] In this most urgent area of the government's concern, however, a functioning machinery could not so readily be appropriated from the old government. An army and navy had to be created. To military preparations President Davis therefore turned his primary attention, out of both personal inclination and probable necessity.

Three hundred twenty-nine of the 1,080 officers of the U.S. Army resigned their commissions during the secession crisis, largely to enter the military service of the Southern states and eventually of the Confederacy. Sixteen of them were Northern men who had married into Southern families. It has been believed that only twenty-six enlisted men deserted the U.S. Army to join the Confederacy, but this figure may be a considerable underestimate. Still, the enlisted soldiers overwhelmingly remained with the old colors. Of 1,457 officers of the U.S. Navy, 237 followed the South.[33] In the old Navy as in the Regular Army, the rank and file remained overwhelmingly loyal to the United States.

The seceded states all began to remedy the military deficiencies of their pretensions to sovereignty before the Montgomery convention assembled. They did so by improving the militia organizations inherited from the English colonial system and later assimilated by both the Constitution and the statute law of the United States, as well as the laws of the states. Under the Uniform Militia Act of May 8, 1792 and its supplement of February 28, 1795, every free, white, able-bodied male citizen between eighteen and forty-five was enrolled in the militia of his state.[34] Since 1808 the Federal government had been distributing $200,000 among the states annually for the purchase of arms and equipment for the militia.[35] Although the universal service obligation, often invoked during the colonial Indian wars, had atrophied in practice even by 1792, the principle of a duty of all able-bodied males to give military service to their states remained established in American history and on the statute books, to be recalled to life when necessary.

Moreover, beyond the paper armies of hundreds of thousands of men enrolled in the muster books of the compulsory-service "common" or "unorganized" militia, the "volunteer" or "organized" militia had enjoyed a precocious growth, North and South, since the War of 1812. As early as the colonial era, men with a special taste or aptitude for military activity had set themselves apart from the mass of the unorganized militia to participate in more or less frequent military drill in organized volunteer companies, which would be the first to enter active service in case of an emergency call upon the militia. In the nineteenth century, the forming of dramatically uniformed militia companies evidently appealed to the romantic spirit of the age, and towns and cities competed with each other in contests of drill and display among such companies, much as they would later compete through their baseball and other sports teams. In the South, trained, armed, and organized volunteer militia companies met the special need for guardians against slave insurrection, in an era when especially in rural areas there were no other police. The companies of volunteer militia had formed the nuclei of the regiments of volunteers for Federal service in the War with Mexico, such as Colonel Jefferson Davis's Mississippi Rifles, and they could play a similar role for the Confederacy. Recruiting and drilling of extant units proceeded briskly in all the seceding states.

On February 28, the Provisional Congress authorized the President to take charge of military activities and to receive into Confederate service for a period of twelve months any military units tendered by the states. On March 6 the Congress followed up with two additional statutes making more detailed arrangements for a Confederate States Army. It authorized a Regular Army of 10,600 men. For immediate emergencies, it authorized the President to call the state militia into the service of the new government for six months and to accept 100,000 volunteers for one year. The volunteers were to furnish their own clothing and when necessary their horses and horse equipment. The states or the Confederacy would provide arms.[36]

By no means wishing to rush into measures that in themselves might imply warlike intent, Davis used these powers with restraint. On March 9 he called for 7,700 men to garrison forts. On April 8 he called for an additional 19,500 men for Confederate service.[37] Otherwise he left mobilization of troops for the time being to the considerable energies of the states. His own special efforts went into creating a military administration to care for and govern the troops as soon as the Confederacy might have to call for them in greater numbers. To establish staff bureaus and a command system, the President had to perform more than his share of the work, for Secretary Walker's appointment was already proving a mistake by any standards, even granting that Davis did not desire a strong character to occupy the War Department.[38]

James Buchanan gave way to Abraham Lincoln as President of the United States on March 4, the day of the Confederacy's flag-raising ceremony. By that time, the Confederate States of America was undoubtedly a going concern, possessing among other attributes a capacity for military defense altogether respectable when measured against the small military force of the United States. The President and Congress in Montgomery accordingly dared hope that the new President in Washington might feel obliged to acknowledge their *fait accompli*. The Confederate Provisional Congress had authorized President Davis to send a three-man commission to Washington to negotiate for friendly relations and the settlement of outstanding questions. To conduct the mission, Davis chose veteran politicians well acquainted in Washington and representing a spectrum of political views: André Bienvenu Roman, distinguished governor of Louisiana as long ago as 1831–1835 and 1839–1843 and a former Whig, more recently a Constitutional Unionist; Martin J. Crawford of Georgia, U.S. Congressman 1855–1861 and a John C. Breckinridge Democrat; and John Forsyth, an Alabama newspaperman who had made the *Mobile Register* a Unionist organ, supported Stephen A. Douglas in 1860, and opposed secession until it was accomplished.[39]

In Washington, however, the commissioners met disappointment. If James Buchanan had been unwilling to receive Southern gentlemen in their claimed official capacity as representatives of an independent republic, the new Republican President, still defining his policies, could hardly yield more. Although they were to talk unofficially with Lincoln's Secretary of State, William H. Seward, the Confederate commissioners were unable to assure themselves that Lincoln was apprised of their presence in town.

## FORT SUMTER: THE CRISIS APPROACHES

Still, Lincoln's aloofness from Davis's emissaries did not prove that the U.S. President intended to test Confederate military preparations by waging war. On the contrary, in his inaugural address Lincoln mixed his inevitable declarations of resolve to uphold the Union and the Constitution and appeals for reunion with the announcement of what could well be construed as a plan for avoiding war. Not only did he remind the world that he had often declared he had no purpose to interfere with the institution of slavery in the states where it existed, while reiterating that stand; not only did he go so far as to pledge enforcement of the constitutional provision for return of escaped fugitives, provided there were adequate safeguards that free men should not be made slaves. He went further, to say that in his defense of the Union, "there needs to be no bloodshed or violence; and there shall be none, unless it be forced upon the national authority." He would hold the property and places belonging to the government, and he would collect duties on imports; but he would do no more unless provoked, and especially he would do nothing to excite a sense of insecurity or endanger peace.[40]

Until 1861 the growth of governmental power in the United States had been so slight that in peacetime most citizens rarely felt the direct touch of any government, and most especially they rarely had contact with the government of the United States. Their principal involvement with any Federal authorities was likely to be through the postal service. Only those directly participating in international commerce met at first hand the import duties that were overwhelmingly the principal form of Federal taxation. These things being true, Lincoln could with relative ease promise that the government would not touch at all any Southern persons or areas not wishing to be touched.

Promptly following his inauguration, he took up with his Secretaries of the Treasury and the Navy and with his Attorney General the question of implementing a suggestion of Secretary of State Seward that where Federal customs collectors could not function in seaports, the import duties might be collected by naval vessels crusing offshore. If Lincoln thus fulfilled his responsibility to collect the revenues without invading the soil of the Southern states, if he refrained as he said he would even from sending the mails if they were resisted,[41] and with no Federal courts or officers functioning in the seceded states and Lincoln promising no invasion to compel their acceptance, then the Federal government simply would not be felt inside the states claiming to be the Confederacy. Lincoln would have avowed no sacrifice of principle, but there would be no occasion for conflict between the Southern people within their states and Federal agents, and a respite might be gained for peace to be assured.

There would be no occasion for collision unless the Confederate States reached out to resist collection of the duties offshore or to seize the offshore property and places that Lincoln had pledged to hold. Consistent with his evident intention to do nothing aggressive and to secure a breathing space between the seceded states and the U.S. government, Lincoln had removed from early drafts of his inaugural address a declaration that he would attempt to repossess Federal property and places already lost.[42] The seceded states had already taken possession of most of the Federal forts located on their soil, most of the forts being accessible enough by land and lightly enough garrisoned that they could be seized by a corporal's guard. There remained in Federal hands when Lincoln delivered his inaugural address four island forts protected by the waters around them as well as by their garrisons: Fort Jefferson on the Dry Tortugas, Fort Taylor at Key West, Fort Pickens near Pensacola, and Fort Sumter in Charleston harbor. The first two were at places too remote to cause an immediate crisis. For Fort Pickens on Santa Rosa Island off Pensacola, various Southern Senators had arranged with President Buchanan a truce, whereby Florida would not attack as long as the United States did not relieve or reinforce the garrison, though it might send in provisions. If not so remote as Forts Jefferson and Taylor, Pickens was also enough out of the way to make such an understanding possible. But Sumter, flying the Stars and Stripes in sight of the nursery of secession, provoked a Southern impatience that threatened Lincoln's whole plan for a respite.[43]

Despite President Davis's relative restraint in implementing his authority to mobilize troops, the busy military preparations of the seceded states and the general haste to put the Confederacy in arms created a momentum toward war and an emotional climate conducive to aggressive military action in the new Southern nation. It was true that after the furor over Major Anderson's removal of his command to Fort Sumter, tempers had cooled sufficiently by the beginning of February that Anderson and Governor Pickens could reach an agreement permitting the women and children of the Sumter garrison to be evacuated to New York, and Pickens allowed Anderson to resume buying meat and vegetables in the Charleston markets, a privilege he had suspended after Anderson's move from Moultrie. Nevertheless, the mounting of guns and other preparations for combat went on busily both inside the fort—Anderson found many more guns at hand than those that had been ready to fire when the crisis began—and on the mainland and islands surrounding it. Meanwhile popular pressure in South Carolina to remove the insulting banner from the state's principal harbor grew so intense that on February 12, the Confederate Congress adopted a resolution to take control of the question of the forts, partly to head off unilateral and precipitate action by South Carolina. At once Governor Pickens wrote to Howell Cobb, still president of the Provisional Congress, urging that Fort Sumter ought to be taken over before the Buchanan administration left Washington. Then the incoming Lincoln administration would have to choose whether or not to make war without the possibility that the South might precipitate a collision at Sumter.[44]

On February 15, the Provisional Congress responded to Pickens's urgings to the extent of resolving that steps should be taken to obtain Forts Sumter and Pickens as soon as possible, by negotiation or by force. Still impatient, Governor Pickens wrote to President Davis asking who should make the demand for the surrender of Sumter. Davis replied on March 1 that he too wanted Sumter in Confederate hands as early as possible, but that the Confederacy must be sure of winning victory in the first clash of arms. Secretary of War Walker told Pickens that a Confederate officer would leave Montgomery that very night to take command at Charleston. The officer was Brigadier-General Pierre Gustave Toutant Beauregard, a dapper disciplinarian from Louisiana who but for secession would have been superintendent of the Military Academy at West Point.[45]

Beauregard promptly reorganized the South Carolina state troops at Charleston into a more coherent force that he hastened into fighting trim, to be sure of the desired victory in the first collision. The conciliatory portions of Lincoln's inaugural address did nothing to retard these activities. Most Southern leaders saw the new President's promise to hold Federal places and property as an intolerable threat.

Promptly after delivering his inaugural address, Lincoln himself received disturbing news about Fort Sumter. He read a dispatch from Major

Anderson dated February 28 and stating that the Confederate fortification of Charleston harbor had gone so far that a force of 20,000 well-disciplined men would be necessary to retain the fort. Furthermore, Anderson's provisions were limited; the Confederates would not allow him to buy a stock of perishables, so that his purchase of meats and vegetables was on a day-to-day basis.[46] When Lincoln's Cabinet held its first meeting on March 9, Fort Sumter was a principal topic, and most of the Cabinet leaned toward evacuation. Seward in particular stirred about officiously in a search for conciliation. He thought he was cast to act as Prime Minister for the inexperienced prairie President, and, taking it upon himself to treat through intermediaries with the Confederate commissioners, he led them and other Southerners to anticipate that Sumter would be evacuated. Newspapers gave the public North and South conflicting guesses about the administration's plans.[47]

By March 14, when two Cabinet meetings over Sumter consumed much of the day, Postmaster General Montgomery Blair was alone among the secretaries in standing unequivocally for holding the fort. Blair was sustained by the Jacksonian tradition still embodied by his father, Francis Preston Blair, a veteran of Andrew Jackson's Kitchen Cabinet. By now General Scott had told Lincoln that with the means at hand, the time to shore up Sumter had passed a month before. Necessarily full of doubts in the face of such counsels, Lincoln nevertheless felt reluctant to abandon Sumter. He wanted conciliation, but only with good odds for eventual reunion, and he thought the latter consideration demanded asserting that he stood firm on the principle of the Union by surrendering no more forts. He hoped that at least he might play for time at Charleston. He decided to send various emissaries there—Gustavus Vasa Fox, until 1856 a lieutenant in the U.S. Navy and now the sponsor of a scheme for reinforcing Sumter from large tugboats; Stephen A. Hurlbut, an Illinois lawyer but a native of Charleston; Ward Hill Lamon, another Illinois lawyer and one of the President's closest friends. These men would report from first-hand observation on the prospects of the fort.[48]

Fox made the trip and still believed Sumter could be reinforced. Hurlbut and Lamon took soundings that were more political than military, and their political conclusions were extremely pessimistic. Hurlbut thought that secession had prospered so well for so long that there was now no possible policy whereby the United States could head off an armed clash. Lamon was told much the same thing by Governor Pickens, except that the one chance for peace was for Lincoln to accept secession, while not reinforcing the forts.

If he believed these tidings, Lincoln could retain little hope for delaying a showdown. To sacrifice Sumter would only strengthen the implied assurance of the Southerners that their revolution was fulfilled and accomplished. Meanwhile the Republican delegation in Congress was growing impatient with conciliatory procrastination; and in a similar spirit, Secretary of the Treasury Salmon P. Chase of Ohio and Secretary of the Navy Gideon Welles of Connecticut shifted to support of holding Sumter, because there no longer seemed to be anything to gain and possibly much to lose by yielding it. Attorney General Edward Bates of Missouri also endorsed at least an end to procrastination; he thought the fort must be either resupplied or evacuated.

As he had stated in his inaugural, Lincoln believed that his oath of office bound him to hold the remaining Federal property. With Fox's assurance that Sumter could still be held, on March 29 Lincoln ordered Secretary of War Simon Cameron of Pennsylvania and Secretary of the Navy Welles to prepare a relief expedition for Sumter, to be ready to move by sea by April 6, and to be commanded by Fox. As Lincoln's plans matured, they still aimed at buying time if possible. The President decided to notify the secession officials in Charleston of his intention to supply Fort Sumter, but to tell them he would send provisions only, "and that if such attempt be not resisted no effort to throw in men, arms, or ammunition will be made without further notice, or in case of an attack upon the fort."[49] Robert S. Chew, a Department of State clerk sent to Charleston, so notified Governor Pickens on April 8, reading to him and then handing him an unaddressed, unsigned copy of Lincoln's message. Pickens called in General Beauregard to hear the news. There would still be no hint of official communication between Lincoln and the secessionists that might imply recognizing them; Lincoln's emissary told Pickens he had no instructions to receive an answer.

Southerners lingering in Washington continued to provide the Confederates with much information about attitudes in the old capital, including word of the hardening determination to try to hold Fort Sumter. This information alarmed President Davis's government. If in response to it the Confederacy did not act to force the United States out of Charleston harbor, the restive South Carolinians might well take matters into their own hands. If not, then a continuing Federal presence at Charleston would surely undercut Confederate bids for international recognition, and a persistent impasse marked by the failure of the Confederacy to open its principal Atlantic seaport might gradually erode secessionist sentiment even within the South — as Lincoln hoped. In light of such fears, General Beauregard had already cut off Major Anderson's purchases in the Charleston market the day before Governor Pickens received Lincoln's message about the intention to provision Sumter. Some Confederate officers feared that a strong expedition to relieve Fort Sumter would succeed. Davis conferred with his own Cabinet, and while it like Lincoln's was divided — Secretary of State Toombs warning of incalculable consequences — the majority opinion in the Cabinet and in the Confederate government generally was that inaction would dangerously revive Southern Unionism. This opinion itself testified again to the uncertainty of the Southern psyche. But it was a judgment with which Davis agreed. On April 10, Secretary of War Walker ordered Beauregard: "If you have no doubt of the authorized character of the agent who communicated to you the intention of the Washington Government to supply Fort Sumter by force you will at once demand its evacuation, and if this is refused proceed, in such manner as you may determine, to reduce it."[50]

## FORT SUMTER: THE BOMBARDMENT

On the afternoon of April 11, two of Beauregard's aides were rowed out to Sumter to present Anderson with the general's message: "I am ordered by the Government of the Confederate States to demand the evacuation of Fort Sumter."[51] Anderson replied that his sense of honor and his obligations to his government prevented his complying; but in conversation with Beauregard's aides he remarked that in any event, the garrison would be starved out in a few days. Beauregard and the Confederate authorities in Montgomery with whom he promptly communicated were quick to see in this remark a hope that they might not have to take the initiative after all. On further instructions, Beauregard sent messengers to tell Anderson: "If you will state the time at which you will evacuate Fort Sumter, and agree that in the mean time you will not use your guns against us unless ours shall be employed against Fort Sumter, we will abstain from opening fire upon you."[52]

But Anderson recognized that such an agreement would forbid his opening fire to support a relief expedition. He replied that he would evacuate by noon of April 15, unless he received new instructions or supplies, but with the proviso that he would have to fire in reply to a hostile act against the fort "or the flag it bears." These terms could not satisfy the Confederates; hastening Sumter's capture before its guns could aid a relief expedition was one of the main purposes of their demands. Beauregard's messengers, principally ex-U.S. Senator James Chesnut of South Carolina and ex-U.S. Congressman Roger A. Pryor of Virginia, consequently rejected the answer on the spot and informed Anderson that Beauregard would open fire in one hour.[53]

Just one hour and ten minutes later, at 4:30 A.M. on Friday, April 12,

1861, a mortar on James Island west of Sumter fired a signal shot that burst above the fort. Soon forty-three guns were firing against the fort from the whole periphery of the harbor. By now, Anderson had sixty guns ready; but he was short of cartridges — he had powder but lacked cloth to make cartridges — and he hesitated to risk the lives of his small garrison by firing his biggest guns, eight-inch howitzers and ten-inch Columbiads, which because of their high angle of fire had to be mounted not in the protected casemates but in the open, on the parade and on the parapet. Not until seven A.M. did Abner Doubleday, Company E, the senior captain of the 1st Artillery, fire Sumter's first shot. The fort kept up a slow return fire against a heavier Confederate bombardment until darkness came. Three times during the day Confederate hot shot set fire to the barracks, but the flames were extinguished, and by nightfall little damage had been suffered.

In the afternoon, three U.S. ships appeared off the bar at the harbor mouth: Fox's relief expedition. Neither then nor during the night, however, did Sumter receive any help. The ships were having trouble keeping station in a coastal storm, and heavy seas frustrated Fox's efforts to send in provision boats during the night.

Besides, Fox was waiting for the powerful steam frigate *Powhatan* to arrive before he attempted to fight his way to Sumter's rescue. He did not know that the *Powhatan* would never reach him. Secretary Seward, still pursuing conciliation in the spirit of his implied promises to the Confederate commissioners that Sumter would be abandoned, had contrived with the aid of Lieutenant David Dixon Porter of the Navy to divert the *Powhatan* from the Sumter expedition to another relief enterprise, bound for Fort Pickens, which Seward considered a less sensitive and therefore more appropriate point at which to display a resolve to retain Federal property. Gustavus Fox always believed that if he had received a warship of the *Powhatan's* strength, as his plans had intended, the next events would have been different.

Confederate fire against Sumter kept up at a slackened pace during the night and resumed at full weight on the morning of April 13. Hot shot now set fires that went out of control, raging through the officers' quarters and the barracks and compelling Anderson to close the doors of the magazine. Heat and smoke soon had the defenders crowding to the embrasures for air or lying on the ground covering their mouths with handkerchiefs. Firing from the fort fell off to one shot every ten minutes. At one o'clock the flagstaff was shot down. Before Anderson could get the flag raised again, Louis T. Wigfall, until secession a boastful and posturing U.S. Senator from Texas and now acting as an aide to Beauregard, set out not from the latter's head-quarters but from Morris Island, mainly on his own initiative, to ask the fort to surrender.

Wigfall offered Anderson any terms he desired. Under the impression that Wigfall came from Beauregard, and with the ships off the bar having made no discernible move to assist him, rations down to pork and water, and his means of responding to the bombardment rapidly diminishing, Anderson said he would accept the terms Beauregard had offered before the shooting began. These included evacuation with his command, taking arms and private and company property, the right to salute the U.S. flag as it was lowered, and conveyance to a Northern port. The arrangements apparently being satisfactory, Anderson raised the white flag, firing ceased, and Wigfall went off to report to Beauregard — that Anderson had surrendered unconditionally.

Eventually the resulting confusion was resolved by Beauregard's agreement to the terms Anderson had accepted. The next day, Sunday, April 14, the Sumter garrison marched out with colors flying and drums beating, to be carried to the Federal fleet off the bar. In the course of the artillery salute to the U.S. flag, the premature discharge of a gun and the explosion of a pile of cartridges killed Private Daniel Hough of Company E, 1st Artillery. Private Edward Galloway of the same company died of wounds from the explosion four days later. Four other wounded soldiers recovered.[54]

## MILITANT AMERICA

The firing on the U.S. flags that flew from the *Star of the West* might well have been insult enough to cause war — but evidently the mood of the North was not yet ready in January, and certainly the Buchanan administration was not. The bombardment of a U.S. fort was worse, and with the tension and suspense of the intervening months, public psychology both North and South had also changed since January and grown ripe for a commitment to conflict.

Throughout the North as the news from Charleston arrived, the Stars and Stripes appeared on public buildings and private homes, mass meetings to support the Union replaced meetings anxiously exploring conciliation plans, and newspapers and public men of Southern sympathies received threats of violence. The Confederate attack on the fort provoked Northern anger, and anger galvanized a conviction growing during the months when the secession crisis simmered, that too large a future would be sacrificed if the Union dissolved. Acquiescence in dissolution would invite future secessions by future discontented minorities, and at the end of such a road lay anarchy. The alternative was to fight for the Union, to save it, and thus to secure all the vast economic opportunities of a united continent, the infinite, imperial destiny that Americans believed was rightly theirs as a new chosen people, and as Abraham Lincoln was increasingly to argue, perhaps democracy itself.

To that end, on April 15, Lincoln called upon the loyal states for 75,000 militia, to suppress resistance to the laws in seven Southern states. He also called for a special session of Congress to meet at noon on July 4. In proclamations of April 19 and 27 he declared the ports of the seven seceded states under blockade.[55]

Lincoln's militia proclamation stated that the details of the militia mobilization would be communicated to the states by the War Department. In carrying out this procedure, the War Department assigned each state a quota of the total of 75,000.[56] The call was for three months' service, not because Lincoln expected armed conflict to be brief, but because Presidential authority to call the militia into Federal service rested on the February 28, 1795 revision of the Uniform Militia Act of 1792, which limited such service to three months in any one year. On April 27 the President ordered the creation of a new manufactory for arms at Rock Island, Illinois; this facility would not be ready for many months at best, and the order to establish it belies the notion that Lincoln was deluded into expecting only a short war.[57]

Lincoln called for troops and invited war knowing that to do so would almost certainly add at least four states to the Confederacy. Virginia, North Carolina, Tennessee, and Arkansas were all led by professed Unionists. Their leaders, however, were plainly Unionists only conditionally, loyal to Washington only so long as Washington took no vigorous steps to force back into the Union the seceded states farther south. If the issue should come to war, Virginia, North Carolina, Tennessee, and Arkansas all possessed too many economic ties, too many links of personal and community sentiment, with the lower South to join in an effort of coercion.

In Virginia, a convention to consider the relations of the Commonwealth with the Union had been elected on February 4, and the sentiments of the convention had been shifting toward secession for weeks before the Sumter bombardment. Doubtful evidence has it that Lincoln had offered to abandon Sumter if the Virginia convention would disperse. Lincoln's call for militia pushed Virginia over the brink into secession, which the Virginia convention voted on April 17. The convention provided for a popular referendum to be held May 23, but meanwhile the state formed an alliance with the Confederacy, Confederate troops began entering its borders, and the outcome of the referendum became a foregone conclusion.[58]

North Carolina, a state of relatively few great slaveholders and of many yeoman farmers, hesitated more than Virginia, but finally ties of interest and sentiment similar to Virginia's produced a North Carolina ordinance of secession on May 20. In Tennessee, Governor Isham G. Harris pressed the General Assembly into passing on May 1 a vote of alliance with the Confederacy that was more than dubious constitutionally, along with related military measures. By the time a referendum was held on June 8, the Tennessee electorate like that of Virginia before it was merely accepting accomplished facts. In Arkansas there were fewer ties to the North than in Tennessee, secessionist procedures could be more straightforward, and a secession ordinance was passed on May 6 by a state convention assembled after Sumter.[59]

The course of the other border slave states was in doubt. On April 19, Maryland secessionists attacked the 6th Massachusetts Infantry when it marched through Baltimore.[60] Governors Beriah Magoffin of Kentucky and Claiborne F. Jackson of Missouri rejected Lincoln's call for militia.[61] But it was not clear for how many of their constituents they spoke. The slave state of Delaware was too small to act independently of its neighbors Maryland and Pennsylvania.

In the Northern states where the flags had blossomed everywhere, states and people offered more troops than the Federal government knew how to organize, command, and provision on short notice — the Lincoln administration having carefully avoided all but the most minute military preparations before Fort Sumter to avoid giving the secessionists provocation. Because no Federal appropriations existed to finance a rapid increase of the Army, the states and groups of individuals also provided much of the equipment for the gathering Federal forces. A semblance of a new army rose almost overnight, nevertheless, because the fervor of angry emotion could be joined with the already organized, partially equipped and trained strength of the volunteer companies. The 6th Massachusetts Regiment, whose troubles in Baltimore made it the first famous Union volunteer regiment of the war, was formed from ten volunteer militia companies: the National Greys of Lowell, the Groton Artillery, the Mechanic Phalanx of Lowell, the City Guards of Lowell, the Davis Guards of Acton, the Warren Light Guard of Lawrence, the Worcester Light Infantry, the Watson Light Guards of Lowell, the Lawrence Light Infantry, and the Washington Light Guards of Boston.[62]

In response to the military rising of the North, the Confederacy of course accelerated its own military preparations. In anticipation of Lincoln's prohibition of trade with Southern ports, President Davis on April 17 invited prospective privateers to apply for letters of marque, and a brisk little privateering campaign soon challenged the Federal Navy and threatened the Northern merchant marine.[63] A second session of the Provisional Congress met at Montgomery on April 29 to consider replies to what Davis called Lincoln's declaration of war. Davis told the Congress that he had 19,000 men under arms in various places, with 16,000 more being assembled in Virginia, and that he planned to organize forthwith the 100,000 volunteers authorized by existing legislation.[64] In the Confederacy as in the North, the foundation upon which these military efforts continued to be built was the organized volunteer companies.

Perhaps "the militant South,"[65] with its felt need for armed forces to guard against slave uprisings and its expectations of possible secession, had gone further than the North in recruiting and organizing the volunteer militia during the decade just preceding Fort Sumter — but only perhaps. Massachusetts, having reorganized its whole militia system around the volunteer rather than the common militia in 1840, in 1849 introduced annual training encampments for the volunteers. The encampments both reflected and further stimulated interest in the volunteer movement, and in 1857 the Commonwealth reported that of the 102 Massachusetts volunteer companies in existence, sixty-three had been organized since the passage of the encampment law. Other Northern states, particularly New York, similarly reorganized their militia systems around the growing enthusiasm of the volunteers.[66]

In the rural and Western states of the North, the rise of the volunteers was less marked than in the more urban Northeast, and the states accomplished much less toward reorganizing their militias on a reasonably sound foundation of organized volunteer companies. But no part of the North was untouched by the volunteer movement. In Chicago in 1859, an impecunious law student with a passion for military drill and display, Elmer Ellsworth, was elected captain of the National Guard Cadets. Ellsworth had studied the drill of the Zouaves, French Army units whose distinctive uniforms and rapid evolutions were based on those of Algerian light infantry. He reorganized his company as the United States Zouave Cadets. Properly costumed and tutored under what proved to be Ellsworth's almost fanatical enthusiasm, the Zouave Cadets toured twenty Northern cities in the summer of 1860, setting off a craze for forming Zouave companies and regiments. Many of the units responding to Lincoln's call of April 15, and some that responded to Jefferson Davis's calls, wore the fez, the short blue jacket, and the baggy red trousers of the Zouaves.

Elmer Ellsworth was a romantic posturer, but he was not merely that.

In 1860, the year he led his Zouave Cadets on their tour, he also became associated with the Springfield, Illinois law firm of Lincoln and Herndon. There he urged upon the prominent politician who headed the firm his well-considered plans for a Bureau of Militia in the War Department to reorganize the militia system across the whole country, and he submitted a similar draft of a militia bill to the Illinois General Assembly. He was a serious student of the problems of military organization in a democracy. A parallel mixture of the romantic and the deadly serious characterized the whole volunteer movement of the 1850s and the beginning of the 1860s, the faddishness of the Zouave idea mingling with forebodings of civil war to produce a special growth of volunteer companies in North and South in 1860 and early 1861.[67]

Although when secession came the states did not have the full apparatus of military organization appropriate to independent republics, in their volunteer companies, supervised by the state governments under their own militia laws and the militia provisions of the Federal Constitution and statutes, the states did possess reasonable facsimiles of armies. These forces were sufficient to enable the states to go to war against each other. Beyond the legalistic complexities of constitutional arguments about states' rights, the states in fact enjoyed sovereignty enough to have armed forces able to wage war — and thus possessed in fact one of the foremost essentials of sovereignty. Beyond the legalistic and historical complexities of the causes of secession, the states had the military means to permit secession to lead directly into civil war.

They controlled in the volunteer companies miniature armies strong enough to begin the Civil War, and the companies were significant also of a national mood and spirit that helps explain both why the sectional crisis should have resulted in war, and why the war should have become so intensely violent. Professor Dennis Hart Mahan, in the generation before the conflict the principal instructor in the art of war at West Point, said: "Of all the civilized states of Christendom, we are perhaps the least military, though not behind the foremost as a warlike one."[68] The United States did not have powerful regular armies and navies, but it was a country fascinated by things military and committed to the principle that war is an acceptable means of solving political problems. The rise of the volunteer military companies of the 1850s and early '60s as their generation's equivalent in the life of American communities of the baseball teams and the Rotary Clubs of a later era indicates a national preoccupation with the military and with war verging upon a romantic desire to test the actual experience of war. Elmer Ellsworth, like all the zealots of the volunteer movement, was a romantic play-actor;

but he was so in earnest about the role he played that he pursued it to the death. On May 24, 1861, as Colonel Ellsworth of the 11th New York Regiment of Volunteer Infantry, the New York Fire Zouaves recruited from New York City's fire companies, he was shot dead after he tore a Confederate flag from the Marshall House Tavern in Alexandria during the Union Army's first march into Virginia.[69]

TWO

# The Battle
# Lines Form

## NAPOLEONIC WAR

With the mood of the times and his French name, it took no more than his
conquest of Fort Sumter to establish General Beauregard in the minds of
many Southerners as the Confederate Napoleon.

The era's fascination with war often took the form of idolization of the
great Emperor. The contemporary presence of another Bonaparte on the
throne of France nourishing the legend of the first Napoleon reinforced the
mystique. Not only did the amateur soldiers of the volunteer companies
fancy themselves as legionaries of France, calling themselves Chasseurs and
Zouaves; but the adulation of the French military tradition in general and
of Napoleon I in particular was nowhere stronger than among America's
professional soldiers, the graduates of West Point who had commanded the
Regular Army and now turned to lead the gathering citizen armies. American military uniforms, and particularly the characteristic *kepi* headgear,
were patterned on contemporary French models. The American Army felt
itself closely linked to the French Army through the alliance during the
American War of Independence. The Military Academy at West Point
looked to France as the fountainhead of military learning. Dennis Hart Mahan, West Point's Professor of Civil and Military Engineering and of the Art
of War for a whole generation before the Civil War and through the war,

had studied in France after his own graduation from West Point in 1824 and brought his teaching materials from that country. The principal instructor in the military art to almost all the cadets who were to become generals in the Civil War, he served as president of the faculty's Napoleon Club and urged faculty and students to model themselves upon Napoleon as the foremost ideal of the soldier.[1]

To American soldiers of 1861, Napoleonic warfare provided their image of war. Napoleonic warfare was war in a dramatic style that revolved around the climactic, decisive battle. The Napoleonic general made the bringing of his enemy to battle the object of his campaign. On the battlefield he hoped to emulate the classic Napoleonic method of winning victory, using part of his army to hold the enemy army in a fixed position, then with the remainder of his army executing *la manœuvre sur les derrières*, which would turn the enemy, smite him flank and rear, and by both punishing him with heavy casualties and unbalancing him psychologically, destroy his army. To destroy the enemy army — that was the object of Napoleonic war: in a single battle to strike such devastating physical and psychological blows that the enemy army would lose its cohesion and cease to exist as an effective fighting instrument. So Napoleon had destroyed the Austrian and Russian Armies in a single day in the greatest masterpiece of Napoleonic battle, at Austerlitz on December 2, 1805. So Napoleon had destroyed the feared Prussian Army — the army that had been Frederick the Great's — in the twin battles of Jena and Auerstädt on October 14, 1806. Both Austerlitz and Jena-Auerstädt permitted Napoleon to impose treaties of peace upon enemy governments after a single campaign.[2]

The admirers of Napoleon tended to overlook the later recovery of the defeated armies and governments. For the Emperor's soldierly disciples, the ideal of generalship was to destroy the enemy army so completely in the decisive Austerlitz battle that the enemy government would have to make peace. The prevalence of this ideal of warfare among American generals, and the American public as well, does much to explain the widespread belief in 1861 that the war between North and South would be brief. General Scott like President Lincoln was among the doubters; Scott offered to the President his plan for a prolonged war of strangulation against the Confederacy by naval blockade and a march down the Mississippi River, soon called the Anaconda Policy. But Major-General Winfield Scott himself had waged a swift campaign in Mexico in 1847, compelling the Mexican government to accept a humiliating treaty by means of a single campaign from the Gulf to the City of México, so that his own example encouraged hopes for a short war.[3]

Napoleonic war with its climactic battles between masses of colorfully uniformed troops did not weigh the gross domestic products of rival powers against each other in the fashion of the world wars of the twentieth century. Napoleonic war was not a contest of rival industrial capacities. The equipment of Napoleonic armies was simple, and their muskets and cannon could be provided by relatively simple economic systems. Much of the time, Napoleonic armies fed themselves off the country through which they marched. By 1861, the logistical requirements of armies had not become much more complicated than they had been in 1814. Armies still fought each other with small arms and cannon; they did not use tanks, motorized artillery, and airplanes. Consequently, the war between North and South could well be expected to be not only a brief war but one in which the industrial inferiority of the South to the North would be of no decisive importance.

The inferiority of the South in population was a different matter. The crush of the Napoleonic battle demanded armies large enough to have considerable resiliency to withstand the shock; to destroy the enemy army required willingness to accept heavy casualties even in the victorious army. The image of Napoleonic war helped account for the expectation of a short war, but it also did much to spur both sides to mobilize much larger armies than had ever been assembled in America before. In ability to mobilize mass armies, the North appeared to possess an important advantage over the South. The eleven Confederate states had a total population of 9,103,332 according to the census of 1860; the states that remained in the Union and the territories had a total population of 22,339,991. Furthermore, of the population of the Confederacy, 3,521,110 were slaves.

Yet these population statistics did not need to carry a fatal message for the South. Admirers of Napoleon also believed with their hero that a great general could overcome numerical odds. When Virginia joined the Confederacy following Fort Sumter, moreover, Southerners hoped that all the slave states might yet cast their lot with the Confederacy; that two or three additional border states did not was among the contests decided in the course of the war, not an outcome preordained. Of the total population outside the eleven states of the Confederacy, 3,305,557 (including 432,586 slaves) resided in the border slave states and areas of Delaware, Maryland, Kentucky, Missouri, the District of Columbia, and New Mexico Territory. Much of this population had to be counted as potentially Confederate no matter what their governments did officially. The 525,660 inhabitants of the Pacific Coast and Rocky Mountain states and territories (California, Colorado Territory, Nevada Territory, Oregon, Utah Territory, Washington Territory) did not effectively contribute to the Union's military manpower potential because they were too far away; instead, the Far West was a place to which it proved to be possible to go to avoid social pressures to volunteer and later to avoid the draft. In the Confederacy, the large population of African-American slaves had mixed military implications. If the war proved long, they were a potential source of dissension; but immediately they permitted the South to recruit into its armies a much higher proportion of its white manpower of military age than the North, because the slaves remained at home to sustain the economy with their labor.[4]

## WAR IN A NEW STYLE

The cult of Napoleon and an expectation of waging Napoleonic war reigned among most of the officers of the armies that gathered North and South, but while outwardly the appearance and equipment of armies had not changed much since Napoleon's day, in fact the way had been prepared for important changes in methods of fighting that were to help undo the expectations of a short, quickly decisive war.

In 1841 the U.S. Arsenal at Harpers Ferry, Virginia, had prepared the pattern weapons of the first general-issue rifled shoulder arm of the U.S. Army. Conservative Army leadership and problems in finding suitable ammunition had prevented an Army-wide effort to replace smoothbore muskets with rifles in the infantrymen's hands until after the Mexican War. In 1850, however, the Army adopted the Minié bullet, named for Colonel Claude Étienne Minié of the French Army, the eventually famous "minnie ball" of the Civil War, whose diameter was small enough in proportion to the rifle's bore that it could be loaded easily into a muzzle-loading rifle, but whose hollow base was expanded by the explosion when the rifle was fired so that the missile then fitted tightly into the rifle's grooves. In 1855 an improved model rifle was adopted, using the Minié bullet. The spin imparted to the rifle bullet by the grooves in the rifle's bore greatly increased the bullet's accuracy in flight. The smoothbore muskets previously in use had an extreme range of 250 to 300 yards and very little accuracy at any range. The U.S. Rifle Model 1855 had an extreme range of half a mile or more and an effective range of 200 to 250 yards. Even though these weapons were single-shot muzzle-loaders, they greatly enhanced the lethality of the standard infantry weapon. They made the climactic, decisive Austerlitz battle almost impossible.

At the time of Fort Sumter, there were only 35,335 rifled muskets (muskets altered to rifles) and rifles of the 1855 model in U.S. arsenals, along with 422,325 smoothbore muskets and rifles of older patterns, the overwhelming majority of which were of the former description. On May 7 Major Josiah Gorgas, head of the Confederate Ordnance Bureau, reported that there were 160,000 small arms in the public depositories of the seceded and seceding states, including 120,000 muskets and 15,000 rifles east of the Mississippi.[5] The Confederacy had far fewer rifles and rifled muskets than the Union. Despite this relative shortage of rifles among the small arms immediately available on both sides, enough rifles soon went into use — more rapidly in the East than in the West — to begin making Napoleonic tactics bankrupt.

The moment of decision in Napoleon's day, and long before, had occurred when a heavy mass of the attacker's close-ordered ranks struck or were about to strike the main strength of the defense. To break the defending ranks decisively, it was necessary to throw a heavy mass of troops upon them in one mighty blow. To bring a heavy mass of troops upon them was possible because of the limited destructiveness of smoothbore firearms. Their range was so restricted that defenders could count on getting off only one reasonably effective volley against advancing attackers. By the time that volley was unloosed, the attackers would be so close to their objective that before the defenders could reload, the attacking troops would be upon them.

Against defenders equipped with rifles, however, an attacking force would come under a hail of infantry fire when they were still about half a mile from their target, and the defenders would be able to get off so many shots, and rifle fire would be so accurate, that a tightly packed mass of attackers could be torn to shreds before it could strike home. In such circumstances, the defenders naturally tended to fight behind some kind of protective wall or entrenchment, to shield themselves from the attackers' rifles. If in the course of the charge the attackers paused to fire their own rifles, they would simply increase the time they were exposed to the defenders' fire and would achieve proportionately small results against the protected defenders. As the devastating impact of the rifle became apparent, attacking forces increasingly dispersed, sent skirmishers ahead of their main mass to take cover and pick off defenders, and advanced by short rushes from cover to cover. Yet Civil War officers still had to try at the climax of an attack to hurl a heavy weight of men simultaneously into the enemy's position, or the defenders could not be broken.

In short, the range and accuracy of the rifle made it nearly impossible for a would-be Napoleon to throw upon the enemy a heavy enough mass of troops to inflict upon the defending forces the casualties and the psychological imbalance necessary for the Austerlitz or Jena-Auerstädt kind of victory that wrecked a whole army in a single battle.

The truth of the matter was that, Napoleonic legend notwithstanding, the latter two battles were exceptional for their decisiveness even in Napoleon's campaigns, and that in spite of the military genius of the Emperor most battles of the Napoleonic Wars, especially in the later phases, more nearly resembled stalemates than smashing triumphs. So did most battles throughout modern military history, since the Thirty Years War of 1618–1648. Contrary to the mythology of Napoleon, and in spite of the example of Scott's campaign in Mexico, modern war tended toward a chronic indecisiveness, in which the long duration of conflicts resulting from that indecisiveness tended to make the cumulative cost of waging war intractably disproportionate to the benefits to be gained. But the rifle made matters yet worse, and helped make the Civil War casualty tolls exceptionally appalling even by the horrifying standards of the entire history of war.

The defensive power of rifles was so lethal and so enhanced the confidence of the defenders that even a well-executed turning maneuver was likely to produce only a decidedly temporary advantage in the Civil War. A reasonably experienced and disciplined defending army would respond to it by simply forming a new front against the flankers and again turning them back. The only way to impose heavy enough casualties upon an enemy army to approximate that army's destruction was to accept such heavy casualties oneself that no decisive advantage could accrue.[6]

Napoleon often prepared the way for the assaults of his infantry by moving highly mobile field artillery close to the enemy's lines to pound him before the Emperor's infantry struck home. Rifles made this tactic impractical because if the artillerists so exposed themselves to entrenched defenders, the defending infantry would use their rifles to pick off the gunners before they could do substantial damage. On the eve of the Civil War, rifled artillery had also come into use, increasing the range of the field guns much as rifling increased the range of shoulder arms. Nevertheless, against sheltered infantry, artillery could not achieve decisive effects at the ranges at which it had to operate for the safety of the gunners, especially because fuses could not yet be timed precisely enough to assure that shells would explode over the heads of an entrenched enemy. Rifled artillery served principally to give another advantage to the defender, increasing the range at which his guns could begin to cut down exposed troops advancing to the attack.[7]

By aggravating war's tendency toward prolonged indecision, rifles gave more relevance to the Confederacy's economic and industrial inferiority than most Confederates anticipated. A war of indecisive battle was likely to become a contest of endurance. If armies could not be readily destroyed on the battlefield, then the ability to sustain and supply them indefinitely became critical. If armies could not readily be destroyed, then the will of the people behind them to continue supporting them and to endure the strains of war became an obvious optional target for the enemy. To keep alive the will and ability to endure among the home population also demanded economic strength and resiliency.

In 1860, New York and Pennsylvania each had more industrial establishments than the entire South. Of the 128,300 industrial establishments in the United States, only 18,026 were in the eleven Confederate States. Of the $1,900,000,000 value of annual product of the nation's industry, the output of the Confederate States represented only $145,350,000, or about 7.5 percent.[8] These statistics might tell much about each section's ability to continue equipping and reequipping armies and to maintain the civilian economy over a prolonged and costly war. So might the agricultural statistics, when production of foodstuffs was likely to be of more direct utility to a war effort than cotton production. The North grew 139,816,487 bushels of wheat in 1860, the eleven states that were to form the Confederacy, 31,366,894 bushels; the North, 549,786,693 bushels of Indian corn, the South, 280,665,014 bushels; the North, 152,634,280 bushels of oats, the South, 19,920,408 bushels. The North slaughtered animals valued at $131,389,352, the South, animals valued at $81,482,301.[9] The dangers to the South implicit in the agricultural statistics were all the greater because the richest granaries of the South, and especially the wheat- and meat-producing areas of Tennessee, lay exposed, close to the Confederacy's borders.

Especially significant for a prolonged war also were the transportation statistics. In 1860 the North had some 22,085 miles of railroad, the future Confederate States 8,541 miles. The Northern railroads were approaching the condition of an integrated, coherent system; the Southern railroads lagged behind. The deficiencies of the Southern railroad system were to prove especially critical; cotton fields could be converted to food production, and the South was to show a remarkable capacity to improvise sufficient industry for war, but increasingly goods could not be moved expeditiously — or at all — from where they were produced to where they were needed.[10]

For all that, although the war was in fact to become prolonged, the Confederacy was to lose through deficiencies of supplies and equipment no battles that would not almost certainly have been lost from other causes. While it was no longer a Napoleonic war, the Civil War was not yet a gross-domestic-product war on the model of World War II. As a contest that would be resolved by the soldiers of the opposing armies largely with the guns they would carry in their own hands, it was still to resemble the Napoleonic Wars much more than the contest of industrialization and mechanization of 1939–1945.

## WASHINGTON RESCUED

When Virginia seceded, Vice President Stephens traveled to Richmond to open negotiations with the Confederacy's prospectively richest state, and he urged Virginia to join the Confederacy by suggesting that the Confederate capital should move to Richmond. Virginia merited such recognition as the most populous of the seceded states and the bearer of a unique historic tradition that would add incalculably to the Confederacy's prestige. Although Richmond would be more exposed to Northern attack than Montgomery, Virginia and its capital would have to be defended stoutly in any event, for reasons of pride, because of the manufactories in Richmond, and because of the grainstuffs of the Shenandoah Valley and the Piedmont. While Stephens made his overtures and Virginia awaited its public vote on secession, moreover, the Union seemed to have more cause than the Confederacy to fear for the safety of its capital.[11]

Washington was a city of Southern antecedents and much Southern sympathy, surrounded by the slave states of Virginia and Maryland. A secessionist coup to seize the city had been rumored since Lincoln's election, and General Scott had stationed troops at key locations to protect Lincoln's inauguration on March 4. Before the inauguration, District of Columbia militia companies had begun to be mobilized, but the loyalties of many of their members were questionable. The Regular Army of some 16,000 officers and men was too widely scattered across the Indian frontier and too much needed there to bring many Regulars quickly to Washington. It did not help matters that when Texas seceded, Brigadier-General (Brevet Major-General) David E. Twiggs, commanding the Department of Texas, had surrendered his 102 officers and 2,328 enlisted men, along with the public property except for the personal arms of the troops. By April 13, Scott had only six companies of fully equipped Regulars in Washington, two companies of dismounted cavalry, 200 Marines, and fifteen companies of District of Columbia militia. The militia were still being recruited, and there would be thirty companies a week later, but they remained a dubious reliance. Across the Potomac River, Virginia fire-eaters were clamoring for a march on Washington.[12]

About seven o'clock in the evening of April 18, a train arrived in the capital from the North carrying a few more Regulars and five companies, some 460 men, of Pennsylvania volunteers — the latter mostly unarmed. The volunteers had been jeered at and pelted with stones when they marched between railroad stations in Baltimore, and an old black man called Nick Biddle who habitually accompanied the Washington Artillery of Pottsville was wearing blood-stained rags around his head; hurt in the stoning, Biddle

### THE PRINCIPAL THEATER OF WAR

**Railroads**

1. Alabama and Florida R.R.
2. Alabama and Mississippi R.R.
3. Alton R.R.
4. Atlantic and Gulf R.R.
5. Atlantic and North Carolina R.R.
6. Augusta and Savannah R.R.
7. Baltimore and Ohio R.R.
8. Blue Mountain and Selma R.R.
9. Brunswick and Albany R.R.
10. Central of Georgia Rwy.
11. Central Alabama R.R.
12. Charleston and Savannah R.R.
13. Cheraw and Darlington R.R.
14. Chicago, Burlington and Quincy R.R.
15. Clinton and Port Hudson R.R.
16. Delaware R.R.
17. East Tennessee and Virginia R.R.
18. Evansville and Terre Haute R.R.
19. Florida R.R.
20. Georgia R.R.
21. Hannibal and St. Joseph R.R.
22. Illinois Central R.R.
23. Indiana Central R.R.
24. Indianapolis and Madison R.R.
25. Jackson and Great Northern R.R.
26. Lexington and Ohio R.R.
27. Louisville and Nashville R.R.
28. Macon and Western Central R.R.
29. Manassas Gap R.R.
30. Memphis and Charleston R.R.
31. Memphis and Little Rock R.R.
32. Memphis and Ohio R.R.
33. Memphis, Clarksville and Louisville R.R.
34. Millville and Glassboro R.R.
35. Mississippi and Tennessee R.F.
36. Mississippi Central R.R.
37. Mobile and Ohio R.R.
38. Montgomery and West Point R.R.
39. Muscogee R.R.
40. Nashville and Chattanooga R.R.
41. Nashville and Northwestern R.R.
42. Natchez and Jackson R.R.
43. New Orleans and Ohio R.R.
44. New Orleans and Texas R.R.
45. New Orleans, Jackson and Northwestern R.R.
46. New York Central R.R.
47. Norfolk and Petersburg R.R.
48. North Carolina R.R.
49. Northeastern South Caroline R.R.
50. Northern Missouri R.R.
51. Orange and Alexandria R.R.
52. Pacific R.R.
53. Pennsylvania R.R.
54. Richmond, Fredericksburg and Potomac R.R.
55. Raleigh and Gaston R.R.
56. Richmond and Danville R.R.
57. Rockingham R.R.
58. St. Louis and Iron Mountain R.R.
59. Savannah, Albany and Gulf R.R.
60. Seaboard and Roanoke R.R.
61. South Carolina R.R.
62. Southside R.R.
63. Southern R.R. of Mississippi
64. Southwestern R.R.
65. Tallahassee R.R.
66. Tennessee and Georgia R.R.
67. Virginia Central R.R.
68. Vicksburg, Pacific and Shreveport R.R.
69. Wabash R.R.
70. Weldon and Petersburg R.R
71. West Feliciana R.R.
72. West Jersey R.R.
73. Western and Atlantic R.R.
74. Western R.R.
75. Wilmington and Manchester R.R.
76. Wilmington and Weldon R.R.

was the first war casualty to enter Washington. The next evening brought a more substantial reinforcement but worse news and prospects. The 6th Massachusetts Regiment arrived after fighting its way through a hostile mob in Baltimore; its casualties were four dead and thirty-one wounded, while twelve civilians had been killed and an unknown number wounded in the fray.[13]

After this Baltimore riot, Governor Thomas H. Hicks of Maryland, hitherto a Unionist, telegraphed Lincoln urging him to avoid sending troops through the Old Line State[14] and allegedly began to express secessionist sympathies. During the night of April 19–20, Governor Hicks and the mayor of Baltimore, George W. Brown, gave the city's police force the impression that they thought Baltimore should be closed to Union troops by destroying the railroad bridges between the city and the North. The police promptly accomplished this task, thus effectively severing Washington from the North as well. On April 21, the telegraph wires north from Washington were also cut, and the capital's only communication with the North became the uncertain telegraph line through Harpers Ferry, a place abandoned by the Federal troops who had guarded the arsenal there. Governor Hicks reversed an earlier decision and agreed to call a special session of the General Assembly, which had a secessionist majority.

Fortunately for the Union, these first responses to the beginning of civil war accurately reflected neither the resolve of the Northern states to protect the national capital nor the full sentiments of Maryland. Lincoln and General Scott told a delegation of Maryland leaders that Washington must be protected and Federal troops must cross Maryland. But they wanted no unnecessary trouble, and Scott offered to use routes bypassing Baltimore. Mayor Brown, a member of the Maryland delegation, agreed to try to prevent mob interference with the bypassing routes. On April 21 and 22 two Union regiments, the 8th Massachusetts and 7th New York, arrived at Annapolis in steamboats. With the 8th Massachusetts was Benjamin Franklin Butler, lately vice-presidential candidate of the John C. Breckinridge Southern Democratic ticket of 1860, but now uncompromisingly Unionist and brigadier-general of Massachusetts militia. A reckless and often unscrupulous man who could thrive amid chaos, Butler found the tracks of the Annapolis and Elk Ridge Railroad torn up for several miles west of the Maryland capital, on the way to Annapolis Junction and a meeting with the Washington Branch of the Baltimore and Ohio Railroad. He proceeded to direct rebuilding, aided by experienced railroaders whom Secretary of War Cameron borrowed from his home state's Pennsylvania Central Railroad. At noon on April 25, the 7th New York arrived in Washington by rail from Annapolis.

The 8th Massachusetts and the 1st Rhode Island soon followed, and then a stream of other regiments came from the North, including Elmer Ellsworth's New York Fire Zouaves.[15]

The coming of regiment after regiment helped nourish a change of mood in Maryland. So did a severe business decline in Baltimore following the mob action and the disruption of the city's rail connections. On April 27 Butler became commanding general of the Department of Annapolis, comprising the area twenty miles on each side of the Annapolis-Washington rail line. On May 4 the energetic Bay Stater occupied the Relay House, where the main line of the Baltimore and Ohio from the west joined the Washington Branch. A week later he put 1,000 troops on a train headed toward Washington, then cut the telegraph lines and doubled back to steam into Baltimore. Under heavy rain, his soldiers occupied the commanding eminence of Federal Hill. Butler took these latter steps on his own initiative and risked dangerous provocation, but in fact he cowed secessionists and encouraged Unionists through his boldness.[16]

Meanwhile Unionism asserted itself as dominant in central and western Maryland, where there were few slaves, and with Annapolis a turmoil of moving troops, the General Assembly met in central Maryland at Frederick. The combination of the sentiments of the Frederick area, the massing of Union troops in the eastern part of the state, and an exodus of pro-Southern militants southward and sometimes into the Confederate forces kept the legislative session relatively innocuous. The legislators called for an end to the war and recognition of the Confederacy, they objected to the military occupation of their state, but they discouraged violent interference with the Federal troops and did not move to secede.

Maryland would still bear watching, but for the time being both the state and the Federal capital were safe enough under the guns of the Union volunteers. By the night of May 23–24, the authorities in Washington felt strong enough to respond to Virginia's ratification of secession on the 23rd by sending troops south across the Potomac, for Elmer Ellsworth to meet his death, but to occupy Alexandria and the Arlington heights opposite Washington and thus further assure the safety of the capital.[17]

## CONTENTIOUS MISSOURI: A FAILURE FOR BOTH SIDES

Because volunteers crowded into Washington from all over the North, including some states of the upper Mississippi Valley, to give the Union overwhelming military strength in the capital and in Maryland, and because there could be no thought of compromise where the protection of the Federal capital was concerned, the flexing of Federal muscles was the most appropriate, indeed the only possible response to secessionism in Maryland. In the border slave states farther west, where there was considerably less Unionist muscle, a more cautious and conciliatory response to Southern leanings seems to have been the better method of nurturing loyalty, or so the contrasting experiences of Missouri and Kentucky apparently would indicate.

Missouri and Kentucky each weighed about as much in population as Massachusetts, with some 1,200,000 people in each.[18] Both occupied positions of great strategic importance. Kentucky aligned with the seceding states would award the Confederacy the Ohio River as a frontier; block the passage of the Mississippi, Tennessee, and Cumberland Rivers into the South; and narrow the Midwest of the Union itself to a thin corridor, made thinner yet by much Southern sentiment in the lower counties of Ohio, Indiana, and Illinois. Missouri in the Confederacy would carry with it the great commercial city of St. Louis and flank southern Illinois, surely stimulating the already considerable pro-Southern feelings of Illinois's "Egypt."

Both these border states balanced delicately between North and South before Fort Sumter, and the Confederacy could hope that rather than join in coercion of their sister slave states they would follow Virginia's example and depart the Union after Lincoln's call for militia. In Missouri, Governor Claiborne Jackson had risen to power as a proslavery opponent of the now deceased old Unionist, the increasingly antislavery ally of Andrew Jackson, Senator Thomas Hart Benton. Claiborne Jackson's leadership of the Stephen A. Douglas Democrats in Missouri made Douglas's carrying the state in the Presidential election of 1860 a somewhat deceptive suggestion of Missouri's tilt toward Unionism. The governor moved closer to secessionism with every turn of the screw of the national crisis, and the General Assembly moved in such a way that it remained within hailing distance of his changing positions.

As other states passed ordinances of secession, Governor Jackson persuaded the legislature to call a convention to consider Missouri's relations with the Union, and the General Assembly itself also urged support for the South and resistance to invasion. The voters, however, had chosen an overwhelmingly Unionist convention, which declared by a margin of 89 to 1 that Missouri should stay in the Union and thereupon adjourned on March 22 before the coming explosion in Charleston harbor could project flames westward. On the other hand, the convention also voted 89 to 6 that national troops should be evacuated from Southern forts, and the governor and his fellow secessionists — for such he now was — hoped that in this anti-coercion sentiment lay the leverage with which to pry Missouri out of the Union.[19]

Secessionists and anti-secessionists both hastened to organize military companies. As the units marched and countermarched both sides looked toward the 60,000 muskets, 90,000 pounds of powder, and 1,500,000 ball cartridges in the U.S. Arsenal at St. Louis as the resources that might determine military supremacy in the state and then the state's allegiance.[20] The focus on the arsenal brought to public attention the thin, nervous, red-headed, Connecticut-born captain of the 2nd United States Infantry who commanded its garrison, Nathaniel Lyon. Lyon's outspoken Union sentiments won him the close friendship of the powerful Blair family's representative in the clan's native state, Republican Congressman Francis Preston Blair (Jr.), son of the old Kitchen Cabinet member and brother of Lincoln's Postmaster General. Congressman Blair's support helped Lyon arrange to have Illinois militia descend on the St. Louis arsenal on the night of April 26 and hurry away many of the munitions to the safety of the Illinois capital at Springfield.

Governor Jackson accompanied his angry rejection of Lincoln's call for troops with a summons to the General Assembly to meet in special session, in the process declaring his now confirmed secessionist sentiments without equivocation. Angered by the incident at the arsenal, he arranged to procure munitions from both Northern and Southern sources — some came from as far as Baton Rouge — for militia assembling at Camp Jackson, in Lindell's Grove on the outskirts of St. Louis. Camp Jackson was not well located to defend itself; the intentions of its commanding officer, Brigadier-General Daniel M. Frost, Missouri State Militia, were much more ambiguous than Governor Jackson's; and its armed men were far outnumbered by Unionist companies in the vicinity. The activities at the camp nevertheless aggravated Captain Lyon's nervousness.

One story has it that the captain toured the camp riding in a carriage and dressed in black bombazine skirts and a black veil. On May 10, encouraged again by Blair, Lyon surrounded the place with superior numbers and compelled its surrender. This action was almost certainly more provocative than necessary, and its effect was bound to be to push toward open secessionism some of the Missourians who hitherto shared the ambivalence of General Frost and indeed many of the soldiers of the camp. Worse, Lyon paraded his prisoners through St. Louis, a spectacle that precipitated a mob effort to rescue them, whereupon Lyon's troops fired into the mob. Twenty-eight persons were killed or mortally wounded and many more injured in the melee. Ethnic prejudices further inflamed this crisis; Lyon's Unionist militia included many Germans, and Missouri had been a center of the Know-Nothing movement.[21]

The legislature now empowered Governor Jackson to arm the state under his own command, with every cent in the treasury placed at his disposal and a loan of a million dollars authorized for the purpose. A former governor of the state (1852–1856) and Mexican War brigadier-general of volunteers, Sterling Price, recently the presiding officer of the Unionist state convention, now placed himself at Jackson's service out of exasperation at the bloodshed inflicted by Lyon and Blair. Price received Jackson's commission as major-general commanding the state forces. Frost remained committed to the same forces. While the secessionists of Missouri thus rallied and gained recruits, the Unionists fell into disharmony and bickering over the outrage caused by the precipitate actions of Lyon and Blair.

Brigadier-General William S. Harney, a sixty-one-year-old Louisianan who commanded the Military Department of the West for the Union, repaired to St. Louis and tried to avert civil war within Missouri by negotiating an agreement with General Price. Thereby Price declared he would use his forces only to maintain order in the state, and Harney pledged in return not to engage in military movements likely to create excitement or jealousy. This plan to keep the peace, avoid further inflaming of opinion, and give Unionism time to rally was consistent with the policy Lincoln earlier contemplated for the whole South, and with the policy the President was currently pursuing in Kentucky. But it led only to further confirmation that in distant Missouri the weaknesses of national strategic planning and of effective central power, such as helped nourish violence everywhere in this war, appeared in aggravated form. Lyon and Frank Blair saw the Harney-Price agreement as consigning Missouri to the secessionists. They already felt suspicious of Harney because of his Deep South origins, and Blair used his influence in Washington and the Republican Party to try to inspire doubts about Harney's loyalty and competence in the President's mind. Blair eventually extracted from Lincoln authorization to remove Harney from command if an emergency arose in which removal became indispensable. Blair did not require much of a pretext to invoke this power, on May 31.

As brigadier-general of United States Volunteers, Lyon succeeded Harney as Federal commander in Missouri. On June 11 he and Frank Blair met Governor Jackson and General Price at the Planters' House in St. Louis and demanded agreement that Federal forces might move freely throughout the state. As Lyon and Blair anticipated, Jackson and Price refused to accept this nullification of the Harney-Price agreement, and the truce was off. Lyon raged that before he would make a single concession to rebels, he would see every man, woman, and child in Missouri buried. His policies proved to tend strongly toward that result. The conference adjourned in anger, and Governor Jackson called for 50,000 militia. Confederate troops from Arkansas, Louisiana, and Texas marched into Missouri to reinforce Price.

Already the emotions stirred up by armed clashes around St. Louis had touched off outbreaks of guerrilla war here and there across Missouri. Unionist neighbor and secessionist neighbor began taking arms against each other. At the beginning of July, armed rebels reported to number 2,700 drove much of the Unionist population out of Knox and Lewis Counties, near and on the Missouri River in the northeast part of the state. On the opposing side, antislavery Kansas Jayhawkers thirsty for revenge since the Kansas troubles of the 1850s began to raid Southern sympathizers in western Missouri. The Unionists elected a state convention that met under the protection of Lyon's troops in Jefferson City in July and declared the state offices vacant, named Hamilton R. Gamble governor in place of Jackson on July 31, and moved the capital from its meeting place to the safer confines of St. Louis.[22]

Lyon marched southward to meet Price in battle. Despite his inferior numbers, the hotheaded Yankee courted and found his fight at Wilson's Creek, southwest of Springfield, on August 10. There Lyon lost his life, and without his leadership the Unionist forces had to retreat. Nevertheless, though outnumbered 11,600 to 5,400, the Federals extracted 1,184 casualties from the secessionists in exchange for 1,235 of their own; they killed 257 and wounded 900 while losing 223 killed and 721 wounded themselves, the difference being in the missing (291 Federals, only twenty-seven Confederates).[23] The secessionists were hurt too badly to pursue the Unionist retreat, and the Unionists seemingly remained in control of the greater part of the area of the state.

Still, Claiborne Jackson was able to gather a remnant of the General Assembly at Neosho in the far southwest, where on October 31 this body, though lacking a quorum in both houses, voted Missouri out of the Union. Jackson continued to serve as governor over the rump secessionist legislature. And the Union control of most of the state was altogether superficial. All along the cotton-growing bottomlands of the Missouri River, secessionism refused to die. In St. Louis itself, despite a workingmen's population largely German, Irish, and free-state in origin, the leading families proclaimed their secessionism with impunity and sometimes flew rebel flags. Hardly anywhere in the state were individual Union soldiers or small Union detachments safe from secessionist guerrillas — nor were Unionist families safe, nor secessionist families safe from guerrillas on the Union side.

Thus, in Missouri the absence of consistent, purposeful, and rational rather than impulsive Federal direction of the effort to hold the state for the Union, combined with not much less impulsive conduct and leadership on the opposite side, along with the ways in which distance from Washington and Richmond worsened the capitals' tendency to do no better than muddle through, all led to increasingly unrestrained and indiscriminate violence, perhaps the most promiscuous of the entire violent war. It was not that sectional animosities ran hotter in Missouri than elsewhere; the ability of slaveowners and antislavery men to coexist in the state in relative peace before the war would argue in the contrary direction. The violence of Missouri came to epitomize and carry to some of its worst excesses the violence of the Civil War mainly because the failure of rational strategy and control was even more marked there than elsewhere.

The nadir of Missouri's accumulating chaos was to come in the summer of 1863. On August 3, Brigadier-General Thomas Ewing, Jr., United States Volunteers, commanding the District of the Border in western Missouri, reported to the Department of Missouri that half the farmers in the western tier of counties had previously entered Confederate service, and that of this group half were either dead or still with the Confederate forces while the other half had come home. But the latter had found too much disorder to resume their normal lives, so many of them had become guerrillas. As such they had driven Unionists either out of the district altogether or to the protection of Ewing's posts. Now the guerrillas were extending their depredations further into Missouri and into Kansas. Because some two-thirds of the families still occupying farms in Ewing's district were actively aiding the guerrillas, he proposed that the worst offending families should be forcibly evacuated to a colony in Arkansas, albeit he was willing to have the government temporarily assist them with supplies.[24]

Receiving no contradiction from his superiors, Ewing issued General Orders, No. 10 on August 18:

> . . . officers will arrest, and send . . . for punishment, all men (and all women not heads of families) who willfully aid and encourage guerrillas, with a written statement of the names and residences of such persons and of the proof against them. They will discriminate as carefully as possible between those who are compelled, by threats or fears, to aid the rebels and those who aid them from disloyal motives. The wives and children of known guerrillas, and also women who are heads of families and are willfully engaged in aiding guerrillas, will be notified by such officers to remove out of the district and out of the State of Missouri forthwith. They will be permitted to take, unmolested, their stock, provisions, and household goods. If they fail to remove promptly, they will be sent by such officers, under escort, to Kansas City for shipment

south, with their clothes and such necessary household furniture and provision as may be worth removing.[25]

Union soldiers had in fact already rounded up some secessionist women, upon some of whom a prison building in Kansas City had collapsed, killing several women of the border-area Quantrill family and its connections. Their kinsman William Clarke Quantrill, holding a Confederate States commission as colonel despite the fact that he had participated ambiguously in the proslavery-antislavery border quarrels since 1859, sought vengeance by raiding Lawrence, Kansas on August 21 at the head of nearly 500 guerrillas, burning and looting and killing about 150 unarmed men and boys.[26]

With violence thus begetting violence, General Ewing responded to the sack of Lawrence by issuing General Orders, No. 11 on August 25. He now ordered the full evacuation of Bates, Cass, and Jackson Counties and the northern half of Vernon County, which were supposed to have sustained Quantrill's raiders, with the exception of Independence and a few other settlements. Those residents who could persuade the commander of the nearest military post of their Unionism might be issued certificates permitting them to remain within the state if they moved to military posts. The rest had to go. Hay and grain found in the area after the evacuation would be destroyed or taken to military posts to be credited to Unionists. General Orders, No. 11 may have turned 20,000 people out of their homes.[27]

The vigorous action of Nathaniel Lyon and Francis P. Blair at the outset of the war had kept most of Missouri officially under Union control, but only at the cost of embroiling the state in its own miniature civil war, waged with the peculiar viciousness and exceptional violence of a guerrilla conflict that blurred the distinction between combatants and noncombatants and also between soldiers and bandits. Out of Quantrill's gang came Frank and Jesse James and Cole, James, John, and Robert Younger. In Missouri, the violence of the Civil War became most closely intertwined with the quintessentially American violence of the frontier — both strands of violence grievously abetted by weakness and blunders among the leaders and institutions supposed to provide law and order.

## NEUTRALIST KENTUCKY

Such or worse might have been the fate of Kentucky, for initially this Commonwealth probably harbored more pro-Confederate sentiment than Missouri, and Kentucky had its equivalent to Governor Claiborne Jackson in Governor Beriah Magoffin. But Lincoln cared especially deeply for the state of his birth; and caring, he planned and thought for Kentucky, insisting that Unionism there have a coherence, a rationality, and a restraint never accorded to Missouri. These elements saved the Bluegrass State from the worst of Missouri's ill fortunes.

Kentucky's closest ties of kinship were with Virginia and North Carolina, from which its population had largely been drawn, and to which Kentucky felt strong ties of culture and shared values. In particular, Kentucky was self-consciously the daughter of Virginia. Even today, the visitor to Kentucky will find a Southernness and a nostalgia for the Confederacy unmatched in any other of the border states.

Still, Kentucky was also the state of the great compromiser Henry Clay, and it had gone for the Constitutional Unionist John Bell in the 1860 Presidential election. It was characteristic of the state that when Governor Magoffin tried to secure the call of a secession convention, the General Assembly called instead for a gathering of all the border states to consider how to repair the Union. Yet in Kentucky as in Missouri, the issue of coercion of states farther south carried grave dangers for Unionism; border-state citizens who would not themselves contribute to the disruption of the Union were ready nevertheless to oppose maintaining the Union by coercion.[28]

Governor Magoffin turned down a request for Kentucky troops issued by Jefferson Davis even as he rejected Lincoln's call, though without similar venom. He continued to urge a convention to consider the Commonwealth's relations with the Union, however, and for a time he allowed Confederate recruiting agents to roam the state. (The latter policy was an especially bad mistake, because after Unionist pressure compelled Magoffin to reverse it, then nobody trusted him.) Kentucky's anti-coercionism came to the fore when Magoffin called the legislature into special session after Fort Sumter, and on May 20 both houses resolved to remain neutral in the gathering civil war, taking no part in it except as mediators and friends to the belligerents. No policy could have accorded more closely with the mixed feelings engendered by Kentucky's Southern heritage and the legacy of Henry Clay. Kentuckians gladly proceeded to act as though their state was Switzerland, maintaining their commercial ties across both their northern and southern borders. Still, with Lincoln careful to apply no heavyhanded pressure of the sort that might boomerang, Congressional elections in June chose Unionists, albeit sometimes ambiguous ones, in nine of Kentucky's ten districts; only the First Congressional District, in the extreme west along the Cumberland

and Tennessee Rivers and much in the political orbit of Tennessee, chose a secessionist Democrat.[29]

Under the neutrality policy, Kentucky became a highway down which Northern goods traveled to the Confederacy during the spring and summer of 1861 even as the armies gathered for mortal combat elsewhere: clothing, shoes, provisions, even munitions crossed the Commonwealth. After the Federal Congress assembled in July, its Republican leaders with Lyon-like spirit attempted to legislate a stop to this commerce, but Lincoln saw to it that the Treasury administered with liberality a permit system for continued trade through Kentucky.

The Federal President was not about to behave toward Kentucky as Nathaniel Lyon and Frank Blair had behaved in Missouri, and fortunately for his policy there were no Lyons or Blairs in the Bluegrass State to force his hand. Instead, Lincoln made Kentucky a test of his original policy toward the South, of his conviction that an absence of aggressive action by the Federal government could heal wounds and nourish in time a resurgent Unionism. He believed that to lose Kentucky with its strategic location on the Ohio and the Mississippi and its possible influence on the other border states "is nearly the same as to lose the whole game."[30] He responded to the proclamation of neutrality by assuring the Commonwealth's old Whig and now Unionist Senator Garret Davis that he intended no attack upon the state but rather the defense of it; that he contemplated no invasion of Kentucky unless driven to it by forcible resistance to Federal law and no military operations across Kentucky's territory; that he regretted having had to march troops across Maryland, but had done so only out of the necessity to protect Washington.[31]

As the forbearing President surely recognized, Kentucky could not go on behaving like Switzerland indefinitely; but it would not be Lincoln who gave it the push that might topple it off the fence in the wrong direction. Kentucky was embedded in the heart of the troubled United States, and individual Kentuckians felt drawn either to the Union or to the Confederacy. Sympathizers with both sides organized military companies. Governor Magoffin requested special appropriations for the militia and a firmer control of it for himself and the state adjutant general, Major-General Simon Boliver Buckner, who was in correspondence with Confederate leaders. The legislature reacted by shuffling the militia to put it under the control of Union men and requiring an oath of allegiance to the Union from all its members. The loyalty oath sent Buckner and part of the militia southward into Confederate service, but disgust at this conduct stimulated Unionism among Kentuckians who stayed home. Lincoln sent Robert Anderson, a Kentuckian and from

May 15 a brigadier-general United States Army as a reward for his conduct at Sumter, to Cincinnati across the Ohio River to recruit Kentuckians thence, in his capacity from May 28 as commanding general of the Department of Kentucky.[32] Anderson, however, decided on the scene that he had best recruit no Kentucky regiments so that he could continue giving no affront to the neutrality policy. Nevertheless, Anderson's decision did not prevent another Kentuckian in U.S. service, Lieutenant William Nelson of the Navy, from distributing government arms among the Unionist military companies inside the state.

To maintain his forbearance, Lincoln had to resist considerable pressure from the governors and other Republican politicians of the states just north of Kentucky, as well as from Congress. But it was eventually Confederate leadership that first lost patience with Kentucky. In early September, Federal forces gathered around Cairo, Illinois and St. Louis with what some Confederates thought was the intention of pushing down the Mississippi River. Major-General Leonidas Polk, Protestant Episcopal Bishop of Louisiana and from July 12 the temporary commander of Confederate Department No. 2 along the river, thereupon concluded on his own initiative that he must occupy Columbus, Kentucky. He wanted to control its high bluffs dominating passage of the river. President Davis naturally questioned Polk's risky inclination, but he yielded to the general's plea of military necessity, and on September 3 Confederate troops entered Kentucky and then on the 4th Columbus. The response of the Kentucky General Assembly was a resolution of September 11 calling on Governor Magoffin to demand the immediate withdrawal of the Confederates and to seek Federal aid and protection. When Magoffin vetoed the resolution, the legislature passed it over his veto. When the Confederates failed to move out, on September 18 the legislature created a military force to expel them. Magoffin persisted in his increasingly hopeless pro-Southern efforts until at last he resigned the governorship, to be succeeded immediately on August 18, 1862 by James F. Robinson, a conservative Unionist.[33]

By this time the United States had also responded to the Confederate invasion of Kentucky. Brigadier-General Ulysses S. Grant, U.S.V., commanding the District of Southeastern Missouri with headquarters at Cairo, Illinois, like Polk acting on his own initiative, sent troops into Paducah, Kentucky on September 6.[34]

Nevertheless, Lincoln's policy of patience had been given enough time to work. Kentucky's Unionism had ripened, and the insult of the Confederate invasion served to align the state firmly with the Union cause. Southern sympathizers remained numerous in the Commonwealth, and Lincoln's subsequent advance toward emancipation of the slaves reinforced Kentucky's misgivings. Occasional arrests of pro-Southern Kentucky leaders added further doubts. Union Democrats in Kentucky often had to go out of their way in denunciations of the Lincoln administration to prove that while loyal to the Union, they were not Lincoln Republicans. But unlike Missouri, Kentucky did not become a battleground of guerrilla depredations and reprisals, its economy functioned almost unimpaired for the further strengthening of the Union, and the Commonwealth was transformed from a highway across which Northern goods flowed to the Confederacy (although such traffic never completely ceased) into the highway for Union armies to march toward the Confederate granary of Tennessee.

## WESTERN VIRGINIA: SECESSION WITHIN SECESSION

Up the Ohio River from Kentucky, in western Virginia, rash leadership out of tune with much of the population, abetted again by muddled Federal policy, demonstrated once more its capacity to promote guerrilla war ruinous to any possibility that the area might make a strong positive contribution to the larger effort to save the Union.

In the Virginia secession convention, the only core of unconditional adherence to the Union came from the extreme northwest of the Commonwealth, from the delegates who lived on or near the Ohio River and especially in or near the panhandle reaching far northward between the states of Ohio and Pennsylvania. Economically and culturally, the northwestern Virginia counties were closer to Ohio and southwestern Pennsylvania than to eastern Virginia. Their opposition to secession was not surprising. Of their delegates to the Virginia convention, twenty-four voted against secession, only five voted for it, and two abstained.[35]

Virginia indeed had long been plagued by its own sectionalism, with the western areas complaining that they paid disproportionately high taxes (property in slaves, of which they held little, was favored by Virginia tax laws) in return for disproportionately few internal improvements. The western counties grumbled also about Virginia's exceedingly slow progress during the first half of the nineteenth century toward universal white manhood suffrage and popular election of the principal state officers. A generation before 1860, the sectional rift within Virginia might have aligned the Valley of Virginia and the southwestern counties along with the northwest against Tidewater and Piedmont. In the middle decades of the century, however, extension of the suffrage and of popularly elected officeholding, more generous internal improvements, and most importantly, a westward advance of slaveholding in the Commonwealth, carried the Valley and the southwest into closer ties with eastern Virginia, so that by 1861 only the extreme northwestern counties voted against secession.

The extreme northwest felt different enough from the rest of Virginia, however, that some of its leaders both opposed secession and believed they should use the occasion to carve out a new state. After the Virginia convention passed the secession ordinance, mass meetings of protest took place in many communities in the northwest. A principal organizer of the protest movement, John S. Carlile, pushed through one of the meetings the Clarksburg Resolutions calling for a new convention to meet at Wheeling in the panhandle on May 13, to determine northwestern Virginia's course of action in the secession emergency. Delegates from twenty-four northwestern and three Valley counties attended the First Wheeling Convention, although it was so hastily assembled that it was more a mass meeting than a conclave of duly elected delegates. At this gathering, Carlile attempted to move rapidly toward creating a new state, but more cautious leaders argued that northwestern Virginia should at least await the outcome of the statewide referendum on secession to be held on May 23. Consequently, the convention resolved that if the Virginia voters approved secession, an election on June 4 should choose delegates to a Second Wheeling Convention.

The Virginia voters of course approved secession. With due allowance for the fact that voting on a *fait accompli* might have skewed the results, the referendum showed that secession sentiment reached so far westward in Virginia that the project of carving out of Unionist territory a state large enough to be viable was extremely dubious. Of the fifty counties that later became the new state of West Virginia, twenty-five, comprising nearly two-thirds of the future state's area and holding 40 percent of its population, voted in favor of secession. Secession captured as much as 40 percent of the vote in some of the Unionist counties.[36] Nevertheless, Carlile and other Unionist leaders continued to labor for the divorcement of the northwestern counties from the Commonwealth of Virginia.

They received indispensable assistance from the State of Ohio and the Union Army. Governor William Dennison of Ohio, a Republican, believed that to assure the safety of his own state from raids and invasion, the military boundary of the Confederacy must be pushed back from the Ohio River immediately, preferably at least as far as the crests of the Alleghenies. Dennison named as major-general of Ohio Volunteers the second-ranking graduate of the West Point class of 1842, one of the most promising of the young

Regular Army officers who had distinguished themselves in the Mexican War, more recently a member of a three-man American military commission to Europe to observe the Crimean War, and more recently still president of the Ohio and Mississippi Railroad — thirty-five-year-old George Brinton McClellan. Ohio had a large enough quota of troops for Lincoln's army to be entitled to a Federal major-generalship, and the War Department soon granted this commission to McClellan as well; he would rank from May 14 and be second in seniority only to Winfield Scott. On May 13 McClellan received command of the Department of the Ohio, comprising Ohio, Indiana, Illinois, the western third of Pennsylvania, and upon Governor Dennison's urging, western Virginia as well.[37] Dennison prodded McClellan to use his Ohio regiments to go to the assistance of Unionist Virginia troops by invading western Virginia. After Virginia ratified the secession ordinance on May 23, General Scott added lukewarm support to Dennison's pleading.

McClellan in fact was concocting a grandiose scheme for the penetration of Virginia all the way to Richmond via the Kanawha River valley. In response to Dennison's activities and now with Scott's apparent endorsement, McClellan launched his invasion of western Virginia on May 26. He accompanied the move with a proclamation in a style that was to become familiar. "Soldiers," he began: "You are ordered to cross the frontier & enter upon the soil of Virginia. Your mission is to restore peace & confidence, to protect the majesty of the law & to rescue our brethren from the grasp of armed traitors."[38] On June 3, his vanguard under Brigadier-General Thomas A. Morris, Indiana Volunteers, won the first of the victories from which McClellan was to draw credit and a rapidly growing fame, by driving a Confederate force from the town of Philippi.

McClellan sent Morris onward to confront the main Confederate force in western Virginia, gathering under the command of Brigadier-General Robert S. Garnett on Laurel Hill to block the approach to the Cheat River valley. McClellan planned to turn Garnett out of his position by moving south of him while Morris held him in place. If McClellan could reach Beverly southeast of Laurel Hill, he would cut Garnett's line of communications. "Soldiers! I have heard that there was danger here. I fear now but one thing — that you will not find foemen worthy of your steel. I know that I can rely upon you," McClellan announced as he took personal command of the turning force.[39]

Morris with about 4,000 men was facing Garnett with 4,000 or 5,000. McClellan had about 8,000 with which to dislodge about 1,300 Confederates under Lieutenant-Colonel John Pegram, 20th Virginia Infantry, who barred the road to Beverly at Rich Mountain. To deal with Pegram, McClellan accepted a plan advanced by Brigadier-General William S. Rosecrans, U.S.A., for Rosecrans with about 2,000 men to make a difficult march over poor or nonexistent roads to get into Pegram's rear. This plan worked, and McClellan also allowed Rosecrans's 2,000 to fight a battle that badly mauled Pegram while McClellan and his remaining 6,000 awaited the outcome — curious conduct in a general who had come to share danger. The Federal victory caused Garnett to abandon Laurel Hill, and Morris pursued him briskly; the Federals killed Garnett himself in an action at Carrick's Ford on July 13. McClellan was too busy writing dispatches in praise of his exploits to join in the pursuit with equal briskness, or the Confederate forces might all have been trapped and captured. Nevertheless, northwestern Virginia was now controlled by the Union Army. Confederate Brigadier-General Henry A. Wise briefly checked another of McClellan's columns, moving up the Kanawha Valley under Brigadier-General Jacob D. Cox, U.S.V., in an action on July 17 at Scarey (or Scary) Creek; but Wise was already under orders to withdraw from the Kanawha, and Cox entered Charleston, Virginia on July 25.[40]

McClellan's campaign assured Union control of the Baltimore and Ohio Railroad across northwestern Virginia; it denied the Confederacy the resources of the area, notably the salt of the Kanawha Valley; and it made feasible the idea of detaching the northwest from the rest of Virginia despite the plan's political dubiety.

The Second Wheeling Convention met on June 11 just as McClellan's victories were commencing. Delegates from thirty-two northwestern counties and two near Washington, Alexandria and Fairfax, agreed first to take a step that might provide an essential constitutional preliminary toward carving a new state from Virginia, and that might also serve to offer a counter-attraction to the Confederate state government among all Virginia Unionists. Article IV, Section III, paragraph 1 of the Constitution of the United States provides that "no new State shall be formed or erected within the Jurisdiction of any other State ... without the Consent of the Legislatures concerned as well as of Congress." The convention began shaping a semblance of a Virginia government that might eventually grant the necessary permission for a new state. On June 19, the Wheeling delegates declared all the offices of the Commonwealth of Virginia vacant. They then elected new officers with loyalty to the Union a major qualification. Francis H. Pierpoint (who sometimes signed his name Pierpont) became governor; John S. Carlile and Waitman T. Willey were elected to the U.S. Senate, which recognized them as the proper holders of Virginia's seats. Other northwesterners were seated in the House of Representatives. A Reorganized Government of

Virginia began to function at Wheeling, representing the parts of the state under Union control.[41]

The Second Wheeling Convention continued to meet alongside a new General Assembly. The convention proved far from united in support of the second major project placed before it, the proposed dismemberment of Virginia. Opponents attempted to thwart the plan by means of stratagems that included absurdly large boundaries for the new state, to take in numerous counties that were unquestionably secessionist. The combination of this tactic with the desire of the dismemberment advocates themselves to have a state large enough to be viable produced a somewhat grotesque compromise assigning to the proposed new state a number of counties reaching well eastward beyond the core of Unionist strength along the Ohio. On August 20, the convention resolved that the designated counties should be formed into the State of Kanawha. On October 4, the people of the projected state were to vote on the question of dismemberment and to select delegates to a constitutional convention.

Dismemberment would be decided upon by the whole vote cast, not by the votes county by county. Thus the higher population of the extreme northwestern Unionist district would offset the fact that about half the counties and more than half the area of the proposed new state favored the Confederacy. Any contretemps was ensured against also by the circumstance that only Unionists recognized the election as legitimate and voted. So dismemberment carried on October 4 by a vote of 18,408 to 781, but in an area that had had about 52,000 voters in 1860.[42] Six secessionist counties cast no votes at all, and eleven cast fewer than 1,000 ballots altogether.[43] In the constitutional convention, the juggling of state boundaries persisted, finally giving forty-four counties unconditionally to the new state and seven more if their voters ratified the constitution. Six of these seven counties, located in the secessionist Shenandoah Valley, eventually joined the new state, by the suspicious referendum tallies of 76-0 in Hardy County, 181-0 in Pendleton, 75-9 in Hampshire, 362-0 in Morgan, 665-2 in Berkeley, and 238-2 in Jefferson, counties that had had more than 11,000 voters in 1860. In Frederick County in the Shenandoah Valley, centering on Winchester, the new statehood movement was too transparent a fraud to prevail even under such circumstances, and the referendum was dropped.[44]

The constitutional convention, meeting on November 26 and also at Wheeling, chose to call the new state not Kanawha but West Virginia. On April 4, 1862, the people of the designated counties ratified a new state constitution by a vote giving off as suspicious an odor as the earlier one on dismemberment, 18,862 to 514. The legislature of the Reorganized Government at

Wheeling on May 13 consented in the name of Virginia to the formation of the new state, thus fulfilling the form of the U.S. Constitution's requirement for creating one state from another. The consenting General Assembly, however, had only thirty-five members in its House of Delegates and ten in its Senate, although the Virginia Constitution provided for 152 and fifty members, respectively.[45]

By this time, furthermore, another obstacle to West Virginia statehood had arisen in the form of the slavery question. An effort to include gradual emancipation in the new constitution failed because many northwestern Virginia Unionists were by no means antislavery. When it became apparent that the Republican U.S. Congress was antislavery enough by the spring of 1862 that it would compel West Virginia to adopt an emancipation plan as a condition for admission to the Union, some of the most influential Unionists abruptly reversed themselves on the whole issue of creating a new state, John S. Carlile among them. A conservative strict-construction constitutionalist, Carlile could no more accept Federal dictation of the provisions of a state constitution than he could swallow the disruption of the Federal Union. Rather than agree to what he interpreted as a perversion of the U.S. Constitution by Congressional dictation of the internal policies of a state — with the United States also, as he saw it, repudiating Republican campaign promises of 1860 not to interfere with slavery in the states where it existed — he turned against his own brainchild, the new state.[46]

Nevertheless, West Virginia statehood had accumulated sufficient momentum that it continued to progress. The state constitutional convention, having foreseen the possibility of a Congressional demand to abolish slavery, had made provision to reconvene in such an event. Congress accepted Virginia Senator Willey's suggestion that West Virginia statehood be approved conditionally, subject to approval of gradual emancipation by a constitutional convention and a majority of voters participating in an election on the question. West Virginia completed these conditions, and on April 20, 1863, President Lincoln proclaimed the state admitted to the Union as of the following June 20. The Pierpoint government vacated Wheeling to set up shop in Alexandria, continuing to claim to be the government of Virginia.[47]

That claim, on which Virginia's consent to the formation of West Virginia rested, was so feeble that Republican Congressman Thaddeus Stevens of Pennsylvania remarked in Congress: "I say then that we may admit West Virginia as a new state, not by virtue of any provisions of the Constitution but under the absolute power which the laws of war give us. I shall vote for this bill upon that theory and that alone, for I will not stultify myself by supposing that we have any warrant in the Constitution for this proceeding."[48] After receiving the opinions of a divided Cabinet on both the constitutionality and the expediency of West Virginia statehood, Lincoln accompanied his consent with a reluctant statement of approval:

> The division of a State is dreaded as a precedent. But a measure made expedient by a war, is no precedent for times of peace. It is said that the admission of West-Virginia, is secession, and tolerated only because it is our secession. Well, if we call it by that name, there is still difference enough between secession against the constitution, and secession in favor of the constitution.[49]

There was good reason for the President and Congress to feel concern about the methods that led West Virginia to statehood, apart from the constitutional niceties. Even less effort toward rational, moderating direction from Washington had gone into West Virginia than into Missouri. Here was yet another instance of the war's running out of control, creating its own momentum, with the predictable unhappy consequences. In much of the new state, the Confederacy in fact dominated throughout the war, all the more firmly supported by a local population resentful of attempts to alter its state allegiance against its will. Except in the Ohio River counties, the new state could enforce its writ only under the bayonets of the Union Army. Not only could there have been no West Virginia without military victories such as McClellan won in the late spring and early summer of 1861; it remained true that except along the Ohio River the Unionist state government and Unionist citizens had no safety but in the immediate vicinity of the Army. Confederate sympathies that were intensified by the highhanded dismemberment of Virginia threw up yet another guerrilla conflict, wracking West Virginia much as the similar guerrilla conflict, similarly precipitated, devastated Missouri. Most of West Virginia went throught the Civil War not as an asset to the Union but as a troublesome battleground, while the Unionist Ohio River counties struggled to cope with the tide of refugees fleeing to their sanctuary from the interior.

## MOBILIZING THE UNION

At Washington, the assembling legions of the North bivouacked in the Capitol and among the display cases in the Patent Office until camps could be prepared for them in the hills around the city. Four days after the first crossing of Federal troops over the Potomac into Virginia, the War Department named Brigadier-General Irvin McDowell, U.S.A., a soldier with a good

Mexican War record and the advantage of recent military study in France, to be commanding officer of the newly created Department of Northeastern Virginia. McDowell would organize the gathering regiments into a field force for the defense of the capital and further invasion of Virginia.[50]

Critics of Lincoln's preparations for war could say not only that the three-months term for which he had called out 75,000 militia was too short, but also that the number of troops called was too small — too small to contend with a Confederacy that immediately promised to mobilize 100,000 men with implications of going on to enlist still more, and too small to tap the immense patriotic enthusiasm of the North while such emotion was at its height in the weeks just after Fort Sumter. In this instance, however, the Union government showed better strategic judgment and planning than appeared on the surface.

From everywhere in the North, the state governors reported to Washington that they were overwhelmed with enlistments far beyond the quotas assigned them, and they pleaded with the War Department to accept more troops. With all the Northern states competing in recruiting drives and competing also to buy the equipment for more regiments than the Federal War Department had requisitioned, it added a frenzy of chaos that private individuals and organizations also joined in the scramble to recruit and supply troops, out of a mixture of patriotic motives and ambition to organize units in order to be able to command them. (Naturally, the same sort of thing was occurring in the Confederacy.) But given the limited bureaucratic resources of the War Department in particular and the Federal government in general, there was no alternative to this pandemonium; while out of the chaos there came a burgeoning army, and Lincoln was willing to abide the chaos to get as many troops as the Army could reasonably absorb. In fact, Lincoln did not stop with accepting 75,000 men.

As soon as the President had gauged the national response to his first call and knew that he would have broad support for bold actions, he moved toward further enlargement of the Army. Without legal authority, but trusting that Congress would uphold him after it met, he called on May 3 for 42,034 volunteers to serve not for three months but for three years, unless sooner discharged. At the same time he enlarged the Regular Army by 22,714 men and the Navy by 18,000. On May 6 Secretary of War Cameron suggested to the governors that all regiments accepted hereafter be mustered into Federal service for the three-year term.[51] On July 1, on the eve of the assembling of Congress for its special session, Cameron reported to the President on the condition of the Army, as Lincoln prepared to report to Congress. By that time, the Secretary could tell Lincoln that 310,000 men were under arms. Eighty thousand of them were three-months troops soon to be disbanded, who had, however, in their short service made Washington secure so that Congress could meet there safely and could deliberate in a far calmer atmosphere and with a much clearer conception of the military situation than if Lincoln had called an immediate session in April.

Meanwhile, 230,000 soldiers were already enlisted for three years. Although Lincoln's extralegal call of May 3 had been for only forty regiments, 208 regiments had already been accepted under the call, of which 153 were in active service and the remaining fifty-five were nearly ready to take the field.[52] On July 4, Lincoln asked Congress to "place at the control of the government . . . at least four hundred thousand men, and four hundred millions of dollars." Congress soon approved all the extraordinary measures Lincoln had taken and authorized the enlistment of 500,000 men.

"One of the greatest perplexities of the government," Lincoln told Congress, "is to avoid receiving troops faster than it can provide for them."[53] This perplexity goes far to explain the much criticized instances of the War Department's refusing to accept certain of the troop units offered by Northern governors and citizens. Yet critics often complained not only that Lincoln's government was failing to accept troops as fast as they were offered, but also that suitable accommodations and equipment were not immediately available for those it did accept. How a government that had not maintained an army of much above 16,000 was to house and equip immediately a force of 230,000 and more has never been explained. Surely preparations for such an army could not have been made between secession and the attack on Fort Sumter, without precipitating the civil war that both Buchanan and Lincoln were trying to avoid. Surely the preparations could not have been made before secession, when Southern members still exercised much of the leadership in Congress.

In both of the twentieth-century World Wars, the U.S. government delayed the expansion of the Army, the full mobilization of the National Guard, and the extensive application of the draft for several months until camps and barracks could be prepared, and at that there were many complaints about inadequate accommodations. In the Civil War, the emergency requirement to defend Washington and to match the Confederate forces gathering not across the oceans but a few miles from the capital would permit no preparatory delay. In the haste to equip an army and the confusion of competing Federal, state, and private agencies contracting for supplies, some bad contracts were drawn — often by Simon Cameron's political favorites — and many inferior tents and uniforms were issued. "But the troops were clothed and rescued from severe suffering," said Quartermaster-

General Brigadier-General Montgomery Cunningham Meigs, "and those who saw sentinels walking post in the capital of the United States in freezing weather in their drawers, without trousers or overcoats, will not blame the department for its efforts to clothe them, even in materials not quite so durable as army blue kersey."[54] A commission of scientists and physicians appointed by the President was working with the Medical Department of the Army to establish the best means of guarding the soldiers' health. Before the year was out, General McDowell would draw on his French experience to tell a committee of Congress: "There never was an army in the world that began to be supplied as well as ours is. I believe a French army of half the size of ours could be supplied with what we waste."[55]

## FIRST BULL RUN

As Commanding General of the Army, Winfield Scott proposed that the military strategy to subdue the Confederacy should be his Anaconda Plan. A tightening naval blockade should be combined with an eventual campaign down the Mississippi River, in the fall or winter when the Union troops would be better trained and the Southern climate would have moderated, to envelop the Confederacy in the coils of Northern power and strangle its economy. Lincoln was well disposed toward this plan if the war should prove to be prolonged, as he feared it would, and he had taken the first step to implement it, the proclamation of a naval blockade, just after the attack on Fort Sumter. But the Northern public and press naturally wanted swifter decisive action, and when Congress assembled in July the pressure to take the offensive before the three-months troops were discharged became intense.

The pressure was largely emotional, but it was not ill-judged. Lincoln himself was inclined toward a judicious gamble, that a prompt offensive stood a reasonable chance of preventing the Confederacy from consolidating itself in its new state of Virginia and its new capital at Richmond and might knock out its still questionable underpinnings in popular support. Events in western Virginia seemed to confirm that boldness might pay off. There a hit-and-run raid by a single regiment, Colonel Lew Wallace's 11th Indiana, in the direction of the town of Romney caused Brigadier-General Joseph E. Johnston, commanding the Confederate force at Harpers Ferry, the Army of the Shenandoah, to abandon that strategic place to a Federal column under Major-General Robert Patterson, Pennsylvania Volunteers, commanding the Military Departments of Pennsylvania, Delaware,

Maryland, and the District of Columbia, with a field force of about 18,000. Johnston retreated to Winchester.[56] Perhaps similar aggressiveness might score similar success against the larger Confederate force, the Army of the Potomac, concentrated under Brigadier-General Beauregard, the hero of Fort Sumter, at Manassas and along Bull Run not far southwest of Washington.[57]

General McDowell estimated Beauregard's force at about 25,000, who might be reinforced from others near at hand to 35,000. McDowell was prepared to march 30,000 troops, with 10,000 in reserve, against Beauregard, who actually had about 21,000 men.[58] If the Federal troops for the most part had scarcely had time for military training beyond what they might have learned in prewar volunteer companies, their adversaries were no better trained. McDowell would leave substantial forces behind to assure the protection of Washington and Baltimore. A gamble seemed appropriate. It heeded better than the Anaconda Plan the moral, political, and economic importance of the Confederate East, and the perception that a dramatic military victory in the East carried indeed the best promise of a short war.

Furthermore, the gamble almost worked. It nearly did so despite McDowell's ignoring what French military theory and practice should have taught him and mismanaging his march from Washington to Manassas. He failed to employ his cavalry properly as a screen and therefore repeatedly halted his infantry to permit reconnaissance missions. The continual pauses aggravated his inexperienced soldiers' propensities to break column for independent foraging. It required two and a half days for McDowell's force to march some twenty miles to Centreville, within striking distance of the enemy, by nightfall of July 18. At that, with another day to regroup McDowell should surely have been able to attack Beauregard on July 20. Instead, he hesitated and conducted unproductive further reconnaissance that delayed his attack until Sunday, July 21. Then he made his troops conduct a difficult night march to get into position for the assault he planned.

The delay from July 20 to the 21st was probably fatal. It permitted virtually the whole of Johnston's Confederate force of 12,000 to arrive from Winchester in time to participate in the battle. They came by way of the Manassas Gap Railroad, one of the first contributions of a railroad to the art of military operations. Coordination of the move was made possible by another instrument of technology making one of its first military contributions, the electric telegraph. Johnston's men were not among the reinforcements to Beauregard that McDowell had foreseen; rather, they were supposed to be held in the Shenandoah Valley by Patterson. But Patterson, afflicted by his seventy years of age, an army that was disintegrating because its three-months regiments were beginning to go home, and confusing orders from General Scott that raised the possibility of following Johnston eastward instead of holding him in place, let Johnston get away.

McDowell's plan called for demonstrating against Beauregard's center along Bull Run while sending the bulk of the Federal force on a flanking march across that stream and around the Confederate left. Confederate Brigadier-General Nathan G. Evans discovered and reacted to the flanking march in time to prevent it from producing complete Confederate disaster. Nevertheless, McDowell's troops pushed back the Confederates through the morning and early afternoon and prepared to storm the commanding terrain feature of the field, the Henry House Hill. There, however, they encountered an unyielding obstacle in the form of Brigadier-General Thomas J. Jackson's Brigade from Johnston's army, which stood like a stone wall.

A subsequent period of indecisive struggle shifted abruptly in favor of the Confederates when two Federal batteries, Captain James B. Ricketts's Company I, 1st United States, and Captain Charles Griffin's Company D, 5th United States, were overrun by the 33rd Virginia Infantry of Jackson's Brigade because the Virginians were wearing blue uniforms and the Union gunners did not fire on them in time. Panic then spread to neighboring Federal infantry, and the last brigade of Johnston's army, Brigadier-General Edmund Kirby Smith's, charged into the Federal right flank at just the critical instant to precipitate nearly complete disarray. It was that brigade particularly whose participation meant that a Federal attack one day sooner might have produced a different battle.

McDowell's weary soldiers, who had carried the disadvantages inherent in attacking along with the burden of their night march, now lost heart and streamed away from the field. It is notorious that their retreat from Bull Run turned into headlong flight as Confederate artillery shelled them and rumor flashed through their ranks exaggerating the dimensions of their defeat. Nevertheless, good order and a reasonable determination to fight again if necessary returned quickly once they were within the defenses of Washington.

In spite of the soldiers' rallying, the War Department ordered McClellan from his western Virginia victories to Washington to take command, believing that a fresh hand was needed to restore control and the prospects for another offensive. McClellan later cultivated the impression that he found not an army but a mob and that Washington was ripe for the taking. Much the same version of conditions in the Union capital spread into the Confederacy, so that the rejoicings of triumph were soon marred by recriminations over who was responsible for failing to grasp the full fruits by marching across the Potomac. "Time and tide wait for no man," wrote the South Carolina diarist Mary Boykin Miller Chesnut, whose husband, James Chesnut, was well connected in the Richmond government, "and there was a tide in our affairs which might have led to Washington, and we did not take it, and so lost our fortune, this round. Thing which nobody could deny!"[59] Because President Davis was on the field of Manassas at the climax of the battle, he shared in the blame.

McClellan to the contrary notwithstanding, however, the Confederates were chiding themselves over an illusion. The outcome of Bull Run did not put Washington in danger. With McDowell were three brigades he had not committed to the battle, and they covered the retreat with admirable calm, remarkably unshaken by the flight that passed through their ranks. Some of the battle-weary units also never lost their cohesion, notably McDowell's composite battalion of Regular infantry under Major George Sykes, 14th U.S., which was a rallying point all through the battle and remained one throughout the retreat. A controversial decision of General Scott's had held the Regular Army together as an entity, limiting the extent to which the skills of its officers and noncommissioned officers could be disseminated into the new armies. But the new armies were so large that if the Regular Army had been broken up, its talents would have been spread so thin that they would have been of dubious value anyway, while maintaining steady files of Regulars offered an example to the new soldiers and, as in the retreat from Bull Run, a hope and a consolation.

Bull Run was not to be the last occasion when critics of a victorious Civil War army argued that great prizes went uncollected because the army did not pursue its vanquished enemy with more fervor; the same cry was to be sounded after every victory by either side. But vigorous pursuit practically never occurred — not only in this war, but in any war. A smashing, devastating pursuit of defeated forces retreating from the battlefield was part of the era's vision of Napoleonic war; it was expected to be the climax and completion of the Napoleonic style of battlefield victory. But in truth Napoleon himself almost never contrived the relentless pursuit favored by military theory. Victory in a serious battle invariably cost the winning army too many casualties and with them too much disorganization to permit swift and determined pursuit. If Napoleon and later the victorious veteran armies of the final years of the Civil War could not accomplish such pursuit, it was far beyond the capacity of the inexperienced Confederate army that won at Manassas.

In the Civil War even more than in recent wars, casualty counts were never altogether reliable. Nevertheless, figures that seem reasonably accurate put the losses of the victorious Confederate army at 387 killed, 1,582 wounded, and twelve missing out of 32,232 effectives on the field, or more accurately, out of some 18,000 troops whom Beauregard and Johnston actually put into the battle. No battle in which North American armies had previously fought involved an army or casualties of that magnitude. The psychological effects of the casualties were devastating, for victors as well as vanquished. On the Federal side, the losses were 481 killed, 1,011 wounded, and 1,216 missing of some 30,000 troops available, of whom also about 18,000 were actually engaged. The much higher number of missing among the Federals was testimony to a lost battle and a retreat. The figures for killed and wounded are consistent with the fact that through most of the time the battle was raging, the Federals were winning it. They show that contrary to Southern legend, the Federals in some ways fought more effectively than the Confederates. Every 1,000 Federals in action suffered about eighty men hit, but hit 100 of the enemy; every 1,000 Confederates in action lost about 100 casualties, while killing and wounding abought eighty Federals. Altogether, the Confederates were too badly battered to have marched into Washington, a city already guarded by a formidable ring of fortifications.[60]

The Confederacy took from Manassas a legend of Southern prowess in war. The Union took from Bull Run the humiliation of defeat but also a renewed determination that the war must be won so that the stain on the record of Federal arms would not be permanent. On July 22, the day after the battle, Lincoln signed the act of Congress authorizing him to enlist 500,000 volunteers for three years. On July 25, he was able to sign still another act rushed through after Bull Run, authorizing him to enlist another 500,000 volunteers for the duration of the war.[61]

## THREE

# Groping for Strategy and Purpose

## THE UNION: WAR AIMS AND MILITARY FRUSTRATION

The Federal Congress expressed redoubled resolution to save the Union after Bull Run as much by going calmly about its daily business as by raising additional troops. On July 22, the Monday after Bull Run, the House gave unanimous consent to the first and second readings of a Pacific railroad bill. The Senate took up a tariff bill. Stephen A. Douglas having died of typhoid fever on June 3, a dynamo burned out, Congress also acted on July 22 to pay his widow, Adèle Cutts Douglas, moneys due him.[1]

Of course, the legislators dealt also with a variety of war bills, to lend added force to the statutes that called for a new army. On July 10 and 26 Congress declared that an insurrection existed, the closest the legislature was ever to come to a declaration of war against the Confederacy.[2]

On August 5, Congress passed a number of revenue measures looking to the war's financial support. One employed the constitutionally awkward method of the "direct tax," a levy of $20 million apportioned as Article I, Section IX, paragraph 4 of the Constitution provides among the states according to their population and to be raised by the states (with the Southern states included, and efforts made to collect the tax wherever Federal power reached into the South). The income-tax law—the first United States income-tax law—fixed a tax of 3 percent on incomes in excess of $800 a year (with an $800 exemption). This method was potentially far more efficient than direct taxation, but collection efforts were slow, and the potential of the income tax was never fully grasped during the Civil War. Congress also authorized the Secretary of the Treasury to borrow a quarter of a million dollars through the sale of treasury notes.[3]

On July 22 the House of Representatives and three days later the Senate passed a resolution sponsored by Congressman John J. Crittenden of Kentucky, the standard-bearer of the old Henry Clay Whig tradition, affirming that the contest against the recently declared insurrection was being waged for the preservation of the Union and not to destroy slavery.[4] Nevertheless, the departure of Congressional representatives of the seceded states left the Republican Party in control of both houses, and the antislavery and anti-Southern proclivities of some segments of the party, intensified by war, expressed themselves in the Confiscation Act of August 6, 1861. This measure provided for the seizure of all property used for "insurrectionary purposes," and "that any person held to service or labor, by laws of any State, to another, the holder of such claim to labor loses his claim if person held to labor is employed in hostile service against the Government."[5] It was the first explicit step toward overturning the Crittenden Resolution and intensifying the war by adding an assault upon slavery to the saving of the Union as its purpose.

Military legislation aimed at improving the efficiency in addition to increasing the size of the Army was limited in scope, because the problems of creating a vast army in short order continued to overwhelm efforts to keep the process under careful and rational control. The act of July 22 to increase the Army tried to improve the quality of the officers by providing for military boards to examine the capacity and efficiency of all volunteer officers. The boards soon began weeding out incompetents, approaching the task earnestly enough that substantial numbers appear to have resigned rather than face the examination. Still, eliminating unqualified officers would not produce qualified ones, and there remained no apparent means to find enough such persons for an army of potentially a million men.[6]

The act of July 22 also provided for the election of company-grade officers by members of the company and of field-grade officers by the company officers of the regiment. Election of officers was a method sanctioned by the traditions of the militia companies, and though much criticized by military theoreticians for obvious reasons, the method had the merit of tending to bring forward men with a natural bent for leadership. On August 6, however, Congress reversed itself and reassigned the appointment of officers to the governors of the states raising the regiments, who had generally been making the appointments in the first place. Since this method demanded that the officers have political influence, it was not a much worse way of finding men with some of the attributes of leadership, and it put useful power into the hands of politicians and political parties.[7]

The better candidates chosen by either system tried to get the advice of professional soldiers and studied military texts. Sometimes the conscientious officer somewhat pathetically reviewed during the night the tactical evolutions he intended to teach his troops the next day. Less conscientious officers naturally did not do even that much, but at least they now had to face the U.S. Army's first efficiency boards. Conscientious governors — the adjective, fortunately, fit most in this crisis — tried to find West Point graduates for as many of their regiments as possible. But while the War Department granted leaves of absence to Regulars to accept volunteer commissions with growing liberality, there were just not enough Regular officers to go around, and most of the officers of the old volunteer companies did not know nearly enough to take up the slack.

In any event, McClellan gave his officers plenty of time to learn what they could about tactical maneuvers and to pass on their knowledge to their men. He arrived in Washington four days after Bull Run; on July 27 the President officially gave him command of the Federal Division of the Potomac, including all the troops around Washington. McClellan was slow, however, to initiate any further offensive action that might risk a repetition of the Bull Run defeat. He allowed the enemy to maintain an outpost on Munson's Hill just outside the part of Virginia that until 1846 had been within the District of Columbia, less than ten miles from the Capitol. From there the Confederates commanded the main road southward from Washington and observed much that went on in the Federals' advanced camps. When early in September the Confederates withdrew voluntarily from their exposed position on the hill, the artillery protection of their outpost proved to have been logs painted black.

On October 21, Colonel Edward D. Baker, 71st Pennsylvania Infantry, a friend of Lincoln, Whig Congressman from Illinois 1845–1847 and 1849–1851, Republican U.S. Senator from Oregon 1860–1861, undertook a demonstration and reconnaissance across the Potomac above Washington toward Leesburg. In a battle at Ball's Bluff that he badly mismanaged, Baker lost his own life and those of forty-eight others, plus 158 wounded and 714 missing. Baker's men were trapped between the bluff and the river without enough boats to escape to the Maryland shore. McClellan had agreed to the foray, but it did nothing to enhance his aggressiveness. The Confederates had abandoned Fairfax by now; McClellan did not hasten to occupy it.[8]

Under the Congressional mobilization acts immediately following Bull

Run, 714,231 men were eventually enlisted, all of them for three years rather than for the war despite the act of July 25 (because recruits of course preferred the less indefinite term), and all of them officially credited to the President's call of May 3. By August 3, 485,640 three-year men were already under arms, and 418 regiments of volunteer infantry, thirty-one regiments of volunteer cavalry, and ten regiments of volunteer artillery had been accepted. By September 27, McClellan's strength in the immediate vicinity of Washington was 168,318.[9]

The ostensible reason for McClellan's slowness in initiating offensive action with this host was that it required time to make an army out of the dispirited losers of Bull Run and the recruits, especially when there were not enough trained officers. Whatever may have been the condition of the troops when McClellan found them, however, the remainder of the summer and all of the autumn should not have been necessary to make soldiers. In the Vietnam War, American soldiers went into combat with an average of about twenty weeks' training, including basic training and training for special operations and with larger units. To be sure, the inexperience of McClellan's officers hampered him, but the military training of the 1860s was not nearly so complex as that of the 1960s. The Civil War infantryman had to know how to handle only the muzzle-loading rifle, not varied and complex weapons or other technologically intricate equipment, such as communications gear. To fight effectively within the tactical systems of the time, officers and men had to learn precise maneuvers for going from column of march into line of battle and back again and for turning and wheeling; but these evolutions were easier to learn than the responsibilities of the officer or the soldier fighting as an individual or in small groups on the late-twentieth-century battlefield. By the late autumn, furthermore, McClellan had his troops trained well enough that he could exhibit them in a series of increasingly grander reviews; in the military systems of the 1860s, once troops could perform to the satisfaction of a drillmaster like George McClellan on the paradeground, there was not much more they could learn except through the experience of combat.

## THE CONFEDERACY: RECRUITMENT, FINANCE, BLOCKADE, AND WAR PRODUCTION

After the battle that the Confederates came to call Manassas, Joseph E. Johnston commanded the Confederate Army of the Potomac, his and Beauregard's armies being consolidated under his command. On August 31 Johnston was confirmed as a full general of the Confederate States Army, ranking from July 4.[10] Johnston put up a bold front before McClellan in spite of reliance on wooden "Quaker-gun" artillery and otherwise inferior manpower and resources. Rumors from the North, however, continually predicted an advance by McClellan's army, and against the day when the advance might come, the Confederates had to worry about matching the burgeoning Union armies and their amply growing equipment.

On August 8, the Confederate Congress authorized the President to call up to 400,000 volunteers for up to three years of service.[11] While new regiments recruited, however, the South had to worry about the impending departure of its existing armies during the coming winter and spring, for most of the first Confederate recruiting had occurred under twelve-month enlistment programs. On December 11, Congress voted for reenlistment bounties of $50 and reenlistment furloughs of sixty days with transportation to and from home — or the money value of the trip for those who did not go — to twelve-month men who would sign up for an additional two years, along with the right of the reenlistees to reorganize themselves into companies and regiments as they chose and to elect their own officers.[12]

These inducements and similar efforts brought disappointing results. Where the armies camped in the upper Confederacy, the winter of 1861–1862 proved hard, and already in the autumn the loosely organized rail system of the Confederacy became unequal to the task of carrying foodstuffs and cold-weather clothing to the troops. Procurement of both kinds of supplies for the Army was less than excellently managed, apart from transportation problems. The Confederate Commissary-General of Subsistence, charged with feeding the armies, was Colonel Lucius B. Northrop, an Old Army friend of Jefferson Davis's; he was probably the Confederate President's least fortunate appointment, which proved to be saying a good deal — a master of weaving labyrinths of red tape to stultify all good intentions. The Quartermaster-General, charged with supplying most other military necessities except munitions and medical stores, was Colonel Abraham C. Myers, scion of an ancient and distinguished South Carolina Jewish family; he was better qualified than Northrop, but barely so. Furthermore, some sources of provisions were already running short, notably hogs, for which Colonel Northrop's calculations had counted too heavily upon Kentucky. Neither was the Confederate Medical Department what it should have been. So into the winter months the troops shivered, ate badly, and suffered neglect if they had to enter Army hospitals. None of these circumstances stimulated reenlistment.[13]

Creaky government finances compounded all Confederate military problems. With the U.S. government still so far from perceiving how to meet the revenue demands of a large-scale war that it was relying on the anti-quated method of direct taxation, the Confederacy with its much more lim-ited experience and resources in finance and banking was far worse off. An initial effort to borrow $15 million, authorized by the Provisional Congress on February 28, 1861, went well largely because nearly two-fifths of it was taken up by the financiers of the Confederacy's one large and rich seaport, New Orleans. As early as the late summer, however, a $100 million loan authorized August 19 fared much less well. The government felt obliged to receive the loan partly in paper money and partly in produce; the latter expe-dient, a style of revenue collection yet more obsolete than the direct tax, would prove one to which the Confederacy resorted often.[14]

Secretary of the Treasury Memminger had been chairman of the Ways and Means Committee of the South Carolina House of Representatives, but he possessed limited experience in finance and limited ability and imagina-tion. He and the Confederate Congress also turned to direct taxation. A law of August 19, 1861 taxed real estate, slaves, and other property. Because the permanent Confederate Constitution was not yet in effect, the tax did not have to be apportioned among the states according to population. It was poorly conceived nevertheless, especially in that the states were allowed to avoid the incidence of the tax directly upon their citizens by making pay-ments themselves either in treasury notes or in specie. The states proceeded to meet the tax largely by borrowing money through issues of bonds for paper currency that they passed on to Richmond. Only some $17,500,000 was real-ized from the direct tax.[15]

Memminger urged Congress to levy additional taxes sufficient to meet a major part of the cost of the war; but Southerners were not accustomed to high taxes, and Congress, in the same spirit as that of the state legislatures, preferred to rely on paper money. Over Memminger's protests it promptly authorized treasury notes payable two years after the ratification of a peace treaty between the Confederacy and the United States. Realistically, there was no alternative; Memminger's preference for higher taxes accorded nei-ther with what was politically possible nor with Confederate access to specie. In these circumstances, the conservatism of Memminger and President Davis worsened matters by preventing a declaration that the notes were legal tender. Supposed to demonstrate that the Confederacy was strong enough that it did not need to force its notes upon its citizens, this policy predictably had the opposite effect from the intended one; it weakened confidence.[16]

The inflationary tendencies of paper currency were aggravated by a scarcity of war supplies. The U.S. Navy was small enough at the beginning of the war, and the Federal blockade of Confederate ports initially porous enough, that some of the deficiencies of Southern industry might have been remedied by a crash program of importation from foreign sources, pushing all available economic resources and all the shipping that could be found into the effort. This is what Davis's one exceptionally talented military supply officer, Major Josiah Gorgas of the Ordnance Department, wanted to do. But President Davis and most Confederate political leaders preferred to believe that the Confederacy did not need to play the supplicant for foreign assistance, but rather that with an application of Southern patience the industrial powers of western Europe could be compelled to become supplicants of the Confederacy.[17]

The source of their opinion was the popular Southern belief that the textile mills and with them the whole prosperity of Great Britain and France so much required Southern cotton that the European powers must come to the rescue of the South if Northern oppression endangered the cotton supply. So much did many Confederate leaders believe that cotton was king that they advocated an embargo against cotton exports, to starve the British and French mills and thus force a hastened foreign intervention in their behalf to reopen the cotton trade. An effort to persuade Congress to declare a legal embargo upon cotton failed, but a voluntary embargo had a wide effect— assisted by the tightening blockade. The embargo advocates also succeeded in persuading many Southerners to curtail their cotton planting, and some even to burn their current crop.

Unfortunately for this essay in King Cotton Diplomacy, 1859 and 1860 had been good years for cotton production in all the major cotton-growing countries, and in 1861 the British and French factories held enough of a surplus of raw cotton from earlier years that they could afford to await further developments instead of pressing their governments toward hasty intervention in the American troubles. Such developments might include expansion of already increasing Egyptian and Indian cotton crops to relieve an embarrassing dependence on the American South and its slavery system.

It did not help make the Southern case for European intervention more persuasive that in choosing the first Confederate diplomats, Jefferson Davis demonstrated again that, as with Secretary Walker and Commissary-General Northrop, he could be inexplicably inept in selecting recipients of responsibility. He sent William L. Yancey to London and Pierre A. Rost to Paris. Yancey may have had to be recognized for his stellar role in precipitating secession, but the stridency of this Alabama fire-eater was scarcely appropriate to winning influence at the Court of St. James's, while Rost of Louisiana had no qualifications whatever except a French lineage and the ability to speak the French language. In Europe, no one would receive these gentlemen officially, and their informal overtures to European functionaries failed to accomplish anything either.[18]

Yancey and Rost were concerned particularly with protesting the Federal blockade and trying to secure action against it. They claimed that the blockade was illegal under international law, because to be legal a blockade must be effective, while the Federal blockade leaked badly. The historian Frank Lawrence Owsley, specializing in the issue, emphatically echoed Confederate views. Owsley says that only one in ten of the ships that tried to run the blockade in 1861 fell captive to the Union Navy, and that for the whole war the average was only one capture in six.[19]

Arguments against the effectiveness of the blockade have tended to overlook, however, the fact that Lincoln's proclamation declared under blockade not the entire 3,500 miles of Confederate coast but only the ports of the Confederacy. This limitation was thoroughly consistent with accepted international practice, under which a blockade was officially inaugurated only by the action of blockading ships on the scene, and could legally be limited to the ports where the ships appeared and declared the blockade in effect. Union ships appeared early off the only eight Confederate ports that could accommodate a substantial volume of international trade, Norfolk, Wilmington, Charleston, Savannah, Pensacola, Mobile, New Orleans, and Galveston. Off these ports the Union Navy, despite initially very limited numbers of ships, soon put the blockade into effect.

In this regard, international law did not require that to be effective, a blockade must apprehend every approaching ship, or even nearly every ship. Instead, international practice holds that to be legal, a blockade must simply endanger ships trying to evade it. Thus the British Secretary of State for Foreign Affairs, John Russell, first Earl Russell of Kingston Russell, took the position that the Federal blockade met the essential criterion and was legal. In the autumn of 1861 the British Minister in Washington, Richard Bickerton Pammell, first Earl Lyons, replying to an inquiry from Lord John Russell about the blockade, conceded that many ships ran it but concluded that it was not merely a paper blockade, and that if it had been as ineffective as the Confederates claimed they would not have been so intent on ridding themselves of it.[20] Antoine Édouard Thouvenel, the French Foreign Minister, reached essentially the same conclusion.[21]

Great Britain, to be sure, was the readier to find the blockade legal because after many quarrels with the United States about the rights of a belligerent navy versus those of neutral commerce, the British were gratified to receive from the Americans precedents that they themselves might cite in defense of the Royal Navy's activities in future wars.

The ships passing through the blockade in the late spring and the summer of 1861 did not represent the concerted effort advocated by Chief of Ordnance Gorgas, to use every possible source of foreign exchange, including the available cotton, to procure and bring into the Confederacy as many implements of war as possible before the blockade tightened. Nevertheless, those ships helped begin a commerce whereby 330,000 stand of arms were eventually to be imported by the Confederate Ordnance Department, and another 270,000 by Confederate states and individuals.[22] Gorgas saw to it that the Ordnance Department imports went to the places where they were needed most; the efficiency of this unassuming, unprepossessing Pennsylvanian who had come South because of marriage ties extended to everything he undertook.[23]

But Gorgas's operations also showed that, notwithstanding grave shortages and the Confederacy's failure to follow his advice in accumulating arms, the South possessed respectable economic means for waging 1860s-style war. Gorgas could call on the Tredegar Iron Works of Richmond, expertly managed by Joseph R. Anderson, which became a fountain of cannon, machinery, plates for ironclad ships, propeller shafts, torpedoes (that is, the equivalent of modern explosive mines), locomotive wheels, and all manner of iron products.[24] Gorgas had the advantage also of Thomas J. Jackson's early capture of the rifle-making machinery at the Harpers Ferry Arsenal. An unseemly quarrel between the Confederate government and Virginia led to the division of this windfall between a state armaments facility at Richmond and a Confederate States Arsenal at Fayetteville, North Carolina; but Gorgas surmounted this incident and all the other handicaps implicit in being chief munitions-maker to the Confederacy.[25] He created impressive arsenals at Augusta, Charleston, Columbia, Macon, Atlanta, and Selma as well as Fayetteville, new foundries at various places, and a large powder mill at Augusta. With Josiah Gorgas supplying its arms, whatever the effectiveness of the blockade the Confederacy was never to lose a battle for lack of the tools of war.

## THE INVINCIBLE U.S. NAVY

Still, no one could foresee how successful Gorgas would be in overcoming the South's industrial handicaps, a naval blockade might bring general economic disintegration to a region that had been dependent on an export economy, and from the Union viewpoint the initially imperfect blockade obviously had to have its leaks plugged as much and as soon as possible.

Lincoln's Navy Department was managed energetically by the Connecticut Yankee Gideon Welles as Secretary and by his equally energetic and more technically expert coadjutor, Gustavus Vasa Fox, whom Lincoln appointed Assistant Secretary on August 1, 1861. If there was an outstanding flaw in Welles's and Fox's direction of the Navy Department, it was to prove to be, in fact, that they were too energetic, too little patient with the obstacles confronting officers who had to try to seal the Confederate ports using an initially small fleet and then to attempt to assail the ports against increasingly powerful artillery.[26]

The U.S. Navy began the war with four steam frigates, twenty-three steam sloops, eight sail frigates, seventeen sail sloops, five small steam gunboats, and two sail brigs. This total excludes the vessels burned when Commodore Charles Stewart McAuley gave up the Gosport Navy Yard at Norfolk after Virginia's secession, among which casualties were the steam frigate *Merrimack*, four line-of-battle ships, three sailing frigates (one of them the *United States* of War of 1812 fame), and two sailing sloops. The figures also ignore the fact that at the beginning, many of the vessels were not ready for sea; some were without crews; and of the effective vessels all but the *Powhatan* and *Brooklyn*, the sail frigate *Sabine*, and three gunboats, plus the small iron paddle sloop *Michigan* on the Great Lakes, were on distant patrol in defense of American commercial interests around the world.[27] But Welles's Navy Department forthwith set about building and buying, there was a fortunate reserve of cannon in the navy yards (from experimental castings and old sailing ships), and the *esprit* of the U.S. Navy nourished itself from a tradition of admirable success against odds, reaching back to Commodore John Paul Jones, *Constellation* versus *L'Insurgente*, and *Constitution* versus *Guerriere*. The *esprit* of the officers who remained with Welles along with the ubiquitous schism in the Confederate psyche can both be inferred from the remarks of Mrs. Chesnut about Captain Duncan Ingraham, one of the naval officers who went South: "He is South Carolina to the tips of his fingers, but he has it dyed in the wool — part of his nature — to believe the U.S.N. can whip anything in the world."[28]

Perhaps it could. Flag Officer Silas H. Stringham, a veteran of the War of 1812, commanded the Union Navy's Atlantic Blockading Squadron. On August 26 he led a naval expedition from Fort Monroe, where the Union had retained a toehold on the Virginia coast, toward the Hatteras Inlet entrance into Pamlico Sound on the coast of North Carolina. The Confederates had built two earthwork forts, Fort Hatteras and Fort Clark, to guard Hatteras Inlet. It was a military truism confirmed by generations of experience and as recently as the Crimean War of 1853–1855 that ships cannot defeat forts: forts offered a steady gun platform against the unsteadiness of ships; the wooden walls of ships were likely to be less sturdy than the masonry or earthen ramparts of forts; and a few well-placed shots could knock out a whole ship, while the guns of a fort had to be overcome battery by battery, or even gun by gun.

But Stringham had with him two big steam screw frigates of the *Wabash* class just built in the late 1850s, *Wabash*, flying his flag, and *Minnesota*, as well as a reliable old sidewheeler frigate, the *Susquehanna*, all armed with modern shell guns that outranged the armament of the forts. For the most part, Stringham could bombard the Hatteras defenses from outside their range. When on August 27 he did bring his ships within range of the forts' guns to bombard with best effect, he used his steam power to do what sailing ships had not been able to do in such a contest, to remain in constant motion in unpredictable patterns. On August 27 Federal troops put ashore from the fleet and occupied Fort Clark, and on the 28th the larger Fort Hatteras sur-rendered in submission to Stringham's bombardment. The Navy had given the Union its first major victory of the war. An important blockade-running route was closed, and the way was open for the amphibious invasion of North Carolina.[29]

Stringham failed to follow up his victory by advancing farther into the North Carolina sounds, and when he was criticized for this lack of initiative he asked to be relieved and Secretary Welles obliged him. Nevertheless, his triumph at Hatteras Inlet had provided a dress rehearsal for action against yet more important targets. To maintain the blockade, Union ships badly needed a harbor and coaling facilities on the Southern coast; Stringham had complained that fuel consumption on the trip South cut so severely into his ships' effectiveness that it took six ships in commission to maintain one ship on blockading station. A Navy Department strategy-planning Blockade Board studied the harbors of the South Atlantic coast, decided which ones offered the best possibilities as bases, and outlined plans for amphibious at-tacks against them. Assistant Secretary Fox decided that Port Royal Sound should be attacked first. It lay half way between Charleston and Savannah; it was big enough to float the navies of the world; and it was not so strongly defended as the city harbors of Wilmington, Charleston, and Savannah.[30]

Port Royal did have two forts stronger than those at Hatteras Inlet, Fort Walker on Hilton Head Island and Fort Beauregard on Bay Point Island. But Flag Officer Samuel Francis Du Pont received command of the newly cre-ated South Atlantic Blockading Squadron to conduct the attack, and Du Pont had not only helped select Port Royal as the target while serving on the Blockade Board, but had studied carefully both Stringham's action and the naval operations of the Crimean War. He had decided that the old rule about forts' superiority over ships could be nullified by steam engines and modern naval guns. He planned to keep his ships in continual motion as a protection against the fire of the forts, sailing in an elliptical pattern that would hold both Confederate forts steadily under fire. The British had begun to work out this tactic at Odessa in the Crimean conflict, but they had been made so timid by the old rule that they failed to pass in front of the Russian batteries and had never brought the land defenses under direct fire. Sailing across the bar with a fleet headed again by *Wabash,* flag, and *Susquehanna,* along with three steam sloops and eight gunboats, Du Pont brushed aside a swarm of tiny Confederate defending vessels and in four or five hours' bombardment pounded the forts until their garrisons abandoned them.[31]

Du Pont's victory occurred on November 7. That same day there arrived at the railroad station nearest Port Royal Sound General Robert Edward Lee, sent by President Davis from Richmond to take command of the defenses of the South Atlantic coast. Lee was a nobly handsome Virginia aristocrat of ancient family, the son of Major-General Henry "Light Horse Harry" Lee, and married to Mary Anne Randolph Custis, the daughter of George Washington's adopted son, George Washington Parke Custis. Lee had been esteemed by Winfield Scott as the ablest soldier in the U.S. Army, and while colonel of the 1st Cavalry he was informally offered the Army's field command before he resigned from it on April 25.[32] But he had already suffered one disappointing campaign when earlier in the autumn he failed to dislodge the Federals from their gains in western Virginia. In spite of that, his promotion to full general had been approved August 31, dating from June 30.[33]

Yet now, as in western Virginia, Lee found himself on a thankless mission compromised before he began it. After Du Pont's demonstration of the power of the Federal Navy against relatively strong forts, Lee concluded it was hopeless to try to hold the sea islands and sounds of the South Atlantic coast. He immediately ordered the complete evacuation of Hilton Head and Bay Point, and then of the sea islands generally. He withdrew the defenses inland to where the rivers emptying into the sounds became narrow and shallow enough that their channels could be obstructed. There he set up batteries as well as obstructions, sufficiently strong that he could hope to resist Union advances until the batteries could be reinforced by reserve troops moving along the Charleston and Savannah Railroad, which ran just inside the coast.

But this method of defense yielded a great deal to the Federals. Du Pont's fleet disembarked some 13,000 troops under Brigadier-General

Thomas W. Sherman, U.S.V. The Union not only held securely a deep-water harbor, where Du Pont assembled a remarkable floating base, but through the sounds it had back-door access to a series of additional harbors, and a means of improving the blockade by corking the neck of the bottle out of which blockade runners must come. At places such as Georgetown, South Carolina; Wassaw, Ossabaw, and St. Simons Sound, Georgia; and Jacksonville and Mosquito Inlet, Florida, Du Pont stationed small vessels at inner anchorages to conduct the blockade from within the coast line. Elsewhere he extended Federal conquests outright. On March 4, 1862, he entered the harbor of Fernandina, Florida, with some of his small gunboats leading the way through the intricate channel of Cumberland Sound to bypass the defenses. The fall of St. Augustine, St. Johns, and St. Mary's promptly followed, and Florida was nearly eliminated from the war.[34]

With Du Pont's help, Sherman's troops invested Fort Pulaski on Cockspur Island, the principal defensive work outside Savannah. In doing so they nearly sealed off Savannah from the ocean. Sherman's chief engineer, Captain Quincy Adams Gillmore, Corps of Engineers, thought that further accomplishments beckoned. The nearest firm ground to Fort Pulaski was on Tybee Island, a mile and a half away. This island was too distant, in the opinion of General Lee, for artillery mounted there to bombard the fort effectively. Moreover, Fort Pulaski was one of the most modern and strongest of the permanent coastal fortifications, no improvised earthwork like the forts at Hatteras Inlet and Port Royal but a stout, casemated masonry citadel designed to fend off the fleets of Europe. Captain Gillmore, however, believed that the new rifled artillery, with its superior accurate range and, yet more important, the greater weight of its conical projectiles in relation to diameter as opposed to old-fashioned cannon balls, could smash the masonry walls of the fort.

In a two-day bombardment beginning April 10, he proved he was right and compelled Fort Pulaski to surrender. For a generation and more, since the close of the War of 1812, the United States had laboriously and expensively constructed a chain of forts similar to Pulaski to guard its principal harbors, on which ironically the Confederacy now counted to keep the U.S. armed forces away. Now the final irony favored the Union; for when the day came to use these forts so long abuilding, in a cause the reverse of that for which they had been intended, Captain Gillmore proved that rifled artillery had made them at best obsolescent.[35]

Flag Officer Du Pont believed that yet more accomplishment was possible, that if the War Department had sent enough troops and energetic commanders immediately after the capture of Port Royal to exploit the inner waterways as approaches, Savannah and Charleston themselves could have been entered by their back doors before Lee improved the Confederacy's inner defenses. But many of Sherman's troops soon became tied down in occupation duties, Du Pont felt he could not prod the Army, and the Navy Department was preoccupied at the time with a scheme to close the port of Charleston by sinking ships loaded with stone in the channel — an experiment eventually attempted to little effect. Charleston, more and more heavily defended by a ring of forts that Du Pont feared to challenge with ships even when he received ironclads — the old dictum about forts versus ships was not yet completely exorcised, and rightly not as we shall see — became the most conspicuous and embarrassing source of leaks in the South Atlantic blockade.[36]

## THE *TRENT* AFFAIR AND A PAPER TIGER

The conviction that the U.S. Navy could whip anything produced a less rewarding outcome on the day after Du Pont's Port Royal victory. On November 8, the U.S. screw sloop *San Jacinto*, Captain Charles Wilkes, was cruising on the Old Bahama Channel, awaiting the Royal Mail Packet *Trent* bound from Havana to Nassau. On board the *Trent* were James M. Mason of Virginia and John Slidell of Louisiana, newly designated Confederate emissaries to Great Britain and France, respectively. Captain Wilkes, an ambitious and cantankerous officer who nursed special grievances against Englishmen, whom he blamed for stealing credit that was rightly his for his Antarctic expeditions, and against Southerners, whose Congressional representatives had curtailed appropriations for his astronomical experiments, had resolved to remove Mason and Slidell from the *Trent* and carry them to the United States. His justification for doing so would be his fine-spun theory that because dispatches were contraband of war, subject to seizure from neutral vessels under international law, the Confederate emissaries as living embodiments of dispatches were also subject to seizure. When the *Trent* steamed into view, Wilkes fired a shot across her bow, boarded, and took away Mason and Slidell.[37]

Wilkes returned home to a hero's welcome from the Northern public and most of the press, the House of Representatives when it met in December voting him a gold medal. (He would be promoted to commodore August 4, 1862.[38]) The Lincoln administration confined Mason and Slidell in Fort Warren, Boston harbor, as political prisoners. Nevertheless the administration was not so sure about the legal aspects of the case. Even if Wilkes's notion that persons could be contraband had any legal merit, international law clearly required that for any part of a ship's cargo to be condemned as contraband, the ship had to be sailed into port and the case submitted to a prize court. Seen in this light, through Captain Wilkes the United States had violated the very doctrine of international law for which it had so long resisted British naval procedures into the War of 1812.

Moreover, word from Britain soon brought the predictable news that the British public was infuriated by the *Trent* affair as an insult to national honor, and that Her Majesty's Government was little more tolerant than the public. More than 14,000 British officers and men and appropriate equipment were sent to Canada; the Home Fleet was readied for war; and the Cabinet prepared an ultimatum to Washington demanding an official apology and the surrender of the prisoners within seven days of the date when the British Minister in Washington submitted the demand, or Great Britain would withdraw its legation from Washington with the implied threat of war.

The Confederate government may have intended the Mason-Slidell mission as a trap to bring the United States and Great Britain to war. The itinerary of the two emissaries was suspiciously well advertised. At Havana, they fraternized and dined with the officers of the *San Jacinto*, again publicizing their departure plans. On board the *Trent*, Slidell appeared unduly eager to become a captive.

The U.S. Minister to the Court of St. James's, Charles Francis Adams, palliated the crisis by assuring the British government that Captain Wilkes must have acted without instructions and that, returning as he had been from the coast of Africa, Wilkes could not have been familiar with U.S. policy when he made the seizure. Adams expressed the view that his government would disavow Wilkes's action.

Secretary Seward agreed with Adams that the United States should back off. English liberals who were friends of American democracy and of the North, preeminently including John Bright and Richard Cobden, used their influence on both sides of the Atlantic to try to smooth the ruffled feathers, especially through their correspondence and friendship with the antislavery Senator from Massachusetts and chairman of the Senate Committee on Foreign Relations, Charles Sumner. Sumner said from the beginning that Mason and Slidell would have to be given up, wrote to his British friends urging them to help avoid war, and took his correspondence from Britain to the White House.

In Britain, the Cabinet experienced its own second thoughts about its initial bellicosity. The Prince Consort, Prince Albert of Saxe-Coburg-Gotha, encouraged by the Queen, rose from his sickbed to consult with the Prime

Minister, Francis John Temple, third Viscount Palmerston, and Lord John Russell. The Prince excised passages from the proposed communication with America until what had begun as an ultimatum was toned down into a temperate statement, not putting the United States in the wrong, but assuming that Wilkes had acted without authority and that Washington would spontaneously release the emissaries and offer suitable apology.

Still, the missive that reached Lord Lyons in Washington continued to advise him privately of a seven-day time limit on America's complying with British expectations, and the crisis had not yet passed. The critical American decision was taken at a Christmas Day Cabinet meeting in the White House. Lord Lyons had informed Seward in friendly, confidential fashion that his instructions would require his requesting his passport and a rupture of diplomatic relations, with the likelihood of war, if the United States did not grant satisfaction. Others of Lincoln's Cabinet still opposed any concessions to the trans-Atlantic lion and traditional enemy. Lincoln himself, undecided, was contemplating an appeal for third-party arbitration.

At this juncture, the pivotal impetus toward resolution came from an unlikely source, France. Napoleon III was beginning to display a wartime habit of blowing alternately hot and cold toward the United States, with the cold spells longer than the warm ones; but the Foreign Minister, Thouvenel, was a firm sympathizer. For days, Seward had been awaiting an interposition by Thouvenel on behalf of peace; Seward had learned the substance of what to expect from the French and British legations, which worked closely together, and from the American Minister in Paris, William L. Dayton. At the Christmas meeting of the Cabinet, Seward was able to present Dayton's report of Thouvenel's attitudes, which went far toward destroying Lincoln's arbitration plan by indicating that no arbitrator was available: all the governments of Europe believed that in the *Trent* affair the United States had done wrong under international law. With the White House meeting already in session, however, the French Minister in Washington, Henri Mercier, received the delayed and long-awaited dispatch from Touvenel, which he hurried to the State Department, and which Frederick W. Seward, the Secretary's son and secretary, in turn hurried to the White House.

In it Thouvenel appealed to the United States to release the prisoners, but he emphasized that thereby Washington would be seizing Great Britain's own vindication of those principles of international law for which both the United States and France had often struggled against the mistress of the seas. On this ground, the vindication of American principles, Lincoln was now persuaded, as Seward had already been, the administration could take its stand, releasing the prisoners but avoiding an impossible sacrifice of public support. To the American people, Seward explained that he could not hold on to the prisoners without repudiating the country's traditions.

The rest was anticlimax, for Mason and Slidell released and sent to Europe never again approached the influence they held while languishing in Fort Warren.

Happily defused, the *Trent* crisis nevertheless was not so dangerous as both American and British bluster made it appear. The United States was not Afghanistan, to be punished for misbehavior by British colonial expeditions, and there was little likelihood in fact that in 1861 and 1862 Britain would have gone beyond threats and gestures of military preparation into war with the trans-Atlantic Republic over a single incident of honor in which the issues were obscured by the technicalities of international law. Great Britain had too much to lose in such a war. Not only would there have been the unsettling commercial dislocations of conflict with a prime customer for British manufactures and a prime supplier of grainstuffs, a country in which much British capital was invested. Not only was British North America dangerously vulnerable to American retaliation; during the American Civil War years the differences between the English- and French-speaking inhabitants were to bring British North America to the verge of paralysis without the added strains of war. Beyond such evident perils, war against the United States would have put to risk Great Britain's worldwide political influence and prestige, the whole ability of Britons to bask in the confidence that a *Pax Britannica* reigned around the globe, by revealing that the military foundations of the *Pax Britannica* were illusory. Such a gamble could scarcely be taken in a dubious cause against a kindred nation.

Militarily, Great Britain in the 1860s would have faced insoluble problems in a war against the United States. The military prestige that was a major factor in Britain's claims to global preeminence rested largely upon the contributions of the British Army and Navy to the defeat of Napoleon, but in the decades since 1815 the substance of British military power had to a considerable extent melted away. The Royal Navy retained the appearance of maritime supremacy principally because it existed in a naval vacuum, with no serious rivals except for halfhearted and sporadic challenges by the French. At that, the British Navy would have had a difficult time making itself felt on the North American coast. The coming of steam power had destroyed the ability of its best warships to cruise indefinitely in American waters as the blockading squadrons had done in 1812. Even with a major base at Halifax, or possible aid from Confederate ports, the British Navy would have found it a precarious venture to try to keep station on the U.S. coast. No steam navy operated with success against any reasonably formidable enemy at the distances from its home ports that a trans-Atlantic war would have imposed on the British fleet until the U.S. Navy fought the Japanese in World War II. The British Navy of the 1860s was a hidebound and inefficient service that could not have begun to approximate the American logistical feats of the 1940s. As for the British Army, that institution with its system of officership by purchase of commissions regardless of competence spent the middle years of the nineteenth century parading its ineptitude in a series of colonial military disasters from Afghanistan to Zululand.

Indeed, stumbling, blunders, and logistical failures during the Crimean War, in spite of the power of the Royal Navy — including especially the horrors of the military hospitals — had already dramatized many of the cracks in Great Britain's armor. A war with America would have posed the danger of destroying altogether the façade of British military preeminence. Palmerston surely knew enough about the military realities to sense the risk. It would have been too much to expect the British government to recognize that even the foundations of British economic primacy were also tottering, though we are aware now that the rate of growth of the British economy began to slow and British industry began to lose its inventive and progressive energies from about the middle of the nineteenth century. The British government could nevertheless appreciate some of the economic peril also implicit in a war with the United States, beyond the manifest dangers such as a new wave of American maritime raiders preying upon British shipping as in 1812–1815.

It would have been better for both the Union and the Confederacy if they had been less infatuated with history — both remembered the decisive effect of foreign intervention in the American Revolution, as well as Britain's past strength — and more clearsighted about current power realities. It would have been better here as in all military matters if they had thought and planned more coherently and systematically, instead of lurching from crisis to crisis and from imagined opportunity to imagined opportunity. Then the *Trent* affair need never have occurred, because sending Confederate envoys across the Atlantic and possibly setting a trap for British-American relations would not have seemed so important, and Captain Wilkes also need not have bothered to seize the envoys. Whether feared by the North or hoped for by the South, British intervention in the American Civil War was little more than a chimera.

## THE JOINT COMMITTEE ON THE CONDUCT OF THE WAR

George Brinton McClellan was only thirty-five, and he found intoxicating his sudden elevation to command of the more than 150,000 men in the hosts gathering around Washington and the adulation heaped on him as the savior of the country after the debacle at Bull Run. Small and compactly built but conveying an impression of driving energy, and altogether a magnetic figure in the Napoleonic mode, McClellan galloped through the streets of the capital almost daily, attended by staff and clattering escorts and attracting the applause of the crowds as he swept by. He found Congressmen, Cabinet ministers, and the President himself all deferring to his military expertise and wisdom, on which they counted to restore the Union.

Unfortunately, George McClellan was not a man who could graciously digest being deferred to. He grew impatient with the President for consuming his valuable time, and although Lincoln habitually came to see him at his headquarters rather than asking him to report to the Executive Mansion, and often waited patiently for his return, on one occasion when McClellan found him waiting the general felt obliged to go straight to bed without wasting even a word of greeting. As for saving the nation, McClellan's most conspicuous accomplishment of the autumn of 1861 was his quarreling with and snubbing General Scott, until the old gentleman twice tried to resign, and on the second occasion Lincoln accepted the resignation. On November 1 McClellan succeeded Scott as General-in-Chief of the U.S. Army while retaining the command of the troops immediately around Washington, the Army of the Potomac.[39]

The President and various vexatious Congressmen soon spoiled McClellan's pleasure in his dual command through increasing displays of their impatience that he should do more than ride conspicuously through the capital city and stage grand reviews. The fiasco at Ball's Bluff naturally aggravated their impatience, and the day after that event, on October 22, matters worsened when the Navy announced that the Confederates had erected batteries commanding the Potomac below Alexandria and in effect blockading the river communications of Washington. With traffic on the Baltimore and Ohio Railroad also interrupted at the time in western Virginia, the capital's supply situation again was not good. McClellan's squabbles with Scott had revolved around the question of McClellan's strength vis-à-vis Johnston's Confederate army across the Potomac and by implication McClellan's ability to accomplish anything. McClellan argued that the enemy had first 100,000, then by late October 150,000 men opposite Washington, and that the capital itself was consequently in danger. Scott dismissed any such suggestion, pointing to lower estimates of Confederate numbers, McClellan's own strength, and the fortifications around the city that McDowell had brought well along and for which McClellan on other occasions liked to give himself much credit.

McClellan's impression of Johnston's strength came from a source unusual in military intelligence. He had hired the detective Allan Pinkerton to set up a Secret Service (with Pinkerton trying to enhance the secrecy by calling himself Major E. J. Allen). By whatever means Pinkerton and McClellan arrived at their estimates, they must have ignored both the testimony of travelers who fairly frequently passed from Johnston's army into the Northern lines and the evidence afforded by Northern knowledge of prewar Southern stocks of arms and of Confederate purchasing activities. Gorgas's armament efforts were just beginning, and arsenal inventories available in the North should have shown that there could not be more than about 175,000 well-armed infantry in the entire Confederacy.[40]

The grumbling of individual Congressmen during the fall served as a warning that when Congress went back into session on December 1, it might attempt concerted action to get the war moving forward. As early as December 9 and 10, the Republican majorities of the Senate and House established the Joint Committee on the Conduct of the War, empowered to inquire into the causes of past defeats and expected to push the administration into measures that would avoid the repetition of defeat and secure victory in the future. The selection of a chairman indicated further the spirit in which the committee was formed, for that post went to Senator Benjamin F. Wade of Ohio, "Bluff Ben" Wade, a profane, angry man of emphatic antislavery convictions, who had made himself conspicuous in the prewar days when Southern fire-eaters sometimes challenged their rivals to duels by displaying a brace of horse pistols on his Senate desk. Impatient by nature and incapable of perceiving any other reason why McClellan so hesitated to advance against the enemy, Wade suspected that the General-in-Chief harbored treasonable sentiments. Certainly McClellan's social consorts were overwhelmingly Democrats, and many of them by Wade's lights were of dubious enthusiasm for the prosecution of the war. Wade's committee marched before itself a parade of generals to question them as to why the Army did not move, and McClellan himself, so recently universally deferred to, had to submit to the jarring experience of a sarcastic inquisition.[41]

While the main lines of the committee's investigations concerned McClellan's inaction, Chairman Wade also rode his own hobbyhorse, a special investigation of the Ball's Bluff affair, and particularly of the conduct of Brigadier-General Charles P. Stone, U.S.V. General Scott had called Stone to Washington early in the year, to be from April 16 colonel, Inspector-General's Department, and commander of District of Columbia Volunteers, planning the defense of the capital in the days when virtually no troops were present and a secessionist *coup de main* seemed a distinct possibility. Stone had served more than competently through Washington's dark hours. In return he received a general's star on May 17.[42] In the autumn, however, he commanded Stone's Division on the upper Potomac, whence he sent Colonel Baker on the reconnaissance that ended at Ball's Bluff, and whence he also habitually sent slaves back to their owners. The slaves tended to enter his lines because they held the confused but understandable impression that in a civil war begun over the issue of slavery, the Northern Army represented freedom. But Stone was both conservative in his own politics and anxious to retain the good will of Maryland.

When his policy compelled the 20th Massachusetts to return two runaways, some of the Massachusetts men felt disturbed about playing the part of slave catchers, the Fugitive Slave Act having long been a special bone of contention in their state. Their antislavery governor, John A. Andrew, heard of their unhappiness, whereupon he rebuked the officers of the 20th who were involved in returning the slaves. Stone then took it upon himself to write to Andrew telling the governor to mind his own business. There followed an increasingly acrimonious correspondence between the general and the governor, with Andrew presently passing the documents on to Charles Sumner, who denounced Stone in the Senate. Stone replied with a public letter to Sumner calling him, with implied reference to his 1857 beating by Congressman Preston "Bully" Brooks, "a well known coward."[43]

General Stone had begun with a conscientious if questionable policy and had proceeded into an unwise political imbroglio, which encouraged Ben Wade to believe that Stone, a friend of McClellan, represented specific evidence of the kind of treason he expected from the McClellan circle. For men of Wade's persuasion, it was an easy jump from Stone's solicitude for slaveholders to the conclusion that Stone had deliberately sacrificed the Republican soldier-Senator Colonel Baker by sending him into a trap at Ball's Bluff. Wade brought Stone before his committee and questioned him about Ball's Bluff and about his attitude toward runaway slaves, and then he followed up with a succession of witnesses from Stone's command and the neighboring civilian population. These persons were asked leading questions designed to elicit evidence of the dubiety of Stone's loyalty, his mishandling of Ball's Bluff, and his friendliness with secessionists, with whom he allegedly engaged in correspondence. The committee presented its evidence to Edwin M. Stanton, from January 15, 1862 Secretary of War in succession to Cameron, arguing that the evidence seemed to impeach both Stone's military capacity and his loyalty. On January 28 Stanton gave General McClellan an order for Stone's arrest.

McClellan managed to delay execution of the order until he had secured for his friend another hearing before the committee, on January 31.

Here Wade informed Stone that there were four charges against him: that he had ordered the troops across the Potomac to Ball's Bluff without adequate transportation; that he had failed to reinforce Colonel Baker during the battle; that he had held undue communication with the enemy; and that he had permitted the enemy to erect fortifications that he could have destroyed. But Stone was not informed of the specific evidence behind these charges, nor permitted to learn the identity of the witnesses who presented them. Stone's hearing was conducted in secret, and with the general not permitted to have counsel. Although Stone grew indignant that his loyalty should be questioned, recalling how he had held the fate of the capital in his hands, he was unable to defend himself to the satisfaction of the committee. Stanton returned to McClellan for execution of the arrest order, and McClellan preferred to sacrifice Stone rather than arouse further suspicions against himself. Without a hearing, Stone was imprisoned in solitary confinement in Fort Lafayette, New York harbor.[44]

The death of Colonel Baker, a popular and militantly Republican political figure, had riveted the attention of the Committee on the Conduct of the War upon General Stone, but it was Stone's policy toward the runaway slaves that had nourished their suspicions. In the gloomy winter of 1861–1862 when McClellan's continued inactivity and the President's failure to prod him into motion seemed to have paralyzed the Union war effort, the North in its impatience and dismay began to gnaw at the question of why it was fighting the war at all. The frenzied activity of the summer to assemble and equip a mighty army in a matter of weeks seemed now to have been effort wasted, leading to practically nothing. The Army lay idle. What had been the point of all the summer's exertions? The mood of frustration in which this question arose led inevitably into the larger question: What was the point and purpose of anything—of the war itself? And that question in turn raised the issue of slavery, which meant that General Stone's slave-catching activities were related to the whole search of the North for meaning in its frustrated preparations to fight. The unfortunate General Stone was made to serve as a Franklin's kite, by which Benjamin Franklin Wade hoped to recapture the electricity of the first mobilization.

## THREE ESSAYS ON ABOLITIONISM: BUTLER, FRÉMONT, CAMERON

On December 4, 1861, Congressman Crittenden and his friends sought Congressional reaffirmation of the Crittenden Resolution. It had passed the House by 121 to 2 in July. But the lower chamber now refused to reaffirm, 71 to 65.[45] The Civil War, like all wars, was developing its own momentum and reshaping the political purposes for which it had begun.

The leaders of Congress were often a good deal more militantly anti-slavery than the President: in the House, men such as Thaddeus Stevens of Pennsylvania and Owen Lovejoy of Illinois, brother of the abolitionist martyr Elijah Lovejoy; in the Senate, Ben Wade and his kindred spirit Zachariah Chandler of Michigan. To these Republicans it appeared as the December Congressional session opened that the South had forfeited by rebellion what-ever constitutional protection the peculiar institution had hitherto enjoyed. Therefore an antislavery party in control of the Federal government, though previously faced with the reluctant necessity for constitutional restraint in its policies toward slavery, no longer needed to consider itself so bound. The Republican Congressional leadership could now act forthrightly on the moral principle that slavery was wrong and ought to be eliminated.

The war had surely erupted because of slavery. It was no wonder that the North was beginning to feel overtaken by a sense of purposelessness as it tried to wage the conflict while not touching slavery, the cause of it. The Republican Congress tended toward these conclusions, but relatively few leaped to them directly. Still, the tendency of Congressional thought had revealed itself in the Confiscation Act of August 6, 1861, with its declaration of the forfeiture of claims to labor employed in hostile service against the government, and now in the House's refusal to reaffirm the Crittenden Reso-lution.

The very act of waging war inside the South was continually putting the U.S. government in contact with the institution that the governing party officially abhorred. Before General Stone encountered his troubles with run-away slaves in Maryland, Ben Butler, since May 16 major-general U.S.A., confronted the fugitive problem in the somewhat different setting of Vir-ginia, a state already seceded. After his occupation of Baltimore made the War Department nervous about his recklessness in the delicate environment of Maryland, Butler was sent to Fort Monroe to command from May 22 the new Department of Virginia. Almost immediately he demonstrated that he could formulate policy for himself and make himself conspicuous anywhere.

On May 23 he took custody of three fugitive slaves who entered his lines, declaring he knew that Negroes were being used to aid the enemy cause:

> Satisfied of these facts from cautious examination of each of the negroes apart from the others, I determined for the present and until better advised, as these men were very serviceable and I had great need of labor in my quartermaster's department, to avail myself of their services, and that I would send a receipt to

Colonel [Charles] McClary [their owner] that I had so taken them as I would for any other property of a private citizen that the exigencies of the service seemed to require to be taken by me, and especially property that was designed, adapted, and about to be used against the United States.

Soon slaves thus taken in Butler's department and elsewhere in similar circumstances came to be called contraband; it is not clear whether Butler himself first so described them. The War Department approved his action provided it was confined to military requirements and did not interfere with slavery as a state institution — a distinction difficult to understand and possessing little practical significance.[46]

Butler's policy of welcoming contrabands into his lines was moderate and cautious compared with the antislavery policy of John C. Frémont. Frémont was the Pathfinder of the West who as a second lieutenant, Corps of Topographical Engineers, and major of California Volunteers had played a romantic and undisciplined role in detaching California from Mexico. On March 15, 1848 he had resigned his Regular Army commission as lieutenant-colonel in the Regiment of Mounted Rifles under a cloud thrown up by his chronic and continuing insubordination. He had left the Army with no real tactical experience in command of troops. He had gone on, however, to be the first Republican Party Presidential candidate in 1856, and therefore Lincoln had felt obliged to commission him on May 14, 1861 as a major-general in the Regular Army and to give him command of the Western Department with headquarters at St. Louis.[47] That particular post reflected the Blairs' belief that Frémont's political stature and especially his marriage to Jessie Benton, the daughter of the great Missouri Jacksonian Thomas Hart Benton, would help calm the troubled waters of Missouri.

Frémont was in Europe in May, and he took his time about returning to America and attending to private business in New York, so that he did not actually assume command at St. Louis until July 25. Then followed almost immediately Nathaniel Lyon's death and defeat at Wilson's Creek, to set Frémont's tenure of command off on the wrong foot. Although Frémont could not be directly blamed for Wilson's Creek, he did not do all he might have to push reinforcements to Lyon. Much else soon went wrong. Missouri continued to sink into guerrilla warfare, and there were other Federal defeats, including the surrender of 2,800 men to Sterling Price at Lexington.[48]

Moreover, rumors of inefficiency and corruption in Frémont's military contracting began to surface at every turn. Friends from California received remarkably lucrative contracts, such as one for $191,000 to build forts at St. Louis, three times what detached observers thought the work should have cost, and another to build thirty-eight mortar boats at $8,250 each, when they should have cost under $5,000. Frémont's headquarters refused to obey warnings from General Meigs that it must observe the law requiring advertisement and competitive bidding for supplies except in extreme emergencies. Dubieties of conduct that might otherwise have been borne appeared all the worse because Frémont isolated himself from his military subordinates and the political leadership of Missouri, withdrawing into a mansion that cost the government a rental of $6,000 a year, where he surrounded himself with sycophantic courtiers and a bodyguard of 300 men selected for their imposing physiques.[49]

In these circumstances, and especially because the Blairs discovered they could not control him for their own purposes, Frémont soon fell out with his initial sponsors. Perhaps in part to establish a new base of political support, he issued a proclamation on August 30 assuming administrative powers over the state government. To deal with the guerrillas, his proclamation drew a line diagonally across Missouri from Fort Leavenworth to Cape Girardeau and declared that any person taken in arms north of the line would be tried by a court-martial and if convicted shot by a firing squad. Apparently the ban included properly enlisted Confederate soldiers, and executions would surely invite reprisals and still more chaos than was already consuming Missouri.[50]

Yet more controversial, however, was Frémont's declaration about slavery. Like West Virginia and unlike Kentucky, Missouri had a Unionist faction divided within itself between antislavery partisans and those who thought that for one reason or another slavery should be let alone. The Blairs represented the latter group. Having broken with them, Frémont on August 30 proclaimed as confiscated for the public use the real and personal property of all persons who had taken an active part against the United States, including their slaves, whom the general declared to be free.[51]

While the proclamation received much praise in Congress and in the press throughout the North, even to a surprising extent among Republican moderates, the President decided it obliged him to enter the growing controversy surrounding Frémont. On September 2, Lincoln sent the general by special messenger a confidential letter about the two points of Frémont's proclamation that caused him anxiety. Noting the danger of retaliation, he ordered Frémont to shoot no one under the proclamation without first receiving Presidential approval. Regarding the confiscation of property, Lincoln sent a copy of the August 6 Congressional legislation on the subject and asked Frémont to modify his proclamation to bring it into conformity with the law, which of course provided for the confiscation of property and the forfeiture of slaves only when they were directly used in support of the insurrection.[52]

As Lincoln feared it would, Frémont's proclamation was raising an uproar throughout the whole delicately balanced border area. James Speed, an old friend of Lincoln's, warned from Louisville, Kentucky that Frémont was likely to destroy the Union party in that state. It was at this juncture that Lincoln said: "I think to lose Kentucky is nearly the same as to lose the whole game. Kentucky gone, we can not hold Missouri, nor, as I think, Maryland. These all against us, and the job on our hands is too large for us."[53]

Frémont nevertheless insisted that the exigencies of war required his proclamation, saying that the President must openly direct him otherwise if he disagreed.[54] The general also decided to send his ambitious and formidable wife to Washington to protest to Lincoln, which she did after rushing directly from her train to the White House, threatening the President that if he did not acquiesce in Frémont's policies, her husband might "set up for himself."[55]

Lincoln complied with Frémont's wishes to the extent of publicly ordering him to modify his antislavery proclamation to conform to the Confiscation Act of August 6.[56] Frémont's proclamation also helped precipitate investigative trips to St. Louis first by Montgomery Blair and Quartermaster-General Meigs, then by Secretary of War Cameron and Brigadier-General and Adjutant-General Lorenzo Thomas. The result of these visits was confirmation of mismanagement by Frémont, especially through a detailed report by Thomas that specified failures in operational command as well as in administration and supply. On October 24, General Scott ordered Frémont's relief from command, unless he had fought and won a battle or was about to fight one, replacing him temporarily with Major-General David Hunter, U.S.V. Melodramatic maneuvering was required to spirit the order past Frémont's protective circle of guards. Frémont yielded to Hunter on September 3.[57]

Not profiting from the example, one of the investigators of Frémont, Secretary Cameron, soon made similar use of the ubiquitous slavery question in similar circumstances. Cameron had entered the Cabinet as part of a political bargain stemming from his support for Lincoln's nomination at the Republican National Convention of 1860, and Lincoln neither had a direct part in the deal nor wanted Cameron in the Cabinet. The President's misgivings about Cameron's ability and ethics were soon confirmed by slipshod administration of the War Department and excessive delegation of authority, particularly authority to contract for supplies, to Cameron's political allies. It must be said in fairness that despite many allegations to the contrary,

Cameron was a careless administrator rather than a dishonest one, and that he received blame for a good deal of administrative chaos that was not of his making but unavoidable in the rapid expansion of his department and the Union armies.

When Presidential dissatisfaction and Congressional probing made it clear that his days in the Cabinet were surely numbered, however, Cameron chose to bid for the support of the antislavery militants by inserting into his annual report to Congress in December 1861 a plea for the employment of slaves as soldiers and the granting of their freedom accordingly. He had his report printed and mailed to postmasters for distribution to the press without Lincoln's inspection. Lincoln nevertheless learned of this secret initiative and thereupon had the advance copies of the report recalled and a new version printed, omitting the part about arming black men. Still, the original inevitably leaked out, so that Lincoln's effort to restrain Cameron merely called added attention to the offending passage. On January 17 the Senate confirmed Lincoln's nomination of Cameron to exile as American Minister in St. Petersburg, but once again a headstrong and disgruntled subordinate had been able to embarrass the President by exploiting the slavery issue.[58]

## LINCOLN AND THE PURPOSE OF THE WAR

In his own annual report to Congress on December 3, 1861, Lincoln affirmed the central reason why, beyond even his concern for the border states, he risked such embarrassment and chose not to turn the authority of his office to an assault upon slavery. "In considering the policy to be adopted for suppressing the insurrection," he said, "I have been anxious and careful that the inevitable conflict for this purpose shall not degenerate into a violent and remorseless revolutionary struggle."[59]

Perceiving the inexorable tendency of war to control statesmen and events, Lincoln still sought to retain such control over the direction of the Civil War as he could. To call for the social revolution implicit in the arbitrary abolition of slavery would, he feared, be to yield to the distortion of policy by war and place an immense obstacle in the way of the reunion that was the goal of his policy. "I have, therefore, in every case," he told Congress, "thought it proper to keep the integrity of the Union prominent as the primary object of the contest on our part, leaving all questions which are not of vital military importance to the more deliberate action of the legislature. . . . We should not be in haste to determine that radical and extreme measures, which may reach the loyal as well as the disloyal, are indispensable."[60]

Lincoln believed that in the preservation of the Union lay purpose enough for the war, because, as he had said in his address to the special session of Congress on July 4, "this issue embraces more than the fate of these United States."[61] At the opening of the war, Lincoln had said to his private secretary John Milton Hay: "For my part, I consider the central idea pervading this struggle is the necessity that is upon us, of proving that popular government is not an absurdity. We must settle this question now, whether in a free government the minority have the right to break up the government whenever they choose. If we fail it will go far to prove the incapability of the people to govern themselves."[62] So, Lincoln had gone on in his message of July 4 to argue that the issue involved more than the fate of the United States:

It presents to the whole family of man, the question, whether a constitutional republic, or a democracy — a government of the people, by the same people — can, or cannot, maintain its territorial integrity, against its own domestic foes. It presents the question, whether discontented individuals, too few in numbers to control administration . . . can . . . break up their Government, and thus practically put an end to free government upon earth. It forces us to ask: "Is there, in all republics, this inherent, and fatal weakness?" "Must a government, of necessity, be too *strong* for the liberties of its own people, or too *weak* to maintain its own existence?"[63]

After a lengthy discussion of the constitutional issue of secession, Lincoln returned to the larger theme again in the same message:

This is essentially a People's contest. On the side of the Union, it is a struggle for maintaining in the world, that form, and substance of government, whose leading object is, to elevate the condition of men — to lift artificial weights from all shoulders — to clear the paths of laudable pursuit for all — to afford all, an unfettered start, and a fair chance, in the race of life. Yielding to partial, and temporary departures, from necessity, this is the leading object of the government for whose existence we contend.[64]

When Congress reassembled in December the President reiterated his view "that the insurrection is largely, if not exclusively, a war upon the first principle of popular government — the rights of the people."[65] "The struggle of today, is not altogether for today — it is for a vast future also."[66]

Lincoln's fear of the dangers of "remorseless revolutionary struggle" and his subsidiary belief that he must walk a tightrope rather than risk losing the border states and conservative Unionist sentiment in the North were wise as well as understandable; but also understandable is the growing restlessness shown by that portion of Northern opinion to which Ben Butler, Frémont, and Cameron sought to appeal, whatever the motives of those gentlemen —

the part of Northern opinion that amid the frustrations of McClellan's in-action found itself asking what the war was all about, and received with difficulty an answer that did not confront the slavery issue so inextricably entwined in the origins of the war.

In his message of December 3, 1861, Lincoln did advocate the elimination of slavery in the loyal slave states with compensation to the slaveholders. But was that enough? Would not the preservation of the Union be a hollow triumph unless artificial weights were indeed removed from the shoulders of all? Among the antislavery idealists who had done much to found the Republican Party, such questions could not but be asked.

## McClellan and the Purpose of the War

With the Army of the Potomac, and particularly with its commander, lay much of the power to decide the coming shape and purpose of the war.

McClellan was a general thoughtful about the relationship between military means and political ends, and aware that at his level of military command there could be no easy separation between military strategy and the political purposes of the war: that his choice of military strategy was bound to affect policy, and that it was futile to expect him to divorce himself altogether from policy considerations because he was a soldier.

As might be assumed from his preference for Democratic social companions, McClellan thoroughly favored Lincoln's desire to prevent the war from degenerating into remorseless revolutionary struggle. Following Frémont's removal, McClellan assigned new department commanders to a reorganized Western theater: Major-General Henry Wager Halleck, U.S.A., on November 9 to a new Department of Missouri with headquarters at St. Louis, because Hunter had proven lethargic and permitted a considerable secessionist resurgence in Missouri; and Brigadier-General Don Carlos Buell, U.S.V., on November 15 to the Department of the Ohio with headquarters at Louisville.[67] McClellan strongly reminded both of them, as he put it to Buell, that "we are fighting only to preserve the integrity of the Union and to uphold the Constitutional authority of the General Government." Buell was to assure the people of Kentucky that their "domestic institutions" would not be interfered with but would receive "every Constitutional protection."[68] "I have not come here to wage war upon the defenseless, upon non-combatants, upon private property, nor upon the domestic institutions of the land," McClellan was to assure Virginians. "I and the army I command are fighting to secure the Union & maintain its Constitution & laws, — and for no other purpose."[69]

In the controversial "Harrison's Landing Letter," or "Harrison's Bar Letter," which he was to write to Lincoln on July 7, 1862, McClellan said that the rebellion having become a war, the war

> should be conducted upon the highest principles known to Christian Civilization. It should not be a War looking to the subjugation of the people of any state, in any event. It should not be, at all, a War upon population; but against armed forces and political organizations. Neither confiscation of property, political executions of persons, territorial organization of states or forcible abolition of slavery should be contemplated for a moment.[70]

". . . all private property and unarmed persons," McClellan said, "should be strictly protected. . . . Military power should not be allowed to interfere with the relations of servitude, either by supporting or impairing the authority of the master, except for repressing disorder. . . ." To be sure, slaves defined as contraband by act of Congress and seeking protection should be granted it; and with compensation to the slaveowners, slaves might be appropriated to government service on the ground of military necessity, even to the extent of compensated manumission throughout a state. But "A declaration of radical views, especially upon slavery, will rapidly disintegrate our present armies. . . ."[71]

At length, during the winter of 1861–1862 McClellan unveiled to the President his plans for the time when he should begin to campaign. In doing so he revealed a strategic conception as coherent as any that had yet been formulated in the North, more mindful of the desirability of rapid success than Scott's Anaconda, and consistent with McClellan's views on war policy. Whatever his faults as a military commander, McClellan possessed an admirable strategic grasp, not least, furthermore, in his recognition that the Washington-Richmond area was the critical theater of war.

Rebellion having become war, the Confederate armies obviously had to be defeated; but the object of the war being friendly reunion, the Confederates must be conciliated even as war was being waged. This delicate balance of means and object required, McClellan held, both that scrupulous protection be given to unarmed Southerners and to Southern property, and that the very military actions of the war be so conducted that they would not inflame passions and anger on either side. Accordingly, McClellan planned to avoid head-on military collisions whenever possible, to prevent the heavy casualties that would embitter sentiments. He would not advance directly against the fortifications elaborately prepared by the Confederates around Manassas since the previous summer's battle. Rather, he would wage a war of maneuver. He proposed to move the Army of the Potomac by ship down the Potomac and the Chesapeake and up the Rappahannock River to Urbanna, whence there would be a relatively short overland march to Richmond. Having turned the principal defenses of the Confederate Army of the Potomac, and having utilized Federal sea power to place his troops within ready striking distance of the Confederate capital, he hoped to score a decisive success by the capture of that capital. With good fortune he would bring the war to a prompt and unbloody conclusion much as Winfield Scott had ended the Mexican War by capturing the Mexican capital.[72]

If McClellan should move with reasonable promptness in 1862, and if this design unfolded approximately as he planned it, then the winter's discontent might yet dissolve, and the war might yet end with little enough bitterness to avoid the danger of remorseless revolutionary struggle. The chances for such an outcome were no doubt slim; the very origins of the war too much implied a revolution. But if war could be prevented from reaching such an outcome, then Major-General George B. McClellan, who much deplored any prospect of revolution, held the remaining opportunity to avert it.

# FOUR

# Bloodshed and Indecision

## AN UNHAPPY NEW YEAR

McClellan's plans notwithstanding, the turn of the year carried Lincoln into deepest gloom. Perhaps he did not appreciate the possibilities in McClellan's design as much as an opponent of remorseless struggle might have; perhaps the President was too clearsighted a realist to do so.

Anyway, the shadow of the *Trent* affair hung over Christmas. Of events in the South, Lincoln lamented on January 4: "But my distress is that our friends in East Tennessee are being hanged and driven to despair, and even now I fear, are thinking of taking rebel arms for the sake of personal protection."[1] He referred to the mountainous area of Tennessee that had voted heavily against the secession of the state, and for the rescue of whose loyal citizens by Union arms his desire had become almost obsessive. But a November rising of East Tennessee Unionist saboteurs against Confederate bridges and railroads had brought no answering offensive from the Union forces just to the north in Kentucky, and now the Confederacy was opening a campaign of executions against the Unionist leaders. In Washington, the General-in-Chief of the Union armies took to his bed at Christmas time with typhoid fever. McClellan's chief of staff, his father-in-law Brigadier-General Randolph B. Marcy, U.S.V., also took sick, and no one else as yet knew any details of McClellan's plans. The great army camped around Washington was now headless as well as motionless. Its immense expenses were driving Secretary of the Treasury Salmon P. Chase of Ohio to his own despair by impelling him to endorse a paper currency much against his financial convictions. "General, what shall I do?" asked Lincoln on a visit to Quartermaster-General Meigs. "The people are impatient; Chase has no money, and he tells me he can raise no more; the General of the Army has typhoid fever. What shall I do?"[2]

Meigs was a practical-minded man who would answer such a question though the questioner's intent might be at least half rhetorical. The Quartermaster-General suggested that since McClellan had failed to create an adequate staff to carry on for him when he was incapacitated, the President ought to improvise a substitute in a council of McClellan's principal subordinates. Lincoln responded by holding a series of Executive Mansion conferences with McDowell and Brigadier-General William B. Franklin, U.S.V., eventually bringing in also the Cabinet and Meigs. This procedure had the salutary effect of rousing McClellan out of bed to meet the council on the afternoon of Sunday, January 12. McClellan was resentful, regarding the conferences as an effort to cripple his control of his army and questioning the President's ability to guard military secrets. The general was beginning to display a self-pitying sense of persecution that in time would go far to undercut his impressive strategic abilities. At length he responded to the council's prodding for action by saying at least that, although the enemy in his own front was still too strong in numbers for him to advance, early operations could be expected in Kentucky. Here he was already undercutting his hitherto impressive grasp of the priority of the East.

It was the next day that Lincoln named Edwin M. Stanton to succeed Cameron as Secretary of War; the new Secretary took office on January 20. Stanton had a reputation for energy that he had confirmed during the short time he was in the Buchanan Cabinet. He was a Democrat and a friend of McClellan, so he would presumably be able to work well with the general and infuse into him some of his own drive and forcefulness.[3]

## MILL SPRINGS

For once, action followed McClellan's promise of it, even if in a strategically out-of-the-way place. The Union Army fought a winter campaign in Kentucky, which pleased Lincoln because it might open the gate to East Tennessee.

After General Polk's Confederate invasion of Kentucky cleared the way politically for Federal forces to enter the Commonwealth, the Federal

AREA OF
THE WESTERN CAMPAIGNS

commanders who did so failed for various reasons to respond to Lincoln's prodding them toward East Tennessee. At fifty-six Robert Anderson was too wedded to the leisurely pace of the Old Army, and perhaps too unnerved by the disruption of the country and his own role in it, to provide military leadership adequate to the complex challenges of his native state. On October 8, 1861, Lincoln had felt obliged to remove him from command of the Department of the Cumberland in favor of a younger man. The latter, unhappily, soon betrayed symptoms of losing his mental balance under the weight of his responsibility and fantasized about huge Confederate forces allegedly concentrating against him. Thus a wartime career that had begun promisingly at Bull Run apparently sank to a pathetic ending. On November 9 the younger commander — Brigadier-General William Tecumseh Sherman, U.S.V. — had to follow Anderson into the discard. He yielded his post to General Buell, who suffered from neither advanced age nor nervous instability; but Buell proved simply not interested in mountainous East Tennessee as a theater of military operations.[4]

Although McClellan and eventually Lincoln himself kept Buell well informed of the President's desire to rescue the East Tennessee loyalists, and although McClellan also repeatedly pointed out the strategic advantage to be gained by an advance to cut the Virginia and Tennessee Railroad at Knoxville, thus requiring rail traffic between Virginia and the West to detour through Atlanta, Buell remained preoccupied with a plan for a different offensive, straight southward from Louisville to Nashville. Here the terrain, it must be said, was far better for large troop movements. McClellan of course could have ordered Buell toward Knoxville, and several times under Lincoln's pressure the General-in-Chief couched his communications about going into East Tennessee in the form of virtual commands; but always he diluted his orders with just enough words about a department commander's discretionary authority that Buell paid him no heed. By January, McClellan and Lincoln were close to reconciling themselves to the prospect that Nashville rather than Knoxville would be the target of any advance Buell might soon attempt.[5]

Then, abruptly, Lincoln's outburst about the friends of the Union who were being left to despair in East Tennessee, combined with similar lamentations and admonitions to Buell from McClellan, surprisingly produced a mood of penitence and a partial change of mind. Buell ordered the commander of his First Division, Brigadier-General George H. Thomas, U.S.V., to concentrate the division in such a manner as to force the withdrawal of a Confederate bridgehead north of the Cumberland River opposite Mill Springs, Kentucky. When Thomas advanced with about 4,000 men, Confederate Major-General George B. Crittenden decided to attack him with similar numbers on January 19. Crittenden's decision was a mistake. He had no advantage of any kind sufficient to run the risks of attacking, which ordinarily required superior force in order to succeed. In the resulting battle of Mill Springs or Logan Cross Roads, Thomas turned back Crittenden and then engaged in that military rarity, a pursuit, thereby capturing twelve artillery pieces, many small arms, and much equipment. Although the various parts of his force were not especially well coordinated during these activities — only about 2,500 of his troops got into action — General Thomas, a Unionist Virginian, had taken the first step toward building what would become a distinguished military reputation. Union casualties were only thirty-nine killed and 207 wounded; Confederate casualties are unknown but almost certainly were considerably more. Thomas's opponent, General Crittenden, son of John J. Crittenden, was accused of drunkenness during and mismanagement of the battle. After censure by a court of inquiry he lost his general's wreath from his collar.[6]

Lincoln could now hope for still better things on the road to East Tennessee — except that Buell's penitence turned out to be brief, and there was no Union follow-up of Mill Springs.

## A WESTERN STRATEGY TAKES SHAPE

Mill Springs proved nevertheless a sign of things to come. The obstacles real and imagined that McClellan saw threatening his offensive in the East made it possible for his Eastern priorities to yield by default to a Western strategy, not toward East Tennessee but down the Mississippi. The Western strategy, indeed, was to develop an enviable momentum and coherence that immensely benefited the Union war effort in the long run — but the West required the long run, whereas it was in the East that opportunity lay for a shorter, less ferocious, less remorseless war.

Buell changed his mind again partly because the roads to East Tennessee through the Cumberland Gap proved, as he had expected, extremely bad in the winter season, and partly he was drawn into other leaders' designs. Much as the President's heart went out to the persecuted loyalists of East Tennessee, a campaign that might open to the Union the great Mississippi River and ultimately reunite the President's native Mississippi Valley had to be acknowledged even by Lincoln as far more critical to the outcome of the war; and it was into such a campaign that other leaders drew Don Carlos Buell.

In the beginning, Winfield Scott had looked to an invasion of the Confederacy down the Mississippi as the first grand offensive to be attempted on land, after naval blockade had weakened the Confederacy, and once the summer heat of 1861 had passed to leave the lower Mississippi Valley tolerably hospitable to Northerners. Scott's grand design never materialized. He envisaged the invasion down the Mississippi as being spearheaded by 60,000 to 80,000 men, an immense force compared with any he had led in Mexico; though it was nonetheless small in contrast with the strength eventually required, it was too large an army for the Union to concentrate in one part of the West in 1861, what with all the distractions of Missouri, Kentucky, and western Virginia. Still, the idea of combining Union naval power embodied in river gunboats with land power for an amphibious advance down the Mississippi, to restore the upper Midwest's outlet to the Gulf while splitting the Confederacy in two, was too obvious a strategic design ever to be completely discarded.[7]

Leonidas Polk's foray into Kentucky seemed justified to President Davis despite its political disadvantages precisely because Polk's guns emplaced on the bluffs overlooking the Mississippi at Columbus, Kentucky put a formidable obstacle in the path of the North's obvious strategic design. By the turn of 1861 into 1862, however, a number of Federal officers in the Western theater of war, including both Halleck and Buell, began to elaborate on the project of a Union amphibious advance: not directly down the Mississippi into the teeth of Columbus, but up the Tennessee and Cumberland Rivers from the base established by General Grant at Paducah.

Grant was contemplating his own part in a Western riverine offensive. A West Point graduate of 1843 who won brevets as first lieutenant and then captain of the 4th Infantry for gallantry at Molino del Rey and Chapultepec on September 8 and 13, 1847, he nevertheless suffered from a reputation as a failure in the Old Army. Dull garrison duty and loneliness on the Pacific Coast drove him to drink and neglect of duty, so that he resigned on July 31, 1854 to evade a court-martial. In civil life he became a worse failure, drifting from one occupation to another and into poverty. At the beginning of the Civil War he was dependent on his father, Jesse R. Grant, for whom he helped run a store at Galena, Illinois. When war came, the military Grant nevertheless raised a volunteer militia company at Galena, which impressed Governor Richard Yates enough that in spite of knowing about Grant's recent past, he helped get him elected colonel of the 21st Illinois Infantry on June 17, 1861. The command was not exactly a plum, because the regiment already had a bad reputation for indiscipline; but the new colonel promptly and with amazing dexterity and tact made it shape up so quickly that another political sponsor, Congressman Elihu B. Washburne of the Galena district, on August 7 secured a star for Grant in the Volunteer Army, with the commission dated back to May 17.[8]

In early November 1861 Grant was commanding the garrison at Cairo at the southern tip of Illinois and conducting demonstrations and diversions down both banks of the Mississippi, ordered by Frémont largely to interfere with the latest Confederate activities farther west in Missouri. On the night of November 6–7 Grant received a report that General Polk was shifting troops from Columbus into Missouri. The report happened to be false, but Grant responded to it by deciding to go beyond demonstrations by launching a relatively large-scale raid, into Belmont, Missouri across the Mississippi from Columbus. He brought downriver from Cairo some 3,114 troops, moving in river transports and guarded by the wooden gunboats *Tyler* and *Lexington*. He landed above Belmont, drove back a probably larger body of Confederates to the river bank (where the guns of Columbus could offer them some protection), and destroyed the enemy's camps. In response Polk crossed the Mississippi with 10,000 reinforcements and tried to interpose between Grant and his transports. But the Union brigadier fought his way to safety with six captured cannons along with about 130 prisoners. Each side lost about 600 total casualties. Grant was to be criticized justly for putting his force into a potential trap and unjustly for not holding on to ground where he had never intended to stay. But Belmont brought him to the attention particularly of President Lincoln as a general of bold combativeness, a commodity not in plentiful supply in the North.[9]

## PEA RIDGE: THE GREAT BATTLE
## OF THE TRANS-MISSISSIPPI

Both Grant and his immediate superior, General Halleck, were thinking in terms of Mississippi River–Tennessee River–Cumberland River possibilities by early 1862; but before Halleck could feel free to commit enough troops east of the Mississippi for a substantial offensive into the State of Tennessee, he thought he had to receive some measure of assurance that incendiary Missouri would not erupt uncontrollably. The launching in earnest of the offensive destined to carry U. S. Grant to the forefront of the Union war effort therefore awaited the outcome of much less well known activities, the Pea Ridge campaign.

On Christmas Day 1861 Halleck created as part of his Division of the Missouri the Military District of Southwest Missouri, under command of

Brigadier-General Samuel R. Curtis, U.S.V. Curtis was a West Point graduate of 1831, but except for a year as colonel of the 3rd Ohio Volunteers during
the Mexican War, he had spent his career mainly as a civil engineer, lawyer,
and railroad man in Iowa and Missouri. He was a Republican Congressman
from Iowa from 1856 until he resigned to become colonel of the 2nd Iowa
Volunteers on June 1, 1861. His brigadier's commission was postdated to May
17. His new mission was to drive the Confederates and more particularly the
Missouri State Guard under Sterling Price from his district. Thus he would
both contribute to the vexed task of pacifying Missouri for the Union and
free resources for Halleck's strategic projects elsewhere.[10]

On February 10, 1862, Curtis led his field force, about 11,000 men gran-
diosely titled the Army of the Southwest, out of Rolla toward Price's concentration at Springfield. He moved along the Telegraph Road or Wire Road,
the principal route from north to south across the Ozark Plateau of southern
Missouri and northern Arkansas, so called because in 1860 an electric telegraph line had been strung along this route of John Butterfield's Overland
Mail stagecoaches. The road, however, was barely an unimproved trace, and
it would require logistical ingenuity on the part of Curtis's staff along with a
good deal of belt-tightening by the soldiers to advance the hundred miles
from the Rolla railhead to Springfield in winter, over rugged, wooded terrain
offering little subsistence en route — let alone to conduct a further campaign
to the Arkansas border another seventy-five miles distant, or even beyond.
Curtis enjoyed a stroke of exceptional good fortune when Halleck assigned
as his supply officer a dynamo named Captain Philip H. Sheridan, 13th U.S.
Infantry; but while Sheridan's accomplishments in pushing food and forage
down the Telegraph Road proved remarkable, not the least reason why the
Army of the Southwest deserves to be better remembered than it usually is
lies in its triumphs over logistical adversity that would have caused many
generals and armies to halt not far from Rolla.[11]

General Price, commanding about 8,000 ill-organized (there were too
many small units) and undertrained Missourians, abandoned Springfield in
the face of his opponents' logistical prodigies and retreated into northwest
Arkansas. There the hopes of the Confederacy for the area lay in a convergence of Price's forces with those of Brigadier-General Ben McCulloch, who
was the victor of Wilson's Creek and a hard-bitten veteran of the Texas war
for independence and the Texas Rangers. Those hopes had to be limited
among the knowledgeable by awareness that Price's Missouri parochialism
and McCulloch's similar focus on Texas and Arkansas had already spawned
a nasty dislike between them. Given their relationship, it might have been
encouraging that Major-General Earl Van Dorn received command of a

new Military District of the Trans-Mississippi on January 10.[12] On March 1 Van Dorn arrived at Van Buren, Arkansas, on the north shore of the Arkansas River across from Fort Smith and a hundred miles south from Missouri, to unite Price's and McCulloch's troops. Although a West Point graduate of 1842, however, Van Dorn was sadly lacking in several qualities of professionalism, notably in caring enough about reconnaissance and in establishing himself in command and control.

The concentration of Price, McCulloch, and Pike's Indian Brigade (under Brigadier-General Albert J. Pike, and largely from Indian Territory), gave Van Dorn about 17,000 men. Emulating or exceeding his opponent in pretentiousness of nomenclature, Van Dorn called his force the Army of the West. With this army he went over to the counteroffensive, while Curtis felt sufficiently outnumbered to begin a retreat. He could take satisfaction from already having eased pressure on Halleck enough to permit a partial beginning of the offensive into Tennessee, the Fort Henry–Fort Donelson campaign.

Curtis decided to halt his withdrawal on a good defensive position, an outcrop of the Ozark Plateau just inside Arkansas that he soon learned was called Pea Ridge, where Elkhorn Tavern was a local landmark. The subsequent battle goes alternately by the names of the ridge and the tavern. Curtis's First and Second Divisions, largely Missouri German regiments together commanded by an educated German soldier and German-American political favorite, Brigadier-General Franz Sigel, U.S.V., barely escaped being cut off during a blizzard-plagued phase of the retreat. They escaped thanks to a combination of skillful maneuvering by Sigel — not, unfortunately for the Union, a portent of things to come — with characteristically loose coordination of his units and inadequate reconnoitering on Van Dorn's part.

With Curtis's four divisions reunited, the battle of Pea Ridge on March 7–8, 1862 was nevertheless one of the few major Civil War engagements in which the Federals were substantially outnumbered. Curtis compensated by keeping his force better in hand than Van Dorn. The battle was essentially two separate fights. Van Dorn essayed a decidedly ambitious Napoleonic design in which McCulloch and Pike were to execute a turning maneuver against Curtis's right rear west of Elkhorn Tavern — a *manœuvre sur les derrières*; but that dramatic effort would in fact be the secondary movement, intended to divert the Federals from another, main turning maneuver against positions on the Telegraph Road around the tavern.

The secondary effort turned out to create six hours of fighting on the first day of battle that were secondary in ferocity to very little during the entire war. Missouri's passions seemed to extend themselves from the guerrilla struggle to conventional-style combat. In the process Ben McCulloch was killed, and on the Federal side the First and Third Divisions had to change front by 180 degrees, from facing south to facing north, all under heavy fire and headlong attacks.

Three miles to the east, alert Union intelligence thwarted the element of surprise in Van Dorn's main turning maneuver and led to a spoiling attack by the Federal Fourth Division to try to preempt the shape of the day's events. Van Dorn had too many Confederates on hand to permit Curtis to seize the momentum in this phase of the two-part battle, but the Confederate commander nonetheless failed to take advantage of this circumstance; he deliberately slowed the assault by Price's wing of his army in the mistaken belief — faulty intelligence again — that the patterns of noise in the west showed that McCulloch would soon join Price. Against Van Dorn's pulled punch Curtis's lines held, and during the night he rearranged his troops into a more compact defensive alignment on the correct assumption that Van Dorn would try again and there would be a furious Confederate surge against the Telegraph Road positions in the morning of March 8. Admirably handled Union artillery then not only smashed Van Dorn's renewed effort but proved uncommonly effective by Civil War standards in opening the way for an infantry counterattack, which drove the Confederates from the field.

The battle of Pea Ridge cost the Federals 1,384 casualties out of about 10,250 engaged. Van Dorn claimed that he lost only about 800 killed and wounded and 200 to 300 prisoners, an estimate that he soon reduced to 600 killed and wounded and 200 prisoners, although even his first statistics flew in the face of all experience of combat as fierce as had occurred. The Federals actually counted 475 to 525 unwounded Confederate prisoners.[13] It is reasonably certain that Pea Ridge was a Union victory in its ratio of casualties as well as by other measurements.

Certainly it was a strategic victory for the Union. Van Dorn pulled back to the Arkansas River and then, with his mercurial temperament longing to put the scene of misfortune as far as he could behind him, accepted with undue haste and eagerness instructions to move the Army of the West to the east of the Mississippi River to join a concentration developing there in reaction to Halleck's and Grant's Union strategy. The commander of the Army of the West might at least have put on record an objection that the effect of such a shift would be to open much of Arkansas to the Federals as well as to leave Missouri with little more than the guerrillas to resist Unionism; in short, by coming close to abandoning Arkansas and Missouri the

Confederate concentration would actually help Halleck by easing his way toward a countervailing Federal concentration.

In the spring, Curtis's Army of the Southwest shifted its operations eastward. The Union general wanted to capture Little Rock, but the logistics of an overland campaign so deep into Arkansas would no doubt have been impossible even with Sheridan still helping; now the logistics were doubly daunting because Curtis in one of his rare mistakes had quarrelled with the captain, who had therefore arranged to return to Halleck's headquarters. With his wagon-train supply line stretched more than 300 miles back to Rolla, Curtis decided he had to give up the idea of taking Little Rock until he could open a waterborne line of communications up the White River from the Mississippi. Halleck and the Union Navy attempted to oblige him, but a naval expedition up the White River got stuck in low water at Clarendon.

Finding himself, however, in a countryside much more generously provided than the Ozark Plateau with the provisions for feeding an army, and in summertime at that, in late June 1862 Curtis came to a remarkable decision. He would voluntarily abandon his supply line from Rolla and march through eastern Arkansas some 200 miles, from Batesville down the White River to the Mississippi, living off the countryside until he achieved a firm junction with the Navy. For two weeks his army thus fended for itself, and by doing so it set a pattern that would be followed later by Grant and others with momentous results. In the process Curtis also executed the Union's first large-scale raid against the enemy's economy, providing an equally momentous example for later operations. The troops of the Army of the Southwest confiscated enough supplies to meet their own needs and destroyed great quantities of property potentially useful to the Confederates. They left devastation in their wake, along with a substantial degree of fear of grim Yankee marauders. They also did more to eliminate slavery in their area of operations than the well-advertised proclamations of Butler, Frémont, and Cameron had ever done. In the course of depriving the Confederacy of militarily valuable property, Curtis had printing presses along the way turn out emancipation papers that his soldiers gave to some 3,000 slaves.

So the shape of much that was to come was foreshadowed by Samuel Ryan Curtis, but the Iowa general was a modest man who never laid much claim to the innovations that he could have trumpeted as his own. Pea Ridge earned him promotion to major-general, U.S.V., on March 21, but he remained west of the Mississippi throughout the war, and the big headlines were not to be won there.[14]

## THE FAR WEST

The surrender of David Twiggs in Texas just before the war began helped precipitate a campaign yet farther west than Arkansas, in the Territory of New Mexico. Inspired by Twiggs's surrender to carry the banners of the Confederacy far up the Rio Grande, a Texan named John Baylor acquired a Confederate commission as lieutenant-colonel and on the strength of it recruited a 350-man Regiment of Texas Mounted Rifles. Early in July 1861 he led it from San Antonio to Fort Bliss and thence forty miles upriver into New Mexico to Fort Fillmore. Baylor was not deterred by the presence at the fort of a 7th United States Infantry garrison of twice his numbers under Major Isaac Lynde of that regiment. Nor should he have been; for the Union Regulars had been stagnating in idleness. Lynde ventured out to meet Baylor but was repulsed on July 26 at Mesilla across the Rio Grande from the fort, suffering nine casualties. Easily discouraged, the next day Lynde surrendered 492 men — the rest had already straggled into Confederate hands — along with two cannons, 200 cavalry mounts, and 300 head of cattle. On August 1 Baylor issued a proclamation transforming New Mexico south of the thirty-fourth parallel into the Confederate Territory of Arizona, with Mesilla as its capital and himself as military governor.

Meanwhile, on July 8, Brigadier-General Henry Hopkins Sibley had received War Department orders to take command of Confederate forces in the Far Southwest. Major of the 1st United States Dragoons when he resigned on May 13, Sibley had long served the Old Army in that region and seemed an appropriate choice to fulfill Jefferson Davis's vision of extending the Confederacy all the way to the Pacific through a region that had attracted his special interest when he was Secretary of War. On December 13, 1861, Sibley organized about 3,700 men, largely Texans, into the Army of New Mexico, also called the Arizona Brigade. Six days later he claimed both Arizona and New Mexico for the Confederacy. On January 4, 1862 he started up the Rio Grande from Fort Bliss to enforce the claim.

On November 9, 1861 the Federals had established their own Department of New Mexico, comprising the entire Territory of New Mexico. Its headquarters was at Santa Fe; its commander was Colonel, 19th Infantry, Edward Richard Sprigg Canby. Canby with some 4,000 troops awaited Sibley at Fort Craig, on the Rio Grande about eighty miles north of Mesilla.

On February 20 Canby perceived Sibley as maneuvering to bypass Fort Craig. In fact, Sibley intended not to leave the fort behind but to draw the Federals from it so he could fight them in the open. Because he misunderstood what Sibley was up to, Canby obliged. He blundered into a virtual ambush on the mesa of Valverde north of the fort, where the Confederates beat him badly on February 21, in action climaxed by a mounted cavalry charge. (Sibley himself, however, missed the culmination of the battle, overcome either by the heat or by alcohol.)

Sibley next turned east toward Santa Fe, to gain the political objective of the capital and, of more immediate importance, resupply after long marches across desert wastes. The Federals responded by burning such stores as they could not evacuate from Albuquerque and repeating the process at Santa Fe. Canby had chosen to return to the relative safety of the stockade at Fort Craig, but the 1st Colorado and a smattering of other Federal troops concentrated at Fort Union, sixty miles east of Santa Fe, to deal with Sibley. In spite of hunger and exhaustion among his troops, the latter was not yet willing to abandon the Southwestern dream he shared with President Davis, and he marched east on the Santa Fe Trail toward Fort Union. On March 26 his forces advanced to meet what they believed was a small Federal force riding toward them through Apache Canyon near Johnson's Ranch — the coming battle goes by both names — when the Coloradans, a wild bunch of miners according to Confederate testimony — jumped them from both sides of the pass. The Texans broke, losing seventy-one prisoners and seventeen other casualties to a loss of only nineteen of the Coloradans. The commander of those desperados was Colonel John M. Chivington, destined for less favorable notoriety when his Colorado volunteers massacred some 500 Cheyenne and Arapaho at Sand Creek in his home territory on November 29, 1864.

Despite their success at Apache Pass, the Federals retreated a short distance to a place called Pigeon's Ranch in La Glorieta Pass. There the Confederate advance guard attacked them on March 28. The Texans were gradually winning until Chivington with about 400 men showed up to plunder the wagons and supplies in their rear after a difficult mountain march. The Confederates lost thirty-six killed, sixty wounded, and twenty-five missing, a total of 121 out of about 1,100 engaged. The Federals lost thirty-one killed, at least fifty wounded, and thirty missing, at least 101 of 1,342. But it was Sibley who without adequate supplies and a desert away from help could not afford the casualties.

He retreated, chivied along by Canby with his customary caution, though he now commanded about 1,210 men from Fort Craig in addition to the indeterminate numbers of the Apache Pass–La Glorieta Pass forces. The Confederate retreat was an epic, for when Sibley was still a ten days' march from the Rio Grande he had food and water for only five days. When he staggered into Fort Bliss at the beginning of May with his stragglers stretched out fifty miles behind him, he learned that the California Column of eleven infantry companies, two cavalry companies, and two artillery companies under Colonel James H. Carleton, 1st California Infantry (from April 28 brigadier-general, U.S.V.), was on its way to add to his opponents. He retreated all the way to San Antonio. Of his 1,700 casualties, 1,200 were lost on the march back to Texas. There would be no Confederate empire of the Southwest.[15]

## Forts Henry and Donelson

Before Pea Ridge was fought, Curtis's southwestern Missouri campaign had already sprung Grant loose for the preliminary phases of the Union invasion of Tennessee on which he and Halleck hoped to embark as soon as the latter was free from the worst of the Missouri distractions. By the time Curtis was marching down the White River to the Mississippi, Halleck had long since felt secure enough in the western part of his command area to follow up Grant's beginnings with the most impressive, spectacular, and successful offensive of the war so far. It was executed in the wrong theater to promise a quick end to the entire contest, but it paid large dividends nevertheless.

For Union forces to go up the Tennessee River not much beyond the Kentucky-Tennessee border would almost certainly compel the Confederates to abandon Columbus, by breaking the railroad connection of that place with the principal Confederate concentration in Kentucky, gathered under General Albert Sidney Johnston around Bowling Green. Furthermore, an advance up the Cumberland River would lead to the Tennessee capital at Nashville and to important ironworks and munitions manufactories in the Nashville vicinity, and it would force Johnston to evacuate Bowling Green. Continuing up the Tennessee River would lead the Federals also to the Memphis and Charleston Railroad along Tennessee's border with Alabama and Mississippi. Drives up both the Cumberland and the Tennessee would go far to deprive the Confederacy not only of all of Kentucky but also of central Tennessee, its single richest source of food grains and pork in addition to being a seat of much war industry.

The Confederates recognized these possibilities clearly enough that during the autumn of 1861 they began building earthwork fortifications to command passage of the Tennessee and Cumberland Rivers just south of the Kentucky-Tennessee border, Fort Henry on the Tennessee and Fort Donelson on the Cumberland. On February 2, 1862 General Halleck communicated to Buell his hope of initiating an advance up the rivers by mid- or late February, stating that the offensive would require about 60,000 men, a force he believed it was now feasible to assemble, with the help of Curtis's clearing the main rebel army from Missouri.[16] Even more intent than Halleck on grasping the advantages of the Tennessee-Cumberland route into the South was General Grant, who late in January traveled to Halleck's St. Louis headquarters to urge that he could capture Fort Henry with his own command of only about a quarter of the strength Halleck had projected, with the cooperation of the seven river gunboats, four of them ironclad, commanded by Flag Officer Andrew H. Foote of the Navy. Grant had been diligently gathering information on Fort Henry and could present to Halleck details of its strength and design.

For reasons unclear, Halleck at this time entertained some sort of resentment against Grant, and the lack of cordiality between the two has obscured the subsequent sequence of events. Halleck as a distinguished military intellectual had a far higher reputation than Grant in addition to ranking him, yet the department commander may have felt uneasy over the subordinate's restless eagerness and energy. Grant years later in his *Memoirs* wrote that at St. Louis he was unpleasantly rebuffed by Halleck and that he returned to Cairo disheartened.[17] But it seems unlikely that Halleck was so completely negative, because a few days later, on January 28, Grant telegraphed Halleck: "With permission, I will take Fort Henry, on the Tennessee, and establish and hold a large camp there."[18] Foote informed Halleck that he supported Grant's idea and would collaborate with him. After a final survey of the latest intelligence data, Halleck gave the order to go ahead.[19]

Fort Henry had been badly located, on low ground on the east bank of the Tennessee. The Confederates were busily at work on another fort on the higher ground of the west bank, but Grant and Foote saw to it that these preparations were too late. Grant with about 15,000 soldiers advanced against the Confederate works on both east and west shores, and on February 6 Foote's gunboats opened a bombardment. Brigadier-General Lloyd Tilghman, in command of Fort Henry, saw his situation as hopeless and already had sent most of the garrison to Fort Donelson, leaving only some 100 artillerists. These gunners replied to Foote with vigor and considerable damaging effect, but after an exchange lasting three hours Tilghman rightly considered his judgment of hopelessness to be confirmed, and he surrendered.[20]

Although his instructions did not call for it, Grant characteristically resolved to go on to Fort Donelson, only twelve miles away, and so informed Halleck. Foote's ironclads had been damaged enough that they had to return to Cairo to refit, however, so Grant gave up the idea of an immediate march against Donelson to wait until they were combat-ready again. Meanwhile the wooden gunboats, which had stayed behind the ironclads during the artillery duel, ranged up the Tennessee as far as the beginning of the Muscle Shoals at Florence, Alabama, capturing or destroying Confederate shipping. A river highway into the Deep South was already open to the Union.[21]

Albert Sidney Johnston on the Confederate side reacted to the news from Fort Henry irresolutely. Much was expected of him; many regarded him as the ablest soldier on either side. He was a West Point graduate of 1822 who had served as commanding general of the Texas Army and Secretary of War of the Republic of Texas. From its establishment on March 3, 1855, he was colonel of the 2nd U.S. Cavalry, Secretary of War Jefferson Davis's favored regiment. He became a brevet brigadier-general as of November 18, 1857, for his leadership of the army that invaded Utah in the Mormon War. At the outbreak of the Civil War the Lincoln government offered him appointment as second to Winfield Scott in command of the U.S. Army. But on May 3, 1861 he resigned his commission and made his way eastward from his headquarters as commander of the Department of the Pacific, and without having been in communication with him the Confederacy commissioned him a full general.

Indeed, President Davis had seen to it that Johnston's commission, confirmed like Lee's and J. E. Johnston's on August 31, 1861, gave May 30 as his date of rank, making him second in seniority in the Confederate officer corps only to Adjutant General and Inspector General Samuel Cooper (also confirmed as general on August 31, with the rank dating from May 16). Since September 15, A. S. Johnston commanded Polk's former department, now usually called the Western Department and by the beginning of 1862 encompassing Tennessee, Arkansas, and Mississippi west at the Mississippi Central Railroad.[22]

Johnston looked the part of a hero; he was over six feet tall, solidly built, and darkly handsome. But he fumbled as he faced his first major challenge. He could have used his railroads to muster a concentration of superior force against Grant from throughout his large command area to save Fort Donelson. Instead he sent the 28,000 men he had brought together at Bowling Green as the Central Army of Kentucky along with his other detachments in central Kentucky into retreat, mainly away from Donelson. Into Donelson, however, he sent 10,000 reinforcements for the 11,000 already there, a move whose only likely effect would be to enlarge Grant's coming bag of prisoners.

On February 12 Grant's troops arrived before the fort and began to invest it. On the 14th Foote's gunboats dueled with the fort; but Donelson was better situated than Henry, Foote brought his gunboats in too close, and the fort had the better of the exchange. Still, Grant was receiving reinforcements that brought his strength to 27,000, and the commander of the fort, Brigadier-General John B. Floyd, Buchanan's Secretary of War, perceived that escape for the garrison would soon be impossible, if it was not already.[23] On the 15th, Floyd attacked the southern end of Grant's lines where Grant had not yet anchored himself on the river, hoping to break open a door for the withdrawal of the whole garrison. But the attack failed, and Grant took advantage of it to assault and capture some of the Confederate works on the opposite flank. Lieutenant-Colonel Nathan Bedford Forrest, with about 500 troops of his Regiment of Mounted Rangers and about 200 others, rode through the Union lines in darkness to escape. Floyd himself, fearing legal charges from his conduct of the War Department, followed with another 3,000 including his second in command, Brigadier-General Gideon J. Pillow. Early the next morning, the senior Confederate officer remaining, Brigadier-General Simon Bolivar Buckner, requested of Grant a discussion of surrender terms, to which Grant gave the famous reply: "Yours of this date, proposing armistice and appointment of commissioners to settle terms of capitulation, is just received. No terms except unconditional and immediate surrender can be accepted. I propose to move immediately upon your works."[24]

Buckner had no choice but to accept. The Federals had suffered 2,832 casualties (500 killed, 2,108 wounded, 224 missing). They received the surrender of some 14,000 Confederates, and the Confederates had lost about 2,000 killed and wounded; the remainder of the garrison had been those who escaped as already indicated or wounded men who were sent away before Grant's noose closed tight.[25]

## SHILOH

The Union victories had been accompanied by considerable negotiation over the telegraph wires among Halleck, Buell, and the General-in-Chief, because Grant's campaign occurred near the boundary between Halleck's and Buell's departments, running through west-central Kentucky, and by crossing the Kentucky-Tennessee line Grant had actually entered Buell's department. This complication was resolved for the future, and Halleck was rewarded for his part in the victories, by bringing Buell under Halleck's command in a large new Department of the Mississippi on March 11.[26] It was to be hoped that unity of command in the theater of war, naturally cited as a desideratum by all military critics then and now, would serve the Federals better than it had the Confederates.

Albert Sidney Johnston shared with President Davis responsibility for the decision to try to guard the northwestern boundary of the Confederacy all the way from the Appalachians to the Mississippi with what amounted to a passive defense, based on a cordon of troops spread thinly from the area of Mill Springs through Bowling Green and Forts Donelson and Henry to Columbus. Such a defensive perimeter across Kentucky — the Confederate States regarding that Commonwealth as a rightful member of their union, so the word "defensive" could apply — was consistent with the claim of Southern policy that the South intended no aggression upon the free states but was merely defending its rights. With about 50,000 men in his command east of the Mississippi when the Henry-Donelson campaign began, however, Johnston did not have enough soldiers to cover adequately his whole Kentucky-Tennessee front of 300 miles. Federal concentrations against any part of the line were bound to find weaknesses, as Grant and Halleck did.

Even within the limits of a thoroughly defensive strategy, Johnston performed poorly, and not only by failing to concentrate against Grant after Fort Henry to make the one riposte that might have saved Donelson. By stationing himself in an advanced position at Bowling Green, insufficiently in contact with the rest of his forces, he became practically a local commander. After Donelson, Columbus had to be abandoned, and Johnston had to try to anchor his Mississippi flank at New Madrid and Island No. 10 near the northern boundary of Tennessee. He himself not only fell back from Bowling Green but had to yield Nashville under pressure from converging columns led by Grant and Buell. Johnston halted his retreat at Corinth, Mississippi, on the Memphis and Charleston Railroad, there to attempt to reorganize his forces well enough to hold that rail link between the Confederate East and West.[27]

Would Halleck be a better theater commander for the Union than Johnston had thus far proven for the Confederacy? Although "Old Brains" Halleck possessed much military erudition — his *Elements of Military Art and Science* had been the first published comprehensive American treatise on the art of war[28] — and although he had helped conceive the Donelson-Henry campaign and reinforced and supplied Grant handsomely, the answer could not be sure. There was something of pedantry about his erudition and of pettiness in his character. Refraining from praising Grant for Henry and Donelson, he instead spent early March indulging in an unseemly quarrel with his energetic subordinate based on the charges that Grant had not kept him adequately informed of developments and that he had not always obeyed orders. Halleck complained about Grant to McClellan in terms that gave the General-in-Chief the impression that Grant was irresponsible and untrustworthy. Eventually, in fact, on March 5, the Western commander put Brigadier-General Charles Ferguson Smith, U.S.V., in Grant's place at the head of the advance.

Fortunately, on February 16, before this unpleasantness surfaced, Congress and the President had already acted to reward Grant with a commission as major-general of volunteers. While misunderstandings and delays in communication may have contributed to Halleck's displeasure with Grant, it must appear that the department commander's campaign against his subordinate was rooted in jealousy and perhaps in malice. The truth was that Grant had been thoroughly obedient to every order received and more than faithful in reporting to Halleck. He could point to enough telegrams and letters in the files to demonstrate it, so that Halleck had to relent, and he reinstated Grant in command of his main field force on March 13.[29]

Grant resumed command at Savannah and Pittsburg Landing up the Tennessee, twenty-five miles short of Corinth. There forces from Halleck's former department were gathering to await Buell with his own main field force, the Army of the Ohio. Once Buell arrived, Halleck intended to come forward to take over Grant's and Buell's combined armies for a march upon Corinth. As troops debarked from river steamers at Pittsburg Landing, Grant placed them in camps on a wooded and broken plateau above the river, as far as and somewhat beyond Shiloh Baptist Church not quite three miles southwest of the landing, on the road to Corinth. By the beginning of April, Grant had about 40,000 men, organized into six divisions. Although they conducted periodic reconnaissance toward the enemy, they discovered no unusual activity. Grant's men were not entrenched, and they were encamped in locations chosen more for convenience in relation to roads, level ground, and water than for defensive strength. In the second half of the war, armies tended to entrench wherever they stopped. That was not yet customary. Anyway, while Grant evidently expected no attack, on the other hand he let Halleck know he was not averse to a fight. He may not have wanted to discourage the enemy too much from giving him one.[30]

If so, he would get his wish. By April 5 a Confederate army of approximately the same size as Grant's was almost upon him, hidden in the woods just to the south. To try to retrieve the Henry-Donelson disasters, Albert Sidney Johnston had collected at Corinth troops from as far away as Pensacola. At first dawn on Sunday, April 6, advance pickets of Grant's Sixth Division under Brigadier-General Benjamin M. Prentiss, U.S.V., collided with the attacking hosts of Johnston's Army of the Mississippi. The Confederates swiftly overwhelmed the pickets and were soon pushing through the camps of Prentiss's division and William T. Sherman's Fifth Division, the commander of which had recently returned to active duty, rested from his earlier breakdown and given another chance by Halleck.

Some Federal units broke and fled under the shock of a surprise attack, but although through the morning and early afternoon they were continually driven back, most of the Federals resisted stubbornly. All Grant's divisions except the Third, that of Major-General Lew Wallace, U.S.V., which got lost on back roads, were soon in the fight. The Confederate assault was handicapped by the temptation to break ranks and forage in the overrun Union camps, which contained a wealth of stores unusual by Confederate standards. In addition, Johnston was guilty of tactical mismanagement as bad as his earlier strategic and operational failings. He sent forward the four corps of his army not in line of corps but in column of corps, that is, with the corps following one another in succession, the front of each corps coterminous with the front of the army, so that every corps commander had to be concerned with the whole front, and units became hopelessly intermixed as the battle developed. Johnston himself behaved like a company commander in the forefront of the action, which is not what the leader of an army ought to do but was something he did well because he was brave and charismatic. About two P.M. a shot severed an artery below the knee of his right leg, and he soon bled to death. According to Southern mythology, this loss of the most promising of generals cost the Confederacy the battle and perhaps the war. There is no reason to accept the mythology.

Johnston's second in command, none other than Beauregard, had done at least as much as Johnston to plan and accomplish the concentration for the battle and had been exercising overall direction of the combat from the time early on April 6 when Johnston began leading troops personally; Beauregard simply continued in charge. Already the Confederates were exhausting their strength against a stronghold formed by Prentiss's and parts of two other Union divisions, Sherman's and Brigadier-General, U.S.V., William H. L. Wallace's Second, behind a sunken road — the "Hornet's Nest" of Shiloh. By the time Prentiss surrendered with the 2,200 Federals who remained in the Hornet's Nest about 5:30 P.M., the bulk of Grant's army had formed too strong a position on bluffs above Pittsburg Landing, too powerful in artillery and well supported by the gunboats *Tyler* and *Lexington* in the river, to be carried in what remained of the day.

By that time Lew Wallace's division had joined Grant's line, having spent much of the day marching but being otherwise fresh and intact. The vanguard of Brigadier-General, U.S.V., William "Bull" Nelson's Fourth Division of Buell's army was also entering the line. The prospect for further Confederate progress was practically nil. Buell's other two divisions arrived by the morning of the 7th, and Grant and Buell cooperated in a counterattack that drove Beauregard from the field. The Confederate attempt to reverse the verdict of the Henry-Donelson campaign had failed.

The soldiers who fought at the battle of Shiloh or Pittsburg Landing were still raw and unskilled, but they tore at each other with what was becoming the customary ferocity. The Federals suffered 13,047 casualties (1,754 killed, 8,408 wounded, 2,886 missing) out of 62,682 engaged (about 20,000 of them Buell's). Most of the losses occurred among the 35,118 men of the five divisions of Grant's army that carried the brunt of the battle on April 6. The Confederates lost 10,694 (1,723 killed, 8,012 wounded, 959 missing) out of about 40,000. Just as after Bull Run, there was criticism on the victorious side that the winning army did not pursue vigorously enough; just as at Bull Run, the victorious army was so severely hurt by winning that it could pursue only feebly.[31]

## WESTERN DRUMBEAT: NEW MADRID, ISLAND NO. 10, THE LOCOMOTIVE *GENERAL*, CORINTH, NEW ORLEANS

Federal efforts to gain control of the Mississippi itself had kept pace with those on the Tennessee and the Cumberland. On the same Monday when Grant and Buell were counterattacking at Shiloh, another of Halleck's subordinates, Major-General John Pope, U.S.V., was ferrying men of his Army of the Mississippi from the Missouri to the Tennessee shore of the great river to cut the line of retreat of the Confederate defenders on the strongly fortified Island No. 10. On March 13, using siege tactics, Pope had already captured similarly fortified New Madrid on the Missouri shore, downstream from Island No. 10, Tennessee, but farther north because of an S curve in the river. Pope's effort to isolate Island No. 10 was made possible in part by the ingenious expedient of digging a canal across one of the bases of the S, so that his transport vessels could bypass the Mississippi at the island and get south of it. The canal helped only in part, however, because it proved too shallow for the Federal gunboats. Without armed protection, transports could not carry Pope's troops from Missouri to the east shore south of the island in face of batteries mounted by the Confederates on that shore. In this predicament, Commander Henry Walke of the ironclad gunboat *Carondelet* insisted that he could run past the guns of Island No. 10 as well as the other rebel shore batteries by night. In spite of misgivings on the part of nearly everybody else concerned, Walke did so on April 4–5, immediately after the completion of the canal. The *Carondelet* then escorted Pope's transports on April 7, when they ferried the troops from Missouri to Tennessee to cut the southward exit from Island No. 10. The result was to force the surrender of some 3,500 men and the Confederacy's latest defensive anchor on the Mississippi. The Confederate defense of the river fell back to Fort Pillow, more than half way from Island No. 10 to Memphis.[32]

When Buell marched from Nashville to Shiloh with most of his field force, he detached his Third Division under Brigadier-General Ormsby M. Mitchel, U.S.V., to operate directly south and southeastward from the Tennessee capital. Mitchel was a West Point graduate of 1829 but was best known as an astronomer; before the war he was one of the few members of the infant American scientific community to enjoy an international reputation. The astronomer proved to be a most audacious general. On April 11, the Friday following Shiloh, he came storming into Huntsville, Alabama, after an impressive forced march that had begun forty-seven miles away at Shelbyville, Tennessee, on Tuesday. Huntsville was on the important Memphis and Charleston Railroad. The Confederates, their forces concentrated farther westward, had expected no such advance by a single Yankee division — particularly a division of Buell's army, hitherto better known for the ambition of its intentions than for its success in execution.

Mitchel was not yet finished. The storied ride of James J. Andrews's twenty-two volunteers in the locomotive *General* up the Western and Atlantic Railroad from Big Shanty, Georgia toward Chattanooga took place on the Saturday of the eventful week that had begun with Shiloh. It resulted from a scheme concocted by Andrews and Mitchel, whereby Andrews's raiders were supposed to wreck enough bridges and block enough sections of track with piled-up crossties, while also cutting the telegraph wires, so that Chattanooga would be isolated long enough for Mitchel to enter it. The plan failed, partly because rain during the Shiloh week made it too difficult to burn the bridges, partly because the planning had not been quite meticulous enough and the *General* ran out of fuel. Andrews's raiders were captured, and the leader and seven others were hanged. But Mitchel kept knocking at the door of Chattanooga anyway, operating around Bridgeport where the Memphis-to-Charleston line crossed the Tennessee River.[33]

When that other scholarly soldier H. W. Halleck arrived at Pittsburg Landing to take personal command of a further Union advance from there, he proved considerably less aggressive than Ormsby Mitchel. Removed from the comforts and safety of St. Louis whence he had commanded until now, and placed in the field in the immediate presence of the enemy, Halleck allowed his boldness — which had been considerable in his encouragement of the Henry-Donelson and New Madrid–Island No. 10 campaigns — to evaporate. For added security against Beauregard's army, he called Pope with much of his force from the Mississippi to join Grant and Buell in a huge agglomeration that grew to about 110,000. With this ponderous array, Halleck conducted a slow advance toward Corinth, the junction of the Memphis and Charleston with the north-south trunk line of the Mobile and Ohio Railroad. The Federals entrenched after each day's march to avoid all risk of a repetition of Shiloh. Beauregard, reinforced to 66,000 by troops from west of the Mississippi, conducted a skillful delaying campaign. When at last, after consuming a month to move twenty miles, Halleck was about to grip Corinth in a siege, Beauregard slipped the Confederate army out of the city during the night of May 29–30. He did so while running trains back and forth to the accompaniment of cheers, to suggest that reinforcements were arriving. In the morning the Federals discovered that Corinth was empty and entered the town, while Beauregard prepared to take up a new defensive line along the Tuscumbia River.[34]

Thus, in the aftermath of Shiloh the Federals in the West had mixed occasional operational brilliance — the bypassing of Island No. 10, Mitchel's advance on Huntsville — with a good deal more of stumbling. Nonetheless, their strategic focus on penetrating the South's river system had carried them reasonably quickly into the Deep South. On the Confederate side, the worst kind of strategy had to bear the blame for the setbacks that had begun at Fort Henry. Military wisdom has it that there are three categories of strategy: good, bad, and none at all, the third of which is worse than bad. The Confederates' vacillation between a foredoomed cordon defensive — a bad strategy — and the counteroffensive spasm leading to Shiloh qualified them, in their inconsistency, for the third strategic category.

Meanwhile the Union's better-focused riverine strategy visited yet another disaster upon the Confederacy before the cruel month of April ended. After a futile Federal bombardment of Forts Jackson and St. Philip below New Orleans from mortar boats, Flag Officer David Glasgow Farragut decided to run up the Mississippi River past the forts on the night of April 24–25 with his fleet of twenty-four wooden vessels mounting some 200 guns. He did not lose a ship, although three small gunboats failed to pass the forts. The next morning, he fought and defeated the small and unfinished Confederate defending squadron and captured the city of New Orleans, from which 4,000 Confederate troops had withdrawn in the face of his advance. An occupying force of 15,000 under Ben Butler followed close behind Farragut. Cut off from the Confederacy by Union occupation of the city, most of the garrison troops of Forts Jackson and St. Philip mutinied and compelled their officers to surrender to the Federals. The largest city and greatest seaport of the South fell under a Union occupation conducted by Butler with grim sternness for anyone betraying a hint of disaffection toward the government and armed forces of the United States.[35]

## CONSCRIPTION IN THE SOUTH

Accordingly, the gloom that had permeated Washington when 1862 began shifted to the Confederacy by the time the spring flowers bloomed. To add to the South's Western woes, during April a new Union amphibious expedition was entrenching itself on Roanoke Island and at New Bern, North Carolina;[36] and of course McClellan's grand army would someday advance from the south shore of the Potomac deeper into Virginia, because Federal policy would demand movement whether the cautious Young Napoleon desired it or not.

Against such multiple threats the Confederate Congress turned to a desperate expedient to shore up the armies. The recruiting inducements of 1861 had never adequately filled the ranks or assured that the twelve-month enlistees of 1861 would remain. On April 16, 1862, therefore, the Congress of the states'-rights Confederacy passed the first federal conscription act in American history, the first statute whereby a central government reached beyond the states and their militia systems to enforce a military obligation directly upon the individual.

Under the Confederate Conscription Act, the President was authorized to draft into service for three years all white males between the ages of eighteen and thirty-five. (On September 27, a second conscription law would include men from thirty-five to forty-five.) The terms of service of all men already in the army were extended to three years or the duration, thus retaining the twelve-month volunteers who had come at the Fort Sumter crisis and afterward. The retained men had forty days in which they might elect their own officers while reforming their regiments under new tables of organization. In deference to states'-rights principles, enrollment and drafting would be administered by state officials though under Confederate supervision, and drafted men would be assigned to units from their own states. In deference to a historic custom of the militia system, persons not liable for service could act as substitutes for those who were liable.[37]

A supplementary act of April 21 provided for various exemptions that made the conscription system a selective service system. The exempted occupations included Confederate and state legislative, executive, and judicial officials and their clerks and employees; employees of railroads; telegraph operators; and employees of mines, furnaces, and foundries.[38] The exemption system in time became the bane of the War Department, threatening to cripple the draft, especially after some of the governors began extending exempted state appointments broadside, and especially too after the conscription law of September 27 provoked protests that a rich man's war was being made into a poor man's fight, by exempting one slaveowner or overseer for every twenty slaves.[39]

## THE POTOMAC FRONT

In Washington's dismal New Year's season, McClellan had felt himself ill used, because the gloom implied insufficient confidence in him and his plans. Although as General-in-Chief he contributed only a small measure of encouragement to the Western campaigns that dissipated the Union's malaise, if he would now set the Army of the Potomac in motion against Richmond and its defending army and pile upon the Confederacy's hastening demoralization a climactic, crushing blow, he could vindicate himself completely, make the pessimism of the New Year and the accompanying distrust of his leadership seem without rational foundation, and assure the rescuing of the nation without the remorseless revolutionary struggle that he and Lincoln alike feared.

Lincoln followed up the Executive Mansion military conferences of early January with his General War Order No. 1 of January 27, ordering a coordinated advance of the Union armies on all major fronts beginning on February 22, Washington's Birthday.[40] A special War Order, No. 1, of January 31, specifically directed the Army of the Potomac, "after providing safely for the defense of Washington," to advance beyond Manassas Junction, beginning the movement on February 22.[41] The Western armies proved not to need this prodding and advanced before the stipulated date; but in the East the most notable event of Washington's Birthday was, to Lincoln's chagrin, the inauguration of Jefferson Davis at Richmond as President of the Confederate States of America under the permanent Constitution. The only immediate accomplishment of Lincoln's orders was to precipitate a further discussion with McClellan about a proper route of advance. Lincoln made it clear that he saw in McClellan's projected amphibious movement down the Chesapeake no advantage to compensate for the time and expense of collecting the necessary shipping, while the risks in case of failure would be greater than if the army advanced overland from Washington and thus covered the capital no matter what happened. McClellan insisted, however, that good roads and favorable terrain awaited his army east of Richmond and that success would be "certain by all the chances of war," should his plan be adopted.[42] Lincoln therefore decided he must acquiesce in the general's view. Thus there was at least firm agreement on a line of advance.

## BATTLE OF IRONCLADS

By the beginning of March, General Meigs had collected enough shipping to make McClellan's movement down the waterways seem at last in prospect. But then there appeared a new and dramatic addition to the seemingly endless round of causes for delay: the Confederacy threatened to seize control of Chesapeake Bay.

On March 8 a strange warship nosed out from Norfolk's Gosport Navy Yard into Hampton Roads, a kind of square-cornered iron pot mounted on a frigate hull, with a ram attached to the prow and an armament of six 9-inch smoothbore Dahlgren guns and two 7-inch and two 6.4-inch Brooke rifles. This was the Confederate States Ship *Virginia*, built upon the hull and the engines of the frigate *Merrimack*, which the Union Navy had scuttled when abandoning Norfolk. Commanded by Captain Franklin Buchanan of Maryland, who had resigned from the U.S. Navy when he thought his state was about to secede and then unsuccessfully attempted to return when Maryland stayed in the Union, *Virginia* spent the day methodically destroying the wooden ships of the Union fleet in Hampton Roads, whose shots glanced off her iron sides.

She sank the sail sloop *Cumberland* and forced aground and set afire the sail frigate *Congress*, with Captain Buchanan's brother, Paymaster McKean Buchanan, among the Federals killed. The steam frigate *Minnesota* of the proud new *Wabash* class was helpless to save her consorts. *Virginia* drew away at nightfall expecting to come back to destroy *Minnesota* and the rest of the nearby Federal ships the next morning. When the news reached Washington at dawn, the Cabinet assembled for yet another session in a mood of despair, the most acute despair yet, with Stanton predicting that *Virginia* would shortly appear in the Potomac to lob shells into the White House.[43]

While the Secretary of War, an excitable man, paced the floor, wrung his hands, and forecast doom, the Secretary of the Navy calmly, even smugly — because he did not like Stanton — awaited further news. Welles was confident of the prowess of the counterweapon that he could tell his colleagues had arrived at Hampton Roads to interpose between the Confederate ironclad and the wooden walls of the Union. This weapon was of course the even stranger ironclad *Monitor*, the cheese box on a raft, a revolving ironclad turret armed with two 11-inch Dahlgren smoothbores and perched along with a small pilothouse atop a hull with freeboard so low that the deck was partly awash.

The U.S. Navy had experimented beginning in 1842 with the ironclad Stevens Battery developed by the engineer Robert L. Stevens of Hoboken, but the Navy had not carried such experiments to a fruition comparable to the ironclad frigate *Gloire* launched by France in 1858 or the iron battleship *Warrior* launched by Great Britain in 1859. Confederate Secretary of the Navy Mallory believed that this neglect afforded the Confederacy an opportunity to offset the Union Navy's quantitative superiority with qualitative innovation. Promptly upon taking office he encouraged the creation of Confederate ironclads, including *Virginia*. Learning of what Mallory was doing, however, the Union Navy Department contracted for several ironclads of its own. The design for *Monitor* came to its attention almost accidentally, when an ingenious Connecticut Yankee groceryman turned promoter and speculator, Cornelius S. Bushnell, consulted in New York with the Swedish-American engineer John Ericsson, the inventor of the screw propeller, regarding the seaworthiness of another ironclad designed by Merrick and Sons of Philadelphia. Bushnell came away to tell the Navy Department that Ericsson had a plan for an ironclad of his own. Awarded a contract, Ericsson pushed *Monitor* to completion in 101 working days. He selected the name himself, to admonish the Confederacy of the power of the Union. The ship was launched January 30, 1862 and commissioned February 25, just in time to reach Hampton Roads to face *Virginia* on March 9.

In the famous first duel of ironclad warships that Sunday morning, *Monitor* outmaneuvered her heavier opponent and had slightly the better of the battle in terms of hits scored and accomplishing at least some damage. But *Monitor's* commanding officer, Lieutenant John L. Worden, was temporarily blinded when a shot struck the sight hole of the pilothouse, and his ship withdrew from the fray to reorganize. Thereupon *Virginia* returned to Norfolk, sufficiently checked that McClellan could resume his amphibious planning, but still a cause for nervousness on that diffident general's part because she had not been destroyed.

## MCCLELLAN LAUNCHES THE
## PENINSULA CAMPAIGN

Before the day was out, Washington learned not only of the checking of *Virginia* but also that the Confederates had abandoned their batteries on the lower Potomac and their entrenchments at Manassas. Richmond had decided these positions were too far advanced to be retained against gathering indications that McClellan was steeling himself to open an offensive. Federal joy at these events was promptly tempered by the discovery that the Confederate defenses at Manassas had harbored another set of painted logs, Quaker guns, as part of a strength that McClellan had always described as formidable. The size of the Confederate camps also suggested that Joseph E. Johnston's Confederate Army of the Potomac was considerably smaller than McClellan said it was.[44]

Yet McClellan had indeed finally made up his mind to advance. Assured by the Navy Department that *Virginia* was safely neutralized, he decided, in consultation with the corps commanders whom Lincoln had lately appointed to second him, that the amphibious thrust should go not to Urbanna but to Fort Monroe, a firm Union-held anchor, and thence toward Richmond via the Virginia Peninsula between the rivers York and James. Embarkation began on March 17, McClellan's Federal Army of the Potomac crowding into 405 vessels aggregating 86,278 tons.[45] At the least, however, the continued existence of *Virginia* would deny McClellan secure naval protection on both flanks; from his first contemplation of a campaign on the Peninsula, he had anticipated safe communications and protected flanks on both the York and the James.

Moreover, McClellan and the Lincoln administration evidently had grown altogether incapable of working in harmony, even on this long-awaited occasion. The general sailed for the Peninsula in a black mood; just as he was about to advance, on March 11, Lincoln removed him from the office of General-in-Chief, leaving that post vacant and restricting McClellan to the command of the Army of the Potomac.[46] Lincoln's reasoning was that when McClellan took the field he would have more than enough to occupy him in the command of one army—a sound enough conclusion, but one that might have been thought of before naming Little Mac to replace Scott, to avoid the embarrassment of McClellan's ill-timed demotion. While the change still further soured McClellan's opinion of the President, Lincoln for his part worried lest the movement of most of the troops around Washington to the Peninsula might open the way to a Confederate raid on the capital. McClellan and his friends thought that Lincoln's fears were excessive, that against the Peninsula expedition the Confederate Army surely had to look to the defense of its own capital, which it did. But Lincoln had to consider public morale in the North and the possibly devastating effect if enemy soldiers took possession of Washington even briefly. Moreover, the Confederates were soon to demonstrate that they had a remarkable capacity for executing diversionary raids. Despite the auspicious campaigns in the West, Union confidence was still compromised by McClellan's long sedentary autumn and winter. If now it should turn out that Union arms could not unquestionably hold Washington, the issue of whether those arms could conquer the South would again appear highly doubtful.

McClellan thus should not have been surprised that when he decided to move most of his army around to the Peninsula by sea, Lincoln insisted that an adequate force must be left behind for the defense of Washington and accepted as meeting his requirements a more recent calculation by McClellan and his generals that such a shield should comprise 25,000 men as a covering force in Virginia, in addition to the Washington garrison. After McClellan had departed for Fort Monroe and while the embarkation of the army was continuing, the Military Governor of Washington, Brigadier-General James S. Wadsworth, U.S.V. (perhaps significantly, given McClellan's politics, a former Free Soil and Republican politician), reported to the War Department that McClellan was leaving him only 26,700 men at both Washington and Manassas, many of them undisciplined. Lincoln thereupon decided that an army corps ought to be held back from McClellan's field army, choosing the First Corps of Major-General, U.S.V. (from March 14) Irvin McDowell (minus its First Division). The Second and Third Divisions of this corps presently marched from Alexandria to Fredericksburg, whence McDowell might aid McClellan if the latter's army should eventually reach around to encircle Richmond from the north. The commander of the Army of the Potomac, however, acutely sensitive to the attacks he had received from Congress, now opened his campaign suspicious that the administration also trusted him too little to support and cooperate with him as it should.[47]

McClellan took to the Peninsula some 121,500 men, which should have been an ample force without McDowell. When the Confederates learned of his embarkation, they were at first uncertain whether he intended to land on the Peninsula or to attack Norfolk. General R. E. Lee, ordered by the President on March 2 to return to Richmond from the South Atlantic coast and henceforth serving as Jefferson Davis's principal military adviser, soon concluded that Norfolk was not the target and arranged for reinforcements from Joseph Johnston's army to hasten into the defenses guarding Yorktown, astride the path from Fort Monroe to Richmond. The bulk of Johnston's army soon followed to the Peninsula. Nevertheless, the commander at York-town, Major-General John Bankhead Magruder, leading the Army of the Peninsula, for a time had only about 17,000 men to hold an eight-mile front against a Union advance guard of some 60,000 — and it was important to delay McClellan at Yorktown to allow Johnston's army time to gather rein-forcements for the defense of Richmond.[48]

Fortunately for the Confederacy, "Prince John" Magruder had a theatri-cal bent that he utilized to stage elaborate charades convincing McClellan of the great strength of the Yorktown defenses. McClellan reacted to Ma-gruder's performances with a characteristic onset of caution. The Union commander prepared for a formal siege. For a month, from April 5 to May 4, the Army of the Potomac stood before the Yorktown lines, laboriously em-placing guns.

Then, abruptly, on the morning of May 4 the Federals discovered that the defenses had quietly been abandoned. Johnston was ready to occupy stronger positions closer to Richmond, with an army of 60,000, and he did not propose to sacrifice any of his valuable troops to McClellan's artillery at Yorktown once the Union general was ready to open fire. General Johnston's verdict on Yorktown was: "No one but McClellan could have hesitated to attack."[49]

McClellan had somehow convinced himself that Yorktown's defenders outnumbered him, a conclusion that led Brigadier-General and Brevet Major-General John E. Wool, U.S.A., the seventy-eight-year-old War of 1812 and Mexican War veteran who commanded Fort Monroe, to say to Stanton: "The desponding tone of Major-General McClellan's dispatch of last eve-ning more than surprises me. He says his entire force is undoubtedly consid-erably inferior to that of the rebels. If that is the fact I am still more surprised that they should have abandoned Yorktown."[50]

Made of sterner stuff than McClellan, Wool had a hand in a more im-pressive Maytime achievement than the Young Napoleon's Yorktown activi-ties. Encouraged by the President himself when Lincoln visited Fort Monroe for a personal inspection of the Peninsula forces, and not only encouraged also by the ambitious and militant Republican Secretary Chase of the Trea-sury — a bitter critic of McClellan — but with Chase as virtual co-com-mander, Wool launched an amphibious assault upon Norfolk. The Confed-erate retreat from Yorktown had by then left Norfolk dangerously exposed and its garrison needed at the capital. With Wool supplying the final push, the Confederate commander, Major-General Benjamin Huger, evacuated the Virginia seaport on May 9. The James River was too low at the time to allow *Virginia* to escape upstream. Confederate Flag Officer Josiah Tatnall consequently ran the ironclad aground near the mouth of the Elizabeth River and set her afire. She blew up when the flames reached her magazine early on May 11. McClellan thus had his desired security and communications on both flanks as a present from General Wool; but in the meantime *Virginia* had inflicted further grave damage upon his distrustful attitude toward the Lincoln administration, whose Navy Department he blamed for allowing *Virginia* to menace him in the first place, as if practically everybody in Washington was conspiring against him.[51]

For all McClellan's sense of grievance, however, Johnston allowed him to advance practically to the gates of Richmond. By the end of May, McClellan's soldiers could listen to the church bells of the city. Moreover, however long it had taken McClellan to advance this far, the military condition of the Confederacy had become appalling. On May 10, the day after the evacuation of Norfolk, out in the West the Confederate River Defense Fleet on the Mississippi made a foray against Flag Officer Charles H. Davis's mortar boats and seven ironclad gunboats that were bombarding Fort Pillow. In the resulting battle of Plum Run Bend, eight Confederate rams, armored with cotton bales and planking but fast and maneuverable, embarrassed the Union by sinking the gunboats *Cincinnati* and *Mound City;* but Commander Walke and his redoubtable *Carondelet* saved the day, disabling the rams *Price* and *Sumter* and sending the Confederate squadron scurrying to the protection of the Memphis batteries. The imminent fall of that city became a virtual certainty. Two days more, and Farragut, steaming up the Mississippi from New Orleans, occupied Natchez. The two prongs of the Union naval attack upon the Mississippi would soon unite. The sort of consistent strategic focus that was lacking in the East continued to pay dividends in the West, though not as rich ones as McClellan might have grasped.[52]

The faltering Confederate war effort was suffering also from bad administration, which compounded the effects of the defeats. President Davis having reluctantly and partially discovered that he had too many problems to become so completely his own Secretary of War as he would have liked, Leroy Pope Walker had had to be dropped from the War Office the previous September 16. Walker's successor, Davis's friend Judah P. Benjamin, was one of the ablest men in the Confederacy but also one of the most widely disliked, and he was incapable of harmonious relations with too many of the generals, notably Joe Johnston. So on March 18 Benjamin was transferred to the Department of State, and beginning May 22 Davis tried still a third War Secretary, George Wythe Randolph, Thomas Jefferson's grandson, son of Jefferson's daughter, Martha, and Thomas M. Randolph, governor of Virginia from 1819 to 1822. The new War Secretary had military experience as a brigadier under Magruder, but the shuffling meant that the Confederate War Department was in disarray within sound of McClellan's guns. Even in nearby Virginia, it could not concentrate its attention on McClellan lest it open doors to other Union columns in the western counties, at Winchester in the Valley, and at Fredericksburg.[53]

## STONEWALL JACKSON'S VALLEY CAMPAIGN

President Davis's military adviser General Lee was widely distrusted in the Confederacy since his failure to retrieve western Virginia in the autumn of 1861 and his retreat from the sea islands of the South Atlantic coast after the Union victory at Port Royal in November. In both campaigns his conduct was in fact open to criticism. He had too often failed to give his subordinates clear and decisive orders in western Virginia, and there was merit in the charge that the coastal waterways need not have been so readily yielded to the Federal Navy if concealed batteries and bodies of troops had been stationed near narrows and shallows to take advantage of the enemy warships' limited turning ability.

Lee himself was troubled by the recollection of his recent campaigns, but especially because of their implications for Confederate defense in general. Whatever mistakes he might have made in western Virginia, the basic reason for his failure there was simply that he did not have enough troops, or enough transport for the mountainous terrain. On the South Atlantic coast, his plans had put almost 25,000 soldiers to work guarding the sea frontier of Georgia and South Carolina, and no scheme of defense different from his would have required fewer. Still, the defenders had to be spread so thin that in spite of the availability of the Charleston and Savannah Railroad paralleling the coast to move reinforcements and support them, there was no assurance of success against additional concentrated Federal offensive thrusts.[54] The Confederate land and sea frontiers stretched so far that spreading defenders throughout their length would open the way to innumerable Fort Henry–Fort Donelson strokes by the Federals against the inevitable weak points. In Virginia alone, the effort to interpose between Richmond and every Federal column was well along toward depriving the Confederacy of adequate defense against any one of the enemy penetrations.

Reflecting on these considerations, Lee moved toward a decision that the Confederacy would surely succumb to the military disaster that already seemed imminent—unless the Confederate armies seized the initiative, at least tactically, if possible strategically in certain of the theaters of war. If the Confederacy could grasp initiatives, then the Southern command could choose where troops should concentrate. If it remained on the defensive, then its dispersed troops would have to yield before Union concentrations. If the South went over to the attack, then by concentrating its forces at chosen points it might compensate for its overall numerical inferiority with local superiority at the places of attack. "It is only by the concentration of our troops," Lee was to say, "that we can hope to win any decisive advantage." The Confederacy must abandon the passivity of defense for the activity of the offensive: ". . . we must decide between the positive loss of inactivity and the risk of action."[55]

Lee's growing conviction that the only way to halt the hitherto inexorable tightening of an iron Federal ring was to take the risk of offensive action found a ready response when he communicated with the Confederate commander in the Shenandoah Valley, Major-General Thomas J. Jackson, the "Stonewall" of Manassas.[56] Major-General Nathaniel P. Banks, U.S.V., a Republican businessman and politician-soldier from Massachusetts, commanded the Federal Department of the Shenandoah.[57] Banks had begun transferring men to McClellan in March, whereupon Jackson had attacked him at Kernstown just south of Winchester on the 23rd of that month to halt such activity. Jackson suffered a tactical setback but nevertheless prompted the Union government to defer reinforcing McClellan from the Valley and contributed to the decision to withhold most of McDowell's corps.[58] By May, the principal part of Banks's 20,000 were at New Market, with an advanced post at Harrisonburg, near the southern end of the Massanutton Mountain range that divides the Valley into eastern and western troughs between Harrisonburg and Strasburg. The Union force in western Virginia, the Mountain Department, since March 29 commanded by Frémont, and was in part making threatening motions in the direction of Staunton in the Valley.[59] "I have hoped," Lee wrote to Jackson, "in the present divided condition of the enemy's forces that a successful blow may be dealt them by a rapid combination of our troops before they can be strengthened themselves either in position or by reinforcements." Lee was able to arrange for Jackson's reinforcement from about 7,000 to 17,000 men, mainly by detaching from Johnston's army Brigadier-General Richard S. Ewell's Division. Thus was formed what came to be called the Army of the Valley.[60]

Despite his Manassas fame, Stonewall Jackson to most Confederate observers did not appear to be any more promising a general than the disappointing Lee. No plantation aristocrat, Jackson had been a poor boy from the mountains of northwestern Virginia who went to West Point to get a free education, suffered at the academy from the handicaps of a previously primitive schooling, nonetheless graduated seventeenth in a class of fifty-nine in 1846, won the limited distinction open to a young officer in the Mexican War — earning promotion to first lieutenant and brevets as captain and major in the 1st Artillery — and went on to become an apparently uninspired professor of mathematics at the Virginia Military Institute. He was a dour, deeply religious Presbyterian, uncommunicative either in social life or with military subordinates, whom he left so completely in the dark about his intentions that in early 1862 some doubted his competence and others his sanity. Lee at least looked like a general; Jackson in contrast was a slight, vaguely seedy man who rode unimpressive little horses.[61]

Encouraged and reinforced by Lee, however, Jackson was to prove a marvel. He first marched against Frémont's vanguard west of Staunton and dealt it a hard blow in the battle of McDowell on May 8. Frémont was sufficiently stunned that Jackson could turn upon Banks, whose force had been reduced to 8,000 in consequence of Washington's latest vacillation, a decision to reinforce McClellan from the Valley after all. Using the Massanuttons to mask his movements and confuse Banks, Jackson fell upon a Union detachment of 1,000 at Front Royal at the northeastern end of the Massanuttons on May 23 and nearly destroyed it. With Jackson thus threatening the Federal line of communications back to the Potomac, Banks hastened northward to Winchester, reaching that town safely thanks to skillful Union rearguard fighting that kept Jackson out. Nevertheless, Jackson defeated Banks in a battle at Winchester on the 25th, and the next day Banks retreated to the north shore of the Potomac.[62]

The faint of heart in the North could perceive this disconcerting Confederate thrust as the prelude to a raid into Maryland and even on to Washington. Lincoln and Stanton, however, reacted mainly with a determination that Jackson's force ought to be repaid for its effrontery with destruction, not only to head off the immediate danger but to preclude any repetition of it. Not yet having decided upon a replacement for McClellan in his vacated role as General-in-Chief, the President and the Secretary of War were at this juncture playing that role themselves. The two lawyers did not do so in any spirit of arrogance, for they were both acutely aware of their lack of specialized military knowledge, but only because they saw no appropriate alternative. Yet they did not perform badly. They ordered Frémont from western Virginia and McDowell from Fredericksburg, the latter commanding 40,000 men in what from April 4 was designated the Army of the Rappahannock, to send converging columns into the Valley to block Jackson's line of retreat. They hoped to destroy him.[63]

Unfortunately for their design, while Lincoln specifically ordered Frémont to march on Harrisonburg, that incorrigibly self-willed officer sent his advance toward Strasburg instead, a place where he was obviously less likely to catch Jackson if the Confederates should withdraw from the Potomac area promptly, even apart from the fact that Frémont was much closer to Harrisonburg to begin with. This disobedience was compounded by heavy rains, which slowed Frémont's and McDowell's progress over the mountains more than they hampered Jackson's movement on the macadamized Valley Pike. Jackson in fact hastened southward to avoid being trapped, and he succeeded. At Port Republic, where the North River and the South River unite to form the South Fork of the Shenandoah, the vanguard of Brigadier-General, U.S.V., James Shields's Division of McDowell's army caught up with Jackson, and the Confederate general himself was almost caught by a Federal cavalry foray on June 7. But the next day most of Shields's force was not yet on the scene, and Jackson held off what there was with Ewell's Division while striking Frémont's advance at nearby Cross Keys. He then turned to hit Shields on the 9th. Shields's troops mauled Jackson's attack, but Lincoln and Stanton, worried because the Federal columns were widely strung out and scattered by their chase, and disappointed because their trap had not sprung, ordered both Shields and Frémont to withdraw. The quiet calm that Jackson had exhibited, first when Frémont and McDowell were both closer to Strasburg in his rear than he was, and second when he seemed to be caught between two enemy columns, was not the least of the reasons why his Valley Campaign propelled him into the first rank of American generals — to say nothing of the aggressiveness with which he resolved the second predicament.[64]

Although Lincoln and Stanton had responded to Jackson's challenge energetically and on the whole creditably, the Confederate campaign went beyond transforming its drab commander into a hero by amply serving the purpose Lee had in mind for it. It halted reinforcement of McClellan from the Valley and ended the prospect that McDowell might be about to advance promptly from Fredericksburg to link up with McClellan.

## THE CLIMAX ON THE PENINSULA: THE SEVEN DAYS

Meanwhile Joe Johnston attacked McClellan just seven miles outside Richmond in the battle of Fair Oaks, or Seven Pines, on May 31. Confusion among the attacking Confederate divisions, attributable largely to inexperienced commanders and too complex a scheme of maneuver, along with stout fighting by McClellan's soldiers, prevented the effort from accomplishing much, however, and in the course of the fight General Johnston suffered multiple wounds from an exploding artillery shell. On June 1, President Davis named Lee to replace Johnston in command of the force that Lee promptly designated the Army of Northern Virginia.[65]

Previously able only to advise, Lee could now invoke his offensive designs for himself. Jackson fell within his army command, and having used Jackson to prevent a Federal concentration under McClellan, Lee now summoned Jackson from the Valley for a Confederate concentration against McClellan. Lee proposed by seizing the initiative to relieve the Federal pressure upon Richmond and, more than that, to do nothing less than destroy McClellan's army as an effective fighting force.

The good roads and good terrain that McClellan had promised Lincoln the army would find east of Richmond had proven to be abominable roads across marshy bottomlands bordering the Chickahominy River. In June, McClellan's army was awkwardly astride the Chickahominy, with most of its strength on the south side facing Richmond, and with only Brigadier-General, U.S.V., Fitz-John Porter's newly organized Fifth Corps north of the stream. Porter's corps was both reaching out toward McDowell and guarding McClellan's line of communications, which followed the Richmond and York River Railroad north of the Chickahominy, back to a base at White House on the Pamunkey River, a tributary of the York.

On June 12–15, Lee's principal cavalry commander, Brigadier-General James Ewell Brown Stuart, led his brigade-strength force in a complete circle around McClellan's army to enhance Lee's knowledge of the Federal dispositions. Lee meanwhile set his men to digging trenches so diligently in front of Richmond that the soldiers called him, with sardonic intent, "the King of Spades."[66] Lee's purpose was to strengthen his defenses on the direct approach to Richmond enough that he could move the bulk of his army to the north side of the Chickahominy. He would then strike heavily against Porter's corps, while Jackson's Valley army, brought secretly to the scene, turned Porter's right flank. Jackson would cut off McClellan's army from its base, and it would be destroyed while it tried to fight its way back or to open a new line of communications.

Lee's assault became the Seven Days Battles of June 25 to July 1. The action at Oak Grove on June 25 was a minor preliminary bout, precipitated by an exploratory probe by McClellan south of the Chickahominy. The battles began in earnest on the 26th. Jackson had originally told Lee he would be ready to join in the attack on the 25th, but delays in his journey from the Valley caused postponement by a day. On the 26th, the Confederate divisions of Major-Generals Ambrose Powell Hill, James Longstreet, and Daniel Harvey Hill waited impatiently opposite Porter's position at Mechanicsville for A. P. Hill to learn that Jackson was about to attack, an event that would signal the beginning of their own attacks. But Jackson fell far behind his latest schedule, and in mid-afternoon A. P. Hill's impatience overcame him, and he sent his division forward on his own initiative. The battle of Mechanicsville became a futile struggle by the Hills and Longstreet to break Porter's lines. It confirmed the message of Seven Pines that whatever else was true of McClellan's leadership, under him the Federal Army of the Potomac had become a tough, resilient fighting organism. It was also one of the war's early illustrations of the devastating effect of the rifled musket in the hands of steady and well-positioned defenders against a frontal attack.

During the night Porter withdrew to Gaines's Mill nearer the crossings of the Chickahominy that tied him to the rest of the Union army. Because Lee's plan demanded it, and because faulty intelligence work by the Confederate staffs and cavalry and faulty maps misled Lee about Porter's position, causing him to believe there were opportunities for turning movements where none existed, the Confederates advanced and ended up attacking nearly head-on again. Also again, the assaults of their various divisions were poorly coordinated, which was becoming habitual; and again Stonewall Jackson was disappointingly slow in getting into position, although on this Thursday his troops did join in the final charges. What ailed him has never been clear, whether fatigue following his swift movement to Tidewater after the gruelling Valley campaign, or difficulty in working in harness after autonomous command, or misunderstandings of Lee's instructions, or some more shadowy quirks of an admittedly eccentric personality. At last, at the close of the day, the superior numbers of the Confederates north of the Chickahominy forced Porter into retreat across the river; but Lee's battles were scarcely developing as he had intended.

While the fighting at Mechanicsville and Gaines's Mill raged north of the Chickahominy, south of the river some 60,000 Federals stood transfixed and idle before the diversionary movements of only 25,000 Confederates commanded by the showman Magruder in Lee's trenches before Richmond. Far from considering the possibilities of smashing into the enemy capital, McClellan let his mind dwell upon his conviction that Lee's total force badly outnumbered his, and upon the injustice of Washington's withholding McDowell's men and various other formations from him (though by now the Second as well as the First of McDowell's original three divisions had in fact joined him, and he had been given command of the 12,000 troops at Fort

Monroe as substantial compensation for his other deprivations; his muster rolls at the beginning of the Seven Days carried only 1,581 fewer men than he had had with McDowell's corps included when the campaign commenced).[67] By about midnight on the 27th, McClellan's dark musings had driven him to such an emotional state that he telegraphed to Stanton:

> I feel too earnestly tonight — I have seen too many dead & wounded comrades to feel otherwise than that the Govt has not sustained this Army. If you do not do so now the game is lost.
>
> If I save this Army now I tell you plainly that I owe no thanks to you or any other persons in Washington — you have done your best to sacrifice this Army.[68]

As a matter of fact, McClellan had seen remarkably few dead and wounded for a Civil War army commander; he had not been present at the principal combats on the Peninsula or in western Virginia, and he was to continue making such absence his custom. Laboring under the terrible responsibility of dispatching men to die, he apparently found the prospect of actually witnessing many of the deaths more than he could bear. Such a sensitive humanity may have done him credit as a man, but habitual distance from the front did nothing to improve his tactical management of battles, because without personal observation he never adequately knew what was going on.

Meanwhile the telegraph operator in Washington who received his late message of June 27 showed it to the military supervisor of telegraphs, Colonel Edward S. Sanford, assistant aide-de-camp, who saw fit to delete the section beginning, "If I save" from the copy given to Stanton.

His assumption of martyrdom did not help McClellan to think with clarity about how to proceed next. Before Lee attacked him, McClellan had already been pondering a change of base from the Pamunkey southward across the Peninsula to the James, where he could be more directly protected by the guns of the Union Navy and would not have to rely on the vulnerable West Point Railroad. He now ordered this idea put into effect. Unfortunately for him, his contemplation of the shift had not led him to have the roads across the Peninsula behind his army explored to discover the best routes, or the practicality of the entire notion. Nor was he alert enough to move quickly to correct this neglect now. His whole army therefore would probably have to move clumsily over the only good road with which the Federals were familiar, thus awarding Lee the opportunity to strike the army in disarray. In the course of the change of base, the consequent road congestion was to be relieved only occasionally, when various of McClellan's subordinates on their own initiative found sections of the other passable roads that did exist.

McClellan was saved from the worst consequences of his own carelessness by the circumstance that Lee's efforts to wreck the Federal army by hitting it on the march were almost as badly bungled as the Federal commander's contingency planning. Uncoordinated Confederate attacks at Savage Station on June 29 and Glendale on the 30th, during which Jackson twice more failed to go into action when expected, hindered but did not disrupt the Federal retreat.

The battle of Glendale, Frayser's Farm, or White Oak Swamp was pivotal. McClellan's army was so strung out along its single main line of retreat that Lee might have broken it in two or more parts, but furious attacks by Longstreet and A. P. Hill again received inadequate support. By the next day, July 1, the Army of the Potomac was in firm contact with the Union Navy in the James, and the Federal rear guard was strongly emplaced, with excellent artillery coverage, on a rise of ground called Malvern Hill. Lee felt unwilling to abandon the campaign without one last attack, but it had to be a frontal assault. Porter, again the Federal commander on the scene — with McClellan as usual well to the rear — mowed the attack down as he had A. P. Hill's first assaults almost a week before.

Throughout the Seven Days, therefore, the Army of the Potomac had fought well, and unlike its rival, it suffered from no severe blunders on the part of its principal subordinate leaders. But its good tactical management owed little to McClellan directly, and under Lee's pressure he had practically abandoned the offensive purposes for which the Peninsula Campaign had been designed. At Harrison's Landing on the James, McClellan and his army rested, and the inhabitants of Richmond could breathe easily again. So completely had McClellan allowed Lee to dominate his army's movement and position, however, that the respite on the James came without enough space for proper sanitation, as the hottest weeks of the Virginia summer came on.

But Lee's own satisfaction with the Seven Days was far from complete. He knew that if he merely saved Richmond from the Army of the Potomac, the Federals would find a way to return. His object had been to fight a Napoleonic Austerlitz or Jena-Auerstädt battle: to destroy the enemy army. He himself was new to the command of a large field army, however; he had made mistakes, and the organization (into too many separate divisions directly responsible to army headquarters), the divisional leadership, the staff work, and the intelligence gathering of the Army of Northern Virginia were all far from what he would have wanted them to be. These shortcomings he blamed for the incompleteness of his triumph. "Under ordinary circumstances," he told President Davis, "the Federal army should have been destroyed."[69]

Other generals struck Napoleonic poses; R. E. Lee, the austere aristocrat, never merely posed. He was to prove the most Napoleonic general of the war. His strategy was an offensive strategy, and his aim, through all the war as long as his strength was enough to let him entertain the possibility, was the destruction of the enemy army.

But Lee was a Napoleon come to warfare too late, as the Federal rifles showed at Mechanicsville, Gaines's Mill, and Malvern Hill. At Malvern Hill, the Army of Northern Virginia suffered 5,500 casualties to no good purpose. In the whole Seven Days, Lee lost 3,286 dead, 15,909 wounded, and 946 missing, totaling 20,141 of somewhat over 80,000 men in the army with which he began his attacks. In the Civil War, no more than half the wounded could be expected to return to the army; of the other half, many would die under the limited medical treatment of the day, and many of the rest would be forever crippled. With the South's inferiority in manpower, casualties of nearly one-fourth of the army were a terrible price to pay even for Richmond. (The Federals lost in the Seven Days 1,734 dead, 8,066 wounded, and 6,055 missing, for a total of 15,855, less than the Confederate toll in absolute numbers and far less in proportion to population resources.)[70]

# FIVE

# The Confederacy Takes the Initiative

## CEDAR MOUNTAIN AND SECOND BULL RUN

The failure to trap Stonewall Jackson in the Valley when the chances to do so had seemed so fair taught Lincoln and Stanton that they ought to establish unity of command over the scattered Federals forces in northern Virginia that had contended against Stonewall. On June 26, John Pope, the victor of New Madrid and Island No. 10, received command of the forces of Frémont (who resigned because Pope was his junior in rank), Banks, and McDowell, consolidated into a new Army of Virginia. Pope's initial mission was to march overland to help McClellan.[1]

The Union victories in the West also gave Lincoln and Stanton, they believed, an officer promising enough to fill the vacant post of General-in-Chief. On July 11, they summoned "Old Brains" Halleck from the Department of the Mississippi to assume that responsibility.

Halleck's first decision had to be what to do with the Army of the Potomac, in its constricted positions around Harrison's Landing. He did not hesitate over the decision. Arriving in Washington from the West and taking command on July 23, he departed for a visit to McClellan and the Army of the Potomac the next day.[2] McClellan asked him for reinforcements and another chance against Richmond from his present position, but he continued to insist that Lee had an army of 200,000 opposite him. Halleck evi-

dently interpreted this insistence as meaning either that no feasible reinforcement would give McClellan enough men to capture the Confederate
capital, or that McClellan was so overawed by the enemy that there was no
chance of his mustering the determination within himself to take it. Yet no
officer capable enough, senior enough, and sufficiently acceptable in the
East seemed available to replace McClellan, so he had to be retained in his
command. On July 30, Halleck, back in Washington and having reported to
Stanton, ordered McClellan to remove his sick and wounded from Harrison's Landing, as the first step toward shifting the whole Army of the Potomac back to northern Virginia.[3]

It required moral courage of Halleck thus to throw away the huge
investment that the North had committed to McClellan's Peninsula Campaign, and a clearsighted appraisal of McClellan underlay the General-in-
Chief's first assertion of his new responsibilities. Nevertheless, it was regrettable for the Northern cause that the step probably had to be taken. With
the formation of Pope's Army of Virginia, the tools were at hand for the kind
of two-pronged application of the operational art that so rarely occurred in
the Civil War, if the Army of the Potomac had remained in southeastern
Virginia. Halleck was jettisoning not only the Peninsula Campaign but also
the prospect of exploiting the North's superior resources to close on Lee a
vise so powerful that all Lee's skills might not have sufficed to resist it — to
trap the main Confederate army in the decisive Eastern theater of war.

Moreover, the transfer of the Army of the Potomac from the Peninsula
was sure to expose the Army of Virginia to grave peril. Once Lee discovered
that McClellan was moving away, both the diminishing remnant of the Army
of the Potomac on the Peninsula and Pope's relatively small army in northern
Virginia would be vulnerable to him, until the evacuation was complete and
enough of McClellan's army had reinforced Pope's to make Pope reasonably
safe. Halleck chose to meet the difficulty first by having Pope, with some
56,000 troops, show a front of bold activity, which Pope initiated down the
Orange and Alexandria Railroad toward and beyond the Rappahannock.
Halleck sought also to hasten McClellan's withdrawal from the James, but
the painfully deliberate pace that the Young Napoleon had by now made his
hallmark frustrated Halleck's efforts in that direction. McClellan received
the orders to depart altogether from Harrison's Landing on August 3. The
last of his troops did not actually leave until August 16. His army marched
eastward toward transports at Newport News at an average pace of eight miles
per day. The embarkation did not begin until August 19. McClellan himself
sailed for Aquia Landing near Fredericksburg on the 23rd, with the evacuation at length nearly complete. The last corps of the Army of the Potomac

to reach northern Virginia, the Second, disembarked at Alexandria on August 28.[4]

Pope's advance meanwhile threatened the junction of the Orange and Alexandria with the Virginia Central Railroad at Gordonsville, which in turn endangered Richmond's connection with the Shenandoah Valley, a major source of food grains. On July 12 Lee learned that a large Federal force had occupied Culpeper, south of the Rappahannock in the triangle between that river and the Rapidan, and only twenty-nine miles from Gordonsville. The next day Lee ordered Jackson to take his own division and Ewell's, about 12,000 men, to Gordonsville to oppose Pope's advance.[5]

His aggressive spirit evidently recharged by his return to autonomous command, Jackson urged Lee that if reinforced he could handle Pope roughly. Although Lee could not yet be completely certain that McClellan was harmless, because the Army of the Potomac remained dangerously close to Richmond, on July 27 he sent Jackson A. P. Hill's Division. This formation was coming to be called the Light Division because of its rapid marching and promptitude in action; it raised to 24,000 what through the remainder of the campaign against Pope was to be Jackson's Command or presently the Left Wing of the Army of Northern Virginia. On August 7 Jackson learned that the Second Corps of the Army of Virginia, General Banks's force, stood relatively isolated at Cedar Mountain eight miles south of Culpeper. He decided to begin his work by hitting his old adversary Banks.

Renewed aggressiveness did not translate, however, into much-improved tactical handling of Jackson's troops; Stonewall managed only a short march on August 8 that delayed his attack on Banks until the 9th, and then Banks with only 8,000 men proved to have the better of the fight for several hours at Cedar Mountain. The politician-general from Massachusetts lacked professional skills but not fighting spirit, and he tried to compensate for his inferior numbers with a sharp preemptive attack against the Confederate left flank. The Stonewall Division itself, the original nucleus of the Army of the Valley, had to struggle hard to maintain its cohesion; its commander, Brigadier-General Charles S. Winder, was sick and insisted on riding into the battle in an ambulance, only to be mortally wounded by an artillery shell. Banks's shortcomings made themselves felt in his ability to keep his attack organized, so that Jackson was able to counterattack and by day's end assert his numerical preponderance. He did not do much to pursue, however, because he learned that enough Federals were in Culpeper for at least an even numerical balance. Jackson's casualties amounted to 314 killed, 1,062 wounded, and forty-two missing, for a total of 1,418. The Federals' considerably higher losses — 320 killed, 1,466 wounded, and 617 missing, a total of 2,403 — reflected particularly in the missing the loss of the battle-ground, but they also indicated admirably hard fighting if not the best of leadership. Cedar Mountain reaffirmed one of the principal messages of the Seven Days and extended it to demonstrate that George B. McClellan could not have been the only effective trainer of soldiers in the Union Army: the combat power of the Union infantry and artillery in the East was of at least as high a quality as that of the Confederates.[6]

Jackson's men tended to the wounded and buried their comrades, but on August 11 they retreated lest Pope come out of Culpeper to turn the tables on them. That possibility and the overall aggressiveness of Pope and Banks went far toward convincing Lee that he should reunite most of his army to snuff out the Army of Virginia before the Army of the Potomac could substantially reinforce it. Lee's thinking was confirmed when on August 7 he learned that the Federals had evacuated outposts they had reoccupied on Malvern Hill and were again in retreat down the Peninsula. On August 13 Lee ordered Longstreet to entrain ten brigades for Gordonsville to begin the movement of the other wing of the Army of Northern Virginia to join Jackson.[7]

Lee's opportunity to crush Pope while McClellan's troops remained far away was now at hand. In mid-August, Pope withdrew behind the Rappahannock to fend off an attempt to trap him between it and the Rapidan. Then, aided by a rainstorm, he showed considerable skill in maneuver while countering several efforts to turn or penetrate his Rappahannock line. The small First and Second Divisions of Major-General, U.S.V., Ambrose E. Burnside's newly organized Ninth Army Corps reached Pope by August 16, and the remainder of the corps was around Fredericksburg; these troops came with Burnside from the North Carolina coast. By August 22, the first reinforcements from the Army of the Potomac began to reach Pope. He had apparently escaped the crisis; the shield thrown up by his energy and alertness seemed about to permit the safe completion of the delicate task of uniting the two Federal armies.[8]

But before that consummation should occur, Lee attempted one final and extremely daring maneuver to undo Pope. On the morning of August 25, Jackson's Left Wing set out on a wide march around Pope's right flank, designed to turn that flank, fall upon Pope's principal supply depot at Manassas Junction, and either force Pope to withdraw into the defenses of Washington or bring him to battle in circumstances that would permit the destruction of his army. Pope mistakenly interpreted the evidence he received of Jackson's initial march westward as indicating that Stonewall was returning to the Valley. He was returning only to the fullness of the spirit that had animated his Valley campaign; he led his wing over a march of fifty-four miles in thirty-six hours, so that late on August 26 Pope was to learn that Confederates were astride his principal line of communications, the Orange and Alexandria Railroad, at his great supply depot, Manassas Junction.[9]

Ever energetic, Pope hurried up the railroad to try to catch Jackson while he remained separated from Lee. After his troops had enjoyed an orgy of feasting as well as destruction at Manassas Junction on August 27, Jackson skillfully concealed most of his force among wooded hills north and west of Manassas to avoid such an outcome, until on the evening of August 28 he deliberately provoked a fight because he knew Lee was now within supporting distance and wished therefore to pin Pope in place so both wings of the Army of Northern Virginia could deal with him. That evening Jackson's men emerged from cover to assail the left flank of Brigadier-General, U.S.V., Rufus King's First Division of General McDowell's Third Corps, Army of Virginia, as in the course of Pope's efforts to locate Jackson it marched east along the Warrenton Pike near Groveton.

Jackson's flank march to Manassas Junction had been a Napoleonic manœuvre sur les derrières as brilliantly executed as any by Napoleon himself. With the emergence from the woods at Groveton, however, there opened a repetition of Jackson's recent unhappy tactical pattern of decidedly less dazzling performance. Groveton proved all too much like Cedar Mountain as a combat whose most lasting impression was of the first-rate fighting qualities of the Federals. At Groveton King's Fourth Brigade, the Black Hat Brigade of four Midwestern regiments under Brigadier-General John Gibbon, U.S.V., began the earning of a special fame in the Union Army. One of its regiments — the 2nd Wisconsin — had seen action as long ago as First Bull Run; the others — the 19th Indiana and 6th and 7th Wisconsin — were entering their first big fight; but they had been drilled zealously by Gibbon, uniformed at his requisition in prewar Regular Army–style frock coats and black hats to lend a distinctive appearance for the sake of morale, and now proved able to slug it out for an hour and more of stand-up, head-on fighting with Stonewall Jackson's veterans and not to break. On both sides, one of every three men who fought at Groveton was shot. While Jackson had the numbers readily at hand to overpower the Federals, however, he contrived to insert only three of fourteen brigades into the battle: the Stonewall Brigade under Colonel William S. H. Baylor of the 4th Virginia, and Brigadier-Generals Alexander R. Lawton's and Isaac Ridgeway Trimble's Brigades of Ewell's Division. Against this unnecessarily small force, Gibbon's brigade and the 76th New York and 56th Pennsylvania of Brigadier-General, U.S.V., Abner Doubleday's Second Brigade of King's division, which carried the brunt of it for the Union, were enough to force a stalemate.[10]

The next day, August 29, Pope had most of his army up to assail Jackson's Wing across much of the old Bull Run battlefield, with Jackson's nucleus still near Groveton. The Federals fought hard again, and again Jackson's tactical performance was less than stellar, so that during a long day's combat his line several times came closer to breaking under Federal assaults than it should have, and night fell upon a Confederate Left Wing that was close to the end of its physical and nervous resources. But Pope's tactics were anything but outstanding either, for he repeatedly attacked piecemeal and failed to reinforce drives that appeared to be on the verge of a breakthrough. And he also repeatedly refused to believe accurate reports informing him that by afternoon Longstreet's Right Wing had passed Thoroughfare Gap in the Bull Run Mountains and was massing on his left to assist Jackson.

The second day of this second battle of Bull Run or Manassas began with more of the same. Indeed, Pope so closed his mind to Longstreet's presence, and so fixated himself on how near he had come to breaking Jackson, that he persuaded himself that Jackson must be in retreat and that his task for the day was pursuit and exploitation. To that end he summoned from his left Porter's Fifth Corps of the Army of the Potomac to deliver the knockout blow as only fresh troops can, so that in the new round of assaults against Jackson, Porter joined the Army of Virginia, the two divisions of the Ninth Corps that had come up, and the Third Corps and the Pennsylvania Reserves Division also from the Army of the Potomac (detached August 26 from the Fifth Corps, of which it had been the Third Division). The persistence of the preceding day's pattern extended to a new series of near-misses, breakthroughs that fell just short because Pope fought his battle in too piecemeal a fashion and never sufficiently reinforced success.

Later Pope was to attempt to unload the blame for never quite rupturing the enemy front upon Fitz-John Porter, in one of the bitterest of all the many quarrels among Civil War generals that long outlived the war and even the principals; Porter became Pope's target partly because he was a McClellan man who never much bothered to conceal his distaste for Pope as an undeserving usurper, partly because Porter's attacks were in truth less than wholehearted because he refused to share Pope's delusion that the enemy was about to retreat if not already doing so, and because he was oppressed by the shadow of Longstreet. It had been the presence of Porter's corps on the Federal left that mainly prevented Longstreet from attacking on August 29; Porter had felt Longstreet's presence too closely that day to forget it now — though strangely, a categoric warning from him through General McDowell, whom unlike Porter Pope liked and trusted, did not reach Pope until it was too late.

It was too late by about 3:30 in the afternoon of August 30. At that time Lee and Longstreet independently but simultaneously became convinced that Pope had stripped his left of all but skeleton forces for the attacks on Jackson, and that if Longstreet's Wing hit hard and in the few remaining hours of daylight moved fast, the Confederate Right Wing might roll up the Union left and reach the Warrenton Pike in rear of most of Pope's army, which could accomplish the great desideratum of all Napoleonic battlefield commanders and particularly of Lee, the destruction of the enemy army. So closely attuned were Lee's and Longstreet's minds at this juncture that by the time Lee's order to attack reached Longstreet, the wing commander had his preparations nearly complete, and the climactic effort kicked off at four P.M.

Longstreet was and is often regarded as slow. The reputation sprang partly from his march to join Jackson for this very battle, when his pace had been leisurely compared with Jackson's earlier forced march, but when Lee in fact had set the tempo, knowing that Jackson was not in immediate peril and wishing to spare the stamina of Longstreet's troops for just such an opportunity as now beckoned. So Longstreet's reputation for sluggishness is at least partly undeserved. Moreover, his harshest critics acknowledged that once he was ready to attack, he consistently struck blows as hard as any in the war. Thus Longstreet fell upon and swept away the Union left at Second Manassas, driving the whole Union army into flight and making this battle almost as close to an Austerlitz or Jena-Auerstädt victory as R. E. Lee's Napoleonic style of generalship was ever to achieve. We shall witness only one possibly closer approximation.

But Pope's army was not destroyed. Perhaps there were simply not enough hours of daylight left when Longstreet began; darkness would fall before eight. Also, the skeleton forces on the Union left fought a more stubborn delaying action than Pope had a right to expect: first, the tiny, two-regiment (5th and 10th New York) Third Brigade, Second Division, Fifth Corps under Colonel Gouverneur K. Warren of the 5th; then the not-much-stronger four-regiment Third Brigade of the Pennsylvania Reserves under Lieutenant-Colonel Martin D. Hardin of the 12th Reserves; then somewhat larger — though still overmatched — forces from Major-General, U.S.V., Franz Sigel's First Corps, Army of Virginia; Porter's Fifth Corps; and the bulk of Brigadier-General, U.S.V., John F. Reynolds's division of Pennsylvania Reserves. Probably most important, Stonewall Jackson failed to heed orders from Lee to join fully in the attack. For all these reasons, but especially because out of excessively prolonged fatigue and strain or a more mysterious recurrence of his tactical funk Jackson withheld his hand, the Confederates did not close off the Warrenton Pike, Pope's escape route toward Washington.

The Union army did not panic. By 11 P.M. most of it had crossed Bull

Run, so that henceforth the stream would help shield it from pursuit. At Centreville, four miles beyond the Bull Run crossings, the Sixth Corps of the Army of the Potomac waited, having arrived that evening from Alexandria. The Second Corps of the Army of the Potomac lay behind it. The defeated Federals had plenty of strength upon which to rally, and the Confederates could do no more to encompass their destruction. A halfhearted effort in that direction by Jackson, another march around the Union right flank toward cutting communications between Centreville and Alexandria, fizzled late on September 1 in a dark rainstorm, the battle of Chantilly or Ox Hill. There were more than enough Federals to check Jackson because there were now simply too many soldiers in Union blue crowded into too narrow an area to afford the Confederates new opportunities.[11]

Almost certainly there should also have been more than enough Federals on the field of Second Bull Run by August 30 to deny the Confederates anything like the opportunity that Lee had nearly grasped. McClellan's abysmally slow evacuation of the Peninsula had been matched by a similarly slow shoveling of men forward from Alexandria to reinforce Pope. McClellan had arrived at Alexandria at midday of August 27. He found his Sixth Corps there and ready to march, with the Second Corps to be on hand the next day. Late on the 27th he assured Halleck that he could begin his advance toward Pope promptly. When Halleck tried to accept the offer, however, nothing happened, and late on the 28th McClellan changed his tune to say he was not ready to move. Halleck then peremptorily ordered him to put the Sixth Corps on the road at six A.M. on the 29th; but when McClellan suggested that because of uncertainty about what was happening with Pope, it might be dangerous to exceed a ten-mile march to Annandale, Halleck acquiesced.[12]

Not only did McClellan withhold two army corps from the battle. Again and again since the creation of Pope's Army of Virginia he had made it clear to all his friends that he hoped Pope would fail. He was completely indiscreet and completely petty. It is no wonder that consequently the belief spread among Pope and his partisans, to linger forever after, that McClellan deliberately sabotaged the Army of Virginia. There is no good reason to think that. Looking west and south from Alexandria in the last days of August 1862, the Federals could see only chaos and therefore much that was unknown. Facing the unknown, McClellan always conjured up vast enemy armies to fill it. McClellan did not behave traitorously during the second battle of Bull Run, but only like McClellan.

Halleck deserves at least equal censure. McClellan still commanded the Army of the Potomac, even though the army gradually dwindled as its troops passed into Pope's command. With two commanders of field armies at large in Virginia, only the General-in-Chief had the authority to coordinate their activities. Halleck did the job badly. He must be admired for his courage at the outset of the campaign in assuming the responsibility for cutting the Union's losses on the Peninsula and evacuating McClellan's army. His decision then was the right and difficult one in spite of the risks it entailed and the possibilities it rejected. Through the rest of the campaign, however, Halleck never again did anything comparably correct. He hid from responsibility. The Union would have been better off without a General-in-Chief, with a return instead to the days of the Valley Campaign when Lincoln and Stanton had tried to trap Jackson. The President and the Secretary of War lacked professional expertise and finesse, but they were not afraid of responsibility.

The statistics of Second Bull Run reaffirmed that in spite of the delusional nature of Pope's response to the approach of Longstreet's Wing and his August 30 efforts to complete the supposed defeat of Jackson, he had not fought the battle altogether badly. He had in fact approached breaking Jackson several times, and finally he acknowledged the threat from Longstreet just soon enough to deny Lee the fullness of an Austerlitz triumph. And of course, as was becoming customary, the Union soldiers mostly fought very well. Statistical evidence of the battle's Napoleonic qualities lay only in the large number of Union soldiers missing, an indication of the Federals' abandonment of the field: 5,958 Union missing in contrast to only eighty-nine Confederates missing. Otherwise, the Union army of 75,696 men lost 13 percent in killed and wounded, while the Confederate army of 48,527 lost 19 percent: 1,724 Federals killed, 8,372 wounded, as compared with 1,481 Confederates killed, 7,627 wounded. The total Confederate casualties of 9,197 represented 19 percent of Lee's army; the total Federal casualties of 16,054 represented 21 percent of Pope's army. Considering that Pope was attacking through a day and a half of the two-day battle, even the disparity in absolute numbers of losses is not so discreditable to the Federals. The proportions were as in the Seven Days much in their favor.[13]

Still, of the three principal Federal commanders who were involved, it was Pope who had to go. Halleck could not be shelved so early in his career as General-in-Chief; McClellan retained to an extraordinary degree the loyalty of the senior officers of the army he had shaped and to some extent also of the soldiers (he was charismatic, and he was reluctant to expend their lives); and it could not be denied that Pope had lost the battle. If Lee had defeated John Pope psychologically much more throughly than he had beaten Pope's army physically, the verdict remained the same. On September 2 Halleck relieved Pope, and that morning Lincoln personally asked

McClellan to assume command of the defense of Washington. During the next few days, this assignment evolved into command of the entire field force in the area of the capital, with the troops of the Army of Virginia being amalgamated into the Army of the Potomac.[14]

## LEE'S FIRST STRATEGIC OFFENSIVE: THE MARYLAND CAMPAIGN

As Lee had acknowledged sorrowfully the limitations of his victory in the Seven Days Battles, so he also recognized the essential barrenness of such a victory as Second Manassas. While his campaign of the summer of 1862 had almost cleared Virginia of the enemy (except for western Virginia, the northern Valley, Fort Monroe, and Norfolk), the Federals surely would soon return unless he accomplished something yet more dramatic and decisive to prevent it. The campaign might also have hurt Republican prospects in the coming Northern Congressional elections, but the Lincoln administration would control the executive branch at least until March 4, 1865, and the administration showed no evidence of losing its resolution to conquer the South. To forestall the Federals from returning to Virginia once they had licked their wounds, Lee believed he must go over from the tactical initiative, the attack on the battlefield, to the strategic offensive, the larger initiative designed to win the war. He decided to follow up Second Manassas by crossing the Potomac into Maryland, with the hope of advancing still further into Pennsylvania and perhaps on to Harrisburg, the state capital, and Philadelphia. All through the campaign against Pope he had such an offensive in mind; his maneuvers against Pope's right always carried a northward shift as an immediate option, possibly superseding a battle against Pope, depending on the Federal responses. Lee would not only drive Pope from Virginia; he would move the Eastern theater of war out of the seceded states and into the enemy's country.[15]

The invasion of Maryland and possibly Pennsylvania would, to be sure, be more of a raid than a sustained offensive. Lee would not have the strength to maintain his army in the North for an indefinite period, unless the hoped-for but unlikely eventuality of Maryland's joining the Confederacy permitted him to remain in the Old Line State. Lee believed, however, that an offensive even of a raiding nature might bring profound, even decisive results not to be gained from tactical victories in Virginia. A battlefield triumph comparable to Second Manassas but won on Northern soil might severely, perhaps fatally, weaken the North's resolve. While Lee believed shrewdly

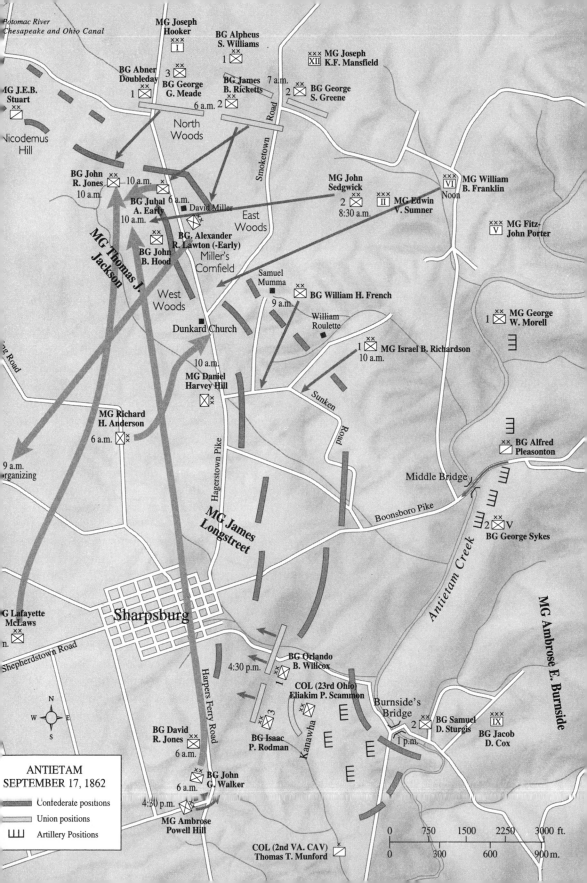

*Potomac River*
*Chesapeake and Ohio Canal*

MG Joseph Hooker
××× I

BG Alpheus S. Williams
××× 1 ××

MG Joseph K.F. Mansfield
××× XII

BG Abner Doubleday
3 ××
1 ×× BG George G. Meade
6 a.m.

BG James B. Ricketts
7 a.m.
2 ×× BG George S. Greene

North Woods

Smoketown Road

MG J.E.B. Stuart
×× 
Nicodemus Hill

MG John Sedgwick
2 ×× II MG Edwin V. Sumner
8:30 a.m.

MG William B. Franklin
××× VI Noon

BG John R. Jones
×× 10 a.m.
10 a.m.

BG Jubal A. Early
10 a.m.
6 a.m.

David Miller

East Woods

MG Fitz-John Porter
××× V

MG Thomas J. Jackson

BG John B. Hood
××
BG. Alexander R. Lawton (-Early)

Miller's Cornfield

West Woods

Samuel Mumma
BG William H. French
9 a.m.

William Roulette

MG George W. Morell
1 ××

Dunkard Church

MG Daniel Harvey Hill
10 a.m.
××

Sunken Road

BG Israel B. Richardson
1 ××
10 a.m.

MG Richard H. Anderson
6 a.m. ××

Road

BG Alfred Pleasonton
××

9 a.m. organizing

Middle Bridge

MG James Longstreet

Boonsboro Pike

Antietam Creek

2 ×× V
BG George Sykes

G Lafayette McLaws
n. ××

Sharpsburg

Shepherdstown Road

Harpers Ferry Road

Hagerstown Pike

BG Orlando B. Willcox
4:30 p.m.
1

COL (23rd Ohio) Eliakim P. Scammon

MG Ambrose E. Burnside

BG David R. Jones
6 a.m.

3 ××
BG Isaac P. Rodman

Kanawha

Burnside's Bridge

2 ×× BG Samuel D. Sturgis
1 p.m.

IX BG Jacob D. Cox

BG John G. Walker
6 a.m.
4:30 p.m.

MG Ambrose Powell Hill

COL (2nd VA. CAV) Thomas T. Munford

ANTIETAM
SEPTEMBER 17, 1862

▬▬ Confederate positions
▬▬ Union positions
ᖚᖚ Artillery Positions

N W E S

| 0 | 750 | 1500 | 2250 | 3000 ft. |
| 0 | 300 | 600 | 900 m. |

that the Confederacy should not count on foreign assistance,[16] it nevertheless seemed possible that a victory in Union territory might bring European recognition and aid. The fortifications of Washington into which Pope's and McClellan's troops had retreated were too strong for Lee to assail them directly, but on September 4 the Army of Northern Virginia began to cross the Potomac farther northwest at White's Ford near Leesburg.

Unfortunately for Lee's grand design, however, the toll of the summer's campaigning prevented him from leading more than about 50,000 men into Maryland. Thousands remained behind in Virginia, many because without shoes, badly nourished, and exhausted from their marches and battles they simply could not keep up, others because they believed it wrong to invade the North when they had enlisted only to defend their own homes and way of life, probably many from a combination of these motives. Inside Maryland, the limitations of Colonel Northrop's Commissary Department and of Confederate transport assured that logistical problems did not much improve. Some soldiers found food given by or purchased from (usually in Confederate currency) more or less willing Marylanders, but others still subsisted on green corn and green apples ruinous to digestion, and many still marched in rags and tattered shoes if they had shoes at all. Nothing in the appearance of Lee's army was likely to inspire fence-sitting Marylanders to join them. Stragglers continued to fall behind by the hundreds, still further depleting Lee's ranks just as his strategic vision approached its fulfillment.

On September 7, when the Confederate army was concentrated around the Maryland town of Frederick, beginning three days of rest, refitting, and attempted recruiting there, a Union army of more than 85,000 began to march northwestward from Washington to meet it. Unfortunately for the Union, public fears and pressure led the administration to retain some 72,500 troops for the direct defense of Washington — Lincoln's concerns when McClellan departed for the Peninsula had been reasonable; demands for so many men in the fortifications now were not — and by September 9, McClellan had again convinced himself that Lee had at least 100,000 men, probably more. Thus the Federal march began with the Young Napoleon's customary slowness and caution, at a pace of about eight miles a day.[17]

The mountain-girt village of Harpers Ferry, where the Shenandoah River meets the Potomac and the scene of John Brown's raid of 1859, now began to assume a disproportionately important part in the Maryland campaign. A Union garrison of more than 13,000 men — the Railroad Brigade, Eighth Corps, Middle Department, commanded by Colonel Dixon S. Miles, 2nd U.S. Infantry — occupied the place. General Halleck believed that the garrison should remain, to protect the Baltimore and Ohio Railroad bridge across the Potomac. McClellan believed otherwise and sought the troops for his army; as he saw it, the garrison was not large enough to do the protecting anyway, and it would be more useful as an addition to his field force. Given the strong possibility that the garrison might be gobbled up as prisoners, McClellan's view made sense; but Halleck's otherwise dubious judgment was inadvertently about to bait a trap for Lee that was comparable to his waning numbers as a threat to his strategic vision.[18]

Lee decided that he could not safely continue his invasion, especially should he proceed into Pennsylvania, with the Harpers Ferry garrison on his line of communications through the Shenandoah Valley. Because the garrison was relatively small, and Miles, its commander, known to be indolent if not downright incompetent, Lee's attitude was questionable. It led him, moreover, into the yet more questionable decision to divide his already much outnumbered army in the face of the enemy, into four and eventually five parts. Against Pope, of course, Lee had prospered mightily by ignoring the military maxim that in the presence of an enemy an army must remain united; but the maxim has merit, and Lee had probably grown overconfident of his ability to defy such dicta.

On September 9 Lee issued Special Order No. 191, for his army to resume its march the next morning with Harpers Ferry as its immediate objective. Stonewall Jackson was to lead six divisions, about two-thirds of the army, in the expedition to capture the town and its garrison. Besides separating these divisions from the rest of the army, the order also divided Jackson's force itself into three parts, to close in on Harpers Ferry from each of the three mountains that overlook it. Two of the parts had to recross to the south bank of the Potomac: Jackson himself with the Stonewall Division, Ewell's Division, and A. P. Hill's Light Division to approach the town from the west via Martinsburg and on to Bolivar Heights; Brigadier-General John G. Walker's Division to capture Loudoun Heights between the Shenandoah and the Potomac and surveying Harpers Ferry from the south. Meanwhile Major-General Lafayette McLaws with his own and Major-General Richard H. Anderson's Divisions would close off the target by occupying Maryland Heights, the highest of the mountains, dominating the town from the north and east. While Jackson carried out this assignment, Lee and Longstreet would be around Boonsboro with Brigadier-Generals David R. Jones's and John Bell Hood's Divisions, while Major-General Daniel H. Hill's Division would be nearby, as a rear guard watching the passes through South Mountain between the Confederates and McClellan. Presently, however, a rumor about enemy militia activity in Pennsylvania led Lee and Longstreet with D. R. Jones's and Hood's Divisions to move to Hagerstown, keeping open

Lee's preferred potential route into Pennsylvania, but by leaving D. H. Hill behind completing the separation of the Army of Northern Virginia into five parts.[19]

Lee had reason to think that McClellan's notorious caution would permit his troops to capture Harpers Ferry and to reassemble before a Federal threat materialized, but even against McClellan he was assuming a large risk. In Unionist central Maryland — there were few slaves here and close ties to Pennsylvania — McClellan's intelligence services functioned predictably better than in Virginia, and the Federal commander enjoyed a pretty accurate idea of the disposition of Lee's formations. If McClellan had simply made the calculations implicit in the many reports he received of how much time each of those formations required to move from one place to another, he could also have formed an accurate estimate of Lee's numbers, though this he did not choose to do. Still, Lee should not have expected the splitting up of his army to go unnoticed.

Furthermore, McClellan was about to receive a famous windfall. On the morning of Saturday, September 13, the Twelfth Corps of the Army of the Potomac[20] made camp on ground recently occupied by the Confederates around Frederick. About ten A.M. Corporal Barton W. Mitchell of Company F, 27th Indiana Infantry, noticed a piece of paper wrapped around three cigars. Retrieving the cigars, he and Sergeant John M. Bloss read the paper and discovered they had found a copy of what appeared to be important Confederate orders — Special Order No. 191, in fact. They quickly passed their discovery up the chain of command, where Captain Samuel E. Pittman, assistant adjutant-general of volunteers and division adjutant of the First Division, Twelfth Corps, to whose Third Brigade the 27th Indiana belonged, saw that the order was in handwriting for which he could vouch. He knew Colonel Robert H. Chilton, assistant adjutant-general to R. E. Lee. Chilton had written out and signed the order on Lee's behalf, and Pittman could authenticate it. Thus even McClellan was willing to believe the order was not a trick and to act on its information.[21]

Not that he acted with much more energy than usual. The order did not inform him of Lee's numbers, so he still believed he must march with caution lest he be overwhelmed by only a part of a much superior enemy force. The order was in his hands before noon on the 13th, but his instructions to his corps commanders did not call for movement in response to it before morning of the 14th. In truth, while he regarded the order as an amazing bonanza, it did not tell him much more than he already knew or would soon have known, considering the high quality of the information already reaching him from Maryland informants. Moreover, his euphoria on receiving the order led him to express jubilation in front of several Frederick businessmen, one of whom was a Confederate sympathizer who promptly rode through the Federal lines to South Mountain and Jeb Stuart. Lee knew by ten P.M. that McClellan probably had a copy of the order, and he therefore warned McLaws that the Federals would probably march to relieve Harpers Ferry.[22]

Because McClellan had shown much concern about the garrison there and wanted it as a reinforcement, that is what the Federals should have done. But it was not exactly what they did. Instead of ordering his major effort on Sunday the 14th to take place in the direction of Crampton's Gap, the southernmost pass through South Mountain and the way to Harpers Ferry, McClellan sent a heavier force toward Turner's and Fox's and adjacent gaps between Frederick and Hagerstown. Not only did McClellan have to be aware that instead of rescuing Harpers Ferry, this emphasis would propel him head-on against Lee and Longstreet — Special Order No. 191 indeed put two Confederate divisions just behind D. H. Hill's Division in the passes — but Lee's awareness that the Federals probably had the order led him to hurry D. R. Jones's and Hood's Divisions eastward again to reinforce D. H. Hill. The upshot was that Ambrose Burnside with McClellan's right wing, the First and Ninth Corps, spent all day Sunday in a hard battle up the steep slopes of South Mountain and around Turner's and Fox's Gaps.

D. H. Hill had his own bad moments that day while his division stood alone awaiting Lee's help, but the reinforcements arrived in time to retain possession of Turner's Gap until nightfall. By then the Federals had taken Fox's Gap and other flanking routes, but the Confederates could stage an orderly retreat, and McClellan would have had access to Lee's plans for a day and a half without effective exploitation of the knowledge. For against Crampton's Gap, to which the logic of his concern for Harpers Ferry should have led him, McClellan directed a lesser force. There Major-General William B. Franklin, U.S.V., with his two-division Sixth Corps and the First Division, Fourth Corps proved not enough to break through three brigades of McLaws's Division that the latter had turned around, along with some stubborn Confederate cavalry support, until late in the day. The Confederates enjoyed strong positions well entrenched, but Franklin conducted the affair in a fashion fully consistent with the habits of his army commander. After he drove the enemy from the mountain line, he halted on Sunday evening in front of a weaker defensive line, professing to have only half the Confederates' strength when in fact his 18,000 men must have given him more than twice the strength of McLaws's and Anderson's Divisions combined. The implication, of course, is that even though McClellan had emphasized the wrong thrust into South Mountain, his southern column should still have been more than enough to save Harpers Ferry. But once Franklin halted, he remained halted until McClellan summoned him away for a different battle on September 17, by which time Harpers Ferry had surrendered.[23]

One of the reasons why Lee had risked dividing his force according to Special Order No. 191 of September 9 was that he expected Harpers Ferry to fall by the night of September 12. The friction customarily attendant upon waging war had prevented such an outcome; unforeseen terrain obstacles, unexpected mishaps, and something less than tireless driving zeal on the part of the Confederate columns kept them from being fully in position on all three heights around Harpers Ferry to Jackson's satisfaction to permit him to order the climactic bombardment and assault even for September 14. That afternoon, however, Walker grew nervous when he heard the sounds of the McLaws-Franklin battle, and he ordered his artillery to open fire on the town and its garrison. Thus stimulated, the other Confederate columns hastened to complete a ring around Harpers Ferry by that evening, ready to send a plunging fire into the town and to follow up if necessary with an infantry assault early in the morning. On the evening of the 14th, Jackson sent off a message to Lee assuring him that victory would occur the next day. When the Confederate guns opened at dawn, Colonel Miles in the garrison quickly decided his position was untenable and after about an hour's firing was ready to surrender. His white flag had gone up when a belated salvo mortally wounded him, but the surrender proceedings continued and reached completion about nine A.M.[24]

That much accomplished, and notwithstanding the favors he had received from McClellan and Franklin, Lee had not yet escaped the perils he had created for himself by allowing Harpers Ferry to shape his campaign. When on Monday the 15th he received Jackson's message promising the capture of Harpers Ferry that day, Lee decided to reconcentrate his army behind Antietam Creek near Sharpsburg, remaining in Maryland just short of the Potomac, where Blackford's or Boteler's Ford crosses a part of the river flowing mainly from north to south. It was a bold decision, not to say another decidedly questionable one, for Lee still had a strength of less than 15,000 in his immediate command — he had lost not many fewer than 3,000 at South Mountain — when the Army of the Potomac began to arrive on the east bank of the Antietam toward noon.[25] Even at McClellan's pace, the bulk of the Union army had to be expected before nightfall. The seventeen miles from Harpers Ferry, in contrast, represented the better part of a day's march. Jackson would have to leave some of his men at Harpers Ferry for the time being to conduct the formalities of paroling Federal prisoners and inventorying supplies; as Lee soon learned, Jackson in fact left A. P. Hill's Light Division, and its 3,000 men would not be able to join Lee until late on Wednesday, September 17. McClellan still had ample time to assail the Army of Northern Virginia while it remained divided because of Harpers Ferry.

And even a reunited Confederate army would now, after all its straggling and the South Mountain casualties, be able to assemble only about 40,000 soldiers against at least twice that many Federals. As usual, Lee's plans in such circumstances rested on his appraisal of McClellan. Still, it is hard to discern a justification for Lee's risking battle on the Antietam at all, let alone while his army remained scattered — except that he had formed by now a resolute confidence that he and his soldiers could defeat McClellan and the Union army under almost any conditions. Furthermore, the campaign meant too much to Lee's strategy to cut it short without a battle. He would have preferred a battle in which he could maneuver in Second Manassas style; if he could not have that, he would prefer to fight on the tactical defensive rather than give up the campaign on which he was staking so much without a fight at all.

Lee's decision to stand along the Antietam offered McClellan the opportunity to attack him during the first half of September 15 with favorable odds of at least four to one. It was only an eight-mile march from Turner's Gap to the east bank of the Antietam, and there was no reason why the bulk of the Federal army should not have been there while the opportunity prevailed. But no one asked the Federal soldiers to march rapidly, and McClellan himself remained east of South Mountain throughout the morning congratulating himself on the mighty victory he had won in the mountain gaps the day before. He did not arrive at the Antietam until three in the afternoon, by which time it was too late to squeeze in a major battle before darkness. Nevertheless, McClellan rode back and forth surveying the Confederate positions and gave some indication that he would attack in the morning.

The morning of Tuesday, September 16 and much of the day still offered golden chances to exploit the consequences of Lee's Harpers Ferry gamble. Jackson himself rode up to Lee and Longstreet as they studied the Federal lines about noon, with two of the three divisions of his own Harpers Ferry force along with Walker's Division not far behind. At the end of the day, however, Lee still had only somewhat fewer than 25,000 men, six of the nine divisions of his army, because McLaws's and Anderson's Divisions had encountered more of the mishaps of war, including trouble exiting Harpers Ferry through a press of paroled Federals. McLaws and Anderson bivouacked for the night a few miles short of Blackford's Ford, which was itself about three miles from the Antietam positions. Learning of the delay, Lee sent a courier summoning the two divisions on a forced march by night, while another courier called on A. P. Hill to depart Harpers Ferry as early as possible in the morning.[26]

But Lee could send those orders without the added pressure of gunfire around him, because McClellan had let another day go by with almost nothing accomplished. Ostensibly, he was again reconnoitering Lee's position, to assure success when he did attack on Wednesday, September 17. In fact, the conduct of the next day's battle was to show that McClellan and his officers still knew little of the terrain and how best to use it.

But there was a battle on the 17th. Not even McClellan could find excuses to delay any longer. And in spite of the opportunities that McClellan had allowed to slip away, it remained true that Lee could have no hope along the Antietam for the Austerlitz victory that the strategic logic of his campaign demanded. With the Potomac just behind him and only one ford practically available for retreat, in a constricted position offering Lee no space for the kind of maneuver that had served him so well in his previous battles, and with McClellan's remaining numerical advantage, the only army that might be destroyed on this occasion was Lee's own. Two and a half months before, in hurling his frontal assaults against Malvern Hill after he had lost his chance to break up McClellan's army along its line of retreat to the James, Lee had revealed a quality of stubborn pugnacity that impelled him to fight even when his strategic or tactical plans had gone awry. Now he displayed that pugnacity again, albeit on the defensive.

Moreover, Lee made a strange tactical judgment when deploying his meager force. He formed a defensive line running from north to south between Antietam Creek and the Potomac River, roughly parallel to the two streams. The observant visitor to the ground will be struck by the presence of a ridge that begins on the north as Nicodemus Hill west of the main part of Lee's left flank, stretching thence southward between Lee's line and the Potomac, and constituting higher ground than the principal Confederate positions. Lee did not post his main force on the high ground. Perhaps his intent was to have strong terrain on which to fall back if he could not hold his line. In fact, however, he made his army exceedingly vulnerable.

It probably would have been too much to expect that McClellan might have gone far enough forward in his reconnaissances to discern that if his opening attack, planned to hit Lee's left, struck instead at Nicodemus Hill behind the left, the whole Confederate position could have been exposed to Federals on the higher ground. When the battle began, Jeb Stuart's Cavalry Division occupied Nicodemus Hill, with its horse artillery ready to harass the Federal attack, but without the strength to defend the hill against a respectable infantry assault. If McClellan did not perceive the opportunity — and even his distant inspections of the ground should not have left him blind to Nicodemus Hill — then surely the possibilities ought to have dawned upon Major-General, U.S.V., Joseph Hooker, who had taken over the First Corps on September 12, who was to lead the opening attack, and who usually demonstrated a keen tactical eye. A relatively slight shift of Hooker's attack to the right would have carried much of his corps onto the exposed high ground. Instead, Hooker plowed straight on into the main strength of Lee's left, southward astride the Hagerstown Road toward Sharpsburg, through David Miller's cornfield toward a simple church building of the German Baptist Brethren.

Largely in consequence, September 17, 1862, the date of the battle of Antietam, or Sharpsburg, became the bloodiest single day of the war so far — a record, in fact, that was not to be surpassed. Through a long day of fighting back and forth across the incongruously green and pleasant Maryland countryside; in Miller's cornfield, which became a trampled, sodden shambles and henceforth *the* Cornfield in memories of the Civil War; around the little church building that many soldiers at first took to be a one-room schoolhouse — hereafter *the* Dunker Church; and later across a sunken road now to be called the Bloody Lane — McClellan's attacks time and again nearly ruptured Lee's thin line, so superior was the pressure of numbers that McClellan could mount. At the end of the day, the final Federal charge, across the Antietam near the far right of the Confederate position over the Rohrbach Bridge — hereafter Burnside's Bridge — and up the adjacent hills, missed turning Lee's right and cutting his road to the Potomac only because Powell Hill and the Light Division arrived from Harpers Ferry at the last desperate moment.

Antietam was McClellan's nadir as a tactician, which is saying a great deal. He directed it as a model of how not to fight a battle. He not only failed to perceive the opportunity presented by the high ground in Lee's rear, but where he did fight he conducted three consecutive uncoordinated assaults, each of them broken into a further series of uncoordinated advances. Thus he permitted Lee all day to shift his scarce troops from one threatened point to another. Meanwhile, McClellan never used his own reserves. Moreover, he never felt the pulse of the battle, because while he positioned himself on high ground east of the Antietam so he could view the fighting west of the stream from a distance, he was never close enough to the action to develop the sense of ebb and flow and thus of the decisive moment for a climactic effort that the greatest military commanders have always gained — even in the twentieth century — from leading at the front.

This distancing of himself from the experience of combat had been McClellan's way throughout his tenure of command. In no battle had he gone to the point of collision in the manner of a Napoleon, a *Generalfeld-marschall* Ervin Rommel, or a General George S. Patton, Jr. He came under fire often enough to demonstrate his physical bravery; but his habitual absence from the crises of combat suggests an unwillingness to face up directly to the mortal consequences for which an army commander must bear responsibility. His soldiers had formed an affection for him no doubt largely because they sensed that he would not readily sacrifice them. But his unwillingness to sacrifice them was in part also an unwillingness to bear a general's burdensome duties. And at Antietam, because he would not confront those duties, because he would not experience combat, and because therefore he was an incompetent tactician, he sacrificed his soldiers' lives after all, in unprecedented numbers. That day the army's confidence in him at last began to disintegrate, perhaps remarkably little among the rank and file, but certainly among his officers.

Evading the ugly realities of combat, McClellan evaded also the opportunity through direct experience to make the timely decisions that in the midst of combat can sometimes turn defeat into victory or marginal victory into smashing triumph. So at Antietam he frittered away numerical strength in timidity and uncoordinated assaults. Repeatedly on September 17, 1862, one more blow might have broken Lee's attenuated line; but all day McClellan kept Fitz-John Porter's Fifth Corps uncommitted, striking no blow with it whatever; and when late in the day Franklin's Sixth Corps also came to hand, only its Third Brigade, Second Division got into serious action.

Still, to save their lines from collapse the Confederates had to fight so desperately that Lee although on the defensive suffered more heavily than McClellan: 13,724 Confederate casualties (2,700 killed, 9,024 wounded, about 2,000 missing) to 12,410 Union (2,108 killed, 9,549 wounded, 753 missing). Almost incredibly, Lee nevertheless remained in his lines still another day, throughout September 18, and McClellan did not attack again on Thursday although he had 26,300 troops who had not fought on Wednesday and another 6,000, albeit raw troops, who arrived on the morning of the 18th. But Lee could do no more in Maryland; on the night of September 18 he retreated into Virginia, little molested in the process.[27]

## Confederate Riposte in the West:
## Iuka and Corinth

Antietam by no means ended Lee's offensive strategy. As soon as he had rested and the stragglers who had never crossed the Potomac returned to replenish his ranks, he turned to thoughts of advancing into Maryland and toward Pennsylvania yet again. If Lee had had his way, the Sharpsburg campaign would have been only the prelude to a more powerful invasion of the North, that same autumn of 1862.[28] And Lee's Sharpsburg invasion had been only part of a rising Confederate offensive tide from the Potomac to the Mississippi that late summer and autumn.

Everywhere the warm months of 1862 brought discouragement to the North and revived hope, coupled with a widespread acceptance of strategic ideas similar to Lee's in spite of Jefferson Davis, all through the Confederacy. For the North, the most imposing army ever assembled in America had reached the gates of Richmond only to be turned back and then forced to defend its own home ground. Even in the West, meanwhile, the North's victories of the winter and the early spring had led not to further triumphs but to frustration. In July, Farragut's river fleet from New Orleans and Charles H. Davis's from upriver united to bombard Vicksburg, Mississippi; but they could not subdue the Confederate batteries on the bluffs commanding the river there, and they parted for their separate bases. After taking Corinth, Halleck had divided his forces to patrol and hold the imposing distances of western Tennessee and the many miles of the Memphis and Charleston and the Mobile and Ohio Railroads that had to be retained against hostile raiders in his rear. After Halleck went to Washington, by the season of Lee's Maryland campaign in mid-September, and on into early October, Grant and Major-General William S. Rosecrans, U.S.V., had to fight hard using part of Halleck's former army simply to hold Corinth against the assaults of Major-Generals Sterling Price and Earl Van Dorn.[29]

The latter Federal problems commenced on September 13, when Price with the Army of the West, some 17,000 men hitherto positioned at Tupelo, Mississippi, drove a small Union garrison from Iuka, on the Memphis and Charleston line about twenty miles southeast of Corinth. To forestall further mischief, Grant decided to attack Price quickly, before Van Dorn, commanding the Army of West Tennessee, could reinforce him with the 7,000 troops he was moving from the west toward Holly Springs, on the Mississippi Central Railroad about forty-five miles southwest of Corinth. Van Dorn had still more Confederates, about 9,000, farther off toward Vicksburg, which he was shielding from overland assault.

Grant directed Major-General Edward Otho Cresap Ord, U.S.V., with three undersized divisions totaling about 8,000 men, to hit Price directly along the rail line from Corinth, while Rosecrans with two divisions aggregating 9,000 turned the Iuka position from the south. A reserve force at Rienzi just south of Corinth was to fend off Van Dorn. Ord was ready to strike by the night of September 18, and he was to do so when he heard Rosecrans's guns. But Rosecrans was delayed by yet another onset of the perennial friction of war and not ready to open his part of the attack until late the following afternoon. By that time Price had become aware of his presence and of the threat he posed to the Confederate rear, so Price sent more than half his troops to drive Rosecrans away. Two Confederate attacks failed but a third made progress, and meanwhile a strong north wind kept Ord from hearing the fight, so that he failed to pitch in. During the night Price discovered that Rosecrans had left one feasible route of retreat open, so he used it, while Rosecrans maintained insufficient vigilance even to harry the retreat. Federal casualties in the battle of Iuka were 144 killed, 598 wounded, forty missing; Confederate losses were 263 killed, 692 wounded, 561 missing.[30]

Van Dorn converged upon Price at Ripley, southwest of Corinth, with the intent of recapturing that strategic railroad junction. Although it was the most obvious target for the Confederates, Grant could not be sure they would hit it rather than another of the garrisons scattered along the rail lines when Halleck broke up his army, either at Memphis — albeit that was unlikely because of the Union Navy in the adjacent Mississippi River — or at Bolivar or at Jackson, Tennessee, both on the Mississippi Central Railroad. Still, the Federals made Corinth more tempting by circulating a false map showing weak outer defenses susceptible to a flank attack and an absence of guns mounted as yet in what was to be the strong point of the defenses, Battery Robinett. Also, Rosecrans, commanding at Corinth, had about 23,000 men by now to Van Dorn's 22,000.

On the morning of October 3 Van Dorn launched an attack against Rosecrans. The Federals withdrew under pressure from an outer to an inner defensive line, where Battery Robinett surprised the Confederates with heavy fire from masked batteries. Van Dorn, an aggressive, even reckless leader, still as at Pea Ridge given to hasty attacks without adequate reconnaissance, tried again the next day with additional headlong as well as head-on assaults. Price actually broke through into the streets of Corinth, where above the hand-to-hand fighting Old Abe, the eagle mascot of Company C,

8th Wisconsin, today immortalized on the shoulder patch of the 101st Airborne Division, swooped and wheeled and screamed.

To exploit the breach, Van Dorn committed all his reserves—he was no McClellan—but they were not enough to make anything decisive of it. About four P.M., when the Confederates were exhausted and had abandoned their assaults, Brigadier-General James Birdseye McPherson, U.S.V., the number one graduate of the West Point class of 1853, turned up with about 5,000 men from Jackson to threaten the rebel rear. Even Van Dorn had to recognize he must retreat, and as Rosecrans and McPherson pursued him on October 5, he also collided at Pocahontas on the Hatchie River with 6,500 troops down from Bolivar under Ord. Van Dorn lost about 300 captured before he slipped away across the Hatchie farther south. Union losses at Corinth were 2,520 against 2,470 Confederates killed and wounded and 1,763 missing, with a large number of missing signifying as usual a disordered retreat.

When Van Dorn himself arrived back at Vicksburg, he learned that as of October 13 Lieutenant-General John C. Pemberton commanded the Department of Mississippi, Tennessee, and East Louisiana. Van Dorn would be permitted reckless use of scarce Confederate manpower no more. Nevertheless, there was not much rejoicing on the Union side either. The ratio of casualties had been favorable at both Iuka and Corinth, and General McPherson had shown the first signs that he was a rising star; but a promising trap had failed to close upon Price at Iuka, and standing fast against Confederate counterattacks was not what the North had anticipated as the sequel to Halleck's assembling his huge concentration in the spring and to Fort Henry, Fort Donelson, Shiloh, and the capture of Corinth.[31]

## CONFEDERATE OFFENSIVE IN THE WEST: THE KENTUCKY CAMPAIGN

For the Confederacy, the consolation implicit in Iuka and Corinth was that they did not constitute the main Western effort of the late summer and early autumn. They were counterattacks, not full-scale strategic initiatives, not strategic offensives. In the West, the Confederacy's hopes for a strategic reversal of early 1862's fortunes of war analogous to the hopes that Lee invested in his invasion of Maryland lay in another part of the vast theater: in Kentucky, where support for the Confederacy ran high enough that Confederates could think of the Commonwealth as rightly their own even more than Maryland, where the compunctions against offensive warfare that helped weaken Lee's army for Antietam therefore did not so much palsy the strategic initiative, and where Confederate prospects could consequently seem still brighter than in Maryland, and for a time appear closer to fulfillment.

The bright prospects here like those farther west sprang largely from the dispersal of the Federal host that Halleck had gathered after Shiloh. Another part of that host, Buell's Army of the Ohio, was reconstituted as a separate force on July 12. Buell spent most of the summer in a cautious advance eastward along the Memphis and Charleston Railroad toward Chattanooga, laboriously rebuilding broken sections of the road as he went. He met little opposition, but that was because the Confederate high command recognized that his ponderous progress through the Tennessee-Alabama border country left central and eastern Tennessee wide open for launching an offensive into Kentucky. They spent their summer largely in assembling men and resources for that purpose. In September, simultaneously with Lee's invasion of Maryland, General Braxton Bragg from the Chattanooga area with much of Sidney Johnston's old Army of the Mississippi, 22,500 men, and Major-General Edmund Kirby Smith from Knoxville with a field force of the Department of East Tennessee, 10,000 men, set off for Kentucky on separate paths.

They were well on their way before Buell awoke to their intent, and Buell's army could only pursue, not stand in front of the invasion. In September 1862 the Confederacy's butternut ranks thus pressed into both Maryland and Kentucky; and if the Eastern theater as always held greater prospects and dangers for the immediate resolution of the war, Bragg and Kirby Smith brought to mind Lincoln's fear that without Kentucky, with the Union reduced in its midsection to the narrow belt between the Ohio River and the Great Lakes, the Union's game was lost. On October 4, Bragg paused at the state capital at Frankfort to preside over the installation of Richard Hawes as provisional Confederate Governor of Kentucky.[32]

Bragg's interruption of military operations for politics was probably a mistake, however, no matter how inspiriting to Confederate morale in the short term. For Buell was badly enough shaken that he had marched north with unaccustomed vigor, and by September 29 he was already at Louisville and able to draw on reinforcements and resupply from directly across the Ohio. In fact, Bull Nelson was there to meet him with no less than 39,721 reinforcements, albeit green ones. Quickly replenishing supplies as well, Buell turned south again only two days later to try to bring the Confederates to battle and end the invasion. He now led 60,000 men.

The particular battle that developed, around Perryville on October 8, was not the one intended by either side. Federal troops were trying to ease a water shortage — the weather was still warm and uncommonly dry — from pools along Doctor's Creek near Perryville when they clashed with Confederates, the vanguard of the combined armies of Bragg and Kirby Smith. The Confederates had the initial numerical advantage, and therefore the action developed into a series of Southern attacks. These reached a climax in late morning and seemed on the verge of breaking the Federals, only to be held off by Buell's arriving Eleventh Division, commanded by General Curtis's former supply officer, since July 1 Brigadier-General Philip H. Sheridan, U.S.V. Sheridan not only stood firm but in a fashion that was to prove characteristic, opened a fierce counterattack that drove the Confederates through the town of Perryville.

Sheridan might have set the stage for a decisive Union victory. But neither the commander and the bulk of the corps to which Sheridan was assigned—Major-General, U.S.V., Thomas L. Crittenden's Second Corps— knew that Sheridan's division was hotly engaged; nor did Acting Major-General and Brigadier-General, U.S.V., Charles C. Gilbert's Third Corps; nor did the army commander. Here was another example of acoustic shadow, similar to the one at Iuka: the failure sometimes of even the sound of a large-scale battle to carry to nearby troops. The battle was now large-scale indeed, because a full corps, the First, under Major-General, U.S.V., Alexander McDowell McCook, was fighting on the Union side along with Sheridan. But probably because of the unevenness of the ground, Buell only two and a half miles away did not know it.

Bragg, however, became aware through reconnaissance that there were enough Federals in the vicinity to beat him badly. He was not a Robert E. Lee; he did not have Lee's pugnacious boldness, and to his credit he did not share Lee's overestimation of the quality of Confederate troops and underestimation of the Federals (which in the West he scarcely could have shared). Unlike Lee at Sharpsburg, therefore, Bragg declined to subject his army to the casualties of a full-scale battle when there was little prospect that he could win it. He contrived to break off the action and to slip away, no small tactical accomplishment even with the help of the quirky passage of sound.

Already, the Confederates had suffered 3,396 casualties (510 killed, 2,635 wounded, 251 missing) against 4,211 Union losses (845 killed, 2,851 wounded, 515 missing). The Union had to accept another half-victory—if that much, considering the disproportion between small Confederate casualties and the political embarrassment and worry that Bragg and Kirby Smith had caused for a while.[33]

Still, Bragg's withdrawal from Perryville meant that the imposing Confederate offensive tide that had swept northward in September had dissolved into anticlimax. For a month, auspicious circumstances had permitted Lee's vision of the strategic offensive as the key to rapid triumph to dominate every major battlefront east of the Mississippi; the lesser Confederate initiatives at Iuka and Corinth were diversionary complements to the major efforts farther east. But the Confederacy's offensive moment had passed almost in the blink of an eye. Because Lee's vision hinged on the Austerlitz victory in battle, moreover, Bragg's retreat from Perryville, however commonsensical, denied the South even the gratification of putting the Western offensive prong to the ultimate test.

But in the East, Lee was not yet done with the strategic offensive and its corollary, the invasion of the North.

## LEE VERSUS McCLELLAN—FOR THE LAST TIME

Less than a week after his withdrawal across the Potomac from Sharpsburg, Lee wrote to President Davis of his desire to resume the offensive:

> In a military point of view, the best move, in my opinion, the army could make would be to advance upon Hagerstown and endeavor to defeat the enemy at that point. I would not hesitate to make it even with our diminished numbers, did the army exhibit its former temper and condition; but as far as I am able to judge, the hazard would be great and a reverse disastrous. I am, therefore, led to pause.[34]

Refitting his army and replenishing his losses took more time than Lee had hoped, and he continued to have to pause until the government at Richmond could be sufficiently persuaded of his strategic wisdom to grant him the means for the renewed offensive. If he could not immediately return in full force to Hagerstown as he wished, however, his zeal for the initiative could still find expression in a preparatory gesture that would also handicap any offensive intentions into which his adversary McClellan might be pushed by Washington. On October 9 Jeb Stuart rode north leading 1,800 of his cavalry, under orders from Lee to destroy the bridge carrying the Cumberland Valley Railroad over a branch of Conococheague Creek just north of Chambersburg, Pennsylvania. Stuart reached Chambersburg that evening. The next day the railroad bridge proved too sturdily constructed of iron to be destroyed, but Stuart proceeded to embarrass the Federals with another ride all the way around the Army of the Potomac. Evading Union cavalry, his troopers recrossed the Potomac at White's Ford on October 12, carrying with them 1,200 captured horses and having ruined about a quarter of a million dollars' worth of Federal stores. The raid covered 126 miles, and in the eighty miles after the railroad bridge the Confederates did not halt.[35]

While Lee continued to importune President Davis for the means to resume the strategic offensive, the opposite course of events played out on the Union side, with Lee's counterpart resisting the President's efforts into pushing him to do just what Lee wished to do. McClellan found one reorganizational or logistical excuse after another to avoid recapturing the offensive for the Union, until at the end of October, Lincoln allowed his impatience to break forth in his famous response to a request for fresh horses: "I have read your dispatch about sore tongued and fatigued horses. Will you pardon me for asking what the horses of your army have done since the battle of Antietam that fatigue anything?"[36]

Incessantly prodded from Washington, on October 26 McClellan's army at last began crossing the Potomac southward. The next day, however, the general sent a telegram implying he did not intend to fight at all until his old regiments were restored to full strength — an impossibility, considering the flawed Union recruitment system that generally raised new units instead of filling up old ones. It was yet another prescription for inaction; and McClellan's actual progress into Virginia, in the direction of Gordonsville and thus ironically along Pope's former route of advance, displayed little more energy than the dispatch led Lincoln to expect. On November 5, an exasperated President ordered McClellan relieved of his command and replaced by General Burnside, who had his operations along the North Carolina coast to his credit even if he had been anything but brilliant since returning northward.[37]

More than military considerations were involved in Lincoln's decision. To the end of his command, McClellan had opposed "remorseless revolutionary struggle." He remained the favorite general of those Northerners who, like Lincoln himself at first, would have subdued the South by military maneuver while somehow conciliating Southerners at the same time. But McClellan's halting of the invasion of Maryland had prompted Lincoln to issue a proclamation of emancipation of the slaves in the Confederacy; if McClellan's unrevolutionary methods of war produced nothing better than stalemate, and indeed opened the way to a season of Confederate offensives, then harsher methods had to be tried. In the light of the Emancipation Proclamation, the departure of McClellan signified the failure not only of a glamorous but grievously flawed general, but also of a whole manner of waging war.

So the already bitter and deadly struggle, so much crueler than almost anyone North or South had foreseen in the spring of 1861, moved toward yet more bloodshed and gall. The North would turn to revolutionary struggle after all, to the uprooting of slavery and thereby of the foundation of Southern life. But to save its social order, the South would determine again to carry the conflict onto Northern soil. R. E. Lee, the premier soldier of the Confederacy, felt certain that only through the strategic offensive could the South achieve its independence and preserve its sectional values. In Virginia, Burnside's replacement of McClellan brought to the Union penetration of the Commonwealth enough of Lincoln's aggressive spirit that Lee's strategic designs would for the present have to be postponed. But Lee was sure to invade the North once more in the new year of 1863, because his own vision of war and consequently the actual outcome of the struggle would hinge upon another crossing of the Potomac by the Army of Northern Virginia.

# SIX

# Of Liberty and War

## THE END OF SLAVERY: THE SEA ISLANDS

"Help me to dodge the nigger — we want nothing to do with him. *I* am fighting to preserve the integrity of the Union & the power of the Govt — on no other issue. To gain that end we cannot afford to raise up the negro question — it must be incidental and subsidiary."[1] So General McClellan had written to a friend influential in the Democratic Party, Samuel L. M. Barlow of New York, on November 8, 1861. But McClellan's inability to force the war to a prompt end ensured that the country could not dodge the question of the place of the black race in America.

The prolonged and indecisive war brought more and more Northerners into the South to witness the conditions attending slavery, and many of them who were essentially as conservative as McClellan, but less preoccupied with themselves and therefore more sensitive, could not abide what they saw.

> My ideas have undergone great change as to the condition of the slaves since I came here and have been on the plantations [Flag Officer Du Pont wrote from the deck of the *Wabash* at Port Royal on December 30, 1861]. I have been a sturdy conservative on this question, and am still — nothing can save us but a strict adherence to the Constitution — but I have defended the institution all the world over, as *patriarchal* in the U.S. compared with the condition of the race in Africa. But God forgive me — I have seen nothing that

has disgusted me more than the wretched physical wants of these poor people, who earn all the gold spent by their masters at Saratoga and in Europe. No wonder they stand shooting down rather than go back with their owners.[2]

For all his constitutional caution, too, Du Pont was not without sympathy for those who believed, as even his South Carolinian friend and subordinate Lieutenant Percival Drayton did, that emancipation should come soon because the "war will last as long as slavery": ". . . ideas travel now with electric speed on the subject of slavery, and many who would like to see it [emancipation] gradual and wisely done, for the good of the slave, would go for immediate extinction rather than have the Democrats come into power to reestablish the South again over us."[3]

The Port Royal expedition had carried Du Pont's fleet and T. W. Sherman's soldiers to the sea islands forming Beaufort County, South Carolina. The occupied area included by the end of 1861 Hilton Head, St. Helens, Ladies, Port Royal, and several smaller islands. With the coming of the Federal forces, virtually all the whites had fled inland, taking a few house servants with them, but leaving more than 8,000 slaves to the care of the Federals.[4]

The exodus of the whites also left a large cotton crop, the fine long-staple cotton of the sea islands. To Northern businessmen acutely conscious that war would mean shortages of raw material for their cotton mills and high returns on such cotton as became available, this fact along with the continued presence of African-American labor to harvest the cotton represented exceptional opportunity. Lincoln had placed the Department of the Treasury in charge of such abandoned property as might fall into the hands of Union forces in the South. Governor William Sprague IV of the State of Rhode Island and Providence Plantations was a wealthy cotton manufacturer with ambitions far beyond his grandly named but tiny home base. He was also a friend of the Treasury Secretary and soon-to-be husband of Chase's famously attractive daughter, Catherine Jane "Kate." Sprague persuaded Chase to put another friend of the governor, Lieutenant-Colonel William H. Reynolds of the 1st Rhode Island Artillery, in charge of collecting the sea-island cotton crop.

Reynolds arrived at the town of Beaufort on December 20, 1861, and promptly extended a system already inaugurated by General Sherman, whereby cotton collectors working for generous fees set the black laborers to picking and gathering the crop, paying the African Americans one dollar for every 400 pounds of unginned cotton delivered at the steamship landings. The collectors would also supply the laborers with food and provisions, charged against their earnings. The government received a commission of 5 percent on the abandoned property the agents sent north, which came to include not only cotton but also such items as household furnishings.[5]

To antislavery Northerners, however, the prospects for a lucrative cotton harvest were much less interesting than the implications of Du Pont's having brought a large African-American community under the protection of the Stars and Stripes. The African Americans of the sea islands occupied an indeterminate position now that their masters had fled, somewhere between slavery and freedom. Antislavery partisans learning of Colonel Reynolds's operations were soon disturbed, in fact, by the likelihood that charging the blacks' sustenance against their meager monetary earnings would lock them into a new kind of bondage under Union auspices. Secretary Chase himself, the most zealously antislavery member of Lincoln's Cabinet, and more than any other individual the source of the Midwestern Republican Party's core of antislavery moralism, could not help but consider the antislavery and humanitarian dimensions of the sea-island situation.

Hard on Reynolds's heels, Chase also sent to Port Royal another emissary, an antislavery Boston attorney, Edward L. Pierce. Pierce had already advocated that Ben Butler's contrabands at Fort Monroe be allowed to work for the Union war effort for wages and as soldiers, by which means African Americans could earn "a title to American citizenship, and become heir to all the immunities of Magna Charta, the Declaration of Independence, and the Constitution of the United States."[6] When he surveyed the sea islands, Pierce decided that the African Americans should labor under the supervision of U.S. agents concerned less with profits than with humanity, who would nourish a capacity for self-reliant labor to assist the transition from slavery into full freedom. Chase endorsed this plan, and on February 15, 1862, a preoccupied and somewhat irritated Lincoln, still worrying about the effect of any gesture toward emancipation upon the border states, told Chase and Pierce to go ahead.

Pierce's plan also included private action by humanitarian groups to send teachers among the sea-island blacks to prepare them for citizenship in ways that labor alone, however increasingly self-reliant and independent, could not: by teaching them reading, writing, and Northern moral and patriotic ideals. He quickly gained support for such a project among Boston antislavery circles, where an Educational Commission was established for the purpose under the presidency of Governor Andrew. The members of the commission were mostly veterans of the New England antislavery crusades, characteristically representing other facets of New England values besides humanitarianism alone. Edward Atkinson, for example, had helped finance

John Brown's schemes, but he was also an agent for six Boston cotton manufacturing plants who argued that cotton could be produced more cheaply
and efficiently by free labor than by slaves. Atkinson was eager for a practical
test of this theory. Pierce himself was a thoroughgoing reformer but an un-
sentimental one; when Republican Senator Charles Sumner of Massachusetts recommended three pacifists to him to join his band of teachers, Pierce
rejected them as unsuited to the military environment of Port Royal and,
furthermore, too likely to deprive the African Americans of the "little manhood left them by inculcating the doctrine of non-resistance."[7]

Pierce's efforts to recruit teachers and find financial support for them
among the humanitarian, often Unitarian, reformers of Boston were paralleled in the more moralistic and evangelical reform circles of New York City
by the efforts of the Rev. Mr. Mansfield French. As soon as the Navy won its
Port Royal victory, Lewis Tappan, the financial angel of innumerable prewar
moral reform movements, had persuaded the American Missionary Association to send French to the sea islands to discover what good work should be
done there. French had met Pierce and joined in his plans. A Philadelphia
group centering on a veteran abolitionist disciple of William Lloyd Garrison,
James Miller McKim, also prepared to send teachers to Port Royal. The Boston, New York, and Philadelphia efforts formed an alliance as the Port Royal
Relief Committee.[8]

The first of the new teachers arrived at Beaufort on March 8, 1862. As
Pierce distributed them over the sea islands, friction promptly and inevitably
developed between their efforts to set the African Americans upon the path
toward free citizenship and the profit-oriented activities of Colonel Reynolds's cotton collection agents. Fortunately for the teachers, Secretary Chase
had decided that the cotton agents' work should not extend beyond the collection of the 1861 crop. Planting a new crop and reorganizing the agricultural life of the sea islands would take place under humanitarian auspices.
So in the spring Colonel Reynolds and his agents departed, having earned
the contempt of the reformers as money-grubbers, fees that were no doubt
exorbitant and furthermore complicated by shortages in various accounts,
and a generous fund made up of the government's commissions from which
to finance the official side of the African Americans' preparation for citizenship.

The plans laid in Washington in the spring of 1862 included eliminating possible conflict between the Treasury and the military by turning the
whole administration of the sea islands over to the War Department. No
diminution of humanitarian purpose was implied, because the new Secretary of War, Stanton, was decidedly antislavery. On March 31 General T. W.

Sherman was superseded in the local military command, from March 15 styled the Department of the South, by Major-General David Hunter, U.S.V., who was known to be more sympathetic than Sherman to antislaveryism.[9] On April 29 Brigadier-General Rufus Saxton, U.S.V., who as captain and assistant quartermaster U.S.A. had been Sherman's chief supply officer, but who was unusual among prewar Army officers in unambiguous antislaveryism, became Hunter's deputy in charge of land and labor. Stanton ordered Saxton to "take possession of all the plantations heretofore occupied by rebels, and take charge of the inhabitants remaining thereon within the department, or which the fortunes of war may hereafter bring into it."[10] Saxton operated the plantations in harmony with Edward Pierce's design, though Pierce himself felt obliged to return to his own affairs in Boston.

The sea-islands project was coming to be known as the Port Royal Experiment. An experiment it was, for the transition from slavery to freedom was bound to be a disorienting experience for the African Americans and a tangle of puzzling problems for those who intended to help them in the transition. As the Port Royal Experiment began there did not exist even a clear-cut governmental commitment regarding the slaves' future. No one could yet be sure where the experiment was leading. No one could be sure, least of all in such circumstances, how to instill in the slaves the Yankee values of self-reliant motivation that Pierce's, French's, and McKim's teachers had in mind. Simply to persuade the African Americans to resume agricultural pursuits and particularly to plant and care for a cotton crop, on some plantations their families were encouraged and allowed to work as teams on what became in effect family plots. Elsewhere, however, the old gang system of plantation labor persisted, albeit under Northerners' direction. The tension between hoping to encourage self-reliance and the humanitarians' paternalistic methods of doing it underlay all activities. The African Americans, while usually ostentatiously friendly to their new masters and aware that the currents of the time were carrying them toward freedom despite eddies along the way, also maintained a shrewd and healthy skepticism about the motives animating their new set of white masters.

As department commander, General Hunter proved to be more antislavery than the Lincoln administration intended, for Hunter almost immediately lost patience with one of the most fundamental problems of the experiment, the indeterminacy of the African Americans' status. Within about two weeks of his arrival, he declared certain of the contrabands within his lines to be free men. Then abruptly, on May 9, he flatly declared that the states in his department, South Carolina, Georgia, and Florida, were under martial law, that slavery and martial law in a free country are incompatible (a curious view), and that consequently all slaves in his department were "forever free."[11]

But if this was the meaning of the Port Royal Experiment, it was a meaning that President Lincoln still thought incompatible with the war aim of preserving the Union. Lincoln acted toward Hunter's proclamation just as he had toward the antislavery proclamations of Frémont and Cameron before it.

In revoking Hunter's proclamation, Lincoln nevertheless felt obliged to display his own awareness of the rushing forward of ideas and events regarding slavery. On March 6, the day when the first teachers arrived at the entrance to Port Royal harbor, Lincoln had sent to Congress an appeal for cooperation with and financial aid to any state that would adopt a plan for gradual abolition of slavery.[12] Lincoln coupled his newest rejection of immediate and forcible abolition with another plea for gradual and voluntary abolition. To the people of the South he offered his "earnest appeal": "I do not argue. I beseech you to make the arguments for yourselves. You can not if you would, be blind to the signs of the times."[13]

## THE END OF SLAVERY: CONGRESSIONAL ACTION

The Republican leaders in Congress, men such as Wade, Chandler, and Lyman Trumbull of Lincoln's own home state in the Senate, and Stevens and George W. Julian of Indiana in the House, less trammeled by responsibility than Lincoln as well as more messianic in their antislavery zeal, still regarded opposition to slavery as both a moral duty and a weapon with which to bludgeon the South. In addition, the veteran Republicans in Congress remembered too well the days of Southern members' arrogant threats of violence, and sometimes deeds of violence, against them, the days when Republican Senator Henry Wilson of Massachusetts said he never entered the legislative chambers without putting his affairs in order as if he would never return. Such men could not help but feel impatient for revenge against the slavocrats.[14] With every failure and frustration on the battle fronts, especially with every new fumble by McClellan, whose policies and generalship the Congressional antislavery men despised, the wisdom of taking up antislavery as a weapon seemed more urgent.

In the wake of Simon Cameron's call for arming the slaves, the House of Representatives on December 17, 1861 promptly passed a resolution calling for the emancipation of the slaves in all military jurisdictions — in effect, something like Hunter's policy.[15] In a more immediately practical gesture, on March 13, 1862 Congress put an end to any of the sort of slave catching made notorious in the Stone case by prohibiting the use of the armed forces for the restoration of escaping slaves.[16] On April 16 the President signed into law a bill abolishing slavery in the District of Columbia, although Lincoln had successfully put pressure on Congress to include encouragement of colonization of the freedmen outside the United States and provision for compensation of the slaveholders. A million dollars was appropriated for this purpose, to be administered by an evaluating commission that was to pay no more than $300 per slave.[17]

On June 19 Lincoln signed a bill abolishing slavery in the Federal territories. This time Congress saw fit to omit compensation, for it was Republican constitutional doctrine that slavery had never legally existed in the territories.[18] The specific question that had done most to precipitate secession was thus abruptly disposed of. Under the Dred Scott Decision of March 6, 1857,[19] both the District of Columbia and the territorial emancipation acts were presumably unconstitutional, but such an objection could now be ignored.

On the last day of the 1861–1862 session, July 17, 1862, Congress went on to pass an apparently far-reaching emancipation act on the Frémont model, the Confiscation Act of 1862. This measure provided for the forfeiture of property of persons convicted of treason, or of having incited, set on foot, assisted, or engaged in rebellion or insurrection, or of having given aid or comfort to rebellion or insurrection. Residence in rebel territory was enough to make one a rebel under the terms of the act. In particular, the slaves of such persons were to be "forever free of their servitude, and not again held as slaves."[20]

To the President, however, consistently cautious on the subject of slavery, the Confiscation Act of 1862 appeared to be a bill of attainder, in violation of the constitutional prohibition against forfeiture beyond the life of the offender — this despite the fact that knowing his objection, Congress on July 17 passed a clarifying resolution disclaiming any such intent.[21] Because of his constitutional misgivings as well as for reasons of policy, Lincoln prepared a veto message; but considering the resolution disclaiming unconstitutional intent, he thought it best not to collide with Congress, and he followed the unusual procedure of signing the bill while also submitting the veto message.[22] Still, largely because of the constitutional and policy reservations of the executive, the ambitious Confiscation Act of 1862 proved a fizzle. It was little enforced and had little practical effect. Yet it was one more sign of the times, to which it was impossible to be blind.

## THE END OF SLAVERY: THE PRESIDENT

Lincoln's own policy on slavery was in transition. One antislavery move the executive could surely make without undue political risk was to enforce rigorously at last the ban against the international slave trade, and for that purpose a treaty with Great Britain for cooperative enforcement was signed on April 7.[23] In the more delicate domestic area, however, ever since his revocation of Frémont's emancipation order the President had come under growing criticism from antislavery leaders who accused him of ignoring the sentiments of those who had elected him while favoring his proslavery opponents. Although he was careful always to distinguish between his personal sentiments and what he could and ought to do under the responsibilities of his office, Lincoln's personal antipathy to slavery encouraged him to concede that there was a degree of merit in such charges.

To find an escape from the dilemma posed by his personal conviction of the moral evil of slavery and his political responsibility, as he saw it, to uphold first the Constitution and the Union, and to the latter end to conciliate the Democrats and the border states, he sought to persuade the border states themselves to begin the process of emancipation. He bent Congress to incorporate the compensation and colonization features into the District of Columbia emancipation act because he hoped to persuade the border states to free their slaves voluntarily, under similar assurances of help for the slaveowners and care for the problems of a biracial future. Through the first half of 1862 he pleaded with border-state visitors to begin compensated emancipation and colonization of the freedmen, promising Federal subsidies to speed the effort.

As early as November 1861, Lincoln had written drafts of a compensated emancipation bill for Delaware, which Unionist Congressman George P. Fisher of that state promoted, but which no one proved willing to introduce into the Delaware General Assembly.[24] In a message of March 6, Lincoln recommended to Congress the passage of a joint resolution: "Resolved that the United States ought to co-operate with any state which may adopt gradual abolishment of slavery, giving to such state pecuniary aid, to be used by such state in it's [sic] discretion, to compensate for the inconveniences public and private, produced by such a change of system."[25] Congress adopted the resolution, and the President pointed to it as the proper means of acknowledging "the signs of the times" when he revoked General Hunter's emancipation order: "This proposal makes common cause for a common object, casting no reproaches upon any. It acts not the pharisee. The change it contemplates would come gently as the dews of heaven, not rending or wrecking anything. Will you not embrace it?"[26]

When Congress was about to adjourn in July, Lincoln submitted a draft of a bill to compensate any state that might abolish slavery, and he invited the border-state members of Congress to meet with him, "Believing that you of the border-states hold more power for good than any other equal number of members."

> You prefer that the constitutional relation of the states to the nation shall be practically restored, without disturbance of the institution; and if this were done, my whole duty, in this respect, under the constitution, and my oath of office, would be performed. But it is not done, and we are trying to accomplish it by war. The incidents of the war can not be avoided. If the war continue long, as it must, if the object be not sooner attained, the institution in your states will be extinguished by mere friction and abrasion — by the mere incidents of the war. It will be gone, and you will have nothing valuable in lieu of it. Much of it's value is gone already. How much better for you, and your people, to take the step which, at once, shortens the war, and secures substantial compensation for that which is sure to be wholly lost in any other event.[27]

Lincoln assured the border-state Congressmen that it was a commitment to gradual emancipation that he desired promptly, not quickly completed emancipation. This assurance was consistent with the usual emphasis of his appeals upon the considerations of expediency as well as those of morality — with more of the former than the latter. Expediently both in terms of making his proposals immediately more persuasive, and for the ease of American white people in the future, he recurred repeatedly to his desire that the freed African Americans should be colonized outside the United States. Why should black people leave the United States? he rhetorically asked a delegation of African Americans on August 14, 1862.

> We have between us a broader difference than exists between almost any other two races. Whether it is right or wrong I need not discuss, but the physical difference is a great disadvantage to us both, as I think your race suffer very greatly, many of them by living among us, while ours suffer from your presence. In a word we suffer on each side. If this is admitted, it affords a reason at least why we should be separated.
>
> . . .
>
> I do not propose to discuss this, but to present it as a fact with which we have to deal. I cannot alter it if I would. It is a fact, about which we all think and feel alike, I and you. We look to our condition, owing to the existence of the two races on this continent. I need not recount to you the effects upon

white men, growing out of the institution of Slavery. I believe in its general evil effects on the white race. See our present condition — the country engaged in war! — our white men cutting one another's throats, none knowing how far it will extend; and then consider what we know to be the truth. But for your race among us there could not be war, although many men engaged on either side do not care for you one way or the other. Nevertheless, I repeat, without the institution of Slavery and the colored race as a basis, the war could not have an existence.

It is better for us both, therefore to be separated. . . .[28]

As a historical analysis of the basic cause of the war, Lincoln's statement was perceptive. The appropriateness of the sentiments to the audience may be a different matter; but the African Americans who had to listen to this lamentation on how hard slavery bore down upon white people were probably too gentlemanly, or too aware of their station, to object.

Lincoln meant what he said, and he sought far and wide for a home for colonizing African Americans, attempting to enter into treaties for colonization with Central and South American states and lending his support to several unhappily dubious projects. To his patient black visitors in August 1862 he specifically recommended — if Liberia should seem too distant — Chiriquí on the isthmus of Panama. He later dropped this venue when he learned it lacked resources for economic survival, but he long clung to an equally questionable scheme for the Haitian island of Île à'Vache, to which over 400 African Americans were transported, but from which 368 returned after much hardship and disappointment.[29]

To be sure, not only was Lincoln's judgment about the cause of the war correct; he may have been close to the mark also in another of the arguments from expediency that he offered consistently in behalf of moving toward abolition, that to do so would hasten the end of the war.

The leaders of the existing insurrection [he told Congress on March 6] entertain the hope that this government will ultimately be forced to acknowledge the independence of some part of the disaffected region, and that all the slave states North of such part will then say "the Union, for which we have struggled, being already gone, we now choose to go with the Southern section." To deprive them of this hope, substantially ends the rebellion; and the initiation of emancipation completely deprives them of it, as to all the states initiating it.[30]

On April 10, Congress voted that "the United States ought" to give financial aid to any state that adopted gradual emancipation,[31] but the border states proved deaf to such action and to Lincoln's many appeals. The majority of the border-state Congressmen answered the President's July appeal with a labored list of objections.[32] Even the loyalty of many parts of the border states still hung by perilously thin threads; those states, where Republicanism had been almost nonexistent in the election of 1860, were still a considerable distance from embracing antislaveryism.

If Lincoln could not end the war by persuading the border states to accept abolition, or by employing a conciliatory military commander such as George B. McClellan, then he might have to turn to more drastic expedients. In the same message to Congress the previous December in which he had warned against the danger of remorseless revolutionary struggle, he had also said: "The Union must be preserved, and hence, all indispensable means must be employed."[33] In his message of March 6 on gradual emancipation he reminded Congress of those words,[34] and as spring passed into summer and military frustrations combined with border-state inaction, he found the words compelling him toward new conclusions.

> When, in March, and May, and July 1862 [he said later, on April 4, 1864] I made earnest, and successive appeals to the border states to favor compensated emancipation, I believed the indispensable necessity for military emancipation, and arming the blacks, would come, unless averted by that measure. They declined the proposition; and I was, in my best judgment, driven to the alternative of either surrendering the Union, and with it, the Constitution, or of laying strong hand upon the colored element. I chose the latter.[35]

Until July 1862 Lincoln had struck down the emancipation plans of Frémont, Cameron, and Hunter and rejected all proposals for general emancipation by Federal action that were broached to him. On Sunday, July 13, however, he took a long carriage ride beyond Georgetown with Seward, Welles, and Seward's son, Frederick W., during which he revealed that he was considering a proclamation to emancipate the slaves in the rebel states. He asked the secretaries' opinion and returned to the subject several times in the course of the ride. Both secretaries said only that they would have to give this new proposal mature reflection. Lincoln said that for his part, "he had given it much thought and he had about come to the conclusion that it was a military necessity absolutely essential for the salvation of the Union, that we must free the slaves or be ourselves subdued. . . ."[36]

On July 22 Lincoln presented to the Cabinet the first draft of his Emancipation Proclamation. In it the President recurred still again to the theme of gradual, compensated emancipation; but referring to the Confiscation Act of July 17, he warned those in rebellion against its forfeitures and seizures, and announced that to restore the Union, on January 1, 1863 he would as Commander in Chief of the armed forces order that "all persons held as slaves within any state or states, wherein the constitutional authority of the

United States shall not then be practically recognized, submitted to, and maintained, shall then, thenceforward, and forever, be free."[37]

The responses of the Cabinet members varied predictably. Chase, the antislavery veteran, said he would "give to such a measure my cordial support; but I should prefer that no new expression on the subject of compensation should be made, and I thought that the measure of Emancipation could be much better and more quietly accomplished by allowing Generals to organize and arm the slaves . . . and by directing the Commanders of Departments to proclaim emancipation within their Districts as soon as practicable. . . ."[38] Montgomery Blair, a spokesman of border-state Republicanism whose family opposed the antislavery faction in Missouri, objected that emancipation would hurt the administration in the coming elections, and next day he wrote Lincoln that it would "endanger our power in Congress, and put the power in the next House of Representatives in the hands of those opposed to the war, or to our mode of carrying it on. . . ."[39] Seward approved but said that the proclamation should be postponed; if Lincoln issued it in the midst of the current series of military defeats, it "would be considered the last shriek of the retreat," the government "stretching forth its hands to Ethiopia, instead of Ethiopia stretching forth her hands to the government. . . . I suggest, sir, that you postpone its issue until you can give it to the country supported by military success. . . ."[40]

Lincoln immediately accepted the force of Seward's view, and he waited. While he did so, he proffered the delegation of visiting African Americans his advice to leave the country, engaged in friendly argument with a delegation of Chicago Christians by citing considerations opposed to the very plan on which he had privately settled, and wrote his reply to Horace Greeley's "The Prayer of Twenty Millions" for emancipation, Lincoln saying that "If I could save the Union without freeing *any* slave I would do it, and if I could save the Union by freeing *all* the slaves I would do it; and if I could save it by freeing some and leaving others alone I would do that."[41] While he waited, however, Lincoln also offered some significant and relevant observations on his further thinking about how to fight the war. When Reverdy Johnson of Maryland, a State Department agent investigating consular complaints about military government in New Orleans, transmitted Louisianans' objections to Brigadier-General, U.S.V., John Wolcott Phelps's interest in enlisting African-American soldiers, Lincoln replied:

> The people of Louisiana — all intelligent people every where — know full well, that I never had a wish to touch the foundations of their society, or any right of theirs. With perfect knowledge of this, they forced a necessity upon me to

send armies among them, and it is their own fault, not mine, that they are annoyed by the presence of General Phelps. They also know the remedy — know how to be cured of General Phelps. Remove the necessity of his presence. And might it not be well for them to consider whether they have not already had *time* enough to do this? If they can conceive of anything worse than General Phelps, within my power, would they not better be looking out for it? They very well know the way to avert all this is simply to take their place in the Union upon the old terms. If they will not do this, should they not receive harder blows rather than lighter ones?[42]

To similar complaints from Louisiana about growing Federal harshness, Lincoln responded two days later: "What would you do in my position? Would you drop the war where it is? Or, would you prosecute it in future, with elder-stalk squirts, charged with rose water? Would you deal lighter blows rather than heavier ones? Would you give up the contest, leaving any available means unapplied[?]"[43]

Heavier blows rather than lighter ones were already becoming the evident Federal offering in the South in midsummer of 1862. General Phelps, it happened, resigned on August 21 because Lincoln would not yet allow him to recruit African-American troops,[44] but everywhere the Union was discarding elder-stalk squirts charged with rose water. In Virginia, R. E. Lee tried with special zeal to win a Napoleonic victory over John Pope, because Lee considered him "the miscreant Pope," a barbarous general guilty of discarding the rules of gentlemanly warfare.[45] Lee formed this opinion because of Pope's orders directing his Army of Virginia to live off the country, with his authorized officers to requisition supplies but to reimburse only loyal citizens, and announcing stern penalties for "Evil-disposed persons in rear of our armies." Pope proclaimed that Virginia communities must pay compensation for any damage done by marauders or guerrillas within their bounds; he threatened to destroy any house from which a Union soldier was shot; and he ordered that an oath of allegiance be administered to all disloyal male citizens within his lines, directing the expulsion from his lines of any such who refused to take the oath, and threatening the death penalty for any who returned after expulsion or any person who from within his lines communicated with the enemy.[46] The oath-taking requirements and death penalties trespassed beyond the boundaries permitted by internationally accepted rules of war; Pope's other decrees pressed close upon those boundaries. But while Pope did not carry out his more dire threats, neither did Lincoln repudiate them. The President's acquiescence in them was an earnest of his sincerity in his letters about General Phelps and elder-stalk squirts.

If remorseless revolutionary struggle was the price of victory, in short, then Lincoln had decided the struggle must come. McClellan's checking of Lee's invasion at Antietam gave the President a close enough approximation of the military success for which Seward thought he should wait. On September 22 Lincoln issued to the public the Preliminary Proclamation of Emancipation, announcing freedom for all slaves in states and parts of states still in rebellion on the coming January 1.[47]

Every move that Lincoln had previously made to restrain the advance toward emancipation brought forth a growing clamor of protest from Republican newspapers, Congressmen, and opinion leaders throughout the North, many arguing that in addition to its other faults, the President's policy of hesitance was ruining the political prospects of the Republican Party. Now that Lincoln had proclaimed emancipation, antislavery Republicans were eager to claim credit for having helped push him to his decision, or to attribute credit to the stoutly antislavery Cabinet member Salmon P. Chase, even while they might carp that Lincoln had not gone far enough because he left slavery untouched in the loyal and reconquered areas.

But the political dividends that the antislavery Republicans had predicted from emancipation were not forthcoming, at least not immediately. Northern wage-earners feared the economic competition of emancipated slaves, and the socially insecure dreaded an influx of African Americans into their Northern neighborhoods. In New York State, the gubernatorial election of 1862 between the Republican General Wadsworth and the Democrat Horatio Seymour came to revolve around the emancipation issue, and Wadsworth lost. In the 1862 elections, New York, Ohio, Indiana, and Illinois, all of which Lincoln had carried in 1860, all sent Democratic delegations to the House of Representatives; while the delegation from Pennsylvania, another Lincoln state in 1860, divided evenly. The previous House had included, after the Southern members departed, 106 Republicans, twenty-six Unionists, and forty-nine Democrats. The Thirty-eighth Congress, elected in 1862, included 102 Republicans and Unionists, seventy-five Democrats, and nine border-state men of uncertain allegiance. Throughout the North, Republican majorities of 1860 shrank or disappeared, while Democratic majorities of 1860 everywhere grew. Dissatisfaction with the progress of the war and the tensions of wartime surely contributed to this diminution of Republican electoral strength, but the Emancipation Proclamation apparently did the Republicans little good at the polls.[48]

It did, however, redefine the purposes and nature of the conflict—a conflict that by now could all the more rapidly move toward remorseless revolutionary struggle because it had acquired virtually the full legal status of a war, in both constitutional and international terms.

## THE CIVIL CONFLICT AS FULL-FLEDGED WAR

On September 24, 1862, two days after issuing the Preliminary Proclamation of Emancipation, Lincoln set forth another proclamation, ordering, first, that all rebels and insurgents and their aiders and abettors be subjected to martial law and made liable to trial and imprisonment by courts martial or military commissions, and second, that in respect to such persons the privilege of the writ of habeas corpus be suspended.[49] This declaration could be regarded as merely the latest in a rising tide of suspensions of the writ, and it had the specific purpose of ensuring that the draft included in the Militia Act of 1862 would go into effect and not be swallowed up by public displeasure with the break from voluntarism. In a more general way, however, the second proclamation responded to the rise of political dissatisfaction in the North, now that the initial bellicose fervor precipitated by Fort Sumter had been dissipated by time, military frustration, and the reaction against the shift toward a policy of emancipation. It also embodied President Lincoln's sweeping conception of the executive power to deal with such wartime problems.[50]

Lincoln argued for the constitutionality of the Emancipation Proclamation from a broad conception of the authority of the Presidency in time of war:

> I think the constitution invests its commander-in-chief, with the law of war, in time of war. . . . Is there — had there ever been — any question that by the law of war, property, both of enemies and friends, may be taken when needed? And is it not needed whenever taking it, helps us, or hurts the enemy? Armies, the world over, destroy enemies' property when they can not use it; and even destroy their own to keep it from the enemy. Civilized belligerents do all in their power to help themselves, or hurt the enemy, except a few things regarded as barbarous or cruel. Among the exceptions are the massacre of vanquished foes, and non-combatants, male and female.[51]

From the beginning, Lincoln had waged the war under this doctrine that the office of Commander in Chief vested him during war with all the powers pertaining to sovereignty under the internationally accepted rules of war — and under a loose construction of the international rules at that, with a questionable degrading of the central principle of noncombatant immunity, at least in matters concerning noncombatants' private property. Lincoln believed that as Commander in Chief in war he could do things otherwise unconstitutional, in order to save the Constitution and the Union. He believed that as Commander in Chief and thus the embodiment of the sovereignty of the United States he held war powers exceeding those of Congress.

Accordingly he initiated waging war without recourse to Congress; and even in areas where under the Constitution, Congressional authority was patently preeminent, such as raising armies, he acted first and sought Congressional authorization only retroactively.

Whether the powers of the President to initiate and wage war rightly extend as far as Lincoln stretched them was and remains not only constitutionally debatable but a most vital question for the American Republic. In the Prize Cases decided in 1863, the Supreme Court of the United States had before it challenges to the legality both of the Union blockade of the Confederacy in general, and particularly of the blockade as conducted by President Lincoln under his proclamations of April 19 and 27, 1861, before Congress on July 13, 1861 declared the existence of an insurrection and authorized the closing of ports where the collection of United States revenues was obstructed. Under international law, the right to establish a blockade existed only in time of war, so that between April 19 and July 13 Lincoln had been waging war without assent from Congress. The Supreme Court upheld the legality of Lincoln's actions during that interval, and thus of the President's power to wage war, but only by the precarious margin of five to four, with the Chief Justice, Roger B. Taney of border-state Maryland, dissenting.

The majority of the Court stated that the President had no power to initiate or declare war against a foreign nation or a domestic state; but they pointed out that he was authorized to call for the militia and to use the military and naval forces of the United States in case of invasion by foreign nations or to suppress insurrection. If war was made against the United States, the President was authorized and bound to resist by force, without awaiting special legislative authority. The existing civil war had "sprung forth suddenly from the parent brain, a Minerva in the full panoply of war. The President was bound to meet it in the shape it presented itself, without waiting for Congress to baptize it with a name; and no name given to it by him or them could change the fact."[52] The majority went on to find legislative sanction for the war in every action that Congress had taken since July 4, 1861. Without admitting that the retroactive sanction of Congress was necessary to give legality to the President's initial acts of war, the majority held that the enactments of Congress had cured any defects. The Supreme Court thus held that the civil struggle among the states constituted a war, in international legal and United States constitutional terms.

The four dissenting justices held that any war, including a civil war, can exist only by act of Congress. While the President holds the power to repel invasion and suppress insurrection, he cannot wage war in the sense that proclaiming a blockade entails, until Congress acts. The issue so narrowly decided in 1863 — and with a Southerner, Justice James M. Wayne of Georgia, contributing to Lincoln's majority — remains fundamentally undecided still, though twentieth-century Presidents have followed Lincoln's example and extended it to foreign wars.[53]

A further problem, and a paradox, lay in Lincoln's very belief that the authority for his extraordinary measures such as emancipation derived from the existence of a state of war. The U.S. government objected to the proclamations of neutrality issued by Great Britain and other foreign nations, because such proclamations recognized a state of war and recognized therefore that the Confederacy enjoyed the wartime rights of a belligerent. The U.S. government held that foreign powers should treat the Civil War as a purely domestic affair. The United States objected to foreign powers' granting even the most limited kind of recognition to the Confederacy. In accordance with his government's contention that the Confederacy was not entitled even to recognition as a belligerent with belligerent rights, President Lincoln initially proclaimed that any person who molested a vessel of the United States would be treated as a pirate.[54] Yet the United States itself promptly invoked against the Confederacy a blockade that could be legal only in war. In short, the United States preferred to acknowledge a state of war between itself and the Confederacy only when doing so was convenient to itself, and to deny that there existed anything but an insurrection of solely domestic concern when to acknowledge war was inconvenient.

The United States's objections to British and other foreign recognition of the Confederacy as a belligerent were thus inconsistent and excessive, because the Lincoln administration itself had to treat the Confederacy as a belligerent and to that extent as a sovereign state. When the Supreme Court decided the Prize Cases, all members of the Court, not just the five who upheld the President's actions before July 13, 1861, agreed that a state of war existed after that date, because Congress through various enactments had established the existence of a war. The United States had to concede belligerent rights to the Confederacy. Not only did the legality of its own blockade and many other war measures — eventually including the Emancipation Proclamation — hinge upon the existence of a war and the workings of international law under war conditions; there would have been no end to the barbarous consequences if Confederate soldiers captured by the Union armies had not been treated as prisoners of war, if crews of Confederate privateers as well as warships had not been treated as naval prisoners rather than pirates (despite Lincoln's initial proclamation), and if Southern citizens had not been generally treated as something short of traitors.

In fact, the War Department took the occasion of the Civil War to promulgate in 1863 its General Order 100, *Instructions for the Government of Armies of the United States in the Field by Order of the Secretary of War*, drawn up by Francis Lieber, a German émigré and internationally known legal authority. Lieber's *Instructions* represented the first modern attempt by any of the powers officially to set forth the international rules of war in systematic, written form.[55]

## LIBERTY IMPERILED IN THE NAME OF LIBERTY

President Lincoln's sweeping conception of the wartime prerogatives of his office extended deeply into the area of policing dissent. In this realm, however, except possibly in the border state of Maryland, the President acted less wisely than he did in grasping the full armament of war, because there never arose a widespread and dangerous Northern internal threat to the prosecution of the war. On the other hand, Federal decrees suggested a more stringent curtailment of civil liberties than ever developed in practice.

Lincoln's habeas corpus proclamation of September 24, 1862 was one of a series of such proclamations and similar measures to limit civil liberties in the name of the preservation of the Union, and then of emancipation of the slaves. The Constitution states that "The Privilege of the Writ of Habeas Corpus shall not be suspended, unless when in Cases of Rebellion or Invasion the public Safety may require it."[56] The privilege of the writ of habeas corpus is intended to protect persons from being arrested and held unlawfully, insuring that anyone arrested shall be brought to trial within a reasonable time. By suspending the privilege of the writ, Lincoln made it possible for Federal officers to arrest presumably suspicious or dangerous persons against whom there was insufficient evidence to secure conviction, and to hold them without the embarrassing necessity of a trial. With the writ available, it would be the duty of Federal judges to order, on due application, the release of arrested persons against whom there was not enough evidence to file charges.

While the Constitution states that the privilege of the writ of habeas corpus may be suspended during rebellion or invasion, it does not state who is authorized to suspend it. The relevant clause is to be found in the section of the Constitution enumerating the powers and duties of Congress, which might be taken to imply that it is Congress that has the power to suspend the writ. But the Constitutional Convention debated the subject in connection with the judiciary, and the insertion into the Congressional article was an afterthought by the committee on style.[57]

In the first weeks of the war, when Maryland seemed on the brink of secession and Washington was perilously isolated from the North, Lincoln did not know who was to be trusted and who not to be trusted in rescuing the capital, and the occasion did not appear to be suited to judicial investigation of the subject. On April 25, 1861, therefore, writing to General Scott about the danger that the Maryland legislature might take its state out of the Union, Lincoln raised the possibility of dispersing the legislature. He said that on the whole he disliked the idea but told Scott he should do whatever was necessary to counteract any hostile action Maryland might take, "in the extremest necessity" suspending the writ of habeas corpus.[58] Two days later Lincoln specifically authorized Scott to suspend the writ anywhere on or near the route from Philadelphia to Washington via Perryville and Annapolis, whenever resistance might make such suspension necessary to the public safety.[59]

Chief Justice Taney, anathema to Republicans since the Dred Scott Decision and an old Jacksonian libertarian, soon undertook to challenge the legality of Lincoln's suspension of the writ, in the case *Ex parte Merryman*. John Merryman was a prominent Maryland citizen and captain of a secessionist military company. To halt his military activities, Federal officers arrested him and imprisoned him in Fort McHenry in Baltimore harbor. He petitioned for the privilege of the writ of habeas corpus, and the petition was received by Chief Justice Taney, who apparently went to Baltimore expressly for that purpose, though not in his capacity as Chief Justice of the Supreme Court but rather as a member of the Court on duty in the geographical circuit to which it was then customary for a justice to be assigned, in this instance the United States Circuit Court for Maryland and the District of Columbia. On May 25, 1861, Taney issued a writ directing Major-General George Cadwalader, Pennsylvania Volunteers, commanding in Baltimore, to produce Merryman in court the next day so that the cause of his imprisonment might be judicially examined.[60]

Cadwalader's orders from the War Department forbade him to produce prisoners in response to habeas corpus writs. Therefore he did not obey Taney's directive but sent an aide to read a statement to the Chief Justice, reviewing the facts of the case, reminding Taney of the President's authorization to suspend the writ, and asking for time to consult the President. Taney made no concession, but instead responded to Cadwalader's disobedience by issuing a writ of attachment for contempt against the general. Cadwalader saw to it that the marshal who attempted to serve this writ was denied entrance to the general's presence in Fort McHenry.[61]

Taney thereupon prepared an opinion denying the President's right to suspend the writ, which he put on record in the circuit court, and a copy of which he sent to the President appealing to him to maintain constitutional guarantees. Taney declared that "it was admitted on all hands that the privilege of the writ could not be suspended, except by act of Congress," a judgment he sought to support with detailed analysis of the Constitution. He argued that even an act of Congress could not extend military authority as far as Lincoln was attempting to carry it. Even if Congress had suspended the writ, a person not subject to the rules and articles of war could not be detained in prison by military authority or brought to trial before a military tribunal, because the Sixth Amendment to the Constitution ensures that: "In all criminal prosecutions, the accused shall enjoy the right to a speedy and public trial, by an impartial jury of the State and district wherein the crime shall have been committed, which district shall have been previously ascertained by law. . . ." Despite this guarantee, and although the civil officers of Maryland were currently performing their duties and there had been no resistance or obstruction to the process of any court or judicial officer in Maryland except by the military authorities themselves, the Federal military had substituted military rule for civil government.

The Constitution furthermore forbade the taking of life, liberty, or property without due process of law and prohibited unreasonable searches and seizures. Yet "These great and fundamental laws, which Congress itself could not suspend, have been disregarded and suspended, like the writ of habeas corpus, by a military order, supported by force of arms." Under such conditions, "the people of the United States are no longer living under a government of laws, but every citizen holds his life, liberty and property at the will and pleasure of the army officer in whose military district he may happen to be found." Taney himself had tried to uphold the Constitution but had been thwarted by a force too strong for him to overcome. It therefore remained for the President to cause the civil process of the United States to be respected and enforced.[62]

Chief Justice Taney's defense of the civil power and of constitutional liberties against military authority as long as the civil courts and authorities are functioning was destined to be upheld by the Supreme Court, but only after the war was over.[63] Meanwhile Republicans tended to take his opinion as mere confirmation of his Southern sympathies, and the President ignored him except to make indirect reply in the July 4 message to the special session of Congress. Therein, Lincoln offered two defenses. First, he asked whether he must obey every law to the extent of sacrificing all the laws and the Constitution to save one law:

The whole of the laws which were required to be faithfully executed, were being resisted, and failing of execution, in nearly one-third of the States. Must they be allowed to finally fail of execution, even had it been perfectly clear, that by the use of the means necessary to their execution, some single law, made in such extreme tenderness of the citizen's liberty, that practically, it relieves more of the guilty, than of the innocent, should, to a very limited extent, be violated? To state the question more directly, are all the laws, *but one*, to go unexecuted, and the government itself go to pieces, lest that one be violated?[64]

Second, Lincoln denied that he had acted illegally. The Constitution did not specify whether it was Congress or the Executive that had the authority to suspend the writ of habeas corpus; "and as the provision was plainly made for a dangerous emergency, it cannot be believed the framers of the instrument intended, that in every case, the danger should run its course, until Congress could be called together. . . ."[65]

Holding to such views, Lincoln extended the suspension of the writ to various additional areas,[66] until at last in his proclamation of September 24, 1862, he applied the suspension to all rebels and insurgents and their aiders and abettors, and further defied Chief Justice Taney's Merryman opinion by subjecting all such persons to martial law and making them liable to trial by courts martial or military commissions. Lincoln in fact thought such assertion of the executive power less dubious constitutionally than the concurrent efforts of Congress to punish disloyalty and dissent. The 1861 special session of Congress passed the Conspiracies Act, which called for fine and imprisonment for those who conspired to overthrow the government or to oppose governmental authority.[67] The Confiscation Act of July 17, 1862 sought to encourage prosecutions for treason by reducing the penalty from death to an alternative of death or imprisonment and fine.[68] On March 3, 1863 Congress itself passed a Habeas Corpus Act, granting the President the authority to extend further the suspensions of the writ. The legislation carefully skirted the issue of whether Lincoln's previous suspensions had been legal.[69] Lincoln never cited the act to justify subsequent additional suspensions.[70]

The Attorney General, Edward Bates, actually showed little interest in availing himself of any of these laws; and while grand juries sometimes brought indictments under the first two of them, such cases were generally postponed from term to term by Federal judges, the offenders remaining free on recognizance, until eventually, usually after the war, the indictments were dropped. Merryman himself was eventually released to the civil authorities, indicted for treason, but never brought to trial.[71]

The Lincoln administration's abridgements of civil liberties were in fact modest when measured against the dimensions of the crisis of disunion. Lincoln's expansive interpretation of Presidential powers to wage war and while doing so to arrogate to his office the attributes of national sovereignty and an authority to curb civil liberties helped lay a foundation for imperial assertions of Presidential prerogatives in the twentieth century. Lincoln's own statements regarding his constitutional authority could be taken to imply, however, a much wider invasion of civil liberties than he undertook. He imposed nothing resembling a reign of terror.

Through 1861 it was Secretary of State Seward who had charge of arrests to safeguard the war effort; he conducted them with more zeal and less tolerance than would have seemed to fit his character.[72] After the advent of a Secretary of War in whom Lincoln felt confidence, the control of such arrests was transferred to the War Department on February 14, 1862, by an executive order that also decreed that all political prisoners in military custody should be released after due inquiry. Stanton appointed Edwards Pierrepont, a prominent New York City attorney and Unionist Democrat, and Major-General John A. Dix, U.S.V., as commissioners to review the arrests, and they released most of the prisoners during the first half of 1862. But opposition and resistance generated by the introduction of conscription, however halfheartedly, later in the year soon brought on a new crop of arrests.[73]

Precise statistics on wartime imprisonment without trial or on the subjection of civilians to military government have never been compiled. It is true that in the course of the war, the total of military arrests of civilians evidently approached 14,000.[74] But of those arrested for whom records have been studied, the overwhelming majority were not citizens of the Northern states but of the border states, the District of Columbia, and the Confederate States. In the relevant Baker-Turner Papers in the National Archives, for example — the papers of Lafayette C. Baker, a principal War Department detective, and Levi C. Turner, an influential Associate Judge Advocate — among 5,442 recorded civilian prisoners, only 624 were definitely arrested north of the border states.[75] Of the arrests and military trials of civilians in the border states and the capital, furthermore, unhappy Missouri accounted for by far the largest number; Lincoln's policy there was almost a flat failure, and arbitrary arrests were a natural concomitant of the guerrilla warfare coming out of the failure.[76]

Of the arrests of Northern civilians, the preponderance did not involve issues of constitutional freedoms of speech, the press, and assembly but instead featured draft evasion, desertion, and trading in contraband. Among the 624 Northern arrests represented in the Baker-Turner Papers, 434 occurred in 1862, most of them after August 8, and they sprang from efforts beginning on that date to enforce the draft of 1862. In fact, 287 of them were categorically the results of those efforts.[77]

Suspension of the privilege of the writ of habeas corpus is a more famous Civil War civil liberties issue, but trial of the arrested civilians by military commissions probably presented more serious constitutional issues. Subjecting civilians to military justice was by no means unknown in the Anglo-American legal tradition, but it has nevertheless been regarded by civil libertarians as anathema. Yet such trial was often the fate of those arrested because of war issues if they came to trial at all. Fortunately, the practice of Union military commissions was by no means as detrimental to freedom as Anglo-American legal tradition suggests. The Union's military commissions kept careful written records, conducted their proceedings with remarkably little departure from the customs of civil jurisprudence, found their decisions nevertheless likely to be overturned by Judge Advocate General Joseph Holt for even technical violations of established legal procedures, and in the words of their most careful historian, "embodied mercy as well as military justice."[78]

Furthermore, trials of civilians of military commissions also occurred mainly in the border states, 55.5 percent of those on record in Missouri, Kentucky, and Maryland. Another large proportion took place in Confederate territory occupied by the Union Army, 31.9 percent.[79] Citizens of the Confederacy caught up by the Union system of military justice were usually accused of guerrilla activity or related destructive behavior.[80] Other civilians arrested in the South tended to be those accused of blockade running — which accounts for many arrests by the Navy Department; but the Lincoln administration's determination to conduct the blockade within the provisions of international law caused it to set most blockade runners free, as persons conducting a legitimate activity under such law and the American tradition of freedom of the sea.[81]

Altogether, Lincoln's dedication to preserving the Constitution extended to the Bill of Rights as well as to the principle of national Union. His assumption of extraordinary wartime authority to arrest without accepting writs of habeas corpus and then to try prisoners before military commissions was directed mainly toward his opponents' warlike actions and toward draft resistance, not toward the suppression of constitutional liberties.

## THE END OF SLAVERY: ARMING AFRICAN AMERICANS

Still, while war may have been the only feasible instrument with which to strike the fetters from the victims of American slavery, war so much tends to manufacture fetters of its own that it is a most unsatisfactory means for advancing the cause of liberty, even when waged by an Abraham Lincoln. No-where did the tension between the purpose of emancipation and the unlib-eral tendencies of war reveal itself more starkly than in the forcible impressment of slaves into the Union Army.

Immediately after General Hunter issued his order of May 9, 1862 that all slaves in South Carolina, Georgia, and Florida were forever free, he pre-pared another order decreeing that all able-bodied male Negroes between the ages of eighteen and forty-five within his lines who were capable of bear-ing arms were to be sent to Hilton Head at once.[82] There he planned to organize them into military units. He kept the second order confidential, so that black men would not run away, until his troops scattered through the sea islands began to enforce it on the morning of May 12. Throughout many of the sea-island plantations the impressment created "the loudest lamenta-tions" and an "agony of separation,"[83] as blacks discovered that safety from the dismemberment of families on the auction block brought with it the penalty of a new kind of separation, to meet the government's appetite for soldiers. Hunter tried to assuage the pain by giving each impressed man a half dollar and a plug of tobacco.

Five hundred African Americans were gathered at Hilton Head, where Hunter's officers instructed them in the school of the soldier and the school of the battalion and transformed them into the 1st South Carolina Regiment. Protests from the teachers and missionaries of the Port Royal Experiment persuaded Hunter to return plowmen and foremen who were essential to the operating of the plantations, but the protests of reformers on the scene were undercut by applause from many abolitionists in the North, who saw Hunter's policy as an assurance that the war would destroy slavery. Men who fought for the Union could scarcely be reenslaved, and arming African Americans could be the most appropriate of all means to tear down the South's slave empire. Soon even the misgivings of the local reformers began to dissipate as they saw gleaming rows of steel above the black faces of the 1st South Carolina on parade. Hunter used the troops mostly for guard duty, but also for occasional raiding.[84]

In the spring and early summer of 1862 the Lincoln administration, which had revoked Hunter's emancipation order, had to be less happy than the abolitionists about Hunter's unofficially created African-American regi-ment as well. The inevitable wave of criticism rose from the border states and from Northern conservatives. Presently Hunter was obliged to disband his regiment except for one company because the War Department refused to send funds to pay the black soldiers. But by that time sentiments were changing in Washington. African Americans had also been recruited in Louisiana and Kansas. On July 17 Congress authorized recruitment of Negroes.[85] In August, General Saxton sent Mansfield French to the capital to try to persuade the government to allow him to reconstitute an African-American regiment. French took along Robert Smalls, who had been inspired by Hunter's emancipation order to lead a group of slaves who sailed the two-gun Confederate steamer *Planter* out of Charleston harbor under the noses of the heavy harbor defenses. Smalls delivered the *Planter* to Du Pont at Port Royal and thereafter served as a pilot for the Union Navy. He was a most persuasive object lesson in both the magnetic attractions of emancipation and the possible utility of freed slaves to the Union. With the President's own course now privately set toward emancipation, Stanton sent French and Smalls back to Saxton with authority dated August 25 for the general to enlist volunteers of African descent up to 5,000 in number.[86]

Saxton recruited more gently than Hunter had done, and he reorganized the 1st South Carolina, on November 5 officially asking a famous Massachusetts abolitionist and friend of John Brown, Thomas Wentworth Higginson, to be its colonel. Higginson accepted.[87] When the Confederate States did not cease resistance to the Union by New Year's Day of 1863, and Lincoln accordingly followed up his Preliminary Emancipation Proclamation with the Emancipation Proclamation of January 1 putting the policies he had announced in September into effect, the new proclamation declared that freedmen, "of suitable condition, will be received into the armed service of the United States to garrison forts, positions, stations, and other places, and to man vessels of all sorts in said service."[88]

Many Massachusetts men believed that their Commonwealth, so long in the forefront of the abolitionist movement, ought to be the first of the Northern states to send an African-American regiment into the field. Governor Andrew envisaged the forming of a black Massachusetts regiment as the crowning achievement of his tenure, and in January 1863 Stanton authorized him to attempt to do it. The War Secretary assured the governor that black soldiers would receive equal treatment with whites in all matters relating to pay and status. "Every race has fought for Liberty and its own progress," Andrew told the African Americans of his state. "If Southern slavery should fall by the crushing of the Rebellion, and colored men should have no hand and play no conspicuous part in the task, the result would leave the colored man a mere helot."[89]

Andrew wanted black commissioned officers, but Lincoln and Stanton believed the country was not yet ready for them—although African-American company officers were quietly being commissioned for the 1st, 2nd, and 3rd Louisiana Native Guards, which Ben Butler was raising among the free blacks of New Orleans.[90] Massachusetts had to turn to white officers, but Governor Andrew was determined to have committed antislavery men with military experience. For colonel he chose Robert Gould Shaw, a native of Boston, son of the wealthy Massachusetts and New York abolitionist and philanthropist Francis George Shaw, a Harvard graduate, and a captain of the 2nd Massachusetts who had made a good combat record especially in that regiment's one great battle so far, Antietam.[91]

Massachusetts was so Northern a state in every sense that finding recruits for a full regiment was another obvious problem; in 1860 there had been only 9,602 free Africans in the state — of all ages and both sexes. Massachusetts blacks filled less than two companies. Consequently Governor Andrew commissioned George Luther Stearns, still another veteran abolitionist and friend of John Brown, to head a group to recruit all over the North. Stearns gained the aid of prominent black abolitionists, notably Frederick Douglass, toured the country, met many of the expenses himself, and carried to African Americans Douglass's message: "Liberty won by white men would lack half its lustre. Who would be free themselves must strike the blow."[92]

Stearns's strenuous efforts succeeded so well that by late spring Andrew could form a second black regiment, the 55th Massachusetts. Colonel Shaw's regiment, the 54th Massachusetts, marched over Beacon Hill and through Boston Common on May 28, with the regimental band setting the pace and 20,000 spectators lining the route. Abolitionist leaders were conspicuous among the latter, William Lloyd Garrison resting his hand on a bust of John Brown as he took Shaw's salute. The regiment was about to embark for the Union foothold on the coast of South Carolina.[93]

Meanwhile other governors, most of them hitherto far less friendly to African Americans than Andrew, were deciding the time was ripe to raise black regiments of their own — for besides meeting the spirit of the hour, African-American troops would count against the states' enlistment quotas and reduce the military burden for white men. But the relationship of black troops to the states' quotas was already causing trouble, because the other states naturally resented that the men recruited from within their borders for the 54th and 55th Massachusetts should count against the Massachusetts quota rather than their own. To head off acrimony, the War Department on May 22, 1863 established a Bureau of Colored Troops to organize and supervise African-American units.[94] Stearns, offering himself and his recruiting organization to the Federal government, became on June 13 major and assistant adjutant-general of volunteers,[95] in charge of black recruitment. Although some state recruiting continued, for the most part the War Department hereafter enlisted African Americans in regiments of United States Colored Volunteers, or soon more simply United States Colored Troops.

Worse troubles persisted than arguments about enlistment quotas. Despite Stanton's promise to Andrew, the black soldiers received less pay than white soldiers: $10 a month, minus $3 for clothing, in contrast to $13 a month, plus a clothing allowance of $3.50. The relevant statute, said the War Department, was the Militia Act of July 17, 1862, which had merely contemplated the employment of African Americans as laborers, not as soldiers, but whose standards for payment were applied nevertheless.[96] The men of the 54th and 55th Massachusetts refused on principle to accept any pay whatever unless they received the promised equal pay with whites. When the General Court of Massachusetts acted to equalize their pay, they held out for equal pay from the Federal government. In December 1863 Stanton asked Congress for equal pay for black and white soldiers, but Congress was not yet ready to act.[97]

The South responded to the enlistment of African Americans with predictable outrage, as a confirmation of the worst fears that Lincoln was another John Brown intent on raising up legions of murderous Nat Turners. Jefferson Davis told the Confederate Congress that unless it directed otherwise, he would order Union officers captured while leading colored troops to be delivered to the states to be dealt with under the laws for punishing servile insurrection. When in the autumn of 1862 General Beauregard referred the question of a captured black soldier to Davis's latest Secretary of War, James A. Seddon, the latter replied: ". . . my decision is that the negro be executed as an example."[98] President Davis advised against it in this instance, but at least four executions did occur,[99] and it was largely the threat of Union reprisals that thereafter gave African-American soldiers a modicum of humane treatment.

The best evidence indicates that the "massacre" of black soldiers at Fort Pillow, Tennessee on April 12, 1864 was a genuine massacre. Major-General Nathan Bedford Forrest at the head of Brigadier-General James R. Chalmers's Division of Confederate cavalry, some 1,500 men, captured the fort and inflicted casualties of about 231 killed, 100 wounded, and 226 captured or missing among a garrison of 557 Federals, 262 of whom were blacks. Many were shot down in cold blood after the fort surrendered.[100]

The revulsion of the South against African Americans wearing uniforms and bearing arms also had the byproduct of assuring the breakdown of an already crumbling prisoner exchange program. Early in the war, once the Union government had changed its mind about treating Confederate privateersmen as pirates and decided to regard them as prisoners of war, it became possible to arrange an agreement for exchange of prisoners, the Dix-Hill cartel of July 22, 1862, negotiated by General Dix for the Union and General D. H. Hill for the Confederacy.

Under the cartel, prisoners of war were to be released by exchange, and surplus prisoners on one side or the other were to be released under parole not to take up arms again until they could be exchanged.[101] But the cartel early ran into trouble. Some time before it had been drawn up, Ben Butler executed one William B. Mumford in New Orleans after Mumford was condemned by a military commission for tearing down the Stars and Stripes from the United States Mint.[102] The upshot of this event was that on December 23, 1862, President Davis proclaimed Butler an outlaw and announced that there would be no more paroles of Federal commissioned officers until Butler was punished for his crime. Thereupon Secretary Stanton suspended all exchanges of commissioned officers. Then difficulties arose over the alleged Confederate employment of prisoners paroled at Vicksburg and Port Hudson in July 1863. Finally, the refusal of the Confederates to exchange black soldiers completed the ruination of the Dix-Hill cartel. Negotiations dragged on for its renewal, but Union policy in 1864 came to recognize that the status quo worked to Federal advantage. The South needed the return of captured soldiers more than the North did. Thus it was not until January 1865, when the Union could regard the war as practically won, that a new agreement could be reached to resume prisoner exchange.[103]

These difficulties did not deter the North from proceeding with African-American recruitment. Considering the slow start, the impediments, and the climate of opinion of the period, the ultimate achievement was impressive. The black regiments of the Union Army aggregated 120 of infantry, twelve of heavy artillery, one of light artillery, and seven of cavalry, altogether 186,017 men, of whom 134,111 were from the slave states.[104] An indeterminate but large additional number were less formally organized.

As such numbers might in part suggest, too often, and despite the best efforts of George L. Stearns, these regiments were filled from the swarms of confused and frightened refugees in the same manner in which General Hunter had gathered his 1st South Carolina Regiment. Most recruiting of African Americans was conducted in the Mississippi Valley, directly by officers of the Union Army, whose principal motive was not philanthropy but the filling of the ranks, especially the ranks of labor troops to do hard and inglorious work along the supply lines of the army, and of garrison troops who could be kept busy digging trenches. Liberty still moved forward in harness to the exigencies of political and military power.

Yet liberty did move forward. The same Militia Act of 1862 that was cited to justify discrimination against black soldiers in their pay also assured the emancipation of blacks who became soldiers, because it declared free any enemy-owned slave who rendered military service to the United States, and freed his family as well.[105] For black men to march through the slave states wearing the uniform of the U.S. Army and carrying rifles on their shoulders was perhaps the most revolutionary event of a war turned into revolution.

## THE END OF SLAVERY: THE EMANCIPATION PROCLAMATION OF JANUARY 1, 1863

It has become proverbial that with the Emancipation Proclamation, Lincoln freed only the slaves it was not in his power to free. The final proclamation of January 1, 1863 followed the terms of the preliminary proclamation by applying only to areas actively in rebellion, so that not only were the border slave states omitted, but so were most of the formerly Confederate areas now occupied by the Union Army. Various Virginia counties and Louisiana parishes were excluded from the terms of the proclamation, as well as the whole State of Tennessee. Occupied South Carolina, however, was not excluded — so the African Americans of the Port Royal Experiment became free.[106]

It is not even certain that the Emancipation Proclamation materially hastened the exodus of slaves from the Confederacy into the lines of the Union Army. Contrabands by the thousands had already been crowding into those lines whenever they could, because they saw that to be a contraband was much like being free. We know that the "grapevine telegraph," the slaves' communication network throughout the South, promptly buzzed with the news of the Emancipation Proclamation; some white Southerners first heard of it from their slaves. Probably, therefore, the proclamation did stimulate the already swelling flight of slaves into the Union camps; but we cannot be sure.

The outcome of the 1862 elections notwithstanding, the proclamation fulfilled some of the political purposes for which Lincoln intended it. For the time being, at least, it won him the applause of most of the antislavery militants of his party who had previously been losing patience with him. Governor Andrew had been enlisting other Republican governors in a campaign to force Lincoln's hand on enlisting black soldiers as well as on emancipation; but Lincoln began to head off Andrew when he persuaded governors more friendly to himself, most notably Pennsylvania's Andrew Gregg

Curtin, to participate in Andrew's movement but in such a way as quietly to slow it down. In the end a conference of the Republican governors in the Pennsylvania mountains at Altoona on September 24 proved to be perfectly timed not to embarrass the President but to be obliged to praise his proclamation.[107]

The proclamation went a long way toward ensuring that there would altogether certainly be no foreign intervention in behalf of the Confederacy. While Napoleon III, Emperor of the French, already taking advantage of the Civil War to meddle in Mexico, continued to flirt with the possibility of intervention, France would not act alone, without assistance from the naval power of Great Britain. But for Britain to try to rescue the Confederacy henceforth would be too much like rescuing slavery for the British electorate to stomach it. The risks that foreign intervention was ever likely to occur and the dangers it would pose for the Union if it did occur were no doubt exaggerated by Lincoln's government; but the mere fact that much of the North perceived foreign intervention as a grave risk meant that the psychological effect would have been highly damaging if interference had occurred, especially while the North was still being dealt frustrations aplenty by the Confederacy alone. Now all of that danger was gone.

Altogether, the Emancipation Proclamation transformed the war, almost in spite of Lincoln and in spite of its specific terms. The role of emancipators was now thrust upon the soldiers of the Union Army. Henceforth, wherever the Union Army advanced, black slaves became not contrabands in some ambiguous world between slavery and liberty, but free people. The victories of the North became undoubtedly victories for freedom. At first, thousands of Union soldiers grumbled about their new role; but it was also true that the horrors of slavery were such that Northern boys confronting the scarred bodies and crippled souls of African Americans as they marched into the South experienced a strong motivation to become antislavery men, even as Flag Officer Du Pont had done. Men do not need to play a role long, furthermore, until the role grows to seem natural and customary to them. That of liberators was sufficiently fulfilling to their pride that the soldiers found themselves growing accustomed to it all the more readily.

War had become revolution, and more bitter and therefore more likely to enlarge its violence.

# SEVEN

# Armies and Societies

## FREDERICKSBURG, THE MISSISSIPPI RIVER CAMPAIGN, AND STONES RIVER

It is a truism that armed forces are mirrors of the societies they serve. If a society is healthy and vigorous, it can usually build healthy and vigorous armies and navies to defend itself. If a society becomes weak with internal discord and economic stagnation, its armed forces cannot long remain strong. Truisms, however, are likely to be too glib to be altogether true. Because force counts for so much in politics, a state that devotes a disproportionate effort to its armed forces can sometimes go far toward masking other weaknesses. The Union of Soviet Socialist Republics long did so. When Frederick II came to the throne of Prussia in 1740, his country was only tenth in area and thirteenth in population among the states of Europe, but by dint of extraordinary effort poured into its army Prussia had built the fourth largest army in Europe and thereby attained rank as one of the great powers.[1] Frederick II was to become Frederick the Great, because while he ruled an otherwise backward country, the Prussian Army in combination with his own genius provided him the means to be one of the principal arbiters of Europe. Even in the First World War, when social cohesion and economic strength would have seemed to count for much more than they had in the eighteenth century, the armies of the Russian and Austro-Hungarian Empires were able to fight from 1914 to 1917 or 1918 with remarkable endurance and creditable skill and valor all out of proportion to the decrepitude of the states and societies behind them. These armies were not merely mirrors of their societies.

Similarly, the American Civil War was a *war* — a military contest, a contest of armies — and the outcome did not hinge simply upon the relative health of the Union and Confederate economies, societies, and governments, nor did the Union and Confederate armies simply mirror the peoples and the strength of the national organizations behind them.

Major-General Ambrose E. Burnside, who replaced McClellan at the head of the Army of the Potomac, was a hearty, kindly gentleman and an uncomplicated soul utterly incapable of the dark imaginings of conspiracies against him that had poisoned McClellan from within. But Burnside protested to Lincoln that he lacked the capacity for army command, and he was right.

He tried to give Lee the slip on the road to Richmond with a rapid march to Fredericksburg south of the Rappahannock while Lee lay around Culpeper Court House and in the Shenandoah Valley recuperating from the summer's costly battles. Rapid marching almost achieved Burnside's purpose; but when his pontoon train failed to arrive in time to permit him to bridge the Rappahannock before Lee entrenched on the opposite side, Burnside could think of nothing to do but cross straight on against Lee's defenses. In the battle of Fredericksburg on December 13, 1862, Lee's soldiers had mainly to stand behind walls, swales, and breastworks on a naturally strong line of hills to mow down wave after wave of blue infantry who hurled themselves forward. The close-ordered ranks, the banners, and the glistening bayonets of the Army of the Potomac offered so glorious a spectacle that Lee uttered his famous remark, "It is well that war is so terrible — we should grow too fond of it!" — but the Confederates inflicted 12,653 casualties (1,284 killed, 9,600 wounded, 1,769 missing) against 113,987 while losing 5,309 (595 killed, 4,061 wounded, 653 missing) out of 72,497.[2]

When Halleck came east to be General-in-Chief of all the Union armies, Grant could emerge in the West out from behind the shadow of Halleck's jealousy. On October 16, 1862 Grant assumed command of the Department of the Tennessee, encompassing Cairo, Forts Henry and Donelson, much of Kentucky and Tennessee west of the Cumberland River, and as much of northern Mississippi as he could conquer and hold.[3] Already he had concentrated the hitherto scattered forces in that area enough that he and his subordinate Rosecrans could blunt the efforts of Price and Van Dorn in October to recapture for the Confederacy the railroad junction at Corinth. Grant now continued the process of consolidation to prepare for an offensive of his own. It was not in him to be a passive general. His obvious objective was the increasingly fortified city of Vicksburg high on its bluffs overlooking the Mississippi River. The naval bombardments of the combined New Orleans and Memphis squadrons had not sufficed to capture the city during the summer, implying that a major land expedition would be necessary for the purpose. Meanwhile Vicksburg represented the principal remaining obstacle to complete Union control of the Mississippi; and via the Vicksburg, Pacific and Shreveport Railroad, which ran westward to Monroe, Louisiana from opposite Vicksburg, the city linked the Confederate East with the trans-Mississippi West.

While Grant restored to independent command was as aggressive a general as ever, the Confederates soon showed that in the Deep South they were prepared to use a geography favorable to them, as well as the experience gained from their own year of failures, to render further Union conquests far more difficult to come by than Forts Henry and Donelson had been at the opening of the year. In December, Grant tried to march toward Vicksburg down the Mississippi Central Railroad. The long, thin rail line behind him proved too precarious an umbilical cord, however, when it ran through intensely Confederate territory in West Tennessee and Mississippi. On December 19 Nathan Bedford Forrest, who had escaped with his cavalry from Fort Donelson and subsequently received promotion to brigadier-general on July 21, led his cavalry brigade against Grant's rail line near Jackson, Tennessee and began tearing up many miles of track.[4] The next day Van Dorn's Cavalry Division of the Army of Tennessee struck Grant's principal advanced supply depot, at Holly Springs, Mississippi. Van Dorn captured about 1,500 Federal soldiers and destroyed about a million and a half dollars' worth of supplies. Grant had to abandon his advance down the railroad.[5] W. T. Sherman, rewarded for his role at Shiloh by promotion to major-general of volunteers on May 1 and since July 21 commanding the District of Memphis, had sailed toward Vicksburg on the river to converge with Grant.[6] Sherman landed to attack the Walnut Hills north of the city out of Chickasaw Bayou above Vicksburg on December 29 in ignorance that his superior officer had retreated. In frontal attacks much like those of Fredericksburg, his force suffered 1,776 casualties (208 killed, 1,005 wounded, 563 missing) out of 30,720 engaged, to 207 Confederate losses (63 killed, 134 wounded, ten missing) out of 13,792.[7]

Rosecrans's reward for his major role in fending off Price and Van Dorn from Corinth in the early fall came on October 30 in the shape of command of the army over which Buell's cautious leadership had exhausted Lincoln's patience. Hitherto the Army of the Ohio, this force was redesignated on October 24 as the XIV Corps but took to calling itself the Army of the Cumberland.[8] One of the crowning blows to Lincoln's forbearance had fallen when Buell, following Bragg's retreat from Perryville, chose to head for the by-now familiar and comfortable precincts of Nashville, although there had been a good chance he might have been able to hurry into East Tennessee instead, that area of Lincoln's long-deferred hopes. Rosecrans consequently began his campaign from Nashville, and in December he marched straight down the turnpike and the Nashville and Chattanooga Railroad southeast toward Chattanooga, but also toward Bragg's defenses around Murfreesboro on the way.

Rosecrans planned to attack Bragg by falling on his right flank on the last day of the year, but Bragg anticipated him by attacking Rosecrans's own right flank earlier in the morning of that day. The mental set of the Federals was so directed toward their own planned attack that Bragg's assault stunned them, and through the day their right kept falling back from one position to another, while their center was caught up in the accumulating dismay and disaster, and their left also came under enemy pressure and wavered as well. Finally in the winter twilight they rallied and held their line of retreat, the Nashville Pike, on a line mainly perpendicular to the one with which they had begun the day. The losses were so heavy that during the night Rosecrans's senior generals counselled retreat, with the conspicuous exception of the commander of the Centre Division, Major-General, U.S.V. (since April 25), George H. Thomas. Encouraged by the sturdy, unflappable victor of Mill Springs, the more mercurial Rosecrans felt confirmed in his own inclination to hang tough. After both armies spent New Year's Day repairing exhaustion, the Federals were able to turn back another series of Confederate attacks, this time against their left, on January 2.

This battle of Stones River, or Murfreesboro, was yet another demonstration, like Lee's attacks during the Seven Days, that against a well-trained opposing army no advantage gained by stratagem, not even the advantage of complete tactical surprise, could long sustain the momentum of the attacker. However skillful the maneuvers with which combat might begin, a battle between reasonably well-trained armies tended to resolve itself into a slugging match of mutual slaughter. Rifles made the case worse, but in Middle Tennessee they were not yet by any means universal. For both sides, the casualties at Stones River were staggering — a quarter to nearly a third of those committed. The Federals lost 12,906 (1,677 killed, 7,543 wounded, 3,686 missing) of 41,400 engaged; the Confederates lost 11,739 (1,294 killed, 7,945 wounded, about 2,500 missing) of 34,739.[9]

## LINCOLN AND THE REPUBLICAN PARTY

A second successive golden autumn of uncommonly bright, warm days had gone wasted for the Federals, and to be followed not by Fort Henry–Fort Donelson victories but by Fredericksburg, Holly Springs, and Chickasaw Bayou defeats and at best the bloody stalemate of Stones River. The Emancipation Proclamation with all its limitations could not long still the impatience of Congressional Republicans in the face of setbacks such as these. Three days after the battle of Fredericksburg, on December 16, the Republican members of the Senate met in secret caucus, and Lyman Trumbull of Illinois posed the question of what the Senate could do to save the nation.

A succession of laments about the inefficiency, lethargy, and pusillanimity of the administration came to a focus upon Seward. Lincoln could not well be removed from the scene, but if the Secretary of State was the principal Cabinet influence upon him, as many believed, then the moderate, cautious Seward might be removed and a more vigorous adviser, presumably responsive to the Congressional leadership, might take his place at the President's side. Senator William Pitt Fessenden of Maine, as Chairman of the Committee on Finance the titular Republican leader of the Senate, spoke to the caucus about Seward's pernicious influence. This assessment was nurtured by the Secretary of the Treasury, who was the source of much of the belief that even so far into his term Lincoln was not his own man, but rather Seward's puppet, and that a reconstituted Cabinet could steer the President to a better course. Secretary Chase had two motives for spreading such ideas; he was both as impatient as any zealous Republican could be for victory and the triumph of antislaveryism, and ambitious to rise to the head of the Cabinet in order to pave the way for the succession of a stronger President — himself — in the election of 1864.

Senator James W. Grimes of Iowa suggested a Senate resolution expressing want of confidence in Seward, but others friendlier toward Lincoln diverted the party caucus instead to a proposal that a delegation should call on the President to express the Republican Senators' misgivings. Senator Preston King of New York then privately warned Seward of what was happening, whereupon the Secretary of State declared that he would not be the instrument of putting the President in a false position, and wrote out his resignation.

Apprised of these developments by both King and Seward, Lincoln attempted to persuade Seward to withdraw the resignation. Seward demurred, and with the specific issue of the resignation in abeyance, Lincoln met with the delegation from the Senate caucus on the evening of December 18. Though the caucus had selected a conservative Republican, Jacob Collamer of Vermont, the oldest member of the upper house, to head the delegation, discontent with the Executive was amply represented among the nine-member delegation by Ben Wade, Sumner, Grimes, Trumbull, Fessenden, Jacob M. Howard of Michigan, and Samuel C. Pomeroy of Kansas; Ira Harris of New York was the sole additional moderate. On behalf of the delegation, Collamer presented to Lincoln a document calling for more vigorous conduct of the war and for the President to rely more upon the counsel of a Cabinet chosen to assure national unity.

Lincoln responded that the Cabinet had always functioned harmoniously and invited the Senators to meet with him again the next evening to discuss their problems further; but with his spirits already weighed down by Fredericksburg and further troubled by Seward's discontent and the Congressional démarche, he knew that his assurance to the Senators was less than the truth. For the present, however, his first goal must be to regain a semblance of control over his own administration, to present a united front to a political world also deeply disturbed by Fredericksburg and its apparent message that removing McClellan had done little military good. Toward regaining control, Lincoln planned to bring his Cabinet as well to the second meeting with the Senators, to create a forum in which he could observe all parties even if he could not dominate all.

On the day of December 19 he consulted with his Cabinet, including Chase, preliminary to the larger meeting. Chase disclaimed knowledge of the activities of the Senators, while Lincoln received the consent of the Cabinet to a joint session with the caucus delegation. When the Senators arrived at the White House that evening, Lincoln in turn sought their agreement to meet with the Cabinet, upon receiving which he invited in his ministers except for Seward. He believed that by bringing together Chase and the disgruntled Senators he was in the presence of the principal source as well as of the exploiters of the charges against Seward and himself.

Consequently he opened with a renewed statement of his version of how his administration was accustomed to functioning. He did not pretend that the Cabinet decided all policies, for everyone knew that the President made the critical decisions. In emergencies, Lincoln acknowledged, he had acted without Cabinet consultation, as when he appointed Halleck General-in-Chief and when he restored McClellan before Antietam. But all the Cabinet members had acquiesced in his policies. All this he asked them to confirm.

His asking put Chase on the spot. The Treasury Secretary either had to make an open break with the President or back away from the very charges he had been making to the Senators in the room. Trying to straddle as much as he still could, Chase agreed that questions of importance had usually been discussed by the Cabinet, but not he thought so completely as they might have been; acquiescence had in fact been the rule, with no member opposing a policy once it had been decided. Chase had at least partially maintained his position, but when several of the Senators now raised questions about the influence of the Secretary of State, it became apparent that Chase had not left them enough ground from which to pursue this issue effectively.[10]

Having been maneuvered into an equivocal position before some of the men he had to count on to advance both his antislavery principles and his Presidential ambitions, Chase returned to the White House the next day to tell Lincoln he had drawn up his resignation. Evidently he was not yet ready to hand it over without a measure of discussion and persuasion, but Lincoln asked him for it impatiently and when Chase produced it snatched it from his hand. "This cuts the Gordian knot," said the President.[11] Holding Chase's resignation as well as Seward's, he could let his Senatorial critics know that if Seward left the Cabinet, Chase would go too. "If I had yielded to that storm and dismissed Seward," Lincoln told his secretary John Hay, "the thing would have slumped all over one way, and we should have been left with a scanty handful of supporters" — that is, the administration would have surrendered itself to the zealous Republican faction Hay called the Jacobins, and only the Jacobin wing of the party would have remained as a base of support.[12] Lincoln kept both Seward and Chase. He had achieved at least his short-term objective.

Whether called Jacobins or Radicals, the antislavery zealots of the Republican Party might be perceived because of such events as a cabal in opposition to Lincoln, more and more impatient with him as he pursued his gradual course toward an unambiguous antislavery commitment and, somewhat less gradually, toward ruthless prosecution of the war. But in fact Lincoln steered his way carefully to avoid either imprisonment by the Radicals, as he feared would result if he sacrificed Seward in favor of Chase, or outright collision with them. If he became their prisoner, he would be left with inadequate partisan support, because the number of categorical Radicals in the Republican Party across the nation and even in Congress, notwithstanding the actions of the caucus, was too small to sustain Lincoln's government through the multiple pressures of war and forthcoming elections. Although it must be remembered that factional boundaries in Congress then as almost always were not clearly demarked, an authoritative historian of the first Civil

War Congress lists only twelve Senators and twenty-five House members as indubitable Radicals.[13]

If on the other hand Lincoln launched into outright opposition to the Radicals, he would have found himself quarrelling much of the time with men who nevertheless were among the most influential Republican Congressional leaders; while the unambiguous Radicals were relatively few, Radical opinions shaded off gradually into the opinions of the bulk of the Republican Party. Many more Republicans in Congress than were fully Radical acted in concert with the Radicals on many occasions, those who enlisted in the effort to get rid of Seward offering a case in point: Wade, Sumner, and Pomeroy can surely be classified as Radicals, but Fessenden, Trumbull, Grimes, and Howard more often restrained themselves from joining the Radicals so openly as they did in the Seward affair.

The Republican Party, especially in the Midwest and New England, was founded upon antislavery principles considerably more forthright than the conduct of the Lincoln administration, with its desire for the cooperation of border-state Democrats and Lincoln's own lingering fondness for compensation of slaveholders and foreign colonization of the slaves. In Congress, the policies and conduct of the administration were bound to provoke challenges on behalf of firmer antislavery action from more than half of the Republican membership. In Congress, lost military campaigns were also bound to provoke Republican challenges to the administration's conduct of the war.

Nevertheless, to describe the political history of the Lincoln administration in terms of a growing conflict between the President and his Congressional allies on the one hand and the Radicals on the other is misleading. Most Republicans preferred to cooperate with Lincoln whenever they could, even while many of them sought to hasten his policies forward. And Lincoln took care never to move too much less rapidly than the vanguard of his party toward the elimination of slavery and, if necessary, a harsh war of conquest. In their voting records, Republican Senators in particular formed a continuum, all but a very few of the most conservative of them consistently voting on issues involving support of the war and emancipation in ways that differentiated their party from the Democrats. The conspicuous breaking point in Senatorial voting was not between Radical Republicans and the rest of the Senate but between Republicans and Democrats.[14]

The Republican Party remained as unified as any major American political party is likely to be; Lincoln kept his lines open to all factions. Characteristically, he remained on terms of close political friendship with the difficult and egotistical, as well as Radical, Charles Sumner, and one effect was that Sumner periodically reassured others of the Republican vanguard that Lincoln was coming along not far behind them. With the Radical Thaddeus Stevens in the House, Lincoln never found a comparable personal rapport. But while he and Stevens saw each other rarely and confided in each other less, there was never an open breach between the two. Stevens served the administration usefully, especially in the contribution that as chairman of the Committee on Ways and Means he could make to the financing of the war.

Although he remained in reasonable harmony with his party's delegations in Congress, Lincoln was not an effective legislative leader on the model of Woodrow Wilson, shaping legislative programs in the White House and persuading Congress to accept them. Taking his own initiatives within the broadest definitions of executive power and independently of Congress, as he did when he recruited the 1861 armies, suspended the writ of habeas corpus, and issued the Emancipation Proclamation, was of the essence of his Presidential style. Nor did he contribute anything but occasional encouragement to the large program of Federal sponsorship for the further economic growth of the nation enacted by Congress in 1862.

## CONGRESS REFASHIONS THE UNION

This program fulfilled major pledges of the 1860 Republican platform, met the ambitions of various of the groups comprising the Republican coalition, and withal expressed a fundamental confidence in the prosecution of the war despite all its frustrations and setbacks. Although Northern Democrats sometimes cooperated in passing economic legislation not directly related to the war, such legislation mainly reflected the long-standing Republican determination to exploit the electoral defeat of the South to establish governmental support for an expanding economy of free soil, free labor, and free men, in particular, freely competitive businessmen.

Since the 1850s, the Republican cry for free soil had implied not only a West free from the blight of slavery but also the policy at last enacted in the Homestead Act of May 16, 1862. Where public lands had previously been open to private entry only at a minimum price of $1.25 per acre, the Homestead Act provided that after January 1, 1863, any citizen or intended citizen over twenty-one, or any head of a family or person who had served fourteen days' military service though under twenty-one, could file for a 160-acre quarter section of public land and receive title to it for $10 plus small legal fees and five years' actual residence and cultivation of the land.[15] Thus the end of Southern control of the Federal government brought realization of a

dream that long antedated the Republican Party, reaching back to the workingmen's movement of Andrew Jackson's day and beyond, of the West as a
domain fully open to the plows of a free yeomanry, able to earn title to the
land as a right that came from working it.

In fact, relatively little Western land remained that was suitable for cultivation by the small holder of a 160-acre plot. In fact, other legislation of the
same Congress was to undercut the Homestead Act by inaugurating a program of generous land grants for other purposes, to agricultural colleges and
to railroads, which immediately removed much and often the most desirable
land from free entry. In fact, through grants to railroads and through a multi-
tude of other devices both legal and fraudulent, speculators still obtained
vast tracts of the best remaining land. Land claims were transferrable, and
settlers could continue to buy land for $1.25 an acre after only six months'
occupancy; under these provisions speculators moved "settlers" onto much
of the most likely acreage and acquired it. Meanwhile the Pre-emption Act
of 1841 still permitted anyone, in practice especially including speculators,
to take up unsurveyed land and buy it at $1.25 an acre as soon as it was
surveyed. Few Eastern workingmen could find the means to transport themselves and their families to the West and acquire tools for farming there even
though the Homestead Act might make some land almost free. Yet for all
that, the snares awaiting the homesteader were not altogether evident in
1862, and the Homestead Act seemed to much of the Northern electorate
a statute of great symbolic importance, affirming the displacement of the
Southern planter by the Western yeoman as the representative American
agriculturalist.[16]

It was as part of the same symbolic turning that Congress passed the act
of May 15, 1862, giving agriculture for the first time a specific voice in the
government through a Department of Agriculture (though not of Cabinet
rank until 1868),[17] and more important, though somewhat contradictory to
the Homestead Act in its specific results, that Congress also passed the College Land-Grant Act. Republican Congressman Justin S. Morrill of Vermont
had long campaigned for this measure. An earlier Morrill Bill had been vetoed in the days of Buchanan's Southern-oriented Presidency; Federal centralization in any degree, even for the benefit of agriculture or agricultural
education, had become anathema to the South. Now the Morrill Act gave
each state a right to select 30,000 acres of land, valued for pre-emption at
$1.25 an acre, for each of its Senators and Representatives, as an endowment
for colleges "where the leading object shall be (without excluding other scientific and classical studies, and including military tactics) to teach such
branches of learning as are related to agriculture and the mechanic arts."[18]

The proceeds from the sale of the land had to be invested in safe bonds yielding at least 5 percent interest; the income could not be used for the erection of buildings; colleges had to be established within five years.

It would be possible at this point to rhapsodize over democratic education; but too often the states proved miserly in their continuing support of the land grant institutions, and for a long time many of the schools were underfunded centers of narrowly defined technical studies. Still, few of the institutions representing the state university movement, which dated back to Jefferson's day, would have attained the greatness that some have found, had it not been for the Morrill Act.

Lincoln signed it on Wednesday, July 2, 1862, as the news of Malvern Hill and the final frustration of McClellan's Peninsula Campaign was filtering into Washington. He had signed the bill to subsidize a transcontinental railroad the day before, while the guns were roaring at Malvern Hill. Southern victories in battle could not stem the confidence with which the North adopted policies to foster national growth on an imperial scale now that Southern obstruction had absented itself from Congress.

A transcontinental railroad was another of the promises of the Republican platform of 1860 and another dream of the free-soil, free-labor, free-men syndrome, held up before the war by Southern insistence that such a railroad should follow a southern route. Now Congress could readily agree on a central transcontinental route. Lincoln's signature authorized the Union Pacific Railroad to build westward from the 100th meridian across the Rockies, while the Central Pacific would build eastward from San Francisco and Sacramento across the Sierra Nevada, until the two should meet. Each of the railroads received a 400-foot right of way, 6,400 acres of public land for each mile of track (an amount doubled two years later), and loans of $16,000 in U.S. 6-percent bonds for every mile of track laid on the plains, $32,000 for every mile in hilly country, and $48,000 for every mountainous mile. If these subsidies can be interpreted as portending lavish Republican generosity toward corporate business and thus the Gilded Age, they also represent the only inducement that could have built a railroad across vast territories that would not generate adequate passenger and freight business for some years to come. Lincoln chose Omaha, facing the Council Bluffs on the Missouri River, as the actual eastern terminus of the line, although it was well east of the 100th meridian. Similarly he gave generous interpretation to what constituted mountainous country.[19]

On July 14, 1862, Lincoln signed a bill expected to offer still additional aid to free labor and free men, fulfilling the wishes of many who had voted for him and his party in 1860 especially in the Middle Atlantic industrial states: the first thoroughly protective tariff since the time of Henry Clay. The Morrill Tariff Act of March 2, 1861 had raised the import duties during the final days of the Buchanan administration, but it was much more a revenue than a protective measure, being described accurately by its advocates as a return to the moderate rates of the Walker Tariff of 1846, with such changes as were necessitated by shifting from *ad valorem* to specific duties.[20] A tariff act of August 5, 1861 had extended the list of dutiable articles, notably adding tea and coffee, but as the inclusion of such commodities implies, it did so mainly to add new sources of revenue in the first weeks of the war.[21] Not until July 1862 did the next Morrill Tariff, still further shortening the free list and taxing solicitously the foreign competition to numerous articles made in America, render the duties candidly protective.[22]

## THE UNION PAYS FOR ITS WAR

Congress and the President could cooperate in building toward the nation's postwar future, and the differences between them were never great enough to prevent an effective cooperation for the war itself either. Secretary Chase, ambitious as he was in the Cabinet crisis of December 1862, did not let his ambition or his policy differences with Lincoln obstruct his dedication to the effective financing of the war. His shortcomings as manager of the Treasury were rather those following from a limited knowledge of finance and from a certain carelessness, curious in a moralist, about the ethics of his associates.

From the fumbling Buchanan administration Lincoln and Chase inherited a nearly empty Treasury and a remarkable peacetime indebtedness of $90 million. Habitually, less than 25 percent of the revenues of the United States had derived from taxation, the rest coming from land sales and short-term borrowing, the latter of which was a way of life for the Federal Treasury. The tax legislation of the 1861 special session of Congress did little to improve this financial system so inadequate to the support of a great war. The direct-tax law was cumbersome, the appointment of assessors and collectors for the new income tax was postponed until the following spring, and despite the 1861 tariff increases just mentioned, customs revenue declined because the war caused a drastic reduction in imports. But while many bankers thus hoped that Chase would propose a better tax system, the Secretary feared that stiff taxes would undermine public support for the war. Chase preferred to continue reliance on borrowing, a balloon, however, that the *Trent* affair deflated at the close of the first calendar year of the war.[23]

The impact of the *Trent* affair upon the marketing of U.S. bonds brought to a climax a financial crisis already developing. To equip the Federal armies that had grown so immense at so unprecedented a rate during 1861, suppliers customarily borrowed from their banks the funds needed for their materials and payrolls and then paid their loans when the Treasury paid them, borrowing anew for their next orders. The pace of supplying the armies so outran the Treasury's means, however, that by the end of 1861 contractors were having trouble procuring either materials for old commitments or loans for new ones. To make matters worse, Chase was a traditional Western-style hard-money man who insisted that all payments to the Treasury be in coin, despite the fact that in the National Loan Act of August 5 the special session of Congress had suspended the part of the Independent Treasury Act of 1846 that required him to do so.

The special session had also authorized Chase to pay the government's creditors in demand notes. The Jacksonian suspicion of any paper circulating medium was still strong enough in Congress, nevertheless, that despite what they were called, these notes were not redeemable in gold on demand. Because they also bore no interest, they were an altogether unsatisfactory medium of payment.[24] If a government contractor refused to accept them, he seemed unpatriotic; if he did accept them, his bank might very well refuse to receive them in turn, whereupon he could neither repay his debts nor borrow more. If the bank accepted the notes, it could neither earn interest on them nor count on using them to discharge its own debts to its customers or its clearing house. Common law required banks to repay depositors in legal tender, which in practice meant gold. In order to retain their most important asset in these circumstances, when incoming payments could not meet the demand for fresh loans and the gold withdrawals of nervous depositors, the New York banks suspended specie payment on December 30, 1861, and banks in other cities quickly followed. This emergency move posed new difficulties, both because of the common-law requirement to repay depositors in gold, and because of various state laws penalizing banks if they suspended specie payment, sometimes by threatening them with the loss of their charters.[25]

There was no escape from this multiplicity of predicaments except in an issue of government notes declared by law to be legal tender, however obnoxious paper money might be to large numbers of Americans conditioned not only by the Jacksonian hard-money faith but also by prejudices reaching back at least as far as the bursting of the South Sea Bubble in 1720. Bankers themselves now threw most of their weight behind a legal-tender issue, although a minority of conservatives urged instead that the Treasury raise money by selling bonds at whatever market price it could get. Thaddeus Stevens in his role as chairman of the House Ways and Means Committee felt reluctant to abandon the hard-money gospel but believed that if there had to be a resort to paper currency, it should consist of the Federal government's notes and not state bank notes.[26]

Anyway, Stevens was preoccupied with the collateral function of the Ways and Means chairman as House floor leader, and he left the principal responsibility for preparing a legal-tender bill to Congressman Elbridge G. Spaulding, himself a banker of Buffalo, New York and twice treasurer of New York during the 1850s. Congressman Samuel Hooper, a Massachusetts banker and sponsor of his state's general banking law, and Congressman John B. Alley, a Massachusetts shoe manufacturer, contributed much also to the effort, as did the financially conservative John Sherman of Ohio in the Senate, where Fessenden, the chairman of the Committee on Finance, opposed legal tender. The array of such support is worth emphasis because legal tender was later to seem a radical and irresponsible experiment, especially among conservatives during the financial debates of the greenback and Populist eras.

In January 1862 Alley and Spaulding urged Congress to enact a legal-tender bill as part of a comprehensive package of financial legislation including new taxation and, to provide for a more adequate currency for the long run, a national currency of bank notes issued by a system of national banks and secured by government bonds purchased by the banks. The banks' purchases of bonds to guarantee their note issues would provide an additional supply of funds for the government. The legal-tender notes were to be only an emergency measure, which had to be effected quickly because all of the Treasury's other means of payment would be exhausted by the time the notes could be prepared. Secretary Chase joined reluctantly in the call for the notes, driven by the inescapable specter of an empty Treasury.[27]

On February 25, 1862, Congress authorized an issue of $150 million of non-interest-bearing U.S. notes declared to be "legal tender in payment of all debts, public and private, within the United States, except duties on imports and interest [on the public debt]." These greenbacks could not be redeemed in coin, and they bore no interest; but they were to be interchangeable for 6-percent twenty-year bonds, of which the act authorized an issue of $500 million.[28]

The legal-tender act was not only a milestone in its departure, however much forced upon its authors, from a deeply engrained national hard-money tradition. By providing the first genuine national currency of the United States, and moreover a currency not immediately redeemable in coin but established by Federal fiat, it represented also a notable advance toward national economic unity and enhanced Federal power, suggesting an instrument for Federal intervention in the management of the economy that was to become a rallying point for the greenback and Populist movements of the later part of the century and an active weapon of the twentieth-century national state.

Once he had choked down his first dose of paper money, the Western hard-money traditionalist Chase soon felt obliged to ask Congress for more of it, and the legislators responded with the authorization of another $150-million issue on July 11, 1862. This second legal-tender act lowered the minimum denomination of the greenbacks from five dollars to one dollar.[29] Legislation of March 3, 1863 raised the total authorization of greenbacks to $450 million, of which actual issues eventually reached $432 million. The reason for these further issues lay of course in the continuing unforeseeable rise of the costs of prolonged war, and in the persisting resolve of Congress and administration together to do anything necessary to win the war. Still more thoroughly confirmed hard-money traditionalists than Chase saw in his conversion the fatal addiction to which they believed soft money leads; but the acceptance of greenbacks by both Chase and Congress was in fact reluctant.[30] Necessity remained their justification.

Since the New Deal and the Second World War, in a time when the United States has engaged in finance by fiat on a scale that nineteenth-century hard-money men would have thought impossible without precipitating an awful cataclysm, the Civil War greenbacks have generally come to be regarded with more tolerance than their own sponsors were willing to accord them, as an acceptable supplement to taxation. Through the inflation they stimulated, they imposed a measure of universal confiscatory taxation that distributed throughout the North the burden of paying for the war. Anyway, in proportion to the eventual total cost of the war the greenback issues were moderate, amounting to somewhat under one-sixth of the total public debt at the end of the conflict.

The issuance of greenbacks could eventually be limited because the greenbacks did in time become part of a more comprehensive — and a reasonably sound — financial program, as Congressmen Alley and Spaulding had urged. Somewhat paradoxically, while Chase was unhappy about accepting the necessity for greenbacks so that the Treasury might have funds with which to make its payments, he also remained slow to offer an adequate program of taxation. At length the Treasury leadership cooperated with Congress, however, to produce the Internal Revenue Act of July 1, 1862, an enactment of a wide and heavy variety of excise taxes, running to 20,000 words detailing its provisions and approaching taxation upon everything — every kind of manufacturing, virtually every business transaction, the practice of every profession except the ministry. Basic manufactures were taxed 3 percent, while luxury goods paid higher taxes. At the same time the income tax was revised upward to 3 percent on incomes between $600 and $10,000 and 5 percent on amounts over $10,000.[31] (On June 30, 1864, furthermore, the rates were raised again, to 5 percent on incomes from $600 to $5,000, 7½ percent on incomes from $5,000 to $10,000, and 10 percent on incomes over $10,000.)[32] Unlike the 1861 income tax, the new rates became operative. With gradual increases of the excise as well as the income-tax rates once they were accepted by the citizenry, the internal revenue receipts of the United States rose from nothing in fiscal year 1862 to $209,464,215.25 in fiscal 1865. The bulk of these receipts derived from the excise taxes; during the war years the income tax produced a total of $55 million. In spite of upward revision of the tariff, wartime customs receipts averaged $75 million a year, which with adjustment for inflation was not impressively above the $60 million annual average in the mid-1850s. Nevertheless, the Union raised 21 percent of its wartime funds by taxation, in contrast to 5 to 6 percent in the Confederacy. The rise of Federal taxation represented another noteworthy expansion of central political power.[33]

Once the North entered the long months of frustration following First Bull Run, and especially after the wasted autumn of 1861 and the *Trent* affair, Secretary Chase continued to experience difficulty in marketing the various bond issues that Congress periodically authorized. Chase meanwhile had formed an ethically questionable connection with the brothers Henry D. and Jay Cooke, natives of his own state of Ohio. Henry Cooke, the former editor of the *Ohio State Journal* of Columbus, a newspaper in which Chase had a financial interest, received an appointment as an assistant to Chase at the Treasury, whence he could conveniently dispense information about impending Treasury actions to his brother Jay, a financier in Philadelphia who in 1861 left the banking firm of Enoch W. Clark to establish his own house, Jay Cooke and Company. Chase's pursuit of the Presidency was expensive, the more so because his young daughter and hostess, Kate, thought it required elaborate entertaining in the capital. Jay Cooke served Chase in part by extending loans to him, investing the amount of the loans, and paying Chase generously out of the dividends and profits, without either man's bothering to keep a careful accounting of whether the money reaching Chase was merely what was owed him from investment of the loans. In any event, Cooke's investments for Chase had a happy habit of returning proceeds just at those times when Chase's financial needs were greatest.[34]

Cooke also served Chase, his own firm, and the government by acting as a temporary Treasury agent for the sale of government bonds. By doing so Cooke advanced the prominence and profits of his new firm in its competition with older New York and Philadelphia houses, but he did so with remarkable utility to the government as well, by widening greatly the market for the bonds. He undertook publicity campaigns that made a buyer of the man in the street, not simply the wealthy financier and financial firm. Cooke established sub-agencies throughout the country, used much newspaper advertising, and appealed to the ordinary citizen to put his savings into Federal bonds. In October 1862 Chase named Jay Cooke the sole private agent for a large issue of bonds. With some reason, Jay Cooke came to be regarded as the financier of the Civil War.[35]

The national banking system was also designed to promote the sale of bonds, though it took shape slowly enough that its usefulness came mainly after rather than during the war. Chase found the national banking portion of the financial package first offered to Congress in December 1861 less contrary to his old Jacksonian opinions on finance than either greenbacks or vigorous taxation. A system of national banks under Federal supervision, issuing bank notes secured by U.S. bonds and guaranteed by the Federal government, might strike down at last the state bank notes of bewildering variety and uncertain security that had plagued the Jacksonian conscience ever since Andrew Jackson himself had destroyed the Bank of the United States only to spawn an inadequately regulated congeries of state banks in its place. Despite Chase's support, however, the national banking plan faced severe opposition from conservative Congressmen who felt distaste for still another Federal encroachment upon states' rights and saw in this issue none of the urgent necessity that had overridden objections to the legal-tender notes.[36] Not until February 25, 1863 did a National Currency Act creating a national banking system become law, and then the statute proved so defective that it had to be redrafted to make a new law of June 3, 1864.

Under the latter, Congress authorized the formation of banking associations under U.S. charters. Their organization and management were to be supervised by a Bureau of Currency in the Treasury, headed by a Comptroller of the Treasury. The minimum capital for a banking association varied with the population of the city or town in which its bank was located. To assure soundness, each shareholder was to be doubly liable for the obligations of the bank. Every national bank was to purchase U.S. bonds to an amount not less than $30,000, nor less than one-third of its paid-in capital. The bonds were to be deposited in the Federal Treasury, and against the security they represented, the Comptroller of the Currency was to issue to the banks the new national bank notes, equal in amount to 90 percent of the U.S. bonds they held, to a maximum amount of $300 million. The banks were to benefit both from the interest they received on their bond holdings and from the further interest they could earn by lending the notes they received, two sources of interest from a single investment of capital. In return, the act required the member banks' maintenance of a relatively high reserve against both bank notes and deposits and the depositing of the reserve in certain reserve cities. It prohibited real-estate loans and branch banking. It provided for the appointment of nationally supervised receivers of failed banks, and for the use of the member banks as depositories and financial agents of the United States.[37]

Despite the benefits to member banks and a 2-percent tax now levied on the notes of state banks, the banks at first were slow to enter the new system, the large Eastern banks because they depended little on note issues for their profits and saw little reason to change, many Western banks because they did not want their note issues curbed by Federal regulation, banks in general because of the stringent regulations established by the law. On March 3, 1865, however, Congress imposed a prohibitive 10-percent tax on state bank notes, effective July 1, 1866. This tax at last forced most of the state banks to enter the new system; during 1865, 1,014 new national banks were organized, for a total of 1,601.[38]

The national banking system eventually did much to bring order and rational regulation to the hitherto chaotic American banks. But the system had serious defects that contributed to subsequent financial panics, including an elasticity of the bank notes that tended to run counter to the needs of business, expanding and contracting at the wrong times; a tendency for reserves to concentrate excessively in New York City, where the largest banks often used such funds to finance stock speculation; and the absence of a central regulating agency so designed that it could curb the defects. Nevertheless, in the Federal rules and the unity that it did provide for American finance, the national banking system was still another war-born step toward wider Federal power.

## DISSENT IN WAR:
## THE OPPOSITION IN THE NORTH

In an atmosphere in which the South's unprecedented experiment in secession seemed to imply that none of the previously familiar rules of the American political game could necessarily be counted on, and that disloyalty to the Union might turn up anywhere, Republicans increasingly concluded that the bulk of the Northern Democratic Party was no longer a loyal opposition, and that it did not want the government to carry on the war but preferred to concede victory to the South. This judgment greatly exaggerated the depths of Democratic opposition, but it was not altogether unwarranted. Lincoln might be able to find cooperation in Congress from all segments of the Republican Party, but in the organized Democratic Party, as distinguished from rank-and-file Democratic citizens, he met little but obstruction, in Congress and throughout the country.

The initial fervor of popular support for the government that followed Fort Sumter perished among most Democratic leaders soon after the physical death of the most prominent Democratic embodiment of that spirit, Senator Stephen A. Douglas of Illinois. After Douglas died on June 3, 1861, the core of the Democratic delegation in the House of Representatives, thirty-one members, agreed to a pact of party unity conceived by Congressman Clement L. Vallandigham of Dayton, Ohio. A man of Southern sympathies, Vallandigham also believed that Democratic support of Republican methods of waging war would put the Democrats into indefinite eclipse. Therefore the circumstances under which the pact was formed suggested that its subscribers would consistently dissent against Republican conduct of the war. For a substantial part of the Democracy in the House to acquiesce in Vallandigham's leadership gave weight almost as soon as the war began to fears that the Democrats would become at best a party of simple obstruction, at worst a nest of treason.[39]

Hundreds of thousands of Democrats nevertheless joined the Union Army and fought its battles as bravely as any Republicans, and surely most of the active leaders as well as the general adherents of the Democratic Party in the North felt outraged over any charge that they were less loyal to the Union than Abraham Lincoln himself. Yet the political style of the times was one of intense partisanship and of a literal interpretation of the maxim that the role of the opposition is to oppose. Even apart from the peculiar bitterness of a civil conflict, no previous American wartime experience had yet developed clearly the concept that the opposition party might oppose the administration's methods of conducting a war without opposing the war itself. Among the opposition Federalists during the War of 1812, and even among the opposition Whigs during the War with Mexico, the entire war tended to be a focus of opposition inseparable from the methods and the party that conducted it. Without a precedent in American history for doing otherwise, and in extraordinary circumstances that called the old rules into question whatever those rules might have been, the Northern Democratic

Party in the Civil War was never able clearly to separate opposition to Lincoln's methods of conducting the war from a tendency to oppose the war, despite its members' overwhelming conviction of their own loyalty to the Union.

A favorite wartime Democratic slogan was, "The Union As It Was, The Constitution As It Is, And The Negroes Where They Were."[40] The slogan implied that the Republicans were doing as much as the secessionists to overturn the old Union and the Constitution. Moreover, the secessionists had taken themselves off into another political universe, where they could not be opposed by conventional political methods; but Lincoln and the Republicans were present in the same political arena with the Northern Democrats and available to be opposed. Naturally, Democratic opposition focused on them in a way it could not focus on the secessionists.

The Democratic Party tended to let opposition to war measures become opposition to the entire war especially in areas where much of the population was of Southern descent, notably the southern counties of Ohio, Indiana, and Illinois. Democratic policy tended to encompass comprehensive opposition to everything Lincoln and the Republicans stood for also in the economically most backward regions of the North, particularly the poorer agricultural areas that had little to gain from the Republican program of subsidizing industry, railroads, banks, and scientific agriculture. But the core of Northern opposition to the war appears to have been neither Southern descent nor a depressed economic status but simply Democratic partisanship. Opposition in Iowa, for example, entailed no geographic or economic pattern whatever, save that hard-core opposition to the war was strongest where the Democratic Party had been strongest before the war. Probably the same pattern prevailed throughout the North.[41]

The accepted mid-nineteenth-century style of partisanship could produce this result all the more readily because the historic ideology of the Democratic Party was consistently opposed to the kind of expansion of governmental power that the Republicans invoked both to fight the war and to advance Northern industrial, commercial, and financial interests in the midst of it. American political parties are proverbially regarded as nonideological, but nevertheless the history of the Democratic Party was that of a party of negative democracy, supporting a democratic political system but opposing any but a negative role for government in economic and social matters. Negative democracy had been the program of the Democratic Party's political ancestors in the time of Thomas Jefferson. Negative democracy was the consistent program of the Democratic Party from its birth as such under Andrew Jackson. The party was bound to object to the centralizing and positive governmental power of the Republican economic and financial programs. It was bound to object to the suspension of habeas corpus and of civil liberties more generally. It was bound to object to such vast and arbitrary assertions of Federal power as the confiscation acts and the Emancipation Proclamation. The Democratic Party was bound to oppose the Republican government on those issues out of both partisanship and ideology — but probably out of partisanship first, because former Democrats serving in the Confederate Congress were by no means so quick to oppose the incursions upon civil liberties and the expanding powers of the Confederate States government, with which they identified, as were Northern Democrats to oppose the similar measures of the Lincoln government.

The Democratic Party was especially bound to oppose the steps toward emancipation because both its opposition to positive government and its historic affinity with the South prepared it to abhor government action to free the slaves. Thus it made itself the political voice of Northern dislike of African Americans. After Antietam, the Emancipation Proclamation, and the habeas corpus proclamation, General McClellan wrote to one of his Democratic friends, William H. Aspinwall of New York: "I am very anxious to hear how you and men like you regard the recent Proclamations of the Presdt inaugurating servile war, emancipating the slaves, & at one stroke of the pen changing our free institutions into a despotism — for such I regard as the natural effect of the last Proclamation suspending the Habeas Corpus throughout the land."[42]

Before the war, Republican Free Soil doctrine had sometimes gone hand in hand with anti-Negro racism, on the ground that the mere presence of African Americans in a state or territory undermined the opportunities of free labor.[43] The role in which the war cast the Republican Party, however, as well as the influence of some of its antislavery idealists, gradually softened the Republican position on the race question, while the opposition role hardened the Democratic Party into the self-proclaimed white man's party. The Pennsylvania Democratic State Convention in 1862 "Resolved, That this is a government of white men, and was established exclusively for the white race; that the Negro race are not entitled to and ought not to be admitted to political or social equality with the white race."[44]

The Emancipation Proclamation combined with the stalemated war, in which the conquest of the South could well appear hopeless to those who did not believe in its merit anyway, to bring Democratic opposition to the Lincoln administration and to the war itself inextricably together and into an angry boil at the turn of 1862 into 1863. Defeatism reinforced all the other sources of Democratic discontent. The intensification of opposition to the administration and the war brought into general circulation among the supporters of the war a nasty term of opprobrium to describe their enemies within the North, the name of a silently striking poisonous snake, the copperhead. In response, some antiwar Democrats affirmed their opinions proudly by wearing on their lapels heads of liberty punched from copper pennies.

In New York, the Democrats elected Horatio Seymour governor in 1862 after he had called emancipation "a proposal for the butchery of women and children, for scenes of lust and rapine, and of arson and murder, which could invoke the interference of civilized Europe."[45] After he took the oath of office, Seymour reaffirmed his opposition to emancipation and his support for states'-rights arguments reminiscent of those of the men now leading the Confederacy.[46]

In Indiana, the Democratic majority in the General Assembly elected in the fall of 1862 met at Indianapolis early in 1863 amid threats from some of its leaders that they would give neither another man nor another dollar for the support of the war. They embarked on a program of intransigent opposition to virtually everything that Republican Governor Oliver Perry Morton was doing to advance the war. Their efforts culminated in a bill to take control of Indiana's military affairs away from the governor and to give it to a military board established by the legislature. Behind this proposal there may have been, however, as much a desire to control patronage as to obstruct war-making. Whatever the true motives, Morton was a militant Republican who thought the local Democrats were deep in a conspiracy with their brethren of New York, Pennsylvania, and sundry other states to assure Confederate independence. Taking no chances therefore that the Democrats might be able to override a veto of the military bill, the governor encouraged the Republican legislators to take advantage of a provision in the state constitution that defined a quorum of each legislative house as not less than two-thirds of its members. The Republican legislators went home, leaving the Democrats with no quorum. After trying for a time to act as a legislature anyway, the Democrats also disbanded, believing that the need for appropriations would compel Morton to recall them and to bring the Republicans back.

Morton, however, appealed to Republican towns and counties to help him, received loans amounting to $135,000 from such communities and private sources, and drew help also from Secretary Stanton's special funds, with a Treasury warrant for $250,000. Creating an extralegal Bureau of Finance to administer such monies, Morton took Indiana most of the rest of the way through the war with himself as a kind of dictator. According to the state constitution, the General Assembly did not meet again until January 1865.

In the context of the expansion of Federal power, it should not be forgotten that the financial dependence of the Indiana dictator was largely upon Washington.[47]

Neighboring Illinois suffered a similar crisis. There the Democratic General Assembly elected in 1862 disappointed the ambition of Republican Governor Richard Yates to become a U.S. Senator. The legislators went on to investigate alleged corruption in Yates's administration, to pass resolutions condemning arbitrary arrests and the conduct of the war, and to demand an armistice and a national convention to make peace. Unlike the Indiana legislature, the Illinois body did pass routine appropriation bills; but when it reassembled in June 1863 it considered a habeas corpus bill to prevent illegal arrests and threatened to reorganize control of the militia. The possibilities for obstruction so frightened Governor Yates that when the two houses disagreed about a date of adjournment, the governor stretched a clause of the constitution regarding such a disagreement and prorogued the General Assembly. The Illinois legislature like Indiana's did not meet again until after the election of 1864 had assured that the war would be fought to a conclusion.[48]

Governors Morton and Yates both believed that behind their troubles with their legislatures lay not only an interstate conspiracy of Democratic politicians but a yet more sinister plot among secret societies under Democratic leadership to overthrow their governments and assure the victory of the Confederacy by *coup d'état*. Evidence reaching the governors indicated that there were hundreds of lodges of secret societies and tens of thousands of members in the Midwest alone. The 109th Illinois Infantry helped confirm Yates's fears by becoming insubordinate at Holly Springs, Mississippi, many of its men declaring that they would not fight for emancipation; General Grant had to disband the regiment and arrest many of its members.[49]

At the center of the antiwar and antigovernment plottings, the governors and their counterespionage agents held, were the Knights of the Golden Circle, organized before the war to promote filibustering around the Caribbean and now enlisted in the cause of the Confederacy. A secret empire grouped around the Knights of the Golden Circle was believed to encompass a phalanx of other organizations of pompous ritualistic procedures and nefarious intent, variously denominated the Order of American Knights, the Order of the Sons of Liberty, the Circle of Honor, and what not.[50]

The Confederate government gave enough credence to the same sort of reports that it sent agents to cooperate with the secret societies in their plotting. Clerk John B. Jones in the Confederate War Department imagined that 1863 would bring "the spectacle of more Northern men fighting against the United States Government than slaves fighting against the South."[51] But the Confederate agents became sadly disappointed as they found pitifully small numbers of active society members and an absence of resolution even among those. *Coups d'état* were mainly the delusions of dreamers conditioned by civil war to listen to any rumor, no matter how melodramatic.

Antiwar sentiments in the North actually ranged across a spectrum from concocting skulduggery against the government, through Copperhead determination to obstruct the war by means of legislative and legal procedures, to a reluctant acquiescence in seeing the war through while opposing many of the Lincoln administration's methods of waging war, especially emancipation. The blurring of these viewpoints and of countless intermediate variations into each other could well mislead supporters of the war into exaggerating their more sinister implications, and did. In fact, the leadership of the Democratic Party went too far for most of the Democratic following on those occasions when it yielded to partisan bitterness and defeatism by obstructing war appropriations or militia organization. To the extent that the Democratic Party acted on the assumptions that the war was wrong and could not be won, the principal effect was to dig its own political grave: to bestow upon the Republicans the opportunity to enjoy a generation of political success gained largely by mere waving of the bloody shirt. There was never a formidable Northern conspiracy against the war.

But the Northern state and Federal governments, confronted by a frightening and unprecedented rebellion, could not feel sure of that, and they persisted in behaving nervously. On September 3, 1862 Lincoln appointed Joseph Holt of Kentucky Judge Advocate General under Stanton; Holt had been the vigorously antisecessionist Secretary of War in the last days of the Buchanan administration, and he now conducted the business of suppressing disloyalty with equal vigor, continuing the policies of military arrests and trial by military commissions, if there were trials at all, for persons suspected of disloyalty, no matter whether the civil courts were in full operation.[52]

On March 3, 1863 Congress passed the bill authorizing the President to suspend the privilege of the writ of habeas corpus throughout the United States or in any part of the country, carefully worded to avoid the question whether the President had acted legally when he suspended the privilege previously. While ensuring the legality of the suspension, however, Congress acted to curb indefinite imprisonment by providing that lists of political prisoners were to be sent to the Federal courts, and that if grand juries found no indictments against them, the prisoners were to be released. If the lists were not provided, a Federal judge might discharge prisoners on habeas corpus. But the executive authorities proved negligent in presenting the lists, the courts were reluctant to assert themselves, and the Habeas Corpus Act made little difference.[53]

On the other hand, the common-sense attitude of the President himself preserved an element of moderation in the government's response to antiwar activity. At the beginning of December 1862 the administration ordered a release of all persons confined on charges of discouraging enlistments or impeding militia drafts — concern over enforcement of the draft of 1862 rather than vague conspiracies having been the main cause of arbitrary arrests in the first place.[54] Early in May 1863 Lincoln learned that General Burnside, since March 25 commanding the Department of the Ohio, had arrested Congressman Vallandigham for making a speech at Mount Vernon, Ohio about the "wicked, cruel and unnecessary war." Burnside said the speech violated his General Orders No. 38, which declared that assertions of sympathy with the enemy, or any other opposition to the war, would no longer be tolerated.[55] A military commission found Vallandigham guilty of disobeying Burnside's order. Lincoln expressed to Burnside his regret at and disapproval of his conduct and then escaped the dilemma imposed on the other hand by the undesirability of appearing to be weak: he commuted Vallandigham's sentence to banishment into the Confederacy. Vallandigham predictably made himself look ridiculous by protesting the tyranny of an administration that would force him to enter a country whose principles he so much professed to admire.[56]

As a counter to disloyalty, the Union League movement spread through much of the North, to organize the business and professional leaders of the cities in support of the Republican Party, its program of economic advancement, and the Union.[57] In the autumn of 1862 the Confederacy looked to the Knights of the Golden Circle to assist its cause in the North; by the early summer of 1863 the antiwar leaders of the North felt obliged to turn to the armies of the Confederacy in the hope of new rebel victories that might reinvigorate their cause.

Unfortunately for the Union, in the early summer of 1863 the armies of the Confederacy seemed all too capable of rewarding that hope. In June, Lee's Army of Northern Virginia took the offensive again and invaded Pennsylvania.

## INSIDE THE CONFEDERACY

It was those same Confederate armies to which the Northern Copperheads were looking in the summer of 1863 that had given the Confederacy such nationhood as it attained by the turn of 1862 into 1863. Under the strains of two years of war, the deep fissures in Confederate unity were beginning to erupt above the surface of Confederate life — fissues far deeper than those manifested by Democratic opposition politics in the North, and rooted in the lack of unanimity behind secession itself, and in the profound schism in the Confederate psyche that prevented the very leaders of the government from abandoning altogether their attachment to the United States. (Jefferson Davis had been inaugurated as constitutional, rather than provisional, President of the Confederate States, it will be remembered, on the occasion of Washington's Birthday; he took the oath and delivered his inaugural address under the equestrian statue of the first President of the United States in Richmond's Capitol Square.) In the Confederacy, the one sure source of national unity was the bond felt by nearly all citizens with the Confederate States Army — with Lee and Jackson and the Confederacy's paladins in butternut gray.

By the summer of 1863, unhappily, 35.1 percent of those paladins themselves were absent from the ranks without leave, 65,594 of 473,058.[58] Most were not deserters, although the numbers of deserters from the Union and Confederate armies were high through most of the war. Rather, in the South's loosely disciplined armies of individualists, many went home at Christmas time and after Fredericksburg and Murfreesboro to look after the needs and safety of their families — especially to do what they could to remedy want. Christmas of 1862 in the South was the cold-water Christmas, because government requirements for grainstuffs, emphasized by prohibitionists for their own purposes, had restricted the availability of grains for distilling, so that patriotism decreed the toasting of the season in nothing stronger than water. But the Confederacy was also facing serious deficiencies of nutriments, and the prices for available basic foods as well as luxuries were mounting beyond the reach of the ordinary citizen's pocketbook. Not least of the causes of these predicaments, of course, was the loss of territory to the Union; most of the rich grain-growing state of Tennessee, for example, had gone in 1862.[59]

Already the Confederacy was overmobilized — taking too high a proportion of its manpower into its armies for the balance of the economy, even granting its wealth in black manpower. Too many of its farms had to be worked by women, children, and old men. Too many of the plantations that did have a labor force were still or again neglecting food crops for cotton, hoping to find markets through the blockade or across Union lines. Too much of the foodstuffs that were raised could not reach potential markets, because the railroads of the South, never a coherent, well-organized system, were overstrained with the carrying of war matériel and unable to accomplish adequate maintenance work and repairs. Blockade runners specialized in bringing in goods of high value but limited volume, not bulky foodstuffs, and efforts to establish government control of their cargoes to assure maximum benefits from their voyages bore little success. Because the Confederacy, far more than the Union, failed to impose adequate taxes and could not command enough credit, the Richmond government was financing the war with the printing press, fueling a runaway inflation.

Since October 1861 the general price index of the Confederacy had been rising at a rate of about 10 percent a month.[60] In the spring of 1863 butter in Richmond cost four dollars a pound, calico $4.50 a yard, and coal $1.25 a bushel. The Confederate infantry soldier was paid eleven dollars a month, which by early 1863 barely fed two people for a day. Workers in Southern armories received three dollars a day.[61] The pace of inflation worsened scarcity by causing speculators to buy up foodstuffs to hoard them in warehouses for the still higher prices sure to come. There were demonstrations verging on riot to demand food in several cities during the winter and spring, and on April 2 a mob mostly of women formed on Capitol Square in Richmond and made its way to speculators' stores on Cary Street, where the participants broke in and helped themselves. The mob then embarked on a more general course of property destruction, until Governor John Letcher called out the City Battalion and threatened to open fire, while President Davis himself appeared before the rioters and mounted a dray to speak reassuringly. Despite suffering loaves of bread thrown at him, the President succeeded in quieting the worst of the excitement, although there was another day of demonstrations before the "bread riot" subsided completely.[62]

By now President Davis had plenty of critics, who were quick to blame him for everything that went wrong. Davis contributed to his own vulnerability by responding to criticism with a deeper retreat into cold, proud aloofness that could make him appear unfeeling in the face of his nation's troubles. His hypersensitivity to criticism perversely tempted his opponents to press their attacks harder and harder, because they could enjoy the satisfaction of knowing that they drew blood.

But as his climbing into the dray to placate the bread rioters suggests, it was wrong to charge that Davis made no effort to reach the people and to communicate with them. His remoteness was an inner remoteness, which he could not conquer despite sometimes pathetic efforts to break out at least from the physical part of his isolation. Mrs. Chesnut found him riding alone and informally through the streets although "It must be unsafe for him, when there are so many traitors, not to speak of bribed negroes."[63] In December of 1862 he swung around the nation to meet with local government officials as well as his army commanders and to address assemblages of the people along the way.[64]

He had to return to face the January 12 session of an increasingly faction-ridden Congress, where the appearance of patriotic unity conveyed by an absence of formal party divisions was paid for in a lack of any substitute for party discipline, and where the strongest personalities, such as Henry S. Foote of Tennessee in the House and Louis T. Wigfall of Texas in the Senate, were to be counted among Davis's enemies. In time, parties might have formed along the old boundary between eager and reluctant secessionists; there were growing indications that such a development was latent, another evidence of the split in the Confederate psyche. For the present, Davis was intent upon securing Congressional support for more effective prosecution of the war. For that purpose the rule of thumb was that he could count on affirmative votes in direct proportion to the exposure of any Congressman's district to the peril of Union invasion. Unfortunately, this rule extended to its logical conclusion, that the Congressmen most ready to call for public sacrifice represented districts already invaded and conquered, so that the most zealous Congressmen spoke effectively for no constituents.[65]

Davis hoped he might also alleviate the country's economic ills, a purpose that might be advanced if Congress would accept his call for more stringent war taxes. No comprehensive taxation measure had yet been adopted to replace the direct tax that the inauguration of the constitutional government had rendered invalid. On April 24, 1863 Congress at length enacted a tax bill whose very prolixity gave it a certain impressiveness. Like the Federal tax law of July 1, 1862, it seemed to tax everything: it imposed an 8-percent *ad valorem* tax on farm produce held from 1862; a 10-percent tax on profits made during 1862 from the purchase and resale of practically any kind of goods; a license tax ranging from $50 to $500 on practically every civilian occupation; a graduated income tax ranging from 1 percent on salaries over $1,000 to 15 percent on incomes over $10,000 from sources other than salary; and a 10-percent tax in kind on agricultural produce of the current year, beyond an allowance of food crops for the farmer's own use. But the law favored the large planters in its lack of levies on land and slaves, the income tax was mild compared with the levies on the produce of small farmers and was not diligently enforced, and the tax law proved highly unpopular as well as too cumbersome to meet the needs of the war.[66]

During its first year, the tax in kind yielded goods valued at some $40,000,000 in current prices, but much of what was collected merely spoiled in warehouses or on slow trains, while farmers close to railroads and navigable rivers rightly complained that the tax collectors hit them hard while ignoring their counterparts in remote areas. The complicated internal revenue and income levies yielded only $82,262,350 in their first year.[67] Just before passing the tax law, indeed, on March 23, 1862, Congress had authorized another $50,000,000 a month in Treasury-note issues.[68]

It was an implicit confession of weakness that the Confederacy was willing to seek a foreign loan based on the proposals of Émile Erlanger & Cie. of Paris. Those proposals may have been related to the interest of Fréderic Erlanger, son of Émile, in John Slidell's daughter Matilda; but the Erlanger firm envisaged few risks for itself, contemplating marketing in Europe $25,000,000 in Confederate 8-percent bonds backed by cotton, the Erlangers to receive the bonds at a 30-percent discount and to enjoy a generous commission, eventually fixed at 5 percent. Slidell believed the plan might assure the commitment of Napoleon III to the success of the Confederacy. Secretary of State Benjamin doubted that any such result, or much good of any kind, would come of it, and he acquiesced only after the issue was trimmed to $15,000,000, the interest rate on the bonds to 7 percent, and the Erlangers' discount to 23 percent. At that, the Confederacy had to use the proceeds of the sale of the first installment of the bonds to buoy up the price of the second installment; but the price of the bonds crashed anyway, and out of the transaction the Confederacy retained only $2,599,000 in cash, though it was able to use the repurchased bonds to pay off some $5,000,000 in older debts to British bankers. Purchasers of the bonds, largely sympathetic British subjects, eventually found their investment worthless, but the marketing terms netted a substantial profit for the Erlangers. By this time, however, it was no doubt only through some such terms that the Confederacy could have marketed bonds in Europe at all.[69]

It was another implicit confession of weakness that when in his Presidential message Davis asked for stronger taxes, he also felt obliged to ask Congress to regulate impressments of private property by the military. Congress felt it must respond with the legislation of March 26. Inflation was carrying from difficult to impossible the task of Confederate commissary officers who had to try to purchase food at government-fixed prices. Impressment of foodstuffs at rates of compensation set by the military became the only apparent remedy, but this practice naturally led to spurious commandeering for the profit of some of the impressing officers, a number of whom carried bogus commissions. The inefficiency and waste that were the hallmarks of General Northrop's department did nothing to foster a more cheerful acquiescence when the impressment detachments did their work. The new statute required that price schedules for goods to be impressed be regularly published, and that arbitration boards be set up to decide the just prices of such goods. This measure was obviously no more than a palliative. Impressment ranked with conscription and the tax in kind among the banes of the Confederate agriculturalist.[70]

The President also called on Congress to do something to improve the workings and particularly the fairness of conscription, but here too he got only a feeble palliative. A new exemption law of May 1, 1863 seemed to repeal the twenty-slave exemption, but its further provisions retained the exemption for farms owned by minors, the feeble-minded, women alone, or soldiers in the field. In effect, one overseer could still be exempted for every twenty slaves, and the law aggravated the appearance of an intent to favor the rich by stipulating that this exemption was to be accompanied—or in practice purchased—by the payment of $500 into the Treasury annually for each person exempted. Congress also gave the President authority to exempt men in areas already hard hit by the draft, and all state officials classified as essential by the governors became exempt; this latter provision was also far from an improvement, but rather an eventual source of gross abuses.[71]

The assertive individualism fancied by Southerners as a key to their character and the assertive claims of states' rights and even local rights related to Southern individualism had done much to create the Confederacy, but by the spring of 1863 they were also threatening its undoing. That spring, while the United States Congress was legalizing the suspension of habeas corpus, the Confederate Congress was rejecting a similar bill to empower the Confederate President to suspend the writ at his discretion anywhere in the Confederacy. After the fall of Forts Henry and Donelson the year before, on February 27, 1862, the Confederate Congress had approved suspension of habeas corpus in areas invaded or threatened by the Federal Army, but the furor over suspensions in large parts of Arkansas, Louisiana, and Mississippi as well as in Richmond was too noisy to permit extension of the law.[72]

By the January 1863 session of Congress, Vice President Stephens was spending less and less of his time presiding over the Senate and more and more time at home in Georgia condemning President Davis's alleged usurpations of power in general and those that limited the state's rights of Georgia in particular. Stephens and Georgia Governor Joseph E. Brown were loud in calling a military suspension of the privilege of the writ of habeas corpus in the Atlanta area under the 1862 law unconstitutional.[73] States' rights had been at least as much a mere means to an end as an end in itself when Southerners first took up the concept as a battle cry in their disputes with the North over slavery. By the spring of 1863, men such as Stephens and Brown had been sounding the states'-rights cry so long that with them it had become an end in itself. In the name of states' rights, Brown also made a specialty of obstructing Confederate conscription, first by trying to suspend its application in Georgia pending judicial review, then by taking advantage of the new exemption law to appoint Georgians wholesale to supposedly essential state offices and thus to gain their exemption.

Assailed by this host of troubles, Southerners had to worry more and more about the effects of Lincoln's Proclamation upon their slaves — "the crowning act of the series of black and diabolical transactions which have marked the entire course of his administration," as First Lieutenant Charles Colcock Jones, Jr. of Captain Joseph S. Claghorn's Company, the Chatham Artillery, 1st Volunteer Regiment Georgia Artillery, called the proclamation in a letter to his father. "I look upon it as a direct bid for insurrection, as a most infamous attempt to incite flight, murder, and rapine on the part of our slave population."[74] The threat of runaways and even of slave insurrection could be offered as a kind of justification for the twenty-slave exemption in the draft laws. Watches against slave restlessness had to be reinforced. Mrs. Chesnut found that Dick, her mother's butler, whom she had taught to read, "looks over my head, he scents freedom in the air."[75] The family of the elder Charles Colcock Jones, who had spent much of his career as a Presbyterian clergyman in labors to carry the good news of Christianity to the slaves, found it puzzling that black people should be so ungrateful despite such work on their behalf that they would now desert to freedom. Yet as Mrs. Chesnut also noted, at least for the time being most African Americans "go about in their black masks, not a ripple or an emotion showing," still performing their assigned tasks as always.[76]

## CHARLESTON HARBOR AND CHANCELLORSVILLE

For the African Americans knew that their future remained unclear and their freedom unsure. In spite of scarce food and high costs, a Congress unwilling to equalize or even to demand wartime sacrifices, and a cold, aloof, and dubiously effective President, white Southerners need not yet despair. The fate of the Confederacy rested with its armies, and Marse Robert and the armies still stood unbroken guard around the country's besieged ramparts.

On April 7, even the mighty Federal Navy broke its iron teeth against those ramparts, and General Beauregard, commanding the South Carolina and Georgia coast defenses, won the laurels of a hero again at the scene of his first triumph. The Charleston defenses turned back an attack by nine Federal ironclads — seven monitors, the ironclad frigate *New Ironsides*, and the light-draft *Keokuk*. The Federal commander, S. F. Du Pont, holding since July 16, 1862 the newly created rank of rear-admiral, U.S.N., had assaulted Charleston without enthusiasm. He feared that even with their defensive armor, the staying power of his ships was inadequate to compensate for their limited gunnery strength against the multiple batteries of Beauregard's forts, in a narrow harbor where they could not remain in motion as his fleet had done at Port Royal. Du Pont's fears were well founded. In an hour and forty minutes of action the forts rained 2,206 shots, 439 of them hits, on the ironclads, while the ships' twenty-three guns were able to fire only 139 rounds. The monitors were heavily damaged, and Du Pont's captains believed another half hour of fighting would have disabled all of them.[77] Impatient Gideon Welles, who had insisted that Du Pont make the attack, now relegated the admiral to shore duty, his career ruined. The Confederates rightly took cheer from the conclusion that Charleston was safe against assault from the sea.[78]

There was less happy news for the Confederacy from the West, where on April 30 General Grant emerged from his winter of futility to cross to dry ground on the Vicksburg side of the Mississippi below the city, in effect turning the main Vicksburg defenses and putting the place in greater peril than ever before. But Joe Johnston had gone west to command the Department of the West against Grant, he had potentially greater numbers than Grant's, and Vicksburg was not lost yet. What might not Confederate arms accomplish against far worse odds than those confronting Vicksburg? Lee and Stonewall Jackson showed how heartening were the possibilities when in the first days of May, with the Army of Northern Virginia outnumbered by more than two to one because Longstreet's First Corps headquarters and two of its divisions were detached to guard the southeastern Virginia coast, they dealt the Army of the Potomac under Major-General Joseph Hooker, U.S.V., its most humiliating defeat yet, stunning its right flank and paralyzing the will of the whole army with Jackson's great flanking march at Chancellorsville.

The Army of Northern Virginia had been reorganized before Fredericksburg, on November 6, 1862, with the infantry and much of the artillery, aligned since just after the Seven Days as Longstreet's Right Wing and Jackson's Left Wing, now formed into the First and Second Army Corps. Their commanders had already been promoted to lieutenant-general, Longstreet on October 9, Jackson on October 10. When the First Corps divisions of Major-Generals George E. Pickett and John Bell Hood went with Longstreet to defend the area of Suffolk on the South Side of Virginia — below the James River — where from February 17, 1863 Longstreet assumed command of the Department of North Carolina and Southern Virginia, Lee was left with fewer than 60,000 men to face the Army of the Potomac.[79]

Hooker had succeeded Burnside at the head of the army on January 26. An outwardly bold and hearty man, as well as usually a good tactician, Hooker had been able to restore some measure of the confidence that the army trained by McClellan, and in some degree always belonging to him, had lost when the Young Napoleon gave way to Burnside. In spite of a penchant for bombast that was the less fortunate side of his heartiness — Lincoln had heard of his incautious remark about the country's need for a military dictator — Hooker's improvement of morale and his sound administration of the army also won the confidence of the President and the War Department enough that they saw to the reinforcement of the army to about 134,000 by the end of April.[80]

To take advantage of the greatest numerical preponderance the Union had enjoyed in the East since McClellan confronted Joe Johnston's Manassas defenses early in 1862, Hooker devised an impressive plan. Lee's truncated army still occupied the defenses on the south shore of the Rappahannock behind and below Fredericksburg where Lee had defeated Burnside on December 13. On April 27 Hooker sent the Fifth, Eleventh, and Twelfth Corps, under Major-Generals, U.S.V., George Gordon Meade, Oliver Otis Howard, and Henry Warner Slocum on a turning movement up the Rappahannock, to cross at Kelly's Ford the next day, to cross the Rapidan at Ely's and Germanna Fords on April 29, and to arrive on the last day of the month in Lee's rear.

While about one-third of Hooker's army was occupied with this march of some forty miles, the Federal Second and Third Corps of Major-Generals, U.S.V., Darius N. Couch and Daniel E. Sickles would feint toward United States Ford, on the Rappahannock just below its confluence with the Rapidan, to distract Lee's attention from the principal turning movement. Thereafter these two corps would form a reserve. If Lee took the bait that they offered, the principal turning movement would still be deep behind him. To limit the possibility of his shifting even as far west as the area of United States Ford, however, Major-General John Sedgwick, U.S.V., with his own Sixth Corps and the First Corps of Major-General John F. Reynolds, U.S.V., would launch a diversionary attack across the Rappahannock straight against the Fredericksburg lines. Already the Cavalry Corps of Major-General George Stoneman, U.S.V., was to be raiding deep into Lee's lines of communication with Richmond.

The Union cavalry raid fizzled, however, because of storms and high water, which delayed its Rappahannock crossings, supposed to have begun on April 14, until the 29th. Irresolute leadership by Stoneman contributed to this miscarriage. Nevertheless, the main operations moved like clockwork until April 30, the day the principal turning force reached Chancellorsville, a crossroads where the Ely's Ford Road met the two main east-west roads through the area, the Orange Turnpike and the Orange Plank Road. At Chancellorsville, Hooker was near the eastern edge of a difficult area of scrub timber called the Wilderness, about to emerge into more open country the better to strike Lee. With his Napoleonic *manœuvre sur les derrières* seemingly about to culminate in a devasting crash into Lee's rear, however, Hooker's grand design began to unravel.

It did so because Hooker's boldness and bluster were a façade hitherto masking a deep absence of self-confidence. Lee took away the mask.

Jeb Stuart, a major-general since July 25, 1862 and since that summer divisional commander of all the cavalry of Lee's army, had committed only token forces to counter Stoneman,[81] so that most of Stuart's troops were available to reconnoiter against Hooker. From Stuart's information, Lee quickly perceived the diversionary character of Sedgwick's movement. Lee left only Major-General Jubal A. Early's Division plus Brigadier-General William Barksdale's Brigade of McLaws's Division, just over 10,000 men, to deal with it. The bulk of the Army of Northern Virginia turned west. During Friday morning, May 1, Hooker's corps commanders at Chancellorsville were impatient to resume their eastward advance, in order to clear the Wilderness altogether. Already Hooker was developing misgivings, however, over the approaching prospect of a direct confrontation between himself and the formidable Lee. He procrastinated until late morning. At this juncture only two Confederate divisions, McLaws's and Major-General Richard H. Anderson's of the First Corps, lay in his immediate front, and there was still time to maul these divisions with overwhelming numbers before Lee arrived to discover he commanded a still further weakened army. But when the heads of the Federal columns actually collided with McLaws and Anderson, Hooker lost his nerve altogether. He ordered a retreat into a defensive horseshoe perimeter around Chancellorsville.

To this point he had used his extraordinarily large field army as an inspiration for thinking operationally. His plan had gone beyond a tactical battlefield conception to encompass coordinated maneuvers across if not an entire theater of war nevertheless a relatively wide arena. His multiple columns should have assured that a setback suffered by one of them should not have been a setback to all. More than any other Federal design since McClellan's 1862 offensive that ranged from the Shenandoah to the Peninsula, Hooker's plan broke free from nineteenth-century categories of tactics and strategy to impale the enemy upon dilemmas created by applying what the twentieth century would regard as the operational art intermediate between battlefield tactics and general war strategy. Yet Hooker's innovative plan collapsed under the character flaws of its own author.

Naturally, Lee was quick to seize the resulting advantage. Before Friday ended, Stuart informed him that Hooker's right flank, Howard's Eleventh Corps, lay about a mile west of Wilderness Church on the Orange Turnpike, hanging in air without good defensive ground to anchor it. Lee, unlike Hooker a genuinely bold leader, decided to divide his small army yet again, thereby responding to Hooker's turning maneuver with an equivalent maneuver of his own. That night Lee conferred with Jackson, the two of them deciding that Jackson's Corps would conduct the attack, first marching about twelve miles, largely across the enemy's front, to get into its launching position. Lee would retain only 14,000 men to conduct holding thrusts to fix Hooker in place, while Jackson took 28,000.

Jackson's column marched at dawn on a clear, warm Saturday. The column was about six miles long, and its route along little-used trails lay only about two and a half miles in front of the Federals. Sickles's Third Corps had now taken position immediately to the left of Howard, and early in the day Union observers high in treetops reported considerable movement in front of Sickles. The latter, the only non-West Pointer commanding a corps in the Army of the Potomac, and a New York Democratic politician known for his dubious morality sexual and otherwise and for recklessness in every conceivable sense, lived up to the latter aspect of his reputation by urging Hooker to allow him to go forward and attack whatever lay before him. Both Sickles and Hooker interpreted the enemy's activity as evidence that Lee was retreating from the field, but they drew differing conclusions about the appropriate response. Hooker, having abandoned the idea of attacking at least twenty-four hours earlier, put off Sickles's importunities altogether until noon. Then at last he authorized a most cautious harassing movement. By 2:30, when Sickles consequently encountered Jackson's rear guard, well to the west the 5th Alabama Infantry of Major-General Robert E. Rodes's Division, the vanguard of the Second Corps, was already forming across the Orange Turnpike to strike Howard's dangling flank. Sickles hit the 23rd Georgia of A. P. Hill's Division hard enough to capture most of the regiment, but Hooker permitted him to do no more.

Howard shared the prevalent delusion that Lee was in retreat, so he ignored several reports of enemy activity on his front and right. Soon after five o'clock Jackson's Corps came hurtling down upon his flank, and the result was the shattering of the Eleventh Corps into disorganized and demoralized fragments. By dusk, however, Jackson's pursuing Confederates were also disorganized, by the very rapidity and momentum of their victory as well as by the density of the Wilderness through which they charged. Scattered Federal units, indispensably aided by artillery concentrations on two elevated positions called Hazel Grove and Fairview, rallied enough to slow the rebel advance. Thereupon Jackson rode forward in the gathering darkness to reconnoiter and to organize a night attack through Chancellorsville to cut off Federal retreat to the nearest fords. As he and an escort turned back toward their own lines, Confederate troops, probably of the 18th North Carolina Infantry of Brigadier-General James H. Lane's Brigade of Hill's Division, fired at the knot of horsemen emerging from the shadows. Three balls struck Jackson, in his left arm between shoulder and elbow, in his left wrist, and in his right palm. He had to be carried from the field.[82]

Stuart took temporary command of the Second Corps and resumed the attack on Sunday morning, May 3. Hooker, his ever-growing timidity compounding his mistakes, did the Confederates the favor of withdrawing Sickles from the Hazel Grove plateau, which opened the way for Stuart's and Lee's troops to reunite as well as turning a superb artillery platform over to the rebels. Under gunfire from Hazel Grove, Hooker withdrew the main portion of his army to a new defensive perimeter near the Rappahannock.

The 75,000 men of this Federal main force did not have to bear prolonged new attacks from Lee's somewhat over 40,000, because Sedgwick, ordered to seize Marye's Heights behind Fredericksburg with his force of some 40,000, did so by driving out Early's Division and then marched westward to assist Hooker. Lee divided his army in the face of the enemy yet again, leaving Stuart with 25,000 to face down Hooker while he himself with the rest of the army halted Sedgwick. Lee struck Sedgwick's van near Salem Church some six miles east of Chancellorsville late on Sunday afternoon, and Sedgwick halted to await his entire force. On Monday, Early reentered the picture by assailing Sedgwick from the east while Lee hit him from the west and south. Sedgwick had to retreat that night across Scott's Ford on the Rappahannock. Lee moved west to bludgeon Hooker yet again; the inveterate pugnacity of the Confederate commander might have carried his men into another Malvern Hill in the form of an attack planned for May 7, had not Hooker in spite of his numbers and by now exceedingly well-constructed defenses withdrawn to the north of the Rappahannock during the night of the 6th.

Chancellorsville has been rightly regarded as Lee's masterpiece battle, the Napoleonic *manœuvre sur les derrières* of Second Manassas raised to a yet higher degree of perfection by the still greater disparity in numbers. No military commander since Napoleon himself had surpassed or ever would surpass Lee's exercises in Napoleonic battlefield tactics at Second Manassas and Chancellorsville. No wonder that Confederate leaders and citizens to-gether could take heart that whatever the internal troubles of the Confeder-acy, their army and especially its greatest chieftain could save them from all military dangers. The Army of Northern Virginia under R. E. Lee was hardly a mirror of Confederate society. Its strengths far transcended those of the beleaguered society.

Nevertheless, Chancellorsville should not have been so heartening as most Confederates appear to have found it. Lee had defeated not so much the Army of the Potomac as Joseph Hooker, who in fact had gone a long way toward defeating himself, albeit because of Lee's psychological ascendancy over him. Whenever the soldiers of the Army of the Potomac were given a fair chance to fight, they did so with tenacity and ferocity, and with their army's customary tactical skill at every level save that of the highest head-quarters. Union casualties were some 1,575 killed, 9,594 wounded, and 5,676 missing for a total of 16,845. Confederate casualties are estimated at 1,665 killed, 9,081 wounded, and 2,018 missing, a total of 12,764. Thus all Lee's skills in generalship could not prevent his casualties from numbering about 22 percent of his army, with his total force estimated at 57,352; while the Union army lost only 16 percent of an aggregate present of 104,891, or 13 percent if Hooker is credited with his full 134,000.[83] Even in his greatest battle, Lee had imposed on the scarcest and most indispensable Confederate resource — the lives of Confederate soldiers — a cost that could foreshadow only a downward spiral of Southern military fortunes.

## LEE TURNS NORTH

Nevertheless, the victory at Chancellorsville made it possible for Lee to re-turn to the strategy that he believed could assure the ultimate triumph of Confederate arms in defiance of the weaknesses of Southern society, the strategy that could win the war: an offensive strategy of invasion of the North. Ever since his retreat from Sharpsburg, Lee had chafed to march northward across the Potomac again. Less than a week after his retreat into Virginia from Maryland in September of 1862 he had told President Davis that his best move would be to return to Hagerstown, but that his army required refitting. By the time he defeated Burnside at Fredericksburg in Decem-ber, he had rebuilt the Army of Northern Virginia to a new crest of self-confidence and to its highest numerical strength, 75,513 soldiers, since the Seven Days.[84] He would have turned his troops northward with the first warmth of spring in 1863 had not a Federal threat to the Virginia and North Carolina coast compelled Longstreet's detachment to Suffolk. This diversion at least allowed the detached formations to renourish themselves and their horses in a region not yet exhausted by war. But the diversion also obliged Lee to parry Hooker's offensive at Chancellorsville, and Lee did not believe that such defensive victories as Fredericksburg and Chancellorsville could win the war.

As early as February, Lee had directed Jackson's talented mapmaker Captain Jedediah Hotchkiss, Topographical Engineers, to prepare a map of the routes from the Valley of Virginia to the Pennsylvania capital at Harrisburg and on to Philadelphia.[85] With the moral ascendancy of his own Army of Northern Virginia over the rival Army of the Potomac seemingly redoubled by the triumph over odds at Chancellorsville, Lee summoned Longstreet back to him, cajoled Davis for other reinforcements from scattered garrison troops, and on June 3 took the road to Pennsylvania.

Stonewall Jackson would not march with him. After a seemingly successful operation to amputate Jackson's left arm, pneumonia set in, and Stonewall died on May 10. Richmond's largest wartime crowds watched the body being borne through the streets and passed in mourning before it as it lay in state in the Capitol Rotunda. On May 15 Jackson was buried, as he had asked, back home in the Valley, "at Lexington, and in my own plot."[86] The Confederacy's most popular and most beloved military hero was gone — the Presbyterian warrior so grim and stern in his service to his Cromwellian God of war, yet also a modest backwoods western Virginian more human and comprehensible than the aristocratic demigod Lee.

Stonewall Jackson was gone; but the superb infantry of the Army of Northern Virginia still marched, and solid "Old Pete" Longstreet, and impetuous Powell Hill, and gallant Jeb Stuart, and Dick Ewell returned from his wound. All prepared to join Lee on the roads to Pennsylvania. Why should they not repeat Fredericksburg or Chancellorsville on Northern soil? And if they did, what would the sorrows, the discords, and the privation within the Confederacy count for, after all, in the outcome of the war?

# EIGHT

# Three Seasons of Battle

## PAYING THE TOLL OF WAR: THE MILITARY DRAFT IN THE NORTH

Economic vigor and relative political unity notwithstanding, for the North to overcome the remarkable military vitality of the Southern Confederacy — to go on to lay conquest to the South, as the war aims of the North required it to do — the North must transform more of its potential strength into actual, mobilized military power. It must approximate the mobilization effort of the Confederacy, with a conscription of manpower. Otherwise, the mere population and economic superiorities of the North were proving insufficient to produce victory. Economic strength alone could not be brought to bear directly enough on the war effort. Superiority in population tended to be offset by the greater difficulties of achieving Northern war aims as compared with Southern, by the requirements of outright conquest as compared with self-defense. Even when Lee made the Confederacy's military strategy an offensive strategy, he did not aim to occupy Northern territory permanently, but rather to raid into the North, to gather supplies there, and to reap the psychological harvest of victories on Northern soil. The offensives of the North, in contrast, aimed at the military occupation of the South. As Union armies penetrated the Confederacy, they tended to dissipate their manpower in police activity, in garrisoning cities, and in guarding railroads and supply depots. It was the demands of occupying and holding the territory they had conquered that nearly paralyzed the Union armies in the West after Corinth in the spring of 1862.

In the spring and early summer of 1862, the manpower requirements brought on by victories in the West had been almost as crippling to the Union cause as McClellan's defeat before Richmond in the East. Both the Western and the Eastern Union armies needed more men. One year after the first massing of the Northern armies, Lincoln's government faced the necessity of another mass recruitment campaign in 1862.

The manpower problems of the Union approached crisis proportions in the early summer of 1862 when the losses of Shiloh and the Peninsula followed close after an excess of zeal on Secretary Stanton's part in his early efforts to economize in the War Department. When the Army approached 700,000 men by the end of 1861, Secretary Cameron apparently concluded that henceforth new regiments need not be formed and that it would be enough to win the war if replacements kept the existing units up to full strength. On December 3, 1861, Cameron ordered that after units in process of organization were completed, troops should thereafter be recruited only when requisitioned by the War Department; a War Department general superintendent of recruiting should take control of recruiting activities in each of the states on January 1, 1862, commanding regimental recruiting parties and thus considerably reducing the states' role in recruiting; and recruits should be assembled at central depots to be equipped and instructed before being taken to their assigned regiments.[1] On April 3, 1862, however, Secretary Stanton, optimistic after victories in the West and over the apparent weakness of the Confederacy in contrast to the Union's Grand Army, closed down the whole recruiting system.[2]

After Shiloh proved the folly of Stanton's decision, on May 1 the War Department directed the principal commanding officers to requisition the governors for recruits to maintain the regiments in the field.[3] On June 6, the Federal recruiting service was restored,[4] but the sound idea of filling up the old regiments rather than promiscuously forming new ones became lost in an emergency effort to find more men after the casualties and increased military requirements of the spring and early summer. The War Department sought to whip up an atmosphere of patriotic fervor for the salvation of the Union, similar to that of the previous summer, by arranging for the governors to appeal to Lincoln to issue a new call for 300,000 three-year volunteers. The call went out on July 2, the day after Malvern Hill.[5]

The country, however, had already seen too much of grim war to rally to the colors with the innocent enthusiasm of 1861. A War Department bounty of $100, $25 to be paid on enlistment and the rest at discharge, failed to compensate for lost innocence. Recruitment proved so sluggish, in fact, that the government responded with a step in the direction of conscription.[6] Congress passed the Militia Act of July 17, 1862, reiterating the principle of a military obligation for all able-bodied male citizens aged eighteen to forty-five, which had been asserted in the Uniform Militia Act of May 25, 1792 and was deeply embedded in American colonial and in English history; authorizing the President to call the militia into Federal service for up to nine months; and further authorizing him to establish Federal rules to govern the militia where state procedures were not adequate.[7] On this basis Lincoln on August 4 announced a draft of 300,000 militia for nine months. The draft would be applied in any state that failed to meet its quota of volunteers by August 15. Where no state machinery for conscripting militia existed, the War Department would cooperate with the governors to establish such machinery.[8]

Despite an ancient American tradition, dating from the earliest English colonies, of a universal military obligation at least in legal theory, the actual enforcement of such an obligation seemed so contrary to the American customs and virtues of the nineteenth century that the prospect of conscription provoked a howl of protest, from the governors as well as newspapers and much of the public. The Northern people did not perceive the kind of danger to their way of life that had steeled the South to accept conscription a little over three months earlier. In consequence, the Union draft of 1862 was never more than minimally enforced. Under the threat of possible enforcement, nevertheless, voluntary enlistment accelerated, and recruits were accepted either as three-year volunteers or nine-months militia. For determining whether a state met its quota of recruits, the War Department rated four nine-months militiamen as the equivalent of one three-year volunteer. Eventually the department credited 431,958 volunteers and 87,558 militia to Lincoln's calls of July 2 and August 4, 1862.[9]

In the spring of 1863, obviously, the nine-months militia would go home. Clearly, a volunteer system could no longer maintain the Army of 918,191 men in service at the beginning of the year.[10] Facing this prospect, the Federal government felt obliged to move farther toward conscription in the spring of 1863, however much the spirit of individualistic democracy might be violated. On March 3, unaided in this distasteful step by any particular executive leadership, Congress passed "An Act for enrolling and calling out the national Forces, and for other Purposes," commonly known as the Enrollment Act of 1863.[11] It was the first direct Federal conscription statute in U.S. history, providing the first Federal compulsion upon individuals to

enter directly into the military service of the United States, without intermediate employment in the militia systems of the states.

As such, the Enrollment Act found its constitutional warrant not in the
militia clauses but simply in the power of Congress "To raise and support
Armies."[12] In an expression of opinion not published during his lifetime,
Lincoln took the view implicit in the law, that because the Constitution gives
Congress authority to raise and support armies, then Congress "must pre-
scribe the mode, or relinquish the power."[13] Chief Justice Taney prepared a
contrary opinion, written as though he intended to incorporate it into a decision of the Supreme Court. He believed the Enrollment Act unconstitutional, especially because it transgressed against the reserved powers of the
states by causing the militia of the states to be of no practical value and
enabling the Federal government to disorganize the state governments by
drafting their officers.[14] Like Lincoln's opinion, however, Taney's remained
unpublished during his lifetime, for a judicial test of the draft did not reach
his court. The Supreme Court never ruled on the Enrollment Act of 1863,
but the Court eventually upheld the constitutionality of the similar Selective
Service Act of May 18, 1917 in a unanimous decision.[15]

The Enrollment Act was based solely on the sweeping constitutional
power to raise and support armies, and it boldly imposed a military liability
upon all male citizens and declarant aliens between twenty and forty-five
years of age, exempting only the physically and mentally unfit, certain high
Federal officials and the state governors, only sons of dependent widows,
only sons of infirm parents, and persons convicted of a felony. It divided the
enrollees into two classes, Class I consisting of all enrollees between twenty
and thirty-five and all unmarried enrollees, Class II consisting of the married
enrollees between thirty-five and forty-five, and provided for the drafting of
the Class I pool before the Class II group should be tapped. The enrollees
were subject to draft for two years after enrollment. Once drafted, they would
serve for three years or the war, whichever ended first.

Having set forth these bold principles, however, Congress compromised them in practice, making the Enrollment Act a limping, only partially
effective measure. The Selective Service Act of 1917 and subsequent American conscription laws were to emphasize the value to the whole nation of
*selective* service — of the government's choosing from among enrollees those
who should serve in the armed forces and those who should be deferred to
serve the economy as civilians. Registering under the draft law to offer oneself for selection was presented by the government to the public as a patriotic
act as well as an obligation — a means of assisting the government to make its
rational, selective choices for the best allocation of manpower to the various
national requirements.

In the 1863 act and the government's methods of presenting it to the public, however, there was little to suggest the value of selective allocations of manpower among the armed forces and civilian occupations. Instead, being conscripted was presented as bearing a stigma. Only the compulsion of the conscript's service was stressed, with no effort to suggest that the conscript might share the patriotism of the volunteer. Consistent with the implications permeating the Enrollment Act and its enforcement that the conscript was unpatriotic, under the 1863 law men were not expected to come forward to enrollment offices, as they have done since 1917; rather, Federal provost marshals would seek them out by conducting house-to-house inquiries. The very process of enrollment took on an aura of Federal snooping and suggested that the potential conscript was attempting to hide. When this method in fact encouraged concealment of potential conscripts in some households, the provost marshals took to examining private employers' payrolls, which angered labor by adding the implication that the draft authorities were particularly seeking out workingmen.

Worse yet as obstacles to an effective draft were the substitution and commutation provisions. As exemptions hobbled the Confederate draft, so substitution and commutation imperiled the Federal draft. The Enrollment Act permitted any person drafted to escape service by providing an acceptable substitute. Or a drafted man might simply purchase exemption by paying the commutation fee of $300. These features gave the Federal draft the same sort of disrepute borne by the Confederate draft, of making the war a poor man's fight. The $300 commutation fee approximated a year's wages for an average industrial worker; the average farmer or laborer could not afford to pay it.[16]

The origins of substitution and commutation lay in the ancient militia system. These practices had made some sense, however invidious they were in discriminating between rich and poor, when a community's militia might be called on to provide men for an expedition against the Indians, but only one call was anticipated and there was no need to mobilize nearly the whole potential military manpower. If the Indian expedition required twenty men out of a militia pool of a hundred, it did not matter which twenty took up arms. In the Civil War, however, a succession of draft calls would be needed, and the government might require almost the whole potential military manpower. In 1863, substitution and commutation were not only invidious; they made no military sense whatever.

The tendency to regard a drafted man as stigmatized by having been drafted and the persistence of the outmoded practices of substitution and commutation both reflected a reluctance to turn from volunteering to conscription as the source of the Army's manpower, even on the part of those governmental leaders who thought conscription had become essential. Volunteering still seemed the American way to raise an army, conscription undemocratic. Neither Congress nor the executive was yet willing to face up to a thoroughgoing Federal control over the nation's manpower. With such attitudes, the draft functioned less as a direct source of soldiers than as a stimulus to volunteering. Communities could avoid the imposition of the draft within their boundaries by meeting their quotas with volunteers, and political and business leaders staged new recruiting drives to find the requisite volunteers. Enrollment under the draft act began on May 25, 1863. The first drafting took place from the beginning of July into August. This effort provoked the famous July 13–15 draft riots in New York City and similar disturbances elsewhere, and yet the conscription machinery was so inefficient and the intentions of the Enrollment Act so diluted that the effort netted only 35,883 men — albeit along with $15,686,400 in commutation fees.[17]

To the end of the war, only 6 percent of the 2,666,999 men who served in the Union Army were directly conscripted. Commutation fees were paid by 86,724 men, 116,188 substitutes served, and only 46,347 men were directly obliged to enter the ranks.[18]

## THE MARCH TO GETTYSBURG

Even this limping draft came too late to assist the Union in the crisis created by Lee's offensive strategy in the late spring and early summer of 1863. As nearly one-fifth of the Army of the Potomac folded its tents and drifted away because of expired enlistments, no replacements were available. The new campaign would reach its climax with that army and Lee's reorganized and reinforced Army of Northern Virginia more nearly equal in numbers than in any other major contest of the war, some 75,000 Confederates against 88,289 Federals.[19]

On the Confederate side, President Davis spent a worrisome May as the campaign for Vicksburg took more and more ominous shape, while Lee simultaneously urged him that the only solution to the Confederacy's military problems was to invade the Northeast. Davis and James A. Seddon, Secretary of War since the previous November 21,[20] believed that their best move might be to draw reinforcements from Lee's successful army to rescue Vicksburg. The President and Lee debated the strategic issues by correspondence and in two visits by Lee to Richmond.

As Lee saw matters, no feasible reinforcement could any longer assure the relief of Vicksburg; diminishing the Army of Northern Virginia was likely only to endanger Richmond as well. If the Army of Northern Virginia took the offensive, however, any Federal plans for a summer offensive in the East would be disrupted; this achievement could be expected at the very least. The Army of the Potomac occupied too strong a position on the north bank of the Rappahannock to be attacked there with advantage, but if it could be drawn away, more favorable ground for an attack might well be found. An advance by the Army of Northern Virginia into Maryland and Pennsylvania would relieve Virginia of the burden of armies through the summer and permit Virginia farmers to harvest their crops, while the army replenished its commissary stores from the rich fields and herds beyond the Potomac River.

Victory after victory won in Virginia had not sufficed to win the war for the Confederacy; but victory over the Army of the Potomac on northern soil might well turn the Northern political balance in favor of the Peace Democrats, enough to force the Lincoln administration into a negotiated settlement. A decisive victory in battle on Northern soil might even strike a hard enough moral as well as physical blow to achieve at last the long-sought object that had been eluding Lee since his first pursuit of it in the Seven Days, the destruction of the enemy army. "So, if General Lee remained inactive," Major Charles Marshall of his staff summed up, "both Vicksburg and Richmond would be imperilled, whereas if he were successful north of the Potomac, both would be saved."[21]

Davis acquiesced and took the risk of reinforcing Lee with troops from the Atlantic coast. On June 3 the Second Corps of the Army of Northern Virginia broke its camps around Fredericksburg. Stonewall Jackson's Corps was now commanded by Jackson's old coadjutor of the Valley Campaign, Richard Stoddert Ewell, promoted to lieutenant-general May 23 as was appropriate to his assuming corps command.[22]

On June 9 a hard-fought cavalry battle at Brandy Station near Culpeper—sabres flashing in mounted charge and countercharge in the old style—failed to unveil the nature of Confederate movements and intentions to the Union horsemen who crossed that day to the south shore of the Rappahannock.[23] The Army of the Potomac still focused much of its attention on the Confederate camps remaining around Fredericksburg, aware that some kind of movement was going on to the westward, but unsure where Lee's center of gravity lay, and fearful of committing itself in a probing attack against Fredericksburg lest Lee then descend from the west upon its line of communications.

"I would not take any risk of being entangled upon the river," Lincoln warned Hooker when he considered a large-scale Rappahannock crossing, "like an ox jumped half over a fence, and liable to be torn by dogs, front and rear, without a fair chance to gore one way or kick the other."[24] But with the Federals' caution, on the evening of June 13 Ewell's Corps appeared among the hills overlooking Winchester far away in the Shenandoah Valley, and Longstreet's Corps was on the march following Ewell. The Army of the Potomac was still opposite Fredericksburg, watching Lieutenant-General A. P. Hill's new Confederate Third Corps (created May 30, with Hill commanding since June 1; he ranked as lieutenant-general from May 23).[25]

During the next two days Ewell seized Winchester and battered its fleeing garrison. On June 14 the Army of the Potomac at last began marching northward toward Centreville, to pursue a Confederate vanguard that began crossing the Potomac near Williamsport, Maryland the next day. Lee then called on Hill's Corps to hasten to rejoin the rest of the army.

On June 12 Governor Curtin of Pennsylvania had issued a proclamation confirming the rumors that his state was in danger of invasion and calling on the citizens to rally to the defense of their homes and firesides by enlisting in an emergency force of home guards.[26] Much that occurred in Pennsylvania and the North during the next few days might have gratified Lee's hopes that the Northern will was fragile enough for his invasion to break it and win the war. When Lee threatened Pennsylvania and the North in the Antietam campaign the year before, the patriotic zeal of the first period of the war was not yet dead, McClellan still embodied that first flush of enthusiasm in the popular ardor he aroused as commander of the Army of the Potomac, the Emancipation Proclamation had not yet embittered a significant segment of Northern sentiment against the Lincoln administration, and appeals for home guards had readily produced a rush of enlistments. Now calls for emergency troops fell flat; only a trickle of men enlisted in Pennsylvania or elsewhere.

The raising of home guards was complicated, moreover, by an effort on Stanton's part to escape dependence on the states and their militias by creating a Federal emergency force under Federal command and committed to serve whenever the North might be threatened for the duration of the war. Northern men who might have signed on for the immediate emergency did not want to risk being called to active duty repeatedly. At Governor Curtin's pleading, Stanton reduced his goal to enlistment for a maximum of six months, and President Lincoln called for 100,000 six-month volunteers on June 15, with Pennsylvania's quota set at 50,000. But this call still asked for too much.[27] Not until June 26, when Curtin called for 60,000 men for a maximum of ninety days and for state rather than Federal service, with a promise of discharge as soon as the emergency ended,[28] were the terms of enlistment in the home guard liberal enough to bring forward significant numbers of Pennsylvania emergency volunteers. Within three weeks some 24,000 joined up.[29] The response in neighboring states was similar, although New York distinguished itself as the only state to have an organized militia force ready at hand; over 10,050 militiamen from New York City and Brooklyn reached Harrisburg by June 25.[30]

At the time of Curtin's June 26 call, Ewell's Corps was in Pennsylvania and about to march in two main columns from Chambersburg to Carlisle and York, A. P. Hill's Corps had reached Chambersburg, and Longstreet's First Corps was a day's march behind Hill. Although home-guard enlistments were about to pick up, Pennsylvania still exhibited a remarkable apathy as the invaders regrouped inside its boundaries. The Confederates thought many of the Pennsylvania German farmers they encountered had decided "a plague on both your houses," and sometimes Confederate troops seem to have been more generously offered cold water, coffee, and other refreshments than the Union soldiers who began to reach Pennsylvania — partly out of fear, to be sure. Philadelphia in particular presented a contrast to its aroused response to the Antietam campaign the year before. George W. Fahnestock, a businessman of the city, reported a strange indifference:

> The archives and records of the State are loaded in cars, and now upon the sidings in West Philadelphia, dangerously near to large quantities of barrels of petroleum. Bailey & Co. sent me a circular yesterday, notifying their friends that all silverware and valuables deposited with them for safe keeping, will be at the owners risk. And yet the people are as quiet and apathetic as if it was all a false report. Thousands of able bodied young fellows are ever parading the streets, but no enlistments go with spirit. These chaps can lounge and dress, swinging canes, or twirling moustaches, but they have no patriotism in their souls.[31]

The apathy prevailed, Fahnestock found, even though, as early as June 25,

> [r]eports of the most exaggerated character flew from mouth to mouth, and it grew so improbable towards evening, that I was obliged to resort to argument and convince the children that the rebels were not astride of the telegraph wires. One came in with the report that Harrisburg had been surrounded, another that martial law had been proclaimed here. As I walked through Chestnut St, on my way home, and saw the moving crowds of able bodied young men lounging around, I wished that some compulsory way could be used to arouse their patriotism. The rebels have undisputed possession of the Cumberland Valley almost to the town of Carlisle. They have ravaged the crops, and stolen all the horses and cattle.[32]

The last statement was scarcely an exaggeration. Ewell and Lee had issued orders that goods needed by the Confederacy were to be requisitioned by properly appointed officers and paid for at current market prices, and that when Northern citizens refused to sell on those terms, the goods were to be seized but their owners were to be given specific receipts for later redemption. It was the Confederates, however, who determined the current market prices, and they paid in Confederate currency that was badly depreciated in the South and almost worthless in the North. In south-central Pennsylvania the Confederates arrived when the wheat was ripe for the harvest, and they stripped the region of newly harvested and stored foodstuffs. Many Pennsylvanians fled from the invasion path with their horses and cattle as well as their movable goods, jamming the bridges across the Susquehanna at Harrisburg and Wrightsville. Nevertheless, one reasonably reliable Confederate estimate had it that Lee's army drove 26,000 cattle and 22,000 sheep from Pennsylvania and Maryland into Virginia. Black people had special reason to flee, for having been born and lived free in Pennsylvania was no protection against the Confederates' practice of sending south into slavery every African American who fell into their hands. By the hundreds African Americans also crossed to the east shore of the Susquehanna.

On June 28, having destroyed Thaddeus Stevens's Caledonia Furnace — along with saw mill, forges, and rolling mill in addition to the iron furnace — along the way from Chambersburg in retribution for Stevens's "most vindictive spirit toward the people of the South,"[33] Major-General Jubal A. Early imposed a ransom of $100,000 on the city of York, threatening to sack the place if his demands were not met. (The citizens could raise only $28,000, but Early did not fulfill his threat.) The vanguard of Early's Division of Ewell's Corps reached the Susquehanna at Wrightsville, though the Pennsylvania home guard burned the bridge there before the Confederates could cross the river. (Confederate soldiers of Brigadier-General John B. Gordon's Brigade of Early's Division labored valiantly and with success to prevent the spread of the fire into the town of Wrightsville.) On the same day, Brigadier-General Albert G. Jenkins's Brigade of cavalry in advance of the other prong of Ewell's Corps skirmished with some home-guard outposts outside Harrisburg and viewed Pennsylvania's capital from the west shore of the Susquehanna, a few miles away.

That same Sunday, however, Lee learned from a spy hired by Secretary of War Seddon, Henry Thomas Harrison, that the Army of the Potomac was in Maryland and closing in on him. He heard the news from a spy because Jeb Stuart, having become infatuated with the romantic risks and consequent popular applause associated with riding around the rear of the enemy army after his previous experiences in doing so, was performing that trick again and had ridden out of touch with army headquarters. Nevertheless, Lee would now have to halt his farflung activities in gathering supplies and sowing Northern demoralization, to concentrate to meet the Army of the Potomac.[34]

General Hooker's response to Lee's march northward had been no better than barely adequate. As Hooker's troops began to close in on the Confederates north of the Potomac, his dispatches to Washington soon betrayed the same symptoms of loss of nerve that had overcome him when he was in proximity to Lee at Chancellorsville. He had long been conducting a quarrel via telegraph with General-in-Chief Halleck over sundry grievances real and imagined, and he now involved himself in a debate with Halleck over his freedom to control the garrison at Harpers Ferry. On June 27, Hooker used this dispute as a reason to resign. Perhaps he fancied that he was merely blackmailing the War Department to give him control of the garrison, but his insecurity could have impelled him toward an escape from his responsibilities. Be that as it may, on the eventful Sunday of June 28, Hooker learned that Lincoln had accepted his resignation and put Major-General George G. Meade, U.S.V., in his place.

Meade, a sobersided, scholarly engineer officer who was appropriately enough a Philadelphian, displayed in his first days of army command an understandable uncertainty and even hesitancy about when and where he wanted to challenge Lee and the Army of Northern Virginia to battle. Nevertheless he kept pressing his formations northward into Pennsylvania and reaching out with his cavalry to feel where Lee's columns were located. On July 1 the First and Second Brigades of the First Division of his Cavalry Corps clashed with infantry of Major-General Henry Heth's Division of A. P. Hill's Corps along the Chambersburg-Gettysburg Pike just northwest of the borough of Gettysburg, seat of Pennsylvania College, a Lutheran Theological Seminary, and the County of Adams. Hill's and Ewell's Corps were converging toward Gettysburg because it was a road junction and a suitable place for Lee to effect his concentration now that he knew the enemy army was nearby. The Federal First Corps infantry was close behind the First Cavalry Division and promptly joined in its fight against Heth's Division, and before July 1 was over a major battle had flared up around Gettysburg between Hill and Ewell on the Confederate side and the First and Eleventh Corps of the Army of the Potomac for the Union.

## GETTYSBURG: THE BATTLE

The great battle of Gettysburg: General Reynolds of the Union First Corps arrived to find Brigadier-General, U.S.V., John Buford's First Cavalry Division deployed west of the town astride the Chambersburg Pike on a low height called McPherson's Ridge. Buford was beginning a holding action to prevent the Confederates from seizing what he and then Reynolds quickly recognized as a ridge line superb for defense on the opposite side of the town, south and east of it. Here, the two Federal leaders thought, and Reynolds so informed Meade, an anvil might be formed on which to break the hammer of Lee's army. Buford had compelled Heth's Division to take the time to deploy from column of march into line of battle as it approached along the Chambersburg Pike, and the cavalry stand gave Reynolds the opportunity to hasten the van of his infantry into line on McPherson's Ridge. The Iron Brigade of Midwestern troops, the old Black Hat Brigade renamed for its stout fighting qualities particularly as displayed at South Mountain in the Antietam campaign, and formally the First Brigade, First Division, First Army Corps, appropriately was the first Federal infantry unit into line.[35]

Reynolds was killed as he led the brigade's deployment in McPherson's Woods. Succeeding him as temporary corps commander was the leader of his Third Division, Abner Doubleday of Fort Sumter, a veteran of the Eastern battles since Second Bull Run, and since November 29, 1862 major-general, U.S.V. As hazy morning gave way to a bright, hot summer's afternoon, the magnetic pull of Gettysburg as a road junction, along with the accumulating perception on both sides of the possible tactical value of the adjacent hills, drew more and more troops into the fight.

Rodes's Division of Ewell's Corps approached from the north, whence it had been called from the foray to Carlisle and the west shore opposite Harrisburg. Its advance threatened the right flank of the Federal First Corps, anchored on an eminence called Oak Hill where McPherson's Ridge converged with another north-south rise of ground to the east of it, Seminary Ridge. Rodes's approach was imperfectly countered by the arrival of Howard's Eleventh Corps, which came too late to tie its left flank into the First Corps right, leaving a gap between the two Union corps for Confederate exploitation. Moreover, Early's Division of Ewell's Corps quickly followed Rodes's from the north, extending the latter's line eastward across the Harrisburg Pike. Early overlapped the Eleventh Corps right flank while Howard's left was also threatened. A question mark shadowed the reputation of the Eleventh Corps not only because of its rout at Chancellorsville, but also because its men were largely German-Americans, and in the mid-nineteenth

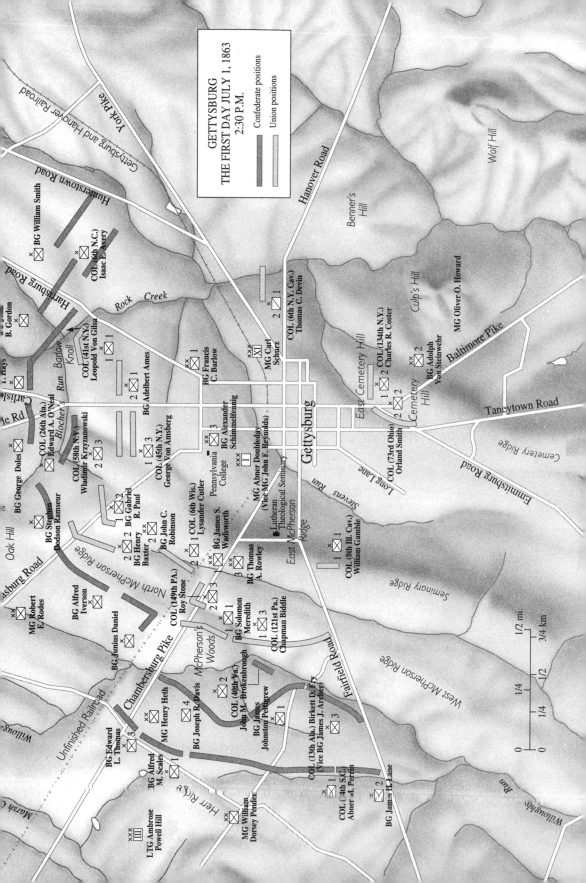

GETTYSBURG
THE FIRST DAY JULY 1, 1863
2:30 P.M.

Confederate positions
Union positions

York Pike

Gettysburg and Hanover Railroad

Hunterstown Road

Hanover Road

Wolf Hill

Benner's Hill

Culp's Hill

MG Oliver O. Howard

Baltimore Pike

BG Adolph Von Steinwehr

Taneytown Road

BG William Smith

COL (6th N.C.) Isaac E. Avery

Hartsburg Road

B. Gordon

Rock Creek

COL (6th N.Y. Cav.) Thomas C. Devin

East Cemetery Hill

COL (134th N.Y.) Charles R. Coster

Cemetery Hill

Cemetery Ridge

T. Hays

Barlow Knoll

COL (41st N.Y.) Leopold Von Gilsa

BG Francis C. Barlow

MG Carl Schurz

COL (73rd Ohio) Orland Smith

Blocher's Run

BG Adelbert Ames

BG Alexander Schimmelfennig

Carlisle Rd

COL (26th Ala.) Edward A. O'Neal

COL (58th N.Y.) Wladimir Krzyzanowski

COL (45th N.Y.) George Von Amsberg

Pennsylvania College

Long Lane

Gettysburg

BG George Doles

Oak Hill

BG Stephen Dodson Ramseur

BG Henry R. Paul

BG Gabriel R. Paul

BG John C. Robinson

COL (6th Wis.) Lysander Cutler

BG James S. Wadsworth

Lutheran Theological Seminary

MG Abner Doubleday (Vice MG John F. Reynolds)

East McPherson Ridge

Stevens Run

Emmitsburg Road

MG Robert E. Rodes

BG Alfred Iverson

BG Junius Daniel

North McPherson Ridge

COL (149th PA.) Roy Stone

BG Solomon Meredith

BG Thomas A. Rowley

COL (121st Pa.) Chapman Biddle

COL (8th Ill. Cav.) William Gamble

Seminary Ridge

Chambersburg Pike

McPherson's Woods

Dysasburg Road

MG Robert E. Rodes

Willoug

Unfinished Railroad

BG Edward L. Thomas

BG Alfred M. Scales

MG Henry Heth

COL (40th Va.) John M. Brokenbrough

BG Joseph R. Davis

BG James Johnston Pettigrew

Herr Ridge

Fairfield Road

West McPherson Ridge

COL (13th Ala.) Birkett D. Fry (Vice BG James J. Archer)

Marsh C

LTG Ambrose Powell Hill

MG William Dorsey Pender

COL (5th S.C.) Abner J. Perrin

BG James H. Lane

Willoughby Run

0    1/4    1/2    3/4 km
0    1/4    1/2 mi.

century everybody knew that Germans have a talent for music and poetry but not for war. The corps was also unlucky; today it fought stubbornly but crumbled under superior numbers and the turning of both its flanks. Its retreat southward through the streets of Gettysburg exposed the rear of the First Corps at a time when Doubleday's troops were already having to give ground before the superior numbers represented by Major-General William Dorsey Pender's Division added to Heth's Division as A. P. Hill's Corps renewed its pressure from the west. The Federal First Corps had to join in the retreat through Gettysburg.

The nucleus of the potential defensive line beyond the town was Cemetery Hill, just south of the grid of streets. Here retreating Federal troops were met and rallied by Major-General Winfield Scott Hancock, U.S.V., whom Meade had dispatched northward ahead of his command, the Second Corps, to try to assure retention of the ridge line whose value Reynolds had urged upon Meade by messenger just before he died. On Cemetery Hill General Howard also rallied the troops. There was a brief contretemps because Hancock claimed Meade's authority to take charge but Howard was senior in rank. Fortunately for their cause, the two Union generals agreed to cooperate, and they quickly made Cemetery Hill a stronghold, building upon the hitherto uncommitted Second Division of Howard's corps. Hancock also sent the Iron Brigade to hold the west slope of Culp's Hill, which rises just to the east and south of Cemetery Hill.

Cemetery Hill promptly became the focus of what has been one of the war's most vexed tactical controversies, as well as of the Union defense. General Lee, arriving on the battlefield in late afternoon, could not fail to observe the importance of the hill but gave General Ewell only discretionary orders to capture it. Lee preferred to deal with his principal subordinates using that kind of light touch of command; he regarded them as fellow gentlemen to whom peremptory orders would have been demeaning. This approach had usually worked well enough with Stonewall Jackson — although as the Seven Days showed, not always even with him. Now Lee had to lead subordinates of lesser capacity, and his kid-glove approach would often create trouble. Similar discretionary and indeed ambiguously phrased instructions to Jeb Stuart had contributed to Stuart's believing he had Lee's permission to ride off the chessboard earlier in the campaign, and Stuart's absence still plagued the Confederates on July 1 with ignorance of the whereabouts of much of the enemy army.

With Ewell, however, Lee's method of command on this occasion probably had little effect on the outcome of the battle. Admirers of Jackson have always preferred to think that Stonewall unlike Ewell would have swept the bluecoats off Cemetery Hill and made their subsequent defense of the Gettysburg high ground impossible. This notion became a major part of the dogma of the postwar religion of the Lost Cause: if Jackson had lived, the Confederacy would have won the war. In fact, Cemetery Hill was naturally so strong a position, Hancock and Howard had so promptly prepared its defenses, Confederate redeployment of units disrupted by the street pattern of the town would have had to require so much time on a day already far gone, and anyway Ewell's troops were sufficiently frayed by an afternoon's hard fighting under the July sun as well as by the rush of pursuit, that by the time the Confederates could have mounted a serious assault on Cemetery Hill the Federals could almost certainly have defied their tired efforts to take it.[36]

Meade reached Cemetery Hill about midnight. His troops were already extending the Cemetery Hill position into the famous fishhook line of Gettysburg. The point of the hook formed on Culp's Hill, where Union troops mainly of Slocum's Twelfth Corps joined the Iron Brigade during the night and the morning hours of July 2. The shank of the fishhook extended almost directly south from Cemetery Hill along Cemetery Ridge, where Hancock's Second Corps stacked arms as its men arrived. Cemetery Ridge almost fades away into a marshy lowland just before the ground rises up again about a mile and a half south of Cemetery Hill in two elevations, Little Round Top and immediately south of it Round Top. During the night of July 1–2 there were not yet enough Federals available to occupy the Round Tops in any strength. Initially the Second Division, Twelfth Corps was on Little Round Top, then as morning came Sickles's Third Corps extended the Second Corps line southward toward the Round Tops as it reached the field.

None of these hills or ridges is particularly lofty. Round Top rises about 350 feet above the surrounding countryside, and the other hills are all at least 100 feet lower. Nevertheless, the hills are steep enough, and they dominate the surrounding fields enough, that they provided a major advantage for their defenders, as all the principal leaders on both sides had recognized from Buford and Reynolds onward. Even gentle Cemetery Ridge could afford concealment and a degree of shelter to troops on its reverse slope.

As the Army of Northern Virginia came up, it formed a line a mile or so away from the Union positions, along Seminary Ridge and other ridges, continuing it south of the town, through Gettysburg from west to east, and bending southward to Benner's Hill opposite Culp's Hill. The Confederate line was concave and about four miles in length; the Union line was convex and about and about three miles long. The Federals thus enjoyed the military advantage of the interior lines. They could shift troops from point to point over much shorter distances than the Confederates.

The strength of the Union position notwithstanding, Lee resolved to attack it. To attack on this battlefield was the logical extension of the offensive strategy that had brought Lee to Gettysburg. Moreover, circumstances gave Lee little choice in the matter. He could not stand in position for any appreciable length of time waiting for the enemy to attack, because his army was subsisting off the country and had to continue to move to continue feeding its men and horses. When he conferred with Longstreet, his senior corps commander proposed an effort to slip around the left flank of Meade's army, get astride Meade's communications with Washington, and oblige Meade to do the attacking. This idea reflected Longstreet's preference for the defense over the attack, about which he was probably more clear-eyed than Lee; but the particular suggestion was less realistic. Lee felt reluctant to accept it because he did not know the roads and the countryside as he did in much of Virginia, and Jed Hotchkiss notwithstanding, he was not sure his maps of Pennsylvania and Maryland were reliable enough. Moreover, if he succeeded in turning Meade's army, he would at the same time leave Meade astride the Confederate line of communications. The Army of Northern Virginia fed itself by foraging, but should it need resupply of ammunition, it depended on the long wagon journey from the Virginia Central Railroad at Staunton in the Shenandoah Valley.

Furthermore, Meade could supply his army from other bases in addition to Washington and would not necessarily attack even if Lee took up a new position southeast of Gettysburg. Thereupon Lee would again confront his own need either to fight or to move. The strong defenses of Washington precluded a quick descent on the Federal capital with the Army of the Potomac immediately in his rear. The only practical alternative to fighting at Gettysburg, as Lee saw it, was to retreat, which meant abandoning the purposes for which he had marched north, except for the secondary one of gathering in the produce of Pennsylvania and Maryland while sparing Virginia. He could not bring himself thus to throw away his central strategy for winning the war. He must at least test that strategy in battle. He must fight at Gettysburg.

Therefore he planned for July 2 a two-pronged effort against the Union flanks. He persuaded a reluctant Longstreet to attempt to roll up the Union's Cemetery Ridge line south to north from its left. When Longstreet's First Corps commenced this main attack, Ewell's Second Corps would mount a secondary strike against the Federal right on Culp's and Cemetery Hills. A. P. Hill's Third Corps in the Confederate center, much of it badly battered the day before, would assist as opportunity offered.[37]

Partly because Lee consumed much of the morning of July 2 in deciding upon this plan, partly because Longstreet dragged his feet to resist

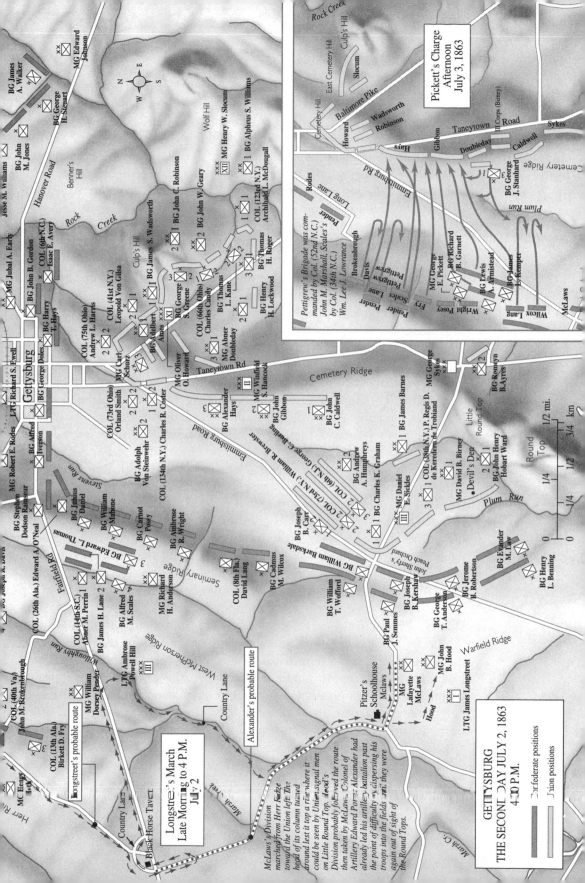

**Pickett's Charge Afternoon July 3, 1863**

Rock Creek

Culp's Hill

East Cemetery Hill

Slocum

Cemetery Hill

Baltimore Pike

Wadsworth

Howard

Robinson

Taneytown Road

Hays

Gibbon

Doubleday

Sykes

III Corps (Birney)

Caldwell

Stannard

Cemetery Ridge

Plum Run

BG George J. Stannard

I

Emmitsburg Rd

Long Lane

Rodes

Pettigrew's Brigade was commanded by Col. (52nd N.C.) John M. Marshall, Scales's by Col. (34th N.C.) Wm. Lee J. Lowrance

Pender

Scales

Pettigrew

Brockenbrough

Davis

Fry

Lane

MG George E. Pickett

BG Richard B. Garnett

BG Lewis A. Armistead

BG James L. Kemper

Wright

Posey

Wilcox Lang

McLaws

Lane

Pender Posey

---

BG James A. Walker

MG Edward Johnson

BG George H. Steuart

BG John M. Jones

Jesse M. Williams

MG Henry W. Slocum

1 BG Alpheus S. Williams

XII

MG Jubal A. Early

BG John B. Gordon

COL (6th N.C.) Isaac E. Avery

BG Harry T. Hays

Hanover Road

Benner's Hill

Wolf Hill

Rock Creek

1 BG James S. Wadsworth

1 BG John C. Robinson

2 BG John W. Geary

COL (123rd N.Y.) Archibald L. McDougall

Gettysburg

LTG Richard S. Ewell

BG George Doles

COL (75th Ohio) Andrew L. Harris

COL (41st N.Y.) Leopold Von Gilsa

Adelbert Ames

1 BG James S. Wadsworth

BG George S. Greene

COL (66th Ohio) Charles Candy

BG Henry H. Lockwood

BG Thomas L. Kane

BG Thomas H. Ruger

MG Robert E. Rodes

BG Alfred Iverson

COL (73rd Ohio) Orland Smith

MG Carl Schurz

BG Adolph Von Steinwehr

MG Oliver O. Howard

Taneytown Rd

MG Abner Doubleday

Cemetery Ridge

Stevens Run

BG Stephen Dodson Ramseur

COL (26th Ala.) Edward A. O'Neal

Fairfield Rd

BG Junius Daniel

BG Alfred M. Scales

BG Edward L. Thomas

BG William Mahone

BG Carnot Posey

BG Ambrose R. Wright

BG Alexander Hays

BG John Gibbon

BG John C. Caldwell

MG Winfield S. Hancock

II

Emmitsburg Road

Seminary Ridge

COL (8th Fla.) David Lang

BG Cadmus M. Wilcox

MG Richard H. Anderson

COL (14th S.C.) Abner M. Perrin

BG James H. Lane

West McPherson Ridge

Country Lane

BG Andrew A. Humphreys

COL (73rd N.Y.) George C. Burling

William R. Brewster

BG Joseph B. Carr

Peach Orchard

John Sherfy's

BG William Barksdale

BG William T. Wofford

BG Joseph B. Kershaw

BG George T. Anderson

Warfield Ridge

COL (38th N.Y.) P. Regis D. de Keredem de Trobriand

MG David B. Birney

BG Charles K. Graham

MG Daniel E. Sickles

III

MG George Sykes

BG Romeyn B. Ayres

Little Round Top

Round Top

BG John Henry Hobart Ward

Devil's Den

Plum Run

BG James Barnes

BG Evander M. Law

BG Henry L. Benning

BG Jerome B. Robertson

BG Paul J. Semmes

MG Lafayette McLaws

MG John B. Hood

LTG James Longstreet

Pitzer's Schoolhouse

McLaws

Hood

1 km

1/2 mi.

3/4

1/2

1/4

1/4

1/2

3/4

0

LTG Ambrose Powell Hill

III

MG William Dorsey Pender

BG James H. Lane

COL (44th S.C.) Abner M. Perrin

Willoughby Run

COL (40th Va.) John M. Brokenbrough

COL (13th Ala.) Birkett D. Fry

MC Henry Heth

Herr Ridge

Black Horse Tavern

Marsh Creek

Country Lane

Marsh Cr.

**Longstreet's March Late Morning to 4 P.M. July 2**

Longstreet's probable route

Alexander's probable route

McLaws's Division marched from Herr Ridge toward the Union left. The head of its column turned around lest it top a rise where it could be seen by Union signal men on Little Round Top. Hood's Division probably followed the route then taken by McLaws. Colonel of Artillery Edward Porter Alexander had already led his artillery battalion past the point of difficulty, dispersing his troops into the fields until they were again out of sight of the Round Tops.

**GETTYSBURG THE SECOND DAY JULY 2, 1863 4:00 P.M.**

Confederate positions

Union positions

initiating attacks that he regarded as a foredoomed Fredericksburg in reverse, partly because of problems of terrain encountered when the First Corps marched toward its launching position — Longstreet conducted a time-consuming countermarch when part of his original route proved to be visible from a Union Signal Corps station observed to be on Little Round Top, and at that did so not by simply turning around and letting his rear become his front but by ordering a laborious U-turn — for these reasons the main Con-federate attack did not jump off until about four in the afternoon.

When James Longstreet at length committed himself to an attack, how-ever, he dependably hit hard, and July 2 at Gettysburg presented no excep-tion. He struck from south-southwest to north-northeast generally parallel to the Emmitsburg Road, which runs into Gettysburg from Emmitsburg, Maryland. Longstreet's right flank took up an alignment such that only a slight deviation from its natural line of advance — to say nothing of the evi-dent attraction of high ground — would carry it up the slope of Little Round Top. Such an advance could compromise the strong position for the safety of which the Union had fought on the previous day. Round Top was too heavily wooded to be of much tactical utility, but the summit of Little Round Top was clear enough of trees to accommodate a battery or two of artillery, so that Confederate guns would be able to enfilade the Union left flank. As Longstreet's drive began, there were no Union troops on the Round Tops except for the signal station.

The Second Division, Twelfth Corps had occupied Little Round Top during the night, and Meade's instructions to Sickles called for his Third Corps to take up the same ground that division had held. Meade therefore believed well into July 2 that Federal troops occupied the hill anchoring his left. Sickles, however, was more concerned about the low-lying, wooded nature of the ground he was to hold just north of the Round Tops, if he extended the Cemetery Ridge line directly southward from the Second Corps. Just west of the low ground lay somewhat higher terrain, a V-shaped ridge extending from the rocky outcropping of the Devil's Den near the foot of Little Round Top west to its apex in John Sherfy's peach orchard, then sharply bending to the north along the line of the Emmitsburg Road. After Sickles during the morning failed to receive the permission he requested from Meade to move forward to the higher ground — Meade was not paying as much attention to his left as he should have — and after Sickles's recon-naissance efforts detected Confederate movement southward across his front, the impetuous politician-commander of the Third Corps ordered his corps into the Peach Orchard Salient. About 1 P.M., consequently, Sickles's corps not only left the Round Tops behind, but also took upon itself the vulnerability to crossfire always inherent in a salient, while breaking any firm connection between itself and the rest of the Union line to its right.

Sickles had just arrived at Meade's headquarters behind the Second Corps near the Union center for a conference of corps commanders when firing broke out on his front. Meade called off the conference and immediately rode with Sickles toward the Peach Orchard. Sickles offered to withdraw from the salient, but Meade rightly told him it was too late. The army commander promptly returned to his command post to try to guard against the perils he had perceived in his belated tour of his left.

He ordered troops from the newly arriving Fifth Corps into the gap between the Third and Second Corps. He also ordered his chief engineer, Brigadier-General Gouverneur K. Warren, U.S.V., to Little Round Top to observe the whole scene of battle on the left and particularly to assure the safety of the hill. From the crest Warren saw rebels approaching, and after ordering the signalmen to make a show with their flags to suggest the heights were occupied, he hastened back down the slope to divert troops to the top. He met Colonel (83rd Pennsylvania) Strong Vincent's Third Brigade, First Division, Fifth Corps moving up to fulfill Meade's order to plug the gap vacated by the Third Corps, and by authority of the commanding general he ordered it to the summit.

As a result, Colonel Joshua Lawrence Chamberlain's 20th Maine deployed on the slope facing Round Top just in time to meet Colonel William C. Oates of the 15th Alabama leading his own regiment and most of the 47th Alabama, also of Brigadier-General Evander M. Law's Brigade, Major-General John Bell Hood's Division, as they crossed the saddle between the two Round Tops. Meanwhile Warren also grabbed Brigadier-General, U.S.V., Stephen H. Weed's Third Brigade, Second Division, Fifth Corps, from which Colonel Patrick O'Rorke led his 140th New York to be first to seize the crest. Vincent and Weed deployed their full brigades, with First Lieutenant Charles E. Hazlett's Company D, 5th U.S. Artillery, accompanying Weed to the top. On the Confederate side, the Texas Brigade of Brigadier-General Jerome Bonaparte Robertson followed Law's Brigade into the fight for the hill. Weed, O'Rorke, and Hazlett all died in the struggle, and Vincent was mortally wounded, but Warren's swift action, brought about by Meade's quick dispatch of him to the scene, had saved a key to the Union line. The Federals held.

In the valley below, Longstreet's hard-driving attack by some 13,000 Confederates in the remainder of Hood's Division and in McLaws's Division gradually crushed the 10,000 or so troops of the smaller divisions of the Third Corps, Major-General, U.S.V., David B. Birney's First Division attempting to hold from the Devil's Den to the Peach Orchard, Brigadier-General, U.S.V., Andrew A. Humphreys's Second struggling from the Peach Orchard northward. Meade busily pushed more and more reinforcements into the battle, most of Major-General, U.S.V., George Sykes's Fifth Corps and other troops drawn from all along the fishhook line. The Federals withdrew sullenly from the Peach Orchard salient and back toward the original Cemetery Ridge line. Sickles's left leg was shattered and would have to be amputated. Meade sent Hancock to take command of all the various troops fighting on the left. Toward dusk Sedgwick's Sixth Corps arrived, 15,000 men, the largest corps in the army, having marched through the night and the long hot day, thirty-five miles from Manchester, Maryland, "Uncle John" Sedgwick seeing to it that the bands played as much as the musicians' stamina would permit, to help keep up the cadence and to cheer the boys along.

When the first elements of Sedgwick's corps filed into position, the Union line was secure from Cemetery Ridge to the Round Tops. Afterward one of those nasty Civil War command controversies — akin to the one among the Confederates about the failure to capture Cemetery Hill on July 1 — developed between Meade and Sickles and among their partisans, over Sickles's alleged folly as well as insubordination in moving his corps forward to the Peach Orchard. The affair was aggravated by the temperamental differences between the dour Philadelphia aristocrat who commanded the army and the rough Tammany Hall New Yorker who had led the Third Corps. At the distance of more than a century, even an admirer of Meade's overall conduct of the battle has to concede, however, that the elevation of the ground at the Peach Orchard went a long way toward compensating for the weaknesses of a salient, and more importantly, that Sickles's advance to the Emmitsburg Road provided the Federal army with a useful cushion of ground: Longstreet's Corps had to fight all evening with no more to show for it than driving the Federals back to the position from which they had started. If the contest had begun on the Cemetery Ridge line, the Union army would have had no acreage that it could safely yield. The name of Daniel Edgar Sickles may just possibly belong with those of Buford, Reynolds, Hancock, Warren, and the like among the saviors of the army at Gettysburg.

Meade had been able to pour reinforcements from his right as well as his center into the battle on his left because Ewell did not open his part of the Confederate attacks until twilight. He may well be more truly blameworthy on this account than for his controversial decision not to try for Cemetery Hill on the evening before. When Ewell did advance on July 2, Cemetery Hill proved too strong both by nature and in the resolution of its defenders — largely the Eleventh Corps Germans, along with fragments of the First

Corps, reinforced by Colonel (18th Ohio) Samuel S. Carroll's First Brigade, Third Division, Second Corps — to be taken. From Culp's Hill, Meade had withdrawn all of the Twelfth Corps except Brigadier-General, U.S.V., George Sears Greene's Third Brigade, Second Division. Greene had his men make as conspicuous nuisances of themselves as possible to suggest greater numbers, but the Confederates generally occupied the abandoned defenses. They might have achieved still more had it not been that, for reasons unknown, Culp's Hill was the only place at Gettysburg where the Federals had dug a strong system of earthworks. Anyway, it was too late at night for the Confederates to exploit their gains.

Meade conferred with his corps commanders, received agreement that the army should remain to fight a third day at Gettysburg, and predicted that Lee would attack his center, upon which he concentrated those parts of the Second Corps that had roamed elsewhere during July 2. Meade judged Lee's intentions correctly, because the Confederate commander was not yet ready to give up the climactic expression of his strategy, and having tested the Union flanks, he resolved to hit the center on July 3. Late on July 2, in A. P. Hill's only contribution to that day's battle, Anderson's Division had advanced eastward across the Emmitsburg Road on Longstreet's left, and the northernmost brigade of the division, Brigadier-General Ambrose R. Wright's, had moved a considerable distance up Cemetery Ridge not far south of a conspicuous copse of trees without meeting strong resistance. Wright's experience strengthened Lee's judgment that the Union center was the next appropriate target.

Major-General George E. Pickett's Division of Longstreet's Corps had just arrived from Chambersburg. Lee designated this fresh formation to be the core of the coming attack, joined by Heth's and two brigades of Pender's Divisions of Hill's Corps.[38] Longstreet would command the entire assault.

There was a contest on the Union right during the morning, when the Twelfth Corps returned to retake its old entrenchments. By about eleven A.M., General Slocum's men had succeeded in doing so.

The wandering General Stuart had reported to Lee on the night of July 2, and the commanding general had dispatched him with the three brigades that made up the heart of his division, that had just completed his ride around the Federals with him, and in which he felt the greatest confidence, to move around the army's right flank for an effort against Meade's line of communications to assist the projected infantry assault. Meade's rear was guarded against such a stroke by Brigadier-General David McM. Gregg, U.S.V., with the First and Third Brigades of his own Second Division, Cavalry Corps, plus the Second Brigade, Third Division under twenty-three-year-old George Armstrong Custer, somewhat mysteriously jumped from first lieutenant, 5th U.S. Cavalry, to brigadier-general, U.S.V., on June 29. It was fitting that the flamboyant Custer should have made his debut as a ranking cavalry officer in one of the rare actions of the war that, like Brandy Station, featured an old-fashioned clash of mounted men.

About five miles east of Gettysburg, along and north of the Hanover Road, with some of the fighting on foot as well as on horseback, Gregg's troopers repeated another aspect of Brandy Station: they showed that Federal cavalry, so inferior to their Confederate rivals earlier in the war as to be regarded with contempt, could now meet mounted charge with mounted charge, saber stroke with saber stroke. With numbers slightly inferior to his adversary's, perhaps 3,000 engaged out of 5,000 against 5,000 of 6,000–7,000, Gregg repulsed Stuart to protect the Union rear.[39]

On the main battlefield there was a lull from the close of the morning's Culp's Hill fighting through about the next two hours, while the Confederates completed the emplacing of some 160 guns for an artillery barrage to soften the way for the infantry attack, and the slightly fewer than 5,000 men of Pickett's Division and about 8,500 of Hill's Corps who were to make up the infantry assault formed up in sheltering woods on the reverse slope of Seminary Ridge. To the east, eighty guns took the available good positions in the shorter Union line to reply to the expected artillery and infantry attacks.

The Confederate artillery barrage began just after 1 P.M. and lasted almost two hours. Its thunder could be heard many miles away, perhaps even in Philadelphia, but it did relatively little harm to the Union's front-line defenders. The guns were firing high, and their shells generally exploded in the rear areas behind the crest of Cemetery Ridge, while the Union Second Corps infantry were behind low stone walls on the forward slope. Eventually Brigadier-General Henry J. Hunt, U.S.V., Meade's chief of artillery, ordered the Federal guns to cease firing, to conserve ammunition for repelling the infantry attack. General Hancock countermanded this order within his Second Corps, as was his prerogative, for the sake of the moral effect on his troops of the guns' firing. The cease-fire by many of the Federal cannon, however, persuaded Colonel Edward Porter Alexander, commanding the Artillery Reserve of Longstreet's Corps and in charge of the barrage, that if the infantry assault could succeed at any time, the time was now. He so informed Pickett. Asked by Pickett whether he should therefore charge, Longstreet gave a grudging nod of apparent assent.

The 13,500 Confederate attackers emerged from the woods where they had formed up, to be taken almost immediately under enemy artillery fire. The copse of trees near the Federal center had been the focus of Alexander's gunfire, and toward it Pickett's Division now marched, to do so executing a left oblique while maintaining paradeground precision under cannon fire. Thus they closed up on the right of Brigadier-General James Johnston Pettigrew's temporary command, Heth's Division, which also came on steadily in spite of its heavy losses on the first day. On Pettigrew's left, however, the small Second Brigade of Colonel (40th Virginia) John M. Brockenbrough, commanded this day for reasons unknown by Colonel (47th Virginia) Robert M. Mayo, and to its right Brigadier-General Joseph R. Davis's Fourth Brigade, inexperienced except for the July 1 battle and severely mauled then, were without the support they were supposed to have from Pender's Division, now commanded by Major-General Isaac Ridgeway Trimble. Through an unexplained error, the two brigades of that formation had lined up not *en échelon* behind Pettigrew's left as Longstreet intended but behind Pettigrew's right. Raked by Federal shells, Mayo's and Davis's troops soon began to waver. Such Federal cannonading of both left and right caused the Confederates still more to bunch up toward the copse.

The Confederates climbed the fences bordering the Emmitsburg Road, and Union guns changed their ammunition from shell to case shot, antipersonnel charges that on bursting propelled a hail of deadly pellets into the rebel ranks. Union infantry added their musketry fire. The Confederates nevertheless paused to dress their lines on the east side of the Emmitsburg Road. Then they charged the last few hundred feet on the double. A compressed spearhead of Pickett's Division penetrated the Second Corps front into a westward-jutting angle of the protective stone walls just north of the clump of trees — henceforth the Bloody Angle. The 26th North Carolina of the First Brigade (Pettigrew's) of Heth's Division pushed somewhat farther eastward to reach the stone wall north of the Angle. So probably did others from Hill's Corps.

But Federal reinforcements also converged on the copse and the Angle, while to the north and the south Federal infantry emerged from the main line to assail the Confederate flanks. At most it was a few hundred Confederates who achieved the penetration of the Angle. Their tide receded from what the North soon came to call the High Water Mark of the Rebellion. The casualties of the charge numbered nearly two-thirds of the participants.

## GETTYSBURG: THE ASSESSMENT

Overall, Confederate casualties in the three days' fighting amounted to 28,063: 3,903 killed, 18,735 wounded, 5,425 missing. With more than a third of his army *hors de combat*, Lee could not resume his attacks. As he had done along the Antietam, he held his position long enough the next day to express his defiance, this time waiting until about 1 P.M. to begin his main withdrawal, although he had called Ewell back to Seminary Ridge and Longstreet away from the Devil's Den on the evening of July 3. For Meade to have attacked him, of course, would still have been for the Federals to risk Pickett's Charge in reverse. In a rainstorm, the Army of Northern Virginia began plodding toward the Potomac on the afternoon of the 4th of July, the downpour growing more torrential with the passing miles.

As usual, the victor's casualties were too high to permit the desired pursuit, although in President Lincoln's judgment Meade was to forfeit much of the luster he had won on the battlefield by failing to harass Lee to destruction. It was as unfair an assessment as Lincoln ever made. The Army of the Potomac lost 3,155 killed, 14,529 wounded, and 5,365 missing, a total of 23,049.[40] Moreover, its command structure was shattered; and because a pursuit is an offensive action and one likely to demand rapid and even intricate maneuver under adverse circumstances, it requires more from commanders even than a fighting retreat, one of the most difficult activities in war. Three of Meade's seven infantry corps were without the commanders who had begun the battle: the First, minus Reynolds; the Second, minus Hancock, because he went down badly wounded in the groin during Pickett's Charge; and the Third, without Sickles. Meade needed time to reorganize his army.

Meade's conduct of the pursuit not only detracted from his credit for the Gettysburg victory, especially with Lincoln, but also helped prevent him from rising to the highest circle among Civil War commanders in public esteem and historical stature afterward. That second circumstance is also unfair, because in the battle Meade had thoroughly outgeneraled Lee. Lee's failure to obtain the actions he expected of them from Stuart, Ewell, and Longstreet could serve as an object lesson in how not to command an army and how not to deal with subordinates. Meade in contrast put the right subordinate in the right place with the right understanding of his mission throughout the battle, with almost uncanny consistency.

The only exception was his handling of the unruly Sickles and his odd neglect of Sickles's sector, the left flank, through much of July 2. Otherwise the positive record includes Reynolds's presence when the battle began, to choose and defend the Gettysburg hills and ridges for the showdown with Lee, because Meade had chosen Reynolds to command the infantry reaching out closest to the Confederates as battle grew imminent (with Reynolds actually commanding the Left Wing of the army, including the Eleventh and Third Corps as well as his own First Corps). It includes Meade's dispatch of Hancock to hold the hills and ridges after Reynolds had reported on them but then died. It includes the dispatch of Warren to Little Round Top and the availability of Sykes's Fifth Corps at the foot of the hill to provide Warren with the troops he needed to hold it. The record includes sending the dependable Hancock to restore order from the chaos on the left during Longstreet's assault of July 2. There is also good reason to assume that, foreseeing Lee's attack against the Federal center on the third day, Meade would have made other arrangements had not Hancock already commanded there. While thus deftly handling his subordinates, Meade also saw to the shifting of his troops from one threatened portion of the field to another with virtuoso timing.

George Gordon Meade was by no means the equal of Robert Edward Lee in overall capacity as a military commander. He was never to show a comprehensive grasp of strategy. While Lee himself displayed only occasional grasping of the operational art, Meade was never to do that much. In tactics, Meade never approached anything resembling the Napoleonic qualities of Lee at Second Manassas and Chancellorsville. At Gettysburg, nevertheless, Meade not only chose the right subordinates at the right times with nearly unerring consistency. He himself was the right general for the battle that Lee's strategy dictated must be if not the climactic battle of the entire war, then at least a principal competitor for that distinction.

For all that, Confederate defeat at Gettysburg was also the logical outcome of Lee's own generalship. Because Lee believed that the Confederacy must invoke the strategic offensive notwithstanding a defensive national policy, he led the Army of Northern Virginia into Pennsylvania under conditions such that it had no choice but to fight a battle there, and such that it was likely to lose the battle if the enemy produced reasonably competent generalship. On July 2 Lee had to attack — but to attack under the limiting conditions imposed by the geography of the field and the geography of the rival army's lines of communications was to court defeat.

Beyond the immediate fatal conditions of Lee's fighting at Gettysburg there lay the larger flaws in his strategic conceptions. A strategy that required Napoleonic victories on the battlefield was a most dubious strategy for the Confederacy, in spite of Lee's capacity to deliver sometimes tactical triumphs worthy of the great Emperor. Such a strategy was dubious because to win Austerlitz or Jena-Auerstädt triumphs that shattered enemy armies, even Napoleon had to pay the price of huge casualties in his own army to impose crippling losses upon the enemy. The Confederacy did not have Napoleon's reserves of manpower (and in the end, the toll of casualties he extracted from his own forces had ruined Napoleon himself). Lee had lost nearly one-fourth of his army in the Seven Days, 18,852 of 85,500; nearly 20 percent of his army at Second Manassas, 9,197 of 48,527; 13,724 of 51,844 at Antietam; 12,764 of 57,352 at Chancellorsville.[41] And now at Gettysburg the toll was 28,000.

The Army of Northern Virginia could not bear this succession of costly battles. The Confederacy, already overmobilized at the beginning of 1863, lacked the manpower to fill its depleted ranks. By 1864, Lee was to discover that his army had lost the power to conduct effective offensive maneuver; but it was his own expensive mode of war that did most to bring it to that plight. The great Southern military historian Douglas Southall Freeman said of his study in command, *Lee's Lieutenants*: "The connecting thread of this book well might be that of the effort to create and to maintain competent senior officers."[42] In the end, the Army of Northern Virginia was crippled because Lee could not obtain them; but the excessive battlefield attrition among his competent lieutenants was another product of Lee's own mode of war.

On the other hand, if not Lee's strategy, then what strategy could have won for the Confederacy? Criticism of Lee should not evade the painfulness of his and the Confederacy's strategic dilemma, that a defensive strategy was all too likely to multiply the advantages of the Union by allowing it to concentrate men and matériel at places of its choosing, and that consequently to stand on the defensive was even less promising than Lee's offensive strategy. The Confederacy lacked strategic options. Moreover, Lee was so deadly an opponent on the tactical level that he merits his place in the pantheon of great generals whatever his flaws.

When Lee retreated from Gettysburg to the Potomac, he did so with such tactical skill that he gave Meade no opening for any but a frontal assault upon him. Meade was a decidedly cautious commander, perhaps too cautious; perhaps Lee's army had suffered so badly that a reconnaissance in force against its defensive perimeter when it stood around Williamsport and Falling Waters on the Maryland shore of the Potomac on July 13 might have been developed into a successful attack. Yet the whole history of Civil War frontal attacks offers no good reason to think so. Cautious though he was, Meade nevertheless planned an attack for the following day, July 14 (and he had had nothing in particular to gain from one day's postponement). On the night of July 13–14, however, Lee retreated across the river, and the Gettysburg campaign ended.

## VICKSBURG: PREPARATIONS

Lee gave the Confederacy in the Eastern theater of war a consistent strategy even if an expensive one. Lee had a design for winning the war that might have worked, if only he had triumphed at Gettysburg. In the West, the Confederacy suffered from a worse handicap than a possibly mistaken strategy.

It had no consistent strategy at all, no design to which it adhered for winning the war. General Albert Sidney Johnston began the Western Confederate war with a defensive strategy more passive than even the defensive-minded Confederate President would have employed, and Johnston passively allowed the Union to reconquer the better part of Tennessee in the Fort Henry–Fort Donelson campaign. Stung by this setback, Johnston then reverted to a Napoleonic effort to destroy the enemy army in an Austerlitz battle: the Shiloh campaign. Strained by the casualties of Shiloh, the Western Confederate armies returned to a passive defensive against Halleck's Corinth campaign. With Corinth lost and the Memphis and Charleston Railroad broken, the Confederacy again sought to recoup its disasters with an offensive stroke, Bragg's campaign into Kentucky coupled with the Van Dorn–Price assault upon Grant's and Rosecrans's troops around Corinth. This alternation between passive defense and convulsive attack afflicted the Western Confederacy with heavy battle casualties without the compensating advantage of curbing the enemy's inroads as Lee did.

The alternation between defense and attack in the West without consistent purpose was in part a product of the Confederacy's lack of unified command. Jefferson Davis, proud of his military education and his military exploits in the Mexican War, persisted in being an active Commander in Chief and refused to appoint a professional leader for all the Confederate armies. Confederate command tended to break down into command by a multiplicity of heads of geographical departments, the departmental boundaries often being drawn in such a way that they fragmented control of a single campaign.

President Davis of course had too many preoccupations to be able to correct such fragmentation, and without a professional chieftain overall, the Confederate war effort lacked as much unity as Scott, McClellan, and Halleck as Generals-in-Chief were able to give to the Union war effort, in spite of the failings of the three Generals-in-Chief. Furthermore, after Albert Sidney Johnston's death and his successor, Beauregard's, departure from the West in June 1862 just after the loss of Corinth, the Confederacy lacked any semblance of a Western theater command to coordinate its defenses against multiple Union thrusts from Middle Tennessee, West Tennessee, and Missouri. The Union had also lost such a theater command when Halleck departed for Washington; but Halleck continued to offer the Union forces in the West at least a modicum of strategic coordination from the capital. The Confederate armies too often were coordinated nowhere, and as the weaker armies they were in more need of coordination to hold Chattanooga, Vicksburg, and the area between those cities and on westward.

In the autumn of 1862 Confederate Secretary of War George W. Randolph concluded that the Confederacy had to give more attention to the defense of its West, and that coordination of the armies from the Appalachians to Arkansas was an essential first step. Believing he had persuaded President Davis of the need for such coordination, Randolph ordered Lieutenant-General Theophilus Hunter Holmes of the Trans-Mississippi Department to bring his army east of the Mississippi to cooperate in the defense of Vicksburg. When Davis learned of the order, however, he suspended its execution, objecting both that every department commander must remain in his own department, and that all appointments of department commanders and movements of troops among the departments must be authorized by the President. Randolph believed that this policy reduced the Secretary of War to an errand clerk for the President, and he resigned on November 15 to be succeeded six days later by Seddon.[43]

Randolph happened to have discovered the truth about Davis's perception of the office of Secretary of War, which explains why Davis now had to look for his fourth Secretary of War in less than two years. Remarkably, Seddon was to hold the office for more than two years to come. He managed to do so partly because he was an apparently unassertive semi-invalid, who managed through indirection. On the other hand, Seddon was no Leroy Pope Walker simply filling a chair. He was an able and experienced Virginia politician who had once had the ear and confidence of John C. Calhoun, and he had his own shrewd perception of how to get along with Davis and at the same time be more than a cipher, by being a good and patient listener and by insinuating his ideas quietly enough into Davis's discussions that the President could imagine the ideas were his own.[44]

Furthermore, Seddon shared Randolph's belief that to save itself the Confederacy must save the West — Lee could take care of the East — and that the first essential instrument must be a unified Western command. He began to demonstrate his remarkable qualities, moreover, not only by leading Davis to accept this principle, but by persuading him to appoint General Joseph E. Johnston as commander of a reconstituted Department of the West on November 24, 1862.[45] Davis required considerable persuading. Johnston was far enough recovered from his Seven Pines wound to be able to accept another command; but he and the President, excessively touchy and sensitive men, had quarreled increasingly from First Manassas to Seven Pines, and during Johnston's long recuperation each had formed the fixed opinion that the other was in league with his enemies and intriguing against him.

There were limits to Seddon's ability to insinuate distasteful ideas into Davis's mind. Johnston opened his tenure of command by renewing the suggestion that Holmes's army be brought from the Trans-Mississippi to the defense of Vicksburg, by far the most vital object within Holmes's reach; but Davis again rejected the idea. The department commanders serving under Johnston continued, moreover, to receive orders direct from Richmond, so that no one knew the boundaries of Johnston's responsibilities, and his nominal subordinates tended to obey him only as much as they chose to do. When Davis made a personal swing through the West in December, he reinforced the Vicksburg defenders not from Holmes's forces close by but from Bragg's distant army in Middle Tennessee, which not only strained the Confederate rail transport system unnecessarily but deprived Bragg of Major-General Carter Littlepage Stevenson's strong Division. The division arrived on the Mississippi too late to help stop Grant's and Sherman's December thrusts against Vicksburg, while it might have been of decisive assistance to Bragg in the closely fought battle of Murfreesboro.[46]

The transfer of Stevenson's Division exasperated Johnston, for it emphasized the problems of distance in his command, already a source of severe anxiety. Good as the idea of the Western geographical command was in principle, it was also true, as Johnston pointed out, that the Vicksburg "troops are farther from Bragg's than Lee's are. It takes about six days now to come from Jackson [Mississippi] to Chattanooga, four from Richmond. But to move troops, so long a time is required that any emergency for which they might be needed would certainly have passed long before their arrival."[47] Distances so magnificent, perhaps combined with a lingering debilitation from his old wound, unstrung Johnston so badly that, along with Davis's persisting interference, the effect was to render his new command almost a nullity. He continued to harp on the desirability of reinforcing Vicksburg from Holmes's department (which, it might be added in Davis's defense, would have amounted to abandoning Arkansas immediately instead of perhaps only after Vicksburg might fall); but he did little of practical value as Grant prepared to test again the Confederate citadel on the Mississippi.[48]

Vicksburg in Confederate hands closed the Mississippi River to any Union navigation except occasional dashes by naval vessels past the batteries on the Vicksburg bluffs, and it retained for the Confederacy a valuable if tenuous contact with the Trans-Mississippi, whence the grain and cattle of the Confederate Far West and war supplies smuggled in through Mexico and Texas could be transshipped eastward. Shielded on the north by Vicksburg's batteries high on the hills above the Yazoo River as well as the Mississippi, in the winter of 1862–1863 the stretch of the Mississippi that was still Confederate received protection toward the south through the construction of fortifications at Port Hudson, Louisiana. The latter defenses were strong enough that when in the spring General Banks, since October 27 Butler's successor commanding the Department of the Gulf, tried to move upriver from New Orleans to cooperate with Grant, he was stopped short by them.[49] Between Vicksburg and Port Hudson, and especially at Natchez, goods and communications between the Trans-Mississippi and the rest of the Confederacy still moved relatively freely.

From the beginning of the war, Northern strategists had nourished a design to recapture the Mississippi River through its whole length with the aid of naval power and thus to begin carving up the Confederacy into separated slices. As long as this design was not accomplished, Vicksburg's blockage of navigation up and down the Mississippi exerted psychological pressure upon the Northwest still greater than its real importance warranted. The people and even the business communities of the Northwestern states had not yet altogether digested the fact that the railroads completed from the East Coast to Chicago and the Mississippi during the 1850s now constituted their principal commercial avenues to the world. With the Mississippi blocked, they felt deprived of their rightful commercial outlet. The belief that the Northwest could not endure indefinitely a suspension of its traffic through New Orleans to the Gulf had much to do with the various schemes for a Northwestern confederacy seeking its own terms with the Southern Confederacy, independent of the Northeast, which were frequently bruited about by Peace Democrats.[50] The discontent of the Northwest with nearly two years of impeded navigation on the Great River had much to do also with the readiness of Lincoln and Stanton to cater to the large ambitions of Major-General John A. McClernand, U.S.V.

McClernand was a political general who had not demonstrated any particular strategic or tactical talents, but he was also a Kentucky native now resident in Illinois, an old Jacksonian legislator and Congressman — the leading Democratic contender in the prolonged 1860 contest to be Speaker of the House — who might be able to do much to keep his fellow Illinois Democrats in harness with the administration and the war effort. At the opening of the war he had been a successful recruiter, which further helped explain the stars on his shoulders, and during the summer and fall of 1862 he was roaming Washington trying to find support for a plan whereby he would take to the recruiting circuit in the Northwest again, raise a new army, and with no fewer than 60,000 men and a fleet of river gunboats strike down the Mississippi to capture Vicksburg and restore to the Northwest its traditional outlet to the sea.

On October 21, Stanton gave McClernand an order to organize the troops remaining in Indiana, Illinois, and Iowa plus such as might be raised by volunteering or draft, and when they exceeded in number the requirements of Grant's command, to lead them himself against Vicksburg. The only major qualification Stanton attached to McClernand's powers was that "[t]he forces so organized will remain subject to the designation of the general-in-chief, and be employed according to such exigencies as the service may in his judgment require." Lincoln attached to the order an endorsement affirming his deep interest in the project and stating that although the order was marked confidential, it might be shown by McClernand to governors and others whose assistance he might require.[51]

Grant soon heard rumors about McClernand's activities and authority. On November 10 he telegraphed Halleck: "Am I to understand that I lie here [at La Grange, Tennessee] while an expedition is fitted out from Memphis, or do you want me to push as far south as possible? Am I to have Sherman move subject to my orders, or are he and his forces reserved for some special service?"[52] Whatever his differences with Grant, Halleck preferred professional officers to nonprofessionals; he did not like the McClernand affair, and he replied to Grant: "You have command of all troops in your department, and have permission to fight the enemy where you please."[53] Nevertheless, little more than a month later, on December 18, Halleck was obliged to send Grant another telegram with somewhat different significance, stating that the troops in Grant's department would henceforth be organized into four corps, and that "It is the wish of the President that General McClernand's corps shall constitute a part of the river expedition and that he shall have the immediate command under your direction."[54] Although Halleck saw to it that Grant retained his department, McClernand apparently would be the direct commander of a Vicksburg expedition.

Halleck was in no hurry to send this latest interpretation of the Western command arrangements to McClernand and hasten him to the field of campaign from his activities recruiting and mustering in troops at Springfield, Illinois. The Grant and Sherman expeditions of December 1862 got under way before McClernand could act on the latest directive. (McClernand was in fact doing much more mustering in and shipping forward than recruiting; there is no evidence that he raised substantial numbers of new troops.) When Sherman failed to break open the door to Vicksburg through Chickasaw Bayou, however, McClernand joined him on the Yazoo to take command of his force and transform it into the Army of the Mississippi, with McClernand as commanding general and Sherman one of two corps commanders under him (leading the army's Second Corps; its First Corps was under Brigadier-General George W. Morgan, U.S.V., hitherto commander of Sherman's Third Division).[55] Unfortunately for McClernand, Sherman's method of trying to reach Vicksburg by climbing out of the bayou from the Yazoo was the very method he himself had had in mind. The attempt having failed, McClernand turned his army away to seek easier success by attacking Fort Hindman, a Confederate defensive work at Arkansas Post some fifty miles up the Arkansas River from the Mississippi.

This expedition produced an ironic dénouement. On January 11, 1863 a combined attack by McClernand's troops and Commander and Acting Rear-Admiral David Dixon Porter's gunboats won the anticipated easily obtained surrender of Arkansas Post. The expedition had the prior approval, however, neither of the War Department nor of General Grant. When Grant heard of it he quickly ordered McClernand to return to the real business at hand, the reduction of Vicksburg, and complained to Halleck that McClernand had "gone on a wild-goose chase to the Post of Arkansas."[56] This dispatch gave Halleck a club with which to hit McClernand as he had wanted to do all along.

Halleck was able to secure Lincoln's and Stanton's assent to his telegraphing Grant: "You are hereby authorized to relieve General McClernand from command of the expedition against Vicksburg, giving it to the next in rank or taking it yourself."[57] By going off "on a wild-goose chase," McClernand had undercut the President's ability to protect him from the professional soldiers. What no one outside the Arkansas Post expedition knew was that the idea for the chase had originated not with McClernand but with Grant's friend General Sherman, who thought that gaining control of the lower Arkansas River would help protect the rear of future Vicksburg operations against Confederate forays from the Trans-Mississippi. When Grant learned of Sherman's authorship, he changed his mind about the wisdom of the expedition; but by then the damage to McClernand was done.

The beneficial result of all this maneuvering for prestige and power was to hasten Grant himself downriver from Memphis, thinking that only by taking personal command of Vicksburg operations could he be sure that McClernand was pushed aside. Under Halleck's order of December 18, McClernand still challenged Grant's authority to issue orders directly to any corps commander except himself; but Grant now had the War Department behind him, and from January 31 McClernand had to subside into the role of commander of the Thirteenth Army Corps in Grant's Army of the Tennessee.[58]

Sherman was inclined to doubt that a feasible approach to Vicksburg's high bluffs could be found from the level of the Mississippi, and to believe that the army should return to Memphis to try another, but stronger, push down the Mississippi Central Railroad, which Grant had attempted to travel in December. But Grant sensed that the ferment of Northwestern discontent which accounted for Lincoln's tolerance of McClernand forbade his risking the psychological impact of a long retreat to Memphis after his troops had reached the mouth of the Yazoo. Grant would try to find a route into Vicksburg from the Yazoo or the Mississippi.

The Confederates had obstructed the Yazoo to prevent Union boats from navigating upriver far enough to turn the flank of the Chickasaw Bayou–Walnut Hills defenses. Still further to limit possible approaches to Vicksburg, the flooded mouth of the Yazoo was merely the southernmost part of a vast network of wooded swamps and bayous that laced the Mississippi delta country through all the 250 miles back to Grant's base at Memphis. A Federal attack on Vicksburg not only had to overcome the stout defenses of the city's surrounding hills; when Grant took command to push the advance against Vicksburg at the beginning of 1863, it seemed more than the Federals could do even to reach dry ground from which to mount an attack — except by means of the politically and psychologically unacceptable retreat to Memphis before trying again the long, vulnerable railroad route through the interior of the State of Mississippi.

The railroad route would lead eventually to a platform of dry ground east of Vicksburg from which the city might be attacked; but was there a way to reach that platform without retreating to Memphis and offering Confederate cavalry raiders the target of a delicate line of communications along the railroad? Grant's first efforts concentrated on finding a way either to bypass the city and land troops on the east shore of the Mississippi south of it, or to get into the Yazoo above the obstructions in order to turn the defenses on Chickasaw Bayou and the Walnut Hills. Toward the first of these two possible routes of advance, he launched three projects; toward the second, two.

First, he reopened an effort of the previous year to dig a canal across the base of the big northward-pointing loop of the Mississippi on which Vicksburg stood, thus opening a channel of navigation that would bypass the city and permit the Navy's gunboats and transports to sail safely to the south of it, whence they could ferry troops to a dry area of the east bank. Unfortunately, the earlier canal-digging efforts had revealed a clay soil that would not wash in such a way that the river itself would deepen an artificial channel and render it navigable. Grant's renewed attempts simply accumulated additional proof that a bypass canal was a more formidable project than available time and resources permitted. Similarly, a more lengthy canal from Duckport on the Louisiana shore nearly opposite the mouth of the Yazoo into bayou systems reaching below Vicksburg failed to sustain a water level deep enough for navigation.

Also, Grant tried by still further digging to open a water route from the Mississippi just south of the Arkansas-Louisiana border into an oxbow lake, Lake Providence, and thence into a series of bayous that eventually led into the Red River far to the south and thence back into the Mississippi. Here heavy late winter rains so flooded the bayous that there were not enough footholds to permit trees to be cleared away to open navigable channels.

East of the Mississippi, yet more digging opened a water route from the big river into another oxbow lake, Moon Lake, and thence via Yazoo Pass into the Coldwater River, which entered the Tallahatchie, which in turn entered the Yazoo and might permit the gunboats and transports to land troops on dry ground beyond the right flank of the Chickasaw Bayou defenses. But as usual, there was a crippling obstacle: in this instance, a sharp bend where the Coldwater turned to enter the Tallahatchie; here the Confederates built a battery strong enough to turn back the Union Navy's advance.

A similar effort to enter the Yazoo above the right flank of the Vicksburg defenses by way of Steele's Bayou, Black Bayou, Deer Creek, Rolling Fork, and the Sunflower River failed when the Confederates rushed troops to pepper with fire Union ships that were already contending against overhanging trees and destructive limbs in an excessively narrow waterway.

Added to Grant's failure to reach Vicksburg by the rail line in December and Sherman's repulse at Chickasaw Bayou, these five efforts made a record of seven failures on the way to Vicksburg. It is little wonder that patience ran short both in the headquarters of Grant's army and at Washington, that rumors of Grant's drinking began to circulate again, and that the War Department sent out Assistant Secretary Charles A. Dana as Stanton's special observer and Adjutant General Lorenzo Thomas to keep an eye on Grant and report on his competence. Fortunately for Grant and the Union, however, they arrived not long before Grant transformed the Vicksburg campaign from a fiasco into one of the masterpieces of military history.

## VICKSBURG: GRANT'S GREAT CAMPAIGN OF MANEUVER WARFARE

It is not clear how much Grant had expected from his various bypassing projects. They kept his army busy and therefore healthy through the winter, and there was always a chance that one of them might pay off. When spring brought back reasonably reliable campaigning weather, Grant resorted to bolder means.

He persuaded Admiral Porter to try to run past the Vicksburg batteries with enough vessels to guard and ferry the army across the Mississippi south of the city. On the night of April 16 twelve vessels, including seven gunboats, went downriver with their boilers protected by bales of cotton and hay. The Confederate guns erupted, and the rebels also lighted large fires on the west bank to illuminate the passing ships. All the vessels were badly hit, but only the transport *Henry Clay* failed to get through. On the night of April 22, six transports towing twelve barges tried the run, protected like their predecessors and manned for the most part by volunteer crews from the Army. Half of the barges were lost, but the rest of the flotilla reached Porter downstream.

To sow confusion, on April 17 Grant had sent Colonel Benjamin H. Grierson, 6th Illinois Cavalry, south into the interior of Mississippi from La Grange with some 1,700 cavalry and light artillery. Grierson's raid eventually covered 600 miles in sixteen days, reaching Banks's forces at Baton Rouge on May 2, losing only three killed, seven wounded, and five left behind sick on the way despite many skirmishes (although Grierson early culled out and sent back about 175 men he thought could not survive the pace). The raid also thoroughly achieved its objective of diverting Confederate attention.[59]

Meanwhile Sherman's Fifteenth Corps resumed moving against the defenses on the hills north of Vicksburg. Both Grierson and Sherman provided feints while McClernand with the Thirteenth Corps and James B. McPherson (since October 8 brigadier-general, U.S.V.)[60] with the Seventeenth Corps moved down the west bank of the Mississippi to meet Porter. At dawn on April 30, Porter's vessels ferried the vanguard of McClernand's corps across the river to Bruinsburg, the desired dry ground on the east bank. "When this was effected," said Grant, "I felt a degree of relief scarcely ever equalled since. . . . I was on dry ground on the same side of the river with the enemy. All the campaigns, labors, hardships and exposures from the month of December previous to this time that had been made and endured, were for the accomplishment of this one object."[61] So far so good; but a still more demanding duel of generalship remained ahead.

Porter had bombarded in vain the defenses at Grand Gulf, nearly ten miles north of Bruinsburg, where Grant had wanted to cross; but the landing at Bruinsburg was unopposed. McClernand's advance pushed north toward Port Gibson, near which it collided on May 1 with Brigadier-General John S. Bowen's Confederate troops from Grand Gulf. The Federals brought up superior numbers and drove Bowen from Port Gibson, whereupon the Confederate commander at Vicksburg decided to abandon Grand Gulf and draw back Bowen's force lest it be cut off from the main body of Vicksburg's defenders.

Since October 13, 1862 the Confederate commander at Vicksburg had been Lieutenant-General John C. Pemberton,[62] a West Pointer from Philadelphia but married to Martha Thompson of Old Point Comfort, Virginia; he had decided he could not invade his wife's native state.[63] Although his command constituted the Department of Mississippi, Tennessee, and East Louisiana, Pemberton believed that the defense of Vicksburg was his most important responsibility, and that he must so deploy his forces that the shielding of the city would be assured. This conviction was to shape his whole conduct of the campaign. On May 1, Joe Johnston telegraphed Pemberton: "If Grant's army lands on this side of the river, the safety of Mississippi depends on beating it. For that object you should unite your whole force."[64] But Pemberton thought that to have united his army and marched it against Grant "would have stripped Vicksburg and its essential flank defenses of their garrisons, and the city itself might have fallen an easy prey into the eager hands of the enemy."[65] The effect was to give Grant the opportunity to defeat the Confederates in detail.

Once McClernand's and McPherson's corps were safely across the Mississippi, Grant brought Sherman's corps down, for a total force of some 45,000 men. Pemberton had about 50,000.[66] Grant initially intended to base himself at Grand Gulf, send some of his troops to help Banks at Port Hudson, and after taking Port Hudson return reinforced by Banks to attack Vicksburg. He now learned that most of Banks's mobile force was west of the Mississippi and not yet ready to operate against Port Hudson, and that by moving to Port Hudson he would give the Confederates a respite in which to accumulate more men around Vicksburg, while he himself would eventually receive only 12,000 additional troops from Banks.[67] Knowing that reinforcements for Pemberton were being assembled at Jackson, the Mississippi capital forty-five miles east of Vicksburg, Grant accordingly decided to strike inland to get between Pemberton and his reinforcements, and then to use his resultant interior lines to defeat first one Confederate force and then the other. To do so he would have to cut loose from his base on the Mississippi:

> It was necessary to have transportation for ammunition [he said]. Provisions could be taken from the country; but all the ammunition that can be carried on the person is soon exhausted when there is much fighting. I directed, therefore, immediately on landing that all the vehicles and draft animals, whether horses, mules or oxen, in the vicinity should be collected and loaded to their capacity with ammunition. Quite a train was collected during the 30th, and a motley train it was. In it could be found fine carriages, loaded nearly to the top with boxes of cartridges that had been pitched in promiscuously, drawn by mules with plough-harness, straw collars, rope-lines, etc.; long-

coupled wagons, with racks for carrying cotton bales, drawn by oxen, and everything that could be found in the way of transportation on a plantation, either for use or pleasure. The making out of provision returns was stopped for a time. No formalities were to retard our progress until a position was secured when the time could be spared to observe them.[68]

McPherson led the van — the thirty-five-year-old military engineer who had proven too good a troop leader to be kept on the staff as Grant's chief engineer. On May 12 McPherson spent much of the day fighting and driving back Brigadier-General John Gregg's Brigade at Raymond, part of the Jackson force. The next evening Joe Johnston arrived in Jackson, ordered by Richmond to take personal command of the efforts to save Vicksburg though he protested that his health still made him unfit for field service. When he learned that Grant's army was pushing through Raymond and on toward Jackson, already between him and Pemberton, Johnston wired Richmond: "I am too late."[69] Nevertheless, he sent a dispatch to Pemberton ordering him to fall on Grant's rear if he could.

Johnston found only about 12,000 troops at Jackson,[70] with which he tried to hold Grant at bay on May 14 long enough to evacuate supplies northward toward a point whence he might link up with Pemberton. After a day of fighting in a heavy rain, McPherson and Sherman broke into Jackson in late afternoon, in time to capture thirty-five guns and much equipment. Meanwhile Grant had intercepted a copy of Johnston's dispatch telling Pemberton to fall on his rear, so the next morning Grant quickly turned his men back westward to deal with Pemberton's Army of Vicksburg. Pemberton, still believing his first duty must be to shield Vicksburg, had declined to obey Johnston's order lest he expose the city. Instead he spent the 14th probing for Grant's line of communications with the Mississippi, which unfortunately for the Confederates was a line that did not exist. Thus Pemberton marched southeastward while Johnston was retreating northward from Jackson, and the Confederate forces became further separated. On the morning of the 15th, new and peremptory orders from Johnston caused Pemberton to countermarch, but he had not gone far before he struck Grant's troops at a crescent-shaped ridge called Champion's Hill.

The battle of Champion's Hill was the most severe of the campaign. McClernand failed to attack the Confederate south flank aggressively, and therefore Pemberton was able to concentrate against McPherson on the opposite flank and put up a stout battle for the hill. But Pemberton's obsession with leaving troops in Vicksburg and on all the approaches gave Grant the advantage of numbers, and the Federals eventually carried Champion's Hill and cut off Major-General William W. Loring's Division from Pemberton's main body. On May 17 trying to hold a crossing for this division exposed part of the Army of Vicksburg to another defeat at the Big Black River.

The Confederates did succeed in destroying the bridges over the Big Black in the face of the Union advance, but this achievement did not delay the Federals long. All three of Grant's corps were crossing the river by fording it by the morning of the 18th, and that morning Sherman on the right reached a road that would lead him to the Yazoo between Vicksburg and the forts that had defied him in December. Pemberton's army retreated into another ring of forts that had been seven months in preparation around the circumference of the city. Johnston believed Vicksburg was doomed, and characteristically he sent Pemberton a dispatch on the 17th saying that "instead of losing both troops and place, we must, if possible, save the troops. If it is not too late, evacuate Vicksburg and its dependencies and march to the northeast."[71] Just as characteristically, when he received this message on the 18th Pemberton did not attempt to exploit the possible remaining routes out of town.

The terrain around Vicksburg had been greatly to the advantage of Pemberton's engineers when they built the city's final defenses, for the loess soil of the area possesses great tenacity except when eroded by running water, and consequently the watercourses had formed the loess into thin, twisting ridges with abrupt faces, separated by deep ravines. The Army of Vicksburg moved into entrenchments along one such ridge system, with nine strong points in the line commanding every negotiable approach. On the 19th Grant's army closed in to take position on a parallel ridge system several hundred yards away, meanwhile making contact with Porter's vessels on the Yazoo to establish a new base of supply.

With Johnston roaming the countryside behind him and gathering reinforcements, Grant wanted to seize Vicksburg quickly, and he ordered an assault for two o'clock in the afternoon. When the strong defenses turned the assault back, he ordered another one, more thoroughly prepared, for May 22. This one also failed, though at several places the Union soldiers planted their flags on the Confederate parapets, and McClernand's corps for a moment breached Pemberton's line. When McClernand exaggerated his success and misled Grant into renewing the attack, and then some time later issued a bombastic order to his corps claiming most of the credit for the campaign, Grant at last replaced him with General Ord on June 19 and sent him back to Illinois. His own accomplishments had made Grant invulnerable to McClernand's inevitable protests to Lincoln.

Grant had to settle down to a siege. The War Department sent him men and supplies from all over the West, including the Ninth Corps, since June 5 commanded by Major-General John G. Parke, from as far away as the Department of the Ohio. Eventually Grant mounted 220 guns to deny the Vicksburg garrison security and sleep. His ranks swelled to 71,000, enough to face some of them eastward to hold off Johnston.[72] His soldiers labored under the early-summer Mississippi sun to press closer upon Vicksburg, digging increasingly elaborate entrenchments and shelter caves and ten major approaches toward the Confederate lines.

Still, Johnston persisted in gathering reinforcements to the east, and reports came in describing Confederate efforts toward a major attack on Union holdings west of the Mississippi in Arkansas and Louisiana. Under pressure from Halleck both out of concern over Johnston's activities and because much of the West had been stripped of troops to reinforce the Army of the Tennessee, Grant planned another assault for July 6.

In the city, however, Pemberton had to fend off not only Grant's army but also starvation. On July 1 the Confederate commander asked his lieutenants whether their army should attempt to fight its way out. They replied that the physical condition of the men would not permit it. On July 3, Pemberton met Grant under a flag of truce between the lines and arranged the surrender of his troops and the city. On July 4, the Confederate defenders marched out to stack their arms, 2,166 officers, 27,230 enlisted men, and 115 civilian employees, with 172 pieces of artillery and between 50,000 and 60,000 muskets and rifles.[73] Rather than strain Federal transport capacities, except for 709 Confederates who preferred to go north as prisoners Grant paroled the rebels, not to fight again until exchanged.[74] This arrangement proved not only to save the Federal government expense but to spread discouragement wherever in the South the men roamed.

In its climactic phases, from Porter's running past the Confederate batteries on April 19, Grant's Vicksburg campaign was one of the most admirably conducted in world military history. It signaled Grant's emergence as the most capable general of the Northern armies and laid the foundation for his eventual ranking as probably the most capable general of the war.

The campaign is especially noteworthy because in it Grant demonstrated his exceptional talent as a general of maneuver warfare. Later in the war he would have to fight in such a fashion that he was to come to be unfairly categorized as a butcher, a reckless spender of lives. His Vicksburg campaign should always be weighed against such charges. Following General Curtis's example set in the closing part of the Pea Ridge campaign, Grant broke free from his own communications to confound those enemies who tried to break his supply lines. He marched rapidly, shifted direction deftly, hit hard when fighting became necessary, but achieved his objectives less through battle with its casualties than by deceptive maneuver. From the battle of Port Gibson on May 1 to the surrender of Vicksburg, Grant lost 9,362 casualties: 1,514 killed, 7,395 wounded, and 453 captured or missing, more than half of them at Champion's Hill. His losses were well short of the Federal casualties of the two-day battle of Shiloh or in the battle that was ending at Gettysburg just as Pemberton surrendered.[75]

Grant hurried news of the surrender of Vicksburg downriver to Port Hudson, where Union soldiers promptly shouted the word across the lines. Port Hudson had proven a tougher nut to crack than the Union in its somewhat offhanded approach to the place had anticipated. After commencing a siege on May 23, Banks mounted three unsuccessful assaults. In the first, on May 27, two of the regiments of free Louisiana African Americans, the 1st and 3rd Louisiana Native Guards, recruited originally for the Confederate government of Louisiana and then the objects of the controversy surrounding General Phelps when they tried to join the Union Army in New Orleans, assailed the Confederate fortifications with a conspicuous display of courage. (The date was just one day before the 54th Massachusetts paraded in Boston.) By the beginning of July, however, the Confederate garrison numbered only 5,500 men, and it could not hold on if part of Grant's force should join Banks. Major-General Franklin Gardner, commanding the garrison as part of what had been Pemberton's department, asked Banks to confirm the news from Vicksburg. After Banks did so, Gardner surrendered on July 8.[76] The fall of Port Hudson sealed the truth of Lincoln's observation that "The Father of Waters again goes unvexed to the sea."[77]

## THE TRANS-MISSISSIPPI

On July 4, while Vicksburg was surrendering, a Federal garrison at Helena, Arkansas, upriver from Vicksburg, repulsed an attack by General Holmes's troops of the District of Arkansas. Similarly, in the Confederate District of Western Louisiana, although the district commander, Major-General Richard Taylor — son of Zachary Taylor — added suspense to the siege of Port Hudson by means of threatening gestures in the direction of New Orleans, the rebels were unable to accomplish anything of consequence toward delaying the Union conquest of the entire length of the Mississippi River.

Since February 9, 1863, both Holmes and Taylor had been subordinates of Edmund Kirby Smith, promoted to lieutenant-general the previous October 9 as a reward for his part in the invasion of Kentucky, and now in charge of the overarching Trans-Mississippi Department; Holmes had been in this higher command until he pleaded ill health and resigned in favor of Smith, who had been in Richmond advising on Army reorganization.[78] Unfortunately for Smith and the Confederacy, Holmes's and Taylor's misfires were characteristic of the fate of the new Trans-Mississippi chieftain's strategic enterprises all through the war. Smith was a soldier of intelligence and character, but he was somehow wanting in the ingredients of successful generalship in the field.

While often frustrated in his military campaigns, however, Smith went on to a different kind of success after the fall of Vicksburg and Port Hudson substantially cut him off from the eastern Confederacy. Thereafter the demands of the war upon his strictly military talents were minimal: Union military efforts largely turned elsewhere; and while the Union's trans-Mississippi military strength to the north of him still looked as if it should be able to overwhelm him, this strength was held at arm's length by the cloud of Confederate irregulars who by now swarmed over Missouri and sometimes carried the war into Kansas. These worthies included tough, ruthless guerrillas such as Colonel William C. Quantrill, whose band burned, plundered, and killed citizens in Lawrence, Kansas on August 21, 1863.[79]

Behind the protective screen of the guerrillas, Smith developed a talent for governmental administration and economic and financial improvisation. Confiscating cotton in the name of the Confederate States of America, presently he had his agents in every conceivable channel trading cotton for commodities and military supplies with Yankees and rebels alike, trading through Mexico and through agents in the West Indies who in turn traded with Europe and the world. A thriving arsenal grew up at Tyler, Texas; a Confederate Medical Laboratory at Arkadelphia, Arkansas; and the Confederate Trans-Mississippi Department, "Kirbysmithdom," became a surprisingly viable and practically independent satrapy. It was destined to be the last outpost of Confederate power on land, holding on to existence briefly after everything else collapsed. But in its isolation and its independence, Kirbysmithdom did the rest of the Confederacy very little good.

## CHICKAMAUGA

In the short span of late spring and early summer, 1863, the war had taken a dramatic turn, from the Union's frustrations of the past winter and the hopes the Confederacy had nourished when Lee led the Army of Northern Virginia into Maryland and Pennsylvania. Before Vicksburg surrendered, Lincoln, Stanton, and Halleck were already looking beyond Gettysburg and Vicksburg toward Rosecrans's army centrally located between Grant and Meade. If Rosecrans could add to the triumphs of the East and West a successful march from Murfreesboro to Chattanooga, then the Confederacy, already split along the Mississippi, would be nearly split again. In addition, the long-coveted Unionist domain of East Tennessee would be ripe for Union reoccupation, the Union Army would stand poised to descend from the railroad center at Chattanooga upon the Confederacy's last remaining southeastern rail center at Atlanta, and the shape of final Union victory would become visible despite the disappointments of Meade's pursuit of Lee.

On January 9, 1863, the Federal Army of the Cumberland was reorganized into three infantry corps and a cavalry corps, with Rosecrans then promptly assembling a fourth infantry corps.[80] This brisk realignment immediately after Stones River might have seemed to herald a prompt follow-up to that battle, but in fact none occurred. For nearly six months thereafter, Rosecrans licked his army's wounds and complained that he lacked the necessary horses or weapons or accumulated provisions to resume his advance. His army had been badly injured at Stones River to be sure, but not enough to explain a paralysis persisting for half a year, especially when Bragg's rival and smaller Army of Tennessee had been damaged approximately as much.

Sometimes, as after Gettysburg, Lincoln and the War Department underestimated the shattering impact of a major battle and expected too much renewed action too soon; but Rosecrans's prolonged idleness approached the ridiculous. That adjective is used advisedly, because in the spring and summer, when Lincoln and Halleck were prodding him to do something for the sound reason that Bragg ought to be discouraged from sending reinforcements to Johnston for use against Grant, Rosecrans replied that he must do nothing until after the Vicksburg campaign was over, because military science forbade fighting two battles in one day![81]

The military scholar Henry Wager Halleck liked to quote maxims of war but not to have them quoted against him, and he was quick to inform Rosecrans that while it was true that there was a maxim against fighting two battles simultaneously, it applied to a single army and not to two separate armies such as Rosecrans's and Grant's. Furthermore, Halleck underlined that telegraphic lesson in the art of war dated June 12 with a wire of June 16 saying to Rosecrans: "Is it your intention to make an immediate movement forward? A definite answer, yes or no, is required."[82] Rosecrans responded: "In reply to your inquiry, if immediate means to-night or to-morrow, no. If it means as soon as things are ready, say five days, yes."[83] Thus prodded, on June 24 Rosecrans's army at last moved.

William Starke Rosecrans was one of the enigmas of the Civil War. As the War Department had gradually come to perceive, he had been the principal architect of victory in McClellan's western Virginia campaign of 1861, and he continued to give good service in holding and expanding Unionist West Virginia after McClellan departed from that theater. Dispatched to the West, he was the senior commander on the field at Iuka and Corinth in the autumn of 1862, though at Iuka his success was marred by his failure to put troops across the enemy's line of retreat when he could readily have done so. At Stones River he fought stubbornly but handled his troops clumsily. After his perplexing lassitude of six months following Stones River, he waged one of the most skillful campaigns of maneuver of the war, and by means of deceptive turning movements chivied Bragg out of the Duck River line around Tullahoma without a major battle and without serious casualties. By July 7, the Confederate Army of Tennessee had retreated before him all the way to Chattanooga.

Another interval to try Lincoln's and Halleck's patience unhappily followed, with Rosecrans resting his army along a line from Winchester to McMinnville, Tennessee, through July and into August, and beyond the apparent requirements following a not excessively strenuous campaign. On August 15, however, the admirable side of Rosecrans emerged again with his issuance of orders for another campaign of deceptive maneuver, designed to pry Bragg out of Chattanooga. Like the Tullahoma campaign before it, this one worked almost to perfection. Bragg was gulled by ostentatious Union movements along the Tennessee River above Chattanooga into thinking that Rosecrans intended to cross the river there. In fact the Army of the Cumberland crossed without opposition below the town and marched into northwest Georgia threatening Bragg's line of communications, the Western and Atlantic Railroad to Atlanta. On September 6, Bragg decided he must abandon Chattanooga, and troops from Rosecrans's left wing entered it three days later.

But Rosecrans never ceased to be inconsistent, and success nearly ruined him. The wide, rugged obstacle of Lookout Mountain stretches southwestward from just west of Chattanooga deep into Alabama, directly across Rosecrans's path toward the Western and Atlantic Railroad. To cross the mountain without undue congestion, Rosecrans split his army into three columns and moved forward with his flanks more than forty miles apart. He thought he could afford to do so because he imagined that Bragg was in full retreat. Instead, Bragg turned at bay at LaFayette, Georgia, to receive reinforcements, counterattack against Rosecrans's scattered columns, and defeat the Army of the Cumberland in detail.[84]

After Rosecrans began his advance against Chattanooga, Bragg had ordered Major-General Simon Bolivar Buckner to bring his corps from Knox-ville to join Bragg's army. In addition, Bragg received Major-Generals John C. Breckinridge's and William H. T. Walker's Divisions from Johnston in Mississippi. About September 9 Hood's and McLaws's Divisions of Long-street's Corps of the Army of Northern Virginia began leaving Orange Court House for a railroad trip to Bragg. When the Confederate government de-cided to send Longstreet with the bulk of his corps, the plan was to use the Virginia and Tennessee Railroad through Knoxville; but Buckner's with-drawal from that place prompted Burnside to move into it with troops from his Department of the Ohio. Consequently Longstreet's 6,390 men had to make a roundabout trip of some 900 miles through the Carolinas and Geor-gia, using sixteen different railroad lines, all in more or less decrepit condi-tion. Nevertheless, three of his brigades under Hood joined Bragg on Sep-tember 18, and Longstreet himself with two more brigades reached Catoosa Station, focus of a now-extinct Georgia village just behind Bragg's army, on the 19th.[85]

Like his opponent, Bragg was among the war's enigmas, alternating be-tween outstanding performances, such as his march around Buell's army into Kentucky the year before, and fumbling ones, such as his feeble con-duct of the same Kentucky campaign once Buell marched north to confront him. With Bragg, however, at least one of the causes of periodic failures can be specified: Bragg's irascible personality, which eventually antagonized everyone he dealt with (except, strangely, Jefferson Davis), from corps com-manders to the private soldiers of his army. Incompatible personalities prob-ably account for the otherwise incredible series of departures from Bragg's orders by his principal subordinates, the effect of which was to give away a glittering opportunity to defeat Rosecrans in detail among the craggy peaks and isolated coves of Lookout Mountain and its adjuncts.

Bragg's first target was to be Major-General, U.S.V., James S. Negley's Second Division of Thomas's Fourteenth Corps, while it lay alone in McLemore's Cove. He ordered against this single division the full weight of Lieutenant-General (since July 11, 1863) D. H. Hill's Corps plus Major-General Thomas C. Hindman's Division of Lieutenant-General (since Oc-tober 10, 1862) Polk's Corps. Hill inexplicably neglected to follow Bragg's instructions. An exasperated Bragg thereupon directed Buckner to join with Hindman against Negley, but instead Buckner and Hindman decided they had a better scheme than Bragg's for doing so, and they delayed in order to send it to the army commander rather than acting against the enemy. Predictably, by the time this military debating society had concluded its pro-ceedings, Negley was gone.

Two days thereafter, on September 12, Bragg discerned another opportunity, in the isolation of Major-General, U.S.V., Thomas L. Crittenden's Twenty-first Corps and its dispersal across some ten miles from Ringgold to Lee and Gordon's Mills. Bragg sent Polk's Corps and William H. T. Walker's Reserve Corps to crush Crittenden with superior numbers, but this time it was Polk who stalled, seeing chimeras, going over to the defensive, and requesting reinforcements. If Polk and the others had not detested Bragg but had cared to exert themselves on his behalf, probably none of the impediments to their acting would have put in an appearance. As it was, Rosecrans's careless overconfidence had been dissolved by his perceiving that Bragg had turned back to fight. The Federal commander thus hastened to call together his detachments, which he assembled along the West Branch of Chickamauga Creek from Lee and Gordon's Mills on his left through McLemore's Cove and thence to Stevens Gap in Lookout Mountain.

With at least two beckonings of fortune spurned, Bragg moved northward on the east side of the creek in the hope of crossing it north of Lee and Gordon's Mills and inserting himself between Rosecrans and Chattanooga, not only to rupture the Federal line of communications and recapture the city, but also to drive the Army of the Cumberland into a hopeless trap among the mountains. During September 18 most of Bragg's army, including Longstreet's three advanced brigades, crossed Chickamauga Creek in quest of those objects. Notwithstanding his summertime complaints about poor and insufficient horses, however, Rosecrans had some of the best-trained cavalry in the Union Army, and his mounted troops obstructed the rebel flanking maneuver, slowed it, and informed army headquarters. Rosecrans, thoroughly reawakened, promptly shifted the Fourteenth Corps northeastward to block the enemy maneuver altogether. By dawn of September 19 the rival armies confronted each other across the West Branch of Chickamauga Creek. The battle of Chickamauga opened early in the day when a reconnaissance from Thomas collided with troops of Nathan Bedford Forrest's Corps of cavalry.

The collision developed into a day-long struggle drawing in most of both armies. As was usual with head-on grappling, the result was a costly stalemate. The next morning Bragg could think of nothing better than to resume the unsubtle slugging match, though still with hopes of eventually working his way past the Federal left. The recent lost chances had apparently exhausted Bragg's supply of tactical ingenuity. Late in the morning of the 20th, however, confused orders from Rosecrans moved troops out of line and created a gap in the Federal right-center, in Crittenden's Twenty-first Corps front just to the right of Thomas's Fourteenth Corps. At this juncture Longstreet, commanding the five divisions of Bragg's Left Wing, departed from Bragg's routine of launching successive attacks by single divisions to hurl the concentrated strength of his entire wing at the Federals — sturdy Longstreet at his hard-hitting best. His assault chanced to strike the hole that had just opened; and although Rosecrans's rarely beaten, self-confident Midwesterners rallied to resist so stubbornly that Longstreet could not altogether recognize how opportune his timing had been, Federal cohesion had been too badly disrupted to prevent Longstreet in the end from shattering the Union right and sending about half the Army of the Cumberland fleeing for Chattanooga: much of the Twenty-first Corps, Major-General, U.S.V., Alexander McD. McCook's Twentieth Corps, and Rosecrans himself. Unable to stem the flight, unfortunate Old Rosy thought his whole army was being destroyed.

Yet another superb stroke of fortune had come Bragg's way. But his frustrations had driven him too deeply into his shell of surly gloom, and he closed his eyes to it. He convinced himself that his own Right Wing had been fought out by Chickamauga's two days' hard pounding, and from that wing he dispatched little help when Longstreet and the Left pressed on against the remaining nucleus of Federal resistance. Moreover, such a nucleus survived, for a Federal commander as sturdy and dependable as Longstreet rallied everyone who had not panicked into a strong, horseshoe-shaped redoubt around Snodgrass Hill: George Thomas, with Negley's Second and Brigadier-General, U.S.V., John M. Brannan's Third Divisions of Thomas's own corps, and Brigadier-Generals, U.S.V., Thomas J. Wood's First and Horatio P. Van Cleve's Third Divisions of Crittenden's corps. In violation of his latest orders from Rosecrans, furthermore, Major-General Gordon Granger, U.S.V., marched from a reserve position to the sound of the guns with Brigadier-Generals, U.S.V., Walter C. Whitaker's First and John G. Mitchell's Second Brigades of the First Division of his Reserve Corps.

Granger arrived just in time to head off Longstreet from enveloping Thomas's right. Through the afternoon and until nightfall, Thomas held on against a succession of Longstreet's attacks, delivered with all the ferocity to be expected of Lee's old paladin. Thomas found his ammunition running low because someone had mistakenly sent his wagons away, and his troops therefore sometimes had to do battle with clubbed muskets and bayonets; but the commander of the Fourteenth Army Corps earned his fame as the Rock of Chickamauga. After 5:00 P.M., Thomas conducted an orderly retreat toward Chattanooga through Rossville Gap, which he held the next day before withdrawing on Rosecrans's orders into Chattanooga itself. His stand on the horseshoe line had saved the Army of the Cumberland and made Bragg's victory Pyrrhic.

The Federal and Confederate armies had traded losses of about 28 percent on each side, the familiar sort of proportions that the Confederacy could not go on enduring. These percentages were rendered even worse than usual for the South because the Confederates lost more heavily than the Union in absolute terms: 18,454 casualties in gray (2,312 killed, 14,674 wounded, 1,468 missing), against 16,170 in blue (1,657 killed, 9,756 wounded, 4,757 missing — the latter figure signalling the shattering of the right wing).[86] More victories like Chickamauga would be as fatal to the Confederacy as a few more Gettysburg defeats.

## CHATTANOOGA

Still, Bragg's near-rout of Rosecrans made Chickamauga a dreadful ending to a Union campaign that had begun so auspiciously on the Duck River in July. Bragg now occupied the heights commanding Chattanooga, notably the point of Lookout Mountain to the southwest and Missionary Ridge to the east, to make the conquered city more a prison than a prize for the Army of the Cumberland. The Confederates interdicted all save the most meager flow of supplies from the terminus of the Nashville and Chattanooga Railroad at Bridgeport, Alabama, where the railroad met the Tennessee River. Thence Union supplies had to be carried about sixty miles by wagon, over Walden's Ridge by way of a narrow and precipitous road, soon rendered worse by October rains. The Federal army's horses and mules could not bring adequate tonnages of foodstuffs over that road and still carry enough forage to feed themselves. While the army went on reduced rations, its animals slowly starved and hauled less and less into Chattanooga.[87]

But it was a measure of how much had been accomplished during the summer that in the autumn of 1863 the war power of the Union was far too great to permit the Army of the Cumberland to starve and wither away. After Vicksburg, Sherman had pushed Johnston eastward past Jackson with part of Grant's army but had been halted short of further substantial achievement by extreme heat and dryness. The same summer heat of the Deep South, along with a strategic debate over whether to strike from Vicksburg next toward Mobile or, for political reasons having to do with the French intervention in Mexico, into Texas, prevented Grant's and Banks's armies from doing much in the months just after Vicksburg and Port Hudson. In consequence, however, four of Grant's divisions were available to be dispatched promptly toward the Army of the Cumberland.

Brigadier-General, U.S.V., John E. Smith's Second Division, Seventeenth Corps, en route from Vicksburg to Helena, Arkansas, was dispatched instead to Memphis. Sherman brought the First Division (under Peter J. Osterhaus, since June 9, 1862 brigadier-general, U.S.V., largely because of Pea Ridge),[88] the Second Division (Brigadier-General Morgan L. Smith, U.S.V.), and the Fourth Division (Brigadier-General Hugh Ewing, U.S.V.) of his Fifteenth Corps back from the Big Black River to Vicksburg to embark northward on the Mississippi. From Memphis, these four divisions rode eastward on the Memphis and Charleston Railroad. Because they had to repair track as they went along through countryside much traversed by marauding rebel cavalry, it was not until November 15 that 17,000 of them were assembled at Bridgeport.[89]

Meanwhile Grant himself, rewarded for Vicksburg with a major-generalship U.S.A. dated July 4, could be called to Louisville to meet Secretary Stanton and be placed in command of a new Military Division of the Mississippi created October 16. The command united all the Federal troops from the Appalachians to the Mississippi except for Banks's forces in Louisiana.[90] Though still in pain from a recent fall from a horse and consequent injury to his left side and leg, Grant promptly took the railroad to Bridgeport and thence the winding mountain trace to Chattanooga to direct the rescue of the city and of the Federal army inside it.

Already the War Department had also sent reinforcements toward Chattanooga from the East—the Eleventh and Twelfth Corps from the Army of the Potomac, with Fighting Joe Hooker recalled to active duty to lead them. On the better managed and maintained railroads of the North, these troops readily surpassed Longstreet's pace in coming westward. In the largest-scale railroad movement thus far in military history, the Union transported 20,000 soldiers and more than 3,000 horses and mules with their equipment and baggage about 1,150 miles, most of the infantry making the trip to Bridgeport in nine days.[91]

Grant arrived in Chattanooga on October 23 to find that the chief engineer of the Army of the Cumberland, Brigadier-General William F. "Baldy" Smith, U.S.V., had devised a plan to open a better supply line using a converging movement of Hooker's men from Bridgeport and troops from Chattanooga. Smith's scheme necessarily took shape from the configuration of the Tennessee River and the mountains between Chattanooga and Bridgeport. Below—west of—Chattanooga, the river loops southward around hilly Moccasin Point, to flow past towering Lookout Mountain. Next the stream makes a longer, northerly loop around Raccoon Mountain, before flowing south to Kelley's Ferry, then west to Bridgeport. Smith's idea was to forge an essentially straight west-to-east connection, cutting the loops at their bases, from Kelley's Ferry through the Wauhatchie Valley at the northwest foot of Lookout Mountain, cutting across the bottom of the Raccoon Mountain peninsula, then across to the east bank of the Tennessee at Brown's Ferry, and then across the top of Mocassin Point to cross the river yet once more and into Chattanooga. The route ran deeply enough through gorges to be protected against plunging fire from Lookout Mountain, but it would have to be established stealthily and swiftly because until Federal troops were stationed strongly in the Wauhatchie Valley, the Confederates could easily move there to interdict the proposed line of communications.

Grant immediately ordered Smith's plan executed. On the night of October 26–27 Brigadier-General, U.S.V., Adolph Von Steinwehr's Second Division — the initial defenders of Cemetery Hill at Gettysburg — and Major-General, U.S.V., Carl Schurz's Third Division of the Eleventh Corps crossed the Tennessee at Kelley's Ferry and advanced to within two miles of Brown's Ferry. Geary's Second Division of Slocum's Twelfth Corps deployed across the Wauhatchie Valley to shield Howard's Eleventh Corps troops from a counterattack. Meanwhile some 1,500 picked men under Brigadier-General, U.S.V., William B. Hazen of the Second Brigade, Third Division, of General Granger's Fourth Corps[92] quietly cast boats loose at Chattanooga to drift downstream, disembark on the west bank at Brown's Ferry, and drive away Confederate pickets of Evander M. Law's Brigade. Brigadier-General, U.S.V., John Basil Turchin's[93] First Brigade, Third Division, Fourteenth Corps had marched across the neck of Moccasin Point and now built a pontoon bridge at Brown's Ferry to link up with Hazen's men and the next day with Howard's.

On the night of October 28–29 Evander McIvor Law's and Jerome Bonaparte Robertson's Brigades — the formidable assailants of Little Round Top and the Devil's Den — spearheaded an attack by Hood's Division[94] against Geary's division at Wauhatchie. A night attack was rare in the Civil War, and the fighting was confused, but Geary's troops held their ground under the heavy pressure to be expected from soldiers nurtured under Longstreet and Hood. Twenty-four hours after the end of this battle the steamboat *Chattanooga* arrived at Kelley's Ferry from Bridgeport with 40,000 rations and much forage. The lifeline to save Chattanooga and the Army of the Cumberland — the Cracker Line, the troops called it — was open.

President Jefferson Davis now lent Grant unintended assistance by visiting his good friend Bragg and suggesting that the way to counter the ominously converging Union strength in the West was to shift the focus of the campaign from Chattanooga by detaching a force to attack Burnside at Knoxville. Bragg, knowing that in any event the Cracker Line almost certainly terminated his chance of capturing Chattanooga, acquiesced in the President's scheme. On November 4 he sent Longstreet's troops and Major-General Joseph Wheeler's Corps of cavalry against Burnside. While Bragg was realistic enough in his appraisal of the Chattanooga situation, it was still a bad idea to divide his army against an increasingly stronger enemy. Doing so killed whatever small chance against Chattanooga there might have remained, without creating much prospect of defeating Burnside either. Grant certainly possessed too steady a gaze to have it so easily diverted from his business at hand.

Grant recognized, in fact, that the best way to assist Burnside was to deal with Bragg quickly and then concentrate against Longstreet. Because Bragg's line of communications ran along the Western and Atlantic Railroad behind his right flank, and because this northern flank also gave Bragg his connection with Longstreet via the Tennessee and Georgia Railroad, Grant proposed to strike against Bragg's right. To speed such a move, he ordered Sherman to suspend his laborious railroad repairs and hasten to Bridgeport, making arrangements for Sherman to be supplied by water from St. Louis up the Mississippi and the Tennessee to Bridgeport. When he arrived at Bridgeport, Sherman was to march shielded by the surrounding mountains from the sight of the Confederates, to a crossing of the Tennessee River north of Chattanooga. Thence his troops of the Army of the Tennessee would cross their namesake stream via pontoons prepared by Baldy Smith and descend upon the enemy right flank on Missionary Ridge. Simultaneously, the Army of the Cumberland would entertain the Confederates with a demonstration against the front of Missionary Ridge, to be converted into a full-scale attack if opportunity warranted. Hooker meanwhile would stage still another diversion against the Confederate south flank on Lookout Mountain.

The major attack had to await Sherman's arrival, because losses of animals before the opening of the Cracker Line had almost immobilized the Army of the Cumberland. Still, when Sherman was delayed yet again, this time by muddy roads, and when reports suggested that Bragg might be withdrawing, Grant sent the Army of the Cumberland forward toward the Confederate positions between Chattanooga and Missionary Ridge. Grant wanted to pin Bragg down so he could not escape unpunished.

Stanton having given him the choice to retain Rosecrans or put Thomas in command of the Army of the Cumberland, Grant had chosen the Rock of Chickamauga, effective October 20. Seven days later Thomas had received an additional reward for Chickamauga, in the form of promotion to brigadier-general, U.S.A. The general who had been the strong man of the Union Army in middle and east Tennessee from the beginning — and who had refused an offer to succeed Buell after Perryville — would now at last lead the army most closely identified with this theater of war.[95]

On November 23 Thomas's troops drove the Confederates from an outpost at Orchard Knob west of Missionary Ridge. By becoming entangled in a struggle worthy of the name battle, the Federals learned that Bragg evidently proposed not to withdraw but to stay and fight. Now Thomas, disturbed by Sherman's continuing slow march into attacking position, suggested to Grant a return to an earlier plan for Hooker to attack Lookout Mountain in earnest, to be surer of holding Bragg's attention away from his right. On November 24, consequently, Hooker led a mixed force consisting of one division from each of the Federal armies represented at Chattanooga to drive the Confederates from a saddle of relatively level land about halfway up the lofty mountain, whose summit rises some 1,100 feet above the valley below. Geary's division would attack from Wauhatchie on the right; Brigadier-General, U.S.V., Charles Cruft's First Division, Fourth Corps would advance in the center; Osterhaus's division would drive from near Brown's Ferry on the left.

Ringed by mountains, Chattanooga was a great amphitheater where the rival armies could witness nearly all that occurred along the length of their hostile lines. This theatrical setting gave a peculiarly dramatic quality to all the actions of the battle of Chattanooga, but the drama and suspense were still more enhanced when low-lying clouds on the slopes of Lookout Mountain obscured the usual visibility just as Hooker attacked. The Federals below and the Confederates along Missionary Ridge could see only flashes of eerie red light as their comrades struggled in what inevitably came to be called the battle above the clouds. In midafternoon, however, there was a brief break in the clouds and a momentary glimpse of Confederates retreating and Federals pursuing — for Hooker had dislodged the Confederates from their defenses on the level saddle. The Confederate garrison, Brigadier-General Edward C. Walthall's Brigade of Major-General Benjamin F. Cheatham's Division, along with Stevenson's Division, both of Lieutenant-General William J. Hardee's Corps, abandoned the summit during the night. The next morning, men of the Union 8th Kentucky Infantry were raising the Stars and Stripes on the mountain peak just as the sun penetrated the clouds again.

That same morning Sherman opened the crucial attack against the main Confederate position by advancing against the north flank of Missionary Ridge. His veterans of Grant's Army of the Tennessee fought their usual good fight, but they were unable to make headway after they met unexpected obstacles of terrain and strong enemy entrenchments at a knob of the ridge called Tunnel Hill. By afternoon they were stalemated, and meanwhile Hooker's effort to reopen his drive against the opposite Confederate flank stalled when the Confederates were able to burn a bridge across Chattanooga Creek. Grant had expected to attempt a frontal assault up the steep slopes of Missionary Ridge only if his other attacks were already succeeding, for otherwise such an assault seemed likely to be suicidal in the usual pattern. But to relieve the pressure upon Sherman's flank attack, Grant now ordered the Army of the Cumberland to demonstrate against the front of Missionary Ridge by attacking the rifle pits at its base.

The result was one of the most extraordinary events of the war, "as awful as a visible interposition of God," said Charles A. Dana, who was a witness. The men of four divisions of the Army of the Cumberland seized the rifle pits: from left to right, they were Major-General, U.S.V., Absalom Baird's Third Division, Fourteenth Corps; Major-General, U.S.V., Thomas J. Wood's Third Division and Major-General, U.S.V., Philip H. Sheridan's[96] Second Division, Fourth Corps; and Brigadier-General, U.S.V., Richard W. Johnson's First Division, Fourteenth Corps. In the rifle pits, however, the Federals found themselves under an intolerable fire from the ridge above.

> Most of them halted there [wrote Quartermaster General M. C. Meigs, who was watching from Orchard Knob]; but the colors of three Regiments pushed on and up the slopes of a projecting spur, too steep to be seen from the summit. Mission Ridge is here five hundred feet in height. Slowly the three red silken flags ascended and the regiments swarmed up after them.
>
> General Grant said it was contrary to orders, it was not his plan — he meant to form the lines and then prepare and launch columns of assault, but, as the men, carried away by their enthusiasm, had gone so far, he would not order them back.
>
> Presently he gave the order for the whole line, now well formed to advance and storm the ridge. It extended some two miles in length, and it pressed forward with cheers. . . .
>
> The line ceased to be a line. The men gathered towards the points of least difficult ascent, for very steep is this hill-side — a horse cannot ascend or descend except by the obliquely graded roads. . . . The men swarm up, color after color reaches the summit, and the rebel line is divided and the confused, astonished and terrified rebels fly this way and that to meet enemies, every way but down the rear slope of the ridge and by this open way they mostly escape.
>
> Bragg whose Head Quarters are in a house in plain sight to the right of

our front, astonished at our success leaves the house, passing from the porch through and out the back door, mounts his horse and rides down the hill-side. Our men then crowned the summit, and had they known it, could by a volley, have put an end to this traitors career, as he fled down the road.[97]

Bragg had so thinned his center to meet Sherman on his right that he had opened the way for this remarkable exception to the rule that frontal attacks could not succeed. Furthermore, he had deployed half his center force at the bottom of the hill, and many of these troops evidently were not informed that they were supposed to fire one volley and then withdraw; so they stayed, were overrun, and could not participate in the fight for the summit. At the top, moreover, the Confederate line followed the topographic crest rather than the military crest, which is the highest place from which the enemy can be seen and fired upon; therefore the Confederates left an area through which the attackers could climb without exposing themselves to the defenders' fire.

Another rule of Civil War battles did, however, prevail even after the near-miracle of Missionary Ridge: the most overwhelming victories left victorious armies in a condition too little better than the defeated armies' to pursue for the kill as military theory suggested they should. General Hardee, commanding Bragg's right against Sherman, held his wing of the Army of Tennessee together in an orderly retreat that screened the flight of the rest of Bragg's army. The next day the vanguard of the Union pursuit struck a strong position held by Major-General Patrick R. Cleburne's Division of Hardee's Corps at Taylor's Ridge near Ringgold, Georgia, and the Federals were repulsed. Grant gave up the chase, to detach troops to Knoxville for the relief of Burnside, which they accomplished.

After Chattanooga, it was less the rate of casualties than the fatigue of the armies that explained both the Confederate defeat and the failure of the Federal pursuit. The Confederates had been wearied and disheartened by their inability to capitalize fully on the Chickamauga victory, by Bragg's continual quarrels with his subordinates, and by the gradual slipping away of their imprisoning grip upon the Army of the Cumberland. The Federals bore the debilitating effects of the weeks of siege or long journeys and were tired by the exertions of victory itself (another general cause of failure in pursuit is the intense physical exhaustion brought on by battle). The casualties of Chattanooga were relatively low: 5,824 Federals (753 killed, 4,722 wounded, 349 missing) versus 6,271 Confederates (361 killed, 2,160 wounded, 4,146 missing), for casualty rates of 10 and 14 percent, respectively.[98]

The effects of Chattanooga, in contrast, were mighty. One of the Confederacy's few east-west railroad connections was broken completely and forever. East Tennessee was at last restored to the Union. Grant's armies could prepare to advance on Atlanta and the remaining Confederate east-west rail linkages.

To some degree, the coordinated movements of three Federal armies in the Chattanooga campaign represent an exception to the general neglect of theater-wide application of the operational art during the Civil War, to insert between the strategic and the tactical levels of war an intermediate dimension of military activity whereby advantages may be gained before the tactical engagement, the better to assure that battle will advance strategic ends. Certainly the appointment of Grant to theater command, making him in effect the leader of what in the twentieth century would be called an army group, was a step toward creating an operational rather than a simply tactical command. Moreover, in the sequel the Federals realized the advantages possible to theater-wide operational command far more effectively than the Confederates had done with Joe Johnston's loosely conceived, half-aborted theater command in the Vicksburg campaign — to say nothing of Jefferson Davis's misguided essay in unified theater operations when he led Bragg to send Longstreet to Knoxville.

Nevertheless, the Federals continued only to grope toward a concept of the operational art. Creating Grant's theater command in the form of the Military Division of the Mississippi as well as Grant's own subsequent maneuvering of elements of three armies were not so much positive advances in the Federal understanding of the conduct of war as measures of desperation. They were reactions to the emergency that erupted when the Chickamauga defeat threatened to undo a dangerously large part of the accomplishments of the Gettysburg-Vicksburg summer, which Rosecrans had crowned with his initial capture of Chattanooga only to have the crown nearly turn to ashes. Troops from the Army of the Tennessee and the Army of the Potomac were drawn to Chattanooga in desperation, to save the Army of the Cumberland.

Once there, moreover, their cooperation was more tactical than operational. They became virtually a single army. Grant used them as contributors to his tactical plans to rescue Chattanooga and in the tactical battle to drive Bragg away. No criticism of Union tactical leadership at Chattanooga is intended in these observations. Grant's tactical conduct of the Chattanooga campaign was on the whole sound if not quite on the level of his immediately preceding campaign. In opening the Cracker Line, Union tactical leadership attained a high standard indeed — with Baldy Smith earning the largest share of the credit. Beyond tactics, however, the Union high command had grasped only the rudiments of the operational art.

## CODA

Just before the battle of Chattanooga had begun, but at a time when Grant's actions had assured the breaking of the Confederate siege, President Lincoln tried to invest all the bloody battles of 1863 with a significance beyond the mere glory of military triumph. On November 19 he dedicated the Soldiers' Cemetery on the battlefield of Gettysburg. He interpreted the military struggle as one to determine the whole fate of democracy not only in America but throughout the world.[99] If we compel ourselves to think about the words of the Gettysburg Address as if we had not already heard them too often, they can still offer inspiration as well as a fuller understanding of the transformation of America by the Civil War; but it is noteworthy that they say nothing about the roots of the war in slavery or about the issue of the African Americans' future, however pertinent to the fate of democracy that issue may seem in the perspective of our own time.

# NINE

# On the Horizon: The Postwar World

## ASSURING FREEDOM

"We are too victorious," Senator Sumner wrote to John Bright on July 21; "I fear more from our victories than our defeats. If the rebellion should suddenly collapse, Democrats, copperheads, and Seward would insist upon amnesty and the Union, and 'no question asked about slavery.'"[1] It was an idle fear to expect the Confederacy's collapse so soon, but Sumner's plaint underlined one tragic dimension of the war: only with prolonged bloodshed could the African American go free. If McClellan's Peninsula Campaign had captured Richmond and in doing so won the war, the Emancipation Proclamation would not have been issued. If McClellan had crushed Lee's army at Antietam and thereby won the war, the Emancipation Proclamation also might well not have been issued. Were Lincoln and the Union people and government committed enough to emancipation that the Civil War would have eliminated slavery if Meade had been able to fulfill Lincoln's hope of winning the war just after Gettysburg? Sumner was right to believe that this issue was at least doubtful.

What did it say of Lincoln's own resolution that in the very interval between his preliminary and final Emancipation Proclamations he had seemed to offer the Southern states a new means of escaping from the latter, by devoting much of his annual message to Congress to a proposition for

Federal compensation for states that would adopt a program to free their slaves by January 1, 1900? He also reiterated that "I cannot make it better known than it already is, that I strongly favor colonization."[2]

Congress did not act on the compensated emancipation plan, and consequently Lincoln followed through with his final Emancipation Proclamation of January 1, 1863. Some of his abolitionist critics then set out to assure emancipation by affording it a firmer legal foundation than a constitutionally challengeable assertion of the war powers of the Commander in Chief. They called for a Congressional emancipation statute, and the Women's Loyal National League, organized by Elizabeth Cady Stanton and Susan B. Anthony, opened a massive petition-gathering campaign for such an enactment. Women abolitionists, long in the forefront of the abolition movement, feeling special sympathy for the slaves because of their own legal and cultural disabilities, and always searching for outlets that would not injure abolitionism by unnecessarily antagonizing men, eventually recruited some 2,000 workers who aimed at securing the unprecedented total of one million signatures by the end of the 1863–1864 session of Congress. By the fall of 1863 continuing doubts both about Lincoln's long-run resolution and about the possible constitutional challenges to an emancipation statute converted the drive into one on behalf of a constitutional amendment. By the target date of mid-1864, the women abolitionists and their male helpers had collected some 400,000 signatures, a total without parallel despite its distance from their original goal.[3]

At the same time in early 1863 when the petition campaign got under way, certain abolitionists together with a circle of less radical antislavery campaigners opened another route toward assuring black people's emancipation. Although some of the backers of the Port Royal Experiment both in the North and on the scene believed fervently that they would prove that free labor could grow cotton more profitably than slave labor, the missionaries at Port Royal and Northern workers among African Americans elsewhere in the South increasingly concluded that the freed slaves had been so robbed of education, initiative, and responsibility by their enslavement that government assistance was needed to guide and protect them on the way to freedom. Without such assistance, emancipation even if legally upheld might become a practical sham. A questionnaire distributed by the Boston Emancipation League in December 1862 among persons working with blacks in the South had generally brought responses favoring some kind of government protection of the freed people during a transition period and until stability returned to the South. James Miller McKim, a Garrisonian and a pillar of the Pennsylvania Anti-Slavery Society, had visited Port Royal in June 1862, and in December he had similarly urged a government protective agency upon such political leaders as Sumner, Stevens, and Stanton. McKim's pleas led directly to Stanton's creating an American Freedmen's Inquiry Commission in the War Department in March 1863.

To the A.F.I.C. Stanton appointed Samuel Gridley Howe, a veteran abolitionist and a friend of John Brown who had suggested the December questionnaire of the Boston Emancipation League, and Robert Dale Owen and James McKaye, both of whom had been converted to emancipation in the course of the war, though Owen had an impressive record of other kinds of reformist activity. The commissioners inspected freed people's camps in several parts of the South, McKaye visited Port Royal, Howe visited free blacks in Canada, and Owen in particular made a careful study of emancipation in the West Indies and of black history more widely. A preliminary report of June 30, 1863 commented optimistically on the freed people as wage workers but acknowledged faults that were legacies of slavery. It said the former slaves must be taught self-reliance and recommended a government freedmen's bureau to assist in the transition to liberty.[4] Owen was the principal author of the final report, submitted to the War Department on May 15, 1864. It emphasized that the West Indies experience indicated freedom should come unconditionally and absolutely, not partially and gradually, but it also argued the need for "a freedmen's bureau, but not because these people are negroes, only because they are men who have been, for generations, despoiled of their rights."[5]

As this latter statement implies, the A.F.I.C. members and most antislavery leaders who advocated a freedmen's bureau recognized that they were skating dangerously close to paternalism if not advancing it outright. The issue of paternalism was already sensitive; the black abolitionist Frederick Douglass insisted that people of color wanted nothing but justice, and otherwise to be left to make their own way by their own strength and intelligence. Most white abolitionists held similar views, partly because the concept of the welfare state whether for freed slaves or for anybody else was virtually beyond the ken of Americans of the 1860s, partly because some of them also shared Samuel Gridley Howe's sound perception that guardianship or apprenticeship however well intentioned was likely to be merely slavery in a new guise.

Already a number of private freedmen's aid societies were joining in bringing philanthropic aid and education to the African Americans who entered Union lines, but all tended to find the demands upon them too large for private activity supplemented by only sporadic government aid. In November 1863 a delegation representing the Boston, New York, Philadelphia, and Cincinnati freedmen's aid societies visited Lincoln to seek his support for a freedmen's bureau. The President expressed sympathy and suggested the delegates prepare a memorandum that he would transmit to Congress. They did so and sent it on December 1, but Lincoln's accompanying message stated merely that the subject "is one of great magnitude, and importance, and one which these gentlemen of known ability and high character, seem to have considered with great attention and care. Not having the time to form a mature judgment of my own, as to whether the plan they suggest is the best, I submit the whole subject to Congress deeming that their attention thereto is almost imperatively demanded."[6]

Congressman Thomas Eliot of Massachusetts reintroduced into the House a freedmen's bureau bill that had died in committee in the preceding session. Providing for a bureau in the War Department that would offer relief and education to freed blacks, supervise their labor, make rules and regulations for their treatment, establish special courts for them, and settle African Americans on abandoned and confiscated lands, the bill met predictable Democratic opposition claiming it was unconstitutional and would create excessive centralization of power. The bill passed the House anyway, but in the Senate it ran into trouble among its own friends, when Sumner insisted the bureau ought to be in the Department of the Treasury. The Senate passed a version different from that of the House, and the 1863–1864 session of Congress adjourned without resolving the differences. Like the movement for an emancipation amendment to the Constitution, the effort to assure an emancipation that would be more than simply formal and legal appeared to be making headway, but its final success was still uncertain.[7]

## THE BURDEN OF RACE

In the 1860s, how complete could emancipation become, how far above paternalism could the best intentions rise? Most probably, no freedman's bureau and no efforts by the most militantly equalitarian abolitionists could have moved the nation to advance African Americans very far beyond the mere legal status of free people toward genuine equality with whites and genuine citizenship. Belief in the inherent inferiority of black people to white in all the basic attributes of humanity was too pervasive; all but a handful of abolitionists themselves believed if not in the inferiority of African Americans, then at least in inherent differences in racial aptitudes such that they were not prepared to perceive blacks as capable of becoming the same kind of citizens as whites.

The exceptional minority among the abolitionists who held to different views inadvertently complicated black people's course toward complete acceptance in American citizenship by failing to recognize the full dimensions of the obstacles in the way. The most radical abolitionists, largely led and typified by William Lloyd Garrison, had drunk deeply of the perfectionist stream within nineteenth-century reformism. To them slavery was primarily a moral issue. All considerations such as race and economics that were not moral considerations were irrelevant to the real problem, and the real problem was the moral imperative to grant full freedom and full equality to all people, on moral grounds alone. Because the issue was moral, no solution short of perfection would do: the complete elimination of slavery, the absolute achievement of citizenship for African Americans. The perfectionist moral abolitionists for whom the race and color of the slaves were irrelevant could not perceive how important race could be to the majority of Americans for whom morality was not everything.

Consequently, Garrison went so far as to deny that race prejudice was an important part of the slavery problem; ". . . the color of the skin," he said, even after the Civil War, "has nothing to. do with prejudice. It [prejudice against blacks] is the offspring of slavery, it is not to be found anywhere in the world excepting where slavery has victimized those of the Negro race."[8] To say that was to display a surpassing blindness to the difficulties that would beset emancipated blacks; to believe such things inhibited the efforts of the very abolitionists on whose help the African Americans might have been expected to count most strongly in the ascent upward from simple legal emancipation.

Although he did not have the benefit of modern historical research into the deep roots of white Americans' prejudice against blacks, if Garrison had been only a little less moralistically earnest and a little more worldly he should have recognized readily enough the broad truths about racial feelings: that in the cultural inheritance in which nearly all Americans shared, blackness connoted everything that was evil, unclean, and impure, and people whose skins were black had become identified inseparably with all the connotations of blackness. The concepts of whiteness as purity and blackness as evil were firmly planted in the English folk mind long before the English enslaved blacks or even encountered enough Africans for them to be more than an oddity. When the English actually met dark-skinned humans in considerable numbers, the shock of the meeting was so severe, the experience so disconcerting, that Africans were perceived as being darker than in fact they were and called blacks as if they were literally black. It was the blackness of slaves in America and the meanings of blackness in the white mind that made the problem of American slavery peculiarly recalcitrant. If the slaves had been white, the perplexities of freeing them would have been vastly smaller; but it was this key fact that Garrison stood on its head.[9]

For most Americans, progress in thinking about the race issue was bound to be a halting progress. Not least, for Lincoln. But the abolitionists and the A.F.I.C. pushed him forward. It was probably on August 26, 1863, that the President wrote for himself a memorandum on emancipation, setting forth his latest thoughts. By this time he had at least moved beyond his idea of the previous December that under some circumstances he might willingly rescind the Emancipation Proclamation. "Suppose those now in rebellion should say," he wrote: "'We cease fighting: re-establish the national authority amongst us—customs, courts, mails, land-offices—as before the rebellion—we claiming to send members to both branches of Congress, as of yore, and to hold our slaves according to our State laws, notwithstanding anything or all things which have occurred during the rebellion.'" His answer, Lincoln reflected, would probably be that the rebels having begun the war, they could end it, in that one side could hardly fight alone. Remaining questions ought to be settled by the peaceful means of courts and votes. Whether Southerners sent to Congress should be seated must be left to each house to decide. But, he also reflected, he himself could not look with indifference on any return of "the disturbing element" to Congress, and on one point he must be firm: "During my continuance here, the government shall return no person to slavery, who is free according to the proclamation, or to any acts of congress, unless such return shall be held to be a legal duty, by the proper court of final resort, in which case I will promptly act as may then appear to be my personal duty."[10]

The same day on which he probably composed this note to himself, Lincoln also made a public reaffirmation of his commitment to the Emancipation Proclamation in his response to an invitation to attend a Unionist meeting in his home state of Illinois.[11] In his annual message to Congress of 1863, moreover, one year after he had rearoused emancipationists' fears in the 1862 message, he reaffirmed the same commitment. In both these public statements he pointed with particular emphasis to still another development of the past year that he believed must bind him to his commitment: "Of those who were slaves at the beginning of the rebellion," as he said to Congress, "full one hundred thousand are now in the United States military service. . . ."[12]

It was a major part of white beliefs about African Americans that they were a docile, unaggressive, feminine kind of race (even if black men were also feared as sexual predators). However slowly, by 1863 the war was bringing blacks opportunities to refute the kindly intended as well as the less benevolent stereotypes of them.

All through the year 1863, Charleston, the first citadel of secession, continued the same successful defiance of Union arms that had thrown back Admiral Du Pont's ironclads from the walls of Fort Sumter on April 7. New Union commanders, for the Navy Rear-Admiral John A. Dahlgren, for the Army Brigadier-General, U.S.V., Quincy Adams Gillmore, promoted April 28, 1862 for his Fort Pulaski victory of April 10–11,[13] sought to reopen the attack on Charleston in July. They began by landing on the south end of Morris Island, thence to assail Fort Wagner farther north on the island. If they captured Fort Wagner, their guns could command the central channel into Charleston harbor and bombard Fort Sumter. The approach to Fort Wagner, unhappily, lay hemmed in between the sea and a marsh, so that an attack would have to be made head-on across a deep ditch against a redoubt with strong bastions at its corners.

On July 11 Brigadier-General, U.S.V., George C. Strong's First Brigade, First Division, Tenth Corps attacked the fort. It gained the parapet but fell back with casualties of 339 against only twelve lost in the 1,352-man garrison. On July 18, following an afternoon's bombardment by twenty-six rifled guns and ten siege mortars, Strong's and Colonel, 7th New Hampshire Infantry, Haldimand S. Putnam's Second Brigade tried again. The regiment that led the charge was the 54th Massachusetts. Strong, a Massachusetts man, had requested the regiment for his brigade for this very purpose after it had fought impressively in its first action, on nearby James Island on July 13. Colonel Shaw welcomed the opportunity for his black soldiers to prove themselves, though they had suffered forty-nine casualties on James Island and since then had been marching through sand and marsh for two days in intense summer heat. The 54th briefly planted its flag in the interior of Fort Wagner, but it was turned back with losses of about 25 percent including Robert Gould Shaw killed. In their general repulse, the two assault brigades lost 1,515 (246 killed, 880 wounded, 389 missing) of 5,264, including Strong mortally wounded and Putnam killed. The defenders, 1,785 men under Brigadier-General William Taliaferro, lost 174 (thirty-six killed, 133 wounded, five missing).[14]

The charge of the 54th Massachusetts at Fort Wagner loomed up behind President Lincoln's public statement of August 26 upholding the Emancipation Proclamation:

You say you will not fight to free negroes. Some of them seem willing to fight for you; but, no matter. Fight you, then, exclusively to save the Union. . . .

I thought that in your struggle for the Union, to whatever extent the negroes should cease helping the enemy, to that extent it weakened the enemy in his resistance to you. Do you think differently? I thought that whatever negroes can be got to do as soldiers, leaves just so much less for white soldiers to do, in saving the Union. Does it appear otherwise to you? But negroes, like other people, act upon motives. Why should they do any thing for us, if we will do nothing for them? If they stake their lives for us, they must be prompted by the strongest motive — even the promise of freedom. And the promise being made, must be kept.

. . . And then, there will be some black men who can remember that, with silent tongue, and clenched teeth, and steady eye, and well-poised bayonet, they have helped mankind on to the great consummation; while, I fear, there will be some white ones, unable to forget that, with malignant heart, and deceitful speech, they have strove to hinder it.[15]

For the time being, nevertheless, the black soldiers would have to continue helping toward the great consummation for less pay than whites; for about two weeks earlier, Lincoln had given no immediate encouragement to Frederick Douglass when he visited the White House on behalf of equal pay. It was not until nearly a year after the assault on Fort Wagner that on June 15, 1864, Congress at last enacted equal pay, and then with the proviso that it was retroactive only to January 1, 1864, except for men who had been free on April 19, 1861, who might receive equal pay retroactive to the date of their enlistment.[16]

It was about the same time in the summer of 1864, furthermore, that the freedmen's bureau bill was dying for lack of agreement between the two houses of Congress, and although the Senate had adopted an emancipation amendment on April 8, the amendment to perpetuate and complete the Emancipation Proclamation failed to obtain the necessary two-thirds majority before the summer adjournment of the House.[17] Charles Sumner surely had had reason to fear that Northern victories might be coming too soon for the good of the slaves.

## FROM BATTLEFIELD TO POLLING PLACE (I)

But while the benefits of military victory were still slow in coming for the slaves, they were highly gratifying for the political prospects of Lincoln and the Republican Party. It was true that the Northern voters had given heart to

Lincoln and his party with Republican triumphs in elections in New Hampshire, Rhode Island, Connecticut, Ohio, Indiana, Michigan, and Iowa even before the 1863 tide of military successes began to roll in.[18] It was also true that the New York draft riots of July 13, 14, and 15 revealed the persistence of American urban turbulence — a familiar phenomenon long before the war — and of the anti-black, anti-abolitionist, and anti-war bitterness of parts of the urban working classes even after the military triumphs of Gettysburg and Vicksburg.[19] Still, Republicans believed that if only the armies could win in the field, the currents of Northern political opinion would run surely to Republican successes at the polls. When the military victories came to pass in 1863 and electoral triumphs in previously doubtful states followed closely thereafter, these contemporary observers perceived a relationship of cause and effect, and their perception was probably right.

In July of 1863 Confederate Brigadier-General John Hunt Morgan, already a famous raider, led 2,500 picked cavalrymen from Bragg's army into Ohio near Cincinnati and rode northeastward across the state toward Pennsylvania. Federal troops and militia harried this raid more effectively than they did most earlier Confederate cavalry excursions, and on July 26 they captured Morgan near New Lisbon with the 700 or so troopers who remained with him.[20] Not the least of Morgan's disappointments and one of the causes of his capture was the failure of Ohio copperheads to rise to his aid. Morgan had hoped for such aid not only because he had heard many general reports of copperhead plotting in the southern Midwest, but also because on July 11 the Ohio Democrats had nominated the exiled Clement Vallandigham as their candidate for governor. As usual, nevertheless, Ohio Democrats for the most part joined as enthusiastically as anybody in repelling the invader, and it was a misreading of their sentiments to believe that they nominated Vallandigham because most of them agreed with him.

Rather, they nominated him in the first flush of their resentment at his arrest, regarding him as a martyr in the cause of civil liberties and hoping to capitalize on that cause at the polls. Nominating him for any reason was perverse enough, of course, and an index to the sorry deterioration of the ability of a once-mighty party to judge even political expediency. The civil liberties issue was the theme of the acceptance address delivered on behalf of Vallandigham by George Ellis Pugh, who became the candidate for lieutenant governor, and a committee of prominent Ohio Democrats promptly followed up the nomination with a letter to Lincoln about Vallandigham's banishment, seeking to embarrass the President by accusing him of countenancing punishments unknown to the Constitution.

Vallandigham himself soon surfaced at Niagara Falls, Canada West, to address the people of Ohio from that outpost across Lake Erie. Curiously, he incorporated into his speech on the subject of liberty and freedom of expression a warning that voting for the administration meant forfeiting one's own rights when the opposition party came to power. The Democrats announced that if Vallandigham should be elected, a huge force of armed men would escort him from Canada to the Ohio state house. This threat enabled the Republicans to counter with a warning that Vallandigham's election would precipitate civil war in Ohio, an exchange that helped the Republicans more than the Democrats. Still better for the Republicans, they nominated as their Union candidate for governor a respectable War Democrat, John Brough, a newspaperman, railroad executive, and as state auditor a politician known as an opponent of political corruption. Still better again, by the time the balloting occurred, the Union armies had knocked the props from under the fundamental assumption of Vallandigham's campaign, that worse than unconstitutional the war was futile. In the Midwest, it could not seem futile when the Father of Waters again went unvexed to the sea. In the voting on October 13, Brough was elected by a majority of 101,000.[21]

The Democrats of Pennsylvania indulged themselves in only slightly less perversity than their Ohio brethren when they nominated for governor Chief Justice George W. Woodward of the Supreme Court of Pennsylvania. Woodward denounced both the legal tender laws and the Enrollment Act as unconstitutional, had obstructed state militia enrollment, and was widely known for commenting in 1861 that if the Union should be divided, he hoped the line of separation would run north of Pennsylvania. Republican Governor Curtin was in poor health and not eager for a second term, and he had proposed a plan to unite Pennsylvania in support of the war by granting both the Republican and the Democratic gubernatorial nominations to a professional soldier who was also a War Democrat and a friend of McClellan, Major-General William B. Franklin. When the Peace Democrats killed the plan within the Democratic Party, Curtin, popular as the Soldiers' Friend, yielded to the demands of many Republican county organizations that he run again. His factional enemy Simon Cameron felt obliged to fall into line. Curtin represented moderate Republicanism — he had argued, for example, that only Congress could suspend the writ of habeas corpus — but the Democrats so conducted their campaign that it became almost a referendum between the supporters and the opponents of the war.

With the contest turning upon what the voters thought of the war, in Pennsylvania there was Gettysburg to do for the Republican campaign what Vicksburg could do in the Midwest. Before the war, Pennsylvania had been predictably Jeffersonian and then Jacksonian, with its key city of Philadelphia only slightly less predictable than the state. In going for Lincoln in 1860, and through the early years of the war, Pennsylvania moved toward a new political allegiance, but from 1860 through 1863 this movement was hesitant and tentative. Lee's invasion then transformed secession from a matter of abstract political debate by presenting secessionists as tangible, plundering raiders. As long as the outcome of the invasion retained all the uncertainty added to it by the hitherto seemingly futile conduct of the war, discouragement and fear combined with old Democratic loyalties to create the doubtful and apathetic mood with which Pennsylvania and Philadelphia faced peril in the month of June. But once Gettysburg turned the military course of the war, the new assurance that the war would not be futile reaffirmed Pennsylvania's shift toward a new political allegiance. Curtin defeated Woodward by 269,000 votes to 254,000, not a spectacular margin, but in light of Pennsylvania's ancient allegiance a heartening one.[22]

New York's Democratic Governor Horatio Seymour, who by his opposition to the draft contributed at least a spark to the July draft riots, and who continued to urge that the draft not be applied, especially in New York City, did not have to stand for reelection in 1863. In a campaign to elect various other state officials and the Legislature on November 3, however, the Republicans won most of the victories and carried both the Senate and the Assembly.[23] Predictably, the Massachusetts Republicans reelected Governor Andrew — and by a margin of 70,000 to 29,000 over a relatively uncontroversial but little-known lawyer, Henry W. Paine.[24] Less predictably, in Maryland contests between "conservative" Union men and "unconditional" Union men, the latter moving more rapidly toward emancipation than the former, the "unconditional" Unionists proved stronger.

The Maryland election was marred by charges of partisan judging of voters' qualifications and of the Union Army's supporting the partisanship of the election judges;[25] this ingredient made it similar to an earlier, August 4 election in Kentucky, where the military had intervened with a generous interpretation of their mandate to prevent Confederate conspirators from subverting the voting, but where the margin for the Union Democrats over the Peace Democrats (there being no effective Republican Party in Kentucky) was nevertheless wide enough to indicate a heartening coalescence of border-state support for the war. The victory of the Kentucky Unionists was genuine enough that in it as in all these electoral triumphs, the champions of carrying on the war rightly believed themselves charging forward at the polls in response to the echoes of the trumpets of Gettysburg and Vicksburg.[26]

## THE BEGINNINGS OF RECONSTRUCTION

"Another year of health, and of sufficiently abundant harvest has passed," the prairie-state President in a characteristic vein began his annual message to Congress of December 8, 1863. "For these, and especially for the improved condition of our national affairs, our renewed, and profoundest gratitude to God is due."[27] With this improved condition of the national affairs in mind, and "[l]ooking now to the present and future, and with reference to a resumption of the national authority within the States wherein that authority has been suspended," Lincoln "saw fit to issue a proclamation, a copy of which is herewith transmitted."[28]

The proclamation embodied Lincoln's plan to capitalize upon the victories of his armies to hasten the political reconstruction of the Union. Pointing to the constitutional power of the President to reprieve and pardon offenders against the United States, he proclaimed a full pardon to all persons who had participated in the rebellion, with restoration of all rights of property except as to slaves, when such persons should take an oath to support, protect, and defend henceforth the Constitution and the Union and to abide by and support the acts of Congress and proclamations of the President issued during the war, except as the acts and proclamations might be modified by the Supreme Court. Certain categories of Confederates were excepted from the proclamation, including high Confederate civil and military officials. Otherwise, Southerners could regain the rights and privileges of citizenship by taking the oath to support the Constitution, the Union, and, in effect, the Emancipation Proclamation. Furthermore, when in any Confederate state the oath-takers numbered as many as 10 percent of the votes cast in that state in 1860, such persons might reestablish a state government.[29]

Such was the program often called Lincoln's 10-percent plan of reconstruction. Although the Union victories of 1863 made the time ripe for the plan, Lincoln was well aware that the war was not yet won, and his program was designed less to outline permanent arrangements for peace than to press the Union's military advantages by grasping additional political successes, these in the Confederacy itself. If Lincoln could establish in the South state governments capable of contesting the legitimacy of the secessionist state governments, he would add to the Union's military weapons the political weapon of Unionist magnets tugging upon the allegiance of Southern citizens, generating increasing power as each new military victory increased their political credibility and decreased that of their Confederate rivals.

When the citizen of Louisiana, or Arkansas, or any other Southern state saw a Unionist state government actually functioning again, while the failures of Confederate arms steadily narrowed the effective domain of his secessionist state government, especially if he had harbored doubts about secession in the first place the citizen was more and more likely to turn his allegiance to the Unionist government — provided a Unionist government existed to claim his allegiance.

Thus arose Lincoln's haste to establish such Unionist state governments quickly, and with minimal requirements placed upon them. Lincoln knew that 10 percent of the voters of a state offered a perilously small foundation on which to erect a government, and he would not have been likely to expect 10 percent of the voters to form a foundation for permanent state government and permanent reconstruction. But if his purpose was to undercut the Confederate state governments, then it made sense for the creation of rival state governments to be as easy as possible, not difficult. "In some States," he said, "the elements for resumption [of state government] seem ready for action, but remain inactive, apparently for want of a rallying point — a plan of action. . . . By the proclamation a plan is presented which may be accepted by them as a rallying point, and which they are assured in advance will not be rejected here. This may bring them to act sooner than they otherwise would."[30]

But Lincoln was not committing himself to a fixed, permanent plan of reconstruction:

> The objections to a premature presentation of a plan by the national Executive consists in the danger of commitals on points which could be more safely left to further developments. Care has been taken so to shape the document as to avoid embarrassments from this source. Saying that, on certain terms, certain classes will be pardoned, with rights restored, it is not said that other classes, or other terms, will never be included. Saying that reconstruction will be accepted if presented in a specified way, it is not said that it will never be accepted in any other way.[31]

The military situation at the end of 1863 made the moment opportune for presenting a general plan, but Lincoln had already been acting to undercut the Confederate state governments with rival Unionist governments wherever he could do so with any semblance of conviction. In Virginia, fortunately for his purposes, a Unionist government had presented itself at the outset of the war; he had encouraged its claims to legitimacy, and when somewhat to his chagrin it turned itself into the government of a new state, Lincoln continued to nourish as best he could the claims of the small remaining rump to represent the Commonwealth of Virginia, although he omitted it from the terms of his proclamation by requiring that the boundary and subdivisions of a state must remain unchanged for it to qualify.[32] In Tennessee, Lincoln had more to build upon, even though the most fervently Unionist section of the state remained so long and so frustratingly in Confederate control. Much of Middle and West Tennessee, including the state capital at Nashville, fell to Union arms early, and Lincoln appointed Andrew Johnson, hitherto the one Senator from a seceded state to remain at his desk in Washington, military governor of his home state, with the rank of brigadier-general, U.S.V., dating from March 4, 1862.[33]

Despite his stout Unionism, however, Johnson was not a good choice to seize Tennessee's rebuilding materials with skill. He combined an irascible disposition with a hatred of the prewar social and economic leadership of the state, born of his origins as a poor, illiterate tailor, but intensified by a personality suspicious of nearly everyone. His Democratic affiliation disqualified him for cooperation with the very group on whom Lincoln was counting for the political restoration of Tennessee as well as the whole South, the Old Whigs. With this group Lincoln himself had been in political alliance through most of his career, until belatedly and reluctantly he became a Republican. Nevertheless, the Old Whigs, often the wealthiest plantation owners and business and professional men of the prewar South, were anathema to Johnson. Beyond that, the annoying recalcitrance of the Confederates in not completely relinquishing Tennessee also hampered Johnson's reconstruction efforts; Forrest's raid in December 1862, for example, did much to break up Congressional elections Johnson had planned for that time. But Johnson himself did even more to delay reconstruction. His loathing for the plantation aristocracy made him an early champion of emancipation, and he pushed this cause hard enough to divide Tennessee Unionists into bitterly feuding factions.

When Lincoln offered his 10-percent plan and amnesty to the previously disloyal, moreover, he was proposing to restore political power to more of the people Johnson despised. The military governor thereupon devised his own oath in place of Lincoln's, asking Tennesseans to declare not mere loyalty but their outright opposition to the rebellion. When local elections in March 1864 still produced too many victories for nonemancipationist, conservative Unionists to suit Johnson's taste, he saw to it that no important statewide elections for state offices were held through the rest of 1864. He so rigged the election machinery for the 1864 Presidential canvass that the Democratic electors withdrew from the contest.

Throughout these setbacks to reconstruction, however, Lincoln remained remarkably sanguine that Tennessee's Unionism was so firm that all would turn out well in the end, and the outcome proved him essentially right. Statewide elections held at last on March 4, 1865 chose the ardent East Tennessee Unionist "Parson" William G. Brownlow as civil governor. Thenceforth Tennessee moved rapidly to become the first Confederate state to be restored to full participation in the Union.[34]

In Louisiana, the early Union conquest of New Orleans permitted efforts to restore Unionist government almost as soon as in Tennessee, and for a time progress seemed more rapid there. Under Lincoln's urgings, Brigadier-General George F. Shepley, U.S.V., military governor from June 1862, conducted elections on December 3, 1862 for members of Congress in two districts in and around New Orleans. Remarkably in light of later reconstruction contests, the House voted to seat the two members who were thus chosen, Georg Michael Hahn and Benjamin F. Flanders, albeit this House decision occurred on February 17, 1863, when the Thirty-seventh Congress was soon to pass out of existence.[35] Less fortunately, Ben Butler, the recent Breckinridge Democrat whom Lincoln appointed to the military command in Louisiana partly in the hope that he would have the political background and adroitness to conciliate Louisianans, disappointed Lincoln's expectations much as Andrew Johnson was doing. Butler failed not only because of the famous alleged harshness of his treatment of still defiant rebels in New Orleans, or because of the odor of peculation that surrounded his regime, but because like Johnson he offended the very people on whose help Lincoln was counting. In New Orleans there was an Old Whig mercantile and professional group who had done much to bring about the early surrender of the city and were eager to reestablish their familiar trade connections along the whole length of the Mississippi River, but who were soon antagonized because Butler, turned Radical Republican, favored the black and white poor of the city by turning taxes and fines into a poor fund and work relief.[36]

On December 12, 1862 Nathaniel P. Banks presented to Butler the President's order of November 8 naming Banks to succeed Butler in command of the Department of the Gulf.[37] Lincoln's purpose was largely to mend fences with Louisiana moderates and hasten political reconstruction. Banks, however, became preoccupied with the mighty military events that occurred on the lower Mississippi in the first half of 1863; did not get along with Shepley, who had become a disciple of Butler; and allowed most of 1863 to pass without political accomplishment in Louisiana. At length, prodded by Lincoln directly as well as by the general announcement of the 10-percent plan, at the beginning of 1864 Banks proclaimed elections both for governor under the old state constitution of 1852 and for a constitutional convention.

On Washington's Birthday, 1864, the oath-taking voters of Louisiana selected Georg Michael Hahn as governor; he was the moderate candidate favored by Lincoln and Banks. Hahn received 6,183 votes. Less encouragingly, John Q. A. Fellows, an avowedly proslavery candidate, received 2,996 votes, while B. F. Flanders, the favorite of the Butler-Shepley forces, received 2,232 votes. Banks inaugurated Hahn on March 6.[38] Presently the oath-taking voters also chose the delegates for the constitutional convention, though a Congressional investigation was later to charge that if there had not been fraud, the number of participants would have been less than 10 percent of the 1860 voters. The convention sat from April to July: abolishing slavery; moving back and forth over a plea from Lincoln to Hahn that would have selected African Americans of high intelligence and those who had fought for the Union to be granted the suffrage, until the issue was evaded by empowering the General Assembly to grant black suffrage; and creating an interracial militia. On September 5, 1864, 6,836 Louisianans voted to ratify the new constitution, while 1,566 opposed. Members of Congress and of the legislature were then chosen, and the latter elected two U.S. Senators.[39]

Arkansas like Tennessee was a state where the breadth and depth of secessionism had always been dubious. Among the military activities that scattered Grant's army after Vicksburg and helped prevent any further major effort by that army in the summer of 1863 was an expedition into Arkansas, led by Major-General Frederick Steele, U.S.V., and marching up the Arkansas River from Helena. This expedition originated in General-in-Chief Halleck's desire to help the commander of the guerrilla-beset Department of Missouri, Major-General John M. Schofield, U.S.V., to fend off the latest marauding foray by Sterling Price, and if possible to capture Price. Schofield and through him Halleck proved to be misinformed about Price's current intentions and location, and so Steele's expedition missed its mark. Skillfully conducted nevertheless, it entered Little Rock on September 10, and to Lincoln capturing the capital of a state was about as good as capturing Price.[40] Lincoln could now apply his 10-percent plan to Arkansas almost as soon as he announced it. On March 14, 1864, Arkansas voters who had taken Lincoln's oath of allegiance approved by 12,179 votes to 226 changes in the state constitution to declare secession void, repudiate the Confederate debt, and abolish slavery. They also elected Isaac Murphy governor, and a Unionist state government was soon in business.[41]

Of course, as the astonishing dimensions of the Arkansas electoral margin imply, Union bayonets played a direct role in all these events, on voting days as well as other days. It was also true that others of Lincoln's reconstruction efforts, including those in Virginia, produced less encouraging results than Tennessee, Louisiana, and Arkansas. Early in 1864 Lincoln sent one of his private secretaries, John Hay, to Florida to administer oaths and enroll voters there, but Hay enjoyed little success even before the Confederate troops in Florida delivered a smart setback to the Union invaders of the northeastern part of the state on February 20, 1864, in the battle of Olustee, the only combat of any considerable size to be fought in Florida during the war. The prospects for Florida were so dim even before Olustee that Lincoln's sending so close an associate as Hay could not help but encourage suspicions, already widely shared among Republicans who were less than enthusiastic about the President as well as among Democrats, that a principal motive for Lincoln's entire reconstruction program was to set up pocket boroughs on which the President could count in the nominating convention and Presidential election of 1864.[42]

This consideration was surely not absent from the President's mind, though there is no cause in that to dismiss his most obvious motive, of trying to undermine the Confederate states' claims to legitimacy and allegiance, reorganize the South, and thus win the war — on which his best hopes for reelection as well as so many other things rested. Granting that in his desire to undermine the Confederacy it was to Lincoln's advantage to make it easy rather than difficult to set up Unionist rivals to the secessionist state governments, which explains why he could be satisfied with only 10 percent of a state's voters to get Unionist government under way, the easiness of his terms for welcoming ex-Confederates back into the Union remains the most striking feature of his plan. His easiness and generosity are especially striking when it is remembered that the Southern states seceded in the first place ostensibly to escape the drastic reorganization of their politics and society that this Republican President presumably had in store for them. How little the South might have had to fear if a long and bloody war had not occurred to infuriate the North, how tragically unnecessary secession was, is suggested also by the fact that even after nearly three years of war, the initial response of most Republicans to Lincoln's amnesty and 10-percent plans was one of applause. Of course, while in 1861 Lincoln and most Republicans had been willing to guarantee slavery in the states where it existed, the war had now provoked the President's Emancipation Proclamation, which called for drastic reorganization indeed; but throughout 1863 at least, there was a certain thinness even in the Northern commitment to emancipation.

## THE UNION: THE WAR,
## THE ECONOMY, AND THE SOCIETY

At more than a century's distance from the war, the hope of finding in it more than tragedy still dies hard, and in large part for that reason so does the belief that the Civil War was a turning point in the economic history of the United States. But the weight of the evidence suggests that the Civil War had no substantial positive effect on American economic development. In much of the South it set back economic development for decades. Even in the North, if there was a perceptible economic effect at all, it may well have been to slow industrialization.

The United States had achieved Walt W. Rostow's takeoff stage in the process of industrialization during the 1840s, and Rostow actually finds the takeoff period completed by 1860. In a nation already well launched into the Industrial Revolution before the war began, every important statistical series tracing industrial and economic growth tends to refute the idea that the war was a major stimulus to growth and suggests instead a retarding effect. Unlike the twentieth-century world wars, the Civil War did not strike at a time of high unemployment; therefore it did not return a large part of the work force to productive occupations, but rather diverted much of it away from activities that contributed to economic growth.

In Robert E. Gallman's statistical series for both "total commodity output," including agriculture, and "value added by manufacture," the decade ending with 1869 shows a very low rate of increase in commodity output compared with all the other decades between 1839 and 1889. "Value added by manufacture" expressed in constant dollars shows an increase of 157 percent from 1839 to 1849, 76 percent from 1849 to 1859, only 25 percent from 1859 to 1869, 82 percent from 1869 to 1879, and 112 percent from 1879 to 1889. Annual pig-iron production in tons, a crucial index to nineteenth-century industrialization, increased 24 percent from 1850 to 1855; 17 percent from 1855 to 1860; 1 percent from 1860 to 1865; and 100 percent from 1865 to 1870. Indices for bituminous coal and copper production show similar patterns. Even in the woolen industry, which we might assume to have benefited from the troubles of cotton, the middle years of the nineteenth century, from 1830 to 1870, did not exhibit a rate of growth comparable with that of the immediately preceding and following periods. The mechanization of American agriculture was closely related to industrialization and urbanization; but the average value of machinery per farm in constant dollars actually fell 25 percent during the decade of the 1860s.[43]

Railroad track mileage had increased at a rate of over 200 percent per decade in the twenty years before the Civil War. The increase slowed to 70 percent for the decade of the 1860s, with only a 15 percent increase during the war years. In the next two decades the increase rose to 75 percent. Building construction in the United States similarly showed a declining rate of growth throughout the latter two-thirds of the nineteenth century; but in this area also, the war period brought a more abrupt decline: Gallman's statistics show a 90 percent growth for 1849–1859, 40 percent for 1859–1869, 46 percent for 1869–1879.

In 1866, total bank loans in the United States were 35 percent lower in constant dollars than they had been in 1860. By 1870, the value of loans was still 15 percent below the 1860 level, and total bank assets were 10 percent lower than in 1860. The collapse of Southern banking is reflected in these statistics, but nevertheless they do not indicate a boom period for the short-term loans that were a principal source of finance for mid-nineteenth-century business expansion.[44]

Certain areas of industrialization did enjoy wartime stimulation. An example is shoemaking. In 1858 Lyman R. Blake had patented a machine to overcome the principal obstacle to mass production of shoes, by machine-sewing the uppers to the soles. In 1862 Blake patented an improved machine, and his promoter, Gordon McKay, organized a company with a capital of $250,000 to distribute the machine, leasing it to manufacturers for a down payment of $500 and a royalty of five cents for each pair of shoes sewn. The demand for mass production of sturdy shoes for the Union Army now encouraged the transformation of the shoemaking industry from one still organized around artisans to a factory industry dominated by entrepreneurs who could afford to pay royalties to the McKay Sewing Machine Company and to provide the steam power necessary to use Blake's machine most profitably. On the other hand, shoe production actually declined during the war years, in part because Southerners were no longer buying Northern shoes for their slaves.[45]

It is true that the business depression precipitated by the opening of the war proved fleeting. This depression was occasioned largely by the failure of banks whose note issues were based on Southern bonds; the problems of firms to which Southerners owed large debts; the troubles of commission houses acting for Southern shippers and of businesses trading in Southern cotton, sugar, and naval stores; and the perils of the Northern cotton manufacturing industry. Some of the largest cotton mills closed down completely; by late 1861 only about half the Northern mills seem to have been operating at more than a limping pace.[46] Border cities suffered especially heavy business losses when the war began. In the year before the war, Cincinnati had butchered twice as many hogs as Chicago, but by the end of 1861 it held pork it could not sell.⁴⁷ Even Chicago, moreover, found its commerce initially disrupted by the cutting off of its trade down north-south railroads and the Mississippi. But by the second year of the war, demands for war material, combined with an unprecedented sale of Northern farm products to Europe because of trans-Atlantic crop failures, carried most of Northern business back to a satisfactory level of prosperity.⁴⁸

It is true also that wartime demand for certain goods and unprecedented government military spending would have created a currency inflation even without the inflationary effect of greenbacks, and that the inflation resulting from these combined sources generated evident prosperity and even a feeling of boom times. As usual, currency inflation transferred income from wage and salary earners and interest recipients to profit makers. Inflation thus stimulated stock-market activity and provided profitable opportunities for speculators in stocks, in gold values, and in commodities such as wool, cotton, wheat, and corn. These opportunities, along with those of contractors in war goods, produced a class of newly rich conspicuous consumers, and it was the expenditures of the relatively small group of war contractors and speculators that especially generated the appearance of a business boom.

It is not surprising that urgent purchasing of uniforms, arms, and equipment in quantities hitherto undreamed of also offered opportunities for the practice of large-scale frauds, selling shoddy goods to the War Department at swollen prices. Although Secretary of War Stanton and Quartermaster General Meigs tried to police frauds strictly, even harshly, they could never eliminate them. Other officers of the government itself were less puritanical than Stanton and Meigs in their attitude toward profiteering. Trading in cotton in occupied areas and along the Southern border was supposed to be regulated by Treasury agents to prevent war supplies from reaching the Confederacy in return, but the agents protected a considerable illicit trade in which Secretary Chase's prospective (and from November 12, 1863 actual) son-in-law, Governor and from March 4, 1863 Senator William Sprague IV of Rhode Island, was heavily involved.

Often we have perceived the Civil War not only as a mighty stimulant to industrialization but also as a spawning ground for the dubious business ethics so prominent in the Black Friday and Credit Mobilier scandals of the postwar era. The postwar business buccaneers almost all spent the war years not in the Army but in private commerce laying the foundations of their subsequent fortunes. This was true of Andrew Carnegie, John D. Rockefeller, and John Pierpont Morgan as well as of the conspicuously unsavory rascals like Jay Gould and James Fisk. Still, if skepticism about the war as an impetus to industrialization is necessary, the idea that the Civil War added new dimensions to business immorality deserves equal skepticism. The financial scandals of the postwar years found precedents in stock-market manipulations of the 1850s as well as during the war. The deleterious effect of war on morality is a well-worn stereotype, but why a war in which few of them participated should have been peculiarly detrimental to the morals of businessmen has yet to be clearly explained.[49]

By removing Southern agrarians from power in Washington, the Civil War of course assured Northern industrialization a friendlier Federal government and a friendlier political climate in general than before the war. The economic legislation of the Civil War Congresses consistently favored Northern business enterprise. The tax legislation of the Civil War Congresses placed the burden of Federal taxation minimally upon business and profits and with disproportionate weight on consumers, an effect that was accentuated after the war when the mildly progressive income tax and manufacturers' taxes were eliminated and the protective tariff and excise taxes remained. Nevertheless, the argument that the war stimulated industrialization by this indirect influence of a friendly government can also readily be pushed too far.

For one thing, the Republican Party of the war years was not yet so completely a business-oriented party as it was later to become. The party's most powerful member of the House, Thaddeus Stevens, quarreled with business interests on a number of occasions. If he had had his way, the interest on government bonds, which bankers purchased in currency, would also have been paid in currency, rather than in gold, and a major source of investment profit would have been removed.[50] Of course, the Republican Party, if not yet so business-minded as it became later, was hardly anti-business. Stevens did not have his way, and many wartime bonds were purchased in greenbacks for what amounted to forty cents on the dollar.[51] Except for the increasingly protective tariff and the general placement of the tax burden not on business but on consumers, however, few Republican policies of the war years were immediately conducive to business growth. The sounder banking system of the National Banking Act did not necessarily encourage business and industrial growth, when local banks had been generous in their credit policies, and when in any event the strongest Eastern banks were so reluctant to subject themselves to any Federal regulation that few of them joined the national system until coerced by the 1865 tax on state bank notes.[52] The building of the transcontinental railroads probably had an adverse effect on industrial growth for the time being, by pouring capital into projects that were economically ahead of their time, offering services for which the demand was not yet commensurate with their consumption of capital.

More important is the question of the long-run influence of Civil War changes on industrial and business development. Did the shifting of political power and of American attitudes associated with the war stimulate the rapid economic growth that occurred after the war? Once more it was not the war that was so important as events already in progress before Fort Sumter. When it is the long run that is examined, the transfer of political power from the agrarian aristocracy to the industrial capitalists had become inevitable by the middle of the nineteenth century. For that matter, even at the height of pre–Civil War Southern political power, the political climate of the United States can scarcely be said to have been hostile to the advance of capitalism. It never was. Not only was industrialization already well advanced before the Civil War, but the increasing inclination of both major political parties, Democrats as well as Republicans, to befriend industrial business was already becoming apparent and would surely have accompanied continuing industrial progress without the war. Although the war led to an unprecedented expansion of the activities of the Federal government and an unprecedented centralization of political power, it is unlikely that even these developments went far enough into areas relevant enough to business activity to have much effect on American industrialization, or on the general organization of American society either.

Allan Nevins argued in his monumental history of *The War for the Union* that the Civil War brought a decisive turn in the United States from an amorphous, amoeba-like society with multiple clusters of life centers in market towns and cities large and small — an "invertebrate society" — toward an organized, structured, vertebrate society. The thesis of his volumes, he said at the beginning,

> is that the war measurably transformed an inchoate nation, individualistic in temper and wedded to improvisation, into a shaped and disciplined nation, increasingly aware of the importance of plan and control. The improvised war of 1861–62 became the organized war of 1863–64. The invertebrate country of Bull Run days, goaded by necessity, gathered its energies together, submitted to system, and became the partially-structured country which heard the news of Five Forks.[53]

"Probably the greatest single change in American civilization in the war period," Nevins went on to say at the end of his final completed volume, "directly connected with the conflict, was the replacement of an unorganized nation by a highly organized society — organized, that is, on a national scale."[54]

Yet this thesis, too, has to be regarded as of only limited applicability. The long *Search for Order* — the phrase that Robert H. Wiebe perceptively made the title of his history of the United States from 1877 to 1920 — still lay ahead. Wiebe found America in 1877 still "the distended society," much like Nevins's "invertebrate society."[55] The expanded Federal government of the Civil War years for the most part faded away. For a generation after the close of the war, national organization, business, political, and social, mainly had yet to be achieved. The war might have helped turn the United States in the direction of national organization — the belief that some mystical great consummation lay ahead may have helped to do that — but at most it assisted a turn in a direction already amply chosen with the country's industrial takeoff.

## THE CONFEDERACY: ACCELERATING BREAKDOWN

Nevins's thesis suggests that the tendency of the South to centralize political power in spite of states'-rights doctrine under the pressures of war somehow contributed lastingly to the incorporation of the South into an organized nation after the war. "The South, in especial, which was rural and in large part crudely developed, had been in 1860–61 ineffectively organized," he says. But the South also changed, though the transformation has not been properly studied: "The growth of organization in the South would be better understood if prompt and comprehensive attention had been given to the subject in Southern memoirs and monographic histories, and if the records of the bureaus . . . [of the Confederate government] had been better preserved."[56] But Southerners were in fact slow to accept even the reluctant centralizing tendencies of the Confederate government, and it would be difficult to argue that after the failure of the Confederacy their experience with those tendencies hastened their acceptance of similar policies in the United States.

By the autumn and winter of 1863–1864, the war gave enough evidence of business boom in the North to lend credence to the later thesis that it was an economic turning point; but in the Confederacy the war was clearly leading to economic ruin. A feat of transportation such as the movement of Longstreet's divisions from Virginia to Chickamauga could be accomplished now only by cannibalizing the less important railroads to find equipment to keep the major ones rolling. Traffic on the major lines moved only at a crawl at that. Engines were sputtering toward exhaustion; in the fall of 1863 some fifty precious locomotives were estimated to be standing idle in the Confederacy for lack of tires;[57] by the next spring the fastest train between Richmond and Wilmington, North Carolina was operating at an average speed of ten and a quarter miles per hour.[58]

Confederate centralization of power, such as it was, never reached adequately into the railroads to form them into a Confederate system. With railroads breaking down, more primitive wagon transport was also nearing paralysis because the armies were well on their way to destroying the South's stock of horses and mules. Without transport, the agricultural and industrial products of the Confederacy too rarely reached their destination. Food prices and shortages in the towns and cities were worse than those that had caused riots the winter before. New clothing was almost impossible to buy.[59]

The Confederate armies themselves eked out an existence in rags and on rations little above bare subsistence levels. Fortunately, Josiah Gorgas's administration of the Ordnance Department still shone as a beacon light of rare Confederate administrative efficiency, and the armies still had the weapons they needed to fight. Perversity ruled in the other supply departments. Davis stubbornly defended the inept Lucius Northrop in the Commissary Department because he liked him, but he secured the resignation of the slightly more effective Quartermaster General, Colonel Abraham C. Myers, on August 10, 1863, because he disliked him. Davis at least found a fairly effective replacement for Myers in Brigadier-General Alexander R. Lawton, but not until February 17, 1864, and the affair worsened the President's tenuous relations with Congress while doing nothing to improve logistics.[60]

Two of the Confederacy's main sources of hope for independence had evaporated in the course of 1863. After Gettysburg, the Confederate armies could no longer expect to win the war with the sort of positive, aggressive strategy that had carried Lee northward in September 1862 and June 1863, to seek a Napoleonic victory on Northern soil that would crush Northern morale and compel the Lincoln government to negotiate a peace. After Gettysburg and Vicksburg, the last hope of foreign intervention to assure Confederate independence also disappeared.

There had no longer been a real chance of such intervention after the Emancipation Proclamation. Napoleon III nevertheless continued to see John Slidell occasionally and to profess his willingness to act on the Confederacy's behalf if Great Britain would only join him,[61] and Britain had remained friendly enough that the Confederacy could by legal subterfuge build warships in British yards and get them to sea and fitted out and manned with the help of British subjects. Thus the Confederates had obtained their commerce-raiding cruisers: *Alabama, Florida, Georgia, Shenandoah*. Truth to tell, however, even as early as 1862 the launching of the *Alabama* into Confederate hands had been less a result of friendly British policy than of the dilatoriness of the Queen's law officers in searching out legal grounds for detaining the vessel. The immediate issues of the Civil War aside, it would never do for Great Britain to sanction a general principle allowing neutral states to build warships for belligerent powers. By the spring of 1863, the British government had resolved to act more decisively to prevent still another cruiser, the *Alexandra*, from hoisting a Confederate ensign after sailing out of British waters. On April 5 the ship was seized; it was later released but never served the Confederacy.[62] Meanwhile the government adopted a tolerant and patient attitude toward the United States over the seizure of a British merchantman, the *Peterhoff*, by none other than Captain Charles Willkes, while bound for Matamoros, Mexico. The United States asserted the international-law doctrine of continuous voyage, arguing that the cargo was clearly intended for the Confederacy. The Americans eventually retained the part of the cargo consisting of contraband, and the British could take satisfaction in American adoption of a principle toward which the United States had been customarily hostile when it was Great Britain that was the belligerent.[63]

For the Confederacy, worse was to follow. Napoleon III's flirtations with the South included a meeting with John Slidell on June 18, 1863, after the news of Chancellorsville had arrived, at which the Emperor replied to Slidell's urgings that he act independently of England on behalf of the Confederacy by saying that he agreed in principle, although the present moment was too dangerous because of the risk of a European war over the Polish insurrection. Two days later, moreover, Napoleon met with two members of the British Parliament who were anxious to help the Confederacy, William S. Lindsay and John A. Roebuck. He told them that while he would not again make a formal overture to England for cooperative action toward America, because when he had done so before Lord John Russell had revealed his initiative to the United States, he continued to favor recognition of the Confederacy. He authorized his visitors so to inform Parliament.

Unfortunately for the Confederacy, Roebuck was a bungler and something of a butt of ridicule — a man of inflated pretensions laughingly called Don Roebucco. On June 30 he offered a motion that Her Majesty should join with the other great powers to bring about recognition of the Confederacy. With numerous allusions to his having been taken into the confidence of Napoleon, he succeeded in conveying the impression that he was an errand boy for the French. Thereby he ensured that his efforts would by no means be taken seriously. The stout friend of democracy John Bright mangled him in debate. He met disapproval from the members both of the Government and of the Opposition, and on July 13 he withdrew his motion.[64]

Significantly, the news of Gettysburg had not yet reached Great Britain. But after word of the great Union victory seemed definite by July 25, Palmerston took up the news to remark that it would not be logical to recognize the Confederacy at a moment when the Confederate war effort was less successful than ever before. Against the background of Gettysburg, furthermore, another possible crisis in Anglo-American relations approached its conclusion, with Gettysburg guaranteeing an outcome already foreshadowed by the *Alexandra* affair: the case of the Laird rams.

Thomas H. Dudley, the U.S. consul at Liverpool, was ably gathering information that he sent on to Charles Francis Adams at the American Legation, detailing the construction progress and the ownership arrangements of two ironclad warships building in the yards of Messrs. John Laird & Co. at Birkenhead under a contract negotiated by Captain James Dunwoody Bulloch, C.S.N., the Confederate naval agent who had been principally instrumental in securing the Confederacy's earlier British-built commerce raiders. The rams were powerful enough that they might at least threaten the blockade. Seward and Adams became careful to warn Great Britain that their entrance into Confederate service could mean an Anglo-American war. On September 2, Dudley and Adams learned, one of the rams had her rigging completed and her engines in working order. Adams responded on September 5 by writing an emphatic protest to Russell, but it happened that the Foreign Secretary had already given orders to prevent the sailing of the rams. On the very day of Adams's note, and before he received it, Russell ordered their detention. At his urging, the law officers had gathered appropriate evidence to warrant this step.[65]

These events of July to September provoked the despairing Confederates practically to break off their diplomatic efforts in Great Britain. Already on August 4, Secretary of State Benjamin had instructed James M. Mason that his continued residence in London would no longer be consistent with the dignity of the Confederate government. On September 30 Mason left London to join Slidell in Paris.[66] In October, at a meeting presided over by Benjamin in the President's absence, the Confederate Cabinet decided to expel all British consuls. The situation of these officials had always been anomalous, because they lacked exequaturs addressed to the Confederate States and received their orders through the British Legation in Washington. Nevertheless, their expulsion was something of a dying gasp of King Cotton diplomacy, an abandonment of the once confident Confederate hope that Europe's appetite for cotton would compel intervention to assure Confederate independence.[67]

Ironically, cotton came to serve the overseas requirements of the Confederacy better now that the hope was abandoned. The Confederacy could feel free to use its cotton simply as an article of commerce, and use it the Confederates did to intensify their efforts to bring war materials through the blockade. Collin J. McRae, an Alabama businessman who had arrived in England in May 1863 to manage the Erlanger loan, proceeded to organize blockade-running efforts on the eastern side of the Atlantic. On February 6, 1864 the Confederate Congress gave the President sole control over cotton shipments and required private blockade runners to place half their cargo space at the disposal of the government, at fixed rates. Under Thomas L. Bayne a Bureau of Foreign Supplies organized cotton procurement east of the Mississippi to exploit cotton in foreign trade and regulated blockade running on the western side of the Atlantic in a manner that complemented McRae's efforts overseas.[68] The blockade continued to wind its coils ever tighter — Frank L. Owsley's conservative estimates have one blockade runner in three falling to the Union squadrons in 1864, as contrasted with one in eight in 1862;[69] but the Confederate war effort now benefited more than before from the ships that escaped the blockade, and cotton commerce in 1864 suggests that much more might have been accomplished if the Confederacy had tried to use cotton as a commercial asset rather than a diplomatic bludgeon from the first.

Two Confederate hopes were gone, but a third remained. The gray legions would not conquer a peace in the North, and the Old World would not intervene in the New to revise the balance of power in the South's favor. But the Army of Northern Virginia still stood unbroken along the Rappahannock and the Rapidan, and in the winter after Chattanooga Joe Johnston seemingly rediscovered the vigor he had lacked since his long-ago wounding at Seven Pines, and succeeding Bragg in command on December 27,[70] he marvelously restored the morale and the fighting edge of the Army of Tennessee.

Neither of these Confederate armies was altogether what it had been in its youth. In the autumn of 1863, when Meade's Army of the Potomac jousted with Lee across the now familiar battlegrounds between the Potomac and the Rappahannock, a number of disconcerting lapses confirmed that the Army of Northern Virginia no longer possessed either the aggressive power to smash enemy columns as it had done at Second Manassas or the finely honed capacity for deceptive maneuver it had displayed at Chancellorsville.

An action at Bristoe Station on October 14 gave disappointing evidence to Lee that his army's strength in attack had been drained to a dismaying degree. The Federals checked Confederate assaults with disturbing ease.[71] When the Federals also snuffed out two Confederate bridgeheads over the Rappahannock, at Rappahannock Station and Kelly's Ford on November 7, inflicting 2,023 Confederate casualties while losing only 419 themselves, they gave Lee similar evidence that his army no longer possessed its old flexibility and quickness of maneuver.[72]

The deficiencies of the Confederate armies were at bottom those of sheer manpower. The accumulated casualties of Lee's aggressive battles from Mechanicsville through Gettysburg were too much for the limited Southern reservoir of potential soldiers to replace. But it was not simply numbers that had been lost; still more irreplaceably, the best and the bravest of the Confederate fighting men had gone, particularly the best officers. The lapses at Bristoe Station, Rappahannock Station, and Kelly's Ford were principally lapses of command among Lee's corps and division leaders. Here again was the problem that D. S. Freeman made the theme of *Lee's Lieutenants:* the difficulty of sustaining the roster of adequate commanders.[73] Admiring Lee as he did, Freeman did not probingly ask the question whether Lee's own costly strategy of attack was principally responsible for the crippling depletion of the officer corps; but he did conclude that the depletion of good officers was imposing a creeping paralysis on Lee's army.

Still, despite disappointments, through the autumn campaigns of 1863 Lee consistently checked Meade's rival efforts in offensive maneuver, notably in the Mine Run campaign of November 26–December 1,[74] and he did so notwithstanding the absence of much of Longstreet's First Corps. Without hope of mounting another invasion of the North, Confederate troops could still fight stubbornly on the defensive — and herein lay the third and final hope. If the Confederate armies could not win the war in the North, they might yet win it in the South, by rebuffing every Federal invasion, rolling up the butcher's bill of the Northern armies, convincing the North that the Confederate will to independence was unquenchable — and especially by doing these things through the coming Presidential election of 1864, when the Democrats might capture the White House and agree to a negotiated peace.

This reckoning assumed, of course, that the Confederate will to win would outlast that of the Union, itself a point on which the evidence was uncertain. Elections for the Confederate Second Congress had stretched on over a period of months in 1863, while the Confederate armies were suffering their setbacks of the year. The outcome was to strengthen the representation in Congress of men of Whig and Unionist background—among active Confederate politicians, the two characteristics tended to run together, four-fifths of the former Whigs in Congress having been opponents of secession until late in the 1860–1861 crisis—against former Democrats and secessionists. About three-fifths of the First Congress had consisted of the latter group; the Second Congress was about evenly balanced, and the Whig-Unionists were distinctly more inclined than the Democrat-secessionists toward defeatism now that the experiment in independence was encountering deep troubles. The 1863 Congressional elections indicated, therefore, at least the beginnings of a revulsion against the Confederacy, one most noticeable among middle-income districts of middle-sized farmers.[75] The center of the revulsion was North Carolina, the one Confederate state where the old prewar party lines had never been abandoned, and where since 1862 Governor Zebulon B. Vance had been obstructing conscription, withholding North Carolina supplies from any but North Carolina troops, and resisting all efforts at centralization of power in Richmond.[76]

On the other hand, only the barest minority of the newly elected Congressmen seem to have felt a mandate to try to make peace, and none openly opposed a war to the finish.[77] Furthermore, a lame-duck session of the First Congress met in December 1863, in a mood to quarrel with the President because the elections could be interpreted as a protest against his leadership, but in a mood also to assist the President in tightening belts and facing up to a supreme effort to hold off the Federals until after the Northern elections. To this end Congress established control over cotton and blockade running, restored the power of the President to suspend the writ of habeas corpus, and dealt with the overriding problem of manpower for the armies by strengthening the draft laws.

Particularly, on December 28, 1863 Congress modified the draft to eliminate the hiring of substitutes and to make those who had employed them eligible for enrollment.[78] A new conscription law of February 17, 1864 provided for the drafting of seventeen-year-olds and men between forty-five and fifty into state reserves, to free men between eighteen and forty-five for the Confederate armies. Congress also extended the term of military service from three years to the duration of the war, thus retaining the men who had enlisted in 1861; reduced the number of offices and occupations granted exemptions; provided for the conscription of agricultural and industrial workers whom the President might then assign to war production; curbed abuses of the exemption for slaveowners and overseers; and authorized the use of both free blacks and slaves in labor units.[79]

The habeas corpus act of February 13, 1864 was intended largely to strengthen the Executive's hand in apprehending deserters and dealing with organized bands of opponents of the war and especially of the draft. Such bands were growing in the mountain counties of Virginia and North Carolina and the hill country of Georgia, Alabama, and Mississippi. Inevitably, the act was bemoaned by extreme states'-rights men and strict constitutionalists such as Vice President Stephens, who said it meant the end of constitutional liberty throughout the continent; but it was obstruction of the draft by states'-righters of this stamp that helped drive Congress into Davis's arms on the civil-liberties question in the first place.[80]

Some Confederates thought the manpower crisis desperate enough and its solution so essential to the last remaining hope of Confederate independence that they were willing to attempt a truly drastic solution. On January 2, 1864 Joe Johnston called a conference of his principal subordinates in his new command, and one of them, Irish-born Pat Cleburne, who had successfully led the rear-guard action at Taylor's Ridge after the battle of Chattanooga, read to the assemblage a memorandum proposing the arming of the slaves. Most of Johnston's lieutenants reacted with horror, and one of them, W. H. T. Walker, collected a sheaf of negative letters that he sent to the President in order to nip such dangerous ideas in the bud. Davis thanked Walker for the information and had the Secretary of War inform Johnston that no publicity about Cleburne's notion should be allowed to reach the public. Significantly, however, Davis added no expressions of horror of his own, leaving an opening to his possible future acceptance of black soldiers.[81]

For the present, nevertheless, some things just could not be done, no matter that Confederate independence might hang on them, and for all the belt tightening of the winter session of the Confederate Congress, the observer must be impressed again by the quantity of perversity with which the Confederates hindered their own efforts toward independence. The unwillingness even in a desperate winter to legislate reasonably adequate taxation, the persistence of Vice President Stephens and his friends in opposing small sacrifices of personal liberties for the liberty of the South,[82] the connivance of state officials in the obstruction of the draft,[83] all are additions to a larger series of self-defeating actions and attitudes each probably understandable on some more or less rational ground, but taken together raising again the suspicion of a fatal rift in the psyche of the South. "The fact was," say the most recent authoritative historians of the Confederate Congress, "that most Confederates, at least subconsciously, placed a limit on the price they would willingly pay for independence; and for a considerable number of those who had initially gone along with secession, that price was ridiculously low."[84]

And while the dedication of President Davis to the Confederate cause was unquestionable, the President contributed his personal perversities. For the coming military contests that might determine the outcome of the Northern Presidential election and on which the Confederacy's final hope rested, during the winter season both sides made changes in their high commands. In the Federal Congress, the House on February 1 and the Senate on February 24 acted to revive the grade of lieutenant-general, vacant since George Washington had held it during the Quasi-War with France. Lincoln signed the measure into law on February 29, and the Congress and the President both obviously had in mind bestowing the grade on the officer whose record of success was virtually unbroken for two years from Fort Henry to Chattanooga — U.S. Grant. Lincoln promptly nominated Grant on March 1, the Senate confirmed him the next day, Grant was commissioned on March 9, and on the 10th Lincoln ordered him to take command of all the armies of the United States.[85] In Richmond, meanwhile, on February 24, Jefferson Davis ordered the conduct of military operations of all the Confederate armies entrusted to his close friend, but unfortunately the general whom Grant had defeated at Chattanooga, Braxton Bragg.[86] For the climactic campaigns, Davis was choosing failure to contend against success.

# TEN

# Traditional Politics and Modern War

## LINCOLN RENOMINATED

Salmon P. Chase thought it imperative both for the approaching crisis of the war and for the redemption of America in the postwar era that the banners of the Republican Party and the country be carried by the only available leader of moral and intellectual stature commensurate with the coming challenges: himself.

Chase was indeed a highly moral man, as proved by his prewar achievements in providing the Midwestern Republican Party with its uncompromising core of moral dedication to antislaveryism. He was so aware of his moral superiority, however, that he was able to acknowledge realistically the merit of almost any expedient, however dubious otherwise, if it might contribute to installing him in the Executive Mansion.

Presidential ambitions cost money, and Chase was not a rich man. Therefore early in the war he consented to his curious private financial arrangements with Jay Cooke. But he was so conscious of his own inability to do wrong that he displayed none of Cooke's sensitivity lest the arrangements become public knowledge. Later, Chase exhibited still less sensitivity and still fewer critical perceptions when his daughter, Kate, saw to the satisfaction of still greater financial demands than the Cooke relationship could meet, through her marriage to William Sprague, the Rhode Island textile heir, politician, militia soldier, and speculator in illegal cotton trading with the Confederacy shielded by complaisant Treasury agents.

It was meritorious in the quest for appropriately moral Presidential leadership also that Chase should have transformed the employees of the Department of the Treasury into an army of political agents maneuvering for his Presidential nomination. This Chase political machine in the Treasury would have its work cut out for it, however, because President Lincoln, though he often gave the appearance of carelessness about political details as well as about day-to-day administrative matters generally, had astutely manipulated the patronage of the rest of the government to create indebtedness to him among key Republican functionaries in every state that would send delegates to the party's national convention, especially including those Southern states that were in the process of Presidential reconstruction. Lincoln apparently believed that allowing the Chase Treasury machine to work at cross purposes with the larger Lincoln political machine was a price worth paying to help maintain cooperative relations with the zealously antislavery wing of the party in waging war and making policy.[1]

The Chase machine not only had a larger political engine against which to contend for the 1864 Republican Presidential nomination, fueled by all the power of the wartime Presidency, but it was also a handicap that Chase's political acumen, particularly in so fine a matter as his sense of timing, did not match his moral grandeur. He launched his campaign too early. A meeting of Chase partisans to arrange Presidential organization and strategy took place in Washington on December 9, 1863, just after the opening of Congress. The meeting appointed central, state, and local committees.[2] On February 22 Senator Samuel C. Pomeroy of Kansas, signing himself "Chairman, National Executive Committee" of the Chase forces, issued a letter marked "Private" that immediately became public knowledge. Soon called the "Pomeroy Circular," it presented a catalog of Lincoln's deficiencies, said that his reelection was practically impossible and that even if it could somehow be achieved it would result in the continued languishing of the war effort, and in contrast listed Chase's sterling qualities.[3]

The prematurity of the Pomeroy Circular as the opening salvo of the Chase campaign lay in the fact that it gave the Lincoln partisans every warrant to train their guns upon Chase as an open rival. Chase became as visible a political target as Lincoln himself, while if he had continued to lie low for a time, leaving it to his agents to collect delegates quietly, the President would have gone on accumulating the scars of political combat while Chase remained relatively sheltered. A strategy of lying low might all the more have commended itself because Chase had no rival worth fearing as a Presidential contender among the Republican Radicals. The Pomeroy Circular, however, both made Chase highly conspicuous and contributed to the Lincoln faction the advantage of being able to charge Chase with disloyalty to the administration of which he was a member. In the House of Representatives, Francis Preston Blair, Jr. of Missouri launched forth a vitriolic attack upon the ungrateful Chase.[4]

The Secretary of the Treasury felt sufficiently embarrassed by the imputation of disloyalty that once again he handed Lincoln his resignation, claiming at the same time that while of course he had consulted with his partisans, he had known nothing of the Pomeroy Circular before it was issued. This denial seems to have been untrue, but with Chase once more in a subdued mood, just as when he had submitted his earlier resignation, Lincoln decided the time was not yet ripe to part with his services. So subdued was Chase, in fact, that on March 5 he wrote a letter publicly withdrawing his Presidential candidacy.[5]

This letter represented an adoption of the low-profile strategy that would have served Chase better in the first place. Chase did not abandon his Presidential ambitions — which would have been an impossibility — nor did his agents cease a more discreet search for delegates; but the public withdrawal from contention caused those Radicals who felt utterly unwilling to swallow another dose of Lincoln to elevate John Charles Frémont as a substitute candidate. Thus Frémont, rather than Chase, might become the Lincoln faction's most conspicuous target, while Frémont's military record and general history of incapacity were such as to assure Chase he could push the Pathfinder aside if the national convention should reach the point of dropping Lincoln.

An *ad hoc* convention calling itself the Radical Democratic Party and meeting in Cleveland in May went through the formal motions of nominating Frémont for the Presidency. The members of the convention were a mixed bag of abolitionists, radical German-Americans, and restless Democrats.[6] But the characteristics that left Chase unworried about Frémont were all too apparent even to those who grasped at the straw of his candidacy. As the spring of 1864 unfolded, the patronage proved to have placed the President so unassailably in charge of his party that the only better hope than Frémont for those who thought Lincoln deficient seemed to be to try postponing the nominating convention, on the chance that with the passage of time something useful might turn up. The Lincoln men had set the convention date unusually early, June 7, on the converse theory that as long as they were in control, they ought to strike quickly.

Assembling in the border city of Baltimore, the convention officially took the form of a National Union Convention, not simply a Republican gathering; supposedly it sounded the trumpet for all who were loyal to the Union, Republican or Democrat. The disguise, however, was thin. This was a meeting of the Republican Party, and its proceedings were shaped by the balance of power among the political professionals of that party.

Presidential power still had a long way to go to reach mid- and late-twentieth-century dimensions, and such centralization of power in the Federal Executive as the Civil War had produced was not destined to be permanent. Nevertheless, as William B. Hesseltine argues in his history of *Lincoln and the War Governors,*[7] while in 1860 the national Presidential nominee had been dependent on the state governors to mobilize party workers on his behalf, by 1864 the growth of the Federal bureaucracy and Lincoln's careful use of it had made the governors and the state party organizations so dependent on the President for loaves and fishes that Lincoln could dominate his party's convention as no President had dominated a modern multifactional party before him. Lincoln could draw also on a considerable though not precisely measurable reservoir of growing popular regard. But in the convention, it was his party strength that was decisive. The roll-call count on the first ballot was 484 votes for Lincoln, 22 for General Grant, whereupon Missouri changed its vote for Grant to make Lincoln's renomination unanimous.[8]

Turbulent Missouri had sent two delegations, one conservative and one Radical, and the Committee on Credentials had recommended seating the Radicals. The Lincoln forces could readily afford such a concession to the factions that would have preferred a different Presidential candidate. The platform drafted mainly by a man close to Lincoln, Henry J. Raymond, editor and co-founder of *The New-York Times,* was also intended to close ranks with the radicals.[9] It called for a vigorous prosecution of the war, a constitutional amendment to abolish slavery, gratitude to the country's soldiers and sailors, and with reference to the recent massacre at Fort Pillow and related events, affirmation "That the Government owes to all men employed in its armies, without regard to distinction of color, the full protection of the laws of war — and that any violation of these laws, or of the usages of civilized nations in time of war, by the Rebels now in arms, should be made the subject of prompt and full redress."[10] The platform also endorsed a liberal immigration policy, speedy construction of the Pacific railroad, economy in expenditures, a just system of taxation, and the Monroe Doctrine (the latter with an eye to current French activities in Mexico).[11]

Apparently Lincoln had sent out overtures to Ben Butler as a possible Vice-Presidential candidate, as another means of clasping hands with the Radicals. Butler turned down the offer, however, and the Vice-Presidential nomination then was put to a different use, that of underlining the claim that Republicanism had given way to a National Union Party. The incumbent, Hannibal Hamlin of Maine, represented old Republicanism and a safe state, and he could not add much strength at the polls. Although Lincoln's role is not clear, almost certainly the President was the prime mover in giving the nomination instead to the lifelong Southern Democrat Andrew Johnson, the Unionist military governor of Tennessee.[12]

With that work done, the convention adjourned and sent a delegation to inform Lincoln officially on June 9 of his renomination. The President with typical caution responded by saying that perhaps he should not definitely declare his acceptance before reading and considering the whole platform. (Indeed, not until June 27 did he say categorically: "The nomination is gratefully accepted, as the resolutions of the convention, called the platform, are heartily approved."[13]) Meanwhile, however, Lincoln gave special notice to the plank advocating an antislavery amendment to the Constitution, with emphasis indicating that here was a new but permanent commitment grown out of the unfolding of the war, and not merely a concession offered up to the Radicals:

> I will now say, however, I approve the declaration in favor of so amending the Constitution as to prohibit slavery throughout the nation. When the people in revolt, with a hundred days of explicit notice, that they could, within those days, resume their allegiance, without the overthrow of their institution, and that they could not so resume it afterwards, elected to stay out, such amendment of the Constitution as now proposed, became a fitting, and necessary conclusion to the final success of the Union cause. Such alone can meet and cover all cavils. Now, the unconditional Union men, North and South, perceive its importance, and embrace it. In the joint names of Liberty and Union, let us labor to give it legal form, and practical effect.[14]

## THE UNION ARMY RETAINED

In the joint names of Liberty and Union, Lincoln prepared to seek reelection and the power to carry the war to a victory that he now explicitly pledged would include the final elimination of slavery everywhere within the borders of the United States.

But reelection could not be managed as renomination had been. Not Lincoln's power within his party but the uncertain measure of his public stature would be decisive now. As the military setbacks of the Union in 1862 had doubtless contributed to that year's Republican setbacks at the polls, furthermore, and as the Union military victories of 1863 had doubtless gone far to ensure that year's Republican electoral successes, so the outcome of the Presidential and Congressional elections of 1864 might well depend on the course of events on the battlefields. On this dependence the Confederates were counting. The dependence was all the greater because the price of continued military victory in 1864 would have to be another sifting of the manpower of the North into the ranks of the Federal armies, the most direct means of aggravating the very war-weariness and discouragement that were the factors most likely to defeat Lincoln's bid for reelection.

Even the victories won by the Federal armies in 1863 complicated Lincoln's problems, because those victories themselves continued to add to the manpower demands upon the North. The areas conquered by the Union armies had to be garrisoned. To make continued advance and conquest possible, conquered cities had to be patrolled and held securely as bases of supply, and especially the railroad lines on which the armies depended for sustenance had to be guarded against Confederate raiders. The railroads gave new strategic and operational mobility to Civil War armies, permitting armies of great size to campaign without having to live off the country through which they passed, but the railroads were also extremely delicate sources of dependence when they ran through hostile territory. If rail communications were wrecked, a whole campaign could be ruined also, like Grant's overland drive on Vicksburg in 1862. To hold conquered territory and safeguard bases and lines of communications, therefore, the Union armies forever dropped off segments of themselves as they advanced. Each new penetration deeper into the South tended to leave the striking spearhead of the Union advance smaller while increasing the size of the logistical and supporting tail dragging behind. The disproportion of the supporting tail to the fighting vanguard of the armies did not reach the dimensions of World War II and later American armies, but the problem was already heightened by an effort to maintain among the Union soldiers a standard of living comparable to the comfortable one they had known at home. In consequence, when the 1864 campaigns began, the three field armies that would carry the brunt of the Union effort against Joe Johnston and Atlanta, for example, showed 352,265 men on their muster rolls, but took only about 100,000 directly into the campaign.[15]

On February 1, 1864 President Lincoln called for 500,000 three-year volunteers by March 10, with the draft to fill the quotas after that date.[16] On February 24, Congress attempted to strengthen the draft law by modifying the substitution and commutation features. Henceforth, substitutes had to be men not liable to the draft themselves; the drafted man who hired a substitute would be exempt only as long as his substitute remained in service; and payment of the commutation fee would exempt the payer from service only for the specific draft call at hand — if his name was drawn in a subsequent call, he would have to pay again or serve. In addition, the new draft law abolished the distinction between Class I and Class II enrollees, and it made African Americans eligible to be drafted.[17]

The Enrollment Act of 1863 had failed to provide for conscientious objectors, particularly for those whose consciences forbade their paying a commutation fee that would contribute to the war effort even if they more directly did not, and some objectors had been imprisoned and otherwise treated harshly by the military. When such cases came to Lincoln's attention, he issued paroles, and eventually, on December 15, 1863, the War Department directed that conscientious objectors who refused to pay commutation or provide substitutes should be put on parole until called for. Mainly, Lincoln saw to it that they were simply let alone. The new draft law of February 1864 stipulated, however, that conscientious objectors should serve in hospital work or in caring for freedmen, and that if they chose to pay commutation, the money should be used for medical purposes. These provisions solved the problems of all but the most purist of pacifists.[18]

Unfortunately, Army veterans considered the recruits being brought in by the draft, directly or indirectly, a sorry lot. The brokers who supplied substitutes inevitably dealt in the dregs of humanity, often crimping drunkards as the old British Navy press gangs had done — or they found immigrants fresh off the boat, who might someday become good soldiers, but who often began ignorant of the English language and utterly befuddled. The best of the conscripts, furthermore, good men who simply could not pay the commutation fee or buy a substitute, so labored under a stigma as conscripts and were so consistently regarded by the veterans as bad soldiers by definition, that it was hard for them not to fulfil the expectations of their officers, sergeants, and comrades: they often turned into bad soldiers.

Because the draft carried so unhappy a stigma, moreover, communities trying to avoid its imposition within their boundaries offered increasingly higher bounties to volunteers. The going rate for a man who would sign up for three years was $300 by 1864 (with an additional $100 for a veteran) — like the commutation fee, a whole year's wages for a workingman. The effect was to create a class of professional bounty collectors, who signed up intending to desert, and who when they could be held in the Army at all proved to be still worse soldiers than the substitutes. With cutthroats and hoodlums entering the ranks in growing numbers, disciplinary methods in the volunteer regiments more and more took on the worst attributes of peacetime Regular Army discipline, with bucking and gagging or spread-eagling a man on a caisson wheel becoming standard punishments.[19]

After postponing enforcement of his draft call to permit volunteers to take advantage of new bounties included in the law of February 24, Lincoln on March 14 increased his call from 500,000 to 700,000 volunteers and again ordered a draft, to fill quotas remaining after April 15.[20] Given the Army's judgment of the low quality of its current recruits, however, it seemed all the more important to solve a difficult problem: the imminent expiration of the three-year enlistment terms of most of the 1861 recruits. The volunteers of 1861 had now become — those who survived — the veteran core of the Union armies, and if they should depart en masse before the 1864 campaigns got well under way, then the prospects for decisive military success before the Presidential election would evaporate, and also very likely the Union's chances of winning the war.

Before the campaigning season resumed, therefore, the War Department mounted a drive in the camps of the veteran regiments to woo their soldiers to reenlist — preferably by regiments, to keep tested units as much as possible intact. If three-fourths of the soldiers of a regiment should reenlist, they might go home together for a thirty-day furlough and return to keep their organization and their flag. Every individual soldier who reenlisted received, in addition to the thirty-day furlough, a bounty of $400 plus state and local rewards that often added up to a total bounty of $700. The reenlistee became a veteran volunteer, with an appropriate chevron for his sleeve. The veterans had seen much more of war than they had ever imagined in 1861, and there was a natural inclination among them to think they had done their share of fighting and that it was now somebody else's turn — much as in the Korean and Vietnam Wars, when soldiers expected to be and were rotated out of combat after a stipulated term. Nevertheless, the U.S. government believed it needed a large portion of these men. It made its offer to them often amidst patriotic oratory, band music, and sometimes generously flowing alcohol, and eventually 136,000 veterans signed on for another three years or the war, a fairly remarkable figure. In the Army of the Potomac, 26,767 veterans reenlisted by the end of March, enough of a nucleus to hold the army together.[21]

## THE GENERALSHIP OF U. S. GRANT

By that time, the new General-in-Chief of the U.S. Army was present with the Army of the Potomac north of the Rapidan, and plans for the coming campaigns were well advanced. Grant had decided to keep Meade in command of the Army of the Potomac; the Philadelphian was a brigadier-general in the Regular Army as of July 3, 1863 as a reward for Gettysburg.[22] But Grant would make his own headquarters at Meade's side to supervise directly the campaign against the most formidable Confederate adversaries, Lee and the Army of Northern Virginia. Halleck was to remain in Washington with the title of Chief of Staff, subordinate now to Grant but otherwise continuing to do much what he had done before, communicating with and coordinating the various Union armies and acting as a link between the armies on the one hand and the War Department, Stanton, and Lincoln on the other.[23] In the West, the Military Division of the Mississippi, which had been created for Grant to command in October, passed on March 18 to Sherman, who was a Regular Army brigadier as of the date of Vicksburg's surrender.[24] On March 26 McPherson succeeded Sherman at the head of the Army of the Tennessee.[25] With that army, Thomas's Army of the Cumberland, and the small Army of the Ohio, since February 9, 1864 commanded by Schofield,[26] Sherman would wrestle against Joe Johnston and the Army of Tennessee.

After visiting Washington and the Army of the Potomac early in March to receive his new commission and assume command, Grant had returned to the West for two weeks to confer with Sherman and outline a strategy for winning the war.[27] No overall strategic design for the whole Union war effort had gained a semblance of official acceptance and execution since Scott's Anaconda Policy. To the extent that the blockade and the gradual constriction of Confederate territory and resources represented the Anaconda in action, this strategy was winning the war too slowly to assure that the Northern people's patience would endure, that a President committed to the complete defeat of the Confederacy would be elected in 1864, and that the North would push the contest through to the restoration of the Union and the extinction of slavery.

Beyond the only partially successful Anaconda Policy, the Federal efforts to reopen the Mississippi and to break the Confederacy's east-west railroad communications through Chattanooga had given a measure of at least regional coherence to Union strategy west of the Appalachians; but no coherent strategic design had guided the principal Union army in the East since the departure of McClellan. When McClellan commanded the Army of the Potomac, he did have a strategy: while conciliating the Confederates by refraining from all unnecessary harshness and destruction, he would dishearten them by outmaneuvering their armies and seizing their capital city, and with this combination of the carrot and the stick he would bring them to peace talks and end the war. None of McClellan's successors in command of the Army of the Potomac, however, had given evidence of possessing a strategic concept for winning the war. Burnside and Hooker concentrated all their attention on winning the climactic, Napoleonic battles they intended to fight against Lee. So much did they point their efforts toward winning a battle that if somehow either of them had succeeded at Fredericksburg or Chancellorsville, the victory might have done the Union little more good than a defeat, because it is difficult to believe that Burnside or Hooker would have known what to do next. This concentration on the battle as the central object of war was a product of the Napoleon cult so prevalent among nineteenth-century soldiers, of which the obsession with the grand Austerlitz or Jena-Auerstädt battle was in turn a part. One of the best things that can be said about Meade as commander of the Army of the Potomac is that he did not share in the Napoleonic battle mania. In his late summer and autumn campaigns of 1863 he drew away from confrontations with Lee's army when the confrontations were likely to produce nothing but bloody battle. But Meade did not have a design for winning the war either.

From the beginning of the conflict, Lincoln's efforts to find his own strategic recipe for victory if his generals could not do so had included the idea that one essential ingredient would be to apply pressure all around the circumference of the Confederacy, by having all the Union armies, or at least several of them, attack at once.

> . . . I state my general idea of this war to be that we have the *greater* numbers, and the enemy has the *greater* facility of concentrating forces upon points of collision [because of his interior lines]; that we must fail, unless we can find some way of making *our* advantage an over-match for *his*; and that this can only be done by menacing him with superior forces at *different* points, at the *same* time; so that we can safely attack, one or both, if he makes no change; and if he *weakens* one to strengthen the other, forbear to attack the strengthened one, but seize, and hold the weakened one, gaining so much.[28]

To this idea, Halleck as the military scholar replied by citing the scholastic military principle that strategy consists of the *concentration* of one's forces against decisive points, and thus rejecting Lincoln's proposed multiple attacks. "To operate on exterior lines against an enemy occupying a central position will fail, as it has always failed, in ninety-nine cases out of a hundred," said Halleck. "It is condemned by every military authority I have ever read."[29]

Halleck had read almost all of them. Grant had not, and one of the first of Grant's decisions regarding a strategy to win the war was that all the Union armies should advance nearly simultaneously, at the beginning of May, to apply pressure against the Confederacy everywhere. The Army of the Potomac would move against Lee. Sherman's armies would move against Johnston. The lesser Union armies would advance also. Ben Butler was back at Fort Monroe where he had been early in the war; since December 11, 1863 he had commanded the Department of Virginia and North Carolina, in which during April he organized the Army of the James.[30] He was to lead this army toward Richmond from the southeastern approaches. Major-General Franz Sigel, commanding the Department of West Virginia since March 10, would lead the Federal forces in the Shenandoah southward up the Valley.[31] Banks in the Department of the Gulf would advance on Mobile.[32] Scattered detachments too small to undertake offensives were as much as possible to be consolidated into one of these attacking columns.

But Grant had a fuller strategic vision than simply that of attacking on all fronts. At least since the dawn of modern military history in the Thirty Years War of 1618–1648, and certainly since the French Revolutionary and Napoleonic Wars, the standard objective of military strategy had been the destruction of the enemy army, if not its literal, physical destruction, then the imposition of casualties so severe and psychological shock so unsettling that the enemy army would cease to exist as an effective fighting force. Such was the objective sought and attained by Napoleon in his Austerlitz and Jena-Auerstädt battles, and such of course was the objective that Lee had consistently pursued. Now Grant's orders to his principal subordinates made it clear that his also was to be a strategy of annihilation, that the Federal armies were also to adopt as their overriding objective the destruction of the enemy armies.

All other objectives, including territorial ones and even the capture of Richmond, were to be secondary. If Atlanta or Richmond or any other territorial objective should be attained, the Confederate armies might fight on; but if the armies were destroyed, obviously they could no longer fight. So to Meade, Grant said: "Lee's army will be your objective point. Wherever Lee goes, there you will go also."[33] To Sherman, campaigning in a wider geographic sphere, Grant wrote of the destruction of enemy resources as an additional objective — a theme to be much developed later — but he made the enemy army the first objective: "You I propose to move against Johnston's army, to break it up and to get into the interior of the enemy's country as far as you can, inflicting all the damage you can against their war resources."[34]

There was to be a difference, however, between Grant's strategy of annihilation and Lee's. Lee was a fully Napoleonic general in his quest for the decisive battle of annihilation, the climactic single engagement in which the enemy army was to be destroyed in one grand thunderclap of war. To destroy the enemy army in one stroke had been Lee's aim in his first battle at the head of the Army of Northern Virginia, and the quest for the Austerlitz battle continued to guide Lee as long as the quality of his own army gave the slightest reason to hope for such accomplishment, through Gettysburg and even later. In the course of the coming campaign of 1864, he was to say to Major-General Jubal A. Early: "We must destroy this army of Grant's before it gets over James River."[35] But Grant was too realistically clear-eyed to hope for so rapidly decisive an outcome.

No large, resolute modern army, backed by the resources and will of a nineteenth-century democratic state, was likely to be destroyed completely and finally in a single battle or campaign. After all, even Napoleon's most powerful enemies, the Austrians, Russians, and Prussians, though dependent on possibly less resilient, autocratic governments, had risen up to fight again. Therefore Grant would not pursue the illusion of destroying the enemy army in a single battle. Grant's approach to strategy, unlike Lee's, is typified not by a regret that the enemy army had not been destroyed in one battle, but by his famous resolve "to fight it out on this line if it takes all summer."[36] To fulfill that resolve, in fact, was destined to take not only all the summer of 1864, but the autumn and winter and part of the next spring — yet Grant was hardly surprised by this prolonged endurance contest.

Grant's strategy of destruction of the enemy army did not necessarily imply its literal, physical annihilation, the killing or disabling of so many of its soldiers that it could fight no more. Grant initially had in mind rather the destruction of Lee's Army of Northern Virginia in the way he had eliminated Pemberton's Army of Vicksburg, by compelling its surrender. The intent with which he and Meade were to open their campaign of 1864 was to turn Lee's right flank and thus to interpose between Lee and Richmond. Grant hoped to conduct a campaign not of bloody battles but of maneuver against Lee as he had done against Pemberton, and to maneuver Lee like Pemberton into an untenable position in which he would have to surrender his army.[37] As the campaign unfolded, successive efforts to maneuver the Army of the Potomac in such a way as to place it between the enemy army and Richmond all met frustration. Thereupon Grant shifted his purpose to that of a larger turning movement to cut the lines of communications of both the Army of Northern Virginia and Richmond with the deeper South. Unfortunately for Grant's aspirations, Lee was not Pemberton.

The commander of the Army of Northern Virginia was too skillful a general to allow himself to be outmaneuvered as Pemberton had been. Eventually, then, Grant was to have to settle for the second-best version of his strategy of destruction against Lee's army. When he could not destroy it through a campaign of maneuver forcing its surrender, he turned to the much grimmer method of annihilating it through attrition, by trading casualties with it, locking Lee in combat not in brief episodes of battle but nearly continuously, day after day, week after week, knowing that the result of a prolonged exchange of losses must be the arrival of a day when the Army of the Potomac would still have men and would still exist, but the Army of Northern Virginia would not.

One more aspect of Grant's planning must be discussed. It is customary and justly so to praise him for his orchestration of the movements of all the principal armies into a single strategic design. Beyond its strategic virtue, this orchestration moved Union military planning closer than ever before toward embracing a conception of the operational art in war, to develop on a level between battle tactics and war strategy plans for defeating the Confederates not only along their entire defensive perimeter but also in theater-wide settings, by coordinating the maneuvers of several forces in each major theater. In Virginia, the Confederates would have to defend against Butler's Army of the James and Sigel's force in the Valley in addition to Meade's Army of the Potomac. In the West, Johnston would have to guard Georgia and its capital city against three armies rather than one.

Yet the concept of the operational art remained imperfectly grasped, and as a result the Union would not fully exploit the possibilities of this situation. Grant was to fail to coordinate effectively the activities of the Army of the Potomac and the Army of the James until almost a year had passed. He was to allow Butler to blunder into an operational and tactical dead end, so that for several months almost all of Butler's potential to aid Meade would be lost; nor did he use the Army of the Potomac in such a way that it might have contributed promptly to the relief and release of the Army of the James. Perhaps Grant might have served the entire Virginia theater better if he had not personally traveled with the Army of the Potomac, which tended to constrict his vision. Similarly, Sherman proved to use his three armies much as if they had been one. He advanced no further toward exploiting his command system's potential for three formations to engage in autonomous maneuver than sometimes to use his separate armies as Napoleon I had used separate corps, to spin a web whereby the enemy was threatened from several directions — but mainly on a tactical rather than a theater-wide, operational scale. The Union was not yet ready, in fact, to approach as close to an application of the operational art as Lee and Jackson had done in 1862 when Jackson's Valley Campaign featured the autonomous but coordinated activities of the Army of the Valley and Joe Johnston's army in front of Richmond.

Nevertheless, the Confederacy must now contend against a far more formidable Union coordination of forces than before, and through his idea of continuous combat Grant was soon to add a new and to the Confederacy extremely dangerous dimension to tactics as well.

## THE WILDERNESS, SPOTSYLVANIA, AND COLD HARBOR

Grant and Meade led the Army of the Potomac across the Rapidan on May 4 to open the 1864 campaign. They had about 118,000 men to 62,000 in the Army of Northern Virginia.[38] The Union army marched into the Wilderness around Chancellorsville, where Hooker had fought Lee exactly a year before. When Grant moved, Lee was upstream around Gordonsville. Aiming to get around Lee's right and to slip between Lee and Richmond, Grant hoped to pass through the tangled second-growth timber and underbrush of the Wilderness before he had to fight; in the Wilderness, his advantages of numbers and superior artillery would be much offset by the barely penetrable forest.

On May 5, however, Lee struck Grant's columns around Wilderness Tavern, and for two days the rival armies grappled amidst the trees and brush in one of the most horrifying battles of the war. The woods were dry, and the shooting set off forest fires that stalked the helpless wounded and consumed them, sometimes torturing them by exploding their cartridges around their bodies.

Lee and the Army of Northern Virginia fought with flashes of the Confederate Army's old skill. On May 6 Longstreet almost drove home a flank attack comparable to Jackson's of the year before — like Jackson, Longstreet was wounded by his own men in the process, a bullet passing through his right shoulder, severing nerves and nearly his arm. After three days of it, the Federals had lost 17,666 (2,246 killed, 12,037 wounded, 3,383 missing) to about 7,750 Confederate casualties.[39]

Held to at best a deadlock, Grant began to draw his army away during the night of May 7–8. But the soldiers of his vanguard, the Fifth Corps, soon found themselves marching not northward as had been habitual after such battles, to rest and refit, but southward, with Grant and his staff riding past them in the night to hurry them along. Grant nullified the setback in the Wilderness by refusing to acknowledge it as a setback. Instead he pressed on again around Lee's right flank. It was a defining moment of the campaign.[40]

Again Lee was alert to the move, and by morning of May 8 Confederates confronted the Union flanking column around Spotsylvania Court

House. Here began another battle, which lasted a week and a half.[41] Grant's method of seeking the destruction of the enemy army if he could not turn and trap it now became clearer. So far was Grant from sharing the cult of the Austerlitz battle that shaped the usual Civil War generalship that a battle lost or won meant relatively little to him. The purpose of a given battle was not to achieve decisive results in itself; a battle could no longer do that, anyway. Rather, Grant's design was to fight Lee day after day, grasping the Army of Northern Virginia with a bulldog grip and never letting go, fighting and fighting again as days led into weeks and weeks into months, all the while inflicting the casualties that would finally destroy Lee's army. To destroy Lee's army was the essential means to the winning of the war, and if Lee could not be outmaneuvered and trapped as Pemberton had, and if the elimination of an enemy army could no longer be achieved by a single spectacular Napoleonic battle, then Grant would destroy Lee's army by the less spectacular but grimly effective method of extracting casualties until it died. As Grant himself described his method:

> Soon after midnight, May 3d-4th, the Army of the Potomac moved out from its position north of the Rapidan, to start upon that memorable campaign, destined to result in the capture of the Confederate capital and the army defending it. This was not to be accomplished, however, without as desperate fighting as the world had ever witnessed; not to be consummated in a day, a week, a month, or a single season. The losses inflicted, and endured, were destined to be severe; but the armies now confronting each other had already been in deadly conflict for a period of three years, with immense losses in killed, by death from sickness, captured and wounded; and neither had made any real progress toward accomplishing the final end. . . . The campaign now begun was destined to result in heavier losses, to both armies, in a given time, than any previously suffered; but the carnage was to be limited to a single year, and to accomplish all that had been anticipated or desired at the beginning in that time. We had to have hard fighting to achieve this. The two armies had been confronting each other so long, without any decisive result, that they hardly knew which could whip.[42]

When Lee's skill prevented maneuver warfare from succeeding for Grant in 1864 as it had succeeded in the Vicksburg campaign, hard fighting became the essence of Grant's generalship. His method was to earn him an unfortunate reputation as a butcher; but Grant was no mere butcher, as he had demonstrated conclusively in the West. In the Vicksburg campaign, moreover, Grant's objective had been first a territorial one, and maneuver sufficed to capture that objective. Because his rival, Pemberton, was unskillful, maneuver also sufficed to capture a large Confederate army. But when Grant became General-in-Chief, the objectives before him were different. He must not only capture territorial objectives; he must win the war. To do that he must destroy Lee's army. If Lee was too good a general to allow his army to be extinguished in the way Pemberton's had been, Grant saw no alternative but to destroy Lee's army by fighting it.

The 1864 Virginia campaign moved on, consequently, without the respite between battles that had always been customary, but with Grant's and Lee's armies constantly in contact with each other. Because Lee's army had been drained of its former powers of aggressive maneuver — Longstreet's flanking attack in the Wilderness proved a last gasp of that method — Lee regularly entrenched wherever he stood to fight. In deference to the destructive power of the rifle, which tacticians were at last coming to acknowledge, the Federals entrenched, too. The campaign came to foreshadow World War I, with the armies inhabiting increasingly elaborate networks of holes in the ground, shelling and sniping at each other continually, an unwary raising of the head above the parapets likely to produce a fatal result, and any frontal attack more certain than ever to be futile — except as it might contribute to Grant's long-run end of wearing down the enemy army.

Or rather, the futility of a frontal attack was nearly certain, unless extraordinary skill went into the planning and execution. On May 10, the Union Sixth Corps of Major-General Horatio G. Wright, U.S.V., demonstrated such an exception. That afternoon Captain Ranald S. Mackenzie, Corps of Engineers, a twenty-four-year-old officer of exceptional promise and quality, asked Brigadier-General David A. Russell, U.S.V., commanding the First Division of the corps, to share the results of his reconnoitering. He pointed out to Russell an area where an attack force should be able to mass unseen only about 200 yards from the west flank of a northward-pointing Confederate salient, whose configuration on a map resembled a mule shoe, and which was so called by the Confederate troops. The Confederate front was entrenched as usual and was further protected by abatis — sharpened logs thrusting toward the Federals — and logs piled above the parapets. A partially completed Confederate second line supported the first sixty to eighty yards behind it. Mackenzie and Russell believed, however, that assailants forming in the sheltered area should be able to rush the Confederate works and enter them without excessive casualties. General Wright, the corps commander, agreed, and he and Russell selected for the assault what World War II military men would have called a task force, twelve regiments chosen from the Second and Third Brigades of Russell's division, some 4,500 to 5,000 men. To head the task force the generals selected another exceptional twenty-four-year-old, Colonel Emory Upton, 121st New York Infantry, commander of Russell's Second Brigade.

A brilliant tactician who had especially proven himself such at Rappahannock Station in November, Upton formed an assault column consisting of four lines of three regiments each. He brought his twelve regimental commanders to the front to study the route of the assault and the targeted works, and to explain his plan to them as carefully and completely as possible. The first line was to load and cap its muskets, so they would be ready to fire instantly. The other three lines were just to load muskets. All would fix bayonets. There were to be intervals of only ten feet between the advancing lines. There was to be a rush forward by the first line, three regiments from Upton's own brigade, with no pausing to fire. After crossing the enemy's first breastworks, these regiments should widen the penetration, the 121st New York and the 96th Pennsylvania turning by their right flank, the 5th Maine turning left. The second line was to dash on to carry the second Confederate line. The third and fourth lines were to form a reserve, the fourth line initially to advance only to the edge of the trees that shielded the assembly area and there to await orders.

An artillery barrage opened at 6 P.M. to prepare for the assault. The guns fired for ten minutes, whereupon the infantry charged, cheering. The first three regiments apparently covered the open ground in less than two minutes; the defenders — Brigadier-General George Doles's Georgia Brigade of Rodes's Division, Second Corps — got off only individual shots against them, with no volley fired. Thus the assailants were forced to pause only momentarily at the breastworks and promptly went over them in a continuing rush. The first and second Federal lines captured the second Confederate works. Upton poured in his reserves to exploit the breach, and his four lines soon became intermingled. They captured about 1,000 prisoners.

But that proved to be the end of the extraordinary care and skill. Matters were already going awry. Gouverneur K. Warren had been promoted major-general, U.S.V., as of May 3, 1863 but actually as a reward for Little Round Top, and since March 23 he commanded the Fifth Corps. Now Warren sent forward prematurely a supporting attack to the right of the Sixth Corps. Also premature, with the time not yet ripe for exploiting whatever psychological impact Upton might make, was a more direct supporting effort by Brigadier-General, U.S.V., Gershom Mott's Fourth Division, Second Corps, assigned temporarily to Wright's command, on Upton's immediate left. Mott attacked an hour early, perhaps because he did not receive an order postponing his assault. In any event, he showed nothing resembling Upton's tactical proficiency, and his was merely the standard and accordingly foredoomed frontal attack. The admirable Winfield Scott Hancock eventually attempted a diversion on Upton's behalf by the Second Corps on the Federal far right, beyond Warren's Fifth Corps, but he was repulsed all the more readily because Warren's attempt was petering out. The effect of all these failures was to leave Upton's task force isolated. Upton held most of his gains until dark but then had to retire. The colonel from New York had shown that rifled weapons and trenches need not always be fatal to an attack, but replicating his capture of the Mule Shoe, and retaining the advantage, would require professional standards of command a good deal higher than those generally prevailing in the Army of the Potomac, or any Civil War army.

A demonstration of this fact soon followed. At Grant's behest Meade shifted his corps fronts so that Hancock could repeat Upton's methods, also against the Mule Shoe, but with the full Second Corps, supported by the Ninth Corps. In the early morning of May 12 Hancock's men charged in massed columns, and with the assistance of a fog they overwhelmed the Mule Shoe, capturing much of the garrison. The Confederates had earlier removed their artillery from the exposed salient, but when sounds from the Union lines tipped off Hancock's impending attack and thus assured against another surprise, the guns came back. Nevertheless the Federals captured them, while they were still in marching order. But the very density of the big Federal attack promptly generated problems of command and control, the more so because there had not been careful instruction of the principal officers on Upton's model.

On the Confederate side Brigadier-General John B. Gordon, a rare citizen-soldier who had honed his skills to a professionalism nearly approaching Upton's, and who was commanding Early's Division of the Second Corps because on May 8 Early had to replace an ailing A. P. Hill in the Third Corps, swiftly and with remarkable audacity organized out of defeat and chaos a counterattack. Gordon could not drive the Federals completely from the Mule Shoe, but he reestablished a defensible line and held it. When Meade ordered Wright to attack on Hancock's left after the main effort had stalled, the fighting through the rest of the day and into the night became so sanguinary that the northwest corner of the Mule Shoe became forever after the Bloody Angle. The rule of warfare with rifled weapons remained unchanged: without an Emory Upton, frontal assaults would fail to contribute to anything but the forbidding arithmetic of Grant's exchanges of casualties toward the day when he would still retain some troops and Lee would not.

The Federals suffered 4,100 casualties on May 10 (753 killed, 3,347 wounded) and 6,820 on May 12 (6,020 killed and wounded, 800 missing), out of 37,822 and 65,785 engaged on those two days, respectively. By the time Grant and Meade pulled their troops out of the Spotsylvania lines on May 20 to begin a new turning maneuver against Lee's right, the battle of Spotsylvania had cost the Union 17,723 casualties (2,447 killed, 10,821 wounded, 1,411 missing in the Army of the Potomac, 2,454 killed and wounded, 590 missing in the organizationally separate Ninth Corps). A reasonable estimate of Confederate losses is, at a minimum, 6,519 killed and wounded, 5,543 captured, for a total of 12,062.[43]

In the trenches of Spotsylvania, the conditions of the Western Front of 1914–1918 were pretty much already at hand. At least in 1864, however, there were still flanks that might be turned, if only Lee's alertness could be overcome. In several days beginning May 20 the Federals and Confederates shifted southeastward rapidly, with sporadic fighting along the way, racing across the North Anna River toward Hanover Junction, where the Richmond, Fredericksburg and Potomac and the Virginia Central Railroads converged — Lee's best links to Richmond. Lee again discerned Grant's purpose and reached Hanover Junction first, shielding it in the battle of the North Anna from May 23 to 26. Thereupon Grant sidled leftward again, crossing the Pamunkey River, which meets the Mattapony to form the York, and thus returning to the Peninsula where McClellan had campaigned in 1862.[44]

At the end of May, Grant's left was reaching toward a crossroads called Cold Harbor, very near the old battlefield of Gaines's Mill. Through Cold Harbor a road from his new base at White House on the Pamunkey, which had also been McClellan's base, led on across the Chickahominy and into Richmond. On June 1 or in the early morning of June 2 there might have been a good chance to push through Cold Harbor, turn Lee's right at last, and catch the Confederates in a dangerous position against the Chickahominy. But delays in marching, some of them seemingly unaccountable but raising again the issue of competent professionalism in command, postponed an attack on Cold Harbor scheduled for half-past four in the morning of June 2 to the morning of June 3. By that time the Confederates were there in force and entrenched. The attack by the Army of the Potomac reinforced by the Eighteenth Corps from the Army of the James cost 7,000 casualties, mostly in half an hour, with no visible accomplishment. The Confederates probably lost fewer than 1,500.[45]

Grant was to remark in his memoirs that he knew he had been criticized for expending so much effort and so many lives to reach the Peninsula, where McClellan had gone safely on ships: "The criticism has been made by writers on the campaign from the Rapidan to the James River that all the loss of life could have been obviated by moving the army there on transports." But he reminded his readers that: "To get possession of Lee's army was the first great object."[46] For that purpose, the method remained hard fighting, and the worth of the campaign lay in the irreparable bleeding it had imposed on the Army of Northern Virginia. From the Wilderness to Cold Harbor, Grant's forces suffered some 52,000 casualties. With the Union and Confederate infantry grappling against each other for all but two or three days, and the rival cavalries always in contact, that meant day-by-day fighting at an average of some 2,000 Union casualties every day. In exchange, the Federals inflicted some 20,000 casualties on the Confederates. The losses amounted to 41 percent of the strength with which Grant had crossed the Rapidan, against 32 percent of Lee's original strength.[47] Grant's strategy of annihilation by means of attrition was well advanced.

## THE RACE TO PETERSBURG

The loss of Lee's power of offensive maneuver was a most striking testimony to the deterioration of the Army of Northern Virginia. Immediately after Cold Harbor, events suggested that even the skill in defensive maneuver with which Lee had so far countered Grant's flanking movements was fading away.

With the roads to Richmond now blocked before him east of the city as they had been to the north, Grant decided to cross the James River and strike toward the railroad junction city of Petersburg, where converged three of the four rail lines serving Richmond from the south — the Southside, the Weldon and Petersburg, and the Norfolk and Petersburg Railroads. If he could seize Petersburg, Grant would go far toward depriving both Lee's army and the Confederate capital of the supplies they drew from throughout the Confederacy. On June 12 Grant's army began moving away from the Cold Harbor front toward the James, and on the 14th it began crossing the river. Meanwhile the rear guard, and especially the Cavalry Corps, masterfully deceived the Confederates. On June 15 Grant's vanguard was knocking at the door of Petersburg, Major-General, U.S.V. (since March 9)[48] William F. Smith's Eighteenth Corps, with Hancock's Second Corps marching close behind. Lee still believed that the bulk of the Federals were threatening him north of the James.

Unfortunately for the Union, the casualties Grant's army had absorbed in punishing Lee had also left Federal striking power sadly depleted. On June 15, 16, 17, and 18 there were always enough more Federals around Petersburg than Confederates inside that either a determined assault from east

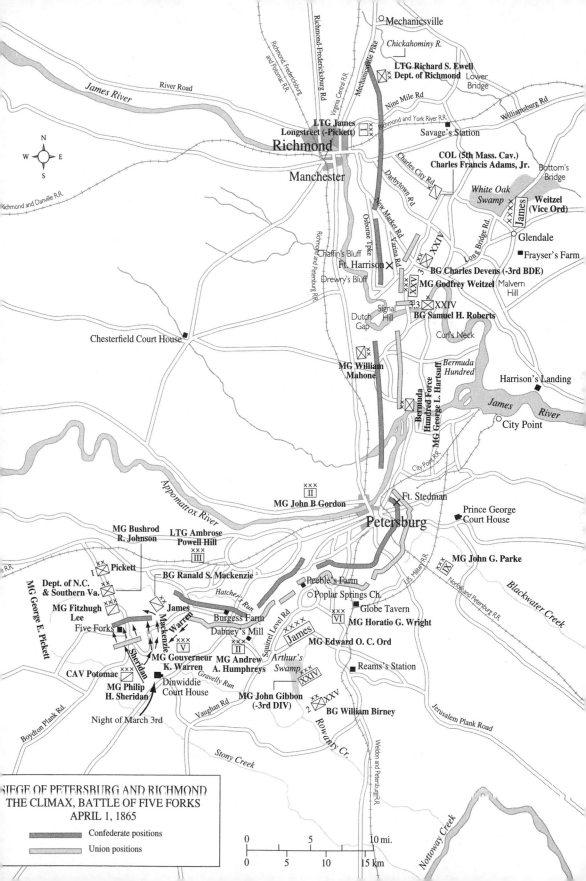

Mechanicsville

*Chickahominy R.*

**LTG Richard S. Ewell**
**Dept. of Richmond**

Lower
Bridge

*James River*

River Road

Nine Mile Rd

Williamsburg Rd

**LTG James**
**Longstreet (-Pickett)**

Savage's Station

*Richmond and York River R.R.*

Bottom's
Bridge

**COL (5th Mass. Cav.)**
**Charles Francis Adams, Jr.**

*White Oak*
*Swamp*

**Weitzel**
**(Vice Ord)**

James

N
W        E
S

Richmond

Manchester

Glendale

Frayser's Farm

**BG Charles Devens (-3rd BDE)**

**MG Godfrey Weitzel**

Malvern
Hill

Chaffin's Bluff

Ft. Harrison

Drewry's Bluff

3.3

XXIV

**BG Samuel H. Roberts**

Signal
Hill

Dutch
Gap

Curl's Neck

Chesterfield Court House

**MG William**
**Mahone**

*Bermuda*
*Hundred*

Bermuda
Hundred Force

**MG George L. Hartsuff**

Harrison's Landing

*James*
*River*

City Point

City Point R.R.

*Appomattox River*

**MG John B. Gordon**

Ft. Stedman

Petersburg

Prince George
Court House

**MG John G. Parke**

*Blackwater Creek*

**MG Bushrod**
**R. Johnson**

**LTG Ambrose**
**Powell Hill**

Pickett

**BG Ranald S. Mackenzie**

Reeble's Farm

Poplar Springs Ch.

Globe Tavern

**MG Horatio G. Wright**

**Dept. of N.C.**
**& Southern Va.**

Hatcher's Run

Burgess Farm

Dabney's Mill

**MG Fitzhugh**
**Lee**

Five Forks

James

Warren

Mackenzie

**MG Edward O. C. Ord**

**MG Gouverneur**
**K. Warren**

**MG Andrew**
**A. Humphreys**

*Arthur's*
*Swamp*

Reams's Station

**MG George E. Pickett**

CAV Potomac

Sheridan

Dinwiddie
Court House

Gravelly Run

**MG John Gibbon**
**(-3rd DIV)**

**BG William Birney**

**MG Philip**
**H. Sheridan**

Night of March 3rd

Vaughan Rd

*Rowanty Cr.*

Boydton Plank Rd.

*Stony Creek*

*Jerusalem Plank Road*

Weldon and Petersburg R.R.

*Nottoway Creek*

**SIEGE OF PETERSBURG AND RICHMOND**
**THE CLIMAX, BATTLE OF FIVE FORKS**
**APRIL 1, 1865**

Confederate positions

Union positions

0        5        10 mi.

0    5    10    15 km

of the city or another maneuver to enter the city from the south would almost surely have caused Petersburg to fall. With every Federal effort of those four days, however, and there were many efforts, something went wrong, and beckoning advantages went unseized. Part of the explanation was that P. G. T. Beauregard had reappeared on stage center. Commanding in Petersburg while Lee was still to the north around Richmond, Beauregard offered a remarkable display of prestidigitation to mesmerize the Federals into thinking he had many more troops than he actually led. (His force grew from 5,400 to 41,499 over the four days beginning June 15; Baldy Smith initially had 16,100, and there were 63,797 Federals by evening of June 18.)[49]

More of the reason for Federal frustration, however, was that the Federal army was exhausted and many of its best soldiers dead or lying in hospitals. Still more of the explanation was that the corps and division commanders were near the limit of nervous endurance under the strain of sending so many men to die in unbroken bitter combat, and their minds were not clear enough to recognize opportunities that in retrospect seem to have been positively shouting at them. Even Hancock had been drained of initiative and will; on June 18 the severe wound in the groin he had received during Pickett's Charge at Gettysburg so completely disabled him again that he had to turn the Second Corps over to David B. Birney until June 27.[50]

By evening of June 18, Lee had thoroughly caught up to the dangers imperiling Petersburg, and there were enough veterans from the Army of Northern Virginia in the city's defenses — the Third Corps arrived beginning that afternoon — to assure that the opportunity to carry Petersburg by assault was gone.

## THE SIEGE OF PETERSBURG: THE FIRST PHASE

The combination of Lee's strength of position for defense and the exhaustion of the Union forces led Grant to settle down to a siege. The preview of 1914–1918 became still more vivid as the rival armies remained in position around Petersburg long enough to dig more elaborate trench systems than ever before, with advanced and main and reserve positions, intricate connecting trenches, increasingly elaborate arrangements for living underground, U.S. Military Railroad supply trackage behind the Union front, and in the absence of barbed wire, satisfactory substitute obstacles in the form of abatis and chevaux-de-frise out in front of the trenches to impale and make stationary targets of troops rash enough to attack. The armies confronted each other now across a front some twenty-six miles long, from White Oak Swamp east of Richmond to the Jerusalem Plank Road south of Petersburg. On the Federal side, Butler's Army of the James, released from immobility by the southward progress of the Army of the Potomac, occupied the front north of the James River; Meade's Army of the Potomac formed up south of the river. Grant continued to reach out gradually with his left, groping now toward the Petersburg and Weldon Railroad which ran south to Weldon, North Carolina.

Grant's army was so nearly worn out, however, that almost any movement entailed high risks — even against the similarly battered and bruised Confederates. At the beginning of the 1864 campaign, the Second Corps had still been able to boast that it had never lost a color to the enemy. On June 22, Brigadier-General William Mahone's and Major-General Bushrod R. Johnson's Divisions of the Confederate Third Corps, since May 21 commanded again by A. P. Hill, hit the corps on the Jerusalem Road at the southwest end of Grant's line and captured 1,700 prisoners — more than the Second Corps had lost at Antietam, Fredericksburg, and Chancellorsville together — along with four cannons and eight stands of colors. But the Second Corps was a shadow of what it had been; its Second Division, which under Brigadier-General, U.S.V., John Gibbon (since June 7, 1864 major-general) had met the spearhead of Pickett's Division at Gettysburg, had begun the 1864 campaign with 6,799 men, and had suffered 7,970 casualties in May and June.[51]

An idea for breaking the deadlock in the trenches reached Meade and Grant from Lieutenant-Colonel Henry Pleasants of the 46th Pennsylvania Veteran Volunteer Infantry. Pleasants was a civil engineer experienced in coal mining; his regiment had been recruited in the anthracite fields of northeastern Pennsylvania. He believed his coal miners could dig a tunnel from the Union lines to a point beneath the Confederate lines, deposit explosives there, and as Pleasants put it: "That God-damned fort is the only thing between us and Petersburg, and I have an idea we can blow it up."[52]

Such tunneling and planting of mines was common enough in the classic routine of siege operations, except that customarily it was preceded by advancing the attacker's main line close to the defender's before tunneling, thus offering warning of what might come. Pleasants's proposed tunnel would be unique in that it would have to be about 500 feet long, which the professional military engineers tended to regard as impossible. But Pleasants was in the Ninth Corps, since April 13 again commanded by its first chieftain, Burnside;[53] and Old Burn, always a curious mixture of strengths and limitations but possessing an inclination toward the innovative, supported Pleasants enthusiastically and secured the acquiescence in the scheme of the much less enthusiastic high command.

Pleasants's miners began digging on June 25 and completed the tunnel on July 23. The Confederates heard something going on beneath them but failed to intersect the tunnel when they dug countershafts, and anyway their engineers were as skeptical about the possibility of a tunnel as their Federal counterparts. The Federals scheduled an attack for July 30, and by that time 8,000 pounds of black powder were ready to blow up.

Grant and Meade entered enough into the spirit of the attempt that they planned an elaborate feint north of the James to tempt Lee into diverting troops from the tunnel area. Nevertheless, the befuddlement that had dogged the Union command since their arrival before Petersburg persisted and plagued the mine project. Burnside detailed his biggest division, Brigadier-General, U.S.V., Edward Ferrero's Fourth, to lead the attack after the explosion went off and carefully rehearsed the division from July 18 onward. But the Fourth Division happened to consist of African-American soldiers, and on the day before the assault Meade told Burnside it would never do to employ blacks on so hazardous a mission, the political repercussions being potentially too dangerous (presumably whether there be success or failure). Meade ordered the African-American division put into reserve. Burnside somewhat understandably lost heart at the need to substitute unrehearsed for carefully prepared troops, but he made matters worse by drawing straws to select the new spearhead division and letting the crucial role go to his weakest, worst-led division, Brigadier-General, U.S.V., James H. Ledlie's First.

The explosion blasted off at 4:45 A.M. on the 30th and accomplished all that Pleasants had promised for it, propelling much of the 19th and 22nd South Carolina Infantry into the air and creating a 500-yard gap in the Confederate defenses. But from that event on the attackers bungled everything. No one had thought to prepare a way for the assault troops through their own abatis. They worked forward in driblets. Then they went down into the crater of the explosion and hesitated there rather than hurrying around its rim. Ledlie did not lead but hunkered down in a bomb-proof shelter with a supply of rum. Beyond the crater "Little Billy" Mahone rallied his Confederates, counterattacked, and restored the line. Lee promoted Mahone to major-general on the spot. The Federals' African Americans were finally sent in, but only after the situation was hopeless.

Union losses in the "battle of the Crater" were 3,793 (2,864 killed and wounded, 929 missing) out of the 20,708 engaged,[54] perhaps a small enough number when compared with the toll from the Wilderness to Cold Harbor, but a last straw in the eyes of the Northern public. With the failure of the mine, Grant could well appear to have achieved nothing in particular, except the slaughter of his own army. He was now no closer to Richmond than McClellan had once been, and seemingly going nowhere.

To compensate for the casualties of his campaign, the Federal draft law had to be stiffened again. On July 4, after much debate in Congress, the President had signed into law a bill limiting commutation to conscientious objectors. The principal immediate effect was the one warned against by the Congressional defenders of commutation; the sequel showed that commutation had actually helped those who were not rich, because eliminating it while retaining substitution inflated the price of substitutes and thus put them still more out of the reach of men who were not well-to-do.[55] Therefore Lincoln and his party faced still greater risks in the coming national elections.

## C.S.S. ALABAMA

Little on the war fronts seemed to be going well for the Union through much of the fateful election year of 1864. Along with the outmaneuvering of factional opponents to assure Lincoln's renomination, the friends of the administration could ease the diet of grim dispatches from the sanguinary Virginia front and take a measure of cheer only from across the seas: the Confederate commerce raider *Alabama* had been destroyed.

Built on the lines of a fast steam sloop of the Royal Navy, *Alabama* had become the terror of the Northern merchant marine since her evasion of the Queen's dilatory law officers and of Charles Francis Adams's restraining efforts by slipping down the Mersey on July 22, 1862.[56] Her captain, Raphael Semmes, one of the most promising and intellectually alert officers of the Old Navy, fresh from eleven captures in the improvised and badly engined raider *Sumter*, had decided that the available sea communications would permit *Alabama* to cruise for two months in any given area before enough news would reach the Union Navy to provoke a concentration of ships against her. So *Alabama* had burned twenty vessels in the North Atlantic — under international law, captures could not be sent to and held in neutral ports, and so because Confederate ports were blockaded the *Alabama's* prizes usually had to be destroyed if they were not to be returned to their owners. The ship had sailed on to the West Indies and thence to Galveston, where she sank the small Union side-wheel armed steamer *Hatteras* while evading combat with the cruiser *Brooklyn*. She had escaped a flying squadron under Commodore Charles Wilkes in the Gulf; took another two prizes in the West Indies, eight more off the hump of Brazil, ten more off Bahía, seven more in the East Indies.

The privateers launched by the Confederacy to considerable fanfare at the beginning of the war had never accomplished much and had mainly been swept from the seas by the end of 1861; but *Alabama* along with her English-built sister ships *Florida* and *Shenandoah* took so many Union prizes, so increased insurance rates for U.S. vessels, and thereby drove so many American ships to foreign registry, that the American merchant marine never in peacetime recovered its prewar dimensions. Altogether the *Alabama* burned fifty-five Union merchant vessels worth more than $4.5 million and bonded and released another ten at $562,000.[57]

Captain Semmes prolonged his stay in the distant East Indies to six months rather than the usual two, however, and in the spring of 1864 *Alabama* badly needed refitting and overhaul. Returning to Europe, Semmes put into Cherbourg on June 11, there to take advantage of French law, which like the maritime law of most nations, allowed a belligerent warship to remain in a neutral harbor beyond the customary twenty-four-hour limit for the humanitarian purposes of escaping bad weather or making essential repairs to remain seaworthy, provided the ship did not add to its crew or armament or otherwise enhance its strength.

Word of *Alabama's* presence quickly reached Captain John Ancrum Winslow, commanding the U.S. steam sloop *Kearsarge*. *Kearsarge* had shared the harbor of Brest with the Confederate raider *Florida* off and on from September 1863 to February 1864 but had been thwarted in her efforts to force an engagement by French neutrality law and vigilant French civil and naval officials. This process had been all very proper under international law, but Captain Winslow was now a disappointed man and determined not to be frustrated again. Fortunately for him, Captain Semmes was prepared to cooperate with him in order to bring on a battle.

Semmes felt goaded by the European and American gossip, which was accurate, that despite his and his ship's fearsome reputation, they had never stood to fight any opponent who could give them approximately equal terms. That conduct had been as it should have been; the purpose of the *Alabama* was not fighting. But when *Kearsarge* took station in international waters just beyond Cherbourg harbor, Semmes withdrew his request for French naval drydock privileges and prepared to steam out to meet his Union challenger. *Alabama* did so on the morning of June 19, with much of the population of Cherbourg lining the bluffs above the harbor to witness the action that developed in plain view.

It was a quixotic chivalric gesture for Semmes to take up the challenge, something out of the medieval chivalric romances of which many Southerners were inordinately fond, but not worthy of his intelligence. *Alabama* fired a broadside of 264 pounds, 101 less than her rival's. Her biggest guns were an 8-inch smoothbore and a 7-inch Blakely rifle, both pivot-mounted, while *Kearsarge's* two pivot guns were 11-inch Dahlgren smoothbores. The Confederate also carried six and the Federal ship five 32-pounders (4.62 inches), but the additional gun was of no appreciable advantage to Semmes. *Kearsarge* wore an improvised armor of sheet-chains. Semmes had skimped on gunnery drill in order to conserve scarce ammunition, while Winslow was a dedicated practitioner of such drill. *Alabama's* ammunition had not been replenished since her commissioning, so percussion caps fired erratically, and the quality of her powder had deteriorated. Although *Kearsarge* was nine months older, she had been refitted just three months before the challenge, and she was more maneuverable and generally more shipshape than *Alabama*, which badly needed the refitting for which Semmes had entered Cherbourg.

The fight lasted sixty-two minutes. *Kearsarge's* gunnery proved far better than *Alabama's*. *Kearsarge* was hit twenty-eight times but never badly. On Winslow's orders, *Kearsarge's* 32-pounders swept the enemy decks, while the 11-inch Dahlgrens aimed for the waterline and repeatedly hulled *Alabama* with their 135½-pound shells.

*Alabama* lowered her flag, but Winslow was suspicious, and he asked for and got another broadside. Thereupon the Confederate raised a white flag. She was already retreating toward the French coast, but she was sinking rapidly and did not make it; she sank in ten fathoms of water about five miles off Cherbourg. Winslow had only two boats that had not been wrecked by the firing. He lowered these and allowed the Confederates to use a surviving dinghy for rescue work; but the three small craft were far from enough, and Winslow appealed to the British yacht *Deerfield*, out from Cherbourg to watch the show. Semmes had jumped overboard, and *Deerfield* rescued him along with forty-one other Confederates.

Two French pilot boats saved another dozen Confederates, and *Kearsarge* took seventy aboard as captives. Thus the loss of life was less severe than might have been expected out of *Alabama's* crew of 150. *Kearsarge* lost one killed and two wounded of a crew of 163. The battle of the *Alabama* and the *Kearsarge* offered the North good news in strong contrast to the reports of bloodletting from Grant's front.[58]

## A Catalog of Union Frustration: Red River, Bermuda Hundred, and Washington

As for good military news in the first half of 1864, *Kearsarge* provided almost all the Union received. In midsummer, Sherman and the Western armies were hung up before Atlanta like Grant in front of Petersburg; Sherman's only superior virtue seemed to be that he was more chary of losing lives than Grant. The subsidiary moves that Grant had intended to keep up pressure against the Confederacy everywhere had all become fizzles or worse.

General Banks never mounted the expedition against Mobile at all, because Lincoln's desire to do something threatening in the direction of Napoleon III's Mexican adventure diverted the Army of the Gulf to a campaign up the Red River instead, beginning early in March. It proved nearly a disaster. Major-General Richard Taylor defeated Banks at Sabine Cross Roads or Mansfield and Pleasant Hill on April 8 and 9, and Banks retreated. Low water in the Red River almost trapped Admiral Porter's accompanying fleet, and by the time the Army and Navy both extricated themselves from Taylor's harassments by safely reaching Unionist territory near the Mississippi, it was past the middle of May and too late to regroup in time to do much to help Sherman. It did the latter no good that Banks failed to create a diversion to shield his right flank as he moved from Chattanooga toward Atlanta, and the Red River expedition also cost Sherman 10,000 good troops, the Detachment, Army of the Tennessee, consisting of the First and Third Divisions, Sixteenth Corps, and the Provisional or Red River Division, Seventeenth Corps, lent to Banks and not returned to Sherman until June.[59]

Ben Butler's Army of the James traveled up the James River in early May. While Butler had earned a reputation for ferocity in policing unorganized and generally unarmed rebels when he commanded at New Orleans, he was a lion who turned quickly into a lamb when he met fortifications skillfully commanded by Beauregard around Drewry's Bluff. Overawed, Butler retreated to Bermuda Hundred, where the Army of the James vegetated in a peninsula formed by the James and Appomattox Rivers. The exception was the Eighteenth Corps, which eventually sailed off to join the Cold Harbor assault. Grant's arrival south of the James at length freed Butler's army to participate in the Petersburg campaign. The fact that the two main Union armies in Virginia were so little coordinated that one of them could be so readily immobilized is an especially damning reflection on the generals' limited understanding of the operational art.[60]

The Shenandoah Valley campaign turned out even worse. Sigel was whipped at New Market on May 15 by Major-General John C. Breckinridge, erstwhile Vice President of the United States and Presidential candidate, in the battle made famous by the participation of the Virginia Military Institute cadets on the Confederate side. General David Hunter, last seen when he was prematurely freeing slaves in the Department of the South, was then taken off the shelf to replace Sigel, on May 21. He resumed the Union advance up the Valley, avenging New Market by putting the torch to V.M.I.[61] But Lee detached Jubal Early, commander of Jackson's old Second Corps since May 29 while Ewell recuperated from an illness, and as of May 31 a temporary lieutenant-general, to march westward with 8,000 veterans of his corps and put a stop to such mischief.[62]

Confronted thus by adversaries of formidable reputation, Hunter decided he lacked enough ammunition to risk a battle and retreated from Lynchburg. He chose to move, however, not northward down the Valley but westward into the West Virginia mountains, which unfortunately for the Union left the Valley open to Early. Depleted though the offensive power of the Army of Northern Virginia might be, Jackson's old foot cavalry could certainly still march against nonexistent opposition, and encouraged by Lee, Early availed himself of Hunter's eccentric movement to strike down the Valley himself.

By July 2 Early was at Winchester with some 10,000 men from the Second Corps and the Confederate Valley forces. By July 5 he was crossing the Potomac into Maryland. On July 9 he pushed aside bits and pieces of Union commands assembled under Lew Wallace to oppose him along the Monocacy River. On Sunday, July 10 he was at Rockville, and refugees from the suburbs were disturbing Washington's sabbath placidity with descriptions of unkempt veterans in butternut bent on revenge in the capital itself for Union depredations in the Shenandoah.

The next day Early burned the Blairs' home at Silver Spring practically on the District of Columbia line. In the capital, residents recalled that it was hardbitten Jube Early who had destroyed Thaddeus Stevens's ironworks and most conspicuously departed from the spirit of Lee's restraints upon property destruction during the Gettysburg campaign.

Since the time when McClellan had exposed Washington by sailing to the Peninsula, through most of the war the administration had insisted that a strong garrison must occupy the ring of fortifications encircling the city. So great was Lincoln's confidence in Grant, however, and so great the appetite of the 1864 campaigns for manpower, that following the early heavy casualties of Grant's Virginia battles the President had allowed the General-in-Chief to strip the fortifications of many of their defenders. Especially, Grant had taken into the field many of the heavy artillery regiments, temptingly oversized units, which had been trained as infantry as well as artillery but until the spring of 1864 had led a safe and often decidedly comfortable life in and near the capital. Grant thought he was running no undue risks. It was central to his strategy that the Army of the Potomac would keep the bulk of Lee's army occupied, and the Union force in the Shenandoah had been expected to bar the Valley approach to Washington. No one foresaw that Hunter would take the Valley force off the board by marching into West Virginia.

Major-General Christopher C. Augur, U.S.V., commanding the Department of Washington, nominally had the Twenty-fourth Corps of 31,000 men; but in fact his troops were so scattered on detachment service that the immediate dependence of the capital was on only 9,600 soldiers, most of them either semi-invalids of the Veteran Reserve Corps or Ohio militiamen serving a brief stint of active duty by guarding the capital. To supplement these men, the War Department hastily mobilized the District militia and detachments of government clerks who had been exposed to a touch of training in arms. Because the strong fortifications of Washington naturally remained, such troops might possibly give a good account of themselves, though the outlook was uncertain at best.

On July 11, President Lincoln and Mrs. Mary Todd Lincoln watched some skirmishing from Fort Stevens in the suburban Brightwood area of comfortable estates, while across the lines Early pondered the risks of pushing into the city. If he broke in through the fortifications, he would not be able to stay, but the briefest Confederate occupation of the Federal capital might pay immeasurable dividends in puncturing the already sagging morale of the North and enhancing the chances of a peace-party victory in the coming Federal elections.

Early pondered too long. Grant and Halleck had been slow to appreciate the danger that Early might drive into Washington itself, and they did not want to play Lee's game by easing the pressure upon Petersburg; but on July 6 they had at length begun shifting troops northward from the Army of the Potomac. At the Seventh Street wharf in the city, on the afternoon of July 11, sun-tanned campaigners wearing on faded blue caps the Greek cross of General Wright's Sixth Corps were disembarking from steamers from the Petersburg front. During the night Early learned that most of what may now well have been the best corps in Meade's army had arrived to resist him.

On Tuesday, Early tapped again at the defenses to make sure they had become as strongly held as he feared, and he found many Greek-cross patches and a considerable stiffening. Lincoln drove out to Fort Stevens to watch the excitement again, and he remained deaf to the entreaties of General Wright to get down from the parapet and out of the line of fire, until Wright asserted his authority as a front-line commanding officer and ordered him to safety. Early had decided he must withdraw, but he said to an aide, Major Henry Kyd Douglas, Assistant Adjutant-General: "Major, we haven't taken Washington, but we've scared Abe Lincoln like hell," which was not quite true.[63]

The truth was bad enough: far from taking Richmond in what was to be the climactic campaign of the war, the Union armies had barely kept a detachment of Lee's skinny ragamuffins out of Washington. On July 18, Lincoln issued another call for 500,000 men, to be raised by the draft if volunteering did not suffice.[64]

## THE POLITICS OF MILITARY DEADLOCK

Pink-cheeked, fuzzy-whiskered Horace Greeley edited the *New York Tribune*, which was probably the most influential newspaper in the United States, especially through its weekly edition which went by mail to farms and small towns all over the North. Greeley had been a member of the Republican factions trying to dump Lincoln as a candidate because the President was not sufficiently ardent in championing the rights of the African Americans and wreaking vengeance upon the South. After the National Union Convention, Greeley was still not satisfied and was busy testing whether a new convention might be called to drop Lincoln after all.

At the same time, Greeley was so appalled by the casualties of Grant's campaigns piled on those of three earlier years of war that he thought Lincoln was also delinquent in not doing enough to explore the possibilities of a negotiated peace. At the very time when Early was barrelling toward Washington, Greeley was demonstrating to the President how much the Union's military difficulties were encouraging a peace movement, by writing to Lincoln that an informant at Niagara Falls, Canada West had told him there were four Confederate emissaries at that place with authority to negotiate, "And thereupon I venture to remind you that our bleeding, bankrupt, almost dying country also longs for peace — shudders at the prospect of fresh conscriptions, of further wholesale devastations, and of new rivers of human blood."

Greeley said there was a widespread impression that the government was not anxious for peace and missed opportunities to get it; that Lincoln should give the Confederate emissaries in Canada the safe conduct they required to come to Washington and "submit overtures for pacification to the Southern insurgents which the impartial must pronounce frank and generous." "Mr. President, I fear you do not realize how intently the people desire any peace consistent with the national integrity and honor."[65]

On the day when Early was brushing Lew Wallace away from the Monocacy, Lincoln passed the ball to Greeley by responding:

> If you can find, any person anywhere professing to have any proposition of Jefferson Davis in writing, for peace, embracing the restoration of the Union and abandonment of slavery, what ever else it embraces, say to him he may come to me with you, and that if he really brings such proposition, he shall, at the least, have safe conduct, with the paper (and without publicity, if he choose) to the point where you shall have met him. The same, if there be two or more persons.[66]

Greeley was reluctant to be the one to run with this ball lest he embarrass not the President but himself. After further prodding, however, and a visit from Lincoln's secretary John Hay, the editor duly set off to Niagara Falls to find the Confederate emissaries. Even though on making contact with these personages Greeley failed to inform them of Lincoln's essential terms — the Union and no slavery — the Confederates refused to go to see Lincoln. They refused on the ostensible ground that they were not properly accredited for that purpose, but in fact because their real mission evidently was not to do anything toward a peace of accommodation but to raise false hopes and stir up dissension in the North. They encouraged Greeley enough, nevertheless, that he telegraphed Lincoln for fresh instructions, whereupon the President sent John Hay bearing a statement to pass "To Whom it may concern":

> Any proposition which embraces the restoration of peace, the integrity of the whole Union, and the abandonment of slavery, and which comes by and with an authority that can control the armies now at war against the United States will be received and considered by the Executive government of the United States, and will be met by liberal terms on other substantial and collateral points; and the bearer, or bearers thereof shall have safe-conduct both ways.[67]

Hay and Greeley together met one of the Confederate agents, John P. Holcombe, who had been a professor at the University of Virginia; but their discussion and the President's latest message produced nothing but a counter-message from the Confederates saying they were shocked both by the way in which the President had addressed them and by his rejection of the peace spirit with unacceptable terms when they had been led to expect better—as in part Greeley had led them. They would feel free to publish the relevant documents to strip away the last delusion that the South could expect peace from the Lincoln administration. Greeley consequently felt obliged to publish his version of the episode, but he quarreled with Lincoln again when the President refused to release every word of the correspondence between the two of them, Lincoln not being eager to advance the idea that the country was "bleeding, bankrupt, almost dying." The affair closed with new recriminations from Greeley, to the effect that Lincoln had continually neglected opportunities to make peace and did not realize that nine-tenths of the people North and South wanted peace on almost any terms.[68]

Horace Greeley was a mercurial man, and his ability simultaneously to join in the Radicals' attacks on Lincoln as a milksop and to rail against him for being insufficiently flexible in the search for peace required a dexterity of thought not shared by all the President's political opponents. Still, Greeley was not unique in his effort to assail the President from both flanks at once. Nerves were strained taut in the battle summer of 1864, and those who thought Lincoln not vigorous enough in the prosecution of the war could convince themselves that he must be doing everything wrong, and therefore that he was not pursuing peace vigorously enough either. Furthermore, some Radical Republicans were not above trying to use Peace Democrats to cooperate toward their own ends, and some Peace Democrats were not above trying to use Radical Republicans as long as both opposed Lincoln and each thought he was the user rather than the used.

An ambivalence akin to Greeley's infected the Frémont Radical Democratic movement. Frémont's Vice-Presidential running mate was John Cochrane, attorney general of New York, a Democrat who had supported Franklin Pierce, Buchanan, and Breckinridge, and who said of General McClellan, whose conciliatory attitudes toward the South as well as his dislike of Lincoln were making him increasingly the most probable Democratic Presidential nominee, that McClellan and Frémont were "twin cherries on one stalk."[69] The Frémont-Cochrane platform denounced the suspension of habeas corpus, both Frémont and Cochrane dwelt more on issues that they shared with the Democrats than on slavery in their acceptance letters, and Frémont seemed as interested in negotiating with the Democrats as with the National Union Party about his possible withdrawal from the Presidential race.

Thus elements of a strange alliance bound together Lincoln's troubles with both Radicals and Peace Democrats, as summer moved toward fall and the elections, little good news came from the battlefronts, and difficulties mounted on both of the President's political flanks.

Radical discontent with Lincoln fueled itself upon a growing restlessness with his reconstruction program as well as upon displeasure with the course of the war under his management. The antislavery militants were quick to note that none of the Southern state governments being reestablished under Lincoln's auspices showed any discernible interest in advancing the civil and political rights of the freedmen, particularly the right to vote. The Tennessee and Arkansas governments took no positive steps whatever.[70] In Louisiana, Lincoln and Banks under Radical Republican pressure tried to dragoon the convention writing a new state constitution into empowering the legislature to enfranchise blacks; but there was no guarantee that the legislature would so act, and the militants could complain that Louisiana was in the hands of conservatives in the first place because Lincoln and Banks had favored the Hahn faction against the Shepley faction, not least by conducting the initial new elections under the prewar state constitution.[71] Moreover, Congress felt concern about Lincoln's reconstruction policy not only for immediate political reasons but on constitutional grounds as well, involving the traditional jealousy between the legislature and the executive: Congress felt inclined to believe that Lincoln was usurping powers properly Congressional.

The constitutional theory behind Lincoln's reconstruction activities was that the whole justification of the War for the Union lay in the constitutional impossibility of secession, so that the so-called Confederate States had never left the Union. Therefore the rebellion was a matter of the misconduct of many Southern individuals rather than of actually seceding state governments, and restoring the Union was not a question of bringing back states — which had never departed — but of bringing numerous individuals back into their proper relationship with government. Thus reconstruction fell within the executive law enforcement and pardoning powers. This view was consistent with Lincoln's inclination to govern as much as he could independently of Congress, avoiding the necessity to cooperate with a sometimes recalcitrant legislature; but it collided inevitably with the Congressional assessment of Congressional prerogatives, and it could well be attacked as placing excessive control over the entire future of the nation in the hands of the President alone — as an almost dictatorial doctrine.[72]

It did not require accepting the still more extreme constitutional doctrines of Thaddeus Stevens, that the Southern states could be dealt with as conquered provinces utterly at the disposal of Congress, or of Charles Sumner, that the seceding states had committed state suicide, to conclude that Congress ought to have a larger part to play in reconstruction and that the Constitution provided such a part.[73] An intermediate constitutional opinion was developing during the war, though it eventually reached its fullest development after the fighting in a speech delivered in the House by Republican Congressman Samuel Shellabarger of Ohio on January 8, 1866. Shellabarger was to point to Article IV, Section IV of the Constitution, enjoining the United States to guarantee to every state a republican form of government. In this provision, Shellabarger pointed out, the Constitution itself contemplates a situation in which a state remains a state and part of the Union but loses its normal relationship to the Union. In Shellabarger's constitutional interpretation, the Southern states had not and could not have seceded, and the war was fought on the same constitutional basis that Lincoln gave it; but by attempting to secede the Southern states had brought upon themselves a necessity for intervention by the United States, by implication including Congress, to guarantee a republican form of government.[74]

Congressmen of the Stevens, Sumner, and Shellabarger persuasions could unite to regain Congressional control over reconstruction policy. When Lincoln first announced his 10-percent plan in December 1863, criticism from among Republican Congressmen and in the Republican press was restrained, except for Stevens and a few other incorrigibles. There was general recognition of the important point that the 10-percent plan was less a blueprint for permanent reconstruction than a war measure. Nevertheless, as Congressmen found time to contemplate the plan's implications for the constitutional balance of power, and as Lincoln's reconstructed governments began to take form and to display their indifference to the freedmen, Congressional dissatisfaction mounted rapidly.

Henry Winter Davis, a newly elected Radical from Baltimore, persuaded the House to refer the reconstruction passages of the President's annual message to a special committee with Davis as chairman. In February 1864 this committee reported a counterplan for reconstruction in a bill guaranteeing a republican form of government to certain states whose governments had been "usurped or overthrown."[75] Davis's bill passed the House on May 4 although it was itself objectionable to part of the Republican left wing; Thaddeus Stevens desired a general land reform in the South to benefit the former slaves, for which Davis's bill did not provide, and more important, the Davis bill entrusted the process of getting proper state government under way again to white male citizens in the South. Ben Wade took charge of the bill in the Senate, and one of his first efforts was to delete the offensive word, *white*; but to most of the membership, Congressional versus executive power proved to be a far more important concern than African-American suffrage, and Wade soon had to reverse himself on the suffrage question, lest he sacrifice the whole bill.

The Wade-Davis Bill passed Congress on July 2. It provided that for the reconstruction of a state government to begin, a majority of all the white male citizens of the state, not merely 10 percent of the 1860 voters, must take an oath to support the Constitution of the United States. Thereupon, however, only those who could further swear that they had never voluntarily borne arms against the United States, nor given aid to persons in armed hostility thereto, nor supported any hostile pretended government, nor held office in such a government, would be entitled to participate in drawing up a new state constitution or to vote or hold office under the new constitution. Thus, while the Wade-Davis Bill would begin the work of reconstruction on a wider political foundation than Lincoln's 10-percent plan, it would drastically restrict participation in Southern state government thereafter by means of the so-called ironclad oath, in contrast to Lincoln's plan which opened the door to political activity to almost any male who would swear to be loyal in the future.[76]

Although he had need of all the support he could find toward reelection, Lincoln proved unwilling to sacrifice on that altar his hopes for winning the war by encouraging and hastening the reconciliation of the South through restored state governments. The Wade-Davis Bill had made its way through a conference committee to final passage in the crowded moments just before the adjournment of the Congressional session. The President was in a room provided for him in the Senate wing of the Capitol, conferring with Congressional leaders and signing other last-minute bills. Senator Zachariah Chandler of Michigan warned him not to veto the Wade-Davis Bill, lest there be disastrous political repercussions in the Northwest, but rumors that Lincoln intended a veto began to circulate. In fact, Lincoln departed the Capitol for the White House without doing anything about the bill.[77]

He still had ten days in which to act positively; but if he failed to take action within that time after adjournment, the bill would not become law. It would become the victim of a pocket veto. Lincoln chose this latter course, but with an unusual twist. On July 8 he announced his intention not to sign the bill and offered an explanation, namely, that he was "unprepared, by a formal approval of this Bill, to be inflexibly committed to any single plan of restoration." He was "also unprepared to declare, that the free-state constitutions and governments, already adopted and installed in Arkansas and Louisiana, shall be set aside and held for nought, thereby repelling and discouraging the loyal citizens who have set up the same." He objected further to the fact that the Wade-Davis Bill required the prohibition of slavery in the reconstructed states; so did his own 10-percent plan, but while he thought emancipation within the war powers of the Presidency, he did not consider it within the competency of Congress. He affirmed, however, that nevertheless he was "fully satisfied with the system of restoration contained in the Bill, as one very proper plan for the loyal people of any State choosing to adopt it." His first reason for rejection therefore all the more seemed to be the binding reason — he would not be confined prematurely to a single plan, at a time when the principal utility of any reconstruction plan remained that of hastening the end of the war.[78]

The pocket veto obviously did nothing to improve Lincoln's relations with the Congressional wing of his party. On August 5 the co-sponsors of the vetoed bill responded with the "Wade-Davis Manifesto," stating their indignation at the message accompanying the veto. "The President," they said, "by preventing this bill from becoming a law, holds the electoral votes of the rebel States at the dictation of his personal ambition." "If electors for President be allowed to be chosen in either of those States [Louisiana or Arkansas], a sinister light will be cast on the motives which induced the President to 'hold for naught' the will of Congress rather than his government in Louisiana and Arkansas." These imputations were not altogether without merit, but having pointed out the dictatorial tendencies in Lincoln's effort to hold reconstruction in his own hands, Wade and Davis proceeded to a more than equally extreme interpretation of Presidential versus Congressional powers from their Congressional perspective, by concluding that if Lincoln "wishes our support, he must confine himself to his executive duties — to obey and execute, not make the laws — to suppress by arms armed rebellion, and leave political reorganization to Congress." Let the supporters of the government, said Wade and Davis, "consider the remedy for these [Lincoln's] usurpations, and, having found it, fearlessly execute it" — an apparent invitation to unseat Lincoln as the Republican nominee.[79]

The Wade-Davis pocket veto occurred just as Early's raid and the Greeley peace initiative were developing, and just as Lincoln was trying to terminate still another difficulty with those to his left in the Republican Party, his loss of whatever credit with the Radicals retaining Chase in the Treasury might have earned. The break in the Lincoln ranks at the National Union Convention for which Chase had hoped when he formally withdrew from the Presidential race had never occurred, and Chase was consequently in an irritable mood during the month of June. At this juncture John J. Cisco, the Assistant Treasurer in New York, chose to resign, another loss to the whole administration because Cisco had done much to placate New York financiers about the preeminence of the Philadelphian Jay Cooke. Rather than continue to defer to New Yorkers with a politically moderate financier from among them, Chase nominated as a replacement a financially ignorant friend, Maunsell B. Field. Secretary Seward, a New Yorker, and his New York–based political right-hand man, Thurlow Weed, objected, and so did the New York Senators, Republicans Preston King and Ira Harris, which raised the issue of Senatorial courtesy. Lincoln tried to mediate by looking for someone satisfactory to all concerned, but the upshot was that with his patience worn thin by the disappointment of his fondest ambition, on June 29 Chase again submitted his own resignation.[80]

Lincoln received assurances that Chase could probably be persuaded to reconsider, but the President responded to Chase's friends that "this is the third time he has thrown this at me, and I do not think I am called on to continue to beg him to take it back, especially when the country would not go to destruction in consequence."[81] So Chase departed at last, and after an abortive effort to replace him with another Ohioan, ex-Governor David Tod, on July 1 Lincoln gave the Treasury to Senator William Pitt Fessenden of Maine, a representative of antislavery views more militant than Lincoln's but a more flexible personality than Chase, and as chairman of the Senate Committee on Finance a man with appropriate experience.[82]

To the Radicals, Chase's departure coming almost simultaneously with the Wade-Davis veto signified the undoubted capture of the administration by the Republican conservatives. The Radicals sought in return the scalp of Postmaster General Montgomery Blair, because the Blairs had been consistently conspicuous as Chase's enemies; but beyond Blair they were aiming at Lincoln himself. From August 14 onward through the rest of the month there met in New York a circle of Republican leaders determined to find means to remove Lincoln from the top of the party's ticket, including Henry Winter Davis and Horace Greeley. Charles Sumner, Ben Butler, and Governor Andrew of Massachusetts worked more independently in the same direction. The Republican dissidents met with representatives of the Frémont party to discuss a possible mutual withdrawal of both candidates on behalf of some new contender. On August 30 the New York group agreed that a new convention should be called, to meet in Cincinnati on September 28. To prepare for it, Greeley, Parke Godwin of the *New York Evening Post*, and Theodore Tilton of the religious antislavery paper *The Independent* addressed a circular letter to all the Republican governors, asking them whether they could carry their respective states for Lincoln, whether Lincoln could be reelected, and whether another nominee should be chosen.[83]

The circular letter was prepared the same day, August 31, that the Democratic National Convention chose General McClellan as its Presidential nominee. The New Yorkers' disgruntlement had reached its climax partly out of fear that McClellan remained so popular as a military hero that the clumsy railsplitter would have little chance against him — particularly in the contest for the soldiers' votes, on which the Republicans had counted. The Democrats, having postponed their convention to an uncommonly late date in the hope that something might turn up to improve their prospects for victory in November and point the direction they should take to assure their electoral triumph, thought that something had done so in the multitudinous setbacks and frustrations suffered by Union arms since the beginning of the 1864 campaigns. The Democratic platform was built upon the assertion that Lincoln's record was one of "four years of failure to restore the Union by the experiment of war."

The remedy, said the Democrats, was a cessation of hostilities "to the end that at the earliest possible moment peace may be restored on the basis of the Federal Union of the States."[84] The platform reflected the influence of the dominant member of the Resolutions Committee, Clement L. Vallandigham, who had returned from Canada while the Lincoln administration thought it most politic to look the other way. The ascendancy of the Peace Democrats was indicated also by the convention's choice of Congressman George H. Pendleton of Ohio as the Vice-Presidential nominee. Once a Douglas Democrat, since the death of the "Little Giant" Pendleton had become almost as stubborn an obstructionist of the war as Vallandigham, and he was a friend and ally of that worthy in his home state. To be sure, all the most prominent Democrats including Vallandigham insisted they wanted no dishonorable peace and no disruption of the Union. Certainly most of them were honest in their insistence; they remained conservatives who desired the restoration of the old Union and old interpretations of the Constitution, and they believed that if they recaptured Congress and the Presidency, there was no reason why the South should not willingly enter into the restoration of such a Union.

Like Southerners, they exaggerated the centralizing, despotic, and revolutionary tendencies of the Lincoln government, which of course they emphasized in their platform. In their calculations they overlooked, however, the fact that the Confederates exaggerated such tendencies in Washington even more than they themselves did, and were thus unlikely to agree to any peace terms except Confederate independence. It was crucial, therefore, that in calling for both peace and the Union the Democrats powerful enough to write their party's platform put peace first. ". . . justice, humanity, liberty, and the public welfare demand that immediate efforts be made for a cessation of hostilities"; they assumed that after they ended hostilities, negotiations between them and the South could restore the Union. This assumption was questionable. But it suited Vallandigham, the single most influential shaper of the platform.[85]

Most of the Democratic Party leaders were willing to acquiesce in a platform written by the Peace Democrats in large part because they shared, or thought it expedient to share, the first premise of the platform, that the war was a failure. Accepting this premise, they could scarcely resist the conclusion that peace ought to be found immediately. Many of these leaders were not willing, however, to go to the length of accepting an outright Peace Democrat for President. The Peace Democrats' urging of Thomas Hart Seymour, former governor of Connecticut and a New England Vallandigham, for first place on the ticket stumbled in part on Seymour's reluctance to take that spot;[86] but most of the delegates believed they had to have the popularity and magnetism that McClellan could bring to the electoral campaign, and a candidate with something like McClellan's identification with the Union soldiers and thus after all with patriotism and the war.

McClellan's attitude toward the peace issue proved ambivalent enough, in fact, that he boggled at the platform's emphasis on peace before the Union. For several days he wrote and rewrote his letter of acceptance, under opposing personal inclinations and opposing pressures from the peace wing and the firm Unionists of his party. On September 8 he issued a letter rejecting the contention that the war was a failure and stating that the restoration of the Union was an essential condition for peace. On the other hand, he was prepared to be generous in the terms he would offer the South, for he said that if "any one State is willing to return to the Union, it should be received at once, with a full guarantee of all its constitutional rights."[87] There seemed good reason to believe that most Northern voters would scarcely reject peace for the sake of emancipation.

As his rivals from opposite camps seemed to labor in harness against him, Lincoln nearly lost hope of his reelection. Just before the assembling of the Democratic convention, he called his Cabinet together and obtained their signatures on a document whose text he did not allow them to read. The document stated:

> Executive Mansion
> Washington, Aug. 23, 1864.
> This morning, as for some days past, it seems exceedingly probable that this Administration will not be re-elected. Then it will be my duty so to cooperate with the President elect, as to save the Union between the election

and the inauguration; as he will have secured his election on such ground that he can not possibly save it afterwards.

This was written, Lincoln later stated, "at a time (6 days before the Chicago nominating Convention) when as yet we had no adversary, and seemed to have no friends."[88]

The contention that the war was a failure was a key element not only in the Democratic platform but in the whole electoral contest. As long as the armies remained clenched in bloody deadlock, the Democrats might well appear to be correct in their estimate of the situation, and it would remain exceedingly probable that the Lincoln administration would not be reelected. Yet Lincoln saw no alternative to the course he was running. By midsummer, Grant had almost expended an entire army and had to replace it with another, but this outpouring of casualties was his only means of imposing enough casualties upon the enemy to win the complete and final victory that Lincoln believed necessary. If the Civil War had come to resemble the later Great War of 1914–1918, and Lincoln's government could be charged as European governments were to be in 1914–1918 with draining away the nation's blood in indecisive battles, the reason was that Lincoln and Grant were in the same terrible predicament that ensnared the Great Powers of Europe just over half a century later. They were using the only feasible military method to pursue the complete and unconditional triumphs their people and parliaments expected of them, peace agitators to the contrary notwithstanding. The revulsion imperiling Lincoln's reelection and the Union itself in 1864 was revulsion at the true face of modern war.

# ELEVEN

# Suspense and Resolution

## CHATTANOOGA TO ATLANTA

In the long run, Grant was to prove that he was achieving more than dead-lock, that he was winning the war in the only way it could be won with the desired totality, by destroying Lee's army. But the Presidential election would not wait for the long run, and the first evidence of a dramatic enough break in the military stalemate to reverse the apparent course of the political campaign came from a Union general less starkly realistic than Grant in his strategic perceptions, better able than Grant to conceal from the Northern people and himself the full horrors of modern war.

William Tecumseh Sherman, commanding the Military Division of the Mississippi, had conferred with his friend Grant about his orders for the 1864 campaigns. It may have been because of Sherman's influence on his own orders that they differed somewhat from Grant's directive to Meade in their statement of objectives. While Grant said to Meade, "Lee's army will be your objective point," and Grant's instructions to Sherman similarly set as his first task "to move against Johnston's army," it will be remembered that the orders to Sherman went on to direct him "to get into the interior of the enemy's country as far as you can, inflicting all the damage you can against their war resources."[1] In practice, Sherman emphasized this second of his responsibilities rather than the first. Of the city of Atlanta he said that "its capture would be the death-knell of the Southern Confederacy," and Atlanta rather than Joe Johnston's army became the principal target of Sherman's campaign.[2] So much did Sherman focus upon territorial objectives and upon enemy resources that he was eventually to allow the opposing Confederate army to slip away while he pursued his preferred objectives exclusively.

Meanwhile, if not quite so essential to the Confederacy as Sherman suggested, Atlanta was nonetheless a worthy target. It was the greatest railroad hub of the Confederacy, from which lines radiated toward all points of the compass. Its capture would leave only one rickety and roundabout railroad route, down the Atlantic coast and westward through Macon, of the already tenuous connections between the Confederate Northeast and the remaining Confederate Southwest, including the iron and coal fields of Alabama and the newly built munitions complex at Selma. Atlanta itself was one of the most productive munitions centers of the Confederacy. Federal troops in Atlanta would be in position to turn toward the Carolinas and threaten Lee's army from the rear.

Sherman's focus not upon the enemy's army but upon the capture of Atlanta as the first purpose of his 1864 campaign combined with the strategic methods of his opponent to develop one of the greatest campaigns of skillful maneuver, on both sides, in American military history. All that was lacking was Sherman's failure to exploit the full potential of his commanding a group of three autonomous armies for operational as distinguished from basically tactical maneuver. During the Vicksburg campaign the demonstration of skill in maneuver warfare had occurred almost entirely on one side. The fascination for the military student of the campaign from Chattanooga to Atlanta lies in the mastery of tactical maneuver displayed by both of the rival commanders.

Joseph E. Johnston, his career in the East cut short by his wounds at Seven Pines, and a grievous disappointment as Western theater commander in 1863, was at last to come into his own, furthermore, as a strategist of distinction. When Grant after the war discussed the inevitable question whether there was any strategy that might have won the war for the Confederacy, he pointed to Johnston's strategy against Sherman in 1864: a strategy markedly different from Lee's, a strategy that avoided battle where Lee sought it, a strategy that traded space to conserve the one most essential resource without which the Confederacy could not persist in the war, its scarce military manpower. Johnston preferred to maneuver rather than to fight, to engage in battle only when he could do so with manifest advantages of position, to withdraw rather than risk heavy casualties, but through careful maneuver to betray his opponent into mistakes and then to fall upon whatever enemy detachments were left vulnerable by the mistakes.

Rather than a Napoleonic strategy of annihilation aimed at the destruction of the enemy army, for which Johnston thought the Confederacy's resources and particularly its manpower too limited, Johnston invoked a strategy of erosion, to wear away the enemy army through strokes against its periphery, and above all to wear away the enemy's patience and will. It was just such a strategy that General George Washington had employed in a similar condition of inferior resources to win the War of the American Revolution. Grant's verdict on Johnston's strategy was: "My own judgment is that Johnston acted very wisely: he husbanded his men and saved as much of his territory as he could, without fighting decisive battles in which all might be lost." ". . . I think that his policy was the best one that could have been pursued by the whole South — protract the war, which was all that was necessary to enable them to gain recognition in the end."[3]

The Johnston-Sherman duel became a great campaign partly because the opposing generals were finely matched in skills, Sherman balancing Johnston's design to draw him into mistakes with an appropriate mastery of discretion to avoid committing many. It was a campaign of high interest for the military student also because their armies were delicately balanced, Johnston having just enough men to play his role of defensive maneuver with effect, but few enough men that effectiveness demanded all the capacities of an able general. As the campaign began, the Confederate Army of Tennessee had been reinforced to some 62,000. Sherman's Armies of the Tennessee, the Cumberland, and the Ohio together, it will be recalled, took about 100,000 into the field.[4]

From May 7 to mid-July the duel ranged from Johnston's initial mountain fortress on Rocky Face Ridge above Dalton, Georgia, through Resaca and across the Oostenaula River out of the Appalachian mountain system and onto a rolling, fertile plateau, through Adairsville and Cassville where Johnston laid ambushes that were narrowly foiled by Sherman's and the Federals' alertness and speed of movement, across the Etowah River and into a country of barren pinelands and occasional towering, abrupt mountains. Here, beyond the Etowah, the nervous, high-strung Sherman impatiently began to expose his men to Confederate gunfire in the manner for which Johnston was hoping, in dubious assaults against entrenchments around New Hope Church, and especially on June 27 in an attack against Kenesaw Mountain that was as hopeless of achieving immediate success and almost as disproportionately costly in terms of long-run results as Grant's attack at

Cold Harbor earlier in the month. In the main action at Kenesaw Mountain, at Cheatham's Hill, the Federals suffered some 2,051 casualties (1,999 killed and wounded, 52 missing) of 16,225 engaged, to about 432 Confederate losses (270 killed and wounded, 172 missing) of 17,733 engaged.[5]

His strategy complementing Johnston's, intent as he was on reaching Atlanta more than on grappling with the Army of Tennessee, Sherman alternately reached out with his right and his left to turn Johnston out of strong positions, while Johnston either lashed out at the maneuvering columns as at Adairsville and Cassville or tempted Sherman to assail his strong points as at Kenesaw. Sherman's ability to maneuver was limited by his dependence on a long and vulnerable railroad stretching through largely unfriendly territory, 185 miles along the Louisville and Nashville from his main supply depot at Louisville to the Tennessee capital, 151 miles mostly along the Nashville and Chattanooga, lengthening constantly down the 140 miles of the Western and Atlantic from Chattanooga to Atlanta.

Confederate cavalry and guerrillas slashed at this line continually. To sustain a fighting army of nearly 100,000 men, 12,000 horses, and 32,600 mules through months of campaigning over this length of railroad was a new challenge in warfare. It was a feat accomplished by means of Sherman's ruthless exclusion of unnecessary baggage and comforts from his army; by his barring of all civilian traffic, freight and passenger, from his rail lines until military needs were met (Sherman successfully overruling Lincoln's protest, by replying: "We have worked hard with the best talent of the country & it is demonstrated that the railroad cannot supply the army & the people too. one or the other must quit & the army don't intend to unless Joe Johnston makes us");[6] and by the mature skills of the U.S. Military Railroad System and the Railroad Construction Corps of the Quartermaster's Department.

The Railroad Act of January 31, 1862 had empowered the Federal government to take possession of any railroad lines in the United States if the public safety required it.[7] This statute both served for bargaining leverage in rate negotiations with Northern railroads and permitted the Union Army to organize captured railroads into its own military railroad system. On February 11, 1862 Lincoln had appointed Daniel C. McCallum, former superintendent of the Erie Railroad, director and superintendent of military railroads, with the rank of colonel, assistant aide de camp. Formally, McCallum's rail system was part of the Quartermaster's Department, which paid its bills and supervised its finances; actually, McCallum worked more directly under the Secretary of War.[8]

In the early part of the war the most famous Union railroad director was Colonel, Assistant Aide de Camp (from September 5, 1862 Brigadier-General, U.S.V.) Herman Haupt, who in turn was almost independent of McCallum and who constructed and coordinated railroads for the Army of Virginia and the Army of the Potomac.[9] Lincoln helped make Haupt famous by describing his remarkable Potomac Creek bridge as constructed of nothing but "beanpoles and cornstalks,"[10] and Haupt's achievements in organizing and reopening the railroads toward and into Gettysburg during Lee's invasion of Pennsylvania were especially noteworthy. On September 5, 1863, however, Haupt resigned, believing himself a victim of excessive interference from soldiers uninitiated in the mysteries of rail transportation.[11] Thus it was McCallum who went west and took personal command of Sherman's railroad supply line. In the course of the Chattanooga-to-Atlanta campaign, to keep the trains moving just behind Sherman's advance the Railroad Construction Corps rebuilt eleven bridges, laid seventy-five miles of completely new track, and made usable again mile after mile of track that the retreating Confederates tried to ruin. The repair of the tracks never fell more than five days behind the vanguard of Sherman's armies.[12]

Tied to the long and tenuous rail line as he was, with his numerical advantage by no means overwhelming, Sherman was also distracted by the busy Nathan Bedford Forrest (since December 4 a major-general),[13] who was able to raid freely beyond the Union right flank because Banks's projected Mobile campaign never got under way. Hoping to end Forrest's threat to his line of communications, Sherman saw to the organizing of a force of 4,800 cavalry and 3,000 infantry under Brigadier-General Samuel D. Sturgis, U.S.V. But on June 10 the rebel cavalryman with 3,000 troopers routed Sturgis's much larger force at the battle of Brice's Cross Roads, Mississippi, also known as Guntown or Tishomingo Creek. Sturgis lost over 2,000 casualties, sixteen of eighteen guns, and 150 wagons.[14] Unschooled except for about six months of elementary education, and thus completely untutored in the academic art of war, Forrest nevertheless employed at Brice's Cross Roads a classic double envelopment that could have come straight from a military textbook. The effect was to leave Sherman's right still almost wide open to enemy raiders.[15]

For all these problems and the skill of his opponent, Sherman had just enough of a numerical advantage that he could go on consistently stretching his flanks beyond Johnston's to turn Johnston out of one position after another. Sherman staged the frontal attack at Kenesaw partly because rains had impeded maneuver. After the attack failed, the rains ended, and Sherman extended his right beyond Johnston's left to force the Confederates into another retreat, the repetitious pattern of the campaign so far.

Johnston had to withdraw into a formidable series of fortifications he had built to guard the crossings of the Chattahoochie, the last major river before Atlanta. The Federals still had just enough superior numbers; while their main body occupied Johnston with demonstrations, and some of the Federal cavalry went riding downriver as if searching for a crossing there, on the 4th of July Colonel, 2nd Ohio Cavalry, Israel Garrard's Second Brigade, Fourth Division of the Cavalry Corps of Sherman's command stole across the Chattahoochie at Roswell far upstream. Meanwhile Colonel, 65th Illinois Infantry, David Cameron's First Brigade, Fourth Division, Twenty-third Corps also crossed, on a fish dam about half way between Roswell and the main armies, to shield the way for the pontoons of the rest of the Twenty-third Corps — that is, Schofield's Army of the Ohio. From the banks of the Chattahoochie, the Federals could see the rooftops of Atlanta. Having crossed the river, they forced Johnston into the immediate defenses of the city itself.

Grant's judgment in his memoirs was probably correct: If there was any way for the Confederacy to win the war, it was by such strategy as Johnston had employed from Rocky Face Ridge to the Chattahoochie, to trade space for men and time, never risking the manpower losses of a major battle except on terms such as those of Kenesaw Mountain, but always watching vigilantly for opportunities created by the enemy's mistakes. Johnston compelled Sherman to consume seventy-four days to advance a hundred miles, and after two and a half months of campaigning Johnston's army remained almost as strong as at the beginning. But the Confederacy should have employed this strategy of erosion from the outset of the war. Johnston attempted it so late in the war that there was no longer enough space remaining to trade for men and time. Johnston was too deep in the South when he began, and when he fell back into the defenses of Atlanta, President Davis not surprisingly concluded that the Confederacy could afford Johnston's retreats no longer. It was too late in the war for Johnston's strategy.

## BATTLING FOR ATLANTA

Davis replaced Johnston on July 18 with the boldest of the army's corps commanders, tall, tawny General John Bell Hood, who had remained in the West when his old division returned to the Army of Northern Virginia. Already Hood had suffered the shattering of his left arm at Gettysburg and the loss of his right leg at Chickamauga, but he remained daring and aggressive, and surely he would fight before the Army of Tennessee retreated again.[16]

But if it was too late in the war for Johnston's strategy, it was too late for any military strategy to save the Confederacy. Hood attacked Sherman as expected, actually adopting for his first strike a plan already developed by Johnston, who was far too capable a general not to have recognized the political and moral necessity of putting up a fight for Atlanta. While Lieutenant-General Stephen D. Lee's Corps held the Atlanta trenches, Lieutenant-General Alexander P. Stewart's and Hardee's Corps fell on Thomas's Army of the Cumberland astride Peach Tree Creek on July 20. Schofield's Army of the Ohio and McPherson's Army of the Tennessee were off trying to maneuver around the Confederate right. Thomas had displeased Sherman on several occasions during the campaign with his alleged slowness of movement; but on defense he was still the Rock of Chickamauga, and he turned Hood back with some 2,500 Confederates killed and wounded to 1,600 Union losses in those categories.[17]

While Hood was thus occupied, McPherson got astride the Georgia Railroad, which ran eastward through Decatur to Augusta. Hood felt obliged to respond with another attack, sending Hardee's Corps against McPherson's left flank on July 22. This action came to be called simply the battle of Atlanta (occasionally the battle of Bald Hill). With Hood also throwing in Major-General, Georgia Militia, Gustavus W. Smith's 5,000 men of the First Division of the state militia behind Hardee, the Confederate Army of Tennessee gave Grant's old Union Army of the Tennessee as hard fighting as it had yet endured. The excellent soldier McPherson was killed, and the Union line broke, until Sherman intervened with a barrage from the massed guns of Schofield's army and then a counterattack by the First and Second Divisions of Sherman's own old Fifteenth Corps. As usual the arithmetic of aggressive battle ran heavily against the Confederates. Hood lost about 8,000 (7,000 killed and wounded, 1,000 missing) of 36,934 engaged, to 3,722 Union casualties (430 killed, 1,559 wounded, 1,733 missing) of 30,477 engaged. The Federals remained across Atlanta's railroad to the northeast as well as the Western and Atlantic to Chattanooga, blocking two of the city's four converging lines.[18]

Sherman had reached as far around the eastern circumference of Atlanta as he profitably could, however, without risking his own hold on the Western and Atlantic. Therefore he next shifted the Army of the Tennessee, commanded from July 27 by Oliver O. Howard, from his left all the way to his newly extended right, reaching west and south as the vanguard of a move against Hood's remaining railroads. These were the Macon and Western Central Railroad to Macon and the Montgomery and West Point Railroad, which divided from the former at Eastport, some five miles below Atlanta, to reach southwestward to Montgomery. Hood's predictable response had been to dispatch two of his three corps, S. D. Lee's followed by Stewart's, on another attacking sortie. The effort produced the battle of Ezra Church on July 28, with the Federals digging in short of the railroads but holding off Confederate attacks from two in the afternoon until dark. In spite of the duration of the battle, Federal casualties were only 732 (559 killed and wounded, 173 missing). The Confederates probably lost at least 4,100 killed and wounded and 200 missing — more bad arithmetic for the South.[19]

Thus Hood had gratified the Confederate government's wish that Atlanta should not fall without a fight, but he had nothing to show for it except a rapid multiplication of his army's casualty rate. Still, Hood's troops had been able to fall back from their futile assaults into the well-prepared fortifications that ringed Atlanta, and an extension of the fortifications held the Federals short of the Montgomery and Macon railroads. Once Hood's impetuosity had exhausted itself, the rival armies settled into a siege along the Atlanta lines, and the month of August passed with the Western armies as stationary around Atlanta as the Eastern armies around Petersburg. This was the month when Lincoln feared he had no friends and wrote his lament that the coming election and the Union both seemed likely to be lost. At the end of the month the Democrats adopted their platform declaring the four years' experiment in war a failure.

Sherman tried to break the Macon railroad with cavalry raids, but two converging cavalry strikes launched under cover of the fighting at Ezra Church ended ingloriously. Major-General George M. Stoneman, U.S.V., with 6,700 horsemen not only failed to tear up track and liberate the Union prisoners near Macon and at Camp Sumter at Andersonville, but became a prisoner himself along with 700 of his men. Brigadier-General Edward M. McCook, U.S.V., with 3,000 troopers destroyed a mile and a half of track but also lost 950 captured, and did no damage that could not be quickly repaired.[20] Hood was so little impressed by Sherman's cavalry, in fact, that he concluded he could send about half of his own mounted men, perhaps 4,000, under Major-General Joseph Wheeler on a long raid against Sherman's vital Western and Atlantic Railroad. This gesture left Hood short of reconnaissance troops, however, when Sherman commenced a new maneuver on August 25.

On the 26th, Hood telegraphed Richmond: "Last night the enemy abandoned the Augusta railroad, and all the country between that road and the Dalton railroad [the Western and Atlantic]. . . . He has not extended his right at all." The next day Hood telegraphed again: "They [the enemy] have drawn back so that their left is now on the Chattahoochie at the railroad bridge; their right is unchanged."[21]

The Confederate commander jumped to the conclusion that Wheeler's raid had so ruined Sherman's supplies that a hungry Union army was abandoning the siege. To confirm the impression, an old woman appealed to some Confederate soldiers for food, saying that inside the Union lines she had been refused by Union soldiers who told her they did not have enough for themselves. The Union troops at the Chattahoochie railroad bridge were Slocum's Twentieth Corps of the Army of the Cumberland (mainly the old Eleventh and Twelfth Corps brought from the Army of the Potomac the previous autumn, the Twelfth Corps with reinforcements having been reorganized as the Twentieth on April 4, 1864, the Eleventh Corps added on April 14).[22] The rest of Sherman's armies were in fact on their way to the Macon railroad, to break up Hood's communications with the South.

On August 28 the Federals reached the Montgomery railroad and began tearing up track. Hood so wanted to believe he had won the campaign that when he heard this news, he convinced himself that Sherman was merely covering his withdrawal, and he sent only a few cavalry brigades southward "to co-operate . . . in repelling raids."[23] Not until the evening of August 30 did Hood become convinced enough of the truth that he sent Hardee's and S. D. Lee's Corps down the Macon railroad toward Jonesboro to try to secure that line. By this time the Federals themselves were within three miles of the Macon railroad. There was another characteristic Hood battle the next day, with Hardee's and Lee's Corps throwing themselves against the Federals in poorly coordinated attacks. By the end of the day the Federals were firmly astride the Macon railroad at Rough and Ready and between that place and Jonesboro.

Even now, Hood refused to believe the whole truth, and he recalled Lee's Corps to Atlanta because he expected an attack on the city by Sherman's main body from the northwest. The effect was to give Sherman an excellent opportunity to isolate and destroy Hardee. The opportunity went lost, however, because Hardee was more alert than some of Sherman's subordinates, particularly Major-General David S. Stanley, U.S.V., commanding the Fourth Corps of Thomas's army. Hardee escaped the trap before the Federals sprang it.

But while Hardee was eluding Sherman's grasp on September 1, Hood was learning at last that it was the bulk of Sherman's armies that blocked the Macon railroad, too strong a force for even Hood to expect to dislodge it with additional headlong assaults. Atlanta therefore no longer had a single dependable line of supply. It had to be yielded.

Hood halted the return of Lee's Corps to the city and ordered Lee instead to cover Hood's own withdrawal from it, which took place during the night of September 1–2. A little after midnight, Sherman far away to the south on the Macon railroad heard explosions from the direction of Atlanta and feared that Hood was falling on Slocum's lonely corps. Actually the explosions were the effect of an only partially successful effort of Hood's rear guard to destroy the ordnance stores and locomotives in the city. Slocum responded to them by probing into Atlanta at daybreak. Not until still the following morning, however, did Slocum's message reach Sherman by a necessarily roundabout route to tell him that Union soldiers had achieved the goal he had set for his campaign. At six A.M. on September 3, Sherman could telegraph Washington: "So Atlanta is ours, and fairly won."[24] Already Sherman had won for himself a commission as major-general in the Regular Army, dating from August 12, 1864.[25]

The Democrats had just drafted their declaration that the war was a failure, and Horace Greeley and his associates were circulating the governors suggesting the desirability of a new Republican nominating convention. By the time the governors could answer, the news from Atlanta had reached them, and their replies indicated that a reconsideration of the Presidential nominee was no longer appropriate.

## MOBILE BAY AND SHERIDAN'S VALLEY CAMPAIGN

Sherman's victory at Atlanta gave new significance to Rear-Admiral Farragut's naval victory at Mobile Bay on August 5, from which dramatic impressions were now reaching the North: Farragut aloft in the rigging of his flagship *Hartford*, his ships outmaneuvering the feared rebel ironclad ram *Tennessee* so that she struck no blow but went to the bottom under Federal gunfire.[26] Farragut's capture of Mobile Bay left only Wilmington, North Carolina as a major nest for blockade runners; and with Atlanta's fall his victory no longer stood isolated but might prove the beginning of a new tide of fortune. The fulfillment of such promise demanded, nevertheless, that the embarrassment of Early's march to the shadow of the Capitol must be washed away. In July the Sixth Corps and additional Federal detachments followed Early northwestward up the Potomac. When, however, the Confederate raiders appeared to have been shooed back into the Valley at a safe distance from Washington, the Sixth Corps countermarched from the Leesburg area to be embarked from the Potomac wharves for Petersburg, and the First and Second Divisions of the Nineteenth Corps, brought up from the Army of the Gulf for the Petersburg front but diverted to oppose Early, also countermarched eastward into Maryland.[27] Because his mission included the responsibility of keeping as many Federal troops as possible away from Lee's front, Early reacted to these developments by dispatching across the Potomac for Chambersburg, Pennsylvania Brigadier-General John McCausland with McCausland's own and Brigadier-General Bradley T. Johnson's Brigades of cavalry (the latter had been Brigadier-General William E. "Grumble" Jones's until his death in action at Piedmont in the Valley the preceding June 5).

McCausland's raid was also intended by Early as a reply to Hunter's burnings in the Valley. Early instructed him to demand from Chambersburg $100,000 in gold or $500,000 in greenbacks for indemnification of persons whose property had been burned by the Federals, and if the indemnity was not forthcoming at once, to set Chambersburg to the torch. McCausland presented his demand to the borough council at 5:30 A.M. on July 30, and at 9 A.M. he ordered the 3,000 inhabitants evacuated and fires ignited. The Confederates withdrew by way of McConnellsburg.[28]

Brigadier-General, U.S.V., William W. Averell's Second Cavalry Division, Eighth Corps achieved a very partial revenge by falling on McCausland's troopers at dawn on August 7 at Moorefield, West Virginia and mauling them; the Federals reported capturing 420 men, 400 horses, and four guns.[29] But the War Department felt obliged to recall the Sixth Corps to block the northern exit of the Shenandoah again. More hot and dusty marching and countermarching by Federal soldiers up and down the Potomac valley followed, until visitors to the Sixth Corps noted markedly deteriorating morale among the disgusted troops of that hitherto excellent organization. Futile maneuvering in response to Early's activities was partly a product of confusion in command, as four military departments (Middle, West Virginia, Susquehanna, and the Defenses of Washington) were involved in the area.

General Hunter, chief of the Department of West Virginia and the senior relevant Federal commander, continued to exhibit discouragement and weariness. The War Department intervened with Halleck's attempting to command field operations from the capital. Grant thereupon decided he must find a new field commander for the whole area, one who would be able and energetic enough to put an end to Confederate raids from the

Shenandoah once and for all. Grant's idea was to "make all the Valley south of the Baltimore and Ohio Road a desert as high up as possible." Desperate to find a suitable commander, he contemplated returning Major-General William B. Franklin, an old McClellan ally, to active duty; but Halleck told him Franklin would not do, either politically or if his record as a corps commander in 1862 should be carefully examined.[30]

The attraction Franklin seemed to hold for Grant is one of the minor mysteries of the war. Once before Grant had proposed calling up Franklin at a time when he was desperate to find the right man for a previously frustrating task — when he had first come east as General-in-Chief and was looking for an officer to transform the cavalry of the Army of the Potomac. Long a whipping boy for Jeb Stuart, in 1863 the eastern cavalry had at last begun to be a fair match for the Confederate horsemen, but Grant believed they needed an exceptional leader to mold them into the clearly superior arm necessary to win the war. The relative neglect of cavalry — even among the Confederates, who relied on sheer luck to find an untutored master in Nathan Bedford Forrest, and on the not always dependable Stuart, and certainly among the Federals — was yet another symptom of a limited conception of the operational art. A reliable mobile arm is invaluable, even indispensable, to the combinations of forces that permit elevating tactical pressure against the enemy into wider threats encompassing an entire theater of war.

On the earlier occasion also, Halleck had objected strenuously to Grant's idea of using Franklin. As a substitute Halleck had offered Philip H. Sheridan. Sheridan had most recently embellished his impressive record when he led his division in the storming of Missionary Ridge. By early 1864, Major-General Alfred Pleasonton, U.S.V., commander of the Cavalry Corps of the Army of the Potomac since the Gettysburg campaign, seemed clearly inadequate for the post; he had no large conception of how best to employ a strong mounted arm. The excellent John Buford had died on December 16, 1863 at thirty-seven from the effects of prolonged exposure to the elements and exhaustion. Grant agreed to try Sheridan at the head of Meade's mounted troops.[31]

In that post, Sheridan had soon quarreled with Meade, because the otherwise capable commander of the Army of the Potomac held the retrogressive belief that cavalry should be diffused around the whole sensitive periphery of the army. Sheridan wanted to concentrate the Cavalry Corps into a powerful striking arm. He desired to do so, first, to deal with the Confederate cavalry, on the theory that "with a mass of ten thousand mounted men . . . I could make it so lively for the enemy's cavalry that . . . the flanks and rear of the Army of the Potomac would require little or no defense."[32]

Second, he wished to create a highly mobile weapon for all purposes, which could move at cavalry speed but, under his plans for training, could fight dismounted against infantry. Sheridan possessed at least the fundamentals of a vision of the operational art of war.

His quarrel with Meade erupted into a raging argument after the Wilderness battle. On May 8, Brigadier-General, U.S.V., James Harrison Wilson's Third Division, Cavalry Corps succeeded in occupying Spotsylvania Court House before the Confederates arrived, but Sheridan's efforts to reinforce the division with his entire corps were thwarted by the cavalry's entanglement with the Fifth Corps on the road. Meade had sent the infantry corps because he believed only infantry could be depended upon to hold a critical place. The result was that neither cavalry nor infantry got to Spotsylvania with sufficient strength or promptness to hang on. Sheridan stormed into Meade's headquarters to protest. His Irish pugnacity — he was famous for it since cadet brawls at West Point — collided with Meade's equally notorious short temper. According to Sheridan he ended the encounter by telling Meade; "I could whip Stuart if he (Meade) would only let me, but since he insisted on giving the cavalry directions without consulting me or even notifying me, he could henceforth command the Cavalry Corps himself — that I would not give it another order."[33]

Meade went to Grant with his version of the story, and Grant responded to hearing of Sheridan's promise that he could whip Stuart: "Did he say that? Then let him go and do it."[34] Accordingly Sheridan was able to concentrate the Cavalry Corps as he wanted. He led it off toward Richmond to draw Stuart after him, and on May 11 at Yellow Tavern near the Confederate capital Sheridan's troopers not only defeated the Confederate cavalry soundly but wounded Stuart mortally while doing so. Sheridan skillfully maximized the Federal superiority in quality of horses by avoiding hard riding en route to his rendezvous with Stuart while pinning Stuart upon the dilemma of deciding whether the Federals' main object was Richmond or the railroads supplying Lee. Thus Sheridan forced much rapid movement on the Confederates as they tried to guard against both threats. Stuart had to fight at Yellow Tavern with tired horses.[35]

On the strength of his elimination of one of the most prestigious of Confederate chieftains and his continued success against enemy cavalry thereafter, Sheridan's name commended itself to Halleck and Grant once again as a substitute for Franklin. On August 1 Grant appointed Sheridan to the field command of the forces watching Early, and when Hunter said he preferred to retire rather than hold merely administrative command, on August 6 Sheridan received the newly created Middle Military Division as well, including a new Department of the Shenandoah and encompassing the area of Early's activities.

Sheridan's field force, which became the Army of the Shenandoah, would consist of Major-General, U.S.V., Horatio G. Wright's Sixth Corps; the First and Second Divisions of Brigadier-General, U.S.V., William H. Emory's Nineteenth Corps; the small Eighth Corps (also known as the West Virginia Corps or the Army of West Virginia), Hunter's former field force, now under Brigadier-General George Crook, U.S.V.; and a Cavalry Corps, consisting of the First and Third Divisions of the Cavalry Corps, Army of the Potomac and Averell's cavalry division of Crook's command, and led by Brigadier-General, U.S.V., Alfred Thomas Archimedes Torbert. In all the Army of the Shenandoah had about 40,000 men, including 6,400 cavalry.[36]

Grant's orders for the new Valley campaign were in part characteristic of all Grant's strategy since he had become the lieutenant-general commanding: "I want Sheridan put in command of all the troops in the field, with instructions to put himself south of the enemy and follow him to the death. Wherever the enemy goes let our troops go also. Once started up the Valley they ought to be followed until we get possession of the Virginia Central Railroad."[37] Here was Grant's familiar strategy of annihilation, with the injunction to get south of the enemy implying, however, that Grant envisaged Sheridan as destroying Early by trapping him as Grant had trapped Pemberton, not by trading casualties as Grant felt compelled to do after failing to ensnare Lee.

But from this accustomed strategy Grant went on to give the war a new turn — by developing his theme of making the Valley a desert:

> In pushing up the Shenandoah Valley . . . it is desirable that nothing should be left to invite the enemy to return. Take all provisions, forage, and stock wanted for the use of your command; such as cannot be consumed, destroy. It is not desirable that the buildings should be destroyed; they should rather be protected; but the people should be informed that so long as an army can subsist among them recurrences of these raids must be expected, and we are determined to stop them at all hazards.[38]

"Give the enemy no rest," Grant instructed Sheridan, "and if it is possible to follow to the Virginia Central road, follow that far. Do all the damage to railroads and crops you can. Carry off stock of all descriptions, and negroes, so as to prevent further planting. If the war is to last another year, we want the Shenandoah Valley to remain a barren waste."[39]

The Valley was an apt route for Confederate advances toward Washington and the North not only because it offered a shielded avenue northeastward, but also because hungry and ill-supplied Confederate troops had always been able to count on rich provisions there, harvested from grain fields unexcelled in fertility anywhere in the South. Although the creakiness of the Virginia Central Railroad prevented Lee's troops around Petersburg from dining so heartily on Valley fare as did Early's men in the Valley itself, the Shenandoah remained the best breadbasket of the Army of Northern Virginia. Now Grant proposed to ruin the Valley as both invasion route and breadbasket, and Halleck and Sheridan agreed, Halleck telling Grant: "I concur with General Sheridan, and think that much greater damage can be done to the enemy by destroying his crops and communications north of the James than on the south."[40] But to destroy crops as well as communications, all provisions, forage, and stock not wanted for the Union command, to make a desert of Virginia's granary, was to carry the war a longer step toward remorseless revolutionary struggle than Lincoln was likely to have imagined when long ago he expressed his fear of such an outcome.

While Sheridan was chosen so that he might bring to the Valley the aggressiveness that had killed Jeb Stuart, at first he jousted against Early with unwonted caution. Lee's pleasure at the success of Old Jube in diverting Federal troops from Petersburg led him to decide on August 6 to send Major-General Joseph B. Kershaw's Division (until December 15, 1863 it had been McLaws's) from Longstreet's Corps and Major-General Fitzhugh Lee's Cavalry Division to assist Early, initially to operate east of the Blue Ridge. All the more because some knowledge reached them that Early had been reinforced, nearly every Federal leader, including Sheridan, greatly overestimated Early's numbers. They could not believe the Confederate general would have threatened Washington itself with so small a force as he actually led. With Kershaw's 4,500 and Fitzhugh Lee's 2,000, Early still commanded no more than 23,000 men.[41] On August 3, nevertheless, Halleck told Grant that the best information put the Confederate Valley army at about 40,000, perhaps a bit more.[42]

In early August, Sheridan advanced cautiously up the Valley to the vicinity of Strasburg. On August 12 Grant told Halleck that two infantry divisions had gone from Lee to Early and that Sheridan would have to turn to the defensive for the time being. Sheridan's information was similar, and included word that Longstreet himself was in the Valley.[43] On the 14th, Grant indicated that his own probings around Petersburg showed that only one infantry division could have gone to Early (which was correct; it was Kershaw's Division). By that time, however, Sheridan was in retreat to Halltown, in front of Harpers Ferry.[44]

The retreat nevertheless was a suitable occasion for obeying Grant's instructions that any provisions the Union Army could not use should be destroyed. A pillar of fire marked Sheridan's route northward. He instructed his officers to spare families enough foodstuffs to subsist through the winter, but the amount necessary for that purpose was left to the officers' discretion. Otherwise, grain, fruits, the generations' accumulation of livestock, and in Sheridan's interpretation of what was necessary to deny sustenance to the rebel army, barns, mills, and corn-cribs, all went to the torch. When occasionally a fire spread from a barn to a farmhouse, that was unfortunate but part of the chances of war. The loyal, of whom there were more than a few in the Valley, especially among the German families who had made their way south from Pennsylvania, had to suffer destruction along with the disloyal; anybody's provisions could nourish the rebels if they came down the Valley again.

Many Union soldiers wrecked farmsteads reluctantly; others were embittered enough by the long war to do so with a will, the more because the Shenandoah Valley was among the borderlands of Mosby's Kingdom, where Lieutenant-Colonel John S. Mosby's Partisan Rangers—the 43rd Battalion of Virginia Cavalry—made life miserable for unwary outposts and stragglers, while less disciplined and more ruthless Confederate irregulars created still more miseries. Sheridan himself commented on his destructive activities: "Death is popularly considered the maximum of punishment in war, but it is not; reduction to poverty brings prayers for peace more surely and more quickly than does the destruction of human life. . . ."[45] Indeed, for a middle-class property-owning family, the loss of a life's accumulation of belongings is a punishment not much exceeded by death. When we read about Civil War depredations and judge their morality, we should not forget that fact.

The new policy of property devastation nevertheless failed to meet the immediate military and political needs of the Lincoln administration. By mid-September Sheridan remained not far beyond Harpers Ferry, and Early, despite Sheridan's depredations, was again occupying Winchester and the Valley south of it. Lincoln had already displayed his impatience with the paucity of Union progress against Early when Sheridan first received the Valley command. At that time the President wrote Grant:

> I have seen your dispatch in which you say, "I want Sheridan put in command of all the troops in the field, with instructions to put himself South of the enemy, and follow him to the death. Wherever the enemy goes, let our troops go also." This, I think, is exactly right, as to how our troops should move. But please look over the despatches you may have received from here, even since you made that order, and discover, if you can, that there is any idea in

the head of any one here of "putting our army *South* of the enemy" or of following him to the "*death*" in any direction. I repeat to you it will neither be done nor attempted unless you watch over it every day, and hour, and force it.[46]

This dispatch had prompted a visit from Grant to Sheridan to impress Lincoln's earnestness upon him. Now in mid-September Lincoln's worrying and appeals that something must be accomplished in the Valley sent Grant traveling to see Sheridan again.

As it happened, Sheridan's inactivity had rendered the Confederates overconfident. Kershaw's Division had departed the Valley by way of Front Royal on September 14, and on the 15th Sheridan learned enough of this movement — though for a time he thought Kershaw was remaining at Front Royal — that he was already planning an attack when Grant visited him on the 17th. The Commanding General's trip proved unnecessary. Hearing Sheridan's plans, Grant said simply, "Go in."[47]

Sheridan made his move on the 19th. Evidently lulled by Sheridan's delay in beginning the campaign, Early had scattered his troops widely around Winchester. Sheridan planned to move on Winchester from the east along the Berryville Road at daybreak, to push through Major-General Stephen Dodson Ramseur's Division, which guarded the road, and in fact to put himself south of the enemy as Grant's orders had directed.

For a time, however, it appeared that Early's lack of respect for Sheridan was well placed. The Berryville Road was the only good easterly approach to Winchester across the steep banks of Opequon Creek. It was inadequate to accommodate Sheridan's attacking force. The road consequently was soon jammed, and Sheridan's design for a smashing attack early in the day miscarried. Instead the Nineteenth Corps, following the Sixth, found itself entangled in the baggage trains of the latter, which had mistakenly moved immediately behind the infantry. Sheridan's assault therefore did not work up a full head of steam until afternoon, by which time the Confederates knew what was happening and had concentrated in the threatened sector. It required stout fighting for the Union to repel a counterattack by Major-Generals Robert E. Rodes's and John B. Gordon's Confederate Divisions into a gap that the confusion on the road caused to open between the Sixth and Nineteenth Corps. In this heavy action Rodes was killed, one of Stonewall Jackson's old champions. Brevet Brigadier-General, U.S.A., and Brigadier-General, U.S.V., David A. Russell was in the forefront of reversing the tide of battle and pushing the Union ranks onward; he was wounded in the chest but insisted on continuing to direct the advance until another hit killed him. The young military intellectual Emory Upton pressed the final sealing of the gap while being carried about on a stretcher, badly wounded in the right thigh.

Once Sheridan's line was intact again, the Federals continued driving forward in a frontal assault, which was already carrying the day by sheer weight of numbers when Crook's Eighth Corps and the Federal cavalry broke and turned Early's left. By nightfall both sides perceived Early's army as disintegrating into panic and rout. But the outcome was hardly astonishing, since Sheridan had opposed 37,711 effectives to about 12,150. After this battle of Third Winchester or Opequon Sheridan held a high reputation among administration, high command, and the Northern public; but he had not fought his first full-scale battle as an army commander with any conspicuous display of skill. Despite the apparent rout, Early was able to halt his retreat in a strong defensive position a little more than twenty miles away, at Fisher's Hill. Sheridan had failed to work his way south of the enemy as Grant desired. Nevertheless, fighting at odds of the sort that confronted Early can be expected to be disproportionately costly to the weaker army. Early had lost some 276 killed, 1,827 wounded, and 1,818 missing, for a total of 3,921 casualties, about 40 percent of his army. (Federal losses were actually higher in absolute numbers: 697 killed, 3,983 wounded, 332 missing, a total of 5,018.)[48]

Fisher's Hill, a steep wooded ridge overlooking Tumbling Run and Strasburg, spans the narrow western part of the Valley between Little North Mountain and the Massanuttons, but it was a long line — almost four miles — to be held by Early's reduced force. Sheridan attacked it on September 22, staging a demonstration on Early's front and right until Crook hit him hard on the left. Once again Early had to retreat with heavy losses, 1,235 in his infantry and cavalry. This time, furthermore, the balance of casualties much favored the Federals — they lost 528, with only fifty-two killed — and Sheridan believed he could have destroyed Early's army altogether if his cavalry had not failed to execute an envelopment and thus to close a trap he had planned. General Torbert of the cavalry lacked Sheridan's own tireless aggressiveness.[49]

All the same, Early had lost enough that the Federal high command considered the latest Valley campaign substantially won, and they discussed how best to return the bulk of Sheridan's troops to the Petersburg front. Grant favored an overland movement through Charlottesville and along the Virginia Central Railroad, but Sheridan thought that Early and the Confederate guerrillas retained enough strength to make so long a march through hostile territory too risky. He preferred to move by way of the Potomac and Chesapeake Bay. Nearly a month after Third Winchester, the Federal authorities were still debating this question, and on the morning of October 19 Sheridan was sleeping in Winchester, some fourteen miles behind the army's camps along Cedar Creek, as he returned from a conference in Washington at which the issue was finally settled in his favor.

That morning Early attacked the Army of the Shenandoah and drove it from its camps. Early's whole campaign since June had been built upon audacity beyond the comprehension of the Federals, and by October he had been beaten so badly at Winchester and Fisher's Hill that he had everything to gain and little to lose in still more audacity—in resuming the attack against Sheridan's army. General Lee agreed, and sent Kershaw's Division to the Valley again to reinforce Early. On October 13, Early reappeared at Fisher's Hill, not far south of Sheridan's Cedar Creek encampment. The Federals were sufficiently alarmed to bring back the Sixth Corps, which had already begun moving out of the Valley. Sheridan's sound hunch that Early still had at least one card to play lay behind his whole discussion with Washington about how to move his troops. Nevertheless, the Federals were disposed carelessly enough on the morning of October 19 that after a stealthy nighttime flanking march by General Gordon with the old Second Corps divisions of himself, Ramseur, and Brigadier-General John Pegram, the whole Confederate army joined in an attack first against the Federal rear and left that rushed through the Eighth and Nineteenth Corps camps in succession and then drove even the veteran Sixth Corps away from its tents.

The acting commander of Sheridan's army, General Wright, was partly to blame for this debacle, especially since to the extent that he had been vigilant at all, he had watched the wrong flank; he imagined that the North Fork of the Shenandoah River so shielded his left as to make that flank invulnerable, which is precisely what Gordon discerned and found a route to exploit. Still, Wright and his fellows rallied the Sixth Corps for a series of firm delaying actions on a succession of hills behind the camps, where General Emory also rounded up more and more men of his Nineteenth Corps. Crook's Eighth Corps, first and hardest hit, was more difficult to rally, and the Valley Pike back toward Winchester was filled with retreating soldiers from nearly all the Union formations.

Sheridan at Winchester awakened at six o'clock to the sound of distant artillery fire, but he thought it too sporadic to signify a major battle. Growing uneasy, however, he hastened his departure southward, and riding through Winchester he heard the gunfire now transformed into a continuous roar and found Virginia women in the streets uncommonly excited and happy. The sounds of battle began to suggest a Union withdrawal. Then, from the crest of a low hill, Sheridan saw stretching before him "the appalling spectacle of a panic-stricken army": hundreds of men and scores of baggage wagons putting distance between themselves and the battle, some simply apathetic, some crying out variations of one chaplain's "Everything is lost, but all will be right when you get there" — though the chaplain did not stop running away.[50]

The day was bright, blue, and glorious in contrast to this dismal scene — cool and brilliant October at its best, the trees yellow and scarlet, a thin haze on the distant hills. And Sheridan remained as cool and bright as the day. The one most distinguishing feature of his generalship thus far, in his whole career from Perryville onward, had been a commanding and inspiring presence wherever the crises of his campaigns were most severe. He was an initially unprepossessing little bandy-legged man, and the pork-pie hat perched atop his oddly shaped head with its phrenologist's dream of a prominent posterior bump could have seemed absurd; but when he shouted, "If I had been with you this morning this disaster would not have happened. We must face the other way; we will go back and recover our camp,"[51] his magnetism was such that many fleeing men abruptly decided to become soldiers again and to rejoin an army that was no longer whipped. Many still retreated, but the tide reversed itself back toward Cedar Creek.

Sheridan's ride from Winchester to Cedar Creek was not a headlong rush but an alternation between dashes and pauses among groups of officers and soldiers to talk with them, receive their impressions of the battle, and urge them to return to the fight. Sheridan reached the battlefield about 10:30 in the morning, when the Sixth and Nineteenth Corps and the cavalry had already formed a line not likely to be broken by the force Early retained. The Union commander spent much of the rest of the day readying his men for a counterattack, which opened about four in the afternoon. Early later complained that he had been unable to complete his victory because too many of his troops had fallen out to plunder the captured camps; but when Sheridan's counterattack rolled back across the camps, the possessions left behind in them proved remarkably intact. Not many of the Confederates could have occupied themselves there. Early simply did not have enough men to best the Army of the Shenandoah when that army was ready to fight.

Early may have led over 18,000 men at Cedar Creek. The Federals had slightly more than 30,000. The odds were better for Early than previously, but not good enough for an attack, even a well-planned and executed surprise attack. The Federals lost 5,665 casualties (644 killed, 3,430 wounded, 1,591 missing). Early's losses included 2,910 men (320 killed, 1,540 wounded, 1,050 missing); forty-three guns — among them Federal pieces taken in the morning as well as most of the Confederates' own artillery; and all of the army's ambulances and ammunition wagons and most of the baggage and forage wagons.[52]

Deficiencies in its own leadership aside, Sheridan's cavalry had become as solid a fighting force as any cavalry of the Civil War. After Cedar Creek it pursued with all the stamina that men and horses could muster. This time the Confederate army in the Valley was indeed almost destroyed, to the extent that Sheridan eventually moved large numbers of his troops back to Petersburg via the overland route he had hitherto opposed. Meanwhile Sheridan followed Sherman and Meade (who ranked from August 18, six days after Sherman) as a major-general, U.S.A., ranking from September 20, the day after Third Winchester.[53]

## FROM BATTLEFIELD TO POLLING PLACE (II)

The day after Fisher's Hill, the politician-soldier Major-General James A. Garfield, U.S.V., wrote that Sheridan had made a speech more powerful and helpful to the Union Party cause than all the speeches the Union stump-orators could make.[54] In spite of Mobile Bay, Atlanta, and the Shenandoah, the rival Democratic Party remained fixated upon its claim that the war was a failure; therefore the Federal military victories were rapidly fastening on the political opposition an air of the ridiculous.

The traditions of American partisanship as they had developed to the time, and Democratic habits of attitude and activity fixedly molded by now through three and a half years of war, still made it impossible for the Democrats to distinguish clearly between opposition to the Republican administration and opposition to the war. Even McClellan, despite his backtracking from his party's peace platform, still talked after the Federal victories in terms of negotiations and conferences that might give the South slavery and the Union as it had been in 1860, as though the recent victories and the whole war with all its sacrifices had never occurred. Although McClellan had rejected the war-is-a-failure plank because of those very sacrifices — "I, for one, could not look in the face of my gallant comrades of the Army & Navy who have survived so many bloody battles, & tell them that their labors and the sacrifice of so many of our slain & crippled brethren had been in vain" — he clung to the possibility of a peace so conciliatory that all the efforts of the war might have gone for almost nothing.[55]

Other Democrats still flirted enough with conspiratorial plans for an anti-Lincoln coup in case ballots did not suffice — in the midst of the Democratic Chicago convention some of the fringe elements of the party had been conferring with Confederate agents from Canada about liberating the prisoners of war from nearby Camp Douglas[56] — so that the Republicans could reap a useful harvest from scare stories about copperhead plots. More than ever, by 1864 copperhead conspiracies were good for nothing except to give campaign ammunition to the Republicans, but they could still be made to do that.

If the Democratic Party at best still hoped to erase many of the efforts of the war and at worst could still dabble in conspiracy, then there was a strong prospect that many formerly Democratic voters, especially with sons in the Union Army, might cast their ballots for Lincoln to uphold the military labors of their kinsmen. After Atlanta and the Shenandoah had altogether punctured the anti-Lincoln balloon within the Republican Party, there was also a more and more irresistible inclination for all champions of the Union to rally to Lincoln, however much they might dislike or distrust him, as far preferable to the only real alternative. Custom forbade Lincoln's campaigning for himself, but doughty old antislavery orators such as Sumner and Garrison put aside their doubts about him to take to the platform on his behalf, and such former arch-rivals in Republican Party factionalism as Simon Cameron and Alexander K. McClure in Pennsylvania buried the hatchet for the duration of the campaign.

At the time of Fisher's Hill, even Frémont's campaign ended, with a public statement from the retiring candidate that he remained as critical of the Lincoln administration as ever, but that a McClellan victory would be intolerable. "The Chicago platform is simply separation," Frémont wrote. "General McClellan's letter of acceptance is re-establishment with slavery."[57]

Senator Zachariah Chandler of Michigan, a close friend and associate of Ben Wade but a highly practical politician, had labored devotedly to bring about this consummation. Chandler's efforts had come to focus on the presence of Montgomery Blair in Lincoln's Cabinet. Blair was anathema to the Radicals, and Chandler concluded after a wide canvass of opinion that if Lincoln sacrificed Blair, not only would Radicals such as Wade feel their views had been paid sufficient respect that they could campaign more diligently for the President, but Frémont might withdraw from the race. Blair was vulnerable, furthermore, because he and his family were such inveterate Machiavellians that neither the conservatives nor the moderates of the Republican Party would be much less happy than the Radicals to see him go. The exact course of Chandler's negotiations to remove Blair from the Cabinet and Frémont from his Presidential candidacy is murky. Frémont apparently thought he had struck no bargain with Chandler; his motives for withdrawal seem mostly to have lain elsewhere (and despite his public statement of his reasons for leaving the race, until almost the last moment he had been in touch with the Democrats and was still considering pulling out in favor of McClellan rather than Lincoln). But the President believed that through Chandler he had made a bargain with Frémont. When Frémont stepped aside on September 22, consequently, Lincoln reminded Blair that he had said his resignation would be available when the President wanted it. He received the resignation on the 23rd.[58]

A reunited Union Party could now concentrate on the mechanics of reelection: on finances and on mobilizing the vote. From Lincoln himself downward, the executive officers of the Federal government busied themselves to ensure that all officeholders would pay the financial assessments expected of them by the party, in a manner that would have offended the laws as well as the sensibilities of a later, perhaps more fastidious age. Cabinet members were assessed $500 each; workers in the New York Customs House were expected to contribute about 3 percent of their yearly pay; other government employees were assessed variously. A few conscientious public servants, such as Gideon Welles, were reluctant to lend themselves to such activity, and the Republican National Executive Committee had a hard time pressuring Welles into firing Democrats who worked for the Navy Department, finally achieving some compliance. Lincoln's political activity embraced the whole Union ticket, and when certain executive officeholders lagged in supporting the party's Congressional candidates, they felt his wrath. Like job holders, recipients of Federal contracts were expected to express their gratitude to the party financially.[59]

To get out the vote, the soldiers presented a special problem of the wartime election. Secretary of War Stanton took pains to stifle any flow of Democratic propaganda into the Army while opening the gates generously to equivalent Union Party materials. Even without this precaution, and despite the affection the Army of the Potomac felt for McClellan, the men in uniform were expected to favor Lincoln overwhelmingly. McClellan and the Democrats verged too close to threatening that the campaigns of the Army would become a waste. Lincoln, in contrast, continued to offer substantive evidence of his concern for the Army and the soldiers, not only by vowing to see the war through to victory, but also by such a gesture as proceeding with a draft in September, the political risks notwithstanding, in order to keep the ranks of the Army filled. Thus Union Party workers saw the problem not as one of how the soldiers might vote but of whether they would be able to vote.

Thanks to diligent Republican efforts, eleven of the twenty-five loyal states made provision for absentee voting by military men, and another eight allowed servicemen away from their homes to cast ballots by proxy. In New York, where the powerful Democrats blocked an absentee voting system, there was evidence that local Democratic officials could and would tamper with proxy ballots, so the administration wanted as many New York servicemen as possible to go home. In the big Midwestern states of Indiana and Illinois, there was no provision for voting away from home, so if Lincoln was to get Army votes there, soldiers had to be furloughed. Pennsylvania permitted absentee voting but was too pivotal to allow for any risks, so the administration wanted Keystone State soldiers to go home also.

Therefore the War Department and Republican politicians leaned heavily on generals in the field to permit the election-day homecoming of all the troops they could conceivably spare. Nothing about the pressure was subtle. Many of the generals complied, out of willingness or a feeling of necessity. Governor Yates's dictum that "Defeat in Illinois is worse than defeat in the field" was the applicable rule.[60] General Sherman had already contributed mightily to the desired political outcome through his achievements in Georgia, but he was contemptuous of politicians and reluctant to spare soldiers for voting. When Governor Morton of Indiana collided with this obstacle, however, the governor persuaded Lincoln himself to twist Sherman's arm to try to bring Indiana men home to the polling places.

"I am just enough of a politician," Lincoln said with exaggerated self-effacement, "to know that there was not much doubt about the result of the Baltimore Convention, but about this thing I am very far from being certain"—meaning his reelection.[61] The renewed military victories came just in time to influence the early elections, and these preliminary auguries for the Presidential contest went well. The Union Party carried the state elections in Maine and Vermont in the second week of September.[62] On October 11, Pennsylvania, Ohio, and Indiana elected state officers and Congressmen. The Pennsylvania returns were close enough to generate suspense for several days, but in the end the Commonwealth would send fifteen Republicans and nine Democrats to the next Congress, while the previous Congressional delegation had been split twelve to twelve. In Ohio and Indiana there were much more sweeping Republican victories. The Ohio Congressional delegation would be Republican by seventeen to two, the Indiana delegation by eight to three. Morton was reelected as governor, and he would have a more friendly legislature with him in Indianapolis.[63]

Two days later, on October 13, the voters of Maryland decided the issue of a new state constitution, one that provided for the emancipation of all slaves, without compensation to the owners. The margin was razor-thin: approval of the constitution by 30,174 votes to 29,979, under conditions whereby a voter was required to take an oath that he had never given aid or countenance to the rebellion, and nearly a hundred who tried to present themselves at the polls — and whose sentiments on slavery can be surmised — refused so to swear and were therefore turned away. Nevertheless, here was another indication of the direction of the tide, on the overriding issue of the era as well as on the immediate political battle.[64]

The same day that Maryland voted, Lincoln made a new private forecast of the November results, different from his apprehensions of late August but still cautious. Placing states and electoral votes in the Union or Democratic columns as he now thought they would fall, he gave himself 117 electoral votes to 114 for McClellan. If Nevada, then in process of acquiring statehood and predictably Republican, could be added, then Lincoln's margin would be six electoral votes rather than three — although in the following weeks Lincoln exhibited no undue haste to complete the admission of Nevada, refused to proclaim Nevada a state until he had seen a copy of the constitution as ratified although he had already read a copy before ratification, and finally issued his proclamation of statehood just eight days before the election.[65]

Lincoln by now was taking a more guarded view of his prospects than was necessary. To be sure, he and his party had to contend with the great residue of Democratic loyalty remaining from the long prewar era of Democratic supremacy. But on November 8, of slightly over four million votes cast, Lincoln received 55 percent, 2,330,552 to 1,835,985, and an electoral college triumph of 234 to 21. He carried every state in the Union except New Jersey, Delaware, and Kentucky.[66] As nearly as can be estimated, he received about three-fourths of the soldier vote. (Where servicemen went home to vote, and in some other states, their ballots cannot be distinguished from the rest.)[67] The Republicans would control Congress again.[68] In Missouri, the voters had elected a constitutional convention that was sure to abolish slavery.[69]

On election day before the outcome was known, McClellan resigned his commission in the Army — a curiously belated step — and subsequently remarked concerning the election: "For my country's sake I deplore the result. . . ."[70] Lincoln responded to a serenade two days after the election by saying, among other things: "We can not have free government without elections; and if the rebellion could force us to forego, or postpone a national election, it might fairly claim to have already conquered and ruined us. . . . But the rebellion continues; and now that the election is over, may not all, having a common interest, re-unite in a common effort, to save our common country?"[71]

The military victories of Mobile Bay, Atlanta, and Cedar Creek and the slow ruination of Lee's army by Grant's campaign of annihilation may well have carried the Confederacy so far toward military collapse by November that the election of McClellan might have made little difference in the outcome of the war—especially because Lincoln was on record as intending, in that event, to spare no effort to win the war before Inauguration Day, March 4, 1865. McClellan's election might have reinspirited the Confederacy enough to hang on beyond the 4th of March despite such efforts, however, and during the electoral campaign Lincoln still professed to believe that a McClellan victory would be fatal to the Union. "My own experience has proven to me, that there is no programme, intended by the democratic party but that will result in the permanent destruction of the Union," he had told former Governor Alexander W. Randall and Joseph T. Mills of Wisconsin, visiting him on behalf of the War Democrats. A Democratic victory, he said, would subtract the black soldiers from the Union Army. "Abandon all the posts now possessed by black men, surrender all these advantages to the enemy, & we would be compelled to abandon the war in 3 weeks."[72] These observations came in the midst of the political campaign, and they are far from carrying complete conviction; but Lincoln's scenario is not altogether implausible either.

In any event, Lincoln won and McClellan lost. With McClellan's defeat the Confederates lost their last chance for a negotiated peace, and Lincoln returned all his energies to the task of saving "our common country."

## TWELVE

# The Relentless War

## SHERIDAN'S WAR AGAINST THE ENEMY'S ECONOMY

Shortly before Cedar Creek, when the President thought that Early's Confederate army was already finished off, Grant had reiterated to Sheridan his orders for destruction of property: "You may take up such position in the Valley as you think can and ought to be held, and send all the force not required for this immediately here [to Petersburg]. Leave nothing for the subsistence of an army on any ground you abandon to the enemy."[1]

On October 7, four days after the dispatch of this order, Sheridan responded to Grant from Woodstock as he withdrew down the Valley:

> I have the honor to report my command at this point to-night. I commenced moving back from Port Republic, Mount Crawford, Bridgewater, and Harrisonburg yesterday morning. The grain and forage in advance of these points up to Staunton had previously been destroyed. In moving back to this point the whole country from the Blue Ridge to the North Mountains has been made untenable for a rebel army. I have destroyed over 2,000 barns, filled with wheat, hay, and farming implements; over 70 mills, filled with flour and wheat; have driven in front of the army over 4,[000] head of stock, and have killed and issued to the troops not less than 3,000 sheep. The destruction embraces the Luray Valley and Little Fort Valley, as well as the main valley.[2]

Even if the territory had not been made quite so untenable for a rebel army as Sheridan thought, at least to support a quick offensive dash, the work of the Army of the Shenandoah in carrying the war into its new dimension of remorseless revolutionary struggle had been exemplary.

Sheridan went on in the same report to say: "[First] Lieut. John R. Meigs [Corps of Engineers], my engineer officer, was murdered beyond Harrisonburg, near Dayton. For this atrocious act all the houses within an area of five miles were burned."[3] The circumstances of John Meigs's death are debatable, and in fact he may well have been shot down after appearing to reach under his poncho for a weapon after he had surrendered. But John Meigs was one of the bright young stars of the Army, an officer of potential comparable to Emory Upton's—the number one graduate of the West Point class of 1863, a paragon of all the virtues soldierly and gentlemanly, a volunteer participant at First Bull Run while on summer furlough from the Military Academy, through his studied mastery of the geography of the Valley an invaluable contributor to the successes of the Army of the Shenandoah, and the son of the Quartermaster General as well. The latter called his son's killers "Virginia hellhounds."[4] Union leaders remained convinced that Lieutenant Meigs was coldbloodedly shot down by guerrillas after surrendering, and while Sheridan relented from the full application of his retaliatory order, he did have all the houses in the immediate vicinity of the incident destroyed and all the nearby able-bodied males made prisoners.

Sheridan retained the characteristics of the meticulous accountant that had commended him to General Halleck when the latter wanted somebody to straighten out Frémont's bookkeeping. As the Army of the Shenandoah completed its campaign, its commanding general submitted a detailed report of property captured or destroyed between August 10 and November 16. His list included 3,772 horses, 545 mules, one woolen mill, eight saw mills, one powder mill, three saltpeter works, 1,200 barns (he had earlier said 2,000, but Sheridan's soldiers did not all count as carefully as he did), seven furnaces, four tanneries, one railroad depot, 947 miles of rails, 435,802 bushels of wheat, 20,000 bushels of oats, 77,176 bushels of corn, 874 barrels of flour, 20,397 tons of hay, 10,918 beef cattle, 12,000 sheep, 15,000 swine, 250 calves, 12,000 pounds of bacon and hams, 10,000 pounds of tobacco, 2,500 bushels of potatoes, and 1,665 pounds of cotton yarn.[5]

Sheridan's devastation spilled over beyond the Shenandoah Valley, especially into Mosby's Kingdom, in the Loudoun Valley just east of the Blue Ridge. On November 27 Brigadier-General Wesley Merritt, U.S.V., of the First Cavalry Division received his instructions for the latter area:

You are hereby directed to proceed to-morrow morning at 7 o'clock, with two brigades of your division now in camp, to the east side of the Blue Ridge, via Ashby's Gap, and operate against the guerrillas in the district of country bounded on the south by the line of the Manassas Gap Railroad as far east as White Plains, on the east by the Bull Run range, on the west by the Shenandoah River, and on the north by the Potomac. This section has been the hotbed of lawless bands, who have from time to time depredated upon small parties on the line of army communications, on safeguards left at houses, and on troops. Their real object is plunder and highway robbery. To clear the country of these parties that are bringing destruction upon the innocent, as well as their guilty supporters, by their cowardly acts, you will consume and destroy all forage and subsistence, burn all barns and mills and their contents, and drive off all the stock in the region the boundaries of which are above described. This order must be literally executed, bearing in mind, however, that no dwellings are to be burned, and that no personal violence be offered to citizens. The ultimate results of the guerrilla system of warfare is the total destruction of all private rights in the country occupied by such parties.[6]

Altogether Sheridan fulfilled with uncommon completeness both missions assigned him by Grant when he took the Valley command. With his preponderance of numbers, he destroyed Early's Confederate army as an effective instrument of war; and he eliminated the Valley as a Confederate granary in which rebel armies could resupply themselves as they marched.

## SHERMAN'S WAR AGAINST THE ENEMY'S ECONOMY AND MORALE

Sheridan's destruction in the Shenandoah Valley was to be overshadowed in the scale of the country devastated by his confrere General Sherman's famous marches through Georgia and the Carolinas. These errands of terrible war had begun to take shape in the mind of the General-in-Chief at the same time that he first contemplated turning the Valley into a desert. On July 15, Grant wrote to Halleck: "Sherman will, once in Atlanta, devote himself to collecting the resources of the country. He will take everything the people have, and will then issue the stores so collected to rich and poor alike. As he will take all their stock, they will have no use for grain further than is necessary for bread."[7]

Sherman had long evinced a belief that Southern civilians should be made to suffer for at least certain of the warlike actions of the Confederacy, on the theory that if public support for those actions could be made to cease, the actions themselves would cease. In 1862, when he was commanding the District of Memphis under Grant before the Vicksburg campaign, Sherman consequently responded to guerrilla risings in the district by issuing Special Orders, No. 254 of September 27:

> Whereas many families of known rebels and of Confederates in arms against us have been permitted to reside in peace and comfort in Memphis, and whereas the Confederate authorities either sanction or permit the firing on unarmed boats carrying passengers and goods for the use and benefit of Memphis, it is ordered that for every boat fired on, ten families must be expelled from Memphis.[8]

The families were to be chosen by lot from a list of Confederate sympathizers.[9]

A few days later steamboats carrying noncombatants and cargo were fired on from the town of Randolph, Tennessee. Therefore, "I have caused Randolph to be destroyed, and have given public notice that repetition will justify any measure of retaliation."[10] "God himself has obliterated whole races from the face of the earth for sins less heinous," he said.[11]

Sherman's temper always exploded readily, but at the autumn of 1862's relatively early stage of the war he could also relent. He expelled several families from Memphis under Special Orders, No. 254 but did not enforce the orders rigidly. Still, the firing upon river boats decreased. And the attitudes Sherman expressed during these incidents were to prove characteristic. After two more years of war he would no longer be so ready to yield.[12]

"What you are to do with the forces at your command, I do not exactly see," wrote Grant to Sherman after the capture of Atlanta. "The difficulties of supplying your army, except when they are constantly moving beyond where you are, I plainly see."[13] Hood proceeded to underline the difficulties of supply by striking out against the Chattanooga-to-Atlanta section of the long railroad at the end of which Sherman's armies dangled, while Confederate cavalry continued to threaten the tracks farther north in Tennessee. Sherman spent much of September and October moving back and forth along the railroad to fend Hood off. These efforts were redeemed by the stoutness of the Union garrisons along the line — after being attacked at Allatoona, Brigadier-General John M. Corse, U.S.V., reported, "I am short a cheek-bone and an ear, but am able to whip all hell yet!"[14] — and by the continued efficiency of the Railroad Construction Corps. When told that cavalry raiders had blown up a tunnel, a disillusioned Confederate soldier is supposed to have responded, "Oh, hell! Don't you know that old Sherman carries a *duplicate* tunnel along?"[15] Nevertheless, Sherman's chases after Hood were contributing nothing positive either to the still-unfinished election campaign or to the ending of the war — the less so when as early as late September, there emerged certain indications that Hood intended to carry his assaults on Sherman's communications north into Tennessee, in an effort to draw Sherman back beyond Chattanooga and even to Nashville.

In response to this development, Sherman on September 28 sent George Thomas to Nashville to gather up a force strong enough to hold the Tennessee capital. As the nucleus of his army Thomas received most of the Fourth Corps from the Army of the Cumberland, and Sherman hoped to pry additional reinforcements for Thomas from Grant. By enabling Thomas to deal adequately with Hood, Sherman intended to free himself for new penetrations deeper into the South. To that end, when he learned on October 30 that new troops promised for Nashville by Grant were moving only slowly, Sherman added Schofield's Twenty-third Corps to Thomas's army.[16]

Also to free himself for further offensive movement, Sherman decided to eliminate any need for retaining a large garrison in Atlanta, or feeding a large number of mouths there, by removing the entire civilian population and transforming the city into nothing more than a military depot. "I had seen Memphis, Vicksburg, Natchez, and New Orleans, all captured from the enemy," Sherman later wrote, "and each at once was garrisoned by a full division of troops, if not more; so that success was actually crippling our armies in the field by detachments to guard and protect the interests of a hostile population."[17] The forced evacuation of Atlanta, moreover, would serve another purpose for Sherman and the Union. "I knew that the people of the South would read in this measure two important conclusions: one, that we were in earnest; and the other, if they were sincere in their common and popular clamor 'to die in the last ditch,' that the opportunity would soon come."[18]

As early as September 8 Sherman ordered the evacuation of Atlanta. It took place from September 12 through 28, when 709 adults, mostly women, 867 children, and seventy-three servants, carrying 1,651 parcels of furniture and household goods, traveled in railroad cars, wagons, and ambulances about ten miles south to Rough and Ready, where Union soldiers transferred them to Confederate escorts and wagons.[19]

Sherman resolved next to impart the same messages yet more strongly to the people of the South by carrying war in earnest still deeper into the Confederacy. For some weeks, however, the Union high command debated the particular direction he should take.

Sherman and Grant considered a march against Mobile, where the city remained in Confederate hands in spite of Admiral Farragut's presence in Mobile Bay. Sherman decided, however, that striking into southern Alabama would entail an excessive further stretching of his already attenuated lines of communications, and without targets of sufficient importance because the Navy nullified any strategic value Mobile might have had. Grant characteristically suggested that the enemy army ought to be the first objective, and therefore after considerable telegraphic discussion of possible movements, the General-in-Chief wired Sherman on November 1: "Do you not think it advisable, now that Hood has gone so far north, to entirely ruin him before starting on your proposed campaign? With Hood's army destroyed, you can go where you please with impunity. . . . If you can see a chance of destroying Hood's army, attend to that first, and make your other move secondary."[20] Sherman insisted, however, that to follow this prescription would be to acquiesce in "Jeff. Davis's cherished plan of making me leave Georgia by manœuvring."[21] His own now-matured plan was "to abandon Atlanta, and the railroad back to Chattanooga, to sally forth to ruin Georgia and bring up on the seashore."[22]

". . . to sally forth to ruin Georgia." Sherman had broached a variation of his eventual plan to Grant as early as September 20. "Where a million of people find subsistence, my army won't starve," he said;[23] but at first he had feared that harassment by enemy forces would require that Union warships and troops be in possession of the Georgia coast to meet him and be penetrating the rivers to threaten his opponents and lend him aid:

> . . . in a country like Georgia, with few roads and innumerable streams, an inferior force can so delay an army and harass it . . . ; but if the enemy knew that we had our boats on the Savannah River I could rapidly move to Milledgeville, where there is abundance of corn and meat, and could so threaten Macon and Augusta that the enemy would doubtless give up Macon for Augusta; then I would move so as to interpose between Augusta and Savannah, and force him to give up Augusta, with the only powder-mills and factories remaining in the South, or let us have the use of the Savannah River. Either horn of the dilemma will be worth a battle.[24]

Sherman's strategic objectives were expanding to include the enemy's economic resources and, by implication in what he said about dying in the last ditch, the will of the enemy people, on a level of importance at least equal to that of the enemy army. By late October he was concluding that he was strong enough to march across Georgia from Atlanta to the sea without the assistance of a Union force waiting on the coast. When Hood definitely turned toward Tennessee, Sherman was sure: "I can make this march, and

make Georgia howl!" "Until we can repopulate Georgia," he said, "it is useless for us to occupy it; but the utter destruction of its roads, houses, and
people, will cripple their military resources."[25] Once he had thus destroyed
Georgia, he proposed to turn north into the Carolinas, toward Virginia,
Richmond, and Lee's army.

Sherman's telegram about not acquiescing in Jeff Davis's efforts to maneuver his armies out of Georgia crossed Grant's of November 1 urging
Hood's army as Sherman's first objective. In response to Sherman's message,
the General-in-Chief for the first time explicitly endorsed the proposed
march through Georgia: Thomas should have enough power to handle
Hood, and "I do not see that you can withdraw from where you are to follow
Hood, without giving up all we have gained in territory. I say, then, go on as
you propose."[26]

Sherman busied the railroads by sending northward "an immense
amount of stores which had accumulated at Atlanta, and at the other stations
along the railroad."[27] He then abandoned his line of communications, including his telegraphic connection with the North along the rail lines, and
consolidated his troops at Atlanta for the plunge away from his previous umbilical cord and on southeastward. He was about to carry to a new plateau
of boldness the device of breaking free from supply lines that Sam Curtis
had pioneered after Pea Ridge and that Grant had employed to dramatic
and decisive effect in the Vicksburg campaign.

With the departure of Thomas and part of Sherman's armies with him,
the force at Atlanta comprised four corps, which Sherman now organized
into two wings: the Right Wing, under General Howard, consisting of the
Fifteenth and Seventeenth Corps, and the Left Wing, under General Slocum, with the Fourteenth Corps, Thomas's old "Rock of Chickamauga"
corps from the Army of the Cumberland, and the Twentieth Corps. The
cavalry, the Third Division, Cavalry Corps, Military Division of the Mississippi, would be commanded by Brigadier-General Hugh Judson Kilpatrick,
U.S.V., an Army of the Potomac veteran who had commanded a foray by
the First Brigade of his Third Cavalry Division against Lee's left flank during
Pickett's Charge at Gettysburg; that effort had been decidedly ill-conceived,
even suicidal, and the troopers sometimes called Kilpatrick Kill-cavalry —
but Sherman desired boldness, and there would be no Army of Northern
Virginia to resist. Total strength was about 55,000 infantry, 5,000 cavalry, and
2,000 artillery with sixty-four guns.[28]

Sherman's directive for the march called for the four infantry corps to
advance generally along four parallel roads. Each regiment was to take along
only one wagon and one ambulance. Each brigade should have a sufficient

but severely limited number of ammunition wagons, provision wagons, and ambulances. Altogether there would be about 2,500 wagons and 600 ambulances. For the most part, the troops would subsist themselves: "The army will forage liberally on the country during the march."[29] Under Sherman's orders, foraging was to be conducted only by foraging parties regularly appointed by the brigade commanders. Soldiers were not to enter dwellings. Only corps commanders would have the authority to destroy mills and houses.

Despite these restraining injunctions, however, Sherman's intent to "make Georgia howl" was widely enough known. Something else of the spirit of the march emerges in other passages of the orders, which specified the conditions under which mills and dwellings might be destroyed:

> In districts and neighborhoods where the army is unmolested, no destruction of such property should be permitted, but should guerrillas or bushwhackers molest our march, or should the inhabitants burn bridges, obstruct roads, or otherwise manifest local hostility, then army commanders should order and enforce a devastation more or less relentless, according to the measure of such hostility.[30]

Furthermore, "As for horses, mules, wagons, etc., belonging to the inhabitants, the cavalry and artillery may appropriate freely and without limit; discriminating, however, between the rich, who are usually hostile, and the poor and industrious, usually neutral or friendly. Foraging-parties may also take mules or horses, to replace the jaded animals of their trains, or to serve as pack-mules for the regiments or brigades."[31]

Sherman's troops set the mills of Atlanta to the torch. Between the effects of the bombardment and fires before the capture of the city and assorted depredations since then, many of Atlanta's houses also were no more. The march away began on the morning of November 15, with the capital of Georgia, Milledgeville, its first target, and Savannah and the sea its eventual destination. During the first few days the wings marched less on parallel lines than would be customary, but rather along roads divergent enough to seem to pose threats to both Macon and Augusta, to prevent an enemy concentration in front of Milledgeville. Sherman set out the next day:

> About 7 A.M. of November 16th we rode out of Atlanta by the Decatur road, filled by the marching troops and wagons of the Fourteenth Corps; and reaching the hill, just outside of the old rebel works, we naturally paused to look back upon the scenes of our past battles. We stood upon the very ground whereon was fought the bloody battle of July 22d, and could see the copse of

wood where McPherson fell. Behind us lay Atlanta, smouldering and in ruins, the black smoke rising high in air, and hanging like a pall over the ruined city. Away off in the distance, on the McDonough road, was the rear of Howard's column, the gun-barrels glistening in the sun, the white-topped wagons stretching away to the south; and right before us the Fourteenth Corps, marching steadily and rapidly, with a cheery look and swinging pace, that made light of the thousand miles that lay between us and Richmond.[32]

A certain suspense attended the disappearance of Sherman and his armies from the direct view of the Northern public and the Washington government as they broke telegraphic communication and marched deeper into Georgia. Wild rumors that Sherman had been destroyed, fed to be sure by Southern claims and fantasies, occasionally surfaced in the North. In fact, military opposition to Sherman proved minimal, coming mainly from about 3,500 troopers of Wheeler's Cavalry Corps who hovered about his flanks. There were also some 3,050 Georgia militia of declining determination. The whole opposition force never amounted to more than 13,000 men — although there was a surfeit of Confederate generals in the neighborhood. Not only did General Hardee turn up on October 5 to command the Department of South Carolina, Georgia, and Florida, but on October 7 Beauregard was dispatched to the area, to become a new theater commander in charge of the Military Division of the West.[33] Confederate and Georgia state officials called for a general uprising to repel the invader, but those Georgians of soldierly inclination and suitable age were almost all gone already. The Georgia General Assembly having joined in the appeal for help, it fled Milledgeville just ahead of Sherman's arrival on November 22. The next day Sherman himself reached Milledgeville, and some of his officers convened a mock session of the legislature to repeal the ordinance of secession.[34]

By early December, Sherman's march had covered more than half the distance to Savannah. On December 3 the Union troops liberated the captives held at Confederate prison camps at and near Millen. They found their comrades emaciated and neglected enough; but Millen was a small prison, and the condition of the men confined there did not match the horrors reported by rumor as prevailing at the Camp Sumter prison at Andersonville, farther south near Americus and the Florida border. Sherman had thought about going to Andersonville, but he decided reluctantly that it was too far off the route to Savannah.[35]

The rumors about Andersonville were largely true. At this prison, established in February 1864 for the ostensible purpose of relieving overcrowding elsewhere, as many as 32,899 enlisted men were herded into twenty-six acres. They were jammed together in an open field and in crude dens and huts.

Their ration was officially that of the Confederate Army, which by this time was bad enough; but because of the crowding and the difficulty of their guards' coming among them, as well as the Confederacy's problems in transporting foodstuffs, they did not receive nearly that much. They suffered from malnutrition, exposure, and complete hygienic neglect. Their water supply was a fetid stream running through the middle of the camp that also served as a bathtub and a latrine. Twelve thousand nine hundred twelve graves are now to be found at the site, but probably the total deaths were much more numerous.[36]

The combination of a collapsing Confederate administration and a nineteenth-century callousness coexisting with Victorian sentimentality, a callousness aggravated by the war but also on display in the factories and urban slums, prevented the authorities in Richmond from doing anything effective to remedy these conditions, of which some of them were partially aware. Like the guerrilla raids on Union outposts that had helped provoke Sheridan's devastation of the Valley, the loathsome Confederate prison pens contributed no little aggravation to the fury with which the Union armies were now thrashing the South. To be sure, the North shared in the public administrative morality of the times, and Northern prisons such as Elmira in New York and Point Lookout in Maryland were little better than Andersonville, despite the affluence of the North.[37]

Revenge for the wrongs of rebel guerrillas and prisons, and the destruction not only of Confederate economic resources but of Confederate popular morale through deliberate terrorism — these were what Sherman's march to the sea was all about. Of course, there were the restrictions on individual foraging and raiding spelled out by Sherman's orders for the march, and enforced with varying laxity by the corps commanders and the exceedingly lax and often vicious Kilpatrick. Of course, the incongruities of Victorian morality were also such that while ruthless destruction of property occurred, there were few murders and it appears remarkably few instances of rape. But whatever the letter of his orders, Sherman obviously gloried in the grim reputation built by the "bummers" who ranged far and wide beyond the main roads on which his corps headquarters marched, foraging liberally off the country and helping themselves to horses, mules, and other movable possessions. The high-strung, nervous general who had once had to retire from the field under a mental and psychic breakdown, now smoldering with the rage generated by three and a half years of war and the tensions of command in interaction with his brittle temper, gloried also in his own growing reputation as almost a depersonalized force of unrestrained nature scouring Georgia, a merciless avenging devil.

A week into December, and Sherman's soldiers were emerging from the Georgia Piedmont into a "country more marshy and difficult, and more obstructions were met in the way of felled trees, where the roads crossed the creeks, swamps, or narrow causeways; but our pioneer companies were well organized, and removed these obstacles in an incredibly short time."[38] By December 10 the last organized opposition had pulled back into the defenses of Savannah, and Sherman stood before that city. By now, Sherman's march had cut the last remaining east-west railroad connections of the Confederacy, his men tearing up the tracks of the Georgia Railroad, the Central of Georgia Railway, and the Savannah, Albany and Gulf Railroad for over a hundred miles altogether.

> We have also consumed the corn and fodder [Sherman reported] in the region of country thirty miles on either side of a line from Atlanta to Savannah, as also the sweet potatoes, cattle, hogs, sheep and poultry, and have carried away more than 10,000 horses and mules, as well as a countless number of slaves. I estimate the damage done to the State of Georgia and its military resources at $100,000,000; at least, $20,000,000 of which has inured to our advantage, and the remainder is simple waste and destruction. This may seem a hard species of warfare, but it brings the sad realities of war home to those who have been directly or indirectly instrumental in involving us in its attendant calamities.[39]

So the Union added to Grant's strategy of annihilation of enemy armies a strategy of destruction of resources and a strategy of terror, to break the will of the enemy people and thus deprive the Confederate armies of the popular support on which they depended. It was not the destruction of resources alone that Sherman expected would win the war. Cutting a swath sixty miles wide through Georgia and the Carolinas would not in itself starve the Confederate armies. It was terror that was to do the job of ruining the Confederate will to fight.

> I attach much importance to these deep incisions into the enemy's country [Sherman said], because this war differs from European wars in this particular: we are not only fighting hostile armies, but a hostile people, and must make old and young, rich and poor, feel the hard hand of war, as well as their organized armies. I know that this recent movement of mine through Georgia has had a wonderful effect in this respect. Thousands who had been deceived by their lying newspapers to believe that we were being whipped all the time now realize the truth, and have no appetite for a repetition of the same experience. To be sure, Jeff. Davis has his people under pretty good discipline, but I think faith in him is much shaken in Georgia, and before we have done with her South Carolina will not be quite so tempestuous.[40]

"If the people raise a howl against my barbarity and cruelty," Sherman could also say, "I will answer that war is war, and not popularity-seeking. If they want peace, they and their relatives must stop the war."[41] "You cannot qualify war in harsher terms than I will. War is cruelty, and you cannot refine it; and those who brought war into our country deserve all the curses and maledictions a people can pour out."[42]

Savannah lay guarded by river and swamp, with five causeways leading into the city. Hardee, in command at Savannah with some 18,000 men he and the Confederacy had gathered together, could defend these few approaches so readily that Sherman sought first to make contact with Union naval power and assurance of resupply, and only then to attack the city. Before leaving Atlanta, Sherman of course had requested that the blockading squadron be on the lookout for his arrival at the coast. Approaching the coast, General Howard made contact with the Navy via the Ogeechee River, in spite of the guns of Fort McAllister commanding the river about five miles above its opening into Ossabaw Sound, where Union ships lay. This fort, Sherman believed, should be the next object of his attentions, to open the Ogeechee and make firm the contact with the fleet.

Fort McAllister had a garrison of some 200 men and held twenty-four artillery pieces, but its strongest armament faced the river and the sound rather than the land side where Sherman would attack it. Late in the short afternoon of December 13, Brigadier-General, U.S.V., William B. Hazen's Second Division, Fifteenth Corps — Sherman's own Fifth Division, Army of the Tennessee at Shiloh — signaled to Sherman that it was completing its preparations to assault the fort. Simultaneously someone in Sherman's entourage discovered a faint cloud of smoke on the horizon: a Federal warship, the gunboat *Dandelion*, steamed slowly into view. "Is Fort McAllister taken?" the vessel signaled, and the army answered: "Not yet, but it will be in a minute."[43] Then Hazen's troops advanced, swarmed over the parapets, smothered the defenders by weight of numbers, and planted their flags. Impatiently Sherman was rowed out in a skiff to the *Dandelion* that same night and got off a note to Rear-Admiral John A. Dahlgren, commanding the South Atlantic Blockading Squadron since the relief of Admiral Du Pont. Sherman had reassured the safety of his armies by transferring his line of communications from the tenuous railroads to the safe ocean controlled by the U.S. Navy.

On December 17 he called upon Hardee to surrender Savannah, saying he enclosed "a copy of General Hood's demand for the surrender of the town of Resaca, to be used by you for what it is worth."[44] The enclosed document, issued by Hood when he was attacking one of the garrisons along Sherman's railway line back in the autumn, had been another downward step in the deterioration of the war into remorselessness, in which Hood had called for the immediate surrender of Resaca saying, ". . . should this be acceded to, all white officers and soldiers will be parolled in a few days. If the place is carried by assault, no prisoners will be taken."[45] Sherman's resurrecting it now was another sign of his mood, however seriously he might have intended Hardee to take it. Hardee did not surrender, however, for he knew that Sherman was not ready to close a trap upon him. By way of a bridge of boats leading to a causeway that connected with the mainland northward, Hardee retained a route of escape. This he used on the night of December 20–21.

Disappointed at not bagging the garrison, Sherman nevertheless sent a dispatch to Lincoln on December 22 saying: "I beg to present to you, as a Christmas gift, the city of Savannah, with 150 heavy guns and plenty of ammunition, and also about 25,000 bales of cotton."[46] With his troops refreshed by a complete refitting sent by the Quartermaster's Department, Sherman could celebrate Christmas Eve by contemplating his next advance:

> When I move, the Fifteenth Corps [his own old corps of Vicksburg days] will be on the right of the right wing, and their position will naturally bring them into Charleston first; and, if you have watched the history of that corps, you will have remarked that they generally do their work pretty well. The truth is, the whole army is burning with an insatiable desire to wreak vengeance upon South Carolina. I almost tremble at her fate, but feel that she deserves all that seems in store for her.[47]

## THE DEATH THROES OF THE CONFEDERACY

To what end was the North wreaking such vengeance, and the South suffering not only the casualties of battle but the spreading devastation inflicted by Union armies turned marauders? What could the South hope to accomplish by fighting on, and thus provoking the depredations of Sherman and Sheridan?

"No hope," wrote Mrs. Chesnut after the fall of Atlanta.[48] Lincoln's reelection further sealed across the South a widespread, and manifestly well founded, conviction that to persist in the war was futile. The Confederate Congress busied itself with measures that could signify only its readiness to give up the ghost: impressment of supplies was largely abandoned, and the

Army would have to purchase most of its needs on the open market; President Davis's appeal to renew the suspension of habeas corpus was rejected.[49]

But President Davis himself, in the words of former U.S. Supreme Court Justice John A. Campbell, "became in the closing part of the war an incubus and a mischief."[50] Davis's unyielding sense of duty and of obligation to his oath of office would permit him to take no step that might lead to denial of Confederate independence and thus no step toward peace. Here the inflexibility of the Presidential system inherited by the Confederacy from the Constitution of the United States displayed itself perhaps at its worst, for the separation of powers permitted no effective Congressional initiatives toward peace, and the President's very permanence in office and dedication to his constitutional duties prevented him from coming to terms with reality, saving lives, and halting the war's destruction.

By the autumn of 1864, over 100,000 and probably about 200,000 Confederate soldiers were no longer present for duty; at the end of the year the muster rolls showed an "aggregate present and absent" of 400,787, and an "aggregate present" of only 196,016.[51] So many had abandoned the cause, or at least gone home to look after their families as Federal armies marched up and down the land. It was another measure of hopelessness that the Richmond government could do almost nothing to bring deserters back, save to issue appeals like those that Davis took to Georgia when he tried to summon up a popular rising against Sherman's advance beyond Atlanta. All through the Appalachian spine and well downward into the hill country, armed bands of opponents of the government now cancelled its writ. Here and there throughout the Confederacy, the local courts refused to enforce measures that would compel men to return to the Army. In many parts of the Confederacy, the will of Richmond had simply become a nullity.[52]

The dissident Georgia triumvirate of Vice President Stephens, Governor Brown, and Robert Toombs constituted an ambivalent bloc of anti-Davis power whose states'-rights inclinations had become almost indistinguishable from a desire for peace. For a time before he left Atlanta, Sherman put himself in contact with some of Brown's friends and tried to meet with the governor to offer to spare Georgia his intended devastation in exchange for Brown's summoning home the Georgia troops of the Confederate Army. While Brown did not respond to Sherman's overtures, at the beginning of November he called on all the states, North and South, to meet in a peace conference, and he granted the Georgia militia a thirty-day furlough with the avowed purpose of preventing General Hood's ordering them out of the state. The practical effect of the latter move was to leave Georgia all the more impotent before the invader; eventually, as we have seen, only a small force of this militia made any effort to oppose Sherman's march. Meanwhile, "Every private in Joe Brown's militia holds an officer's commission," as a somewhat hyperbolic popular saying had it,[53] thus further assuring that reluctant Georgians would not have to enter Jefferson Davis's Army.

On the other hand, Brown and Governor Zeb Vance of North Carolina set an example for other states, nowhere else followed so zealously but still influential, of using state financial resources to alleviate the economic distress of the poor, with welfare outlays remarkable for the nineteenth century. Though North Carolina exceeded Georgia's total of 8,000 men kept out of the Confederate Army, altogether the two states may well have accomplished more to prolong the life of the Confederacy by sustaining morale than their obstruction did to injure it.[54] So far along was the deterioration of Richmond's authority by late 1864 that governors more dedicated to the Confederate cause found themselves being pushed by necessity to set up almost as independently for themselves as Brown and Vance, merely to keep their own states functioning at all.

Although his conscience would not permit him to seek peace, President Davis had to recognize the desperate condition of the Confederacy well enough by the time of Lincoln's reelection that he called on Congress for authority to purchase slaves to be used as cooks and teamsters for the Army, in order to free more white men for combat. He also announced his willingness to go even further if Confederate independence demanded it: "Until our white population shall prove insufficient for the armies we require and can afford to keep in the field, to employ as a soldier the Negro . . . would scarcely be deemed wise or advantageous. . . . But should the alternative ever be presented of subjugation or the employment of the slave as a soldier, there seems no reason to doubt what would then be our decision."[55] Congress accepted the first proposal, but immediately the pressures of declining manpower pushed toward the unpalatable alternative as well. The grave trouble here was, as Howell Cobb put it: "If slaves will make good soldiers our whole theory of slavery is wrong. . . ." By implication, so then was the whole foundation of the Confederacy wrong. (Cobb finished his sentence, however: " — but they won't make soldiers.")[56]

As long as Davis led on, similarly dutiful people followed. The Virginia General Assembly debated arming slaves and called on General Lee for his opinion. Lee replied with words much like Davis's: "I think, therefore we must decide whether slavery shall be extinguished by our enemies and the slaves be used against us, or use them ourselves at the risk of the effects which may be produced upon our social institutions."[57] The implications of Lee's words were decisive. On March 13, 1865 Congress authorized the President to call on the owners of slaves for as many of their slaves between the ages of eighteen and forty-five as he deemed expedient, "to perform military service in whatever capacity he may direct."[58] No more than one-fourth of the slaves in any state were to be called, however, and the law did not force any owner to yield slave property. Nor was there a promise of freedom; but nearly all concerned were sufficiently perceptive that there existed a general understanding that slaves who fought for the Confederacy would be freed by state action. A number of African Americans were enlisted, and some paraded around Capitol Square in Richmond. But none saw action. As the black enlistment bill was pending, a final special emissary, Duncan Kerner of Louisiana, chairman of the House Committee on Ways and Means, was dispatched to Paris to see if the French and British might at last recognize the Confederacy now that a step was being taken to remove the slavery albatross; but the mission was absurdly too late, like the entire black-enlistment maneuver, a testimony to the futility of a vision of duty that demanded continued fighting.[59]

Lee believed that as a military man he had no right to question the President's conception of duty, yet it was Lee's prestige, not Davis's, that carried the enlistment measure through Congress, and Lee's prestige was almost the only attribute of the Confederacy around which a majority of Congress could still be rallied. Davis had consistently resisted any effort to dilute in the slightest his constitutional prerogatives as Commander in Chief of the armed forces. The only professional military assistance he would accept was that of advisers appointed completely on his own initiative and responsible only to himself, Lee early in the war and Bragg from February 24, 1864 until January 31, 1865, when accumulating military disasters seemed to dictate Bragg's joining the generals who were trying to shore up the Confederacy in battle.[60]

It was therefore as both a slap at Davis and an accolade for Lee that on January 23, 1865 Congress acted to create a General-in-Chief who should "have command of the military forces of the Confederate States."[61] Everyone knew that Lee was intended for the appointment. The slap at Davis was also understood by all; Mrs. Varina Howell Davis is supposed to have said that in her husband's place, "I would die or be hung before I would submit to the humiliation."[62] It was too late, of course, for the new Army commander to have much impact on the shape of the war, and the other current activities of Congress suggest discounting the idea that a hope of achieving much militarily was a major motive. Despite pleas from Davis to remain in Richmond and stand by the Confederacy in its climactic hour of trial, Congress adjourned on March 18, and its members scattered forever.

When the bill to enlist black soldiers was still being debated, Davis in support of it replied to the Howell Cobb argument about the bill's contradicting the whole theory of slavery by saying: "If the Confederacy falls, there should be written on its tombstone, 'Died of a theory.'"[63] It did not occur to the earnest, unbending, dedicated Confederate President that he himself was killing not institutions but people for the sake of his own theories, and for the hopeless theory of a powerful President within an independent Confederacy in particular.

He would not end the war. He was the only person in the world with the power to do so — it was no longer possible that Lincoln could have halted the victorious march of the Union armies — but Davis's rectitude demanded that the fighting persist.

The busy Horace Greeley had been at work again to try to restore peace, and in December 1864 he had urged Francis P. Blair, Sr., to try his hand at going south to see what he could accomplish within the Confederacy. Ever as busy as Greeley, Blair needed little urging, because he already had a scheme in mind. He obtained a pass from Lincoln to travel through the Union lines, received one from Secretary of War Seddon to enter the Southern lines on the pretext of looking for family papers lost when Early raided Silver Spring, and wrote President Davis that he wanted to discuss the "state of the affairs of our country" with him.[64] Davis assumed that he came with Lincoln's blessing, and therefore the Confederate President granted the old Jacksonian a private interview on January 12.

Blair's scheme proved to be one for negotiations leading to an armistice that would permit Union and Confederate troops to join together in driving the French and the Emperor Maximilian from Mexico. Together the Union and the Confederacy could vindicate the Monroe Doctrine, perhaps conquer Mexico and Central America, and while fighting a common enemy resolve their differences. The scheme attests that Frank Blair was indeed growing old. Whatever Jefferson Davis thought of it, however, he gave Blair a letter to show to Lincoln, expressing his willingness to appoint commissioners "with a view to secure peace to the two countries."[65] His purpose, judging by his thinking in general and by subsequent events, was not so much to secure peace, which he correctly believed Lincoln would not offer on terms his duty permitted him to accept, but to try to gain a truce, which would permit a respite for the Confederacy; or failing that, to discredit the peace advocates inside the Confederacy by demonstrating the intractability of Lincoln's insistence on reunion.

Blair's travels were soon the talk of both rival capitals, rumors went flying, and Lincoln heard criticism of his apparent willingness to conciliate rebels. Whatever the rumors, Lincoln in fact had given no encouragement to Blair's Mexican fantasy; but on January 18 he did authorize Blair to carry back to Davis an assurance that he would receive any agent Davis might send to him informally, "with the view of securing peace to the people of our one common country."[66] So much for Davis's "the two countries." Nevertheless, after consulting his Cabinet, Davis concluded he should appoint commissioners and continue to explore Lincoln's intentions. The Confederate President went so far as to name three peace advocates: Vice President Stephens; Senator Robert M. T. Hunter of Virginia, president pro tem of the Confederate Senate; and John A. Campbell of Alabama, Associate Justice of the Supreme Court of the United States until on April 29, 1861 he notified Chief Justice Roger B. Taney of his resignation, and since October 1862 Confederate Assistant Secretary of War. Secretary of State Judah P. Benjamin gave the three commissioners an innocuous letter of instruction indicating they should proceed to Washington to confer with Lincoln about the subject of the Union President's letter. Davis predictably altered the instructions to read, "for the purpose of securing peace to the two countries."[67]

The emendation nearly prevented the occurrence of any conference at all. Only the direct intervention of General Grant, who telegraphed Washington that he was convinced of the good intentions of the commissioners and their sincere desire for peace and union, got them through the lines in spite of the instructions they carried.[68] Grant's intervention also brought Lincoln himself, along with Secretary Seward, down to Hampton Roads to meet with the commissioners on board the *River Queen* off Fort Monroe on February 3. But except for some pleasant reminiscing about the past, especially between Lincoln and Stephens, who had been Whigs in Congress together, Davis's policy and sense of duty ensured that this conference could accomplish nothing. The identity of the participants suggested high drama, and word of their meeting fueled a growing popular speculation about peace North and South. But Lincoln could not respond affirmatively to Stephens's version of Blair's Mexico plan, namely, that there should be a truce while the Union armies rescued Mexico from Maximilian and the French; Stephens threw out this strange suggestion because like Davis he assumed that Lincoln had inspired Blair's original idea.

Lincoln indicated he would accept almost any peace terms as long as reunion and emancipation were included. He offered the opinion that when resistance to the Union ceased, the Southern states would immediately be restored to their places in the Union and the concomitant political privileges. He suggested in regard to the project for a constitutional amendment outlawing slavery that the Southern states might ratify it prospectively, that is, to take effect at some such date as five years hence. He held out a strong possibility that if they returned now the Southerners might yet be compensated for their slaves, and he went home to prepare a message to Congress recommending that he be empowered to pay $400 million in government bonds to the slaveholding states as compensation for emancipation. So much did Lincoln's old desire to avoid remorseless revolutionary struggle, or now to reverse the degeneration into it, persist; so long did he cling to the hope that African Americans might go free with minimum inconvenience to white people, even to rebels. But all Lincoln's generosity was useless to wring an agreement from commissioners instructed by Jefferson Davis.

The one major result of the Hampton Roads conference was to demonstrate that there could be no peace of reunion with Jefferson Davis's government—only the complete destruction of its ability to resist through the annihilation of its armies and, perhaps, the ruination of its resources and the terrorization of its people. Davis responded to the report of his commissioners by delivering to a public meeting at the African Church in Richmond on February 6 one of the most impassioned of all his appeals to rally around the Confederacy, claiming that Washington offered nothing but complete submission. His dedication to duty so inspired him to eloquence that for a brief moment he seems to have stimulated a new mood of determination in the capital. At another meeting at the same place on February 9, Senator Hunter, from among the peace commissioners, seconded Davis's sentiments—for somehow Hunter also carried away from the Hampton Roads conference the impression that Lincoln was offering only submission. Secretary Benjamin similarly joined in the spirit of the occasion. Some 10,000 people are said to have tried to get into the auditorium to hear Davis; whether most of them shared the President's zest for continuing the fight seems doubtful. Davis's policies were as good a justification for the new strategy of property destruction and terror as Grant, Sherman, or Sheridan could have wished.[69]

## THE END OF SLAVERY: THE CONSTITUTIONAL ASSURANCE

To what end was the North wreaking its vengeance, and the South suffering not only the casualties of battle but the spreading devastation inflicted by Union armies turned marauders? One positive answer, then and since, might be so that the African Americans should see the gates of freedom opening before them.

The Union Party platform for the election of 1864 called for a constitutional amendment to abolish slavery. Immediately after the election, Lincoln moved to fulfill this pledge, both through efforts to exert his personal influence upon individual Congressmen and through an appeal included in his annual message of December 6:

> At the last session of Congress a proposed amendment of the Constitution abolishing slavery throughout the United States, passed the Senate, but failed for lack of the requisite two-thirds vote in the House of Representatives. Although the present is the same Congress, and nearly the same members, and without questioning the wisdom or patriotism of those who stood in opposition, I venture to recommend the reconsideration and passage of the measure at the next session. Of course the abstract question is not changed; but an intervening election shows, almost certainly, that the next Congress will pass the measure if this does not. Hence there is only a question of *time* as to when the proposed amendment will go to the States for their action. And as it is to so go, at all events, may we not agree that the sooner the better?[70]

The Senate had passed the proposed amendment in its previous session, on April 18, but in the House on June 15 only four Democrats had voted in favor of a resolution that such an amendment ought to be adopted, so that the constitutional two-thirds margin was lacking.[71] As Lincoln pointed out, the same membership was still present when Congress reassembled after the Presidential election. Although the Thirty-ninth Congress elected in 1864 would offer the necessary antislavery margin, that Congress in the normal course of events would not meet until December 1865, or at the earliest, until after March 4, 1865, when the President might call it into special session. Despite his subsequent willingness to offer the Confederate commissioners at Hampton Roads the possibility of postponing the effect of the amendment, Lincoln preferred not to wait for the new Congress but to make another effort to wrest a two-thirds majority from the old House. As he also said in his message to Congress, no doubt truthfully as well as characteristically, his motive was his belief that extinguishing slavery might hasten the restoration of the Union, by extinguishing also the South's last hope that slavery could survive the war.[72]

One Republican Congressman, James M. Ashley of Ohio, had voted against the resolution favoring the antislavery amendment in June in order that under the rules of the House he would be able to move for reconsideration at the session opening in December.[73] Lincoln's efforts to exert personal influence upon individual members to supplement his public appeal apparently included judicious use of the patronage. The President's argument about heeding the will of the people evidently also impressed some Congressmen, for on conferring with Representative James S. Rollins of Missouri, a large slaveowner from a heavily slaveholding district, to appeal to him as a fellow former Henry Clay Whig, Lincoln found Rollins had already changed his mind since the summer, intended to vote for the amendment, and was willing to work in its favor among the other members of the Missouri delegation.[74]

The Congressional debate followed predictable lines. Democratic opponents of abolition returned to their party's familiar theme of defending the Constitution as it is and the Union as it was, and they argued that abolition by constitutional amendment would pervert the Constitution besides bringing along a train of horrendous social consequences. The amending process, they sometimes argued, was never intended to permit change of the substance of the Constitution or to allow constricting the reserved rights of the states. Substantive change affecting the powers of the states would require the unanimous consent of all the states. This argument carried a certain plausibility, because for more than half a century since the passage of the first ten amendments, the only amendments had been procedural; and even the first ten, the Bill of Rights, had not attempted social change on the scale now proposed. On the other hand, this Democratic argument ignored the fact that the reserved rights of the states were themselves guaranteed explicitly not by the original Constitution but by an amendment, the Tenth.[75] It was also strange that many of the most fervent constitutional opponents of an antislavery amendment had themselves advocated fervently in 1861 an amendment to bar forever tampering with the institution of slavery, which implied that without such an amendment tampering was possible.

On the other side of the debate, while some of the more zealous antislavery Republicans stressed the moral evil of slavery, more often than not support for the amendment was couched in the lowest-common-denominator terms that Lincoln had employed in his annual message, the efficacy of the amendment for the restoration of the Union. Like the quoted passage of Lincoln's annual message, moreover, the debate may strike the modern reader as singularly uninspiring in contrast to the momentous nature of the subject, and in contrast to the amendment's possible force not only to help restore the Union but to give a measure of justification to the entire tragedy of the war.

Uninspiring or not, the advocates of the amendment prevailed. Thirteen Democrats who had opposed abolition in June joined the four who had favored it in voting for the proposed amendment on January 31, 1865, and the amendment received more than the necessary two-thirds majority.[76] Lincoln was sufficiently exhilarated by the occasion that on February 1 he signed the Congressional amending resolution, forgetting that he need not have done so because the President is not part of the amending process described by the Constitution.[77] Responding to a serenade that day, he rose to sentiments more lofty than those of his recent message to Congress: "He could not but congratulate all present, himself, the country and the whole world upon this great moral victory."[78]

"It winds the whole thing up," Lincoln also said in response to the serenade.[79] But of course it did not wind up everything, for as he pointed out in the same remarks, ratification by the states remained necessary. Furthermore, the quality and extent of the freedom to be conferred upon the slaves remained to be determined—would they be legally free but still inferior members of the population, or would they rise to all the rights and privileges of U.S. citizenship?

As for ratification, Secretary Seward eventually declared the process complete on December 18, 1865, counting in order to secure three-fourths of the states the actions of eight states that had belonged to the Confederacy, although Congress at that time recognized the legitimacy of their governments for no other purpose.[80]

As for the quality and extent of the African Americans' freedom, events directly relevant to that issue were developing at the very time when Congress approved the amendment, in consequence of Sherman's arrival in the vicinity of the sea islands where the Port Royal Experiment had been going on almost since the long-ago day when Du Pont's black warships steamed into Port Royal Sound.

The course of events toward emancipation under the impulse of the war had generated among antislavery leaders a growing conviction that to be truly forever free, the former slaves residing as they did in an agricultural society must become owners of land. As they thought in such terms, the leaders sought to make the confiscation bills introduced into Congress from early in the war vehicles for the expropriation of Southern land and its redistribution among the former slaves. In the Confiscation Act of July 17, 1862, the Congressional effort to respond in part to this desire fell afoul of Lincoln's belief that permanent confiscation violated the constitutional prohibition of an attainder of treason that forfeited property beyond the life of the offender.[81] On June 7, 1862, however, Congress had authorized the President to appoint tax commissioners to assess the proportion of the direct tax of 1861 owed by occupied areas of the Confederacy and to offer the land of delinquent taxpayers for sale at public auction.[82] This measure opened another avenue toward expropriation and redistribution, one that was followed at Port

Royal. When Federal tax commissioners announced a public auction of lands to take place there early in 1863, the antislavery Port Royal experimenters tried to ensure the African Americans a share in the available lands and persuaded Congress to amend the tax law on February 6, 1863 to permit the tax commissioners to reserve a certain portion of land for educational and charitable purposes.[83]

In March 1863 the tax commissioners put 16,479 acres of the sea islands up for general sale. Freed African Americans who had pooled funds that they managed to accumulate purchased about 2,000 acres. Most of the rest of the land sold, about 8,000 acres, went to a group of Boston capitalists who represented a different, though also partly philanthropic, impulse: they proposed to reorganize Southern plantations as capitalist enterprises and to continue under private auspices the free-labor experiments in cotton culture already begun at Port Royal under the government, completing the transformation of the African Americans into wage earners, believing they would prove that cotton culture could be more productive as well as more beneficial to the worker under a capitalist wage system than under slavery.[84]

Many antislavery leaders were suspicious of this plan as primarily intended to generate profits, and the Port Royal experimenters were disturbed when on September 16, 1863 Lincoln seemed to endorse the plan by ordering the tax commissioners to sell most of some 60,000 acres withheld at the March auction, reserving only 16,000 acres for the freedmen. The experimenters argued that 16,000 acres were not enough to support the 15,000 freed African Americans on the sea islands. It was true that Lincoln also specified that certain tracts were to be sold to freed people in twenty-acre lots at a special price of $1.25 per acre; but while the antislavery experimenters urged the African Americans to try to preempt additional acreage by asserting squatters' rights, and Lincoln on December 16 agreed to allow preemption of up to forty acres by African-American heads of families as part of his special-price plan, the President eventually reversed himself on preemption under pressure from the capitalist group. Utter confusion about which rules governed at any given moment then marred the auction when it took place on February 18, 1864, and freed people purchased only 2,276 acres at the special price. Several groups of African Americans also found means to purchase 470 acres at about $7.00 an acre in the competitive bidding, but the effort to redistribute land through the tax laws was not going well at Port Royal.[85]

Yet at Port Royal something at least was being done, and nothing much was happening elsewhere. African Americans drawn into the magnetic field of Lincoln's armies tended to become the ragged denizens of forlorn camps sprawling behind the armies' lines, unless they were males of military age and therefore hustled into uniform. The black people around the camps eked out a living by doing odd jobs for the soldiers and by scavenging. Various efforts in the various military departments sought to find employment for some of them on the government payroll.

An ambitious and controversial scheme to remove African Americans from the contraband camps and from dependence on charity developed in the Department of the Gulf, when by general orders of January 29, 1863, later supplemented by orders of February 3, 1864, General Banks required able-bodied male freedmen to labor either on plantations or on public works.[86] The plantation labor was likely to be under the blacks' former masters, since many Louisiana planters had taken the oath of allegiance and were continuing to operate their plantations. Nevertheless, Banks's orders regulated wage scales and attempted to ensure healthy working and living conditions. The freedmen were allowed to choose their employers, but they were required to remain with an employer for one year. They were not allowed to leave the plantations without a pass, and provost marshals were to assist in enforcing discipline upon them. To many antislavery partisans, the system looked like slavery under new names, or at least serfdom. But Banks defended the plan as preferable to the contraband camps and as a means of helping freedmen through the difficult transition from bondage to self-reliance. Moreover, Banks also established an ambitious school system for African Americans, including night and Sunday classes for adults, which he offered as an earnest of the sincerity of his intentions to prepare blacks for full freedom. Still, there was nothing here to provide the independence that goes with land ownership.[87]

During 1864 Congressman George W. Julian of Indiana tried to win a homestead act for freed people, making forty- and eighty-acre tracts in the South available free to African Americans, and also to Union soldiers and loyal Southern whites, in return for settling and farming them. The land was to be found by confiscating estates, and to this end Julian tried to dissuade Lincoln from his belief that permanent confiscation is unconstitutional. The President eventually acquiesced, accepting the idea that the constitutional prohibition of attainder of treason involving permanent forfeiture of property[88] does not prevent Congress from confiscating property permanently by legislative action. With Lincoln converted, Julian's efforts produced several resolutions in both chambers to repeal the limiting resolution that Lincoln had insisted be attached to the Confiscation Act of 1862. But the two houses never got together on a common wording, and Julian's efforts foundered on this procedural problem.[89]

The issue of land for the freed people was thus unresolved when Sherman surfaced at Savannah after his passage through Georgia, accompanied by a train of African Americans. The ferocious Sherman might be a kind of radical in his assaults upon the Southern economy, but he was highly conservative in most of his attitudes about slavery and race; for example, he accepted no black combat troops in the armies under his immediate command. He had tried to discourage the African Americans who followed in his wake. He could not, however, forcibly turn them away, and once confronted with hordes of them who had to be kept from starvation, he was willing to adopt drastic experiments to deal with the immediate, pressing problems they posed, and thereby to rid himself of their encumbrance when he should march on.

Secretary Stanton, a man of considerably more radical inclinations, came down to Savannah to confer with Sherman about the refugee problem among other things — the abolitionists were complaining about Sherman's indifference to the welfare of African Americans — and on January 12 the Secretary of War and the general together met with a delegation of black leaders concerning what to do for the refugees. The result was that four days later the conservative Sherman offered, with Stanton's full approval, the most radical approach to the land issue thus far officially advanced, his Special Field Orders, No. 15 of January 16, 1865: "The islands from Charleston south, the abandoned rice-fields along the rivers for thirty miles back from the sea, and the country bordering the Saint John's River, Fla., are reserved and set apart for the settlement of the negroes now made free by the acts of war and the proclamation of the President of the United States."[90]

Whenever three respectable African-American heads of families desired to form a settlement in the designated area, Sherman's orders stipulated, they should receive "possessory title" for the land they might choose from the "abandoned" property of the area, plus assistance toward becoming productive agriculturalists. They were to subdivide their land among themselves and such others as they might desire to bring into their settlement, so that each family should have a plot of not more than forty acres of tillable ground. An African American who enlisted in the Union military service might locate his family in any such settlement and receive all rights and privileges of a settler even if not present in person. In the possession of their land, "the military authorities will afford them protection until such time as they can protect themselves, or until Congress shall regulate their title."[91]

Sherman's order named the abolitionist General Saxton to administer this program as Inspector of Settlements and Plantations.[92] The order also provided that no white persons should be permitted to reside among the

African-American settlements, except for military personnel on duty there, and that under Saxton the freed people should have sole management of their own affairs.[93] When some abolitionists protested that such isolation was a new form of paternalism and that it carried Sherman's plan close to being a new colonization scheme, Secretary Stanton replied that the black leaders themselves had thought isolation necessary for their protection for the time being. Saxton offered assurances that he would still permit white teachers and missionaries to go among the African Americans.[94]

Saxton had become pessimistic over the many frustrations that attended laboring among the freed people and had submitted his resignation from the Army, but Sherman's order and Stanton's assurances that the land program would be permanent buoyed his spirits. He withdrew the resignation and accepted a brevet as major-general dated January 12 to preside over the great new experiment (he became brigadier-general, U.S.A., as of April 9).[95] He held mass meetings to apprise the blacks of the opportunities being offered them, appointed several of the Port Royal experimenters to assist him, and by the end of June 1865 had settled 40,000 freed people on the coastal lands. He assigned as many as 5,000 acres in a single day. Provided with farming tools and seeds and accompanied as Saxton had promised they might be by teachers, missionaries, and advisers from various freedmen's aid societies, the African Americans hurried to their lands to get in the spring planting.

Sherman's order proved to have a decisive effect on the continuing Congressional debates about black land ownership and policy toward the freed people more generally. The bold stroke from the field gave the needed impetus to push at last through the Thirty-eighth Congress in its closing hours on March 3, 1865 an act to create a Bureau for the Relief of Freedmen and Refugees. This measure sought to protect and aid the freed people through a special government agency as recommended long since by the American Freedmen's Inquiry Commission, and it apparently legalized Special Field Orders, No. 15 and promised additional land to the African Americans. It provided that to every male refugee or freedman "shall be assigned not more than forty acres" of abandoned or confiscated land at rental for three years, with an option to purchase at the end of that time with "such title thereto as the United States can convey."[96]

In that last phrase lay the rub, just as all along the discussions of providing land for the freed people had been clouded by questions about how the land was to be obtained and whether the government could properly and constitutionally acquire Southern lands. The dénouement came after the war. When Andrew Johnson became President of the United States at the close of the war, for various reasons he soon announced a policy of general amnesty. His proclamation of May 29, 1865 granted amnesty to all former rebels except for certain categories, mainly high civil and military officials and owners of property valued at $20,000 (who might make individual applications for pardon and amnesty), "with restoration of all rights of property, except as to slaves, and except in cases where legal proceedings under the laws of the United States providing for the confiscation of property of persons engaged in rebellion have been instituted. . . ."[97] Thus property that had never been seized as "abandoned" clearly belonged to its prewar owners; there would be no further confiscation and land redistribution. The fate of land sold to meet direct-tax obligations or assigned under Sherman's Special Field Orders, No. 15 was not immediately clear, but Johnson had shown in which direction the wind was blowing.

In August the President issued a series of executive orders for the restoration of all confiscated property except that which had already been sold under court decrees. This policy left the Northern capitalists who had bought land at the tax commissioners' sales, and the relatively few African Americans who had bought, safely in possession because their lands had been sold to them outright; it did not offer the freed people much. In October, Johnson ordered General Howard,[98] from May 12 commissioner of the Freedmen's Bureau, to travel to the coastal lands involved in Special Field Orders, No. 15 to persuade the freed people to return their settlements to pardoned owners. Howard was appalled, but he obediently urged the African Americans to abandon their farms and find work with their former masters. Some of the freed people resolved to hold on to their lands, by force if necessary, and General Saxton refused to dispossess them. Thereupon, on January 15, 1866 President Johnson removed Saxton from his office, and land repossessions proceeded with the freed people, whatever their resolves, impotent to do much to impede them.

Along with all Sherman's destructiveness had come his Special Field Orders, No. 15, which might have created a major constructive effort, but it was all quickly washed away. When the heavily Republican Thirty-ninth Congress elected in 1864 assembled at last on December 4, 1865, the attempt to revive land redistribution found a place on the agenda. A bill to extend the life and expand the powers of the Bureau of Refugees, Freedmen, and Abandoned Lands, passed over the President's veto on July 16, 1866, included a provision intended to restore some of the coastal lands to dispossessed freedmen.[99] But the land issue became so enmeshed in the larger developing struggle between Congress and the President over reconstruction, and the struggle so paralyzed effective administration of government, that the attempted restoration failed. Land redistribution never recaptured even a shadow of the dream that had opened for it at the beginning of 1865. The freed African Americans would mostly remain landless in an agricultural society.

Therefore the war seemed likely to produce at best a legalistic, limited emancipation of African Americans from the chains of slavery, without affording them the means to rise above continued economic dependence on their former masters. In Congress Representative Ashley, chairman of the House Committee on Rebellious States and sponsor of an effort to assure wider Federal protection to blacks in the Southern states than seemed likely to come from Lincoln's 10-percent plan, had found in the final session of the Thirty-eighth Congress that the friends of the Lincoln administration were strong enough to require him to offer a compromise reconstruction program whereby Louisiana, Arkansas, and Tennessee would be readmitted to the Union under Lincoln's plan, in return for executive acceptance of Congressional regulation of later readmissions. Ashley's hope had been to include in a Congressional plan some guarantee of black voting rights, in the face of the painfully halting progress in that direction in the states already under reconstruction. His further testing of Congressional sentiment, however, indicated that even following his initial compromise with the Republican moderates and conservatives, the best he could do for the freed people would be to secure a reconstruction program similar to that of the Wade-Davis Bill, which was much more radical in its resentment of secessionists than in its support for African-American rights. When Congressman William D. Kelley of Philadelphia had proposed an amendment to Ashley's legislation to assure equal suffrage regardless of race, such voting rights predictably failed.[100]

The closing of the war was about to leave emancipation constitutionally assured but otherwise decidedly fragile and imperfect.

# THIRTEEN

# The Fires Die

## FRANKLIN AND NASHVILLE

Yet the war went on, toward the only military outcome still possible, the conclusive defeat of the Confederate armies.

When Sherman reached Savannah just before Christmas to refit and prepare to invade the Carolinas, the news awaiting him on his resumption of contact with the North included the outcome of his gamble that Thomas could contain Hood and the Confederate Army of Tennessee.

It had truly been a gamble. Sherman would in time be hailed, especially by the twentieth-century British military critic Basil Henry Liddell Hart, as the premier military strategist of the American Civil War, both because he carried war to the resources behind the enemy armies and thus struck at the foundation on which the armies depended, and because the British critic perceived Sherman's campaigns as exemplifying his own favorite strategy of the indirect approach. Unlike Grant, and unlike the generals of the First World War whose strategy on the Western Front produced the enormous casualties that twentieth-century military commentators such as Liddell Hart hoped desperately to avoid, Sherman no longer grappled head-on with the enemy army. He had avoided doing so as much as he thought possible already during his campaign from Chattanooga to Atlanta. From November 1864 he still more emphatically sought a back door, an indirect way, to the enemy's defeat, through the attack on economic resources and popular will.

If enemy states could be defeated in war not by direct confrontation with their armies but through an indirect attack by way of the resources and the public will behind the armies, then Wilderness and Spotsylvania blood-baths and the greater bloodbaths of the Western Front of 1914–1918 might be unnecessary. Armies deprived of their sustenance in resources and morale might fall of their own weight. War's casualties might be reduced enough to make war a reasonably acceptable means of deciding great issues. But as such an interpretation of Sherman's march from Atlanta to the sea began to take shape even during Sherman's lifetime and even while the war contin-ued, contrary-minded military critics argued that to pursue Sherman's strat-egy could pose severe and needless dangers.[1]

Sherman departed from the prime precept of military strategy, so well represented by Grant's campaign against Lee, that the first object should be the destruction of the enemy army. Critics could point out that Sherman was able to apply the strategy of the indirect approach from November 1864 onward largely because the Confederacy was so far along toward defeat that its armies were already well on their way to elimination. General Schofield was to argue, however, that even then, Sherman ran both grave and unneces-sary risks that Hood's army might not be adequately contained by Thomas — unnecessary risks because Sherman could have followed Hood from Geor-gia into Alabama, where the Confederate army resupplied itself before marching north into Tennessee, and thus could have kept the rival army under firm control and, if it was desired, could also have devastated an eco-nomically valuable part of the Confederacy just as well as by marching to Savannah. Sherman might just as well have substituted Alabama for Georgia as the theater of devastation. Moreover, this line of criticism leaves aside the still more fundamental question of the wisdom of making civilian popula-tions rather than armies the direct targets of war.[2]

Schofield knew whereof he spoke when he discussed the risks of Sher-man's indirect approach in leaving Hood's army behind — though Schofield himself contributed to increasing the risks. When persuading Grant of the desirability of marching from Atlanta to the sea, Sherman emphasized the numbers of men he left with Thomas to cope with Hood. By November 14, Thomas had about 70,000 troops, but a large proportion of them were garri-son soldiers or newcomers to the fighting units who were just being trained and equipped for field service. In field forces Thomas had only about 30,000 against Hood's effective army of about 33,000 reinforced by some 6,000 cav-alry under Forrest. Schofield commanded practically Thomas's whole field force, the Fourth and Twenty-third Corps and James Harrison Wilson's Cavalry Corps, Military Division of the Mississippi, of some 5,000 troopers. With these formations, Schofield took position about seventy miles south of Nashville with headquarters at Pulaski, Tennessee.[3]

Fortunately for Thomas and Schofield, Hood was slow to commence his march from Decatur, Alabama, because of time spent gathering supplies; repairing the Mobile and Ohio Railroad from Meridian, Mississippi to Corinth and the Memphis and Charleston between Corinth and Tuscumbia, Alabama; and awaiting Forrest's cavalry. General Beauregard, commanding the Military Division of the West since October 17 with the customary vague authority of overall Confederate commanders between the Appalachians and the Mississippi,[4] later concluded that if Hood had moved with the dispatch he had urged upon him, Sherman would have had no choice but to turn around toward Tennessee. Perhaps so; even with his delay, when Hood did begin moving on November 29 he stole a march on Schofield and almost cut him off from the bridges and fords over the Duck River at Columbia. Then the Confederate commander repeated the process and almost closed Schofield's route of retreat at Spring Hill. In fact, perhaps the greatest of all the military mysteries of the war is why Hood failed to attack when all through the night of November 29–30 Schofield's troops marched straight up the Columbia-Franklin Pike through Spring Hill while the bulk of the Confederate army lay encamped only a short distance away, more than close enough to spring a trap.

Having created a marvelous opportunity for himself through alert maneuvering, and having then forfeited it through his inexplicable lapse into lethargy, Hood followed Schofield in a mood of fury at himself and all concerned. Determined that Schofield should not escape after all, Hood caught up with him on the 30th, at Franklin, where the Federals were delayed by the crossing of the Harpeth River. Here, however, Schofield had time to draw up a strong defensive position, and Hood's current state of mind reinforced his usual impetuosity to provoke him to order a frontal assault. He took no time for artillery preparation, and his troops had to assault the Union works across some two miles of open ground — about twice the distance Pickett's Charge had to travel at Gettysburg, albeit with more troops, about 18,000 in the attack, and on a narrower front. The results were all too predictable: Confederate failure, with 6,252 casualties (1,750 killed, 3,800 wounded, 702 missing) to 2,326 Federal losses (189 killed, 1,033 wounded, 1,104 missing). Confederate leadership tried so desperately to hurl the troops to victory that five of Hood's generals were killed, including the famous and formidable Irish-American warrior Pat Cleburne, along with Brigadier-Generals John

Adams, Otto F. Strahl, States Rights Gist, and Hiram B. Granbury.[5] Schofield later observed aptly: "Was it not, in fact, such attacks as that of Franklin,
Atlanta and Gettysburg, rather than any failures of defense, that finally exhausted and defeated the Confederate Armies?"[6]

The battle of Franklin had surely exhausted Hood's army, and removed
all reason from the Confederate campaign. Schofield withdrew across the
Harpeth and into the defenses of Nashville, where Thomas had received an
additional reinforcement of about 12,000 troops under Major-General Andrew J. Smith, U.S.V., from the old Sixteenth Corps (formally deactivated
November 7, 1864, so that while Smith's troops were generally called the
Sixteenth Corps, they were officially the Detachment, Army of the Tennessee); they had recently been campaigning against Sterling Price and the pe-
rennially pestiferous guerrillas in Missouri.[7] If Hood could not successfully
attack Schofield's force, after the casualties at Franklin he could scarcely
assail Thomas's whole army with any hope of winning. He advanced to face
the Nashville fortifications but then sat down to ruminate upon the unattrac-
tive question of what to do next. While he did so he allowed Forrest and his
cavalry to depart on secondary raiding missions.

Thus passed the first two weeks of December. For although urged by
Grant and the War Department to attack, Thomas with the deliberateness
that had earned him the nickname "Slow Trot" waited for General Wilson
to find horses for 2,000 or so troopers who were dismounted, while Thomas
himself continued organizing garrison troops into provisional tactical units
for the field and in general made sure that when he moved, his disparate
elements would have become an approximation of an army. Somehow the
aloof Virginian Thomas had never won the full friendship, or the full confidence, of Grant or Sherman. Now, unaware either of the true condition of
some of the second-line troops Sherman had bequeathed to Thomas or of
the increasingly bitter weather gripping Nashville, Grant lost patience with
Thomas's preparations and on December 6 peremptorily ordered him to
attack Hood.

Thomas planned to do so, but only on the 8th, to give his cavalry a bit
more time to mount itself. On December 8, however, an ice storm set in to
make movement almost impossible and a battle folly. Still not adequately
informed about the Nashville situation, and apparently distrustful of Thomas
from the beginning, Grant ordered Thomas replaced by Schofield. When
Halleck, learning of the ice storm, delayed transmission of this order and
then got it withdrawn, Grant waited a few more days but on the 13th ordered
Major-General John A. Logan, U.S.V., commander of the Fifteenth Corps
in Grant's favored Army of the Tennessee during much of the Atlanta cam-

paign, to travel toward Nashville with the idea of putting Logan in Thomas's place. Himself prodded by Lincoln and Stanton, Grant then departed Petersburg for Washington on his way to Nashville.

In the capital, the Commanding General learned that on the 15th Thomas had attacked at last and won a resounding victory. When the weather relented, Thomas executed a superb plan that utilized his superior numbers to envelop Hood's left while a demonstration occupied his right. In spite of hard punishment Hood awaited a renewed Union effort from a new line on December 16, whereupon Thomas employed a similar plan to better Hood once more. Wilson's cavalry, for whose remounting Thomas had delayed, played the decisive role in a wider, more ambitious envelopment of the Confederate left. Because numbers and skill permitted Thomas to execute two bold turning movements rather than expend strength in head-on grappling, the killed and wounded were relatively few on both sides: 2,949 Federals (387 killed, 2,562 wounded), along with 112 missing; an unknown but probably not considerably larger number of Confederates killed and wounded — but 4,462 Confederates reported by the Federals as captured. Thomas had commanded 49,773 men, Hood 23,207.[8]

Unable to please Grant thoroughly, Thomas did not pursue vigorously enough to satisfy the General-in-Chief. But as always, pursuit was much more difficult than it seemed from afar — even though Thomas's envelopments had so thrashed and demoralized the already battered remnants of what had been the Confederacy's second greatest army that Nashville ranks as probably the most complete battlefield victory of the war. It is no particular exaggeration to say, as the historian of the campaign Thomas R. Hay did, that after Nashville, "The once powerful army of Tennessee was all but a mere memory."[9]

## THE CAMPAIGN OF THE CAROLINAS

Drowsy Savannah was spared the wrath of Sherman and his armies, for here they must rest and refit. But Sherman soon grew restless in the town; the amenities of urban life seemed almost sybaritic to the puritanically hardened campaigner. He complained of luxurious food and wanted to be rid of it for camp fare, and his temperament responded less well to conferences with Stanton and charitable endeavors for black folk than to punishing white rebels. "My aim then was to whip the rebels to humble their pride, to follow them to their inmost recesses, and make them fear and dread us."[10] When Grant suggested Sherman might bring his troops north by ship to join in the kill against Lee, Sherman treated the aides in his office to a display of his temper.[11] The General-in-Chief promptly abandoned that idea, however, as too expensive and time-consuming and as politically unwise because of the implicit insult to the Army of the Potomac. Sherman received the authorization he wanted to make South Carolina, the nest of secession, feel the hard hand of war.

> Many and many a person in Georgia [he claimed] asked me why we did not go to South Carolina; and, when I answered that we were *en route* for that State, the invariable reply was, "Well, if you will make those people feel the utmost severities of war, we will pardon you for your desolation of Georgia."
> I look upon Columbia [South Carolina] as quite as bad as Charleston, and I doubt if we shall spare the public buildings there as we did at Milledgeville.[12]

The Carolinas were less productive agriculturally than Georgia, and sustenance would be somewhat harder to gather. In part for this reason, the kind of prior preparation for a friendly reception that Sherman had once contemplated as a condition for his march to Savannah was now arranged for the expedition into the Carolinas. An ample penetration of North Carolina from the coast was assured by the capture of the last major port for blockade runners, Wilmington, and its guardian bastion, Fort Fisher.

Ben Butler first received the task of opening Wilmington, because it fell geographically within his Department of Virginia and North Carolina. He steamed down in December with 6,500 troops and two batteries and early on Christmas Eve morning played what he expected to be his trump card, exploding a powder boat — a boat laden with explosives — near the fort. Unfortunately for Butler, the blast had the effect Halleck said he had predicted for it: "Thank God," as the *Official Records* prints Halleck's account to Sherman, "I had nothing to do with it, except to express the opinion that Butler's torpedo ship would have about as much effect on the forts as if he should ———— at them."[13] When on top of this fizzle and after a brief naval bombardment and some preliminary attacks on outworks, Butler learned that Major-General Robert F. Hoke's Division of the Second Corps, Army of Northern Virginia was within five miles on its way as a reinforcement, he gave up and returned to Hampton Roads.

Thereupon Lincoln and Grant reflected on how little they needed Butler now that the election of 1864 was safely over, and they removed him from active command and put Major-General Alfred H. Terry, U.S.V., a competent self-taught soldier who had come up from the ranks, in command of a Provisional Corps to mount a new Fort Fisher expedition.[14] Assisted by Admiral Porter's naval bombardment at point-blank range, Terry's soldiers captured the fort on January 15 in a handsome assault though a predictably costly one, with 955 casualties out of 8,000 engaged. A column of 2,261 sailors and marines failed in a secondary attack, with 300 casualties. The Federals claimed to take 2,083 prisoners.[15]

Wilmington was now sealed off from the ocean, and on Washington's Birthday the Federals occupied it.[16] With it the Confederacy lost practically its last outlet to the world. Terry could march inland to meet Sherman. So would Schofield and his Twenty-third Corps, carried by rail and water from Tennessee to the Neuse River and New Bern.[17]

Sherman began his campaign into South Carolina by transporting his right wing, Howard's Army of the Tennessee (the Fifteenth and Seventeenth Corps), by ship to Beaufort, thence to march inland. The left wing, the Fourteenth and Twentieth Corps, under Slocum and unofficially called the Army of Georgia (officially from March 28), crossed to the north shore of the Savannah River, with the Twentieth Corps on the far left some thirty miles upstream. Again Sherman had some 60,000 troops. To oppose him the Confederacy arrayed perhaps the most impressive assemblage of generals he had yet faced. Beauregard had command of all Confederate troops in South Carolina, Hardee led the field force, D. H. Hill was a senior subordinate. In February Wade Hampton, a hero of Lee's cavalry and freshly promoted to lieutenant-general on the 15th, came south from Virginia to command the cavalry opposing Sherman and to help rally the defenders of his native Palmetto State, of which he was one of the wealthiest citizens and a leading political figure.[18] Generals without troops, however, were likely to be no more effective than the ringing calls for universal resistance that were recycled from the Georgia campaign.

In fact, Beauregard could count about 22,500 soldiers listed on the muster rolls as present for duty at the end of January, including the former Savannah garrison, and he could expect more to arrive eventually from the remnants of the Army of Tennessee. But Sherman formed so wide a front and so deftly appeared to be threatening either of two places, Augusta or Charleston, that the Confederates dissipated their strength hopelessly. Their best reliance against him seemed to be not a scattered army and either worn-out or inexperienced troops, but geography and weather.[19]

Bad weather delayed the start of Sherman's campaign from mid-January to February 1. Then it rained on twenty-eight of the first forty-five days. The Carolina lowcountry through which Sherman began his advance was cleft by major rivers and, even without excessive rains, sodden with smaller streams and marshes between them. Hardee hoped the principal crossings would prove impossible.[20] To the Federals they were not, though Major-General, U.S.V., Joseph A. Mower's First Division of the Seventeenth Corps soon found itself having to cross sixteen streams in two days. To build bridges and corduroy roadways, the division had to work waist-deep in icy waters.

Yet Sherman's veterans had become proof against almost any obstacle in the path of their marches. In its two days of intensive stream crossings, Mower's division constructed a mile and a half of bridges and more corduroy road surfaces than it bothered to tally. At the end of its passage across the sixteen streams, the division reached the Edisto River and stormed breastworks that Hardee thought were the strongest he had ever seen, approaching them through water up to the armpits.[21] In former days this frontal assault would have been futile and suicidal, but the Confederate odds and ends making up Hardee's army were too cowed to hold on. Rebels were coming to abandon resistance simply before such cries as: "You'd better get out, this is the Fifteenth Corps!"[22] Both the inhabitants and Confederate soldiers, said Sherman, "invented such ghostlike stories of our prowess in Georgia, that they were scared by their own inventions. Still, this was a power, and I intended to utilize it."[23]

Such South Carolina acres in the armies' path as happened to be dry were not much more hospitable to farming than the marshes, and to gather enough rations, more Union foragers had to go mounted than in Georgia. The effect was to encourage still more plundering by making it easier to carry the spoils away. There were orders against vandalism as in Georgia, but Sherman seemed even less inclined to enforce them.

> Somehow [said Sherman], our men had got the idea that South Carolina was the cause of all our troubles; her people were the first to fire on Fort Sumter, had been in a great hurry to precipitate the country into civil war; and therefore on them should fall the scourge of war in its worst form. Taunting messages had also come to us, when in Georgia, to the effect that, when we should reach South Carolina, we would find a people less passive, who would fight us to the bitter end, daring us to come over, etc.; so that I saw and felt that we would not be able longer to restrain our men as we had done in Georgia.[24]

Kilpatrick's cavalry found the bodies of eighteen Union soldiers, some with their throats cut, all bearing papers pinned on them saying, "Death to foragers." Sherman ordered his cavalry commander to retaliate man for man and to mark the Confederate bodies in a similar manner. Kilpatrick was just the leader to do it.[25]

Some citizens later claimed that when the Federal forces converged on South Carolina's capital city of Columbia on February 17, Union soldiers warned them there would be hell to pay that night and that it would be wise to leave town. Federals entering Columbia found cotton bales already burning in several places; many of them assumed that the fires had been set by the retreating Confederate forces. Sherman's men extinguished some of the fires, but others continued to burn in a dangerously rising wind. In the afternoon Sherman entered the city, met Mayor Thomas Jefferson Goodwyn at the City Hall, requested a house to use as his headquarters, and assured the mayor that except for the public buildings the city would be safe.

Soon after dark, however, the fires spread out of control across Columbia, driven by the high winds. By this time some of Sherman's soldiers had found stocks of liquor and gotten drunk. Sherman was later to say that drunken soldiers started the worst of the fires, and he blamed the Confederates for leaving alcohol to tempt them. Still later he was to decide that it was Wade Hampton who had deliberately set the fires that had burned his own state capital, and with malicious intent against the Union Army's reputation. General Hazen saw Federal soldiers trying to fight fires as long as their officers watched them, only to scatter and do nothing when their officers left. By the time a shift in the wind in the early morning of February 18 halted the course of destruction, half the city, according to Sherman, or two-thirds, according to the mayor, was in ashes. Columbia had nearly felt "the scourge of war in its worst form."[26]

The same day that the Federals captured Columbia, General Hardee evacuated Charleston on orders from Beauregard. Sherman's armies had approached no closer than fifty miles, but their threat to Charleston's communications inland, and the danger that the garrison would be trapped in the city as Major-General Benjamin Lincoln's had been during the Revolutionary War, led to the order to evacuate. The Union Navy had been bombarding the seaward defenses for almost two years. After Admiral Du Pont's failure in April 1863, Admiral Dahlgren had continued the assault from the footholds he could capture on the neighboring islands. Federal artillery pounded Fort Sumter into rubble, but no direct attack on Charleston from the harbor had been able to succeed. The ease with which this defiant prize fell when its communications were threatened inspired a member of Dahlgren's long-frustrated naval force to reflect upon strategy and upon how little understanding of it the Navy's stubborn battering against Charleston's front door revealed. So that some day naval officers might master not only seamanship but the art of war as well, this officer, Lieutenant-Commander Stephen B. Luce, conceived the idea of a naval war college.[27]

Sherman's resumption of his advance northward from Columbia was slowed again by heavy rains. Meanwhile Lee became General-in-Chief of the Confederacy, and at his request Joe Johnston, the most skillful adversary Sherman had had to face, returned on February 23 as commanding general of the Army of Tennessee, to lead the troops opposing the Northern invader in the Carolinas. In the galaxy of Confederate brass concentrated there, Beauregard moved down to second place under Johnston.[28] The rains gave Johnston time to effect around Fayetteville, North Carolina as considerable an assembly of troops as the Confederacy remained capable of, perhaps 21,000 effectives. Another 5,500 Confederate troops lay at Goldsboro, North Carolina, the field force of the Department of North Carolina and Southern Virginia, of which Braxton Bragg had taken command on October 24, 1864 in response to the first threats against Fort Fisher. Bragg was the third full general in this scene of top-heavy command; Johnston hoped to use him and his men but would not receive authority to command them until March 6. Meanwhile Johnston had to think about parrying both Sherman and the Federals under Schofield and Terry, now advancing inland.[29]

To aggravate Johnston's problems, Sherman repeated the strategy of impaling his opponent on the horns of a dilemma. He advanced on a front that threatened both Raleigh and Goldsboro: if he took the railroad junction at Raleigh he would be well along toward blocking the Army of Northern Virginia's last rail connections to supplies from the deeper South, while if he captured Goldsboro his uniting with Schofield and Terry would be assured.

Johnston nevertheless hoped to use the habitual wide front with which Sherman posed his dilemmas as the means of injuring him, by concentrating against Slocum's left wing which threatened Raleigh. This method also minimized the disadvantage of Bragg's temporary autonomy. The result was Johnston's precipitating the hardest fighting Sherman had faced since the Army of Tennessee slipped away from him after Atlanta. On March 16, the Twentieth Corps collided with Hardee's Corps at Averasboro. Sherman happened to be present with the left wing, and he watched the action, in which despite tough going Slocum pushed Hardee away. Having located Slocum, however, Johnston massed to fall upon him, and on the 19th he did so, at Bentonville. Johnston hit hard, the red battleflags of the Army of Tennessee and of the regiments the Confederacy had grouped around it going forward with almost the zest of the old, early days of uniformed militia companies and romantic illusions — though the source of the zest was now desperation.

Slocum had to summon all the energies of the Fourteenth and Twentieth Corps to contain the Confederate rushes. But Sherman, who was with his right wing on this day, promptly heard the news of battle from a courier and hastened Howard's wing to Slocum's aid. By the 20th, Johnston's strength was spent and Howard was arriving. On the morning of the 21st,

Mower's division attempted to envelop Johnston and cut off his retreat, while the rest of Sherman's forces attacked frontally. Johnston discovered Mower's movement, blocked it, but retreated during the night.

In his memoirs, Sherman says that Mower was breaking through the rebel line in the course of the action and that he, Sherman, made a mistake by not piling his whole right wing in behind Mower at this juncture. At the time, however, Howard believed that Sherman was fighting with deliberate restraint, and Liddell Hart argues that such may well have been the case: that Sherman did not want a full-scale battle and restrained his troops' attacks at both Averasboro and Bentonville because he did not want the problem of caring for large numbers of wounded far from his base, and more than that, because Sherman was sick of bloodshed and believed Johnston would surely retreat upon Goldsboro, where by converging upon that place the Federals would be able to scoop him up.[30]

Ferocious as he was in his marauding marches, Sherman had never shown much taste for battle under any circumstances, and now, with the war obviously nearing its close, it became significant that he had continually assured Southerners that they could count on him for every generosity when the war ended. After all, before the war he had acquired many Southern friends and a considerable sympathy for Southern viewpoints (including those having to do with African Americans) when he was superintendent and professor of engineering at the Louisiana Seminary of Learning and Military Academy at Baton Rouge. "Then," when the war ends, "will I share with you my last cracker, and watch with you to shield your homes and families against danger from every quarter," he had told the citizens of Atlanta.[31] Perhaps he now thought the time for sharing was so close at hand that the killing should stop. Johnston did not fall back on Goldsboro, and the Confederates who were there had to evacuate it. Schofield and Terry thereupon linked up with Sherman, giving him some 80,000 men to confront barely 21,000 after Confederate losses to a growing epidemic of desertion in addition to those of Bentonville.[32] Against any possible human intervention, Sherman's armies were irresistible.

On March 25, Sherman left Schofield in temporary command and set out by the Atlantic and North Carolina Railroad and then the small steamer *Russia* to meet Grant at City Point, the harbor of Petersburg, there to boast a bit about his men's most recent campaign of 425 miles in fifty days—forty days of actual marching—through the rain-soaked Carolinas, and to plan the end of the war.[33]

## THE PETERSBURG CAMPAIGN, SUMMER 1864–SPRING 1865

The results of Grant's campaign against Lee had not been visible enough to assure Lincoln's reelection, and Grant's casualties had been all too visible; but Grant went implacably onward with the one most essential task toward winning the war, the destruction of Lee's Army of Northern Virginia. By the morrow of Lincoln's reelection, little more than Lee and that army propped up the Confederacy.

Not enough Southerners retained sufficient faith in Jefferson Davis and the Confederate civil government to go on with the struggle on their account; but because Davis would not make peace and thus would not release Lee from his perceived duty to continue fighting, and because Lee was above all a man of duty — "There is a true glory and a true honor," he said: "the glory of duty done"[34] — Lee persisted, the Army of Northern Virginia persisted, and the war persisted.

Even Sherman's marches had as one of their principal objects, perhaps the most important object of all, the demoralization of the Southern people so that they would call their soldiers back from the Army of Northern Virginia to rescue their own homes, wives, and children. We cannot be sure how much of the desertion that plagued Lee's and all the Confederate armies during the winter of 1864–1865 can be attributed to Sherman's depredations. Certainly the desertions were many — though we also cannot be sure just how numerous — but poor supplies and a cold winter, along with a generalized loss of confidence, must have accounted for large numbers of them without Sherman's help.[35]

Nevertheless, desertion alone was not going to wipe out the stout core of Lee's army. Only Grant and the Union Army could do that. Because Davis and Lee would not cease fighting though all rational hope was gone, only Grant and the patient soldiers of the Army of the Potomac, with their comrades of the Army of the James, could force an end to the war.

Set back by the fiasco of the Crater in midsummer of 1864, Grant had resumed his now customary shifts toward his left, reaching for Lee's lines of communications. On the night of August 14–15 Meade relieved Warren's Fifth Corps from its positions in the Petersburg trenches and sent it marching south and west to get astride the Weldon Railroad, Lee's most direct route of supply from North Carolina. On the 18th Warren lodged himself on the road around Globe Tavern against only minimal opposition from Brigadier-General James Dearing's Cavalry Brigade, and he set his troops to tearing up the tracks in both directions. Lee inevitably reacted strongly, first with A. P. Hill and most of his corps, then with almost all the Confederate troops who previously had remained north of the James. Grant and Meade responded by sending to Warren's aid first Hancock's Second Corps and then Major-General, U.S.V., John G. Parke's Ninth Corps. Although four days of fighting ensued, this Federal concentration could not be budged. On the other hand, it was symptomatic of Grant's continued limitations in operational rather than tactical thinking that he did not seize the opportunity to strike immediately at Lee's denuded trenches north of the James.[36]

The Confederates tried to make do logistically by using the Weldon Railroad as far north from the Carolinas as possible and employing wagons to haul supplies around the section of Federal destruction and possession. Therefore on August 21 Meade ordered Hancock with the First and Second Divisions of his corps (Brigadier-General Nelson A. Miles, U.S.V., and Major-General John Gibbon, U.S.V.), along with a strong force of cavalry, to destroy the railroad southward even beyond Reams's Station, which was about four miles south of Globe Tavern. A. P. Hill again led the riposte — hitherto a disappointment as corps commander, Hill was somehow finding again the abilities he had shown at the head of the old Light Division — and Major-General Wade Hampton's Cavalry Division piled in also. Together Hill and Hampton mauled Hancock's Federals badly. The proud Federal Second Corps absorbed another battering comparable to the disaster inflicted on it by the same A. P. Hill on the Jerusalem Road in June. This time it lost nine cannon and twelve colors, along with over 3,000 stand of small arms and more than 2,000 prisoners. Nevertheless, the Confederates now had only the Southside Railroad remaining as an iron link between Petersburg and the South.[37]

Through the autumn, Grant patiently probed toward the Southside Railroad, balancing his leftward shifts with occasional — but unfortunately for the Union, not simultaneous and coordinated — movements on the far flank facing Richmond north of the James. Lee responded with a delicate balancing act of his own, carefully judging just the right number of troops to sidle back and forth between his flanks. When his defenders collided with Grant's probes, they fought with the energy of desperation along with the other customary virtues of Lee's soldiery, touching off a series of battles that ought to be better remembered than they usually are: Chaffin's Bluff, Peebles's Farm, Hatcher's Run, the Boydton Plank Road among them.

On the night of September 28–29 Butler's Army of the James struck against the New Market Line on New Market Heights and the Exterior Line just behind and south of it, the outer shell of the defenses of Richmond north of the James. Grant's purpose was to prevent Lee from dispatching additional reinforcements to Early in the Shenandoah Valley as well as to probe the entrenchments weakened by the Confederates during the previous fighting.

In the earliest morning hours of September 29 the Federals pushed through the New Market Line to position themselves for attacks against Fort Harrison at the junction of the Exterior and Intermediate Lines and strong points reaching south and west from Fort Harrison to Chaffin's Bluff overlooking the James. As the initial success had suggested might be true, Fort Harrison was weakly garrisoned in spite of a pivotal location. Just after 6:00 A.M. the First Division of the Eighteenth Corps launched what proved an admirable charge against it. Spearheaded by its Second Brigade under a tough volunteer soldier from Maine, Brigadier-General, U.S.V., Hiram Burnham, the division advanced across 1,400 yards of open ground swept by enemy fire and captured the fort. Burnham was killed by a bullet in the bowels just after he had turned around a Confederate gun inside the fort, either just before or after getting off a shot; but the division commander, another New Englander of similar prowess, the granitic Vermont militiaman Brigadier-General George J. Stannard, U.S.V., would ensure ample preparation against counterattack.

The Confederates had to react swiftly to the loss of Fort Harrison, because it was indispensable to avoid the further loss of Chaffin's Bluff to the right of it. Chaffin's Bluff on the north bank of the James shielded Drewry's Bluff just upstream on the opposite shore, and Drewry's in turn commanded the Confederate pontoon bridge across the river, while its artillery emplacements had long blocked the passage of the Union Navy toward Richmond. Lee hurriedly gathered reinforcements from the southside, but Grant and Butler had achieved surprise, and it would take time for fresh Confederate troops to arrive at the threatened scene. Meanwhile one-legged Lieutenant-General Richard S. Ewell, assigned to command the Department of Richmond when poor health obliged him to leave Lee's Second Corps on May 29, for at least a brief shining hour emulated the rejuvenation of A. P. Hill, rushing to the field to cobble together new defenses between Fort Gilmer and Fort Gregg north of Fort Harrison and the White Battery, Fort Hoke, and Fort Maury reaching to Chaffin's Bluff to the south.

Ewell's personal leadership succeeded; he shored up a line that held. The Confederate situation was probably critical enough to justify the kind of front-line leadership in which an army, department, or corps commander ought not ordinarily to indulge, because his higher direction of affairs should be too valuable to warrant his behaving like a battalion commander. On the

Federal side, there was no equivalent crisis to call for Major General Edward Otho Cresap Ord, U.S.V., commanding the Eighteenth Corps, to take direct charge of the attacks south of the White Battery. Ord's fate vindicated the rule against such activity, because he fell so badly wounded in the right thigh that he had to leave the field. His successor, Brigadier-General, U.S.V., Charles A. Heckman of the Second Division, lacked the capacity to coordinate a corps-sized attack, and the consequent breakdown in Union command contributed much to Ewell's accomplishments.

North of Fort Harrison the loss of the fort compelled the Confederates to fall back into the Intermediate Line hinging on Forts Gilmer and Gregg. Here, too, the Confederate rally succeeded. Fort Gilmer repulsed one of Heckman's indifferently organized attacks. When Major-General, U.S.V., David Bell Birney's Tenth Corps arrived on the scene after playing the principal role in the morning's capture of New Market Heights, Grant, who had also arrived in person, ordered a large-scale attack on Gilmer by elements of both Federal corps. Launched about 3:00 P.M., the effort featured a headlong charge by Brigadier-General, U.S.V., William Birney's (David's brother) First Brigade, Third Division, Tenth Corps. This brigade was African-American, and its troops proved their soldierly merit in an action worthy of comparison with the assault of the 54th Massachusetts on Fort Wagner in July 1863. Unhappily, like the attack on Fort Wagner it failed despite its gallantry, and so did the whole Fort Gilmer effort.

The sequel, the second battle of Fort Harrison on September 30, requires reflection upon the generalship of R. E. Lee. Arriving north of the James around the time of the climactic Fort Gilmer action, Lee immediately began preparing a counterattack against Fort Harrison. At 3:00 P.M. on the 30th Lieutenant-General Richard H. Anderson, commanding the First Corps because Longstreet was still recovering from his Wilderness wound, hurled forward a frontal assault in the style of Malvern Hill and Pickett's Charge. The pugnacious Lee had yet to abandon that method after so many casualties and so many failures. Of course, the same method had worked for the Federals the day before, but then the defense was puny, while now the First Division, Eighteenth Corps stood ready under the eye of George Stannard, who had been there when the Union center turned back Pickett on July 3 at Gettysburg. Anderson had 7,000 men, mostly of Hoke's and Major-General Charles W. Field's Divisions — the latter of which had been John Bell Hood's — but their attack merely repeated the pattern of its sad though brave predecessors, albeit it cost Stannard his fourth wound of the war, the loss of his right arm, which ended his career as a warrior forever.

There were 19,639 Union troops engaged at Forts Harrison and Gilmer and Chaffin's Bluff, and they suffered 3,327 casualties (383 killed, 2,299 wounded, 645 missing). Among some 10,836 Confederates engaged, the losses are unknown, but may well have totaled about 2,000. The fighting in Virginia might be hopeless for the Confederates, but it was no less ferocious than ever before.[38]

Only as the offensive by the Federal right wing sputtered out did Grant thrust again with his left. He had not yet resolved to strike with both wings simultaneously. On the last day of September Grant began a new effort to press his left flank northwestward toward the Southside Railroad, and toward a supplementary supply route, the Boydton Plank Road. The First and Second Divisions of the Fifth Corps (Brigadier-Generals, U.S.V., Charles Griffin and Romeyn B. Ayres) led off, followed by the First and Second Divisions of the Ninth Corps (Brigadier-Generals, U.S.V., Orlando B. Willcox and Robert B. Potter), with Brigadier-General, U.S.V., David McM. Gregg's Second Cavalry Division screening the left rear. Griffin marched along the Poplar Spring Road past Poplar Spring Church until he struck partially completed enemy earthworks reaching southwestward across his path at Squirrel Level Road, intersecting Poplar Spring Road about a quarter of a mile beyond the church. Only cavalry and artillery held the Confederate line, however, the infantry having moved into Petersburg to relieve the troops who had crossed the James. It appeared that Grant had struck blows on both sides of that river nearly enough simultaneously to achieve decisive effects.

Nevertheless, fortifications sufficed for the Confederates though men were in short supply. Warren allowed his troops to halt in front of the Squirrel Level Line, disconcerted particularly by a redoubt called Fort Archer on William Peebles's farm. Not until several hours had passed to give the enemy time to gather reinforcements, at one in the afternoon, did Warren make bold to attack, whereupon Fort Archer fell readily. But much momentum — and much opportunity — was already lost.

The sympathetic observer of the history of the long-suffering Army of the Potomac can scarcely escape exasperation on sensing that, so late in the war, the spirit of George B. McClellan could still palsy the army. Surely the terrible losses of the 1864 campaign also had much to do with a stumble like that at Peebles's Farm; but lost opportunities were too inherent in the entire history of the Army of the Potomac for that explanation to be able to stand alone. Warren's caution in particular was to contribute to a reputation for hesitancy that would eventually cost the hero of Little Round Top dearly. That other and greatest Union hero of Gettysburg, George G. Meade, com-

manded the army with a loose rein on leisurely generals. It would be understandable that Grant might have been thinking that the army much needed
the return of fiery Phil Sheridan.

Warren had delayed partly on the ground that he had to wait for Potter's
division to come up in support of his left. By the time Potter moved forward
west of Peebles's Farm later in the afternoon, however, after another less
than urgent advance, the rejuvenated A. P. Hill was ready with a riposte.
Commanding the entire front south of the James in Lee's absence, Hill
counterattacked about four o'clock with Major-Generals Henry Heth's and
Cadmus M. Wilcox's Third Corps Divisions. He drove Potter back in
enough confusion to cause the Federals embarrassment, until Griffin belatedly—again—intervened and permitted stabilizing the Union front across
Peebles's Farm.

Thus for the time being ended Federal offensive efforts, though not
quite yet Hill's counterefforts. During a rainy and dismal first day of October,
Gregg repulsed an attempt by Wade Hampton to turn the new line, and to
assure the termination of Confederate infantry counterattacks the next day
it was necessary to attach General Mott's Third Division, Second Corps to
the Ninth Corps and bring it up in support. Thereupon the Federals built a
permanent new line between Globe Tavern and Peebles's Farm, an advance
of about three miles, almost halfway to the Southside Railroad and with the
apex of the front within less than two miles of the Boydton Plank Road.

The actions known as Poplar Spring Church, Peebles's Farm, and for
part of the fighting west of Peebles's, (Oscar) Pegram's Farm cost the Federals
2,898 casualties and the Confederates some 1,239. For all the flaws of Federal
command, these actions in combination with those north of the James had
rewarded Grant with not altogether unsatisfactory progress toward the enemy lines of communications while they punished the Confederates with
additional manpower losses they could not afford.[39]

And Grant was sure to prod again. On October 27, he essayed as close
an approximation of simultaneous assaults north and south of the James as
he had contrived yet. South of the river, he pulled 43,000 of an available
57,000 troops out of the trenches to form a mobile force for another attempt
to cut the Boydton Plank Road and the Southside Railroad. North of the
river, Butler was to employ both corps of the Army of the James, the Tenth
and Eighteenth, in a major demonstration to keep the Confederates there
altogether pinned down.

Butler, moreover, as ever ambitious for the political implications of his
military career even if the Presidency had fallen out of the question for the
current year, hoped to accomplish nothing less than to use enemy preoccu-

pation with the Army of the Potomac to drive into Richmond itself. He intended no mere demonstration but a full-scale offensive; often amateurish as a tactician, Butler in his operational vision sometimes seems to have recognized the possibilities implicit in coordinating the two Federal armies on the James more clearly than Grant himself.

Butler was correct to perceive operational opportunity, but his tactical limitations once more undid him. His offensive design was to hold Richmond's defenders firmly in place with vigorous attacks by David Birney's Tenth Corps on his left, while the Eighteenth Corps shifted to the north of the Williamsburg Road and thence turned and crushed the Confederate left flank. On October 1, however, Brigadier-General Godfrey Weitzel, U.S.V., had relieved Heckman of his temporary leadership of the corps in place of the wounded Ord, and while an officer considerably superior to Heckman, Weitzel also had severe limitations as a corps commander in a large-scale endeavor. He was primarily a military engineer, and generally a decidedly able one; he had been chief engineer of Butler's army before taking over the corps; but while he had held divisional command in the Department of the Gulf, he had not had much experience in handling large numbers of troops in intense combat. Now he was slow to move his troops into position north of the Williamsburg Road, and only on arriving there did he begin a serious reconnaissance of the terrain, an odd omission for an engineer that led to the consumption of more than two hours in reconnoitering and deploying troops without any more positive action during the early afternoon.

It virtually assured the usual ill consequences of such delay that since October 19 James Longstreet had been back in the field, commanding his old corps and the defenses of Richmond north of the James. Always a superb defensive fighter, Longstreet promptly discerned that the Tenth Corps activities against him constituted a feint and that the real threat would appear in the Williamsburg Road sector. Consequently he hastened Field's veteran division to that area, having to deploy the division over an excessively long front, the soldiers stationed at intervals of three to six feet and without reserves, but able to take advantage of strong pre-prepared fortifications facing about 1,200 yards of open ground. Therefore, when Weitzel at length launched his attack about 3:30 P.M. on both sides of the road, it quickly broke down in the customary manner of such frontal assaults, and Ben Butler's latest ambitions fizzled with it. Such was the battle of Williamsburg Road or Second Fair Oaks. The Eighteenth Corps lost some 1,064 casualties; the Tenth Corps and cooperating cavalry lost 539; Confederate casualties were, as was becoming increasingly the norm, insufficiently reported to be known.[40]

The big Union push on the left involved the Ninth, Second, and Fifth Corps, along with Gregg's Second Cavalry Division, the latter always busy now that most of the horse soldiers of the Army of the Potomac were away with Sheridan in the Valley. Parke's Ninth Corps was to move out of the entrenchments it had occupied since Peebles's Farm to try to surprise and overrun the current Confederate right flank, at Hatcher's Run just over a mile in front of the Boydton Plank Road. If he was unsuccessful, Parke was nevertheless to go through the motions of persisting in an attack, to divert attention from the other two advancing Union corps. Hancock, with the Second (Brigadier-General, U.S.V., Thomas W. Egan) and Third (Mott) Divisions of his Second Corps, was to move wide to the south and west to hit the Boydton Plank Road from the Dabney's Mill Road, which roughly paralleled Hatcher's Run about a mile south of it. If possible, of course, Hancock was to press on from the plank road to the Southside Railroad. Warren, advancing with his Fifth Corps between Parke and Hancock, was to throw the main weight of his corps to the support of Hancock if Parke's initial attack broke down.

October 27 was another wet and dismal day, like the first of the month. In spite of the weather and a firefight with Confederate cavalry on the way, Hancock's men covered about eight miles from 3:30 A.M., the head of the column coming within sight of the Boydton Plank Road by 10:30. Gregg's cavalry on Hancock's left had to fight off a good deal more enemy cavalry, of Brigadier-General John Dunovant's South Carolina Brigade, and reached the road only about 1:00 P.M.

By that time Parke's attack along Hatcher's Run had thoroughly broken down, notwithstanding the presence since about nine in the morning of both Grant and Meade to urge it on. Warren in the center meanwhile had been enmeshed in woods exceptionally thick even for a generally much-wooded area, and he had not kept pace with either Hancock or Parke. Once Parke was stalemated, Meade's bright, able, and sometimes caustic chief of staff, Major-General Andrew A. Humphreys, U.S.V., found Warren and personally and emphatically ordered him to hurry his march to reinforce Hancock. Presently Grant and Meade caught up with Warren, and they also, on this occasion unlike Peebles's Farm, Meade especially, repeated both the substance and the manner of Humphreys's injunction. Because Warren's Third Division (Brigadier-General Samuel W. Crawford, U.S.V.) was closest to Hancock, Warren personally directed that division's advance.

Good generalship is in no small measure dependent on luck, and Warren was fast becoming an unlucky general for whom nothing any longer went right. His column could not break free from the woods in time to help when the indefatigable A. P. Hill unleashed his predictable counterattack upon the isolated Hancock. This time it was Heth's and Mahone's Divisions that Hill brought out of the trenches to be the assailants, while Wade Hampton similarly belabored Gregg. The advantage shifted back and forth, attack and counterattack, from four in the afternoon until the night became too dark to permit anything more with a semblance of cohesion. Hill's and Hampton's men fought with the now accustomed urgency of desperation, under two senior commanders who could still raise up memories of the Army of Northern Virginia in its prime. But David Gregg was about as dependable as he was ubiquitous; and if Hancock would never again be the dashing corps commander of the days before his Gettysburg wound, and the Jerusalem Road and Reams's Station had exposed a woefully depleted Second Corps, still Hancock was less trammeled by timidity and self-doubt than any other remaining corps commander in the Army of the Potomac, and save for the distant Sixth the Second remained probably the best corps in the army. Hancock and Gregg held on, though the infantry's ammunition fell almost to nothing.

They could obviously not go farther, however, and on October 28 the Federals pulled back to their original positions. They had reached but could not yet hold the Boydton Road. Tactical deficiencies had deprived Grant of operational opportunity south as well as north of the James. Hatcher's Run cost the Army of the Potomac 1,758 men (166 killed, 1,028 wounded, 1,194 missing). Once more, the number of Confederate casualties is unknown — but in Hill's and Hampton's seesaw battle, surely more than Lee could afford.[41]

As usual with Grant, he took this setback as meaning little in itself. From December 7 through 11, the Fifth Corps reinforced by Mott's Third Division, Second Corps, and accompanied as usual by Gregg's cavalry, raided southward along the Weldon Railroad again. The Federals destroyed track as far as Hicksford, forty miles south of Petersburg. Around Sussex Court House, the bodies of Federal stragglers were found stripped and sometimes mutilated by rebel guerrillas, whereupon the Federals' return march northward became punctuated by burning buildings, houses as well as barns, mills, and even corn-cribs. A. P. Hill came south in pursuit, but Warren managed mostly to elude him — good luck for a change — and Meade sent Potter's division south as insurance. Union losses of all kinds numbered only about a hundred. On December 10 Longstreet probed north of the James to make sure that trenches had not been vacated there, but he found the Army of the James in its usual strength and accomplished nothing.[42]

By now Lee was defending a thirty-five-mile front, from the Williamsburg Road east of Richmond, across the James, across Bermuda Hundred neck, across the Appomattox River, and on east and south of Petersburg beyond Peebles's Farm. Obviously, he was stretching his 66,000 or so men ever more dangerously thin, against more than 110,000 Federals.[43] And while the Federals shared with Lee's army the taut nerves of trench life, the perils of sniping and mortar fire, the miseries of damp and cold, they could compensate themselves out of the mountains of supplies shipped to City Point and thence distributed by the line of the U.S. Military Railroad that had been built to circle the rear of their trenches. On an average day forty steamers, seventy-five sailing vessels, and a hundred barges emptied their holds for Grant's army at City Point, where the wharves lined the James River for more than a mile and swung up the Appomattox. In contrast, by autumn the Army of Northern Virginia endured frequent pangs of hunger, and for a time in January 1865 its reserve of food was down to two days' short rations.[44]

In early February, Meade and Grant tried again to reach for the Boydton Plank Road and the Southside Railroad. General Humphreys led the way. On November 26 Hancock had bade farewell to the Second Corps to return to Washington and organize a new First Corps, Veteran Volunteers, in fact a rear-echelon post intended to restore Hancock's burned-out spirit, the flair he had briefly shown a month before on the Boydton Road notwithstanding. So Humphreys had taken the corps that same day, and on February 5 he took it out of its earthworks toward the Vaughan Road crossing of Hatcher's Run.

Warren's Fifth Corps marched also, to take up a supporting position at Monks Neck about two miles south of the Second Corps objective. In part the purpose was to divert attention while Gregg's cavalry division raided from Reams's Station to Dinwiddie Court House, fifteen miles just south of east from the station and on the Boydton Plank Road almost ten miles from the right flank of the Confederate fortifications, there to break up wagon traffic on the road. Unfortunately, there proved to be almost no wagons in the vicinity; Gregg captured only eighteen of them, along with fifty prisoners. The Second and Fifth Corps, however, provoked the usual counterattacks, from Heth's and Mahone's Divisions of the Third Corps and Brigadier-Generals John Pegram's and Clement A. Evans's Divisions of the Confederate Second Corps. There was heavy fighting through February 7, in which Pegram, just married to Hetty Carey of Baltimore on the 2nd, was among the dead of the 6th. The unlucky Fifth Corps might have been routed on the 6th had it not been for the support of Major-General, U.S.V., Frank Wheaton's First Division of the Sixth Corps, back from the Shenandoah. Still, at the price of 1,539 Union casualties (171 killed, 1,181 wounded, 187 missing) to an estimated irreplaceable 1,000 Confederates, this action — called Dabney's Mill, Armstrong's Mill, Vaughan Road, Hatcher's Run (again), Rowanty Creek, or Boydton Road (again) — gave the Federals the Vaughan Road crossing of Hatcher's Run, where they had not been able to hold on in October.[45]

Lee's perimeter had grown to over thirty-seven miles, and Grant's persistent movements even in winter confirmed what was already altogether apparent: that when spring came he would compel his opponent to extend his lines and extend them again until somewhere they broke.[46] Lee remained too aggressive a general to await that outcome passively. He prepared for one more offensive effort, an attack that might shorten his lines. If that much could be accomplished, Lee hoped next to be able to spare some troops to reinforce Johnston against Sherman, aiming at a decisive initiative in North Carolina following which Johnston would be able to join Lee against Grant.

A. P. Hill's indefatigability throughout the Petersburg campaign had been nothing short of amazing to his friends, who could all too readily perceive that he was dying — of prostatitis that was a complication of gonorrhea contracted in the summer of 1844 probably in New York City on cadet leave after his second year at West Point.[47] Now at last Hill had had to go on sick leave, so to command his attack Lee turned to the able Georgia citizen-soldier John B. Gordon, long an outstanding brigade and division commander, a major-general from the preceding May 14, and commanding general of the Second Corps since the return of most of it in December while Early remained behind in the Shenandoah. Gordon selected as the most promising target of attack a strong point called Fort Stedman, occupied by Brigadier-General, U.S.V., John F. Hartranft's Third Division, Ninth Corps. This redoubt was located directly east of Petersburg and only 150 yards from the Confederate lines, which made a rapid and with luck a stealthy approach feasible. The capture of the fort should cause confusion in the right flank of the Army of the Potomac. In consultation with Lee, Gordon prepared the assault carefully.[48]

Gordon had almost all of his Second Corps available for the attack, along with Major-General Bushrod R. Johnson's Division of R. H. Anderson's new Fourth Corps. The initial assault force comprised about 11,500 men largely of Major-General Bryan Grimes's Second Corps Division and Johnson's Division. At 4:00 A.M. this force charged from Colquitt's Salient opposite the fort and carried it. Three columns of 100 picked men each were to advance next on smaller forts behind Stedman from which the Confederates could turn artillery onto the Federal rear and move to widen the penetration.

The attack succeeded in carving out a gap in the Union defenses approaching a mile in width. Nevertheless, the picked troops were unable to find the subsidiary forts. It may well be that Confederate intelligence was faulty and that Gordon had set nonexistent objectives. In any event, confusion and frustration began to infect the Confederate vanguard, and the attack would not have the advantageous artillery sites that Gordon had expected.

In March 1865 the very assurance of possessing overpowering strength generated a certain complacency among the Petersburg besieging force, which goes far toward explaining why Gordon's early morning rush could accomplish as much as it did. Once aroused, however, that overpowering strength lashed back at the Confederates. Heavy concentrations of artillery blasted them, and about 7:30 Hartranft's division launched a counterattack stimulated by embarrassed fury. By eight o'clock the Ninth Corps line was restored. Meanwhile the Union Second and Sixth Corps had taken advantage of the large Confederate concentration away from their fronts to capture the entrenched picket lines facing them. Estimates of Confederate losses at and immediately around Fort Stedman range from 800 to 3,500, while the Ninth Corps lost 1,044 (seventy-two killed, 450 wounded, 522 missing).[49]

Fort Stedman, which was to prove to be the last major attack by the Army of Northern Virginia, thus repeated the old story of Lee's aggressive tactics. The battle expended too much of that resource which the Confederacy could least afford to lose, its military manpower.

## To Appomattox

Lee had hoped that if Gordon failed to plant himself inside Fort Stedman, and Grant did not contract his lines, then nevertheless Gordon's assault would distract the Federals sufficiently to permit the Army of Northern Virginia to slip away intact southward and westward on a march to join Johnston and defeat Sherman before facing Grant again. Although Gordon had not met that minimum objective, Lee would now have to evacuate the Petersburg lines anyway and try to move south to unite with Johnston. The alternative, passivity, would mean slow strangulation at best, and more likely destruction at the hands of Grant's spring offensives. While Lee tried to collect a week's rations in preparation for his retreat, however, Grant hastened to make orderly retreat impossible.

Pitilessly, furthermore, Grant intended at last to strike simultaneously with all his major forces, and more than that, he could throw into the operational balance not two but three armies, any one of which was more than equal alone to the depleted Army of Northern Virginia, and all of which in combination made Lee's plan to go to North Carolina almost certainly chimerical.

On the day after the Fort Stedman battle, Sheridan rejoined Grant from the Valley, bringing with him the First and Third Divisions, Cavalry Corps, of Brigadier-Generals, U.S.V., Thomas C. Devin and George Armstrong Custer, the last large force he had retained in the Shenandoah. Custer had dispersed forever the final remnant of Early's army in an action at Waynesborough on March 2.[50] Now Grant dispatched Sheridan westward and southward toward Dinwiddie Court House with the entire Cavalry Corps under Merritt, including the Second Division, commanded from March 26 by George Crook,[51] and in support the Fifth and Second Corps. The mission was to turn the Confederate right at last and once and for all; to block any Confederate withdrawal to the west; and to break the Southside Railroad, cutting off almost all of Petersburg's remaining trickle of supplies. Sheridan retained the title of Commander in Chief of the Army of the Shenandoah, and the Army of the Potomac troops under him would be independent of Meade. Reflecting events around Petersburg during his absence, he received even the authority to remove Warren from command of the Fifth Corps. Grant wanted all the aggressiveness he could get to be injected into what he intended as the climactic effort of the war. Whatever other qualities Sheridan had displayed as an army commander — he had not fought his battles in the Shenandoah with exceptional tactical skill — he was altogether aggressive.[52]

When Lee's intelligence apprised him of Union movement toward and beyond his right, he sent there all the cavalry he had hitherto retained north of the James, under his nephew Major-General (since August 3, 1863) Fitzhugh Lee,[53] and Pickett's Division of infantry. Fewer than 10,000 men, this force represented Lee's last semblance of a reserve. If it could not hold open an escape route to the west, even the ghost of a hope of Confederate survival that lay in the notion of uniting Lee's army with Johnston's would virtually disappear. There was some small cause for Confederate cheer, then, when heavy rains delayed Sheridan's progress, and on March 31 Pickett actually drove back the vanguard of Sheridan's cavalry on the road northwest from Dinwiddie Court House toward Five Forks.[54]

Five Forks was an important crossroads, because in possession of it Sheridan could choose to move either a mere five miles north to reach the Southside Railroad, or east along the White Oak Road toward the Boydton Plank Road and Lee's right flank. Learning of the action near the crossroads on March 31, Lee instructed Pickett that holding Five Forks was imperative.

Although Pickett had encountered growing Federal forces before he called off his activities at darkness on the 31st, however, and although Union infantry correctly believed to be the Fifth Corps was known to be in the vicinity, Pickett failed to take this injunction altogether seriously. He decided that his entrenchments around Five Forks were strong enough that the place would hold without his personal supervision, and on April 1 he and Fitz Lee retired to a Saturday shad bake.

It was a grievous error. George Pickett was by no means the preeminent division commander of the Army of Northern Virginia, but so far there was nothing in his record to mar the aura of the great charge at Gettysburg. Now he would end the war with a blot against his name that even the magnanimous Lee apparently found hard to forgive. While Pickett enjoyed the shad, Sheridan came crashing into his front with all the weight of the Cavalry Corps, fighting variously mounted and dismounted, and reinforced by Brigadier-General, U.S.V., Ranald S. Mackenzie's Cavalry Division, Army of the James — another evidence of Grant's intentness upon assuring that this campaign must be the last. Late in the afternoon the Fifth Corps, wedging itself between Pickett and the rest of the Confederate army, rolled up his left flank, and ruthless Sheridan drove Pickett's force until it was ruined beyond repair and the Southside Railroad lay open for the taking.

Not that Pickett's forgoing the shad could have changed much; the offensives of Lee's heyday and the continual pounding inflicted by Grant during the past year were reaching their cumulative effect in the utter depletion of the Army of Northern Virginia's last wells of energy and manpower. When a courier gave Grant the news of Sheridan's victory at Five Forks, estimating 5,000 prisoners taken in addition to the opening of the way to the Southside Railroad, Grant finally ordered the Armies of the Potomac and the James to attack simultaneously, and to do so before the nighttime hours of April 1–2 ended.

The Union soldiers who were awakened to go forward at 4:30 A.M. against the Confederate trenches feared another Cold Harbor. Many had seen far too much of war fought with rifled firearms to anticipate anything else. But the effort to hold the road junction at Five Forks had at last stretched Lee's army too thin. There were not enough Confederate soldiers left in the trenches to stand against a determined assault. The Army of the James knocked hard against the eastern door of Richmond, and the door began to cave in. Parke's Ninth Corps broke through against Gordon's defenses around Fort Mahone east of Petersburg. Wright's Sixth Corps ruptured the lines of A. P. Hill's Corps. Union penetrations spread swiftly to the right and the left, the Sixth Corps rolling up the Confederate fortifications all the way westward to Hatcher's Run.

About 10 A.M. of April 2, Lee telegraphed the Secretary of War, since February 4, John C. Breckinridge: "I see no prospect of doing more than holding our position here till night. I am not certain that I can do that. . . . I advise that all preparation be made for leaving Richmond to-night."[55]

That Sunday morning a messenger quietly approached Jefferson Davis while he worshipped at St. Paul's Protestant Episcopal Church just off Capitol Square to tell him of Lee's message. Rumors and then more definite news of Lee's dispatch began to swirl through Richmond almost immediately after the President's departure from the church, and the government offices were moving out through the afternoon and into the evening.

Law and order began to disintegrate as convalescent soldiers from the hospitals tried to take the place of the military guards who had enforced a virtual military regime in the capital through much of the war. During the night the last troops to evacuate the city marched out past drunken, looting crowds and amidst rapidly spreading fires. President Davis moved himself and the official seat of government to Danville, whence on April 4 he issued yet another of his familiar addresses to the people about how the struggle must continue.[56]

The loss of the Southside Railroad dictated that there was no choice for the Army of Northern Virginia but to cross to the north bank of the Appomattox River and there march westward to the Richmond and Danville Railroad, where it might receive supplies and follow the rail line toward North Carolina and Johnston. Lee arranged for a cache of stores to await him at Amelia Court House, on the railroad some eight miles southwest of where his army in following it would recross the Appomattox. But the reason why Five Forks had killed almost any glimmer of a hope for the Confederacy was precisely that it compelled Lee to turn toward his proposed meeting with Johnston with the Federal army already as far west as his own troops. Sheridan was almost certain to be able to block any path along which sustenance for Lee's march might be found.[57]

Sheridan hastened toward the Richmond and Danville Railroad in a fury. Grant was getting all the aggressiveness he could have hoped for from the chief of the Army of the Shenandoah, past the boundary even of irrationality and injustice. On the triumphant day of Five Forks Sheridan had invoked his authority to remove Warren from the head of the Fifth Corps, because a tired, hard-marched, rain- and mud-plagued corps had not performed completely to Sheridan's expectations, and because Warren had committed a mistake in judgment in failing to position his troops for the best possible approach to Pickett's flank. Sheridan's removal of Warren is one of the most dismaying command decisions of the war. Most of Warren's delay on April 1 was caused by bad weather and could not have been remedied by any commander, his approach to Five Forks had been plagued by contradictory instructions from Sheridan and Grant, and his one real misjudgment of that day had been minor and had hardly interfered with routing the enemy. To sack a hero of Warren's stature for dubious reasons when the war was almost won said little for the balance of Sheridan's own judgment, to say nothing of his sense of humanity. And yet, and yet: knowing the background in the form of Warren's conduct of his share of the Petersburg campaign almost creates sympathy for Sheridan's decision, just as the reader of the history of that campaign who empathizes with the Union soldiers feels impelled to shriek with frustration over the way leisurely command often betrayed the best efforts of the men in the ranks. The same fury that spitefully removed Warren could lash onward, at a pace Lee's hungry and weary veterans no longer had the strength to match, both the Cavalry Corps and the Fifth Corps (the latter now under Griffin, promoted to major-general of volunteers to rank from April 2).[58]

On April 5, Sheridan reached the Richmond and Danville Railroad at Jetersville, seven miles southwest of Amelia Court House. Lee could not go down the railroad to meet Johnston.

Moreover, when Lee had reached Amelia Court House the previous day he found that the expected supplies were not there. He waited through the morning of the 5th for the stores that did not appear, and then he concluded he must march on. As Longstreet's Corps led the way farther southwest along the railroad, they found the line blocked.

Nothing remained now but to persist westward toward Lynchburg, in the hope that supplies might be collected there, where the Virginia and Tennessee Railroad met the Southside and the Virginia Central. Then a way might yet be found to move south toward Johnston. Lee's inability to find rations at Amelia was yet another curb on hard marching, however, and if the Federals could continue to move faster and should succeed in reaching to the west to block the Confederates' path in that direction as well as to the south, then the game would be up. Not only Sheridan, but Grant, Meade, and the whole Federal command, furthermore, saw complete and final victory before them as clear as the western horizon of the fine spring days now brightening the land. Having fought so long to destroy the Army of Northern Virginia, they would not now let it slip from their grasp.

Meade kept up with the pursuit on an ambulance sickbed. The troops

trudged forward thirty-five miles a day and more, stragglers dropping everywhere but the armies going on footsore, hungry, and thirsty but drawn by the
scent of triumph. Humphreys's Second Corps was upon Lee's rear guard and
continually snapping at it and biting away bits and pieces. On April 6, along
a tributary of the Appomattox called Sayler's Creek just east of Farmville,
Custer's cavalry division cut into a Confederate wagon train and discovered
that in the process it had separated a considerable part of the enemy army
from Lee's main body. Sheridan was swift as usual to throw in his whole
Cavalry Corps and hurried up Wright's Sixth Corps. The Confederates lost
seven or eight thousand men in killed, wounded, or captured, mostly the
latter. This was about a third of what remained of the Army of Northern
Virginia, and it included two veteran corps commanders, Richard S. Ewell
and Richard H. Anderson.[59]

On April 8, Custer charged into a cache of the Confederates' meager
supplies, aboard some railroad trains filled with rations and parked at Appomattox Station on the Southside Railroad. He drove off the defenders, and
having run the cars far enough away to make sure that the Confederates
would not enjoy this sustenance, he rode on from the station toward Appomattox Court House, about three miles to the north. At nightfall he collided
with fieldworks and saw before him many campfires. He had struck the main
body of the Army of Northern Virginia. He was west of it, across its road
to Lynchburg.

Sheridan promptly joined Custer and hastened up the rest of the Cavalry Corps. But even in its final extremities, Lee's army could not be contained by cavalry alone, and Sheridan's couriers were soon summoning the
nearest infantry to march through the night and close off the only semblance
of an escape route remaining. At 5:00 the next morning, Sunday, April 9,
Gordon and Fitz Lee led Confederate infantry and cavalry forward to break
Sheridan's screen while there were still minutes in which to do it. The rebel
yell rose triumphantly one more time as butternut infantry drove Sheridan's
cavalry before them. But as Gordon's infantry wheeled left to push the Union
troopers off the projected path of Lee's army, word reached him that Federal
infantry wearing the Maltese cross badge of Griffin's Fifth Corps waited in
woods to his right and rear.

These Federal infantrymen began to emerge from the trees, more and
more of them. Thereupon reemboldened Federal cavalry moved threaten-
ingly on Gordon's left. Gordon withdrew to a defensive position. So small
were the Confederate regiments now that their red flags clustered like a field
of poppies. About 8:00 A.M., Colonel Charles S. Venable, aide de camp to
Lee, rode up to ask Gordon what was his progress. "Tell General Lee," said

Gordon, "I have fought my Corps to a frazzle, and I fear I can do nothing unless I am heavily supported by Longstreet's Corps."[60] The word from Longstreet, positioned to the east, was, however, that Meade with the Second and Sixth Corps was opening an attack on his rear guard.

Lee summoned Longstreet, his senior lieutenant since the springtime of the war and the one with whom he had always had a special relationship, to confer with him. He explained that Gordon's path was blocked and that the army seemed to have no feasible choices remaining except to offer itself for slaughter or surrender. He asked Longstreet's advice. Longstreet responded with a question of his own: in Lee's opinion, would the sacrifice of the Army of Northern Virginia help the Confederate cause elsewhere? "I think not," Lee answered. "Then your situation speaks for itself," said Longstreet. Lee's duty at last pointed to a new course.[61]

Two days earlier, on April 7, the Federal Second Corps had captured High Bridge across the Appomattox northeast of Farmville, enabling it to keep in unbroken contact with the Confederate rear guard. At this juncture Grant had decided Lee's prospects were so plainly barren that he might well address the Confederate commander:

> General: The result of the last week must convince you of the hopelessness of further resistance on the part of the Army of Northern Virginia in this struggle. I feel that it is so, and regard it as my duty to shift from myself the responsibility of any further effusion of blood by asking of you the surrender of that portion of the C. S. Army known as the Army of Northern Virginia.[62]

Lee had replied that evening that: "Though not entertaining the opinion you express of the hopelessness of further resistance on the part of the Army of Northern Virginia, I reciprocate your desire to avoid useless effusion of blood," and asked Grant's terms.[63] Further correspondence during April 8 was inconclusive, Grant reiterating that he sought the surrender of the Army of Northern Virginia, Lee stating that he did not yet feel obliged to make such a surrender, but that he wished to meet with Grant the next morning to discuss general terms of peace.

Thinking that a meeting for the latter purpose was to be held, on Sunday morning Lee departed from his interview with Longstreet to cross between the lines under a flag of truce. He met instead a note from Grant emphasizing that the Federal Commanding General did not have the authority to treat for a comprehensive peace but only for the surrender of the army immediately before him. The report from Gordon and the conversation with Longstreet convinced Lee that to this statement he must reply:

General: I received your note of this morning on the picket-line, whither I had come to meet you and ascertain definitely what terms were embraced in your proposal of yesterday with reference to the surrender of this army. I now request an interview in accordance with the offer contained in your letter of yesterday for that purpose.[64]

Lee also requested a truce to end the fighting, and he ordered his corps commanders similarly to seek an armistice on their fronts. For a time it appeared that a "further effusion of blood" might occur nevertheless, because the subordinate Federal commanders on the lines did not feel authorized to grant a truce, and they were under orders to attack promptly. Fortunately, Meade cut short his soldiers' advance before fighting resumed; and one contretemps, when the brash Custer and presently his equally brash superior, Sheridan, attempted to bully Gordon into surrendering the Army of Northern Virginia to themselves, passed because Gordon stood his ground on behalf of the negotiations between Lee and Grant.

Grant acceded to Lee's latest request for a meeting, and so the subsequently famous scene in Wilmer McLean's parlor at Appomattox Court House unfolded: Lee majestic in his best uniform; Grant by comparison stumpy, as well as dusty in a private's coat distinguished only by his three-starred shoulder straps; the opening moments of reminiscence about acquaintanceship in the Mexican War, as though both hesitated to face the business that must be so painful to Lee; Grant's writing out in pencil the terms providing for the surrender of Lee's Army of Northern Virginia, with officers and men to be paroled, the officers to retain their side arms and private horses and baggage; Lee's reminding Grant that in the Confederate Army, cavalrymen and artillerymen owned their horses, so that Grant agreed informally that men claiming to own horses and mules might take the animals home with them; Grant learning that Lee's army had been living for several days mainly on parched corn and offering to send 25,000 rations across the lines.

Then Lee returned to his troops, was thronged by admiring, often weeping soldiers, and the next day composed his formal message of farewell to the Army of Northern Virginia. In the days that followed, officers visited old friends across the lines, and on April 12 Lee's army marched out to stack arms and battleflags, the initial part of it before a detachment of the Fifth Corps. Brigadier-General Joshua Lawrence Chamberlain, U.S.V., who as colonel of the 20th Maine had held the extreme left of the Army of the Potomac on Little Round Top on July 2, 1863, now commanded the special detachment. When he had learned of this assignment on the evening of

April 9, he had requested transfer from command of the First Brigade, First Division, Fifth Corps to the Third Brigade, his old regiment's brigade of which the 20th Maine was still a part. General Griffin granted the request. Chamberlain then arranged for the entire First Division to be present for the ceremony, the First Brigade to be a little behind the Third, the Second Brigade opposite it.

He had also determined upon a gesture of respect from the Army of the Potomac to the Army of Northern Virginia, and he issued instructions to the regimental commanders before the ceremony. General Gordon rode toward Chamberlain's detachment at the head of the Confederate column, his head bowed in gloom. When Gordon came up to the right of the Third Brigade, a Union bugle sounded, ordering Chamberlain's soldiers to raise muskets to the carry, the marching salute. Gordon immediately took the meaning, lifted his head, turned toward the Third Brigade, and dropped his sword point to the toe of his boot in the return salute. He also ordered his own troops to raise muskets to the carry, so that the two rival armies formally parted from each other's company with a mutual expression of honor.

Twenty-eight thousand, two hundred thirty-one Confederate soldiers surrendered and were paroled. By the time of the stacking of Confederate arms and battleflags, Grant, Meade, and Sheridan had departed, in no way making the surrender a personal triumph for themselves. Lee did not witness the surrender of the arms, but he waited until the ceremony was over before going home.[65]

## RICHMOND AND REUNION

Grant's determination to spare no effort to destroy Lee's army once Petersburg and Richmond had fallen, and the accomplishment of that grim mission, had kept the soldiers of the Army of the Potomac for the time being from achieving their secondary goal of four years of war, entry into Richmond. Troops from the Army of the James began to find their way into the burning city during the night following the Confederate evacuation. The first United States flags to fly again over the Capitol were the guidons of Companies E and H of the 4th Massachusetts Cavalry. General Weitzel, commanding the Twenty-fifth Corps and the occupation force, arrived to receive the formal surrender of civic and military officials at the City Hall at 8:15 in the morning. Meanwhile Weitzel had set his troops to extinguishing fires and restoring order. Many of the first occupiers of the city were African-

American troops — the Twenty-fifth was a black corps — which accentuated the joyfulness of the welcome from the African-American population and the glum silence of most white inhabitants.[66]

Close on the heels of the first Union soldiers came Abraham Lincoln. In March, Lincoln had responded to an invitation from Grant to visit Army headquarters, glad for a respite from the Washington routine and aware enough of Grant's plans to know he might be present for the climax of the war. Steaming from Washington on the *River Queen* on March 23, Lincoln made the ship his home until April 9, one of the first instances of a President's establishing in effect a temporary White House and keeping in touch with the business of government in Washington by telegraph.

On April 3, Lincoln accepted another invitation from Grant, to visit him in the streets of occupied Petersburg, whence he returned to City Point to find a telegram from Stanton warning him not to visit Petersburg because of the danger from rebel assassins. Blandly, Lincoln not only informed Stanton that he had already been in Petersburg, but the next day he went with the smallest of escorts to Richmond itself. Admiral Porter's flagship, the *Malvern*, accompanied by the *River Queen* and the *Bat*, took him up the James to where the river was obstructed several miles above Drewry's Bluff, and from there he traveled by Admiral Porter's twelve-oared barge to the wharf at Rockett's. Along with his twelve-year-old son Thomas (Tad), a contraband guide, Admiral Porter, three other officers, and ten armed sailors, he walked up Shockoe Hill to the center of the city. Naturally, many of the city's African Americans crowded enthusiastically around him. There were also whites on the streets, some of them drunk and in an ugly mood, and fires still burned in various places.[67]

Nevertheless, no assassin marred the President's visit, and Lincoln rested for a time in the house on the southeast corner of North Twelfth and East Clay Streets that until two days before had been the Executive Mansion of the Confederacy. There he received the Confederate Assistant Secretary of War, recent peace commissioner, and one-time intermediary for negotiations with Secretary Seward on the Fort Sumter question, John A. Campbell. Campbell said it was obvious that the war was over and the country must be recomposed. He particularly urged Lincoln to consult with the public men of Virginia to restore order in that Commonwealth and bring it back to its normal relations with the Union. Lincoln was sufficiently interested in Campbell's ideas about peace that, after spending the night on the *Malvern*, he conferred with Campbell again the next day. According to Campbell, Lincoln spoke of wanting the Virginia legislature to meet. Most probably,

Lincoln did express a willingness to have the General Assembly come together for a strictly limited purpose, for from City Point on April 6 he wrote to General Weitzel:

> It has been intimated to me that the gentlemen who have acted as the Legislature of Virginia, in support of the rebellion, may now desire to assemble at Richmond, and take measures to withdraw the Virginia troops, and other support from resistance to the General government. If they attempt it, give them permission and protection, until, if at all, they attempt some action hostile to the United States, in which case you will notify them and give them reasonable time to leave; & at the end of which time, arrest any who may remain. Allow Judge Campbell to see this, but do not make it public.[68]

Despite reading the letter, Campbell did not have in mind a meeting of the Confederate legislature of Virginia merely to withdraw the Virginia troops and other support from the Confederate government, and his account of Lincoln's words at the Richmond meetings and during the next few days suggest that Lincoln himself might not have been sure how much he wanted to limit "the gentlemen who have acted as the Legislature of Virginia, in support of the rebellion." On April 7, Campbell met with five members of the legislature in question and discussed with them reconvening for the considerably larger purpose of negotiating with Washington about the terms of Virginia's reentry into the Union, giving the impression that such negotiation was what Lincoln envisaged. Campbell urged General Weitzel that the South Carolina General Assembly ought to be allowed to gather for a similar purpose. By this date, Lincoln was remarking to Assistant Secretary of War Charles A. Dana "that Sheridan seemed to be getting Virginia soldiers out of the war, faster than this Legislature could think."[69] But Lincoln continued to contemplate a session of the Virginia General Assembly nevertheless, for on April 11 he discussed the idea with the Cabinet — and by that date Sheridan, Grant, and Meade had certainly got Virginia soldiers out of the war faster than the Virginia legislature could think.

The Cabinet did not react with enthusiasm. Stanton and Attorney General James Speed especially disliked the notion of bringing together a Confederate state legislature. When Lincoln talked privately with Welles on April 12 and 13, the Secretary of the Navy, a barometer of conservatism in the Cabinet, also expressed doubt. Welles feared that the rebel legislature might still find ways to cause trouble; Lincoln thought the South was too badly beaten for that. The President wanted a temporary authority to conduct the Southern people through the transition from war to peace.

Civil government must be reëstablished, he said [according to Welles], as soon as possible; there must be courts, and law, and order, or society would be broken up, the disbanded armies would turn into robber bands and guerrillas, which we must strive to prevent. These were the reasons why he wished prominent Virginians who had the confidence of the people to come together and turn themselves and their neighbors into good Union men.[70]

Thus Welles, like Campbell, received the impression that Lincoln had in mind a wider purpose than the withdrawal of Virginia troops. It may be that such negotiation with the Virginia legislators and other prominent Southern leaders as Campbell proposed would have proven a more effective method of commencing reconstruction than any method actually attempted. The South might have been more amenable to social changes to which its established political leaders agreed in negotiation than to changes that the Washington government attempted to impose simply by fiat. If the negotiations clearly would have been conducted under duress, the South might nevertheless have been more acquiescent to terms imposed at the time of its most severe consciousness of defeat than it was to Congressional reconstruction imposed much later, after Andrew Johnson's lenient reconstruction program led Southerners to assume that little change was expected of them.

In fact, however, at the time when Lee surrendered, President Lincoln was still groping his way toward a postwar reconstruction program, and the Washington government itself scarcely knew what it wanted of the South. This Lincoln demonstrated by reversing himself on the assembly of the Virginia legislature, and doing so on the ground that he had never considered their attempting anything more than taking Virginia out of the war. On April 12 he telegraphed Weitzel that he observed that Campbell was bringing the Virginia legislature together "as the rightful Legislature of the State, to settle all differences with the United States." But his own intent, said Lincoln in contradiction of some of his other words and actions, was to call the men who had acted as the Virginia legislature only with the specific purpose of withdrawing Virginia troops and other support from the Confederacy. Therefore the President ordered Weitzel not to allow the legislators to assemble.[71]

Lincoln apparently intended to reconstruct the Union on a foundation of generous welcome to the returning Southern white people, with secondary consideration for the advancement of African Americans from the shackles of slavery beyond simple legal freedom. He had already offered in his Second Inaugural his eloquent plea for peace with "malice toward none; with charity for all."[72] The night before he sent his instructions to Weitzel not to allow the Virginia legislators to assemble, he had delivered what was to prove his last public address, to a crowd gathered outside the White House "in gladness of heart" over Lee's surrender two days before. On this occasion he urged the prompt recognition of the Louisiana government established under his 10-percent plan and the extension of the plan to other states — although the need for a means to subvert the Confederate state governments was now gone, and the need for a long-range program of reconstruction had arrived.[73]

On Good Friday, April 14, at midday, Lincoln and the Cabinet considered reconstruction again. Frederick Seward, sitting in for his father, who had been injured in a carriage accident, said that "kindly feelings toward the vanquished, and hearty desire to restore peace and safety at the South, with as little harm as possible to the feelings or the property of the inhabitants pervaded the whole discussion."[74] On the other hand, Lincoln said that he had made a mistake in inviting a meeting of the Virginia legislature, and while suggesting modifications in detail he did not repudiate a proposal presented by Stanton and providing for military occupation as the first step toward reorganizing the Southern states. Stanton's plan emphasized the restoration of Federal authority "without any necessity whatever for the intervention of rebel organization or rebel aid."[75] Lincoln's apparent friendliness toward it encouraged Attorney General Speed to hope that the undecided President was veering in the direction of the Radicals. "He never seemed so near our views," Speed told Salmon P. Chase.[76] Yet Lincoln also stated that he was glad Congress was not in session, so that he could proceed with the reestablishment of Federal authority in the South and the recognition of state governments on his own initiative. Later in the day he told Speaker of the House Schuyler Colfax that he would not call Congress into special session before its scheduled meeting in December.[77]

## DURHAM STATION

Lincoln's contemplation of the idea of negotiating with Confederate officials, at least with members of the state governments of the Confederacy, contributed to a dramatic train of events before his change of mind became generally known. Lincoln's presence at City Point when Sherman came up from Goldsboro to visit Grant led to two conferences on the *River Queen*, on March 27 and 28, bringing the President together with his two most important military commanders. Both generals expressed their confidence that the campaigns about to open would complete the defeat of the Confederate armies, and this discussion led Sherman to inquire "of the President if he was all ready for the end of the war. What was to be done with the rebel armies when defeated? And what should be done with the political leaders, such as Jeff. Davis, etc.?"[78] According to Sherman in his memoirs, Lincoln intimated that he would prefer that Davis escape the country, "'unbeknownst' to him," and he stated more directly:

> that in his mind he was all ready for the civil reorganization of affairs at the South as soon as the war was over; and he distinctly authorized me to assure Governor Vance and the people of North Carolina that, as soon as the rebel armies laid down their arms, and resumed their civil pursuits, they would at once be guaranteed all their rights as citizens of a common country; and that to avoid anarchy the State governments then in existence, with their civil functionaries, would be recognized by him as the government *de facto* till Congress could provide others.[79]

Admiral Porter, who was present at one of Lincoln's conferences with Sherman, confirmed this account and went further. He held that Lincoln was concerned lest Johnston's army escape Sherman's grasp, and while Sherman assured him it could not do so, urged Sherman to accept the surrender of Johnston's army on any terms rather than risk its escape.[80] Porter was inclined toward the dramatic and was not an altogether reliable witness. Furthermore, his and Sherman's accounts do not square with even the most sweeping of other versions of Lincoln's intentions toward the Confederate state governments. Still, the evident uncertainty of Lincoln's intentions toward the white South and his inclination to be generous make it not unlikely that Sherman received at least the overall impression he said he did.

Sherman returned to North Carolina and resumed his march northward, at first feinting toward Raleigh but actually intending to interpose between Lee's and Johnston's armies so they could not unite. When he received word of Lee's surrender, he changed his objective, to capture Raleigh in fact and to block all possibility of Johnston's escaping southward. About that time, naturally, Johnston also heard of Lee's surrender, and he came under conflicting pressures regarding his own subsequent course. President Davis himself arrived in the neighborhood and, as dedicated to duty as ever, insisted Johnston must fight on and spoke of raising new armies. Governor Vance and other North Carolina leaders meanwhile urged Johnston to surrender, Vance in fact making his own contacts with Sherman to try to spare the state. Believing the South beaten, Sherman responded to Vance's emissaries sympathetically and forbade property destruction in Raleigh. When Sherman put his mind to it, he proved able to curb the maraudings of his soldiers with remarkable dispatch, despite his claims that many of the earlier depredations were unauthorized.

Sherman's conciliatory attitude encouraged Johnston's own belief that he ought to surrender. He told Davis that the only feasible task remaining for the Confederate government was to make peace. When Davis replied that the United States would not treat with the President of the Confederacy, Johnston observed that consequently Davis should authorize him to arrange a military convention as the first step toward a general peace. Davis acquiesced, writing a letter for Johnston's signature to propose a meeting with Sherman to arrange an armistice so that the civil authorities might agree on terms of peace.

Sherman agreed, although by accepting a meeting on such terms he was coming dangerously close to including political matters within his purview. Earlier, before Appomattox, Stanton had expressly forbidden Grant to respond affirmatively to an overture from Lee that might involve discussion of civil questions and a general settlement. Grant, said Stanton on March 3, was to hold no conference with the enemy except for his capitulation or for minor purely military matters. Unfortunately, no copy of this directive to Grant was sent to Sherman.[81] Sherman of course was aware of the general boundaries between political and military affairs and of the limits of military authority, but he was given to impulsiveness, and the Lincoln administration had encouraged rather than interfered with his earlier efforts to deal on a limited scale with Confederate state authorities, such as his attempt to persuade Governor Brown to remove Georgia from the war. Furthermore, Grant's own terms at Appomattox had encroached upon policy by widening the scope of amnesty to include everyone in the Army of Northern Virginia; while Lincoln's amnesty proclamation of December 8, 1863 had excluded officers above the rank of colonel and anyone who had resigned from Congress or the Army or the Navy to participate in the rebellion.

When Sherman met Johnston near Durham Station on April 17, the Union general began by saying that he offered such terms as Grant had given Lee. Johnston refused, saying that his army was not in the desperate condition of Lee's. He and Sherman went on to discuss possible terms nevertheless, and both referred to the danger that the remaining Confederate armies might simply scatter and their members go over to waging guerrilla war. Sherman then and later confessed that he feared such an outcome, and his account of the meeting suggests that it was a combination of fear of brutal guerrilla war and recollection of Lincoln's attitudes expressed on the *River Queen* that made him receptive when Johnston went on to suggest that he could suspend hostilities on behalf of all the remaining Confederate armies.

Sherman agreed to meet the next day not only with Johnston but with Secretary of War Breckinridge as well, the presence of the latter obviously a key to the possibility of making peace with all the Confederate armies. Johnston pointed out that Sherman's objection to dealing with a Confederate civil officer could be evaded by having Breckinridge present in his capacity as a Confederate major-general. Sherman was now fully in the mood to share his last cracker. He believed that "[t]he South is broken and ruined and appeals to our pity. To ride the people down with persecutions and military exactions would be like slashing away at the crew of a sinking ship."[82] He had heard of Lincoln's willingness to let the Virginia legislature assemble, but not of the reversal of this policy.

Sherman thus wrote out for Johnston and Breckinridge a proposal for the contending armies to agree to a truce maintaining the status quo, which might be broken on forty-eight hours' notice from either side, and with additional terms to be completed if both governments agreed: the Confederate armies to be disbanded and conducted to their state capitals, where they would deposit their arms in the state arsenals; the President of the United States to recognize the Southern state governments once their officers had taken the oaths prescribed by the United States Constitution, conflicting claims to legitimacy to be resolved by the U.S. Supreme Court; the people of all states to be guaranteed their political rights and franchises and their rights of person and property; a general amnesty for all who remained henceforth in peace and quiet. Nothing was said about excepting slavery from the property rights to be guaranteed, but Sherman's later position was that he and Johnston took it for granted that slavery was extinct. Johnston accepted these terms, and he and Sherman signed the document Sherman had prepared.

It was clear that except for the truce, the terms could not go into effect until approved by the U.S. government, although that government came to regard it as one of Sherman's trespasses that he also acknowledged a need for approval by the Confederate States government. When Sherman's transmission of the agreement, with his enthusiastic endorsement, reached the War Department in Washington, Secretary Stanton exploded. Sherman had guaranteed more generous peace terms than Stanton thought tolerable, but much worse, he had encroached deeply upon the domain of policy-making. Stanton characteristically allowed his private explosive anger to shape his public response. He not only repudiated Sherman's agreement, so informed other generals, and sent Grant to North Carolina to overrule Sherman, all of which was proper; but he also published Sherman's terms along with a statement implying that Sherman had proven false to his trust and was somehow conniving in the escape of Jefferson Davis from Federal capture with a large amount of specie.

The Secretary's action opened what was to become a notorious feud between him and Sherman. When Halleck dispatched orders to the Army of the Potomac and the Army of the James to begin advancing against Johnston before the Confederates could be informed of the repudiation of the truce, Sherman took the orders as an insult, so a feud between Halleck and Sherman also commenced. Fortunately, the Union troops from Virginia did not make hostile contact with Johnston, and thus no worse harm was done.

At least, Stanton's sending Grant to Sherman headed off the eruption of still further disputes and animosities. Grant instructed Sherman to give Johnston the required notice of the cancellation of the truce, informing Johnston that the terms Grant had offered to Lee were still available to him. On April 26, Sherman met again with Johnston at Durham Station, Grant sparing Sherman the humiliation of accompanying him. Johnston had been weakened by desertions since the truce went into effect, and he now believed he had no choice but to accept the Appomattox terms for about 25,000 officers and men remaining in his command.[83] Restricted to Johnston's immediate force, the surrender extended not to the Rio Grande as first contemplated, but only to the Chattahoochee.

## THE TERRIBLE ASSASSINATION, AND THE TERRIBLE WAR

One of the reasons why Sherman feared guerrilla war when he first conferred with Johnston was that on the way to the meeting he received news suggesting the Confederates might resort to a campaign of murder and other irregular violence. The news was that President Lincoln had been assassinated at Ford's Theater in Washington on Good Friday evening, April 14. Sherman, of course, was to believe that if Lincoln had lived, the reception accorded his first agreement with Johnston would have been different. Similarly, when John A. Campbell heard of the cancellation of the invitation to the Virginia legislature to assemble, he sought to travel to Washington to appeal to Lincoln in another personal meeting; but the telegram requesting the meeting was sent from Richmond on the evening of April 14, and it was too late.[84]

Certainly it is futile to speculate further about what Lincoln's subsequent reconstruction policies might have been. The 10-percent plan had been a wartime policy designed to undermine allegiance to the Confederacy, and Lincoln more than once reiterated that he was not committed to it as a postwar reconstruction plan; yet toward the end he sometimes seemed to be returning to it. At the least, the last days of Lincoln's life saw him vacillating about reconstruction, so that he encouraged the hopes of both a Confederate such as Campbell and a Republican Radical such as James Speed. The principal tendency of his thinking may indeed have been grasped accurately by Sherman, who wrote:

> I know, when I left him, that I was more than ever impressed by his kindly nature, his deep and earnest sympathy with the afflictions of the whole people, resulting from the war, and by the march of the hostile armies through the South; and that his earnest desire seemed to be to end the war speedily, without more bloodshed or devastation, and to restore all the men of both sections to their homes.[85]

This assessment means, however, that Lincoln felt at least as much sympathy for the concerns of white Americans, including white Southerners, as of blacks.

It was yet another horror piled upon a superfluity of horrors that the war should have ended with the President's assassination. The North's rejoicing in the warm and green spring over Lee's surrender on Palm Sunday gave way abruptly on Good Friday to mourning, and bonfires and illuminations to black crepe. But the horror of the assassination was symbolically fitting. It underlined the true nature of the Civil War as stark tragedy.

The recitation of casualty statistics barely begins to suggest the dimensions of the tragedy, but the beginning must be made. The Union armies lost some 360,222 dead, including 110,100 battle deaths and the remainder mostly from disease and in prison camps. Union Navy deaths were 1,804 in battle and some 3,000 from other causes. The Confederate armed forces lost some 258,000 dead, including 94,000 battle deaths. Total Federal casualties, Army, Navy, and Marine Corps, amounted to 642,427. Total casualties for the war were at least 1,094,453. The nearest approach to this total casualty figure in any other American war occurred in World War II, with 1,078,162 American casualties, and 407,316 deaths compared with at least 623,026 deaths in the Civil War. The population of the United States during World War II was more than four times that of the 1860s. Some 12 million Americans served in the World War II armed forces; the Civil War casualties were suffered by a total of some 3¼ million men in the Civil War armed forces.[86]

For all the costs, nevertheless, there may well be wisdom in the apparent common judgment of most Americans of the North, and in time of many Americans of the South as well, that the outcome of the Civil War somehow redeemed the costs. The Civil War never spawned the disillusionment that followed American participation in the First World War. The Civil War never generated anything approaching the popular revulsion against the Vietnam War. In American national memory, the Civil War stands with the Second World War as a conflict that was worth fighting, although these two accepted and applauded wars were also our costliest.

In spite of the limitations of the positive results issuing from the Civil War, furthermore, it thus ranks with the Second World War in favorable national memory for ample reason. Just as the outcome of World War II, the destruction of Adolf Hitler's satanic empire and of the brutal Japanese aggression allied with it as threats to all of humane civilization, came to be attainable only through war, so also the elimination of slavery in the United States as an embodiment of evil may have been unattainable except by paying the toll of war. It remains difficult to conjecture a pattern of events that could have caused the South to abandon slavery without war. If we nevertheless conjecture that world opinion would have compelled the abandonment of slavery by sometime in the first half of the twentieth century, how can we balance several decades more of slavery for millions against the costs of the war? And if the emancipation of the slaves fell sadly short of the elevation of African Americans to full U.S. citizenship and to full equality with white Americans, yet it was the indispensable foundation for the attainment of those still-sought-after goals.

If the liberation of African Americans might have been achieved in no way except through war, if almost certainly without the war slavery would have endured through several decades more, then the Civil War calls for a rethinking of the attitude toward war that has become widespread, even predominant, in the United States since the Vietnam War: the belief that war is always futile, that its rewards never match its cost, that any conflict that is accepted at all must assuredly be briefly, immediately decisive and virtually without loss of American lives. Neither side would have gone to war in 1861 had there existed then the refusal to accept American risks of death or injury in battle that appears to prevail in the mid-1990s. Neither side would have gone to war had there existed the current insistence that America must never fight unless it is certain of victory beforehand.

Which does not imply that our generation is so much wiser or more civilized than the generation that initiated the great war of 1861–1865 for the destiny of America. To balance the loss in war of over 600,000 largely white American lives against the gain of freedom for nearly 4 million slaves requires a higher than human capacity to weigh conflicting values. Still, the liberating of so many, and of their descendants, along with the preservation of the American experiment in democracy, may well appear to our rough human calculations as gains not falling short after all of justification for the terrible price of the Civil War.

## THE SUDDEN DEATH OF THE CONFEDERACY

Scattered as the remaining Confederate military strength was after Lee's and Johnston's surrenders, the Federals were able to snap it up readily by bits and pieces.

When Grant began his last campaign, General Wilson, recently Thomas's cavalry chieftain at Nashville and still commanding the Cavalry Corps, Military Division of the Mississippi, was leading a strong cavalry force of three divisions toward the principal remaining enemy munitions center, around Selma, Alabama. Beating back numerically inferior forces under the once redoubtable Nathan Bedford Forrest (from February 28 a lieutenant-general), Wilson captured Selma on April 2 and then moved on to Montgomery, to Columbus, Georgia, and to Macon.[87] Meanwhile Major-General, U.S.V., Edward R. S. Canby's troops of the Military Division of West Mississippi were pressing against the defenses of Mobile, the last major Confederate city, and they entered the place on April 12. Lieutenant-General Richard Taylor, commanding the Confederate Department of Alabama, Mississippi, and East Louisiana, abandoned hope and arranged a truce with Canby on April 30, which he followed up with a formal surrender on May 4 after he heard of Johnston's capitulation. Forrest's troops were included.[88]

Some of Kirby Smith's subordinates in the Trans-Mississippi urged him to keep up the fight in his remote domain, but Smith could see no point in it. On May 26, Lieutenant-General Simon Bolivar Buckner, who had surrendered unconditionally to U. S. Grant at Fort Donelson, acted for Smith to surrender the last Confederate army of any consequence, arranging terms at New Orleans with Peter J. Osterhaus, whom we met long ago at Pea Ridge.[89] Some of the Trans-Mississippi Confederates, feeling far from Federal power, refused to accept the capitulation, notably Brigadier-General Joseph O. "Jo" Shelby, who led his cavalry brigade into Mexico to continue the trade of fighting by taking up the cause of the Emperor Maximilian.[90]

Jefferson Davis continued his flight from Federal arms and his quest for supporters who would interpret duty as he did, until troopers of the 1st Wisconsin Cavalry and 4th Michigan Cavalry detached by General Wilson for this purpose surprised his camp near Irwinsville, Georgia on the morning of May 10. Mrs. Davis was with him. The Confederate President was taken to Fort Monroe, where for a time he was imprisoned in chains. He was never brought to trial, and on May 11, 1867, he was released and allowed to live out the rest of his life undisturbed.[91] Several other Confederate civil leaders were imprisoned for shorter periods, including Vice President Stephens.[92] Major Henry Wirz, the commandant at Andersonville prison, was arrested, brought to trial before a military commission on criminal charges growing out of his management of the prison, convicted, and hanged on November 10, 1865. He was the only person to be executed by judicial decree for his part in the rebellion.[93]

The Confederate banner last flew defiantly at sea. Most of the commerce raiders were long since gone. The *Florida* had been captured on October 7, 1864, when Captain Napoleon Collins of the screw sloop U.S.S. *Wachusett* ignored international law and attacked and seized her in the harbor of Bahía, Brazil. The consequent Brazilian outcry led Secretary Seward to agree that she should have been returned to Brazil, but by that time most regrettable and conspicuous carelessness by Federal officers concerned about the possibility of having to yield their prize had involved the ship in a collision in Hampton Roads on November 19. Consequently she sank on November 28.[94]

That event left of the raiders only the C.S.S. *Shenandoah*, purchased in England in September 1864, equipped and commissioned in the Madeiras, and roaming among the Caroline Islands in the distant Pacific capturing Yankee whalers at the time of Lee's last campaign. The *Shenandoah* took eleven whalers in the Bering Sea as late as June 28. Not until August 2 did Lieutenant Commanding James Waddell learn that the war was over, when he met the British bark *Barracouta* on his way from the Arctic toward San Francisco. He then sailed for Liverpool by way of Cape Horn, surrendering his ship to the British authorities on November 6.[95]

On the same day that Jefferson Davis was captured, President Andrew Johnson proclaimed that "armed resistance to the authority of this Government in the said insurrectionary States may be regarded as virtually at an end."[96] Only a month and a day had passed since Lee's surrender at Appomattox. One of the puzzles of the Civil War is why the Confederacy collapsed so rapidly and so completely. The whole history of nationalist movements in the modern world suggests that nationalism is almost impossible to suppress by force of arms, as the then-still-powerful Russian and Turkish Empires could not permanently suppress the nationalism of small Balkan peoples in the early nineteenth century, and France with all the technology of late-twentieth-century war could not suppress Algerian nationalism in the 1950s. Yet the Confederacy collapsed so fully in the spring of 1865 that the

American Civil War in retrospect seems notable, compared with other modern wars for the elimination of a national independence movement, not for the difficulty of the North's defeat of the South but for its relative ease. Applying this standard casts doubt on whether the Confederacy represented a true nationalist movement. It is not to deny the stubbornness of Southern fighting at Gettysburg and Chickamauga and more than a hundred other fields to call attention to the abrupt deflation at Appomattox and Durham Station.

Just after Lee talked to Longstreet about going to meet Grant on the morning of April 9, Edward Porter Alexander, brigadier-general and First Corps Chief of Artillery since February 26, 1864, proposed to Lee that rather than surrender, the soldiers should take to the woods and eventually report to the governors of their states. The soldiers would become guerrillas. Then the states could go on resisting until each state could make an honorable peace.

"If I should take your advice," Lee asked Alexander, "how many men do you suppose would get away?"

"Two-thirds of us. We would be like rabbits and partridges in the bushes and they could not scatter us."

Lee thought such resistance would still be futile.

> Then, General [he also went on], you and I as Christian men have no right to consider only how this would affect us. We must consider its effect on the country as a whole. If I took your advice, the men would be without rations and under no control of officers. They would be compelled to rob and steal in order to live. They would become mere bands of marauders, and the enemy's cavalry would pursue them and overrun many sections they may never have occasion to visit. We would bring on a state of affairs it would take the country years to recover from. And, as for myself, you young fellows might go on bushwhacking, but the only dignified course for me would be to go to General Grant and surrender myself and take the consequences of my acts."

"I had not a single word to say in reply," Alexander wrote later. "He had answered my suggestion from a plane so far above it, that I was ashamed of having made it."[97]

Thus Lee led his army away from guerrilla war. But if to do so was the only dignified course for Lee himself, it remains less easy to explain why nearly all the other warriors of the Confederacy also abandoned so readily the alternative of the kind of war that has become the customary recourse of nationalist movements unwilling to die but unable to compete with their enemies in regular war, and that parts of the Confederacy, particularly the

Carolinas, had themselves invoked against British arms in the course of the American Revolution.

It may be that Confederate nationalism died so abruptly and so completely because it was never a true nationalism, that the fatal split in the Confederate psyche prevented the national spirit from ever flowering fully enough to nourish a resolve that would have persevered in the contest after all the romance was gone. All the more tragic was a war fought with so much bloodshed around a flag whose opponents did not really want to pull it down.

Yet without the war, who could have destroyed American slavery? How could the United States have rededicated itself to the attainment of human equality, in an ever-growing vision of the meaning of equality?

The Great Valley of the eastern United States marches in a wide arc from southwest to northeast, from Virginia to New Jersey. Their shared possession of it had been among the reasons why during the American Revolution and well into the nineteenth century, the Middle States seemed to constitute a unified bloc, until the slavery issue pulled Virginia into the orbit of the more southerly slave states and propelled the others toward New York and the New England Yankees of whom they had not always felt overly fond.

The artificial divisions created within the geographic unity of the Great Valley were of course especially evident in the spring of 1865. The Shenandoah Valley of Virginia was barely beginning to recover from the devastation wrought by Phil Sheridan the autumn before. It was not so, however, farther north and east. Above the Potomac, though some property damage marking Lee's invasion paths remained evident from the Catoctin Mountains across South Mountain to the Sharpsburg area of Maryland, and in the Cumberland Valley of Pennsylvania, and especially east of South Mountain around Gettysburg — and although compensation claims upon governments would drag on for years — mostly the apple orchards were blossoming fully again, the winter wheat was ripening, and livestock grazed behind restored fences. Some names on the land had changed: the Rohrbach Bridge over Antietam Creek below Sharpsburg was more and more often called Burnside's Bridge, and the two most prominent hills south of Cemetery Hill near Gettysburg were now fixed in nomenclature as Little Round Top and Big Round Top. These alterations did not affect the land itself.

Eastward still and across the Susquehanna, where the Great Valley becomes the Lebanon Valley, and then borders the middle reaches of the Schuylkill before changing its local name again to be the Lehigh Valley, and after that crossing the Delaware below its Water Gap in the Kittatiny Range and rolling on across New Jersey toward New York City — through all this latter region everything looked much as it had in 1861. Even there, though, much that was not visible had changed. Isaac Weigley still enjoyed the plentiful harvests of the limestone-enriched soil of Lebanon County, Pennsylvania; but since the previous September the letters from his son Francis in the distant Army of the Cumberland — with which this book began — had no longer arrived.

Francis Weigley of Company A, 7th Pennsylvania Cavalry, had been captured at Lovejoy Station, Georgia, some twelve miles south of Atlanta, at the beginning of September 1864, just as Atlanta was being evacuated by the Confederates and occupied by the Federals. He died in a Confederate prison camp, perhaps Camp Sumter at Andersonville, perhaps at Florence, South Carolina.

His youngest brother, Jacob, who had written to him about the sightseeing trip to Gettysburg in July 1863, was to name his own first son Francis in the cavalry soldier's honor. The first son of that Francis, Frank, in turn married a Rohrbach, a name much in evidence around the Antietam battlefield; but the Rohrbachs had come from several German and Swiss sources and were scattered through much of the Middle States; and this Rohrbach, Meta, came from the hills on the northern edge of the Oley Valley of Berks County, Pennsylvania, yet another subsection of the Great Valley. Frank's and Meta's son wrote this book, with which these events therefore have much to do.

Throughout his boyhood he often heard how Harriet Boyer Weigley, Isaac's wife and the mother of Francis and Jacob, never stopped grieving over the loss. She believed Francis had died of starvation, an idea she found particularly unsupportable when she contrasted it with the abundance that came to the family of Isaac Weigley in their solid brick house at Richland, from whence her husband went to operate the locally renowned eponymous grist mill of Millbach two miles away. For Harriet, like so many others, the war would never end.[98]

# Notes

**INTRODUCTION**

1. France [Francis Adam] Weigley, [Private,] Com. A, 7. Penn Ca Reg, Whinchester [sic], Tennessee, Camp near Salum [sic], July 25, 1863, to My Dear Brother, Jacob Weigley, Richland Station, Lebanon County, Pa., author's collection.

2. William A. Frassanito discusses the dating of the opening of the General Hospital at Camp Letterman northeast of Gettysburg to replace scattered, more temporary hospitals in his *Early Photography at Gettysburg* (Gettysburg, PA 17325: Thomas Publications, 1995), pp. 355–60. He concludes, p. 360, that the site had been selected and preparations there begun by, or slightly before, July 16, that it was ready for patients on July 22, and that it probably received its first patients July 23. He had earlier reached essentially the same conclusion, that Camp Letterman received its first patients "by and possibly slightly prior to July 23," in William A. Frassanito, *Gettysburg: A Journey in Time* (New York: Charles Scribner's Sons, 1975), p. 37. The larger medical history of the war is not within the scope of the present military and political study but merits careful attention for the advances made toward the modern hospital, in anesthesiology, in the organization of emergency care, and in the rise of the nursing profession. For the military organizational history, see Mary C. Gillett, *The Army Medical Department. 1818–1865* (Army Historical Series, Washington, D.C.: Center of Military History United States Army, 1987). For a greater wartime killer than bullets and shells, see Paul E. Steiner, *Disease in the Civil War: Natural Biological Warfare in 1861–1865* (Philadelphia: Whitmore Publishing Company, 1968). William Quentin Maxwell, *Lincoln's Fifth Wheel: The Political History of the United States Sanitary Commission* (New York, London, Toronto: Longmans, Green & Co., 1956) concerns an indispensable volunteer movement supplementing the Union Army Medical Department. Two specialized studies are Horace H. Cunningham, *Field Medical Services at the Battle of Manassas (Bull Run)* (Athens: University of Georgia Press, 1968; reprint, Baltimore: Butternut and Blue, n.d.), and Glenna R. Schroeder-Lein, *Confederate Hospitals on the Move: Samuel H. Stout and the Army of Tennessee* (Columbia: University of South Carolina Press, 1994). The standard overviews are George Worthington Adams, *Doctors in Blue: The Medical History of the Union Army in the Civil War* (Baton Rouge: Louisiana State University Press, 1952; Baton Rouge and London: Louisiana State University Press, 1980), and Horace H. Cunningham, *Doctors in Gray: The Confederate Medical Service* (Baton Rouge and London: Louisiana State University Press, 1958, 1986).

3. Kenneth P. Williams, *Lincoln Finds a General: A Military Study of the Civil War* (5 vols., New York: The Macmillan Company, 1950–1959), II (1950), 693. Frassanito points out, however, that some of the place names did not become fixed until after the battle; see his discussions of Big Round Top, *Early Photography*, pp. 243, 245; Little Round Top, ibid., pp. 245–46, and Devil's Den, ibid., pp. 266–68.

4. Writers' program, Pennsylvania, *Pennsylvania: A Guide to the Keystone State*, Compiled by workers of the Writers' Program of the Work Projects Administration in the State of Pennsylvania, *American Guide Series* (Co-sponsored by the Pennsylvania

Historical Commission and the University of Pennsylvania, New York: Oxford University Press, 1940), p. 228.

5. Kent Gramm, *Gettysburg: A Meditation on War and Values* (Bloomington, Indianapolis: Indiana University Press, 1994), p. 90.

6. This discussion of the nature of national mythology is based on Richard Slotkin's works *Regeneration Through Violence: The Mythology of the American Frontier, 1600–1860* (Middletown, Connecticut: Wesleyan University Press, 1973), especially Chapter 1, "Myth and Literature in a New World," pp. 3–24; *The Fatal Environment: The Myth of the Frontier in the Age of Industrialization, 1800–1900* (Middletown, Connecticut: Wesleyan University Press, 1985), especially Chapter 2, "Myth and Historical Memory," pp. 13–32; and *Gunfighter Nation: The Myth of the Frontier in Twentieth-Century America* (New York: Atheneum; Toronto: Maxwell Macmillan Canada; New York, Oxford, Singapore, Sydney: Maxwell Macmillan International, 1992), especially "Introduction: The Significance of the Frontier Myth in American History," pp. 1–26.

7. Everette B. Long's estimates are 642,427 total Federal casualties and 378,026 to 383,026 total Confederate casualties; E. B. Long with Barbara Long, *The Civil War Day by Day: An Almanac 1861–1865*, Foreword by Bruce Catton (Garden City, New York: Doubleday & Company, Inc., 1971), p. 711. These figures include 67,088 died in battle and 43,012 mortally wounded, 275,175 wounded, 234,580 died of disease, and the remaining casualties deaths from other causes in the Federal Army; 1,804 killed or mortally wounded, 2,226 wounded, and 3,000 dead of disease and other causes in the Federal Navy; ibid., p. 710, with Long relying for the Navy statistics on William Freeman Fox, *Regimental Losses in the American Civil War, 1861–1865: A Treatise on the Extent and Nature of the Mortuary Losses in the Union Regiments, with Full and Exhaustive Statistics Compiled from the Official Records on File in the State Military Bureaus and at Washington* (Albany, New York: Albany Publishing Company, 1889), p. 537. The Confederate statistics include 94,000 killed in battle or mortally wounded, 194,026 wounded, and 164,000 died of disease in the Army, together with 26,000 to 31,000 died in Northern prisons, and with Navy figures unavailable; Long, *Civil War Day by Day*, p. 711, with Long drawing his estimate of the wounded from "Confederate Losses During the War, — Correspondence Between Dr. Joseph Jones and General Samuel Cooper," *Southern Historical Society Papers*, 7:6 (June 1879), 287–90.

8. Using various sources, Long gives the population of the seceded states as 9,103,332 total, of whom 5,449,462 were white, 3,521,110 slaves, and 132,760 free African Americans. He relies particularly on *The National Almanac and Annual Record for the Year 1863* (Philadelphia: George W. Childs, 1863), pp. 307–10, p. 309 for the numbers of white males, 2,800,969 in the eleven seceding states and 11,068,465 in the rest of the nation in 1860. While pointing out that estimates of the numbers who served in the Confederate armed forces run from 600,000 to 1,400,000, Long suggests 750,000 individuals serving as a likely number. Long, *Civil War Day by Day*, pp. 702, 705. Thus 13 percent of the total white population of the Confederacy, and 26 percent of the total white male population, which included old men and boys, probably entered the Confederate forces.

9. "Address Delivered at the Dedication of the Cemetery at Gettysburg," November 19, 1863, Abraham Lincoln, *The Collected Works of Abraham Lincoln*, Roy P. Basler, ed.; Marion Dolores Pratt and Lloyd A. Dunlop, asst. eds. (9 vols. inc. index, The Abraham Lincoln Association, Springfield, Illinois; New Brunswick, New Jersey: Rutgers University Press, 1953; index, 1955), VII, 17–23, giving various versions; see particularly Final Text, Address delivered at the dedication of the Cemetery at Gettysburg, Autograph Document Signed, owned by Oscar Cintras, Havana, Cuba, known as the Bliss Copy, ibid., pp. 22–23, quotation from 23.

10. See Garry Wills, *Inventing America: Jefferson's Declaration of Independence*

(Garden City, New York: Doubleday & Company, Inc., 1978). For the same author's analysis of the Gettysburg Address, see Garry Wills, *Lincoln at Gettysburg: The Words That Remade America* (New York, London, Toronto, Sydney, Tokyo, Singapore: Simon & Schuster, 1992).

11. All quotations from Basler, ed., *Works of Lincoln*, VII, 23.

12. Ibid.

13. The battle of Iwo Jima in World War II, beginning February 15, 1945 and with the action essentially ending on March 24, 1945, was among the most costly of the war to Americans, with over 6,000 deaths and 25,000 wounded (while of slightly more than 20,000 Japanese defenders of the island, only 200 were taken alive, the rest fighting to the death); Gerhard L. Weinberg, *A World at Arms: A Global History of World War II* (Cambridge; New York; Oakleigh, Victoria, Australia: Cambridge University Press, 1994), p. 868. Jeter A. Isely and Philip A. Crowl, *The U.S. Marines and Amphibious War: Its Theory, and Its Practice in the Pacific* (Princeton, New Jersey: Princeton University Press, 1951), p. 529 gives the similar figures of more than 5,500 American military personnel killed and more than three and one-half times as many wounded or in other ways incapacitated, while stating that the number of men in the main assault forces was 84,000, p. 451. At the time, 31,000 American casualties in a battle lasting somewhat more than a month seemed to push toward the limits of public tolerance. Yet no similar outcry arose during the Civil War when in the three days' battle of Gettysburg, July 1–3, 1863, the Union Army suffered 23,000 casualties out of some 83,000, and the Confederate Army lost 28,000 out of 75,000; Thomas L. Livermore, *Numbers and Losses in the Civil War in America 1861–65* (Boston and New York: Houghton, Mifflin and Company, 1901; reprint, Dayton, Ohio: Morningside, 1986), pp. 102, 103.

14. Henry Wager Halleck, *Elements of Military Art and Science: or, Course of Instruction in Strategy, Fortification, Tactics of Battle &c Embracing the Duties of Staff, Infantry, Cavalry, Artillery, and Engineers. Adapted to the Use of Volunteers and Militia* (Third Edition, with Critical Notes on the Mexican and Crimean Wars, 443 & 445 Broadway, New York; 16 Little Britain, London: D. Appleton & Company, 1862), pp. 37, 38.

15. Richard M. McMurry presents an especially persuasive statement of the opposing view, that the West deserved strategic priority over the East, in his comparative history of the Army of Northern Virginia and the Army of Tennessee, *Two Great Rebel Armies: An Essay in Confederate Military History* (Chapel Hill & London: University of North Carolina Press, 1989). "To those of us who have been converted to its study," he writes, "the western front of the American Civil War was, by far, the most important part of that struggle"; p. x. McMurry's well reasoned arguments deserve to be pondered; his own analysis of the deficiencies of the Army of Tennessee, however, suggests to this writer that they were embedded so deep that the problems of bringing that army to the level of Lee's army were insuperable.

16. Bell Irvin Wiley, *The Life of Johnny Reb: The Common Soldier of the Confederacy* (Indianapolis, New York: The Bobbs-Merrill Company Publishers, 1943), Chapter I, "Off to the War," pp. 15–27, and pp. 123–24 on motives for enlisting, Chapters V, "Heroes and Cowards," pp. 68–89, VIII, "Trials of Soul," pp. 123–50, XVI, "Blue Bellies and Beloved Enemies," pp. 308–21, and XVII, "What Manner of Men?" pp. 322–47, on motives for persisting in the fight; Bell Irvin Wiley, *The Life of Billy Yank: The Common Soldier of the Union* (Indianapolis, New York: The Bobbs-Merrill Company Publishers, 1952), Chapter I, "Southward Ho!" pp. 13–16, on reasons for enlisting, Chapters III, "The Supreme Test," pp. 66–95, XII, "The Men Who Wore the Blue," pp. 296–345, and XIII, "Billy Yank and Johnny Reb," pp. 346–61, on persisting.

17. James M. McPherson, *What They Fought For 1861–1865* (Baton Rouge and London: Louisiana State University Press, 1994), pp. 9–14 on Southern motives for enlist-

ment, pp. 27–34 on Union motives. Reid Mitchell's interpretations are similar to Mc-Pherson's; see his *Civil War Soldiers* (New York: Viking, 1988), especially One, "Wars for Freedom," pp. 1–23, and pp. 24–36; and his *The Vacant Chair* (New York, Oxford: Oxford University Press, 1993), especially 1, "Soldiering, Manhood, and Coming of Age," pp. 3–18. Although his main subject is the different one of studying courage as the sustainer of Civil War armies, Gerald F. Linderman suggests similar conclusions in his *Embattled Courage: The Experience of Combat in the American Civil War* (New York: The Free Press, A Division of Macmillan, Inc.; London: Collier Macmillan Publishers, 1987), especially pp. 2, 8–16.

18. McPherson, *What They Fought For*, pp. 47–48, and for Confederate soldiers, pp. 48–50, 53–56, 58, and for Union soldiers, pp. 57–68. James M. McPherson deals with similar issues, but places greater emphasis on reasons for sustaining the fight, in his *For Cause and Comrades: Why Men Fought in the Civil War* (New York, Oxford: Oxford University Press, 1997); here he examines the Confederate soldier's attitudes toward slavery on pp. 19–21, 106–10, 171–72, the Union soldier's attitudes on pp. 19, 110, 117–30, 146. Mitchell deals with the Southern defense of slavery in *Civil War Soldiers*, pp. 21, 181, and with Union soldiers' attitudes toward it on pp. 14–15, 41–42.

19. McPherson, *For Cause and Comrades*, pp. 22–24 on duty and honor, and on comradeship, especially pp. 6, 13, 85–90, 91, 114, 131, 209–10n. In this book McPherson returns to the theme of the soldiers' commitment to ideology on pp. 13, 18–21, 27–28, 90–94, 104–16, 135, 170–78.

## 1. FROM SECESSION TO WAR

1. For the pre–Civil War coastal defenses, see Emanuel Raymond Lewis, *Seacoast Fortifications of the United States: An Introductory History* (City of Washington: Smithsonian Institution Press, 1970), pp. 1–65; David A. Clary, *Fortress America: The Corps of Engineers, Hampton Roads, and United States Coastal Defense* (Charlottesville: University Press of Virginia, 1990), 1, "Foundations of American Military Engineering," pp. 1–13; 2, "America's First Two Fortification Systems," pp. 14–35; 3, "The Golden Age of Coastal Fortifications," p. 36; Robert S. Browning III, *Two If By Sea: The Development of American Coastal Defense Policy* (Contributions in Military History, Number 33, Westport, Connecticut; London, England: Greenwood Press, 1983), "Introduction: The Colonial and Early National Tradition," pp. 3–21; One, "The Creation of a System," pp. 24–58; Two, "Engineer Training and Fortification Design," pp. 59–77; Three, "Alternatives and Auxiliaries," pp. 78–105; Four, "Technological Change and Coastal Defense," pp. 106–127.

2. The figures here are from "Fort Sumter," Mark Mayo Boatner III, *The Civil War Dictionary* (Revised Edition, New York: Vintage Books, A Division of Random House, Inc., 1991), pp. 299–300, particularly 300, citing John G. Nicolay, *The Outbreak of Rebellion* (New York: C. Scribner's Sons, 1881), p. 63. Companies E and H are identified in William A. Swanberg, *First Blood: The Story of Fort Sumter* (New York: Dorset Press, 1990; first published New York: Charles Scribner's Sons, 1957), p. 38.

3. On the division of Buchanan's Cabinet, see Allan Nevins, *Ordeal of the Union* (8 vols., *Ordeal of the Union*, I, *Fruits of Manifest Destiny 1847–1852*, *Ordeal of the Union*, II, *A House Dividing 1852–1857* [New York, London: Charles Scribner's Sons, 1947], III, *The Emergence of Lincoln*, I, *Douglas, Buchanan, and Party Chaos 1857–1859*, IV, *The Emergence of Lincoln*, II, *Prologue to Civil War 1859–1861* [New York, London: Charles Scribner's Sons, 1950], V, *The War for the Union*, I, *The Improvised War 1861–1862* [New York: Charles Scribner's Sons, 1959]; VI, *The War for the Union*, II, *War Becomes Revolution* [New York: Charles Scribner's Sons, 1960]; VII, *The War for the Union*, III, *The Organized War 1863–1864*, VIII, *The War for the Union*, IV, *The Organized War*

to Victory 1864–1865 [New York: Charles Scribner's Sons, 1971]), IV, *Emergence of Lincoln*, II, 343; Roy Franklin Nichols, *The Disruption of American Democracy* (New York: The Macmillan Company, 1948), pp. 382–88, particularly 382.

4. James Buchanan, Fourth Annual Message, Washington City, December 3, 1860. Fellow-Citizens of the Senate and House of Representatives. United States, President, *A Compilation of the Messages and Papers of the Presidents, 1798–1908 (With Revisions)*, James D. Richardson, ed. (11 vols., Washington: Bureau of National Literature and Art, 1911), V, 626–53, particularly 627, 630–34 deploring secession, 627, 634–25 on the lack of effective power against it.

5. Swanberg, *First Blood*, pp. 83–84, quoting F. W. Pickens, Governor of South Carolina (Strictly Confidential), Columbia, December 17th, 1860, to Hon. James Buchanan, President of the United States, Washington, in William A. Harris, *The Record of Fort Sumter from Its Occupation by Major Anderson to Its Reduction by Confederate Troops* (pamphlet, Columbia, South Carolina, 1862), pp. 7–8; quoted also in Roy Meredith, *Storm over Sumter: The Opening Engagement of the Civil War* (New York: Simon and Schuster, 1957), pp. 47–48. Pickens took office December 16; Swanberg, *First Blood*, p. 83.

6. Philip Shriver Klein, *President James Buchanan: A Biography* (University Park, Pennsylvania: Pennsylvania State University Press, 1962), p. 372.

7. D. C. Buell, Assistant Adjutant-General. Fort Moultrie, S.C., December 11, 1860. Memorandum of verbal instructions to Major Anderson, First Artillery, commanding at Fort Moultrie, S.C. U.S. War Department, *The War of the Rebellion: A Compilation of the Official Records of the Union and Confederate Armies* (four series, 70 vols. in 128, Washington: Government Printing Office, 1880–1901), Series One, I (serial 1, 1880), 89–90, particularly 90. Hereafter cited as O.R.; citations are of Series One unless otherwise noted.

8. Ibid.

9. J. B. Floyd, Secretary of War. [Telegram.] War Department, Adjutant-General's Office, December 17, 1860. To Major Anderson, Fort Moultrie, ibid., p. 3.

10. Klein, *Buchanan*, p. 371.

11. Ibid., p. 372.

12. Ibid., pp. 379–80.

13. Robert W. Barnwell, J. H. Adams, James L. Orr, Commissioners, Washington, D.C., January 1, 1861. To His Excellency the President of the United States, O.R., I, 120–125, quotation from p. 123.

14. Headquarters of the Army, Washington, January 2, 1861. Memorandum of arrangements [In the handwriting of General Scott], to Lieut. Col. Lorenzo Thomas, Assistant Adjutant-General, Washington, D.C., ibid., pp. 128–29, quotation from p. 128.

15. L. Thomas, Assistant Adjutant-General, Headquarters of the Army, New York, January 5, 1861. To Maj. Robert Anderson, First Artillery, Commanding Fort Sumter, "In accordance with the instructions of the General-in-Chief," ibid., p. 132.

16. "Secretaries of War," in Francis B. Heitman, *Historical Register and Dictionary of the United States Army, From Its Organization, September 29, 1789, to March 2, 1903*. Published under act of Congress approved March 2, 1903, 57th Congress, 2nd Session, House Document 446 (serial 4536) (2 vols., Washington: Government Printing Office, 1903), I, 16–17, particularly 16. On the *Star of the West* incident, see Kenneth P. Williams, *Lincoln Finds a General: A Military Study of the Civil War* (5 vols., New York: The Macmillan Company, 1950–1959), I, 27–31; Nevins, *Ordeal of the Union*, IV, *Emergence of Lincoln*, II, 380–81, 432.

17. On the Montgomery Convention, see George C. Rable, *The Confederate Republic: A Revolution against Politics* (Chapel Hill and London: University of North Carolina Press, 1994), pp. 43–59; Emory M. Thomas, *The Confederate Nation 1861–1865* (New

York, Hagerstown, San Francisco, London: Harper & Row, Publishers, 1979), pp. 38–41, 57–66; Nevins, *Ordeal of the Union*, IV, *Emergence of Lincoln*, II, 433–35.

18. For the duration of the Provisional Congress, see Confederate States of America, Laws, statutes, By Authority of Congress, *The Statutes at Large of the Provisional Government of the Confederate States of America, from the Institution of the Government, February 8, 1861, to Its Termination, February 18, 1862, Inclusive. Arranged in Chronological Order. Together with the Constitution for the Provisional Government, and the Permanent Constitution of the Confederate States, and the Treaties Concluded by the Confederate States with the Indian Tribes*, James M. Matthews, ed. (Richmond: R. M. Smith, Printer to Congress, 1864). On the Provisional Congress, see also Thomas, *Confederate Nation*, pp. 57–58; Rable, *Confederate Republic*, pp. 50–51.

19. The permanent Constitution of the Confederate States of America is conveniently available in Confederate States of America, President, *A Compilation of the Messages and Papers of the Confederacy, Including the Diplomatic Correspondence, 1861–1865*, James D. Richardson, ed. (2 vols., Nashville, Tennessee: United States Publishing Company, 1905), I, 37–54, and in Matthews, ed., *Statutes at Large of the Provisional Government of the Confederate States*, pp. 11–23.

20. Doc. 48. — Speech of A. H. Stevens [sic], *The Rebellion Record: A Diary of American Events with Documents, Narratives, Illustrative Incidents, Poetry, Etc.*, Frank Moore, ed., With an Introductory Address, on the Causes of the Struggle, and the Great Issues before the Country, By Edward Everett (11 vols. plus Supplement, I–III, New York: G. P. Putnam, C. T. Evans, General Agent, 1862; IV–VI, New York: G. P. Putnam, 532 Broadway; Chas. T. Evans, 448 Broadway, 1862–1863; VII–XI, 192 Broadway, New York: D. Van Nostrand, Publisher, 1864–1866; Supplement, New York: G. P. Putnam, Henry Holt, Publication Office, 441 Broadway, 1864), I, 44–49, quotation from 45.

21. Article I, Section 8, paragraphs 1 (quotations) and 3, Richardson, ed., *Compilation of the Messages and Papers of the Confederacy*, I, 41–42, quotations from p. 41; Matthews, ed., *Statutes at Large of the Provisional Government of the Confederate States*, p. 14. See Marshall L. DeRosa, *The Confederate Constitution of 1861: An Inquiry into American Constitutionalism* (Columbia: University of Missouri Press, 1991).

22. "Flags, Confed.," Boatner, *Civil War Dictionary*, p. 284; Alyce Billings Walker, ed., *Alabama: A Guide to the Deep South* (New Revised Edition, Originally Compiled by the Federal Writers Project of the Works Progress Administration in the State of Alabama, later called the Writers Program, *American Guide Series*, Harry Hansen, gen. ed., New York: Hastings House, Publishers, 1975), p. 209 (both identifying Nicola Marschall, identified by Walker, ed., *Alabama* as of Marion, Alabama, as designer of the flag); "March 5, 1861 [date thus given], "Mary Boykin Miller Chesnut, *Mary Chesnut's Civil War*, Comer Vann Woodward, ed. (New Haven and London: Yale University Press, 1981), pp. 15–16, particularly p. 16 and 16n.

23. Louis Philippe Albert d'Orléans, comte de Paris, *History of the Civil War in America* (4 vols., Philadelphia: Porter & Coates, 1875–1888), I, 97.

24. Charles P. Roland, *The Confederacy* (Daniel J. Boorstin, ed., *The Chicago History of American Civilization*, Chicago and London: University of Chicago Press, 1960), p. 23.

25. Constitution for the Provisional Government of the Confederate States of America, Matthews, ed., *Statutes at Large of the Provisional Government of the Confederate States*, pp. 1–9, Article II, Section 1, 1, p. 5, for President and Vice President; Section 2, ibid., for Executive Departments; Article I, pp. 1–4 for Congress, Also in Richardson, ed., *Compilation of the Messages and Papers of the Confederacy*, I, 3–14, specifically p. 8 for Article II, Section 1, p. 9 for Section 2, pp. 3–8 for Article I.

26. For those considered for the Confederate Presidency and the election process, Rable, *Confederate Republic*, pp. 65–68; Thomas, *Confederate Nation*, pp. 58–60, Nev-

ins, *Ordeal of the Union*, IV, *Emergence of Lincoln*, II, 433–34. Toombs had resigned from the U.S. Senate January 12, 1861; Ulrich Bonnell Phillips, *The Life of Robert Toombs* (New York: The Macmillan Company, 1913), p. 219.

27. Davis had resigned from the U.S. Senate and delivered his parting address there on January 21; Hudson Strode, *Jefferson Davis* (2 vols., New York: Harcourt, Brace and Company, 1955–1964), I, *American Patriot, 1808–1861*, 389. On Davis, see also Clement Eaton, *Jefferson Davis* (New York: The Free Press, A Division of Macmillan Publishing Co.; London: Collier Macmillan Publishers, 1977). On Stephens, see Rudolph Von Abele, *Alexander H. Stephens: A Biography* (New York: Alfred A. Knopf, 1946).

28. Davis was commissioned thus on January 25, 1861; Strode, *Davis*, I, 397.

29. Richardson, ed., *Compilation of the Messages and Papers of the Confederacy*, I, 32–36. For Davis's learning of his election, his journey to Montgomery, and his inauguration, Strode, *Davis*, I, 401–13; Eaton, *Davis*, pp. 126–27.

30. On Davis's Cabinet and governing style, Rable, *Confederate Republic*, pp. 71–74; Thomas, *Confederate Nation*, pp. 72–80.

31. The Laws of the Confederate States. Public Acts of the Provisional Congress of the Confederate States. Passed at the first session of the Provisional Congress, which was begun and held at the City of Montgomery on Monday, February 4, 1861, and continued to March 18, 1861. Statute I. Chapter I. — An Act to continue in force certain laws of the United States of America. Adopted February 9. Matthews, ed., *Statutes at Large of the Provisional Congress of the Confederate States*, p. 27. Resolutions, First Session. [No. 17.] Resolution providing for a digest of laws. Approved March 12, 1861. Ibid., p. 94. On May 21 Congress resolved that the committee "deposit in the office of the Attorney General the digest, so far as it has progressed. . . ." Resolutions, Second Session. [No. 7.] A resolution rescinding a resolution providing for a digest of laws, approved March twelfth, eighteen hundred and sixty-one. Approved May 21, 1861. Ibid., p. 164. For the Post Office transition, Thomas, *Confederate Nation*, p. 78.

32. Public Acts of the Provisional Congress. Statute I. Chap. XXIX. — An Act for the establishment and organization of the Army of the Confederate States of America. Approved March 6, 1861. Ibid., pp. 47–52, particularly Sec. 29, p. 51.

33. "Loyalty of Regular Army Officers," Boatner, *Civil War Dictionary*, p. 495, citing Richard Ernest Dupuy, *The Compact History of the United States Army* (New York: Hawthorn Books, 1956), pp. 122–23; "Loyalty of Regular Army Enlisted Men," Boatner, *Civil War Dictionary*, p. 495, for the decidedly conservative estimate of twenty-six; for the Navy, "Naval Participation," ibid., pp. 582–83, citing Francis Trevelyan Miller, ed.; Robert S. Lanier, managing ed., *The Photographic History of the Civil War* (10 vols., New York: The Review of Reviews Co., 1911–1912), VI, James Barnes, *The Navies*, 78, for the number of defections.

34. Second Congress. Session I. Statute I. Chap. XXXIII. — An Act more effectually to provide for the National Defence, by establishing an Uniform Militia throughout the United States. Approved, May 8, 1792. U.S., Laws, statutes, *The Statutes at Large of the United States of America, 1789–1873* (17 vols., I–IX, Boston: Charles C. Little and J. Brown, 1845–1854; X–XVII, Boston: Little, Brown, and Company, 1855–1873), 1 (From the Organization of the Government in 1789, to March 3, 1799), 471–74; also in U.S. Congress, [*Annals of the Congress of the United States.*] *The Debates and Proceedings in the Congress of the United States; with an Appendix Containing Important State Papers and Public Documents, and All the Laws of a Public Nature; with a Copious Index* (42 vols., Washington: Printed and Published by Gales and Seaton, 1834–1856), III, Second Congress, Comprising the Period from October 24, 1791 to March 2, 1793, Inclusive. Compiled from Authentic Materials. (1849) Appendix, 1392–95, particularly Sec. 1, 1 *Statutes at Large* 271–72; *Annals*, III, 1392. Third Congress. Session I. Statute I. Chap. XXXVI. — An Act to provide for calling forth the Militia to execute the Laws of the

Union, suppress insurrections, and repel invasions; and to repeal the act now in force for those purposes. Approved, February 28, 1795. 1 *Statutes at Large* 424–25; *Annals*, IV, Third Congress: Comprising the Period from December 2, 1793, to March 3, 1795, Inclusive. Compiled from Authentic Materials. (1849) Appendix, 1508–10. Sec. 4, 1 *Statutes at Large* 424, *Annals*, IV, 1509, limits service to "no more than three months after his [the militiaman's] arrival at the place of rendezvous, in any one year, nor more than in due rotation with every other able-bodied man of the same rank in the battalion to which he belongs." Sec. 2, ibid., provides that "the use of militia so to be called forth, may be continued, if necessary, until the expiration of thirty days after the commencement of the next session of Congress." Sec. 10, 1 *Statutes at Large* 425, *Annals*, IV, 1510, repealed Second Congress. Session I. Statute I. Chap. XXVII. — An Act to provide for calling forth the Militia to execute the Laws of the Union, suppress insurrections and repel invasions. Approved, May 2, 1792. For that act, 1 *Statutes at Large* 264–65, *Annals*, III, Appendix, 1370–72.

35. Tenth Congress, Session I. Statute I. Chap. LV. — An Act making provision for arming and equipping the whole body of the Militia of the United States. Approved, April 23, 1808. 2 *Statutes at Large* (December 24, 1799–March 13, 1813) (1845) 490–91; *Annals*, XVIII, Tenth Congress. — First Session. Comprising the Period from October 26, 1807, to April 25, 1808, Inclusive. Compiled from Authentic Materials (1852). Appendix, p. 2860.

36. Public Acts of the Provisional Congress. Statute I, Chap. XXII. — An Act to raise Provisional Forces for the Confederate States of America, and other purposes. Approved February 28, 1861. Matthews, ed., *Statutes at Large of the Provisional Congress of the Confederate States*, pp. 43–44, particularly Sec. 1 and Sec. 3, p. 43. Chap. XXIX. — An Act for the establishment and organization of the Army of the Confederate States of America. Approved March 6, 1861. Ibid., pp. 47–52, particularly Sec. 1, p. 47. Chap. XXVI. — An Act to provide for the Public Defence. Approved March 6, 1861. Ibid., pp. 45–46, particularly Sec. 1, p. 45, for the calling up of men, Sec. 2, p. 46.

37. L. P. Walker, Secretary of War, Confederate States of America. War Department. Montgomery, March 9, 1861. To His Excellency A[ndrew]. B[arry]. Moore [Governor of Alabama], Montgomery, Ala., and similar letters, simply summarized, calling on Florida, Georgia, Louisiana, and Mississippi, O.R., Series Four, I (serial 127, 1900), 135. L. P. Walker, Confederate States of America, War Department, Montgomery, April 8, 1861. To His Excellency Francis W. Pickens, Charleston, S.C., and similar letters, simply summarized, calling on Alabama, Florida, Georgia, Louisiana, Texas, and Mississippi, ibid., p. 211. The first call was based on the act of February 28, 1861, to raise provisional troops, Matthews, ed., *Statutes at Large of the Provisional Congress of the Confederate States*, pp. 43–44, specifically Sec. 3, p. 43; the second on the act of March 6, 1861 to provide for the public defense, ibid., pp. 45–46, specifically Sec. 1, p. 45.

38. On Davis's creation of the War Department machinery, see Steven E. Woodworth, *Davis and Lee at War* (Lawrence: University Press of Kansas, 1995), pp. 10–12. See Public Acts of the Provisional Congress. Statute I. Chap. IX. — An Act to establish the War Department. Approved February 21, 1861. Matthews, ed., *Statutes at Large of the Provisional Congress of the Confederate States*, p. 32. Chap. X. — An Act to establish the Navy Department. Approved February 21, 1861. Ibid., p. 33. And again, Chap. XXIX. — An Act for the establishment and organization of the Army of the Confederate States. Approved March 6, 1861. Ibid., pp. 47–52.

39. The resolution of authorization is in First Session, Resolutions. [No. 11.] A Resolution for the appointment of Commissioners to the Government of the United States of America. Adopted February 15, 1861. For the experiences of the commissioners, see Nevins, *Ordeal of the Union*, V, *The War for the Union*, I, 40, 49–50; David M. Potter, *Lincoln and His Party in the Secession Crisis* (New Haven: Yale University Press; Lon-

don: Humphrey Milford, Oxford University Press, 1942), pp. 342–49; David M. Potter, *The Impending Crisis 1848–1861*, completed and edited by Don E. Fehrenbacher (New York, Evanston, San Francisco, London: Harper & Row, Publishers, 1976), pp. 572–73, 576; James G. Randall, *Lincoln the President* (4 vols., New York: Dodd, Mead & Company, 1946–1955, IV, *Last Full Measure*, coauthored with Richard N. Current), I-II, *Springfield to Gettysburg*, I, 321–24; Kenneth M. Stampp, *And the War Came: The North and the Secession Crisis, 1860–61* (Chicago and London: Phoenix Books, University of Chicago Press, 1964), pp. 273–74.

40. "First Inaugural Address — Final Text," March 4, 1861, Document and Autograph Document, The Robert Todd Lincoln Collection of the Papers of Abraham Lincoln, Library of Congress, in Abraham Lincoln, *The Collected Works of Abraham Lincoln*, Roy P. Basler, ed.; Marion Dolores Pratt and Lloyd A. Dunlop, asst. eds. (9 vols. inc. index, The Abraham Lincoln Association, Springfield, Illinois; New Brunswick, New Jersey: Rutgers University Press, 1953; index, 1955), IV, 262–71, quotation from p. 266; declarations of resolve to uphold the Union, pp. 264–66; appeals for reunion, especially pp. 270–71; plan for avoiding war, pp. 266–69; reassurance for slavery where it existed, pp. 262–63, 270; pledge on fugitive slaves, pp. 263–64; holding federal property, collecting duties on imports, but doing nothing more, p. 266.

41. Potter, *Lincoln and His Party*, pp. 326–27; see also Randall, *Lincoln the President*, I, 300. In the Inaugural Address, Lincoln stated: "The mails, unless repelled, will continue to be furnished in all parts of the Union." Basler, ed., *Works of Lincoln*, IV, 266.

42. "First Inaugural Address — First Edition and Revisions," Documents, March 4, 1861, from The Robert Todd Lincoln Collection, LC, ibid., pp. 249–61, particularly p. 254 and note 41, that p.; Potter, *Lincoln and His Party*, p. 328.

43. Randall, *Lincoln the President*, I, 316; Stampp, *And the War Came*, p. 86.

44. First Session, Resolutions. [No. 5.] A Resolution in relation to the occupation of the forts and arsenals &c. Adopted February 12, 1861. Matthews, ed., *Statutes at Large of the Provisional Congress of the Confederate States*, p. 71. Printed also with slight variations in punctuation and capitalization in O.R., I (serial 1), 254. F. W. Pickens, Governor of South Carolina. Headquarters, Charleston, S.C., February 13, 1861. To Hon. Howell Cobb, President of the Provisional Congress. Ibid., pp. 254–57.

45. [Resolution.] That the President of the Confederate States be requested to communicate, in such manner as he may deem expedient, to the governors of South Carolina and Florida the resolution of Congress concerning Forts Sumter and Pickens. RESOLUTION in relation to the occupation of Forts Sumter and Pickens. Passed February 15, 1861. O.R., I (series 1), 258. F. W. Pickens, State of South Carolina, Charleston, S.C., February 27, 1861. To the President of the Confederate States, &c., Montgomery, Ala. O.R., I (series 1), pp. 258–59, particularly p. 259. Two communications, L. P. Walker, Secretary of War, War Department, C.S.A., Montgomery, March 1, 1861 [replying for Davis]. To His Excellency F. W. Pickens, Governor, &c. Ibid., pp. 259, 259–60, the first indicating that "An officer [identified in the second as Beauregard] goes to-night to take charge." As captain and brevet major, Corps of Engineers ("Beauregard, Pierre Gustave Toutant," in Heitman, *Historical Register*, I, 204), Beauregard was superintendent of the U.S. Military Academy January 23–28, 1861, being removed after he stated openly that if Louisiana seceded he would follow his state ("Beauregard, Pierre Gustave Toutant," Boatner, *Civil War Dictionary*, pp. 54–55, particularly 55). The standard biography remains Thomas Harry Williams, *P. G. T. Beauregard: Napoleon in Gray* (Baton Rouge: Louisiana State University Press, 1956).

46. Robert Anderson, Major, First United States Artillery, Commanding, Fort Sumter, S.C., February 28, 1861, [to?], O.R., I (serial 1), 197.

47. Randall, *Lincoln the President*, I, 311–24; Potter, *Lincoln and His Party*, pp. 345–49. The intermediaries were Justices of the U.S. Supreme Court John A. Campbell of

Alabama and Samuel Nelson of Pennsylvania, along with Edouard Baron de Stoeckl, the Russian Minister; Randall, *Lincoln the President*, I, 322–24; Potter, *Lincoln and His Party*, pp. 345–45 and, for Stoeckl, p. 347n.

48. Nevins, *Ordeal of the Union*, V, *War for the Union*, I, 43–46, 47–48 (for Blair), 48–49, 53–54; Randall, *Lincoln the President*, I, 320–21 (for Blair), 328–29 (for Fox), 329–330 (for Hurlbut and Lamon); Williams, *Lincoln Finds a General*, I, 38–39 (for Fox), 39–41 (for Hurlbut and Lamon).

49. Simon Cameron Secy of War, to Robert S. Chew [a clerk in the Department of State, who was to deliver the message to Governor Pickens], [War Department.] Washington, April 6. 1861. Autograph Draft, Autograph Document, Autograph Endorsement, from The Robert Todd Lincoln Collection, LC, in Basler, ed., *Works of Lincoln*, IV, 323 (p. 324n for the identity of Chew); also *O.R.*, I (serial 1), 291. On Chew's session with Pickens and Beauregard, Theo. Talbot, Captain, Assistant Adjutant-General, U.S. Army. Washington, D.C. April 12, 1861. To Hon. Simon Cameron, Secretary of War, ibid., pp. 251–52; F. W. Pickens, G. T. Beauregard, April 8, 1861. Statement quoting document communicated to them by Chew, ibid., p. 291.

50. L. P. Walker, Montgomery, April 10, 1861. To General Beauregard, Charleston. Ibid., p. 297.

51. G. T. Beauregard, Brigadier-General, Commanding. Headquarters Provisional Army, C.S.A., Charleston, S.C., April 11, 1861. To Robert Anderson at Fort Sumter, Charleston Harbor, S.C. Ibid., p. 13.

52. Robert Anderson, Major, First Artillery, Commanding. Fort Sumter, S.C., April 11, 1861. To Brig. Gen. Beauregard, ibid., p. 13; G. T. Beauregard, Brigadier-General, Commanding, Headquarters Provisional Army, C.S.A., Charleston, S.C. April 11, 1861. To Maj. Robert Anderson, Commanding, Fort Sumter, Charleston Harbor, S.C., ibid., pp. 13–14, quotation from 14.

53. Robert Anderson, Major, First Artillery, Commanding, Fort Sumter, S.C., April 12, 1861. To Brig. Gen. Beauregard, Commanding. Ibid., p. 14. James Chesnut, Jr., Aide-de-Camp, Stephen D. Lee, Captain, C.S. Army, Aide-de-Camp, Fort Sumter, S.C., April 12, 1861 — 3.20 a.m. To Maj. Robert Anderson, U.S. Army, commanding Fort Sumter. Ibid. For the *Powhatan*–Fort Pickens affair, see Nevins, *Ordeal of the Union*, V, *War for the Union*, I, 6; Potter, *Lincoln and His Party*, pp. 363–68; Potter, *Impending Crisis*, pp. 576–77, 579–80; Randall, *Lincoln the President*, I, 331–39; Williams, *Lincoln Finds a General*, I, 55–56.

54. Swanberg, *First Blood: The Story of Fort Sumter*, p. 328. This book is a good popular account of the Fort Sumter crisis. Still useful and authoritative is a history by an eyewitness, Samuel Wylie Crawford, *The Genesis of the Civil War: The Story of Sumter, 1860–1861* (New York: C. L. Webster & Company), 1887. Crawford, an assistant surgeon at Sumter, was commissioned major, 14th Infantry on May 14, 1861 and ended the war as a major-general of volunteers (August 1, 1864), becoming brigadier-general, U.S.A., on March 3, 1875, to date from February 19, 1873 ("Crawford, Samuel Wylie," in Heitman, *Biographical Register*, I, 337).

55. For the calling of the militia and the convening of Congress, By the President of the United States, A Proclamation, April 15, 1861, Abraham Lincoln, By the President, William H. Seward, Secretary of State, Document Signed, National Archives, Record Group 11, Proclamations, and Autograph Draft, Robert Todd Lincoln Collection, LC, in Basler, ed., *Works of Lincoln*, IV, 331–32; for the blockade, By the President of the United States of America: A Proclamation, April 19, 1861, Abraham Lincoln, By the President: William H. Seward, Secretary of State, Document Signed, NA Record Group 11, Proclamations, ibid., pp. 338–39; By the President of the United States of America, A Proclamation. April 27, 1861, Abraham Lincoln, By the President: William H. Seward, Secretary of State, Document Signed, NA, Record Group 11, Proclamations, ibid., pp.

346–47. For descriptions of the North after Fort Sumter, see Nevins, *Ordeal of the Union*, V, *War for the Union*, I, 74–76; Randall, *Lincoln the President*, I, 354–56.

56. Simon Cameron, Secretary of War. War Department, Washington, April 15, 1861. To the Governors, *O.R.*, Series Three, I (serial 122, 1899), pp. 68–69 for quotas, and p. 69 for the numbers that each state supplied. An excessively critical account of the Union's mobilization and military organization is Fred Albert Shannon, *The Organization and Administration of the Union Army, 1861–1865* (2 vols., Cleveland: The Arthur H. Clark Company, 1928).

57. Simon Cameron, Secretary of War. Washington, April 27, 1861. To J[ohn]. Edgar Thomson, Philadelphia, Pa. *O.R.*, II (serial 2, 1880), 603–604, particularly p. 604.

58. On Virginia's secession, see Henry T. Shanks, *The Secession Movement in Virginia, 1847–1861* (Richmond, Virginia: Garrett and Massie, 1934); Nevins, *Ordeal of the Union*, V, *War for the Union*, I, 46–47, 101–104; Ralph A. Wooster, *The Secession Conventions of the South* (Princeton, New Jersey: Princeton University Press, 1962), pp. 139–48.

59. For the secession of North Carolina, Tennessee, and Arkansas, see, respectively, Joseph Carlyle Sitterson, *The Secession Movement in North Carolina* (Chapel Hill: University of North Carolina Press, 1939); John Milton Henry, "The Revolution in Tennessee, February, 1861, to June, 1861," *Tennessee Historical Quarterly*, 18:2 (July 1959), 99–119; Jack Scruggs, "Arkansas in the Secession Crisis," *Arkansas Historical Quarterly*, 12:2 (July 1953), 179–92; Nevins, *Ordeal of the Union*, V, *War for the Union*, I, 104–105, 105–106, 106–107; Wooster, *Secession Conventions*, pp. 190–94, 173–80, 155–64.

60. Robert I. Cottom, Jr. & Mary Ellen Hayward, *Maryland in the Civil War: A House Divided* (Baltimore: Published by The Maryland Historical Society, Distributed by The Johns Hopkins University Press, 1994), pp. 29–31; George William Brown, *Baltimore and the Nineteenth of April 1861: A Study of the War* (Johns Hopkins University Studies in Historical and Political Science, Extra Volume 3, Baltimore, Maryland: N. Murray, 1887) (Brown was mayor of the city at the time of the riot); Wooster, *Secession Conventions*, pp. 243–51.

61. For Magoffin and Jackson, see, respectively, Nevins, *Ordeal of the Union*, V, *War for the Union*, I, 131, 122; Wooster, *Secession Conventions*, pp. 214, 238.

62. The local volunteer companies that made up the 6th Massachusetts are listed in Marcus Cunliffe, *Soldiers & Civilians: The Martial Spirit in America 1775–1865* (Boston, Toronto: Little, Brown and Company, 1973), pp. 222–23. For the mustering in and organizing of the first Union Army, see Marvin A. Kreidberg and Merton G. Henry, *History of Military Mobilization in the United States Army 1775–1945* (Department of the Army Pamphlet 20–212. Washington: Department of the Army, June 1955), 83–85, 88–93; Williams, *Lincoln Finds a General*, I, 60–61, 64–66.

63. Nevins, *Ordeal of the Union*, V, *War for the Union*, I, 208; William Morrison Robinson, *The Confederate Privateers* (New Haven: Yale University Press; London: Humphrey Milford, Oxford University Press, 1928), pp. 17–20.

64. Nevins, *Ordeal of the Union*, V, *War for the Union*, I, 94–95.

65. The thesis here briefly summarized is that of John Hope Franklin, *The Militant South 1800–1861* (Cambridge, Massachusetts: Harvard University Press, 1956). For a contrary view, see Cunliffe, *Soldiers & Civilians*, 10, "A Southern Military Tradition?" pp. 335–84.

66. For Massachusetts and New York, see Cunliffe, *Soldiers & Civilians*, p. 250, citing for the Massachusetts statistics (p. 464n) *Massachusetts Adjutant-General's Report for 1857* (Boston: Commonwealth of Massachusetts, 1858), p. 26.

67. Ruth Painter Randall, *Colonel Elmer Ellsworth: A Biography of Lincoln's Friend and First Hero of the Civil War* (Boston: Little, Brown and Company, 1960); Cunliffe, *Soldiers & Civilians*, "Elmer Ellsworth," pp. 241–47.

68. Dennis Hart Mahan, *An Elementary Treatise on Advanced-Guard, Out-Post,*

*and Detachment Service of Troops, and the Manner of Posting and Handling Them* (Revised Edition, New York: John Wiley, 1864), p. 36.

69. Randall, *Ellsworth* 24, "Tragedy at Alexandria," pp. 254–63; Cunliffe, *Soldiers & Civilians*, p. 247.

## 2. THE BATTLE LINES FORM

1. For the West Point that molded Civil War officers, see James L. Morrison, Jr., *"The Best School in the World": West Point, the Pre–Civil War Years, 1833–1866* (Kent, Ohio: Kent State University Press), 1986, and particularly for Dennis Hart Mahan, pp. 47–49, 59–60, 94–98, 153. For prewar American military thought as nurtured at West Point and foreign influences upon it, see Herman Hattaway and Archer Jones, *How the North Won: A Military History of the Civil War* (Urbana, Chicago, London: University of Illinois Press, 1983), pp. 11–17, 21–25; Thomas Lawrence Connelly and Archer Jones, *The Politics of Command: Factions and Ideas in Confederate Strategy* (Baton Rouge: Louisiana State University Press, 1973), pp. xii–xiii, and "I, The European Inheritance," pp. 3–30; also p. 176. The reader should note the emphasis of the latter two works on the influence of the Archduke Charles of Austria as well as of the French; *How the North Won*, p. 13; *Politics of Command*, pp. 27–28, 30, 104, 176.

2. On Napoleonic warfare, see Hattaway and Jones, *How the North Won*, pp. 12–14, 22–24, 709–11; Connelly and Jones, *Politics of Command*, pp. 6–16, 21–25; and the best modern overall exposition, David G. Chandler, *The Campaigns of Napoleon* (New York: The Macmillan Company, 1966), especially Part Three, "Napoleon's Art of War: A study of Napoleon's philosophy of war, an analysis of his strategic and battle methods — and the sources of his ideas," pp. 131–201, particularly pp. 162–63 for *la manœuvre sur les derrières*; and Gunther E. Rothenberg, *The Art of Warfare in the Age of Napoleon* (Bloomington and London: Indiana University Press, 1978).

3. Hattaway and Jones, *How the North Won*, p. 35; Allan Nevins, *Ordeal of the Union* (8 vols., *Ordeal of the Union*, I, *Fruits of Manifest Destiny 1847–1852*; *Ordeal of the Union*, II, *A House Dividing 1852–1857* [New York, London: Charles Scribner's Sons, 1947]; III, *The Emergence of Lincoln*, I, *Douglas, Buchanan, and Party Chaos 1857–1859*; IV, *The Emergence of Lincoln*, II, *Prologue to Civil War 1859–1861* [New York, London: Charles Scribner's Sons, 1950]; V, *The War for the Union*, I, *The Improvised War 1861–1862* [New York: Charles Scribner's Sons, 1959]; VI, *The War for the Union*, II, *War Becomes Revolution* [New York: Charles Scribner's Sons, 1960]; VII, *The War for the Union*, III, *The Organized War 1863–1864*; VIII, *The War for the Union*, IV, *The Organized War to Victory 1864–1865* [New York: Charles Scribner's Sons, 1971]), V, *War for the Union*, I, 150–52. Scott had become brevet lieutenant-general as of March 29, 1847; "Scott, Winfield," Francis B. Heitman, *Historical Register and Dictionary of the United States Army, From Its Organization, September 29, 1789, to March 2, 1903*. Published under act of Congress approved March 2, 1903, 57th Congress, Second Session, House Document 446 [serial 4536], 2 vols. (Washington: Government Printing Office, 1903), I, 870.

4. Everette B. Long with Barbara Long, *The Civil War Day by Day: An Almanac 1861–1865*, Foreword by Bruce Catton (Garden City, New York: Doubleday & Company, Inc., 1971), p. 702 for the population of the Confederacy and the number of slaves, p. 701 for the Union population, the border area, and the Far West.

5. For the Federal statistics, H[enry]. K[nox]. Craig, Colonel of Ordnance, Ordnance Office, Washington, D.C., January 21, 1861. To Hon. J. Holt, Secretary of War, U.S. War Department, *The War of the Rebellion: A Compilation of the Official Records of the Union and Confederate Armies* (four series, 70 vols. in 128, Washington: Government Printing Office, 1880–1901), Series Three, I (serial 122; 1899), 42–43. Hereafter cited as O.R.; citations are of Series One unless otherwise noted. For the Confederate statistics,

Nevins, *Ordeal of the Union*, V, *War for the Union*, I, 114, citing Report to Chairman Frederick S. Barstow of the Cong. Committee on Military Affairs.

6. See "United States Rifle Musket, Model 1841," and "United States Rifle Musket, Model 1855," p. 860; "United States Rifle Musket, Model 1855 ('Harpers Ferry')," "United States rifle Musket, Model 1861," "United States Rifle Musket, Model 1863," and "United States Rifle Musket, Model 1863, Type 2," p. 861, in Mark Mayo Boatner III, *The Civil War Dictionary* (Revised Edition, New York: Vintage Books, A Division of Random House, Inc., 1991). On the introduction of rifled weapons into warfare, see Bernard and Fawn M. Brodie, *From Crossbow to H-Bomb* (Revised and Enlarged Edition, Bloomington & London: Indiana University Press, 1973), "Transformation of Land Warfare: Improved Infantry Weapons," pp. 131–39, and "Artillery Changes," pp. 139–44. The tactical impact of the rifle is minimized in Paddy Griffith, *Battle Tactics of the Civil War* (New Haven and London: Yale University Press, 1989), especially 6 "The Infantry Firefight," pp. 137–63. Griffith probably goes too far toward dismissing the effects of rifled weapons; certainly the tendency of warfare to harden into tactical deadlock grew even more pronounced than before during the Civil War, and especially so as rifled muskets increasingly became standard shoulder arms in the East during 1862 and in the West during 1863. Nevertheless, Griffith's arguments cannot be ignored. For an assessment close to the present author's, see Edward Hagerman, *The American Civil War and the Origins of Modern Warfare: Ideas, Organization, and Field Command* (Bloomington & Indianapolis: Indiana University Press, 1988), especially 2. "Tactical and Strategic Reorganization: McClellan and the Origins of Professionalism," pp. 31–69; 5. "Intimations of Modern Warfare: Lee and the Army of Northern Virginia," pp. 126–48; 6. "Maneuver and Tactics: The First and Second Lines of Confederate Defense," pp. 151–74; 7. "The Emergence of Trench Warfare: The Third Line of Confederate Defense," pp. 175–98; and 8. "Trench Warfare and Maneuver," pp. 199–230. It is not necessary to accept the authors' argument that it was because of its Celtic ethnic inheritance that the South fought aggressively to be informed about tactics in Grady McWhiney and Perry D. Jamieson, *Attack and Die: Civil War Military Tactics and the Southern Heritage* (University, Alabama: University of Alabama Press, 1982). There is also much retrospective information about Civil War tactics in Perry D. Jamieson, *Crossing the Deadly Ground: United States Army Tactics, 1865–1899* (Tuscaloosa & London: University of Alabama Press, 1994).

7. On Civil War artillery, see "Cannon of the Civil War," Boatner, *Civil War Dictionary*, pp. 119–21, especially p. 120; Hagerman, *American Civil War and the Origins of Modern Warfare*, pp. xi–xii, xv, 20–22, 92, 146, 334; Griffith, *Battle Tactics*, 7 "Artillery," pp. 165–78.

8. New York had 23,236 industrial establishments, Pennsylvania 21,000. Long, *Civil War Day by Day*, p. 726.

9. Ibid., p. 721.

10. Ibid., p. 723. See Robert C. Black, *The Railroads of the Confederacy* (Chapel Hill: University of North Carolina Press, 1952); Angus James Johnston, *Virginia Railroads in the Civil War* (Chapel Hill: Published for the Virginia Historical Society by the University of North Carolina Press, 1961), which argues that the Confederacy relied too much on its railroads and not enough on waterways; George Edgar Turner, *Victory Rode the Rails: The Strategic Place of the Railroads in the Civil War* (Indianapolis, New York: The Bobbs-Merrill Company, Inc., Publishers, 1953); Thomas Weber, *The Northern Railroads in the Civil War, 1861–1865* (New York: King's Crown Press, 1952); Jeffrey Lash, *Destroyer of the Iron Horse: General Joseph E. Johnston and Confederate Rail Transport* (Kent, Ohio and London: Kent State University Press, 1991).

11. Nevins, *Ordeal of the Union*, V, *War for the Union*, I, 101–102; Emory M. Thomas, *The Confederate Nation 1861–1865* (New York, Hagerstown, San Francisco, London: Harper & Row, Publishers, 1979), 99–101.

12. For the condition of the Regular Army, Marvin A. Kreidberg and Merton G. Henry, *History of Military Mobilization in the United States Army 1775–1945* (Department of the Army Pamphlet No. 20–212, Washington: Department of the Army, June 1955), p. 88, and p. 89 for Twiggs's surrender (Kreidberg and Henry, p. 88, give the strength of the Regular Army as 1,108 officers and 15,259 enlisted men on January 1, 1861, citing Abstract from returns of the U.S. Army, December 31, 1860. *O.R.*, Series Three, I [serial 122, 1899], 22). For the garrison of Washington, Nevins, *Ordeal of the Union*, V, *War for the Union*, I, 79; for a vivid general survey of the Washington situation, Margaret Leech, *Reveille in Washington 1861–1865* (New York and London: Harper & Brothers, Publishers, 1941), pp. 53–57.

13. For the First Defenders, the first troops from the North to reach Washington, see Leech, *Reveille in Washington*, pp. 58–59, particularly 59 for Nick Biddle, also pp. 60–61 for the arrival of the 6th Massachusetts and the Baltimore riot; Nevins, *Ordeal of the Union*, V, *War for the Union*, I, 79, for the First Defenders, and 81 for the Baltimore riot and the arrival of the 6th in Washington. See again also chap. 1, n. 60, p. 469 above for works on the riot.

14. Thomas H. Hicks, Governor of Maryland. [April 19, 1861.] To his Excellency Abraham Lincoln, President of the United States. *O.R.*, II (serial 2, 1880), 12.

15. Robert I. Cottom, Jr. & Mary Ellen Hayward, *Maryland in the Civil War: A House Divided* (Baltimore: Published by The Maryland Historical Society, Distributed by The Johns Hopkins University Press, 1994), pp. 27–35; Nevins, *Ordeal of the Union*, V, *War for the Union*, I, 81–87, and particularly 86 for the arrival of reinforcements, including Ellsworth; Leech, *Reveille in Washington*, pp. 66–70 for the reinforcements.

16. Robert S. Holzman, *Stormy Ben Butler* (New York: The Macmillan Company, 1954), pp. 30–34, particularly 31 for the Department of Annapolis; Cottom & Hayward, *Maryland in the Civil War*, pp. 35, 39; Nevins, *Ordeal of the Union*, V, *War for the Union*, I, 87.

17. Cottom & Hayward, *Maryland in the Civil War*, p. 44; Nevins, *Ordeal of the Union*, V, *War for the Union*, I, 137–139, for Union control of Maryland. For the crossing of the Potomac, Leech, *Reveille in Washington*, pp. 80–81; Kenneth P. Williams, *Lincoln Finds a General: A Military Study of the Civil War* (5 vols., New York: The Macmillan Company, 1950–1959), I, 66.

18. The population of Massachusetts in 1860 was 1,231,066 (1,221,464 white, 9,602 free black), of Missouri 1,182,012 (1,063,509 white, 3,572 free black, 114,931 slave), of Kentucky 1,155,684 (919,517 white, 10,684 free black, 225,483 slave); Long, *Civil War Day by Day*, p. 701.

19. Nevins, *Ordeal of the Union*, V, *War for the Union*, I, 120–21, particularly 121 for the votes; more generally, Thomas, *Confederate Nation*, p. 88.

20. Nevins, *Ordeal of the Union*, V, *War for the Union*, I, 122.

21. "Lyon, Nathaniel," in Boatner, *Civil War Dictionary*, pp. 497–98, particularly 497 for Lyon's background; Michael Fellman, *Inside War: The Guerrilla Conflict in Missouri During the American Civil War* (New York, Oxford: Oxford University Press, 1989), pp. 10–11; Nevins, *Ordeal of the Union*, V, *War for the Union*, I, 122–25, particularly 125 for the number of casualties.

22. "Price, Sterling ('Pap')," Boatner, *Civil War Dictionary*, p. 689; "Harney, William A. [sic]," ibid., p. 376; Long, *Civil War Day by Day*, June 12, Wednesday, 1861, p. 85, for Jackson's call for militia; Nevins, *Ordeal of the Union*, V, *War for the Union*, I, 126–29, 307–311, particularly 310 for Jackson's call; Fellman, *Inside War*, for a survey of Missouri's guerrilla conflict.

23. "Wilson's Creek Campaign," Boatner, *Civil War Dictionary*, pp. 932–35, particularly 935 for the casualties; Albert Castel, *General Sterling Price and the Civil War in the West* (Baton Rouge: Louisiana State University Press, 1968), pp. 39–47; Williams, *Lincoln Finds a General*, III, *Grant's First Year in the West*, 30–34.

24. Long, *Civil War Day by Day*, October 31, Thursday, 1861, p. 133, for Missouri's attempted secession; Nevins, *Ordeal of the Union*, V, *War for the Union*, I, 309–11; James G. Randall, *Lincoln the President* (4 vols., New York: Dodd, Mead & Company, 1946–1955, IV, *Last Full Measure*, coauthored with Richard N. Current), I–II, *Springfield to Gettysburg*, II, 15–16. For Ewing, "Ewing, Thomas, Jr.," Boatner, *Civil War Dictionary*, p. 270, and for the 1863 incident, Fellman, *Inside War*, p. 95; Mark E. Neely, Jr., *The Fate of Liberty: Abraham Lincoln and Civil Liberties* (New York, Oxford: Oxford University Press, 1991), pp. 46–48. For Ewing's report on chaos in his district, Thomas Ewing, Jr., Brigadier-General, Saint Louis, Mo., August 3, 1863. To Lieut. Col. C[alvin]. W. Marsh, Assistant Adjutant-General, Department of the Missouri, O.R., XXII, pt. 2 (serial 33, 1888), p. 428.

25. By order of Brigadier-General Ewing: P[reston]. B. Plumb, Major and Chief of Staff, General Orders, No. 10, Hdqrs. District of the Border, Kansas City, Mo., August 18, 1863. O.R., XXII, pt. 2 (serial 33), p. 461.

26. Fellman, *Inside War*, p. 27 for the prison building, pp. 25–26, 77, 96–97, 135, 207, 214, 254–55 for the raid, particularly 25 for the number of guerrillas, 254 for the number of casualties they inflicted; "Quantrill, William Clarke," Boatner, *Civil War Dictionary*, p. 675.

27. By order of Brigadier-General Ewing, H[arrison]. Hannahs, Acting Assistant Adjutant-General. General Orders, No. 11. Hdqrs. District of the Border, Kansas City, Mo., O.R., XXII, pt. 2 (serial 33), p. 473; Neely, *Fate of Liberty*, p. 47, for the 20,000 estimate; Charles R. Mink, "General Orders, No. 11: The Forced Evacuation of Civilians during the Civil War," *Military Affairs, the journal of military history, including theory and technology*, 27:4 (Dec. 1980), 132–36, particularly 136.

28. Ellis Merton Coulter, *The Civil War and Readjustment in Kentucky* (Chapel Hill: University of North Carolina Press, 1926), pp. 1–30; Nevins, *Ordeal of the Union*, V, *War for the Union*, I, 129–31; Randall, *Lincoln the President*, II, 1–4; Thomas, *Confederate Nation*, pp. 88–89.

29. Coulter, *Civil War and Readjustment in Kentucky*, pp. 30–51; Nevins, *Ordeal of the Union*, V, *War for the Union*, I, 131–34; Randall, *Lincoln the President*, II, 4–11. For the First Congressional District, Stuart S. Sprague, "Civil War," in John E. Kleber, ed. in chief; Thomas D. Clark, Lowell H. Harrison, James C. Klotter, assoc. eds., *The Kentucky Encyclopedia* (Lexington: University Press of Kentucky, 1992), pp. 192–94, particularly 193.

30. A. Lincoln. Private & confidential. Executive Mansion Washington Sept 22d 1861. To Hon. O[rville]. H. Browning. Letter Signed, Illinois State Historical Library, Springfield, and copy, The Robert Todd Lincoln Collection of the Papers of Abraham Lincoln, Library of Congress, in Abraham Lincoln, *The Collected Works of Abraham Lincoln*, Roy P. Basler, ed.; Marion Dolores Pratt and Lloyd A. Dunlop, asst. eds. (9 vols. inc. index, The Abraham Lincoln Association, Springfield, Illinois; New Brunswick, New Jersey: Rutgers University Press, 1953; index, 1955), IV, 531–533, quotation from 532.

31. Randall, *Lincoln the President*, II, 7–8, citing *The Congressional Globe*, XXXII, pt. 4, 37th Congress, 2nd Session, *June 23, 1862 to July 17, 1862*, Appendix, pp. 82–83.

32. Coulter, *Civil War and Readjustment in Kentucky*, pp. 87–92; Nevins, *Ordeal of the Union*, V, *War for the Union*, I, 134–35; for Anderson, "Anderson, Robert," Boatner, *Civil War Dictionary*, p. 15.

33. For the military events, "Department No. 2 (Confed.)," Boatner, *Civil War Dictionary*, p. 236 for the department; Thomas Lawrence Connelly, *Army of the Heartland: The Army of Tennessee, 1861–1862* (Baton Rouge: Louisiana State University Press, 1967), pp. 43, 46 for Polk's command; ibid., pp. 51–54 for the invasion of Kentucky and capture of Columbus; September 3, Tuesday, 1861, and September 4, Wednesday, 1861, in Long, *Civil War Day by Day*, pp. 114 and 114–15 for the dates; Williams, *Lincoln Finds a General*, III, 54–55. For the political repercussions, Randall, *Lincoln the President*, II, 10. On

Robinson and the date of his accession, Lowell H. Harrison, "Robinson, James Fisher," Kleber, ed., *Encyclopedia of Kentucky*, p. 777. The secessionist was Henry C. Burnett, who joined the Confederacy; Leonard P. Curry, *Blueprint for Modern America: Nonmilitary Legislation of the First Civil War Congress* (Nashville: Vanderbilt University Press, 1968), p. 33.

34. Williams, *Lincoln Finds a General*, III, 47, for Grant's command, 55–56 for his actions; Bruce Catton, *Grant Moves South* (Boston, Toronto: Little, Brown and Company, 1960), p. 46 for Grant's command, pp. 49–51 for his taking Paducah.

35. Richard Orr Curry, *A House Divided: A Study of Statehood Politics and the Copperhead Movement in West Virginia* (Pittsburgh: University of Pittsburgh Press, 1964), p. 34, citing Virgil A. Lewis, ed., *How West Virginia Was Made: Proceedings of the First Convention of the People of Northwestern Virginia at Wheeling, May 13, 14 and 15, 1861, and the Journal of the Second Convention of the People of Northwestern Virginia at Wheeling, Which Assembled, June 11th, 1861, With Appendices and an Introduction, Annotations and Addenda.* (Charleston, West Virginia: News-Mail Company, Public Printer, 1909), pp. 29–30.

36. R. O. Curry, *House Divided*, 4, "The First Wheeling Convention (May 13–15, 1861)," pp. 38–45, 5, "Secession Sentiment in West Virginia," pp. 46–54, and particularly 53.

37. 6, "Ohio to the Rescue," ibid., pp. 55–68; "McClellan, George Brinton," Boatner, *Civil War Dictionary*, p. 524; "Ohio, Union Department and Army of the," ibid., 606–607, particularly p. 606; Williams, *Lincoln Finds a General*, I, 104–105.

38. G B. McClellan, Hd Qtrs Dept of the Ohio Cincinnati May 26 1861 [to] Soldiers. Autograph Document Signed, McClellan Papers (A-12:5), Library of Congress, in George B. McClellan, *The Civil War Papers of George B. McClellan: Selected Correspondence, 1860–1865*, Stephen W. Sears, ed. (New York: Ticknor & Fields, 1989), p. 25 ("Your mission . . ." begins a new paragraph); also in O.R., II (serial 2, 1880), 49. For the launching of the campaign, Stephen W. Sears, *George B. McClellan: The Young Napoleon* (New York: Ticknor & Fields, 1989), pp. 69–80; Williams, *Lincoln Finds a General*, I, 105–106.

39. Geo. B. McClellan Major Gen'l Commanding Head-Quarters, Dep't of the Ohio Grafton, Va., June 25th, 1861. To the Soldiers of the Army of the West: Document Printed, McClellan Papers (B-7:46), LC, in Sears, ed., *Civil War Papers of McClellan*, pp. 35–36, quotation from p. 36; also in O.R., II (serial 2, 1880), 196–97, quotation from 197. For Philippi and its sequel, Sears, *McClellan*, pp. 80–84; Williams, *Lincoln Finds a General*, I, 105.

40. Sears, *McClellan*, pp. 86–92; William M. Lamers, *The Edge of Glory: A Biography of General William S. Rosecrans, U.S.A.* (New York: Harcourt, Brace & World, Inc., 1961), pp. 26–35; Williams, *Lincoln Finds a General*, I, 106–12. For the Confederate perspective on the early western Virginia campaign, see Douglas Southall Freeman, *R. E. Lee: A Biography* (4 vols., New York: Charles Scribner's Sons; London: Charles Scribner's Sons Ltd, 1934–1935), I, 519, 532–535; and the same author's *Lee's Lieutenants: A Study in Command* (3 vols., New York: Charles Scribner's Sons, 1942–1944), I, *Manassas to Malvern Hill*, 23–34. For Scarey Creek, Long, *Civil War Day by Day*, July 17, Wednesday, 1861, p. 96.

41. Article. IV. Section. III. U.S. Constitution. 103rd Congress, 1st Session, Senate Document No. 103–6 (serial 14152), *The Constitution of the United States of America: Analysis and Interpretation: Annotations of Cases Decided in the Supreme Court of the United States to June 29, 1992*, Prepared by the Congressional Research Service, Library of Congress, Johnny H. Killian, George A. Costello, co-editors (Washington: U.S. Government Printing Office, 1996), p. 16; R. O. Curry, *House Divided*, pp. 69–72.

42. R. O. Curry, *House Divided*, pp. 79–86, particularly 86 for the voting returns, citing West Virginia, Constitutional Convention, 1861–1863, *Debates and Proceedings of*

*the First Constitutional Convention of West Virginia, 1861–1863,* Charles H. Ambler, F. H. Atwood, and W. B. Mathews, eds. (1 vol. in 3, Huntington, West Virginia: Gentry Brothers, Printers, 1939), I, 239–41.

43. R. O. Curry, *House Divided,* p. 86.

44. Ibid., pp. 88 (for first three tallies and Frederick)–89, 152 for all three statistics.

45. Ibid., p. 97, for ratification vote, citing *The Wheeling Intelligencer,* April 4, April 23, and May 7, 1862, all p. 1; for the legislative vote of May 13, 1862, Curry, *House Divided,* p. 100, and James G. Randall and David Donald, *The Civil War and Reconstruction* (Second Edition, Revised with Enlarged Bibliography, Lexington, Massachusetts: D.C. Heath and Company, A Division of Raytheon Education Company, 1969), p. 240, pp. 240–41 for the contrast between the Reorganized Government's legislature and the General Assembly of Virginia.

46. R. O. Curry, *House Divided,* 10, "Slavery Clouds the Issue," pp. 90–99.

47. Ibid., p. 129.

48. Ibid., pp. 122–23, citing *Cong. Globe,* XXXIII, pt. 1, 37th Congress, 3rd Session, *December 1, 1862, to February 12, 1863,* New Series, No. 4 (Friday, December 9, 1862), pp. 50–51.

49. [Abraham Lincoln, December 31, 1862.] Autograph Draft, Robert Todd Lincoln Collection, LC, in Basler, ed., *Works of Lincoln,* VI, 26–28, quotation from 28.

50. "McDowell, Irvin," Boatner, *Civil War Dictionary,* p. 531; "Northeastern Virginia, Union Department of," ibid., p. 600; Williams, *Lincoln Finds a General,* I, 66.

51. Abraham Lincoln. By the President: William H. Seward, Secretary of State. May 3, 1861, By the President of the United States. A Proclamation. Document Signed, National Archives, Record Group 11, Proclamations; Draft Signed, Robert Todd Lincoln Collection, LC, in Basler, ed., *Works of Lincoln,* IV, 353–54. Simon Cameron, Secretary of War, War Department, Washington, May 6, 1861, to          . Sent to the Governors of Connecticut, Delaware, Illinois, Indiana, Iowa, Maine, Massachusetts, Michigan, Minnesota, New Hampshire, New Jersey, New York, Ohio, Pennsylvania, Rhode Island, Vermont, and Wisconsin. O.R., Series Three, I (serial 122, 1899), 161.

52. Simon Cameron, Secretary of War, War Department, Washington, July 1, 1861. to the President of the United States, ibid., pp. 301–10, pp. 303–304 for the statistics given here.

53. Abraham Lincoln. July 4, 1861 *Fellow-citizens of the Senate and House of Representatives:* Autograph Draft, proof sheets, and revisions, Robert Todd Lincoln Collection, LC, in Basler, ed., *Works of Lincoln,* IV, 421–41, first quotation from 431–32, second from 432. Thirty-seventh Congress. Session I. (Statute I.) Chap. IX. — An Act to authorize the Employment of Volunteers to aid in enforcing the Laws and protecting Public Property. Approved, July 22, 1861. U.S. Laws, statutes, *The Statutes at Large of the United States of America, 1789–1873* (17 vols., I–IX, Boston: Charles C. Little and J. Brown, 1845–1854; X–XVII, Boston: Little, Brown, and Company, 1855–1873), 12 (December 5, 1859–March 3, 1863) (1863) 268–71; *Cong. Globe,* XXXI, 37th Congress, 1st Session, *July 4, 1861, to August 6, 1861,* Appendix, pp. 27–28, and with some typographical changes, in O.R., Series Three, I (serial 122, 1899), 380–83. For the legalization of Lincoln's emergency measures: Thirty-seventh Congress. Session II. (Statute II.) Chap. I. — An Act to refund and remit the Duties on Arms imported by the States. Approved, July 10, 1861. 12 *Statutes at Large* 255. Chap. II. — An Act to provide for the Payment of the Militia and Volunteers called into the Service of the United States from the Time they were called into Service to the thirtieth Day of June eighteen hundred and sixty-one. Approved, July 13, 1861. Ibid., p. 255. Chap. III. — An Act further to provide for the Collection of Duties on Imports, and for other Purposes. Approved, July 13, 1861. Ibid., pp. 255–58. Chap. V. — An Act to authorize a National Loan and for other Purposes. Approved, July 17, 1861. Ibid., pp. 259–61. Chap. VI. — An Act making additional Appropriations for the Support of the Army for the fiscal Year ending June thirtieth, eighteen hundred and sixty-

two, and Appropriations for Arrearages for the fiscal year ending June thirtieth, eighteen hundred and sixty-one. Approved, July 17, 1861. Ibid., pp. 261–64. Chap. VIII.—An Act making additional Appropriations for the Naval Service for the Year ending the thirtieth of June, eighteen hundred and sixty-two, and Appropriation of Arrearages for the Year ending the thirtieth of June, eighteen hundred and sixty-one. Approved, July 18, 1861. Ibid., pp. 265–66. Chap. XIII.—An Act to provide for the temporary Increase of the Navy. Approved, July 24, 1861. Ibid., pp. 272–73. These acts appear also in *Cong. Globe*, XXXI, Appendix, Chap. I, 23; Chap. II, 23; Chap. III, 23–24; Chap. V, 24–25; Chap. VI, 25–26; Chap. VIII, 26–27; Chap. XIII, 28.

54. M. C. Meigs, Quartermaster-General Quartermaster-General's Office, Washington, November 1, 1862 (annual report of the Quartermaster's Department for the fiscal year ending June 30, 1862), *O.R.*, Series Three, II (serial 123, 1899), 786–843, quotation from 803.

55. Thirty-seventh Congress, Third Session, House of Representatives, Rep[ort]. of Com[mittee]. *Report of the Joint Committee on the Conduct of the War* (3 vols., Washington: Government Printing Office, 1863), II, *Army of the Potomac*, 139.

56. Williams, *Lincoln Finds a General*, I, 68–72; Freeman, *Lee's Lieutenants*, I, 12–13, 44; "Shenandoah, Confederate Army of the," Boatner, *Civil War Dictionary*, pp. 738–39, particularly p. 738; "Patterson, Robert," ibid., p. 623. For the estimate of Patterson's numbers, "Bull Run Campaign, Va. 1st," ibid., pp. 99–101, particularly 99.

57. "Potomac, Confederate Army of the," Boatner, *Civil War Dictionary*, p. 664; Freeman, *Lee's Lieutenants*, I, 41–42.

58. Williams, *Lincoln Finds a General*, I, 74; for actual Confederate strength, see note 60 below. The present account of the First Battle of Manassas, as the Confederates usually called it, or First Bull Run, is based on the current standard work, William C. Davis, *Battle at Bull Run: A History of the First Major Campaign of the Civil War* (Garden City, New York: Doubleday & Company, Inc., 1977); Williams, *Lincoln Finds a General*, I, 74–101; Freeman, *Lee's Lieutenants*, I, 41–80; Hattaway and Jones, *How the North Won*, pp. 39–46.

59. Mary Boykin Miller Chesnut, *Mary Chesnut's Civil War*, ed. Comer Vann Woodward (New Haven and London: Yale University Press, 1981), August 1, 1861, p. 125.

60. The casualty estimates are from Thomas L. Livermore, *Numbers and Losses in the Civil War in America 1861–65* (Second Edition, Boston and New York: Houghton, Mifflin and Company, 1901; reprint, Dayton, Ohio: Morningside, 1986), p. 77, as is the figure for 32,232 Confederate effectives (8,884 of whom were the reinforcements from Johnston's Army of the Shenandoah; numbers engaged on each side are those of Williams, *Lincoln Finds a General*, I, 98.

61. Thirty-seventh Congress, Session II. (Statute II.) Chap. XVII.—An Act in addition to the "Act to authorize the Employment of Volunteers to aid in enforcing the Laws and protecting Public Property," approved July twenty-second, eighteen hundred and sixty-one. Approved, July 25, 1861. 12 *Statutes at Large* 274. The act appears also in *Cong. Globe*, XXXI, Appendix, 28–29, and with some typographical changes in *O.R.*, Series Three, I (serial 122, 1899), 383. See Williams, *Lincoln Finds a General*, I, 114, 399–40 n. 30, for a discussion of the confusion over whether the second act authorized 500,000 men in addition to the 500,000 of the first act. Williams concludes, like the present writer, that it did.

## 3. Groping for Strategy and Purpose

1. *The Congressional Globe*, XXXI, 37th Congress, 1st Session, *July 4, 1861, to August 4, 1861.* New Series, No. 14, Tuesday, July 23, 1861. For the Pacific railroad, 224; for the tariff bill, 217; relief for Mrs. Douglas, 221, 222.

2. Thirty-seventh Congress. Session I. (Statute I.) Chap. I. — An Act to refund and remit the Duties on Arms imported by States. Approved, July 10, 1861. Included was the proviso: "*Provided*, The Secretary of the Treasury shall be satisfied that the said arms are intended, in good faith, for the use of troops of any State which is, or may be engaged in aiding to suppress the insurrection now existing against the United States." U.S., Laws, statutes, *The Statutes at Large of the United States of America, 1789–1873* (17 vols., I–IX, Boston: Charles C. Little and J. Brown, 1845–1854; X–XVII, Boston: Little, Brown, and Company, 1855–1873), 12 (December 5, 1859–March 3, 1863) (1863), 255. The act appears also in *Cong. Globe*, XXXI, Appendix, 23. Also, Resolution No. 10, text, ibid., New Series, No. 18, Monday, July 29, 1863, 275, passed by the Senate, July 26, ibid., by the House, July 26, ibid., 288.

3. Thirty-seventh Congress. Session I. (Statute I.) Chap. XLV. — An Act to provide increased Revenue from Imports, to pay Interest on the Public Debt, and for other Purposes. Approved, August 5, 1861. 12 *Statutes at Large* 292–363. For the direct tax, Sec. 8, pp. 294–96; on its enforcement, Secs. 9–51, 53, pp. 296–309, 311–12. Chap. XLVI. — An Act supplementary to an Act entitled "An Act to authorize a National Loan, and for other purposes" (Chap. V. Approved, July 17, 1861. Ibid., 259–61, amount in Sec. 1, p. 259.) Approved, August 5, 1861. Ibid., 313–16. These laws appear also in *Cong. Globe*, XXXI, Appendix, 34–40; Sec. 8, p. 38; Secs. 9–48, 53, pp. 35–39; Sec. 49, p. 39; Secs. 50–51, pp. 39–40; Chap. V, 24–25; Chap. XLVI, 40–41. Article. I. Section. IX., paragraph 4 provides: "No Capitation, or other direct, Tax shall be laid, unless in Proportion to the Census of Enumeration . . ."; 103rd Congress, 1st Session, Senate Document No. 103–6 (serial 14252), *The Constitution of the United States of America: Analysis and Interpretation: Annotations of Cases Decided in the Supreme Court of the United States to June 29, 1992*, Prepared by the Congressional Research Service, Library of Congress, Johnny H. Killian, George A. Costello, co-editors (Washington: U.S. Government Printing Office, 1996), p. 10.

4. Text, *Cong. Globe*, XXXI, New Series, No. 14, Tuesday, July 23, 1861, 222, passed by the House, ibid., 223, by the Senate, ibid., No. 17, Friday, July 26, 1861, 257–65, particularly 265.

5. Thirty-seventh Congress. Session I. (Statute I.) Chap. LX. — An Act to confiscate Property used for Insurrectionary Purposes. Approved, August 6, 1861. 12 *Statutes at Large* 319; *Cong. Globe*, XXXI, Appendix, 42.

6. Thirty-seventh Congress. Session I. (Statute I.) Chap. IX. — An Act to authorize the Employment of Volunteers to aid in enforcing the Laws and protecting Public Property. Approved, July 22, 1861. 12 *Statutes at Large* 268–271, particularly Sec. 10, 270; *Cong. Globe*, XXXI, Appendix, 27–28, Sec. 10, 28. U.S. War Department, *The War of the Rebellion: A Compilation of the Official Records of the Union and Confederate Armies* (four series, 70 vols. in 128, Washington: Government Printing Office, 1880–1901), Series Three, I (serial 122, 1899), 380–83, Sec. 10, 383. The latter is hereafter cited as O.R.; all citations are of Series One unless otherwise noted.

7. Thirty-seventh Congress. Session I. (Statute I.) Chap. LVII. — Public [Law.] — No. 38. An Act to promote the Efficiency of the Engineer and Topographical Engineer Corps, and for other purposes. Approved, August 6, 1861, 12 *Statutes at Large* 317–18, particularly Sec. 3, 318. Also in *Cong. Globe*, XXXI, Appendix, 42; O.R., Series Three, I (serial 122, 1899), 401–402, Sec. 3, 402.

8. For McClellan's being summoned to Washington, Stephen W. Sears, *George B. McClellan: The Young Napoleon* (New York: Ticknor & Fields, 1988), pp. 94, 421 n. 34, and his arrival and assumption of command, p. 95. The Division (or District) of the Potomac became the Department of the Potomac, with its field force the Army of the Potomac, on August 15. "Potomac, Union Department and Army of the," "Potomac, Union Military District of the," Mark Mayo Boatner III, *The Civil War Dictionary* (Re-

vised Edition, New York: Vintage Books, A Division of Random House, Inc., 1991), p. 664. For Munson's Hill, Kenneth P. Williams, *Lincoln Finds a General: A Military Study of the Civil War* (5 vols., New York: The Macmillan Company, 1950–1959), I, 123; Margaret Leech, *Reveille in Washington* (New York and London: Harper & Brothers, Publishers, 1941), pp. 112, 116. For Ball's Bluff, ibid., p. 116; "Balls Bluff," Boatner, *Civil War Dictionary*, p. 41 (giving the Union casualty figures and Confederate casualties of thirty-three killed, 115 wounded, one missing, total 149); Herman Hattaway and Archer Jones, *How the North Won: A Military History of the Civil War* (Urbana, Chicago, London: University of Illinois Press, 1983), pp. 81–82.

9. Jas. Lesley, Jr., Chief Clerk War Department, War Department, Washington, August 26, 1861, to Major-General McClellan, U.S. Army, Washington, August 3, 1861. O.R., Series Three, I (serial 122, 1899), 455–56, particularly Inclosure, Statement of the number of troops accepted by the United States Government since the 8th of July, 1861, War Department. On 455–56, specifically 456. Regarding the September 27 figure, McClellan with a cautiousness that was to prove typical of him pared the number available for offensive action to 76,285. No. 1. Geo. B. McClellan, Major-General. U.S. Army, New York, August 4, 1863, to Brig. Gen. L. Thomas, Adjutant-General U.S. Army [extract from report of operations of the Army of the Potomac], ibid., V (serial 5, 1881), 5–6, specifically 6–8 for 168,318 and 76,285; also quoted letter Geo. B. McClellan, Major-General, to Hon. Simon Cameron, Secretary of War, late October, 1861, ibid., 9–11, specifically 10 for the statistics given here.

10. "Johnston, Joseph Eggleston," Boatner, *Civil War Dictionary*, p. 441, and Douglas Southall Freeman, *Lee's Lieutenants: A Study in Command* (3 vols., New York: Charles Scribner's Sons, 1942–1944), I, *Manassas to Appomattox*, 113, for both dates; Craig L. Symonds, *Joseph E. Johnston: A Civil War Biography* (New York, London: W. W. Norton & Company, 1992), p. 127, for the date of confirmation and the controversy over proper seniority of full generals.

11. Public Laws of the Provisional Congress. [Statute III.] Passed at the third session of the Provisional Congress, which was begun and held at the city of Richmond, on Saturday the twentieth day of July, 1861, and ended on the thirty-first day of August, 1861, Chap. XX. — An Act further to provide for the public defence, Approved August 8, 1861. Confederate States, Laws, statutes, By Authority of Congress, *The Statutes at Large of the Provisional Government of the Confederate States of America from the Institution of the Government, February 8, 1861, to Its Termination, February 18, 1862, Inclusive. Together with the Constitution of the Provisional Government, and the Permanent Constitution of the Confederate States, and the Treaties Concluded by the Confederate States with Indian Tribes*, James M. Matthews, ed. (Richmond: R. M. Smith, Printer to Congress, 1864), p. 176.

12. Public Laws of the Provisional Congress. [Statute V.] Passed at the fifth session, of the Provisional Congress, which was begun and held at the city of Richmond, on Monday, the eighteenth day of November, 1861, and ended on the eighteenth day of February, 1862, Chap. IX. — An Act providing for the granting of bounty and furloughs to privates and non-commissioned officers in the provisional army, Approved December 11, 1861. Ibid., pp. 223–24.

13. "Northrop, Lucius Bellinger," Boatner, *Civil War Dictionary*, p. 601; "Myers, Abraham C.," ibid., p. 577; Emory M. Thomas, *The Confederate Nation 1861–1865* (New York, Hagerstown, San Francisco, London: Harper & Row, Publishers, 1979), pp. 76, 134–35; Steven E. Woodworth, *Davis and Lee at War* (Lawrence: University Press of Kansas, 1995), pp. 8, 48–50 for Northrop, pp. 33, 48–49 for Myers.

14. Public Laws of the Provisional Congress. [Statute I.] Passed at the first session of the Provisional Congress, which was begun and held at the City of Montgomery, on Monday, February 8, 1861, and continued to March 16, 1861, Chap. XXI. — An Act to raise money for the support of the Government, and to provide for the Defence of the

Confederate States of America. Approved February 28, 1861, Matthews, ed., *Statutes at Large of the Provisional Congress of the Confederate States*, pp. 42–43. Also [Statute III.] Chap. XXIII. — An Act to authorize the issue of treasury notes and to provide a war tax for their redemption. Approved August 19, 1861. Ibid., pp. 177–83. James G. Randall and David Donald, *The Civil War and Reconstruction* (Second Edition, Revised with Enlarged Bibliography, Lexington, Massachusetts: D.C. Heath and Company, A Division of Raytheon Education Company, 1969), p. 259; Robert Cecil Todd, *Confederate Finance* (Athens: University of Georgia Press, 1954), pp. 39–41, 140–141.

15. Public Laws of the Provisional Congress. [Statute III.] Chap. XXIII, Matthews, ed., *Statutes at Large of the Provisional Congress of the Confederate States*, pp. 177–83; Randall and Donald, *Civil War and Reconstruction*, p. 257.

16. Public Laws of the Provisional Congress. [Statute III.] Chap. XXIII, Sec. 1, Matthews, ed., *Statutes at Large of the Provisional Congress of the Confederate States*, p. 177; Rembert W. Patrick, *Jefferson Davis and His Cabinet* (Baton Rouge: Louisiana State University Press, 1944), p. 224; Randall and Donald, *Civil War and Reconstruction*, p. 280.

17. Richard D. Goff, *Confederate Supply* (Durham, North Carolina: Duke University Press, 1969), especially pp. 3–19; Frank E. Vandiver, *Ploughshares into Swords: Josiah Gorgas and Confederate Ordnance* (Austin: University of Texas Press, 1952), especially pp. 3–65; Frank Lawrence Owsley, *King Cotton Diplomacy: Foreign Relations of the Confederate States of America* (Second Edition, revised by Harriet Chappell Owsley, Chicago: University of Chicago Press, 1959), p. 19. Gorgas had married Amelia Gayle of Alabama; Frank E. Vandiver, "Gorges, Josiah," Richard N. Current, ed. in chief; Paul D. Escott, Lawrence N. Powell, James I. Robertson, Jr., Emory M. Thomas, editorial board, *Encyclopedia of the Confederacy* (4 vols., New York, London, Toronto, Sydney, Tokyo, Singapore: Simon & Schuster, A Paramount Communications Company, 1993), II, 698–99, particularly 698. Gorgas was promoted to brigadier-general November 10, 1864; Ezra J. Warner, *Generals in Gray: Lives of the Confederate Commanders* (Baton Rouge: Louisiana State University Press, 1959), p. 112.

18. Owsley, *King Cotton Diplomacy*, pp. 134–35 for the 1859 and 1860 crops and the surplus in European factories, pp. 51–52 for Yancey, p. 52 for Rost; Thomas, *Confederate Nation*, p. 172 for the cotton crops and stocks.

19. Owsley, *King Cotton Diplomacy*, p. 261.

20. On international law, the critical importance of major ports, and the Union's blockading them, Lynn M. Case and Warren F. Spencer, *The United States and France: Civil War Diplomacy* (Philadelphia: University of Pennsylvania Press, 1957), pp. 139–40; on Lyons, ibid., p. 145. On Russell, Owsley, *King Cotton Diplomacy*, pp. 222–23.

21. Case and Spencer, *United States and France*, pp. 142–43.

22. Owsley, *King Cotton Diplomacy*, pp. 266, 267.

23. Vandiver, *Ploughshares into Swords*, especially pp. 55–60.

24. Charles B. Dew, *Ironmaker to the Confederacy: Joseph R. Anderson and the Tredegar Iron Works* (New Haven and London: Yale University Press, 1966).

25. Vandiver, *Ploughshares into Swords*, pp. 60–63, 65.

26. John Niven, *Gideon Welles: Lincoln's Secretary of the Navy* (New York: Oxford University Press, 1973). For Fox, ibid., especially pp. 353–55.

27. Fletcher Pratt, *The Navy: A History: The Story of a Service in Action* (Garden City, New York: Garden City Publishing Co., Inc., 1941), "1861, Outbreak of Civil War: Ships, Stations and State," p. 424; also p. 244 for ships in home waters, pp. 247–248 for the destruction at Norfolk. *Powhatan* added to Pratt's list because of use in Fort Pickens expedition.

28. Mary Boykin Miller Chesnut, *Mary Chesnut's Civil War*, ed. Comer Vann Woodward (New Haven and London: Yale University Press, 1981), May 13, 1861, p. 61.

29. Rowena Reed, *Combined Operations in the Civil War* (Annapolis, Maryland:

Naval Institute Press, 1978), pp. 10–16; Allan Nevins, *Ordeal of the Union* (8 vols., *Ordeal of the Union*, I, *Fruits of Manifest Destiny 1847–1852; Ordeal of the Union*, II, *A House Dividing 1852–1857* [New York, London: Charles Scribner's Sons, 1947]; III, *The Emergence of Lincoln*, I, *Douglas, Buchanan, and Party Chaos 1857–1859; IV, The Emergence of Lincoln*, II, *Prologue to Civil War 1859–1861* [New York, London: Charles Scribner's Sons, 1950]; V, *The War for the Union*, I, *The Improvised War 1861–1862* [New York: Charles Scribner's Sons, 1959]; VI, *The War for the Union*, II, *War Becomes Revolution* [New York: Charles Scribner's Sons, 1960]; VII. *The War for the Union*, III, *The Organized War 1863–1864;* VIII, *The War for the Union*, IV, *The Organized War to Victory 1864–1865* [New York: Charles Scribner's Sons, 1971]), V, *War for the Union*, I, 285–86.

30. Samuel Francis Du Pont, *Samuel Francis Du Pont: A Selection from His Civil War Letters*, ed. John D. Hayes (3 vols., Ithaca, New York: Published for The Eleutherian Mills Historical Library, Cornell University Press, 1969), I, *The Mission: 1860–1862*, Introduction, lxvii–lxx; Reed, *Combined Operations*, pp. 8–10, 22–23.

31. Hayes, ed., *Du Pont Letters*, I, Introduction, lxx–lxxii; Frank [S. F. Du Pont], (Journal Letter No. 4), *Wabash*, off Hilton Head, Port Royal, 7 Nov. 1861, to My precious Sophie [Sophie Madeleine du Pont Du Pont], Henry Francis du Pont Collection of Winterthur Manuscripts, Eleutherian Mills Historical Library, Delaware 92410, ibid., pp. 222–26 and editor's n. 1, pp. 222–23; [continued] Nov. 8 1861, pp. 226–28; Reed, *Combined Operations*, pp. 23–32.

32. Douglas Southall Freeman, *R. E. Lee: A Biography* (4 vols., New York: Charles Scribner's Sons; London: Charles Scribner's Sons Ltd., 1934–1935), I, 92–94 for Mrs. Lee's family, 104–107 for the marriage, 431–32 and 432 n. 4 for Scott; Emory M. Thomas, *Robert E. Lee: A Biography* (New York, London: W. W. Norton & Company, 1995), pp. 60–61 for Mrs. Lee's family, pp. 64–65 for the marriage, pp. 187–88 for Scott. For Lee's arrival at Port Royal, Freeman, *Lee*, I, 608; Thomas, *Lee*, p. 211.

33. Freeman, *Lee*, I, 559; Thomas, *Lee*, p. 204. Both sources point out that by date of commission, Samuel Cooper and Albert Sidney Johnston were senior to Lee, Joseph E. Johnston and Pierre G. T. Beauregard junior to him.

34. Hayes, ed., *Du Pont Letters*, I, 228–387; Reed, *Combined Operations*, pp. 46–51; Freeman, *Lee*, I, 608–23; Thomas, *Lee*, pp. 211–14.

35. "Gillmore, Quincy Adams," Boatner, *Civil War Dictionary*, p. 343; "Fort Pulaski," ibid., pp. 296–97; Hayes, ed., *Du Pont Letters*, I, 395–423; Reed, *Combined Operations*, pp. 52–56; Freeman, *Lee*, 623–24, 626–27, 629; Thomas, *Lee*, pp. 215–16.

36. Hayes, ed., *Du Pont Letters*, I, Introduction, lxxiv–lxxvii; Reed, *Combined Operations*, pp. 57, 268–71.

37. James G. Randall, *Lincoln the President* (4 vols., New York: Dodd, Mead & Company, 1946–1955, IV, *Last Full Measure*, coauthored with Richard N. Current), I–II, *Springfield to Gettysburg*, II, 37; Case and Spencer, *United States and France*, pp. 191–93.

38. Charles Wilkes, *Autobiography of Rear Admiral Charles Wilkes, U.S. Navy, 1798–1877*, ed. William James Morgan, David B. Tyler, Joye L. Leonhart, Mary F. Loughlin, With an Introduction by John D. H. Kane, Jr. (Washington: Naval History Division Department of the Navy, 1978), "Wilkes Chronology," pp. xvii–xxii, specifically xxi. This account of the *Trent* Affair owes much to Case and Spencer, *United States and France*, pp. 193–234, and Norman B. Ferris, *The* Trent *Affair: A Diplomatic Crisis* (Knoxville: University of Tennessee Press, 1970). See also Charles Francis Adams, "The Trent Affair," *American Historical Review*, 17:4 (July 1912), 540–62; Owsley, *King Cotton Diplomacy*, pp. 78–85; Randall, *Lincoln the President*, II, 37–51.

39. Sears, *McClellan* attempts to give the Young Napoleon as much sympathy as he merits; see pp. 96–124 for his activities during the autumn of 1861, pp. 122–23 for his quarrel with Scott, p. 125 for his replacing Scott as General-in-Chief. An effusively sympathetic biography is Warren W. Hassler, Jr., *General George B. McClellan: Shield*

of the Union (Baton Rouge: Louisiana State University Press, 1957); see pp. 23–37, 30, 37, respectively, for the same topics. McClellan offers inadvertently generous insights into his own character in George B. McClellan, *McClellan's Own Story: The War for the Union, The Soldiers Who Fought It, The Civilians Who Directed It and His Relations to It and to Them* (New York: Charles L. Webster & Company, 1887); see especially pp. 66–141, 84–86 and 91, 173 for the topics just indicated. Always essential for the Union military issues that it encompasses is Williams, *Lincoln Finds a General*; see I, 113–30 for McClellan during the autumn, 126–27 for his quarrel with Scott, 131 for his replacement of Scott.

40. For McClellan's estimates of 100,000, then 150,000 Confederates facing him, Williams, *Lincoln Finds a General*, I, 126, 127; for Pinkerton, ibid., 129. For similar McClellan estimates of the enemy, Sears, *McClellan*, pp. 103–107, and for Pinkerton, pp. 107–10.

41. Everette B. Long with Barbara Long, *The Civil War Day by Day: An Almanac 1861–1865*, Foreword by Bruce Catton (Garden City, New York: Doubleday & Company, Inc., 1971), December 9, 1861, Monday, p. 147, December 10, Tuesday, 148; Hans L. Trefousse, *The Radical Republicans: Lincoln's Vanguard for Racial Justice* (New York: Alfred A. Knopf, 1969), pp. 93–148; Sears, *McClellan*, pp. 136–38.

42. "Stone, Charles Pomeroy," Boatner, *Civil War Dictionary*, p. 800; "Stone, Charles Pomeroy," Francis B. Heitman, *Historical Register and Dictionary of the United States Army, From Its Organization, September 29, 1789, to March 2, 1903*, Published under act of Congress approved March 2, 1903. 57th Congress, Second Session, House Document 446 (serial 4536), (2 vols., Washington: Government Printing Office, 1903), I, 928–29, particularly 929.

43. Quoted in David Donald, *Charles Sumner and the Rights of Man* (New York: Alfred A. Knopf, 1970), p. 70, citing Stone to Sumner, Dec. 22, 1861, Sumner MSS., Houghton Library, Harvard University (Donald's biography of Sumner during the Civil War and Reconstruction complements his earlier *Charles Sumner and the Coming of the Civil War* [New York: Alfred A. Knopf, 1961]).

44. Thomas Harry Williams, "Investigation 1862," *American Heritage*, 6:6 (December 1954), 16–21; Leech, *Reveille in Washington*, pp. 28–29, 34, 43–44, 64–65, 81, 111–12, 116–17, and especially 126–27 for Stone's trial.

45. *Cong. Globe*, XXXII, pt. 1, 37th Cong., 2nd Sess., *December 2, 1861 to February 26, 1862*, New Series, No. 1, Friday, Dec. 6, 1861, p. 15; for July 22 vote, ibid., XXXI, New Series, No. 14, Tuesday, July 22, 1861, p. 223.

46. For Butler's rank, "Butler, Benjamin Franklin," Heitman, *Historical Register*, I, 268; "Butler, Benjamin Franklin," Boatner, *Civil War Dictionary*, pp. 109–10, specifically 110. For his department command, "Virginia, Union Department of," ibid., p. 879. For his policy, Benj. F. Butler, Major-General, Commanding, Headquarters Department of Virginia, Fort Monroe, May 24, 1861, to Lieutenant-General Winfield Scott, O.R., II (serial 2, 1880), 648–49, [continued] Saturday, May 25, ibid., pp. 649–51, quotation from May 25, pp. 649–50. For the controversy over whether Butler first called the African Americans taken into the Union Army's custody contraband, Hans L. Trefousse, *Ben Butler: The South Called Him BEAST!* (New York: Twayne Publishers, 1957), pp. 79, 274 notes 11 and 17. For Union policy in response, Randall, *Lincoln the President*, II, 130.

47. "Fremont, John Charles," Heitman, *Historical Register*, I, 436, for his rank. "Frémont, John Charles," and "Western Department," Boatner, *Civil War Dictionary*, pp. 314–15, specifically p. 314, and p. 903, for the department command.

48. For Frémont's arrival, Allan Nevins, *Frémont: Pathmarker of the West* (New York, London, Toronto: Longmans, Green and Co., 1955), p. 477; Nevins, *Ordeal of the Union*, V, *War for the Union*, I, 309, 311. For the early period of his command, the same

two works, pp. 477–99 and pp. 311–27, respectively. The Blairs would have preferred Nathaniel Lyon, but they settled on Frémont to avoid antagonizing Missouri's conservative Unionists; Nevins, *Frémont*, p. 475. For the siege of Lexington, September 19–21, ibid., pp. 523–25; K. P. Williams, *Lincoln Finds a General*, III, *Grant's First Year in the West*, 64, the latter for the strength of the Federals surrendered.

49. Randall, *Lincoln the President*, II, 20, for the dubious contracts, 19 for the headquarters. For an account of Frémont's business dealings sympathetic to the general, Nevins, *Frémont*, pp. 489–93; for the headquarters, pp. 493–94.

50. Proclamation, J. C. Frémont, Major-General, Commanding, Headquarters Western Department, Saint Louis, August 30, 1861, O.R., III (serial 3, 1881), 466–67.

51. Ibid., p. 467.

52. A. Lincoln, Private and confidential, Washington, D.C. Sept. 2, 1861 To Major General Fremont, Copy, The Robert Todd Lincoln Collection of the Papers of Abraham Lincoln, Library of Congress, Abraham Lincoln, *The Collected Works of Abraham Lincoln*, Roy P. Basler, ed.; Marion Delores Pratt and Lloyd A. Dunlop, asst. eds. (9 vols. inc. index, The Abraham Lincoln Association, Springfield, Illinois; New Brunswick, New Jersey: Rutgers University Press, 1953; index, 1955), IV, 506. Also O.R., Series Two, I (serial 118, 1898), 766–67.

53. A. Lincoln, Private & confidential, Executive Mansion, Washington Sept 22d 1861. To Hon O[rville]. H. Browning, Letter Signed, Illinois State Historical Library, Springfield, Illinois; Autograph Draft Signed and Letter Signed copy, The Robert Todd Lincoln Collection, LC, Basler, ed., *Works of Lincoln*, IV, 531–33, quotation from 532. See pp. 506–507 on the letter from Speed, 507n on Frémont's response.

54. J. C. Frémont, Headquarters Western Department, Saint Louis, September 3, 1861. To The President, O.R., III (serial 3), 477–78; ibid., Series Two, I (serial 118), 767–68.

55. John G. Nicolay and John Hay, *Abraham Lincoln: A History* (10 vols., New York: The Century Co., 1890), IV, 415, quoting Lincoln on what Mrs. Frémont had said. Frémont's biographer Allan Nevins does not believe she stated anything so extreme; Nevins, *Frémont*, pp. 516–19, quoting, pp. 516–18, undated testimony from her, in the MS. Memoirs by her and the Frémonts' son, Frank P., Jessie Benton Frémont MSS., Hubert Howe Bancroft Library, University of California, Berkeley.

56. A. Lincoln, Washington D.C., Sep. 11. 1861. to Major General John C. Frémont. Autograph Draft Signed, The Robert Todd Lincoln Collection, LC, Basler, ed., *Works of Lincoln*, IV, 517–18; O.R., III (serial 3, 1881), 485–86.

57. Nevins, *Frémont*, pp. 513–14, 537; K. P. Williams, *Lincoln Finds a General*, III, 62, 64–65, for the investigative trips. For the transfer of command, Winfield Scott, By command: E[dwin]. D. Townsend, Assistant Adjutant-General, General Orders, No. 18, Headquarters of the Army, Washington, October 24, 1861. O.R., III (serial 3, 1881), 553; J. C. Frémont, Major-General, U.S. Army, General Orders, No. 28, Hdqrs. Western Department, Springfield, Mo., November 2, 1861. Ibid., 559; D. Hunter, Major-General, Springfield, Mo., November 3 [?], (via Rolla, November 7, 1861.), to Adjutant-General. U.S. Army. Ibid., 561. Thomas had been brigadier-general, Adjutant-General, since August 3, 1861; Heitman, *Historical Register*, I, 954.

58. Nevins, *Ordeal of the Union*, V, *War for the Union*, I, 400–403; Randall, *Lincoln the President*, II, 56–58.

59. Abraham Lincoln, December 3, 1861, to Fellow Citizens of the Senate and House of Representatives, Document Signed, National Archives, RG 233, Thirty-seventh Congress, Second Session, Original Annual Message of the President — Interior, Basler, ed., *Works of Lincoln*, V, 35–53, quotation from 48–49.

60. Ibid., p. 49.

61. Abraham Lincoln, July 4, 1861, to *Fellow-Citizens of the Senate and House of*

*Representatives*, Autograph Document, Robert Todd Lincoln Collection, LC, ibid., IV, 421–41, quotation from 426.

62. Quoted in John Hay, *Lincoln and the Civil War in the Diaries and Letters of John Hay*, Selected and With an Introduction by Tyler Dennett (New York: Dodd, Mead & Company, 1939), May 7, 1861, pp. 19–20, citing the Diary of John Hay in the John Hay Papers in possession of the Hay family.

63. Message of July 4, 1861, Basler, ed., *Works of Lincoln*, IV, 426.

64. Ibid., p. 438.

65. Message of December 3, 1861, ibid., V, 51.

66. Ibid., p. 53.

67. "Halleck, Henry Wager," Boatner, *Civil War Dictionary*, p. 367; "Missouri, Union Department of (the)," ibid., p. 556; "Buell, Don Carlos," ibid., pp. 96–97, particularly 96; and for Buell's date of command, "Ohio, Union Department and Army of the," ibid., pp. 606–607, especially 606.

68. Geo. B. McClellan Maj. Gen. Comd'g U.S.A. Head Quarters of the Army Washington, D.C. Nov. 11 1861 to Maj. Gen. H. W. Halleck, U.S.A. Comd'g Dept of Missouri, Copy, McClellan Papers (D-7:69), LC, George B. McClellan, *The Civil War Papers of George B. McClellan: Selected Correspondence, 1860–1865*, Stephen W. Sears, ed. (New York: Ticknor & Fields, 1989), pp. 130–31; also O.R., III (serial 3, 1881), 568–69. [George B. McClellan,] Head Quarters of the Army Wasn. Nov. 7 1861 to Brig. Gen. D.C. Buell, Copy, McClellan Papers (D-7:69), LC, Sears, ed., *Papers of McClellan*, pp. 125–126, quotations from p. 125; also O.R., IV (serial 4, 1882), 342. McClellan's similar words to Halleck about the purposes of the war in the letter of November 11 are: "In regard to the political conduct of affairs, you will please labor to impress upon the inhabitants of Missouri and the adjacent States that we are fighting solely for the integrity of the Union, to uphold the power of our National Government, and to restore to the nation the blessings of peace and good order." Sears, ed., *Papers of McClellan*, p. 130; O.R., III, 569. McClellan reiterated essentially the same instructions to Buell: [George B. McClellan,], Head Quarters of the Army Washn. Nov 12 1861. To Brig. Gen. D.C. Buell Comd'g Dept. of the Ohio. Copy, McClellan Papers (D-7:69), LC, Sears, ed., *Papers of McClellan*, pp. 131–32; O.R., IV (serial 4, 1882), 355–56.

69. Geo B McClellan Maj Genl USA Comdg Head Quarters, Army of the Potomac July 11/62 to Hill Carter, Esqr Shirley, Copy, McClellan Papers (B-11:48), LC, Sears, ed., *Papers of McClellan*, pp. 352–53, quotation from p. 352; O.R., XI, pt. 3 (serial 14, 1884), 316.

70. Geo B McClellan Maj Genl Comdg (Confidential) Head Quarters, Army of the Potomac Camp near Harrison's Landing, Va. July 7th 1862 to His Excellency A Lincoln Presdt U.S., Letter Signed, Lincoln Papers, LC, Sears, ed., *Papers of McClellan*, 344–345, quotation from p. 344; O.R., XI, pt. 1 (serial 12, 1884), 73–74, quotation from 74; McClellan, *Own Story*, pp. 487–89, quotation from p. 489.

71. Same letter, Sears, ed., *Papers of McClellan*, pp. 344, 345; O.R., XI, pt. 1, 74; McClellan, *Own Story*, p. 488.

72. For the design for the amphibious campaign to Urbanna, Sears, *McClellan*, pp. 131, 140–41, 147, 149–51, 156, 159–60; K. P. Williams, *Lincoln Finds a General*, I, 137–42.

## 4. Bloodshed and Indecision

1. A. Lincoln, Executive Mansion, Washington, January 6th, 1862, to Brig. Gen. Buell, Letter Signed, Oliver R. Barrett Collection, Chicago, Ill. [since broken up], Autograph Draft Signed, The Robert Todd Lincoln Collection of the Papers of Abraham

Lincoln, Library of Congress, Abraham Lincoln, *The Collected Works of Abraham Lincoln* (9 vols. inc. index, The Abraham Lincoln Association, Springfield, Illinois; New Brunswick, New Jersey: Rutgers University Press, 1953; index, 1955), V, 91; also in U.S. War Department, *The War of the Rebellion: A Compilation of the Official Records of the Union and Confederate Armies* (four series, 70 vols. in 128, Washington: Government Printing Office, 1880–1901), VII (serial 7, 1882), 531. The latter is hereafter cited as *O.R.*; all citations are of Series One unless otherwise noted.

2. Montgomery Cunningham Meigs, "The Relations of President Lincoln and Secretary Stanton to the Military Commanders of the Civil War," *American Historical Review*, 26:2 (Jan. 1921), 285–303, quotation from 292.

3. For the conference, Stephen W. Sears, *George B. McClellan: The Young Napoleon* (New York: Ticknor & Fields, 1988), pp. 139–42; Kenneth P. Williams, *Lincoln Finds a General: A Military Study of the Civil War* (5 vols., New York: The Macmillan Company, 1950–1959), I, 137–38. For the appointment of Stanton, the standard biography, Benjamin P. Thomas and Harold M. Hyman, *Stanton: The Life and Times of Lincoln's Secretary of War* (New York: Alfred A. Knopf, 1962), p. 143; Herman Hattaway and Archer Jones, *How the North Won: A Military History of the Civil War* (Urbana, Chicago, London: University of Illinois Press, 1983), p. 90.

4. General Anderson's Department of Kentucky was merged into a newly created Department of the Cumberland on August 15, 1861; "Kentucky, Union Department and Army of," Mark Mayo Boatner III, *The Civil War Dictionary* (Revised Edition, New York: David McKay Company, 1986), pp. 455–56, particularly 456; "Cumberland, Union Department and Army of the," ibid., pp. 212–13, particularly 212. On Sherman's command, ibid., and "Sherman, William Tecumseh," pp. 750–51, particularly 751. On Buell, whose command was redesignated on November 9 as the Department of the Ohio, ibid., p. 212; "Buell, Don Carlos," ibid., pp. 96–97, particularly 96; "Ohio, Union Department and Army of the," ibid., pp. 606–607, particularly 606.

5. Hattaway and Jones, *How the North Won*, pp. 56–57, 61–62; Sears, *McClellan*, pp. 129, 139, 153; Williams, *Lincoln Finds a General*, III, *Grant's First Year in the West* (1952), 139, 141–44.

6. The battle is also sometimes known as Fishing Creek, Somerset, and Beech Grove. For it, Hattaway and Jones, *How the North Won*, pp. 62–63; Williams, *Lincoln Finds a General*, III, 146, 171–76; "Logan Cross Roads," Boatner, *Civil War Dictionary*, pp. 487–89, particularly p. 489 for the numbers and casualties; "Crittenden, George Bibb," ibid., p. 208.

7. Hattaway and Jones, *How the North Won*, p. 35; Sears, *McClellan*, p. 76; Charles Winslow Elliott, *Winfield Scott: The Soldier and the Man* (New York: The Macmillan Company, 1937), pp. 721–24; John S. D. Eisenhower, *Agent of Destiny: The Life and Times of General Winfield Scott* (New York, London, Toronto, Singapore, Sydney: The Free Press, 1997), pp. 385–87.

8. For Grant's ranks, "Grant, Ulysses Simpson," Francis B. Heitman, *Historical Register and Dictionary of the United States Army, From Its Organization, September 29, 1789, to March 2, 1903*. Published under act of Congress approved March 2, 1903. 57th Congress, Second Session, House Document 446 (serial 4536). (2 vols.) Washington: Government Printing Office, 1903), I, 470. For his entry into the Civil War Army, Williams, *Lincoln Finds a General*, III, Chapter I, "Point Pleasant to Galena," 1–9, and Chapter II, "'And Captain Grant,'" 10–41, particularly 11 for Yates, 11–12 for Washburne. See also Bruce Catton, *Grant Moves South* (Boston, Toronto: Little, Brown and Company, 1960), pp. 3–12 for the 21st Illinois, particularly 3 for Yates, and pp. 16–17 for Washburne. *Grant Moves South* continues the biography in which Grant's early years are covered by Lloyd Lewis, *Captain Sam Grant* (Boston: Little, Brown and Company, 1950); Bruce Catton, *Grant Takes Command* (Boston, Toronto: Little, Brown and Company, 1969) in turn continues the narrative through the late 1863–1865 campaigns.

9. "Belmont, Mo.," Boatner, *Civil War Dictionary*, pp. 57–58, particularly 58 for the cannon and prisoners; Williams, *Lincoln Finds a General*, III, 80–98, particularly 98 for an assessment of the casualties; Catton, *Grant Moves South*, pp. 70–84.

10. "Curtis, Samuel Ryan," Heitman, *Historical Register*, I, 347, for Curtis's ranks. William L. Shea and Earl J. Hess, *Pea Ridge: Civil War Campaign in the West* (Chapel Hill & London: University of North Carolina Press, 1992), p. 5 for his command, pp. 5–6 for his background, pp. 3, 7, 9–10 for his assignment.

11. "Sheridan, Philip Henry," Heitman, *Historical Register*, I, 881. Shea's and Hess's *Pea Ridge* is an exemplary campaign history, all the more impressive because its topic was hitherto badly neglected. For Sheridan, p. 10, and for Curtis's logistics more generally, pp. 10–12, 51–52.

12. Van Dorn actually arrived to assume command on January 29. "Trans-Mississippi, Confederate District, Department, and Army," Boatner, *Civil War Dictionary*, pp. 845–46, specifically 845. Shea and Hess, *Pea Ridge*, pp. 15–16 (for Price), 16, 19 (for McCulloch), 19–20, 22 (for Van Dorn), 23 (for the strength of Price's army), 27–28 (for the abandonment of Springfield).

13. This account is based mainly on that of Shea and Hess, *Pea Ridge*. The strength and casualty figures appear on p. 270.

14. 15, "Marching through Arkansas," ibid., pp. 284–306. "Curtis, Samuel Ryan," Heitman, *Historical Register*, I, 347.

15. The standard work is Ray C. Colton, *The Civil War in the Western Territories: Arizona, Colorado, New Mexico, and Utah* (Norman and London: University of Oklahoma Press, 1959). See particularly pp. 13–19 for Fort Fillmore; pp. 21–48 for Sibley's advance; 4, "Glorieta, the Gettysburg of the West," pp. 49–80 for that battle; and pp. 81–98 for the Confederate withdrawal. There is a detailed account of the campaign in Shelby Foote, *The Civil War: A Narrative* (3 vols., New York: Random House, 1958–1963), I, *Fort Sumter to Perryville*, 293–305, particularly 295 for the numbers at Fort Fillmore, 296 for Lynde's surrender of 492 men and Sibley's numbers at the beginning of his advance, and 304 for Sibley's total casualties. See also "New Mexico and Arizona Operations in 1862," Boatner, *Civil War Dictionary*, pp. 590–91, particularly 590 for Lynde's total losses, Baylor's creation of the Territory of Arizona, and Canby's establishment of the Department of New Mexico; "New Mexico, Confederate Army of," pp. 589–90, particularly 589 for the December 14 date; "Valverde, N.M.," ibid., p. 865; "California Column," ibid., p. 114. Everette B. Long with Barbara Long, *The Civil War Day by Day: An Almanac 1861–1865*, Foreword by Bruce Catton (Garden City, New York: Doubleday & Company, Inc., 1971), July 8, Monday, 1861, p. 92 for Sibley's date of assignment; December 14, Saturday, ibid., p. 149, for his assumption of command; February 21, Friday, 1862, ibid., pp. 173–74, particularly 173, for Valverde; March 26, Wednesday, ibid., p. 189, for Apache Pass, including the casualties; March 28, Friday, ibid., pp. 189–90, for Glorieta, particularly 190 for the casualties; November 29, Tuesday, 1864, pp. 602–603 for Sand Creek, particularly 602 for casualties; "Canby, Edward Richard Sprigg," 279; "Carleton, James Henry," p. 282; "Sibley, Henry Hopkins," p. 886 in Heitman, *Historical Register*, I, for their ranks in the United States Army; "Sibley, Henry Hopkins," Boatner, *Civil War Dictionary*, p. 759, for the latter in the Confederacy.

16. H. W. Halleck, Major-General, Saint Louis, February 2, 1862, to Brig. Gen. D. C. Buell, Louisville, Ky., O.R., VII (serial 7, 1882), 578–79. The recent standard history of the Henry-Donelson campaign, another work of exemplary quality, is Benjamin Franklin Cooling, *Forts Henry and Donelson: The Key to the Confederate Heartland* (Knoxville: University of Tennessee Press, 1987).

17. Ulysses S. Grant, *Personal Memoirs of Ulysses S. Grant* (2 vols., New York: Charles H. Webster & Co., 1885–1886), I, 287.

18. U. S. Grant, Brigadier-General. Cairo January 28, 1862. To Maj. Gen. H. W. Halleck, Saint Louis, Mo. O.R., VII (serial 7, 1882), 121.

19. A. H. Foote, Flag-Officer, Cairo, January 28, 1862. to Major-General Henry W. Halleck, Saint Louis, Mo., ibid., p. 120; U.S. Naval War Records Office, *Official Records of the Union and Confederate Navies in the War of the Rebellion* (two series, 30 vols., Washington: Government Printing Office, 1894–1927), Series One, XXII (1908), 524; H. W. Halleck, Major-General. Headquarters, Department of the Missouri, Saint Louis, January 30, 1862. to Brig. Gen. U. S. Grant, Cairo, Ill., *O.R.*, VII (serial 7, 1882), 121–22.

20. Cooling, *Forts Henry and Donelson*, pp. 72–109; Williams, *Lincoln Finds a General*, III, 199–205; Thomas Lawrence Connelly, *Army of the Heartland: The Army of Tennessee, 1861–1862* (Baton Rouge: Louisiana State University Press, 1967), pp. 19, 39, 43, 106–13.

21. Cooling, *Forts Henry and Donelson*, pp. 115–19; Williams, *Lincoln Finds a General*, III, 206–11; Catton, *Grant Moves South*, pp. 145–47.

22. "Johnston, Albert Sydney," Heitman, *Historical Register*, I, 576, for ranks in the U.S. Army; Marcus J. Wright, comp. and preparer, *General Officers of the Confederate Army, Officers of the Executive Departments of the Confederate States, Members of the Confederate Congress by States* (New York: The Neale Publishing Company, 1911), pp. 9–10; "Johnston, Albert Sidney," "Department No. 2 (Confed.)," Boatner, *Civil War Dictionary*, pp. 440, 236; Connelly, *Army of the Heartland*, pp. 59–64. The standard biography is Charles P. Roland, *Albert Sidney Johnston: Soldier of Three Republics* (Austin: University of Texas Press, 1964).

23. "Kentucky, Confed. Central Army of," Boatner, *Civil War Dictionary*, p. 455; Williams, *Lincoln Finds a General*, III, 213–17, 231–32 for Johnston's moves, including the estimate of 28,000 men at Bowling Green from 214, 229–38 for the beginning of Grant's investment; Cooling, *Forts Henry and Donelson*, pp. 122–38 for Johnston's moves, including p. 126 for the numbers of Confederate reinforcements, pp. 138–65 for the actions through the gunboat attack; Connelly, *Army of the Heartland*, pp. 111–21. "Henry and Donelson Campaign," Boatner, *Civil War Dictionary*, pp. 394–97, gives the Union strength at Fort Donelson as 27,000 and the Confederate as 21,000 (p. 397).

24. U. S. Grant, Brigadier-General, Commanding, Headquarters Army in the Field, Camp near Fort Donelson, February 16, 1862 to General S. B. Buckner, Confederate Army. *O.R.*, VII (serial 7), 161. Buckner had received a Confederate States commission as of September 14, 1861; "Buckner, Simon Bolivar," Boatner, *Civil War Dictionary*, pp. 95–96, particularly 96.

25. Thomas L. Livermore, *Numbers and Losses in the Civil War in America 1861–65* (Second Edition, Boston and New York: Houghton, Mifflin and Company, 1901; reprint, Dayton, Ohio: Morningside, 1986), p. 78. See Cooling, *Forts Henry and Donelson*, p. 205, for escapees with Forrest; "Henry and Donelson Campaign," Boatner, *Civil War Dictionary*, p. 396 for escapees with Pillow.

26. Williams, *Lincoln Finds a General*, III, 202, 219, 224, 230–31, 233–34, 248–52, 263–64, for communications among commanders; "Ohio, Union Department and Army of the," Boatner, *Civil War Dictionary*, pp. 606–607, particularly 606; "Mississippi, Union Department of the," ibid., p. 555.

27. Connelly, *Army of the Heartland*, pp. 126–51; Archer Jones, *Confederate Strategy from Shiloh to Vicksburg* (Baton Rouge: Louisiana State University Press, 1961), pp. 54–57; Thomas Lawrence Connelly and Archer Jones, *The Politics of Command: Factions and Ideas in Confederate Strategy* (Baton Rouge: Louisiana State University Press, 1973), pp. 96–99; James Lee McDonough, *Shiloh — in Hell before Night* (Knoxville: University of Tennessee Press, 1977), pp. 6–11.

28. Henry Wager Halleck, *Elements of Military Art and Science; or, Course of Instruction in Strategy, Fortification, Tactics of Battle &c Embracing the Duties of Staff, Infantry, Cavalry, Artillery, and Engineers. Adapted to the Use of Volunteers and Militia* (443 & 445 Broadway, New York: D. Appleton, 1846).

29. Williams, *Lincoln Finds a General*, III, 301–304, particularly 302–303 for plac-

ing Smith in command; "Smith, Charles Ferguson," Boatner, *Civil War Dictionary*, p. 769; for Grant's reinstatement, H. W. Halleck, Major-General, Saint Louis, March 13, 1862, to Maj. Gen. U. S. Grant, Fort Henry, O.R., X, pb. 2 (serial 11, 1884), 32; for Grant's promotion, "Grant, Ulysses Simpson," Heitman, *Historical Register*, II, 470.

30. Williams, *Lincoln Finds a General*, III, 328–35, 336–38, 345–47, 348–54; Bruce Catton, *Grant Moves South* (Boston, Toronto: Little, Brown and Company, 1960), pp. 210–21; McDonough, *Shiloh*, pp. 40–54; Wiley Sword, *Shiloh: Bloody April* (Dayton, Ohio: Press of Morningside Bookshop, 1988), pp. 19–48. Livermore, *Numbers and Losses*, gives the strength of Grant's army as 41,682; p. 79.

31. For the Confederate buildup and intentions, Connelly, *Army of the Heartland*, pp. 145–62; McDonough, *Shiloh*, pp. 11–18, 59–84; Sword, *Shiloh*, pp. 64–116; Williams, *Lincoln Finds a General*, III, 321–24, 354–56. For the opening of the battle, McDonough, pp. 86–104; Williams, *Lincoln Finds a General*, III, 356–59; Connelly, *Army of the Heartland*, pp. 160–63. For Sherman's return, John F. Marszalek, *Sherman: A Soldier's Passion for Order* (New York: The Free Press, A Division of Macmillan, Inc.; Toronto: Maxwell Macmillan Canada; New York, Oxford, Singapore, Sydney: Maxwell Macmillan International, 1993), pp. 169–76 (and pp. 176–78 for the opening of the battle from Sherman's vantage point); Williams, *Lincoln Finds a General*, III, 151, 183, 252, 310, 315. Livermore, *Numbers and Losses*, gives the Confederate strength as 40,335; p. 80.

The account of the course of the battle of Shiloh is based mainly on Williams, *Lincoln Finds a General*, III, 356–95; McDonough, *Shiloh*, pp. 84–225; Sword, *Shiloh*, pp. 139–442; Connelly, *Army of the Heartland*, pp. 160–75; Catton, *Grant Moves South*, pp. 225–47. The casualty figures are Livermore's, *Numbers and Losses*, p. 79 for the Federals, p. 80 for the Confederates.

32. For New Madrid and Island No. 10, Williams, *Lincoln Finds a General*, III, 293–300; James M. Merrill, *Battle Flags South: The Story of the Civil War Navies on Western Waters* (Rutherford, Madison, Teaneck: Fairleigh Dickinson University Press, 1970), 116–32; "New Madrid and Island No. 10," Boatner, *Civil War Dictionary*, pp. 587–88, particularly 588 for Confederates surrendered.

33. Williams, *Lincoln Finds a General*, III, 400–403 for Mitchel, 403–404 for Andrews and the *General*, 403 for the fate of the raiders; George Edgar Turner, *Victory Rode the Rails: The Strategic Place of the Railroads in the Civil War* (Indianapolis, New York: The Bobbs-Merrill Company, Inc., Publishers, 1953), Chap. XIII, "The Saga of the 'General,'" pp. 166–77.

34. Williams, *Lincoln Finds a General*, III, 404–23; Connelly, *Army of the Heartland*, pp. 175–77; Hattaway and Jones, *How the North Won*, pp. 170–71, 187.

35. Merrill, *Battle Flags South*, pp. 142–72; Hattaway and Jones, *How the North Won*, pp. 142–43; Rowena Reed, *Combined Operations in the Civil War* (Annapolis, Maryland: Naval Institute Press, 1978), pp. 60–62, 192–99; Raimondo Luraghi, *A History of the Confederate Navy*, tr. Paolo E. Coletta (Annapolis, Maryland: Naval Institute Press, 1996), pp. 156–63.

36. Reed, *Combined Operations*, pp. 39–43; Hattaway and Jones, *How the North Won*, pp. 111–12.

37. Confederate States, Laws, Statutes, *Public Laws of the Confederate States of America, Passed at the First Session of the First Congress; 1862. Carefully collated with the Originals at Richmond. To Be Continued Annually.* James M. Matthews, ed. (Richmond: R. M. Smith, Printer to Congress, 1862), [Statute I.] Chap. XXXI. — An Act to further provide for the public defence, Approved April 21, 1862, pp. 29–32. Second Session. [Statute II.] Chap. XV. — An Act to Amend an Act entitled "An Act to provide further for the public defence," Approved Sept. 27, 1862, ibid., pp. 61–62.

38. [Statute I.] Chap. LXXIV. — An Act to exempt certain persons from enrollment for service in the Armies of the Confederate States, Approved April 21, 1862, pp. 51–52.

39. Second Session. [Statute II.] Chap. XV, p. 61.

40. Abraham Lincoln, Executive Mansion, Washington, January 27, 1862. President's general War Order no. 1, Autograph Document Signed, the Robert Todd Lincoln Collection, LC; Document Signed, Edwin M. Stanton Papers, LC, in Basler, ed., *Works of Lincoln*, V, 111–12.

41. Abraham Lincoln, Executive Mansion Washington January 31, 1862 President's special War Order, No. 1, Copy, National Archives, RG94, Adjutant General, Letters Received, P1295, ibid., p. 115.

42. Geo B McClellan Maj Gen Comdg USA, Head Quarters of the Army Washington January 31st [February 3] 1862, to Hon E M Stanton, Secty of War Autograph Letter Signed, The Robert Todd Lincoln Collection, LC, in George B. McClellan, *The Wartime Papers of George B. McClellan: Selected Correspondence, 1861–1865*, Stephen W. Sears, ed. (New York: Ticknor and Fields, 1989), pp. 162–70, quotation from p. 169; also in O.R., V (serial 5, 1883), 42–45, quotation from p. 45.

43. This account of the *Virginia* and the *Monitor* is based largely on Robert W. Daly, *How the* Merrimac *Won: The Strategic Story of the CSS* Virginia (New York: Thomas Y. Crowell Co., 1957); William C. Davis, *Duel between the First Ironclads* (Garden City, New York: Doubleday & Company, Inc., 1975); Luraghi, *Confederate Navy*, Eight, "The Battle (I)," pp. 133–54; William N. Still, Jr., *Iron Afloat: The Story of the Confederate Armorclads* (Nashville: Vanderbilt University Press, 1971), 1, "Mallory and the Origin of the Confederate Ironclad Program," pp. 5–17, and 2, "The *Virginia*," pp. 18–40. A classic work on the background is James Phinney Baxter, 3rd, *The Introduction of the Ironclad Warship* (Cambridge, Massachusetts: Harvard University Press, 1933); see Chap. VI, "The First Seagoing Ironclad Fleet," pp. 92–115 on the *Gloire* and other early French ironclads; Chap. VII, "Great Britain Enters the Race," pp. 116–39 on the *Warrior*; Chap. XI, "Mallory's Ironclad Policy," pp. 211–37; Chap. XII, "The North Seeks a Solution," pp. 238–84; and Chap. XIII, "Hampton Roads," pp. 285–301.

44. Sears, *McClellan*, p. 163; Williams, *Lincoln Finds a General*, I, 153–54.

45. Report No. 7, Stewart Van Vliet, Brigadier-General and Quartermaster, Quartermaster's Office, Washington, August 2, 1862, to Brig. Gen. R[andolph]. B. Marcy, Chief of Staff, O.R., XI, pt. 1 (serial 12, 1884), pp. 156–61, specifically p. 158.

46. "Commanders of the Army since 1775," Heitman, *Historical Register and Dictionary*, I, 17.

47. Sears, *McClellan*, pp. 169–77, particularly 170 for the 25,000-man force, p. 171 for Wadsworth's assessment of his strength, pp. 175–76 for the First Corps; Williams, *Lincoln Finds a General*, I, 159–60, and for allowing McClellan to take the First Division, First Corps, p. 165, for McDowell's advance to Fredericksburg, p. 170. "Wadsworth, James Samuel," in Boatner, *Civil War Dictionary*, pp. 882–83; "Corps, Union," "I Corps (Potomac)," ibid., pp. 187–88. For McDowell's promotion, "McDowell, Irvin," ibid., p. 531; "McDowell, Irvin," Heitman, *Historical Register*, I, 664.

48. For the 121,500 men, Report John Tucker, Assistant Secretary of War, April 5, 1862, O.R., V (serial 5, 1881), 46. Davis recalled Lee to Richmond on March 2; Douglas Southall Freeman, *R. E. Lee: A Biography* (4 vols., New York: Charles Scribner's Sons; London: Charles Scribner's Sons Ltd., 1934–1935), I, 628; for Lee's views on the unfolding of McClellan's offensive, ibid., II, 8, 10, 14–18. For Magruder and the defense of the lower Peninsula, ibid., pp. 18–20; Freeman, *Lee's Lieutenants* I, 148–49, 152–53. For Davis's order bringing Lee to Richmond, Jefferson Davis Richmond, Va., March 2, 1862, to General R. E. Lee, Savannah, O.R., VI (serial 6, 1882), 400.

49. J. E. Johnston, General, Headquarters Lee's Farm, April 22, 1862, to General R. E. Lee, O.R., XI (serial 14, 1884), 455–56, quotation from 456. Sears, *McClellan*, pp. 174–82; Williams, *Lincoln Finds a General*, I, 162–67.

50. John E. Wool, Major-General, Headquarters Fort Monroe, May 6, 1862. (Re-

ceived 12.20 pm), to Hon. E. M. Stanton, *O.R.*, XI (serial 14), 143. For Wool, Williams, *Lincoln Finds a General*, I, 160–62; "Wool, John Ellis," Boatner, *Civil War Dictionary*, p. 948.

51. "Peninsular Campaign," Boatner, *Civil War Dictionary*, pp. 632–34, particularly 635; Randall, *Lincoln the President*, II, 78–80; Freeman, *Lee's Lieutenants*, I, 209 and n; and for details on the scuttling, Luraghi, *History of the Confederate Navy*, pp. 164–67.

52. Luraghi, *History of the Confederate Navy*, p. 169; Merrill, *Battle Flags South*, pp. 191–94; Williams, *Lincoln Finds a General*, III, 422–23, for Plum Run Bend. For Natchez, Luraghi, *History of the Confederate Navy*, p. 169. Long, *Civil War Day by Day*, May 12, Monday, 1862, p. 211.

53. "Walker, Leroy Pope," Boatner, *Civil War Dictionary*, p. 885; "Benjamin, Judah Philip," ibid., p. 59; "Randolph, George Wythe," ibid., pp. 678–79, particularly 679 for date of accession.

54. Freeman, *Lee*, I, Chapter XXXVI, "An Easy Lesson in Combating Sea-power," 605–31; Reed, *Combined Operations*, pp. 48–51.

55. R. E. Lee, General, Headquarters Army of Northern Virginia, November 4, 1863, to General S[amuel]. Cooper, Adjutant and Inspector General, *O.R.*, XXIX (serial 51, 1890), 819.

56. Jackson was promoted major-general October 7, 1861 and given command of the Shenandoah Valley; "Jackson, Thomas Jonathan ('Stonewall')," Boatner, *Civil War Dictionary*, p. 432; Robert G. Tanner, *Stonewall in the Valley: Thomas "Stonewall" Jackson's Shenandoah Valley Campaign Spring 1862* (Updated and revised, Mechanicsburg, PA: Stackpole Books, 1996), p. 37 for the designation of Jackson's command as the Valley District and Jackson's appointment to it on October 21. For the conception of the Valley Campaign by Lee and Jackson, ibid., pp. 170–71; Freeman, *Lee*, II, 50–54; Freeman, *Lee's Lieutenants*, I, 337–42; and the latest and now most authoritative biography of Jackson, James I. Robertson, Jr., *Stonewall Jackson: The Man, the Soldier, the Legend* (New York: Macmillan Publishing USA, Simon & Schuster Macmillan; London, Mexico City, New Delhi, Singapore, Sydney, Toronto: Prentice Hall International, 1997), pp. 363–64.

57. "Banks, Nathaniel Prentiss," Boatner, *Civil War Dictionary*, p. 42; "Shenandoah, Union Department of [the]," ibid., p. 739; "V Corps, Potomac," ibid., pp. 190–91, particularly 191.

58. Freeman, *Lee's Lieutenants*, I, 315–20; Robertson, *Stonewall Jackson*, pp. 338–49; Tanner, *Stonewall in the Valley*, 6, "Kernstown," pp. 111–46; Williams, *Lincoln Finds a General*, I, 172.

59. The classic nineteenth-century biography of Jackson by the English military critic George Francis Robert Henderson is not to be ignored: *Stonewall Jackson and the American Civil War*, With an Introduction by Garnet first Viscount Wolseley (New Impression, 2 vols., London, New York: Longmans, Green and Company, 1900), I, 208–21, particularly map, p. 216, for Banks's strength; Tanner, *Stonewall in the Valley*, pp. 167–77; "Shenandoah Valley Campaign of Jackson," Boatner, *Civil War Dictionary*, pp. 739–43, particularly pp. 740–41, the latter for Frémont's assuming command of the Mountain Department on March 29.

60. R. E. Lee, General, Headquarters, Richmond, Va., April 25, 1862, to General Thomas J. Jackson, Commanding Valley District, *O.R.*, XII, pt. 3 (serial 17, 1885), 865–66, quotation from 865. "Shenandoah Valley Campaign of Jackson," Boatner, *Civil War Dictionary*, p. 739 for Jackson's strength before Ewell's reinforcement, p. 741 for Ewell's strength; Freeman, *Lee's Lieutenants*, I, 319–30, for details of the organization of Jackson's army.

61. In addition to Robertson, *Stonewall Jackson*, pp. 1–221, and Henderson, *Stone-*

*wall Jackson,* I, 1–90, see Frank E. Vandiver, *Mighty Stonewall* (New York, Toronto, London: McGraw-Hill Book Company, Inc., 1957), pp. 1–135; Freeman, *Lee's Lieutenants,* I, 303–10; Tanner, *Stonewall in the Valley,* pp. 47–50.

62. Tanner, *Stonewall in the Valley,* pp. 182–289; Robertson, *Stonewall Jackson,* pp. 363–413; Freeman, *Lee's Lieutenants,* I, 329–407; Henderson, *Stonewall Jackson,* I, 213–64; Williams, *Lincoln Finds a General,* I, 171–77.

63. Williams, *Lincoln Finds a General,* I, 177–82, 187–200, 205–13; Henderson, *Stonewall Jackson,* I, 270–77 makes too much of the idea of panic in the Federal high command and not enough of a sense of opportunity but is nevertheless valuable.

64. Williams, *Lincoln Finds a General,* I, 187–205, particularly pp. 187–91 for Frémont's misconduct; Robertson, *Stonewall Jackson,* pp. 416–49; Tanner, *Stonewall in the Valley,* pp. 345–413; Freeman, *Lee's Lieutenants,* I, 412–69; Henderson, *Stonewall Jackson,* I, 270–94. An excellent recent account of the battles of Cross Keys and Port Republic is Robert K. Krick, *Conquering the Valley: Stonewall Jackson at Port Republic* (New York: William Morrow and Company, Inc., 1996). For a fascinating account of Cross Keys in the context of establishing a modern farm there, see Peter Svenson, *Battlefield: Farming a Civil War Battleground* (Boston, London: Faber and Faber, 1992).

65. Freeman, *Lee's Lieutenants,* I, 225–64; Sears, *McClellan,* pp. 193–97; Stephen W. Sears, *To the Gates of Richmond: The Peninsula Campaign* (New York: Ticknor & Fields, 1992), pp. 113–47; Williams, *Lincoln Finds a General,* I, 183–86. For Lee's accession to command, Freeman, *Lee's Lieutenants,* I, 262; Freeman, *Lee,* II, 76–79. For Lee's designation of his force as the Army of Northern Virginia, ibid., pp. 78 and 77–78n; "Northern Virginia, Confederate Army of," Boatner, *Civil War Dictionary,* pp. 600–601, particularly 600, briefly reviews the evolution of the force.

66. Freeman, *Lee,* II (1934), 86. For McClellan's position astride the Chickahominy, Sears, *McClellan,* pp. 200–202; Sears, *To the Gates of Richmond,* pp. 158–60; Williams, *Lincoln Finds a General,* I, 224–25. For Stuart's ride, Freeman, *Lee's Lieutenants,* I, Chapter XX, "Stuart Justifies His Plume," 275–303; Sears, *To the Gates of Richmond,* pp. 167–74.

67. Williams, *Lincoln Finds a General,* I, 216 and 414 notes 11 and 12. The present account of the Seven Days Battles through the June 27 battle of Gaines's Mill is based on ibid., pp. 222–28; Freeman, *Lee,* II, 104–58; Freeman, *Lee's Lieutenants,* I, 494–537; Sears, *McClellan,* pp. 204–13; Sears, *To the Gates of Richmond,* pp. 181–250. The initial battle of the Seven Days at Oak Grove is also known as King's School-House, French's Field, or the Orchard; June 25, Wednesday, 1862, Long, *Civil War Day by Day,* p. 230. The next day's battle, Mechanicsville, is also known as Beaver Dam Creek or Ellerson's Mill; 'June 26, Thursday,' ibid. The third day's battle, Gaines's Mill, is also called First Cold Harbor or the Chickahominy; June 27, Friday, ibid., p. 231.

68. G B McClellan, Savage Station June 28 [1862] 12.20 am, To Hon E M Stanton, Autograph Letter Signed (telegram sent), McClellan Papers (A-71:28), Library of Congress, in Sears, ed., *Papers of McClellan,* pp. 322–23, quotation from 323; also, with slight variations, in *O.R.,* XI, pt. 1 (serial 12, 1884), 61. For the alteration of the telegram in Washington as described below, Sears, *McClellan,* pp. 214–15; Williams, *Lincoln Finds a General,* I, 230. The incident was first recounted by David Homer Bates, *Lincoln in the Telegraph Office: Recollections of the United States Military Telegraph Corps during the Civil War* (New York: The Century Co., 1907), pp. 109–12.

69. Report No. 201, R. E. Lee, General, Headquarters Army of Northern Virginia, March 6, 1863, to General S. Cooper, Adjutant and Inspector-General, Richmond, Va., *O.R.,* XI, pt. 2 (serial 13, 1884), 489–98, quotation from 497. This account of the Seven Days Battles from June 28 through July 1 is based largely on Freeman, *Lee,* II, 159–249; Freeman, *Lee's Lieutenants,* I, 538–667; Sears, *McClellan,* pp. 215–23; Sears, *To the Gates of Richmond,* pp. 252–348; Williams, *Lincoln Finds a General,* I, 231–41.

70. For Confederate casualties, Freeman, *Lee*, II, 230, citing Edward Porter Alexander, *Military Memoirs of a Confederate: A Critical Narrative* (New York: Charles Scribner's Sons, 1907) p. 171. For Federal casualties, Sears, *To the Gates of Richmond*, pp. 344 (for dead and wounded)–45.

## 5. THE CONFEDERACY TAKES THE INITIATIVE

1. "Virginia, Union Army of," Mark Mayo Boatner III, *The Civil War Dictionary* (Revised Edition, New York: Vintage Books, A Division of Random House, Inc., 1991), p. 879; Everette B. Long with Barbara Long, *The Civil War Day by Day: An Almanac 1861–1865*, Foreword by Bruce Catton (Garden City, New York: Doubleday & Company, Inc., 1971), June 26, Thursday, 1862, pp. 230–31, particularly 231.

2. Kenneth P. Williams, *Lincoln Finds a General: A Military Study of the Civil War* (5 vols., New York: The Macmillan Company, 1950–1959), I, 251, 254 for the dates, 254 for Halleck's departure to visit McClellan; Long, *Civil War Day by Day*, July 11, Friday, July 23, Wednesday, 1862, pp. 238, 243 for the dates.

3. For the conference, Williams, *Lincoln Finds a General*, I, 254–57; Stephen W. Sears, *George B. McClellan: The Young Napoleon* (New York: Ticknor & Fields, 1988), pp. 239–41. For the July 30 date, ibid., p. 242; Long, *Civil War Day by Day*, July 30, Wednesday, p. 245.

4. Williams, *Lincoln Finds a General*, I, 257–61, particularly 261 for Pope's strength, 258 for receipt of order to leave the Peninsula; Sears, *McClellan*, p. 242 for that order, pp. 246–47 for August 19, 247 for August 23, p. 251 for August 28; Long, *Civil War Day by Day*, p. 247 for August 3, Sunday, p. 251 for August 16, Saturday.

5. Douglas Southall Freeman, *R. E. Lee: A Biography* (4 vols., New York: Charles Scribner's Sons; London: Charles Scribner's Sons Ltd., 1934–1935), II (1934), 261, 261–62; "Bull Run Campaign, Va., 2d," Boatner, *Civil War Dictionary*, pp. 101–105, particularly p. 102 for Jackson's strength.

6. The definitive account is Robert K. Krick, *Stonewall Jackson at Cedar Mountain* (Chapel Hill and London: University of North Carolina Press, 1990). See also James I. Robertson, Jr., *Stonewall Jackson: The Man, the Soldier, the Legend* (New York: Macmillan Publishing USA, Simon & Schuster Macmillan; London, Mexico City, New Delhi, Singapore, Sydney, Toronto: Prentice Hall International, 1997), pp. 513–39; Douglas Southall Freeman, *Lee's Lieutenants: A Study in Command* (3 vols., New York: Charles Scribner's Sons, 1942–1944), II, *Cedar Mountain to Chancellorsville* (1943), 10–53; George Francis Robert Henderson, *Stonewall Jackson and the American Civil War*, With an Introduction by Garnet first Viscount Wolseley (New Impression, 2 vols., London, New York: Longmans, Green and Company, 1898), I, 402–14; Williams, *Lincoln Finds a General*, I, 265–72. For the casualties, Krick, *Stonewall Jackson at Cedar Mountain*, pp. 372 (Confederate), 376 (Union).

7. Freeman, *Lee*, II, 270, 272 for the dates; for the implications, see also Williams, *Lincoln Finds a General*, I, 273–74.

8. The best book on the campaign is John J. Hennessy, *Return to Bull Run: The Campaign and Battle of Second Manassas* (New York, London, Toronto, Sydney, Tokyo, Singapore: Simon & Schuster, A Paramount Communications Company, 1993), pp. 48–59 for the retreat to the Rappahannock, 60–89 for the immediately subsequent maneuvering, 39–40 for the arrival of the Ninth Corps divisions (and 560 for further information on their identities), 65 for the first reinforcements from the Army of the Potomac; see also Williams, *Lincoln Finds a General*, I, 277–80 for Pope's retreat, 282–86 for the subsequent maneuvering (282–84 for the rain); Freeman, *Lee's Lieutenants*, II, 66–67, 67–80 (and 70–71 for the rain).

9. Hennessy, *Return to Bull Run*, pp. 92–116; Robertson, *Stonewall Jackson*, pp.

547–54; Freeman, *Lee's Lieutenants*, II, 82–93; Williams, *Lincoln Finds a General*, I, 291–98.

10. Hennessy, *Return to Bull Run*, pp. 117–93; Robertson, *Stonewall Jackson*, pp. 556–63; Freeman, *Lee's Lieutenants*, II, 94–111; Williams, *Lincoln Finds a General*, I, 298–320. The battle of Groveton is sometimes called Brawner's Farm, for the establishment of John Brawner on which part of it was fought; for Brawner, Hennessy, *Return to Bull Run*, p. 151.

11. Hennessy, *Return to Bull Run*, pp. 194–471; Freeman, *Lee*, II, 310–49; Freeman, *Lee's Lieutenants*, II, 111–43; Robertson, *Stonewall Jackson*, pp. 564–81; Williams, *Lincoln Finds a General*, I, 320–49. For Chantilly or Ox Hill, Hennessy, *Return to Bull Run*, pp. 446–50; Robertson, *Stonewall Jackson*, pp. 579–81. For the date of detaching the Pennsylvania Reserve Division from the Fifth Corps, "V Corps (Potomac)," Boatner, *Civil War Dictionary*, pp. 190–91, particularly 190.

12. Hennessy, *Return to Bull Run*, pp. 127 for McClellan's arrival, 239 for his assurance to Halleck on the 27th and the latter's subsequent impatience and order and the march to Annandale; see also Sears, *McClellan*, pp. 250–55; Williams, *Lincoln Finds a General*, I, 301, 321–24, 330.

13. Thomas L. Livermore, *Numbers and Losses in the Civil War* (Boston and New York: Houghton, Mifflin and Company, 1901; reprint, Dayton, Ohio: Morningside, 1986), pp. 88 (Union), 89 (Confederate).

14. Sears, *McClellan*, pp. 259–60 for the initial appointment, 263–64 for the evolution of the command. The Army of Virginia was officially merged into the Army of the Potomac on September 12; "Virginia, Union Army of," Boatner, *Civil War Dictionary*, p. 879.

15. Freeman, *Lee*, II, 350–54; Gary W. Gallagher, "The Autumn of 1862: A Season of Opportunity," pp. 1–13, especially 1–10, and Robert K. Krick, "The Army of Northern Virginia in September 1862: Its Circumstances, Its Opportunities, and Why It Should Not Have Been at Sharpsburg," pp. 35–55, especially 35–39, both in Gary W. Gallagher, ed., *Antietam: Essays on the 1862 Maryland Campaign* (Kent, Ohio and London, England: Kent State University Press, 1989); Stephen W. Sears, *Landscape Turned Red: The Battle of Antietam* (New Haven and New York: Ticknor & Fields, 1983), pp. 63–69; James V. Murfin, *The Gleam of Bayonets: The Battle of Antietam and the Maryland Campaign of 1862* (South Brunswick, New Jersey: A. S. Barnes & Co., Inc., 1965), pp. 63–71.

16. Freeman, *Lee*, I, 621.

17. Ibid., II, 353–55, 358–59; Gallagher, "Season of Opportunity," pp. 9–10; Krick, "Army of Northern Virginia," pp. 38–43; Sears, *Landscape Turned Red*, pp. 69–71; Murfin, *Gleam of Bayonets*, pp. 90–98; Freeman, *Lee's Lieutenants*, II, 149–56, for the Confederates. For the Federals, Williams, *Lincoln Finds a General*, I, 351–54; Sears, *McClellan*, pp. 265–69, particularly 266 for the strength of the field and garrison forces; Sears, *Landscape Turned Red*, pp. 102–104; Murfin, *Gleam of Bayonets*, pp. 85–87, 121–25; A. Wilson Green, "'I Fought the Battle Splendidly': George B. McClellan and the Maryland Campaign," in Gallagher, ed., *Antietam*, pp. 56–83, particularly 56–61.

18. Dennis E. Frye, "Drama between the Rivers: Harpers Ferry in the 1862 Maryland Campaign," in Gallagher, ed., *Antietam*, pp. 14–34, particularly 15–17; Sears, *McClellan*, pp. 273–80; Sears, *Landscape Turned Red*, p. 106; Murfin, *Gleam of Bayonets*, p. 106; Williams, *Lincoln Finds a General*, I, 372.

19. Special Orders, No. 191 Hdqrs. Army of Northern Virginia September 9, 1862. By command of General R. E. Lee: R[obert]. H. Chilton, Assistant Adjutant-General, U.S. War Department, *The War of the Rebellion: A Compilation of the Official Records of the Union and Confederate Armies* (four series, 70 vols. in 128, Washington: Government Printing Office, 1880–1901), Series One, XI, pt. 2 (serial 30, 1887), 603–604. Hereafter cited as *O.R.*; citations are of Series One unless otherwise noted. For the shift of Long-

street to Hagerstown, Freeman, *Lee*, II, 36; Freeman, *Lee's Lieutenants*, II, 166; Sears, *Landscape Turned Red*, pp. 95–96.

20. On September 12, 1862, the Second Corps, Army of Virginia, became the Twelfth Corps, Army of the Potomac, with Major-General John Fenno King Mansfield, U.S.V., succeeding Nathaniel P. Banks in command; "XII Corps (Potomac), Boatner, *Civil War Dictionary*, p. 194; "Banks, Nathaniel Prentiss," ibid., p. 42; "Mansfield, Joseph Fenno King," ibid., 508; "II Corps (Va.)," ibid., p. 189. At the same time the Third Corps, Army of Virginia, became the First Corps, Army of the Potomac; "I Corps (Potomac)," pp. 187–88, particularly 188; "III Corps (Va.)" ibid., p. 189. Major-General Joseph Hooker, U.S.V., had commanded this corps since September 6 and retained the command; "Hooker, Joseph," ibid., pp. 409–10, particularly 409. The previous commander had been Irvin McDowell; "McDowell, Irvin," ibid., p. 31; "Corps, III (Va.)," ibid., p. 189. Also on September 12, the Eleventh Corps, Army of the Potomac, was constituted mainly from the First Corps, Army of Virginia; "XI Corps (Potomac)," ibid., pp. 193–94, particularly 193; "I Corps (Va.)," ibid., p. 188. Command remained with Major-General Franz Sigel, U.S.V.; "Sigel, Franz," ibid., p. 761.

21. Sears, *Landscape Turned Red*, pp. 112–13; Murfin, *Gleam of Bayonets*, pp. 132–33.

22. Sears, *Landscape Turned Red*, pp. 117–21; Sears, *McClellan*, pp. 284–88; Murfin, *Gleam of Bayonets*, pp. 134, 160–64. For Lee's learning that the lost order had fallen into McClellan's hands, Freeman, *Lee's Lieutenants*, II, 722–23; Sears, *Landscape Turned Red*, p. 12. For discussions of how the order reached the Federals, Freeman, *Lee's Lieutenants*, II, Appendix I, "Transmission of the 'Lost Order,'" 715–23; Murfin, *Gleam of Bayonets*, Appendix A, "Lee's 'Lost Dispatch,'" pp. 328–38 (with the order printed in full, pp. 328–29).

23. Sears, *Landscape Turned Red*, pp. 117–49; Murfin, *Gleam of Bayonets*, pp. 160–84; Greene, "'I Fought the Battle Splendidly,'" pp. 61–64; Sears, *McClellan*, pp. 285–90; Williams, *Lincoln Finds a General*, I, 376–83; Freeman, *Lee*, II, 366–75; Freeman, *Lee's Lieutenants*, II, Chapters X, "Harvey Hill's Battle," 166–83, and XI, "The Test of Lafayette McLaws," 184–92. For the battle for South Mountain as experienced by the rank-and-file soldiers, see John Michael Priest, *Before Antietam: The Battle for South Mountain*, Foreword by Edwin C. Bearss (Shippensburg, Pennsylvania: White Mane Publishing Company, 1992).

24. The best succinct account of the campaign for Harpers Ferry is Frye, "Drama between the Rivers," especially pp. 17–33. See also Freeman, *Lee's Lieutenants*, II, 161–65; Robertson, *Stonewall Jackson*, pp. 591–605; Sears, *Landscape Turned Red*, pp. 116, 121–24, 143–44, 150–55; Murfin, *Gleam of Bayonets*, 5, "Harpers Ferry," pp. 135–58; Williams, *Lincoln Finds a General*, I, 373–75, II (1950), 445–46.

25. Murfin, *Gleam of Bayonets*, pp. 196–99, particularly 198 for Lee's numbers; Sears, *Landscape Turned Red*, pp. 160–62, particularly 161 for numbers. Livermore, *Numbers and Losses*, estimates Confederate casualties at South Mountain at 2,685 (325 killed, 1,560 wounded, 800 missing), out of 17,852 engaged; p. 91. (He estimates Union losses at 325 killed, 1,403 wounded, 85 missing, for a total of 1,813 of 28,480; p. 90.)

26. Freeman, *Lee*, II, 381–83, particularly 383 for Lee's numbers, 382 for the courier to A. P. Hill; Sears, *Landscape Turned Red*, pp. 162–75, and particularly 174 for the couriers to McLaws and Hill.

27. This account of the battle of Antietam, or Sharpsburg, largely follows Sears, *Landscape Turned Red*, pp. 176–297; Murfin, *Gleam of Bayonets*, pp. 210–91; Freeman, *Lee*, II, 384–414; Freeman, *Lee's Lieutenants*, II, 201–25; Williams, *Lincoln Finds a General*, II, 446–58; Bruce Catton, *Mr. Lincoln's Army* (Garden City, N.Y.: Doubleday & Company, Inc., 1951), pp. 250–327. Focusing on the soldiers' view is John M. Priest, *Antietam: The Soldiers' Battle* (Shippensburg, Pennsylvania: White Mane Publishing

Company, 1989). The casualty figures given here are Livermore's from *Numbers and Losses*, p. 92 for the Union, p. 93 for the Confederacy; Livermore estimates the Union army as 75,316 effectives; p. 92. For McClellan's fresh troops on September 18, Sears, *Landscape Turned Red*, p. 302; the raw troops were Brigadier-General, U.S.V., Andrew A. Humphreys's Third Division, Fifth Corps, ibid., pp. 301–302.

Immediately after the battle of Antietam, Alexander Gardner and his assistant, John F. Gibson, took the first American collection of battlefield photographs made before the dead had generally been buried. For this remarkable photographic record see William A. Frassanito, *Antietam: The Photographic Legacy of America's Bloodiest Day* (New York: Charles Scribner's Sons, 1978); see particularly pp. 51–54 for a discussion of Gardner and Gibson at Antietam.

28. For suggestions of Lee's prompt thoughts of a renewed offensive from his aide Major Walter H. Taylor, see Freeman, *Lee*, II, 409.

29. James M. Merrill, *Battle Flags South: The Story of the Civil War Navies on Western Waters* (Rutherford, Madison, Teaneck: Fairleigh Dickinson University Press, 1970), pp. 206–16; Rowena Reed, *Combined Operations in the Civil War* (Annapolis, Maryland: Naval Institute Press, 1978), pp. 210–20; Williams, *Lincoln Finds a General*, III, *Grant's First Year in the West* (1952), 428–40, IV, *Iuka to Vicksburg* (1956), 1–17, 67–71.

30. Williams, *Lincoln Finds a General*, IV, 72–85; Bruce Catton, *Grant Moves South* (Boston, Toronto: Little, Brown and Company, 1960), pp. 307–12; William M. Lamers, *The Edge of Glory: A Biography of General William S. Rosecrans, U.S.A.* (New York: Harcourt, Brace & World, Inc., 1961), pp. 103–30; "Iuka," Boatner, *Civil War Dictionary*, pp. 428–29, particularly p. 429 for losses.

31. Williams, *Lincoln Finds a General*, IV, 85–102; Catton, *Grant Moves South*, pp. 313–18; Lamers, *Edge of Glory*, pp. 131–69. Livermore, *Numbers and Losses*, estimates the Union forces at Corinth as 23,077, the Confederate at 22,000; he gives Union casualties as 355 killed, 1,841 wounded, 324 missing, for the total of 2,520, and Confederate losses as 473 killed, 1,997 wounded (for the total of 2,470), and 1,763 missing (4,233 overall total); p. 94. For Pemberton's accession to command, "Pemberton, John Clifford," Boatner, *Civil War Dictionary*, p. 631.

32. For the reconstituted Army of the Ohio, "Buell, Don Carlos," Boatner, *Civil War Dictionary*, pp. 96–97, particularly p. 96. For Buell's advance toward Chattanooga, Williams, *Lincoln Finds a General*, IV, 25–43; Thomas Lawrence Connelly, *Army of the Heartland: The Army of Tennessee, 1861–1862* (Baton Rouge: Louisiana State University Press, 1967), pp. 190–94. For the beginning of the Kentucky campaign, ibid., pp. 190–252; Williams, *Lincoln Finds a General*, IV, 43–67, 107–26. For Confederate numbers, "Perryville (Chaplin Hills)," Boatner, *Civil War Dictionary*, pp. 642–44, particularly 644.

33. For Buell's 60,000, "Perryville (Chaplin Hills)," Boatner, *Civil War Dictionary*, p. 643. This account of Perryville is based on ibid., pp. 642–44; Williams, *Lincoln Finds a General*, IV, 121–35; Connelly, *Army of the Heartland*, pp. 256–67; Roy Morris, Jr., *Sheridan: The Life and Wars of General Phil Sheridan* (New York: Crown Publishers, Inc., 1992), pp. 93–99. For casualties, Livermore, *Numbers and Losses*, p. 95; Livermore estimates Federal effectives present at Perryville as 36,940, Confederate effectives 16,000; ibid.

34. R. E. Lee, General, Headquarters, Army of Northern Virginia, Camp on the Opequon, near Smoketown, September 25, 1862, to His Excellency, President Davis, Richmond, Va., O.R., XIX, pt. 2 (serial 30), 626–27, quotation from 627.

35. Freeman, *Lee*, II, 422–23; Freeman, *Lee's Lieutenants*, II, Chapter XVIII, "How to Accomplish 'The Impossible,'" 284–309; Emory M. Thomas, *Bold Dragoon: The Life of J. E. B. Stuart* (New York, Cambridge, Philadelphia, San Francisco, London, Mexico City, São Paulo, Singapore, Sydney: Harper & Row, Publishers, 1986), pp. 173–81.

36. A. Lincoln, Washington City, D.C., Oct. 24 [25], 1862, to Majr. Genl. McClellan, Autograph Letter Signed, Illinois State Historical Library, Springfield, Ill., in Abraham Lincoln, *The Collected Works of Abraham Lincoln*, Roy P. Basler, ed.; Marion Dolores Pratt and Lloyd A. Dunlop, asst. eds. (9 vols. inc. index, The Abraham Lincoln Association, Springfield, Illinois; New Brunswick, New Jersey: Rutgers University Press, 1953; index, 1955), V, 474; also in O.R., XIX, pt. 2 (serial 30), 485. Sears, *McClellan*, pp. 323–34; Williams, *Lincoln Finds a General*, II, 463–74.

37. Sears, *McClellan*, pp. 334–38, particularly 338 for the removal; Williams, *Lincoln Finds a General*, II, 474–75, particularly 475 for the removal.

### 6. OF LIBERTY AND WAR

1. Washington, Nov 8 1861, Geo B McClellan to My dear Samuel L. F. X. Q. Q. [Samuel L. M. Barlow], Autograph Letter Signed, The Henry E. Huntington Library, Art Collection, and Botanical Gardens, San Marino, California, in Stephen W. Sears, ed., *The Civil War Papers of George B. McClellan: Selected Correspondence 1860–1865* (New York: Ticknor & Fields, 1989), pp. 127–29, quotation from p. 128; the editor indicates, p. 129, that "L. F. X. Q. Q." was "A jape at Barlow's use of initials."

2. *Wabash*, Port Royal, 28 Dec, 1861, 30 Dec. 1861, to My dear [William] Whetten [of New York], Winterthur Mss. 9–2449, Winterthur Library and Museum, Winterthur, Delaware, in Samuel Francis Du Pont, *Samuel Francis Du Pont: A Selection from His Civil War Letters*, John D. Hayes, ed. (3 vols., Ithaca, New York: Published for The Eleutherian Mills Historical Library, Cornell University Press, 1969), I, *The Mission: 1860–1862*, 290–95, quotation from 30 Dec, 1861, 294.

3. (Journal Letter No. 52), *Wabash*, Port Royal, 1 May 1862, F. to My precious Sophie [Sophie Madeleine du Pont Du Pont], Winterthur Mss. 9–2572, ibid., II, *The Blockade: 1862–1863*, 22–30, first quotation, 24, second quotation, 25.

4. Willie Lee Rose, *Rehearsal for Reconstruction: The Port Royal Experiment*, With an Introduction by Comer Vann Woodward (Indianapolis and New York: A Brown Thrasher Book, The Bobbs-Merrill Company, Inc., Publishers, 1964), map pp. viii–ix for the area; James M. McPherson, *The Struggle for Equality: Abolitionists and the Negro in the Civil War and Reconstruction* (Princeton, New Jersey: Princeton University Press, 1964), p. 158 for the black population.

5. Rose, *Rehearsal for Reconstruction*, pp. 18–19, particularly 19 for Reynolds's arrival, 24; for Kate Chase and Sprague, Thomas Graham Belden and Marva Robins Belden, *So Fell the Angels* (Boston, Toronto: Little, Brown and Company, 1956), a study of Salmon P. and Kate Chase and their associates, pp. 41, 43, 81–84, 86, 91–99.

6. Quoted in Rose, *Rehearsal for Reconstruction*, p. 22, citing [Edward L. Pierce,] "The Contrabands at Fortress Monroe," *The Atlantic Monthly, A Magazine of Literature, Science, Art, and Politics*, 8:11 (November 1861), 626–640, particularly 633. For the antislavery Northerners and Pierce, Rose, *Rehearsal for Reconstruction*, pp. 21–23; McPherson, *Struggle for Equality*, pp. 159–60.

7. Quoted in Rose, *Rehearsal for Reconstruction*, p. 48, citing E. L. Pierce to Charles Sumner, March 20, 1862, Charles Sumner Papers, Houghton Library, Harvard University, Cambridge, Massachusetts. Rose, *Rehearsal for Reconstruction*, pp. 24–38, particularly 34 for Pierce and Lincoln, 36 for the Educational Commission, 37–38 for Atkinson; McPherson, *Struggle for Equality*, pp. 159–60, particularly 160 for Lincoln.

8. Rose, *Rehearsal for Reconstruction*, pp. 26–28, 30, 40–43, 72–74; McPherson, *Struggle for Equality*, pp. 160–61.

9. "South, Union Department of the," Mark Mayo Boatner III, *The Civil War Dictionary* (Revised Edition, New York: Vintage Books, A Division of Random House, Inc.,

1991), pp. 778–79, particularly 778; Rose, *Rehearsal for Reconstruction*, pp. 43–70, 142–43, particularly 59 and n for the teachers' arrival; McPherson, *Struggle for Equality*, pp. 162–67 on the teachers.

10. Edwin M. Stanton, Secretary of War. War Department, Washington, D.C., April 29, 1862. To Brig. Gen. R. Saxton. U.S. War Department, *The War of the Rebellion: A Compilation of the Official Records of the Union and Confederate Armies* (four series, 70 vols. in 128, Washington: Government Printing Office, 1880–1901), Series Three, II (serial 123, 1899), 27–28. Hereafter cited as O.R.; citations are of Series One unless otherwise noted. For Saxton, "Saxton, Rufus, Jr.," Boatner, *Civil War Dictionary*, pp. 722–23, particularly 722. He became brigadier-general, U.S.V. April 15, 1862; ibid., p. 722, and "Saxton, Rufus," Francis B. Heitman, *Historical Register and Dictionary of the United States Army, From Its Organization, September 29, 1789, to March 2, 1903*. Published under act of Congress approved March 2, 1903. 57th Congress, Second Session, House Document 446 (serial 4536). (2 vols., Washington: Government Printing Office, 1903), I, 862.

11. By command of Maj. Gen. D. Hunter: [Ed(ward). W. Smith, Acting Assistant Adjutant-General] Orders No. 11. Hdqrs. Dept. of the South, Hilton Head, Port Royal, S.C., May 9, 1862. O.R., XIV (serial 20, 1888), 333; printed also, with slight variation, ibid., Series Two, I (serial 114, 1894), 818, and in Abraham Lincoln, *The Collected Works of Abraham Lincoln*, Roy P. Basler, ed.; Marion Dolores Pratt and Lloyd A. Dunlop, asst. eds. (9 vols. inc. index, The Abraham Lincoln Association, Springfield, Illinois; New Brunswick: Rutgers University Press, 1953; index, 1955), V, 222, as part of Lincoln's revocation of Hunter's order cited in n13 below.

12. Abraham Lincoln, March 6, 1862, to Fellow-citizens of the Senate, and House of Representatives, Autograph Draft, The Robert Todd Lincoln Collection of the Papers of Abraham Lincoln, Library of Congress; Document Signed, National Archives Record Group 46, Senate 37A F2, Document Signed, Record Group 233, House of Representatives Original Executive Document No. 69, in Basler, ed., *Works of Lincoln*, V, 144–46.

13. Abraham Lincoln. By the President: William H. Seward, Secretary of State. May 19, 1862 By the President of The United States of America. A Proclamation. Autograph Draft Signed, Robert Todd Lincoln Collection, LC; Document Signed, National Archives, Record Group 11, Proclamations, in Basler, ed., *Works of Lincoln*, V, 222–23, quotations from 223; also in O.R., Series Two, I (serial 114), 818–19.

14. Thomas Harry Williams, *Lincoln and the Radicals* (Madison: University of Wisconsin Press, 1941) remains the basic work on the Radicals as well as Lincoln's relationship with them. Hans L. Trefousse, *The Radical Republicans: Lincoln's Vanguard for Racial Justice* (New York: Alfred A. Knopf, 1969) perceives the relationship as less adversarial than does Williams. Allan G. Bogue, *The Earnest Men: Republicans of the Civil War Senate* (Ithaca, New York: Cornell University Press, 1981) analyzes Republican factions using statistical methods.

15. *The Congressional Globe*, XXXII, pt. 1, 37th Congress, 2nd Session, *December 2, 1861 to February 26, 1862*, New Series, No. 8, Dec. 19, 1861, text, 115–16, passed, 116.

16. Thirty-seventh Congress. Session II. (Statute II.) Chap. XL. — An Act to make an additional Article of War. Approved, March 13, 1862. U.S. Laws, Statutes, *The Statutes at Large of the United States of America, 1789–1873* (17 vols., I–IX, Boston: Charles C. Little and J. Brown, 1845–1854; X–XVII, Boston: Little, Brown, and Company, 1855–1873), 12 (December 5, 1859–March 3, 1863) (1863), 354; *Cong. Globe*, XXXII, pt. 4, 37th Congress, 2nd Session, *June 23, 1862 to July 17, 1862*, Appendix, 340.

17. Thirty-seventh Congress. Session II. (Statute II.) Chap. LIV. — An Act for the Release of certain Persons held to Service or Labor in the District of Columbia. Approved, April 16, 1862. 12 *Statutes at Large* 376–78, including Sec. 7, appropriation of

$1,000,000 to compensate slaveowners, 378; *Cong. Globe*, XXXII, pt. 4, Appendix, 347–48, Sec. 7, 348.

18. Thirty-seventh Congress. Session II. (Statute II.) Chap. CXI. — An Act to secure Freedom to all Persons within the Territories of the United States. Approved, June 19, 1862. 12 *Statutes at Large* 432; *Cong. Globe*, XXXII, pt. 4, Appendix, 364.

19. Dred Scott, Plaintiff in Error, *v.* John F. A. Sandford [Sanford]. [March 6, 1857] U.S. Supreme Court, Benjamin C. Howard, ed., *Reports of Cases Argued and Adjudged in the Supreme Court of the United States* (24 vols., I–III, Philadelphia: T. & J. W. Johnson, Law Booksellers, 1843–1845; IV–XII, Boston: Charles C. Little and James Brown, Law Publishers and Booksellers, 1846–1851; XIII–XVIII, Boston: Little, Brown and Company, Law Publishers and Booksellers, 1852–1856; XIX–XXIV, Washington, D.C.: William H. Morrison, Law Publishers and Booksellers, 1857–1861), XIX, *December Term 1856* (60 *United States Reports*, 1857), 399–454, Opinion of the Court, Mr. Chief Justice [Roger B.] Taney; 454–56, Mr. Justice [James M.] Wayne; 457–68, Mr. Justice [Samuel] Nelson; 469, Mr. Justice [Robert C.] Grier; 469–93, Mr. Justice [Peter V.] Daniel; 493–518, Mr. Justice [John A.] Campbell; Dissents, 525–64, Mr. Justice [John] McLean; 564–633, Mr. Justice [Benjamin R.] Curtis; see particularly 432–52 and most particularly 452. For a comprehensive analysis, see Don E. Fehrenbacher, *The Dred Scott Case: Its Significance in American Law and Politics* (New York: Oxford University Press, 1978); p. 1 for date of decision, p. 248 for the spelling of Sanford's name.

20. Thirty-seventh Congress. Session II. (Statute II.) Chap. CXCV. — An Act to suppress Insurrection, to punish Treason and Rebellion, to seize and confiscate the Property of Rebels, and for other Purposes. Approved, July 17, 1862. 12 *Statutes at Large* 589–92, quotation from Sec. 9, 591; *Cong. Globe*, XXXII, pt. 4, Appendix, 412–13, quotation from 413; excerpted, including quotation, *O.R.*, Series Three, II (serial 123, 1899), 276.

21. Thirty-seventh Congress. Session II. [Resolution No. 63]. Joint Resolution explanatory of "An Act to suppress Insurrection, to punish Treason and Rebellion, to seize and confiscate the Property of Rebels, and for other Purposes." Approved July 17, 1862. 12 *Statutes at Large* 627; *Cong. Globe*, XXXII, pt. 4, Appendix, 423. Article. I. Section. IX. Paragraph 13 of the Constitution provides: "No Bill of Attainder or ex post facto law shall be passed"; U.S. Constitution, 103rd Congress, 1st Session, Senate Document No. 103–6 (serial 14152), *The Constitution of the United States: Analysis and Interpretation: Annotations of Cases Decided by the Supreme Court of the United States to June 29, 1992.* Prepared by the Congressional Research Service, Library of Congress, Johnny H. Killian, George A. Costello, co-editors (Washington: Government Printing Office, 1996), p. 10. Article. III. Section. III., paragraph 2 provides: "The Congress shall have Power to declare the Punishment of Treason, but no Attainder of Treason shall work Corruption of Blood, or Forfeiture except during the Life of the Person attainted"; ibid., p. 16.

22. [Abraham Lincoln,] July 17, 1862, to Fellow-Citizens of the Senate, and House of Representatives, and [additional message] to Fellow Citizens of the House of Representatives, Autograph Draft, Robert Todd Lincoln Collection, LC, in Basler, ed., *Works of Lincoln*, V, 328 and 328–31; explanation of Lincoln's action, 328n.

23. Treaty between the United States and Great Britain for the Suppression of the Slave Trade. Concluded at Washington, April 7, 1862. Ratifications exchanged at London, May 25, 1862. Abraham Lincoln. By the President: William H. Seward, Secretary of State. By the President of the United States: A Proclamation. 12 *Statutes at Large* 1225–36.

24. [Drafts of a Bill for Compensated Emancipation in Delaware] [November 26? 1861], Autograph Draft, Huntington Library, in Basler, ed., *Works of Lincoln*, V, 29–30. For the evolution of Lincoln's views toward the Emancipation Proclamation, see James G. Randall, *Lincoln the President* (4 vols., New York: Dodd, Mead & Company, 1946–

1955, IV, *Last Full Measure*, coauthored with Richard N. Current), I–II, *Springfield to Gettysburg*, II, 126–54; Phillip Shaw Paludan, *The Presidency of Abraham Lincoln* (Lawrence: University Press of Kansas, 1994), pp. 123–35, 142–47; David Herbert Donald, *Lincoln* (New York, London, Toronto, Sydney, Tokyo, Singapore: Simon & Schuster, 1995), pp. 354, 362–65.

25. Abraham Lincoln, message of March 6, 1862, Basler, ed., *Works of Lincoln*, V, 144–46, quotation from 144–45.

26. Abraham Lincoln, proclamation of May 19, 1862, revoking Hunter's order of military emancipation, ibid., p. 223. For the resolution, Thirty-seventh Congress. Session II. [Resolution No. 26]. Joint Resolution declaring that the United States ought to cooperate with, affording pecuniary Aid to any State which may adopt the gradual Abolishment of Slavery. Approved, April 10, 1862. 12 *Statutes at Large* 617; *Cong. Globe*, XXXII, pt. 4, Appendix, 420.

27. [Appeal to Border State Representatives to Favor Compensated Emancipation] July 12, 1862, Autograph Document and Autograph Draft, Robert Todd Lincoln Collection, LC, in Basler, ed., *Works of Lincoln*, V, 317–19, quotations from 317.

28. [Address on Colonization to a Deputation of Negroes] August 14, 1862, ibid., pp. 370–75, citing *New York Tribune*, August 15, 1862, quotations from 371, 372.

29. Ibid., pp. 373–74, though he did not specifically mention Chiriqui; see Randall, *Lincoln the President*, II, 138–39.

30. Abraham Lincoln, message of March 6, 1862, Basler, ed., *Works of Lincoln*, V, 145.

31. 12 *Statutes at Large* 617; *Cong. Globe*, XXXII, pt. 4, Appendix, 420.

32. Randall, *Lincoln the President*, II, 147; Allan Nevins, *Ordeal of the Union* (8 vols., *Ordeal of the Union*, I, *Fruits of Manifest Destiny 1847–1852*; *Ordeal of the Union*, II, *A House Dividing 1852–1857* [New York, London: Charles Scribner's Sons, 1947]; III, *The Emergence of Lincoln*, I, *Douglas, Buchanan, and Party Chaos 1857–1859*; IV, *The Emergence of Lincoln*, II, *Prologue to Civil War 1859–1861* [New York, London: Charles Scribner's Sons, 1950]; V, *The War for the Union*, I, *The Improvised War 1861–1862* [New York: Charles Scribner's Sons, 1959]; VI, *The War for the Union*, II, *War Becomes Revolution* [New York: Charles Scribner's Sons, 1960]; VII, *The War for the Union*, III, *The Organized War 1863–1864*; VIII, *The War for the Union*, IV, *The Organized War to Victory 1864–1865* [New York: Charles Scribner's Sons, 1971], *Ordeal of the Union*, VI, *War for the Union*, II, 148–49.

33. Abraham Lincoln, December 3, 1861, to Fellow Citizens of the Senate and House of Representatives, Document Signed, National Archives, Record Group 233, Thirty-seventh Congress, Second Session, Original Annual Message of the President — Interior, in Basler, ed., *Works of Lincoln*, V, 35–53, quotation from p. 49.

34. Abraham Lincoln, message of March 6, 1862, ibid., p. 145. He quoted himself as having said: "The Union must be preserved; and hence all indispensable means must be employed."

35. A. Lincoln, Executive Mansion, Washington, April 4, 1864. To A[lbert]. G. Hodges, Esq., Frankfort, Ky. [editor of *Frankfort Commonwealth*], Autograph Draft Signed, Robert Todd Lincoln Collection, LC, ibid., VII, 281–282, quotation from 282, identification of Hodges 282n.

36. Gideon Welles, *Diary of Gideon Welles: Secretary of the Navy under Lincoln and Johnson*, Howard K. Beale, ed., Assisted by Alan W. Brownsword, with an Introduction by Howard K. Beale and appendices drawn from Welles's correspondence (3 vols., New York: W. W. Norton & Company, Inc., 1960), I, 70. See Randall, *Lincoln the President*, II, 154; Nevins, *Ordeal of the Union*, VI, *War for the Union*, II, 149–50; Donald, *Lincoln*, pp. 362–63.

37. Emancipation Proclamation as first sketched and shown to the Cabinet in July

1862 [July 22, 1862], Autograph Draft, Robert Todd Lincoln Collection, LC, in Basler, ed., *Works of Lincoln*, V, 336–37, quotation from 337.

38. Ibid., p. 337n, citing Salmon P. Chase, *Diary and Correspondence of Salmon P. Chase (Annual Report* of the American Historical Association, 1902, 2 vols., Washington: Government Printing Office, 1903), II, *Sixth Report* of Historical Manuscripts Commission; With Diary and Correspondence of Salmon P. Chase, Tuesday, July 22d, 1862, 47–49, particularly 48–49.

39. Basler, ed., *Works of Lincoln*, V, 337n, citing Document, Salmon P. Chase Papers, LC.

40. Randall, *Lincoln the President*, II, 155–56, citing Abraham Lincoln, *Complete Works of Abraham Lincoln*, John G. Nicolay and John Hay, eds. New and Enlarged Edition, With a General Introduction by Richard Watson Gilder and Special Articles by Other Eminent Persons (12 vols., New York: Francis D. Tandy Co., 1905), X, 2–3.

41. A. Lincoln, Executive Mansion, Washington, August 22, 1862. To Hon. Horace Greel[e]y, Autograph Letter Signed, Wadsworth Atheneum, Hartford, Connecticut, in Basler, ed., *Works of Lincoln*, V, 388–89, quotation from 388. Greeley had published his "Prayer" in the *New York Tribune*, Aug. 20, 1862, p. 1; he published Lincoln's letter ibid., August 25, 1862, p. 1, together with a response. For Lincoln and the Christian delegation, see Reply to Emancipation Memorial Presented by Chicago Christians of All Denominations. September 13, 1862, in Basler, ed., *Works of Lincoln*, V, 419–25, and 419n.

42. A. Lincoln, Private, Executive Mansion, Washington, July 26, 1862. To Hon. Reverdy Johnson, Copy in John Hay's handwriting, Robert Todd Lincoln Collection, LC, ibid., pp. 342–43.

43. A. Lincoln, Private, Washington, D.C., July 28, 1862, to Cuthbert Bullitt Esq New Orleans La, Letter Signed, Robert Todd Lincoln Collection, LC, ibid., pp. 344–46, quotation from 346.

44. "Phelps, John Wolcott," Boatner, *Civil War Dictionary*, p. 650.

45. R. E. Lee, General, Headquarters, Army of Northern Virginia, July 28, 1862. To Hon. George W. Randolph, Secretary of War. O.R., XI, pt. 2 (serial 12, 1884), 936.

46. By command of Major-General Pope: Geo. D. Ruggles, Colonel, Assistant Adjutant-General, and Chief-of-Staff. General Orders, No. 7. Headquarters Army of Virginia, Washington, July 10[?], 1862, ibid., XII, pt. 2 (serial 15, 1885), 51.

47. Abraham Lincoln, By the President: William H. Seward, Secretary of State, September 22, 1862, By the President of the United States of America A Proclamation. Autograph Document Signed, National Archives, Record Group 11, Proclamations, in Basler, ed., *Works of Lincoln*, V, 433–36.

48. Nevins, *Ordeal of the Union*, VI, *War for the Union*, II, 320 for the New York gubernatorial election; 319 for the Pennsylvania, Ohio, and Indiana Congressional delegations; 320 for Illinois; 318–22 for the 1862 elections generally. For the House in the Thirty-seventh Congress, Leonard P. Curry, *Blueprint for Modern America: Nonmilitary Legislation of the First Civil War Congress* (Nashville: Vanderbilt University Press, 1968), p. 34; for the House in the Thirty-eighth Congress, James G. Randall and David Donald, *The Civil War and Reconstruction* (Second Edition, Revised with Enlarged Bibliography, Lexington, Massachusetts: D.C. Heath and Company, A Division of Raytheon Education Company, 1969), p. 458, citing [New York] *Tribune Almanac* (New York: New York Tribune, 1864), p. 24.

49. Abraham Lincoln. By the President: William H. Seward, Secretary of State. September 24, 1862, By the President of the United States of America A Proclamation, Document Signed, National Archives Record Group 11, Proclamations, in Basler, ed., *Works of Lincoln*, V, 436–37.

50. Mark E. Neely, Jr., *The Fate of Liberty: Abraham Lincoln and Civil Liberties* (New York, Oxford: Oxford University Press, 1991), pp. 51–65.

51. A. Lincoln, Executive Mansion, Washington, August 26, 1863. To Hon. James C. Conkling [of Illinois], Letter Signed, Illinois State Historical Library, Springfield, Illinois; Autograph Draft and Autograph Draft Signed, Robert Todd Lincoln Collection, LC, in Basler, *Works of Lincoln*, VI, 406–10, quotation from 408.

52. Prize Cases. The Brig Amy Warwick, the Schooner Crenshaw, The Barque Hiawatha, The Schooner Brilliante [March 10, 1863], in U.S. Supreme Court, Jeremiah S. Black [ed.], *Reports of Cases Argued and Determined in the Supreme Court of the United States* (2 vols., Washington, D.C.: W. H. & O. H. Morrison, Law Publishers and Booksellers, 1861–1862), II, *At the December Term 1862* (67 *United States Reports*, 1863), 635–99. For date of the decision, Charles Warren, *The Supreme Court in United States History* (2 vols., Boston, Toronto: Little, Brown, and Company, 1926), II, 380; discussion of cases, 380–84. The quotation is from the Opinion of Mr. Justice [Robert C.] Grier for the Court, 2 Black 665–82, specifically 669. For Lincoln's relevant proclamations of a blockade, Abraham Lincoln, By the President: William H. Seward, Secretary of State, April 19, 1861, By the President of the United States of America: A Proclamation. Document Signed, National Archives, Record Group 11, Proclamations, in Basler, ed., *Works of Lincoln*, IV, 338–39; Abraham Lincoln, By the President: William H. Seward, Secretary of State, April 27, 1861, By the President of the United States of America, A Proclamation. Document Signed, National Archives, Record Group 11, Proclamations, ibid., pp. 346–47.

53. Mr. Justice [James M.] Wayne, Mr. Justice [Noah H.] Swayne, Mr. Justice [Samuel P.] Miller, and Mr. Justice [David] Davis concurred with Grier for the majority; 2 Black 665–82. Mr. Justice [Samuel] Nelson dissented, with Mr. Chief Justice [Roger B.] Taney, Mr. Justice [John] Catron, and Mr. Justice [Nathan] Clifford concurring; ibid., pp. 682–99.

54. Proclamation of April 19, 1861, Basler, ed., *Works of Lincoln*, IV, 339.

55. E[dwin]. M. Townsend, Assistant Adjutant-General, General Orders, No. 100. War Dept., Adjt. General's Office, Washington, April 24, 1863. Instructions for the government of armies of the United States in the field; O.R., Series Three, III (serial 124, 1899), 148–64, and excerpted in Series Two, V (serial 118, 1891), 671–82; and ibid., Series Three, III (serial 124, 1899), 148–64; Leon Friedman, comp., *The Law of War: A Documentary History*, With a Foreword by Telford Taylor (2 vols., New York: Random House, 1972), I, 158–86. On the author of the orders, Frank B. Freidel, *Francis Lieber: Nineteenth-Century Liberal* (Baton Rouge: Louisiana State University Press, 1948).

56. Article. I, Section. IX, paragraph 2; U.S. Constitution, 103rd Congress, 1st Session, Senate Document No. 103–6 (serial 14152), *Constitution of the United States*, p. 10.

57. Randall and Donald, *Civil War and Reconstruction*, p. 305. For the obscurity of the writ of habeas corpus before the Civil War, see also Neely, *Fate of Liberty*, pp. xiii–xvi, 4–5; Paludan, *Presidency of Lincoln*, pp. 71–72.

58. Abraham Lincoln, Washington, April 25, 1861. To Lieutenant-General Scott, Autograph Letter Signed copy, Robert Todd Lincoln Collection, LC, in Basler, ed., *Works of Lincoln*, IV, 344.

59. Abraham Lincoln, April 27, 1861, To the Commanding General of the Army of the United States, Letter Signed, owned by Foreman M. Lebole, Chicago, Illinois, ibid., p. 347; O.R., Series Two, II (serial 114, 1897), 19.

60. Nevins, *Ordeal of the Union*, VI, *War for the Union*, II, 310; Paludan, *Presidency of Lincoln*, pp. 75–76; Carl Brent Swisher, *American Constitutional Development* (Second Edition, Boston, New York, Chicago, Dallas, Atlanta, San Francisco: Houghton Mifflin Company, The Riverside Press Cambridge, 1954), pp. 278–79. For Cadwalader's rank, "Cadwalader, George," Boatner, *Civil War Dictionary*, p. 112; Heitman, *Military Register and Dictionary*, I, 272.

61. Randall and Donald, *Civil War and Reconstruction*, p. 302; see also Nevins,

*Ordeal of the Union,* VI, *War for the Union,* II, 310; Paludan, *Presidency of Lincoln,* p. 76; Swisher, *American Constitutional Development,* p. 279.

62. R. B. Taney, Chief Justice of the Supreme Court of the United States. *Ex parte* John Merryman. Before the Chief Justice of the Supreme Court of the United States, at Chambers. [May 27, 1861] In Edward McPherson, *The Political History of the United States of America, During the Great Rebellion, from November 6, 1860, to July 4, 1864; Including a Classified Summary of the Legislation of the Second Session of the Thirty-sixth Congress, the Three Sessions of the Thirty-seventh Congress, the First Session of the Thirty-eighth Congress, with the Votes Thereon, and the Important Executive, Judicial and Politico-Military Facts of that Eventful Period; Together with the Organization, Legislation, and General Proceedings of the Rebel Administration* (Washington, D.C.: Philip & Solomons, 1864), pp. 155–58, quotations from 158; also in *The Federal Cases: Comprising Cases Argued and Determined in the Circuit and District Courts of the United States from the Earliest Times to the Beginning of the Federal Reporter* [i.e., *The Federal Reporter, with Key-Number Annotations,* Permanent Edition, March 1880–November 1924 (300 vols., St. Paul: West Publishing Co., 1880–1925)] [1789–1880], Arranged Alphabetically by the Titles of the Cases and Numbered Consecutively (30 vols., St. Paul: West Publishing Co., 1894–1897), 17 (1886), 144, Federal Case No. 9,487: 1861. See also Swisher, *American Constitutional Development,* pp. 279–81, including 279 for the date of Taney's reading his opinion. Amendment. [V.] of the Constitution provides that: "No person shall . . . be deprived of life, liberty, or property without due process of law. . . ." Amendment. [IV.] provides that: "The right of the people to be secure in their persons, houses, papers, and effects, against unreasonable searches and seizures, shall not be violated. . . ." For these amendments, see U.S. Constitution, 103rd Congress, 1st Session, Senate Document No. 103–6 (serial 14152), *Constitution of the United States,* pp. 26–27, quotations from 27; for Amendment. [VI.], ibid., p. 27.

63. *Ex parte* [Lambdin P.] Milligan [April 3, 1866], in U.S. Supreme Court, John William Wallace, reporter, *Cases Argued and Adjudged in the Supreme Court of the United States* (23 vols., Washington, D.C.: W. H. & O. H. Morrison, Law Publishers and Booksellers, 1867–1878), IV, *December Term 1866* (71 *United States Reports,* 1867), Opinion of the Court, delivered by Mr. Justice [David] Davis, Mr. Justice [Robert Cooper] Grier, Mr. Justice [Samuel] Nelson, Mr. Justice [Nathan] Clifford, Mr. Justice [Stephen J.] Field concurring, 2, 107–31; Dissent by Mr. Chief Justice [Salmon P.] Chase, Mr. Justice [James M.] Wayne, Mr. Justice [Noah H.] Swayne, and Mr. Justice [Samuel F.] Miller concurring, 132–42. See also Warren, *Supreme Court in United States History,* II, 423–27, particularly 423 for date of decision. But regarding the long-run importance of *Ex parte* Milligan, see Neely, *Fate of Liberty,* Chapter 8, "The Irrelevance of the Milligan Decision," pp. 160–184.

64. Abraham Lincoln, July 4, 1861, to Fellow-citizens of the Senate and House of Representatives, Autograph Draft, Robert Todd Lincoln Collection, LC, in Basler, ed., *Works of Lincoln,* IV, 421–41, quotation from 430.

65. Ibid., pp. 430–31.

66. To Florida, Abraham Lincoln, By the President: William H. Seward, Secretary of State. May 10, 1861, By the President of the United States of America. A Proclamation. Document Signed, National Archives, Record Group 11, Proclamations, ibid., pp. 364–65; authorization to suspend the writ "at any point, on or in the vicinity of any military line which is now, or which shall be used, between the City of New York and the City of Washington," Abraham Lincoln, by the President of the United States: William H. Seward, Secretary of State. July 2, 1861, To the Commanding General of the Army of the United States, Document Signed, The New York Public Library, New York City, ibid., p. 419, also *O.R.,* Series Two, II (serial 114, 1897), 19; authorization, "The military line of the United States for the suppression of the insurrection may be extended

so far as Bangor in Maine," Abraham Lincoln. By the President: William H. Seward, Secretary of State, Washington, October 14, 1861. to Lieut. Gen. Winfield Scott, ibid., p. 554, citing O.R., Series Two, II, 109; to Missouri, Abraham Lincoln, By the President: William H. Seward, Secretary of State, December 2, 1861, To Major General, Henry W. Halleck, Commanding in the Department of Missouri, ibid., V, 35.

67. Thirty-seventh Congress. Session I. (Statute I.) Chap. XXXIII. — An Act to define and punish certain Conspiracies. Approved, July 31, 1861. 12 *Statutes at Large* 284; *Cong. Globe*, XXXI, Appendix, 32.

68. Sec. 1, 12 *Statutes at Large* 589–90; *Cong. Globe*, XXXII, pt. 4, Appendix, 412.

69. Thirty-seventh Congress. Session III. (Statute III.) Chap. LXXXI. — An Act relating to Habeas Corpus, and regulating Judicial Proceedings in Certain Cases. Approved, March 3, 1863. 12 *Statutes at Large* 755–56, particularly Sec. 1, 756; *Cong. Globe*, XXXIII, pt. 2, 37th Congress, 3rd Session, *February 12, 1863 to March 3, 1863*, Appendix, 217.

70. Neely, *Fate of Liberty*, pp. 68–69.

71. Nevins, *Ordeal of the Union*, VI, *War for the Union*, II, 313, and for Merryman, 311n.

72. Neely, *Fate of Liberty*, pp. 18–24; Nevins, *Ordeal of the Union*, VI, *War for the Union*, II, 311.

73. Neely, *Fate of Liberty*, pp. 75–76; Nevins, *Ordeal of the Union*, VI, *War for the Union*, II, 315–16, particularly 315 for Dix and Pierrepont; Benjamin P. Thomas and Harold M. Hyman, *Stanton: The Life and Times of Lincoln's Secretary of War* (New York: Alfred A. Knopf, 1962), pp. 158, 248–49, 280.

74. Neely, *Fate of Liberty*, p. 234. Neely carefully analyzes the difficulties of compiling relevant statistics in his Chapter 6, "Numbers and Definitions," pp. 113–38.

75. Ibid., p. 131, citing the Lafayette C. Baker–Levi C. Turner Papers, Record Group 94, The Adjutant General's Records, War Department Division, National Archives.

76. Ibid., Chapter 2, "Missouri and Martial Law," pp. 32–50, and particularly 45–46 and 128 for estimates of numbers of arrests.

77. Ibid., p. 131, again citing the Baker-Turner Papers, National Archives; see also pp. 52–65.

78. Ibid., pp. 162–75, particularly 162–63, 165–66, 171 for Holt, quotation from 166.

79. Ibid., pp. 168, 169.

80. Ibid., p. 169.

81. Ibid., pp. 143–50, particularly 146 for the Navy Department, 150 for the release of most blockade runners.

82. David Hunter, Major General Commanding. Ed[ward]. W. Smith, Acting Assistant Adjutant General. Headquarters Department of the South, Hilton Head, S.C., May 9, 1862. O.R., Series Three, II (serial 123, 1899), 52–53.

83. L. D. [actually Samuel] Phillips, Doctor Pope's Plantation, Saint Helens, Tuesday, May 13 [1862] — 9 a.m. to E[dward]. L. Pierce, ibid., pp. 59–60, quotations from 60. For the correct identity of Phillips, Rose, *Rehearsal for Reconstruction*, p. 146, where the quotations also appear, pp. 146 (first), 146–47, second.

84. Rose, *Rehearsal for Reconstruction*, pp. 147, 194; McPherson, *Struggle for Equality*, p. 195, for more on negative reactions.

85. Thirty-seventh Congress. Sess. II. (Statute II.) Chap. CXCV. — An Act to suppress Insurrection. . . . Approved, July 17, 1862. Sec. 11. 12 *Statutes at Large* 592; *Cong. Globe*, XXXII, pt. 4, Appendix, 413; O.R., Series Three, II (serial 123), 276. For the disbanding of all but one company of the original regiment, Rose, *Rehearsal for Reconstruction*, p. 189; McPherson, *Struggle for Equality*, pp. 195–96. For Louisiana and Kansas, ibid., p. 196; for Kansas, Bernard C. Nalty, *Strength for the Fight: A History of Black Americans in the Military* (New York: The Free Press, A Division of Macmillan, Inc.;

London: Collier Macmillan Publishers, 1986), p. 34; Joseph T. Glatthaar, *Forged in Battle: The Civil War Alliance of Black Soldiers and White Officers* (New York: The Free Press, A Division of Macmillan, Inc.; London: Collier Macmillan Publishers, 1990), p. 7; for Louisiana, ibid., pp. 7–9.

86. Edwin M. Stanton, Secretary of War. War Department, Washington City, D.C., August 25, 1862. To Brigadier-General Saxton, O.R., XIV (serial 20, 1885), 377–78. For the French-Smalls mission, Rose, *Rehearsal for Reconstruction*, pp. 190–91; for Smalls's exploit, ibid., pp. 149–50; Nalty, *Strength for the Fight*, p. 32.

87. McPherson, *Struggle for Equality*, p. 197, including date; see also Rose, *Rehearsal for Reconstruction*, p. 193.

88. Abraham Lincoln, By the President: William H. Seward, Secretary of State, January 1, 1863, By the President of the United States of America: A Proclamation, Autograph Document Signed, Robert Todd Lincoln Collection, LC; Document Signed, National Archives, Record Group 11, Proclamations, in Basler, ed., *Works of Lincoln*, VI, 28–30, quotation from 30.

89. McPherson, *Struggle for Equality*, p. 204, citing Henry Greenleaf Pearson, *The Life of John A. Andrew, Governor of Massachusetts, 1861–1865* (2 vols., Boston and New York: Houghton, Mifflin and Company, 1904), II, 69–70. For the establishing of the black regiment, McPherson, *Struggle for Equality*, pp. 202–203; Luis F. Emilio, *History of the Fifty-Fourth Regiment of Massachusetts Volunteer Infantry* (Second Edition, Revised and Corrected, with Appendix upon Treatment of Colored Prisoners of War, Boston: Boston Book Company, 1894), pp. 3–5.

90. Glatthaar, *Forged in Battle*, p. 809.

91. For Shaw, see Peter Burchard, *One Gallant Rush: Robert Gould Shaw and His Brave Black Regiment* (New York: St. Martin's Press, 1965), particularly 2, pp. 4–8; 3, pp. 9–15; 4, pp. 16–21; 5, pp. 22–28; 6, pp. 29–37; 7, pp. 38–47; 8, pp. 48–60; 9, pp. 61–70 for his background; also McPherson, *Struggle for Equality*, p. 203; Glatthaar, *Forged in Battle*, pp. 13–14, 37; Nalty, *Strength for the Fight*, p. 37.

92. McPherson, *Struggle for Equality*, p. 204, citing a March 1863 broadside by Douglass, *Men of Color, To Arms*. For the Massachusetts black population in 1860, Long, *Civil War Day by Day*, p. 701; for the two companies, McPherson, *Struggle for Equality*, p. 205; for Stearns and Douglass, ibid., p. 205; Nevins, *Ordeal of the Union*, VI, *War for the Union*, II, 513.

93. McPherson, *Struggle for Equality*, p. 206; also Nevins, *Ordeal of the Union*, VI, *War for the Union*, II, 512, including date.

94. Long, *Civil War Day by Day*, May 27, Friday, 1863, pp. 356–57, particularly 357, for date of bureau; McPherson, *Struggle for Equality*, pp. 205–11; Nevins, *Ordeal of the Union*, VI, *War for the Union*, II, 516–19, 523.

95. "Stearns, George Luther," Heitman, *Historical Register and Dictionary*, I, 918.

96. Thirty-seventh Congress, Sess. II. [Statute II.] Chap. CXCV. — An Act to suppress Insurrection. . . . Approved, July 17, 1862. Sec. 11. 12 *Statutes at Large* 592; *Cong. Globe*, XXXII, pt. 4, Appendix, 413; O.R., Series Three, II (serial 123), 276; McPherson, *Struggle for Equality*, p. 212.

97. McPherson, *Struggle for Equality*, pp. 212–17; Glatthaar, *Forged in Battle*, pp. 65, 169–72; Nalty, *Strength for the Fight*, pp. 39–40.

98. [Second Endorsement.], by J. A. S., Secretary of War. To [First Endorsement.], by G. T. Beauregard, General, Commanding, Hdqrs. Dept. of South Carolina and Georgia. Charleston, November 17, 1862. To H[ugh]. W. Mercer, Brigadier-General, Commanding, Headquarters District of Georgia, Savannah, November 14, 1862. To Brigadier-General [Thomas] Jordan, Chief of Staff and Assistant Adjutant-General, Charleston, S.C. O.R., Series Two, IV (serial 117, 1899), 945–46, endorsements 946. See Nevins, *Ordeal of the Union*, VI, *War for the Union*, II, 520–22.

99. Nevins, *Ordeal of the Union*, VI, *War for the Union*, II, 520.

100. John Cimprich and Robert C. Mainfort, Jr., "Fort Pillow Revisited: New Evidence about an Old Controversy," *Civil War History: A Journal of the Middle Period*, 28:4 (Dec. 1982), 293–306; Albert Castel, "The Fort Pillow Massacre: A Fresh Examination of the Evidence," ibid., 4:1 (March 1958), 37–50. The statistics used here are those of "Fort Pillow 'Massacre,'" Boatner, *Civil War Dictionary*, pp. 295–96, 295 for Confederate strength, 296 for approximate losses.

101. Randall and Donald, *Civil War and Reconstruction*, p. 334; Randall, *Lincoln the President*, III, *Midstream* (1952), 243.

102. Robert S. Holzman, *Stormy Ben Butler* (New York: The Macmillan Company, 1954), pp. 69–70; Randall and Donald, *Civil War and Reconstruction*, p. 335.

103. For the repercussions of the Mumford affair, Randall, *Lincoln the President*, II, 243; Randall and Donald, *Civil War and Reconstruction*, p. 335; and particularly for Davis, Holzman, *Butler*, p. 102. For subsequent developments, Randall and Donald, *Civil War and Reconstruction*, pp. 335–36. For the issue of black Union soldiers and their white officers taken prisoner, Glatthaar, *Forged in Battle*, pp. 200–204.

104. Marvin A. Kreidberg and Merton G. Henry, *History of Military Mobilization in the United States Army 1775–1945* (Department of the Army Pamphlet No. 20–212, Washington: Department of the Army, June 1955), p. 114, citing "Final Report Made to the Secretary of War by the Provost Marshal General of the Operations of the Bureau of the Provost Marshal General of the United States from the Commencement of the Business of the Bureau, March 17, 1863 to March 17, 1866; the Bureau terminating by Law August 28, 1866," III, pt. 1, in U.S. War Department, *Messages and Documents, War Department, 1865–1866* (3 vols., Washington: Government Printing Office, 1866), 68–69 for numbers of regiments, 69 for numbers of soldiers; for the latter also, *O.R.*, Series Three, IV (serial 125, 1899), 1269–1279, particularly 1270 for totals given here.

105. Thirty-seventh Congress, Sess. II. (Statute II.) Chap. CXCV. — An Act to suppress Insurrection. . . . Approved, July 17, 1862. Sec. 11. 12 *Statutes at Large* 592; *Cong. Globe*, XXXII, pt. 4, Appendix, 413; *O.R.*, Series Three, II (serial 123), 276. For later recruiting efforts among African Americans. McPherson, *Struggle for Equality*, pp. 209–12; Glatthaar, *Forged in Battle*, 4, "Filling the Ranks," pp. 61–80.

106. Abraham Lincoln . . . January 1, 1863 . . . A Proclamation, Basler, ed., *Works of Lincoln*, VI, 28–30, 29 for excluded areas.

107. William B. Hesseltine, *Lincoln and the War Governors* (New York: Alfred A. Knopf, 1948), pp. 253–62.

## 7. ARMIES AND SOCIETIES

1. Gordon A. Craig, *The Politics of the Prussian Army 1640–1945* (New York and Oxford: Oxford University Press, 1956), p. 8, citing Herbert Rosinski, *The German Army* (Second Edition, Washington: The Infantry Journal, 1944), pp. 12, 16, and Robert R. Ergang, *The Potsdam Führer: Frederick William I, Father of Prussian Militarism* (New York: Columbia University Press, 1941), p. 63.

2. Quoted in Douglas Southall Freeman, *R. E. Lee: A Biography* (4 vols., New York: Charles Scribner's Sons; London: Charles Scribner's Sons, Ltd., 1934–1935), III (1934), 462, citing John Esten Cooke, *A Life of Gen. Robert E. Lee* (New York: D. Appleton and Company, 1871), p. 184. The casualty figures are those of Thomas L. Livermore, *Numbers and Losses in the Civil War in America 1861–65* (Second Edition, Boston and New York: Houghton, Mifflin and Company, 1901; reprint, Dayton, Ohio: Morningside, 1986), p. 96: Union casualties of 1,284 killed, 9,600 wounded, 1,769 missing, for a total of 12,653 out of 113,687 engaged; Confederate casualties of 595 killed, 4,061 wounded, 653 missing, for a total of 5,309 out of 72,497 engaged. For analyses of Fredericksburg by

various authorities, see Gary W. Gallagher, ed., *The Fredericksburg Campaign: Decision on the Rappahannock* (Chapel Hill & London: University of North Carolina Press, 1995). Of special interest is the effort to rehabilitate Burnside's reputation for the conduct of the battle, William Marvel, "The Making of a Myth: Ambrose E. Burnside and the Union High Command at Fredericksburg," pp. 1–25. Marvel earlier applied this rehabilitary endeavor to Burnside's whole career in *Burnside* (Chapel Hill & London: University of North Carolina Press, 1991), with pp. 162–206 on the Fredericksburg campaign; his carefully researched writings ought to be pondered in spite of his somewhat smug adherence to the "everybody before me was wrong" school of historiography. See also Edward J. Stackpole, *Drama on the Rappahannock: The Fredericksburg Campaign* (Harrisburg, Pennsylvania: Military Service Publishing Company, 1957), and the British military critic George Francis Robert Henderson's *The Campaign of Fredericksburg, Nov.–Dec., 1862: A Tactical Study for Officers* (Third Edition, London, Chatham: Gale & Polden, 1891), republished in G. F. R. Henderson, *The Civil War: A Soldier's View: A Collection of Civil War Writings by Col. G. F. R. Henderson*, Jay Luvaas, ed. (Chicago: University of Chicago Press, 1958), pt. II, pp. 9–119. See also the relevant sections of the standard accounts of Union and Confederate command in the East: Kenneth P. Williams, *Lincoln Finds a General: A Military Study of the Civil War* (5 vols., New York: The Macmillan Company, 1950–1959), II (1950), Chapters XV, "A New Commander Marches Well," 480–508, and XVI, "Burnside Fails at Marye's Hill," 509–46; Freeman, *Lee*, II, 429–74; Douglas Southall Freeman, *Lee's Lieutenants: A Study in Command* (3 vols., New York: Charles Scribner's Sons, 1942–1944), II, *Cedar Mountain to Chancellorsville* (1943), 312–13, 325–85.

3. "Tennessee, Union Department and Army of the," Mark Mayo Boatner III, *The Civil War Dictionary* (Revised Edition, New York: Vintage Books, A Division of Random House, Inc., 1991), p. 830.

4. "Forrest, Nathan Bedford," ibid., pp. 288–89, specifically 288 for Forrest's promotion; "Forrest's Second Raid," ibid., pp. 291–92, particularly 291; Williams, *Lincoln Finds a General*, IV, *Iuka to Vicksburg* (1956), 218–221.

5. "Holly Springs," Boatner, *Civil War Dictionary*, pp. 405–406; Williams, *Lincoln Finds a General*, IV, 196–204.

6. "Sherman, William Tecumseh," Francis B. Heitman, *Historical Register and Dictionary of the United States Army, From Its Organization, September 29, 1789, to March 2, 1903. Published under act of Congress approved March 2, 1903. 57th Congress, Second Session, House Document 446 (serial 4536).* (2 vols., Washington: Government Printing Office, 1903), I, 862, for promotion; "Sherman, William Tecumseh," Boatner, *Civil War Dictionary*, pp. 750–51, specifically 751 for promotion and command of the District of Missouri.

7. Livermore, *Numbers and Losses*, p. 96 for Union numbers engaged and losses, p. 97 for Confederate; see Williams, *Lincoln Finds a General*, IV, 206–18; John F. Marszalek, *Sherman: A Soldier's Passion for Order* (New York: The Free Press, A Division of Macmillan, Inc.; Toronto: Maxwell Macmillan Canada; New York, Oxford, Singapore, Sydney: Maxwell Macmillan International, 1933), pp. 202–208.

8. "Rosecrans, William Starke," Boatner, *Civil War Dictionary*, p. 708 for date of command; "Ohio, Union Department and Army of the," ibid., pp. 696–97, specifically 696 for change of name; "Cumberland, Union Department and Army of the," ibid., pp. 212–13, specifically 212 for date of command and change of name. The second entry gives October 24 as the date of Rosecrans's assuming command, but the date October 30 given in the other two entries is confirmed by the evidence presented in Williams, *Lincoln Finds a General*, IV, 141.

9. Livermore, *Numbers and Losses*, p. 97; the Union casualties of 12,906 included 1,677 killed, 7,543 wounded, and 3,686 missing, while the Confederate losses of 11,739

included 1,294 killed, 7,945 wounded, and about 2,500 missing. See also Peter Cozzens, *No Better Place to Die: The Battle of Stones River* (Urbana and Chicago: University of Illinois Press, 1990); James Lee McDonough, *Stones River — Bloody Winter in Tennessee* (Knoxville: University of Tennessee Press, 1980); William M. Lamers, *The Edge of Glory: A Biography of General William S. Rosecrans, U.S.A.* (New York: Harcourt, Brace & World, Inc., 1961), pp. 199–248; Thomas Lawrence Connelly, *Autumn of Glory: The Army of Tennessee, 1862–1865* (Baton Rouge: Louisiana State University Press, 1971), pp. 44–68; Williams, *Lincoln Finds a General*, IV, Chapter IX, "An Indecisive but Timely Victory," 252–85.

10. This account of the Cabinet crisis draws on those of Francis Fessenden, *Life and Public Services of William Pitt Fessenden, United States Senator from Maine 1854–1864; Secretary of the Treasury 1864–1865; United States Senator from Maine 1865–1869, by His Son Francis Fessenden* (2 vols., Boston and New York: Houghton, Mifflin and Company, 1907), I, 233–53; Gideon Welles, *Diary of Gideon Welles, Secretary of the Navy under Lincoln and Johnson*, ed. Howard K. Beale, assisted by Alan W. Brownsword, With an Introduction by Howard K. Beale and appendices drawn from Welles's correspondence (3 vols., New York: W. W. Norton & Company, Inc., 1960), I, *1861–March 30, 1864*, December 19 [1862], Friday, 194–96, December 20, Saturday, 196–204; Leonard P. Curry, *Blueprint for Modern America: Nonmilitary Legislation of the First Civil War Congress* (Nashville: Vanderbilt University Press, 1968), pp. 216–27; David Herbert Donald, *Lincoln* (New York, London, Toronto, Sydney, Tokyo, Singapore: Simon & Schuster, 1995), pp. 401–406; Phillip Shaw Paludan, *The Presidency of Abraham Lincoln* (Lawrence: University Press of Kansas, 1994), Chapter 8, "Cabinet Crisis," pp. 167–81; Allan Nevins, *Ordeal of the Union* (8 vols., *Ordeal of the Union*, I, *Fruits of Manifest Destiny 1847–1852; Ordeal of the Union*, II, *A House Dividing 1852–1857* [New York, London: Charles Scribner's Sons, 1947]; III, *The Emergence of Lincoln*, I, *Douglas, Buchanan, and Party Chaos 1857–1859*; IV, *The Emergence of Lincoln*, II, *Prologue to Civil War 1859–1860* [New York: Charles Scribner's Sons, 1950]; V, *The War for the Union*, I, *The Improvised War 1861–1862* [New York: Charles Scribner's Sons, 1959]; VI, *The War for the Union*, II, *War Becomes Revolution* [New York: Charles Scribner's Sons, 1960]; VII, *The War for the Union*, III, *The Organized War 1863–1864*; VIII, *The War for the Union*, IV, *The Organized War to Victory 1864–1865* [New York: Charles Scribner's Sons, 1971]), VI, *War for the Union*, II, 350–359. Valuable as always for Lincoln and his administration is James G. Randall, *Lincoln the President* (4 vols., New York: Dodd, Mead & Company, 1946–1955, IV, *Last Full Measure*, coauthored with Richard N. Current), I–II, *Springfield to Gettysburg*, II, 241–49; but as Paludan, *Presidency of Lincoln*, p. 344, n15, points out, · Randall neglects the extent to which, beyond the activities of the Senators and Chase's ambitions, "Lincoln, overburdened by his duties and inexperienced as an administrator, also contributed to the crisis."

11. Welles, *Diary*, I, 202.

12. John G. Nicolay and John Hay, *Abraham Lincoln: A History* (10 vols., New York: The Century Company, 1914), VI, 271.

13. Curry, *Blueprint for Modern America*, pp. 15, 29–30.

14. Allan G. Bogue, "Bloc and Party in the United States Senate: 1861–1865," *Civil War History: A Journal of the Middle Period*, 13:3 (September 1967), 221–41; and the same author's "The Radical Voting Dimension in the U.S. Senate during the Civil War," *Journal of Interdisciplinary History*, 3:4 (Winter 1973), 449–74.

15. Thirty-seventh Congress. Session II. (Statute II.) Chap. LXXV. — An Act to secure Homesteads to actual Settlers on the Public Domain. Approved, May 20, 1862. In U.S. Laws, statutes, *The Statutes at Large of the United States of America, 1789–1873* (17 vols., I–IX, Boston: Charles C. Little and J. Brown, 1845–1854; X–XVII, Boston: Little, Brown, and Company, 1855–1873), 12 (December 5, 1859–March 3, 1863) (1863), 392–93;

*The Congressional Globe*, XXXII, part 4, 37th Congress, 2nd Session, *June 23, 1862 to July 17, 1862*, Appendix, 352; see Curry, *Blueprint for Modern America*, "The Homestead Act," pp. 101–108.

16. Nevins, *Ordeal of the Union*, VI, *War for the Union*, II, 204–206; Curry, *Blueprint for Modern America*, pp. 248–49.

17. Thirty-seventh Congress. Session II. (Statute II.) Chap. LXXII. — An Act to establish a Department of Agriculture. Approved, May 15, 1862. 12 *Statutes at Large*, 387–88; *Cong. Globe*, XXXII, pt. 4, Appendix, 350–51; Everette B. Long, with Barbara Long, *The Civil War Day by Day: An Almanac 1861–1865*, Foreword by Bruce Catton (Garden City, New York: Doubleday & Company, Inc., 1971), May 15, Thursday, 1862, pp. 211–12, particularly 212.

18. Thirty-seventh Congress. Session II. (Statute II.) Chap. CXXX. — An Act donating Public Lands to the several States and Territories which may provide Colleges for the Benefit of Agriculture and the Mechanic Arts. Approved, July 2, 1862. 12 *Statutes at Large* 503–505, quotation from Sec. 4, 504; *Cong. Globe*, XXXII, pt. 4, Appendix, 386; Curry, *Blueprint for Modern America*, "The Land-Grant College Act," pp. 108–15; Nevins, *Ordeal of the Union*, VI, *War for the Union*, II, 206–208.

19. Thirty-seventh Congress. Session II. (Statute II.) Chap. CXX. — An Act to aid in the Construction of a Railroad and Telegraph Line from the Missouri River to the Pacific Ocean, and to secure to the Government the Use of the same for Postal, Military, and Other Purposes. Approved, July 1, 1862. 12 *Statutes at Large* 489–98; *Cong. Globe*, XXXII, pt. 4, Appendix, 381–84; Curry, *Blueprint for Modern America*, "The Pacific Railroad Act," pp. 116–26; Nevins, *Ordeal of the Union*, VI, *War for the Union*, II, 208–11.

20. Thirty-sixth Congress. Session II. (Statute II.) Chap. LXVIII. — An Act to provide for the Payment of outstanding Treasury Notes, to authorize a Loan, to regulate and fix the Duties on Imports, and for other Purposes. Approved, March 2, 1861. 12 *Statutes at Large* 178–99, tariff provisions, Secs. 5–33, 179–98; *Cong. Globe*, XXX, Part 2, 36th Congress, 2nd Session, *February 18, 1861 to March 2, 1861, Special Session, March 4–28, 1861*, Appendix, 328–33, Secs. 5–33, 328–33. For this and the next two tariff acts, see Curry, *Blueprint for Modern America*, pp. 149–62; Nevins, *Ordeal of the Union*, VI, *War for the Union*, II, 213.

21. Thirty-seventh Congress. Session I. (Statute I.) Chap. XLV. — An Act to provide increased Revenue from Imports, to pay Interest on the Public Debt, and for other Purposes. Approved, August 5, 1861. 12 *Statutes at Large* 292–314, tariff provisions, Secs. 1–5, 292–94; *Cong. Globe*, XXXI, Thirty-seventh Congress. 1st Session, *July 4, 1861, to August 6, 1861*, Appendix, 34–40, Secs. 1–5, 34–36.

22. Thirty-seventh Congress. Session II. (Statute II.) Chap. CLXIII. — An Act increasing, temporarily, the Duties on Imports, and for other Purposes. Approved, July 14, 1862. 12 *Statutes at Large* 543–61, tariff provisions, Secs. 1–23, 543–60; *Cong. Globe*, XXXII, pt. 4, Appendix, 398–403, Secs. 1–23, 398–403.

23. Bray Hammond, "The North's Empty Purse, 1861–1862," *American Historical Review*, 67:1 (October 1961), 1–18, particularly 2–8 to the end of 1861; Bray Hammond, *Sovereignty and an Empty Purse: Banks and Politics in the Civil War* (Princeton, New Jersey: Princeton University Press, 1970), Chapters 1, "A Stunted Government," pp. 3–34, 2, "Sumter, Bull Run, and the Special Session April to August 1861," pp. 35–70, and 3, "August to December 1861," pp. 107–28.

24. Thirty-seventh Congress. Session I. (Statute I.) Chap. XLVI. — An Act supplementary to an Act entitled "An Act to Authorize a National Loan and for other Purposes" [Chap. V. — An Act to authorize a National Loan and for other Purposes. Approved, July 7, 1861. 12 *Statutes at Large* 259–261; *Cong. Globe*, XXXI, Appendix, 24–25]. Approved, August 5, 1861. 12 *Statutes at Large* 313–14, particularly Sec. 6, 313–14; *Cong. Globe*, XXXI, Appendix, 40–41, Sec. 6, 41. The Independent Treasury Act is Twenty-ninth Con-

gress. Session I. (Statute I.) Chap. XC. — An Act to provide for the better Organization of the Treasury, and for the Collection, Safe-Keeping, Transfer, and Disbursement of the public Revenue. Approved August 6, 1846. 9 *Statutes at Large* (December 1, 1845 to March 3, 1851) (Boston: Charles C. Little and James Brown, 1851), 55–56. See Bray Hammond, *Sovereignty and an Empty Purse*, p. 66, and "The North's Empty Purse," pp. 3–4.

25. Hammond, *Sovereignty and an Empty Purse*, pp. 147–59, and particularly 157 for the suspension, and "The North's Empty Purse," pp. 4–6.

26. Fawn M. Brodie, *Thaddeus Stevens: Scourge of the South* (New York: W. W. Norton & Company, Inc., 1959), p. 173.

27. Hammond, *Sovereignty and an Empty Purse*, pp. 173–207, 221–25 for the House; 211–21 for the Senate and particularly 217 for John Sherman; 168–73 for Chase; Curry, *Blueprint for Modern America*, pp. 181–96; Robert P. Sharkey, *Money, Class, and Party: An Economic Study of Civil War and Reconstruction* (Baltimore: Johns Hopkins Press, 1959), pp. 23–48.

28. Thirty-seventh Congress. Session II. (Statute II.) Chap. XXXIII. — An Act to authorize the Issue of United States Notes and for the Redemption or Funding thereof, and for Funding the Floating Debt of the United States. Approved, February 25, 1862. 12 *Statutes at Large* 345–48; *Cong. Globe*, XXXII, pt. 4, Appendix, 338. See Sharkey, *Money, Class, and Party*, p. 46; Hammond, *Sovereignty and an Empty Purse*, pp. 225–29, and "The North's Empty Purse," pp. 8–14, as well as pp. 14–18 for a digest of interpretations.

29. Thirty-seventh Congress. Session II. (Statute II.) Chap. CXLII. — An Act to authorize an additional Issue of United States Notes, and for other Purposes. Approved, July 11, 1862. 12 *Statutes at Large* 532–33; *Cong. Globe*, XXXII, pt. 4, Appendix, 395; Hammond, *Sovereignty and an Empty Purse*, pp. 246–49; Sharkey, *Money, Class, and Party*, pp. 47–48.

30. Thirty-seventh Congress. Session III. (Statute III.) Chap. LXXIII. — An Act to provide Ways and Means for the Support of the Government. Approved, March 3, 1863. 12 *Statutes at Large* 709–13, particularly Secs. 2–6, 710–12; *Cong. Globe*, XXXIII, pt. 2, Appendix, 203–204, Secs. 2–6, 203–204; Hammond, *Sovereignty and an Empty Purse*, pp. 252–54, particularly 254 for the legislation; Sharkey, *Money, Class, and Party*, pp. 47–49.

31. Thirty-seventh Congress. Session II. (Statute II.) Chap. CXIX. — An Act to provide Internal Revenue to support the Government and to pay interest on the Public Debt. Approved, July 1, 1862. 12 *Statutes at Large* 432–89; *Cong. Globe*, XXXII, pt. 4, Appendix, 364–84; Hammond *Sovereignty and an Empty Purse*, pp. 269–80; Curry, *Blueprint for Modern America*, pp. 162–79.

32. Thirty-eighth Congress. Session I. (Statute I.) Chap. CLXXII. — An Act to provide Ways and Means for the Support of the Government, and for other Purposes. Approved, June 30, 1864. 13 *Statutes at Large* (December 1863, to December 1865) (Boston: Little, Brown, and Company, 1866), 218–306; *Cong. Globe*, XXXIV, pt. 4, 38th Congress, 1st Session, *June 14, 1864 to July 4, 1864*, 206–35.

33. For internal revenue receipts in fiscal 1865, U.S., Treasury, Department of the, *Report of the Secretary of the Treasury on the State of the Finances for the Year 1865*, Thirty-ninth Congress, First Session, House Executive Document No. 3 (serial 1254) (Washington: Government Printing Office, 1865), p. 18; for income tax receipts, James G. Randall and David Donald, *The Civil War and Reconstruction* (Second Edition, Revised with Enlarged Bibliography) (Lexington, Massachusetts: D.C. Heath & Company, A Division of Raytheon Education Company, 1969), p. 345; for tariff returns and percentages of funds derived from taxation, James M. McPherson, *Battle Cry of Freedom: The Civil War Era* (New York, Oxford: Oxford University Press, 1988), p. 443.

34. Thomas Graham Belden and Marva Robins Belden, *So Fell the Angels* (Boston, Toronto: Little, Brown and Company, 1956), pp. 28–32, 38–39, 106; this book is something of a muckraking account of Chase and his personal financial arrangements.

35. Ibid., p. 81, and Hammond, *Sovereignty and an Empty Purse*, p. 289, for Chase's appointment of Cooke. See ibid., pp. 263–64, 289–90, 339, particularly 289 for October 1862; Belden, *So Fell the Angels*, pp. 81, 105–106, particularly 81 for October 1862. The standard biography remains Ellis Paxson Oberholtzer, *Jay Cooke: Financier of the Civil War* (2 vols., Philadelphia: G. W. Jacobs & Co., 1907).

36. Curry, *Blueprint for Modern America*, pp. 197–206; Hammond, *Sovereignty and an Empty Purse*, pp. 285–86, 290–91, 296–317, 321–32, and by the same author, Bray Hammond, *Banks and Politics in America from the Revolution to the Civil War* (Princeton, New Jersey: Princeton University Press, 1957), pp. 723–27; Sharkey, *Money, Class, and Party*, pp. 25–26, 224–25.

37. Thirty-seventh Congress. Session III. (Statute III.) Chap. LVIII.—An Act to provide a national Currency, secured by a Pledge of United States Stocks, and to provide for the Circulation and Redemption thereof. Approved, February 25, 1863. 12 *Statutes at Large* 665–82; *Cong. Globe*, XXXIII, pt. 2, Appendix, 189–94; Curry, *Blueprint for Modern America*, pp. 203–204; Hammond, *Sovereignty and an Empty Purse*, p. 332; Sharkey, *Money, Class, and Party*, pp. 224–26.

38. Thirty-eighth Congress. Session I. (Statute I.) Chap. CVI.—An Act to provide a National Currency, secured by a Pledge of United States Bonds, and to provide for the Circulation and Redemption thereof. Approved, June 3, 1864. 13 *Statutes at Large* 99–118; *Cong. Globe*, XXXIV, pt. 4, 38th Congress, 1st Session, *June 14, 1864 to July 4, 1864*, Appendix, 169–75; Hammond, *Banks and Politics*, pp. 727–32, particularly 731–32 for the terms of the law; Sharkey, *Money, Class, and Party*, pp. 226–29, particularly 227–29 for the terms of the act; Randall and Donald, *Civil War and Reconstruction*, pp. 350–51.

39. Nevins, *Ordeal of the Union*, VI, *War for the Union*, II, 191, 395–96. For Vallandigham in Congress, Curry, *Blueprint for Modern America*, p. 33. The standard biography is Frank L. Klement, *The Limits of Dissent: Clement L. Vallandigham & the Civil War* (Lexington: University Press of Kentucky, 1970). For a scathing depiction of Vallandigham as crossing the boundary into treason, see David E. Long, *The Jewel of Liberty: Abraham Lincoln's Re-election and the End of Slavery* (Mechanicsburg, Pennsylvania: Stackpole Books, 1994) pp. 49–50, 60–61, 77–81, 103–105, 134, 138–39.

40. Richard Orr Curry, "Copperheadism and Continuity: The Anatomy of a Stereotype," *Journal of Negro History*, 57:1 (January 1972), 29–36, quotation from 32.

41. Robert Rutland, "The Copperheads of Iowa: A Re-examination," *Iowa Journal of History*, 52:1 (January 1954), 1–54.

42. Geo B McClellan, Head-Quarters Army of the Potomac, Sharpsburg, Sept. 26, 1862 to Wm H Aspinwall esq New York City, Autograph Letter Signed, Civil War Collection, Henry W. Huntington Library, Botanical Gardens, and Museum, San Marino, California, in George B. McClellan, *The Civil War Papers of George B. McClellan: Selected Correspondence, 1860–1865*, Stephen W. Sears, ed. (New York: Ticknor & Fields, 1989), p. 482.

43. Eric Foner, *Free Soil, Free Labor, Free Men: The Ideology of the Republican Party before the Civil War* (London, Oxford, New York: Oxford University Press, 1970), 8, "The Republicans and Race," pp. 244–315; V. Jacque Voegeli, *Free but Not Equal: The Midwest and the Negro during the Civil War* (Chicago & London: University of Chicago Press, 1967), pp. 1–3.

44. Quoted in Nicholas B. Wainwright, "The Loyal Opposition in Civil War Philadelphia," *Pennsylvania Magazine of History and Biography*, 88:3 (July 1964), 294–315, quotation from 298, citing Democratic Party, Pennsylvania, State Central Committee, *Address of the Democratic State Central Committee, Together with the Proceedings of the Democratic State Convention Held at Harrisburg, July 4, 1862, and the Proceedings of the Democratic State Central Committee held at Philadelphia, July 29, 1862* (Philadelphia, 1862), p. 4.

45. Quoted in Nevins, *Ordeal of the Union*, VI, *War for the Union*, II, citing Stew-

art Mitchell, *Horatio Seymour of New York* (Cambridge, Massachusetts: Harvard University Press, 1938), p. 245, and De Alva S. Alexander, *A Political History of the State of New York* (4 vols., New York: H. Holt and Company, 1906–1923), III (1909), 19.

46. William B. Hesseltine, *Lincoln and the War Governors* (New York: Alfred A. Knopf, 1948), pp. 282–84; Mitchell, *Seymour*, pp. 265–67.

47. Hesseltine, *Lincoln and the War Governors*, pp. 312–15, 315 for War Department funds; Bruce Catton, *Glory Road: The Bloody Route from Fredericksburg to Gettysburg* (Garden City, N.Y.: Doubleday & Company, Inc., 1952), pp. 132–41, 140 for the War Department funds; Nevins, *Ordeal of the Union*, VI, *War for the Union*, II, 391–92, 392 for loans and Federal funds.

48. Hesseltine, *Lincoln and the War Governors*, pp. 315–18; Nevins, *Ordeal of the Union*, VI, *War for the Union*, II, 391–92.

49. Nevins, *Ordeal of the Union*, VI, *War for the Union*, II, 318, and for the 109th Illinois, 390. See also Hesseltine, *Lincoln and the War Governors*, p. 263.

50. David E. Long, *Jewel of Liberty*, pp. 43–48, 73–74, 134–52, 172–74, 243–47, takes the danger of Copperhead conspiracies seriously, regarding them as thwarted by Unionists' vigilance and then, in 1864, by the copperheads' illusion that a Democratic Party committed to peace would win the elections. Long believes the copperheads dealt so closely with Confederate agents that they went beyond mere flirtation with treason. For a more benign view of the Peace Democrats and particularly the secret societies, see Frank L. Klement, *Dark Lanterns: Secret Political Societies, Conspiracies, and Treason Trials in the Civil War* (Baton Rouge and London: Louisiana State University Press, 1984), especially Chapter I, "George Beckley and the Knights of the Golden Circle," pp. 7–33; also the same author's *The Copperheads in the Middle West* (Chicago: University of Chicago Press, 1960). The best overall examination of the Democratic Party during the war, presenting a restrained view of the Peace Democrats, is Joel H. Silbey, *A Respectable Minority: The Democratic Party in the Civil War Era, 1860–1868* (New York: W. W. Norton and Co., 1977).

51. John B. Jones, *A Rebel War Clerk's Diary at the Confederate Capital* (2 vols., Philadelphia: J. B. Lippincott Company, 1866), January 29th [1863], I, 249; also in John B. Jones, *A Rebel War Clerk's Diary*, Condensed, edited, and annotated by Earl Schenck Miers, complete in one volume (New York: Sagamore Press, Inc. Publishers, 1958), January 29th, pp. 157–58, quotation from 158.

52. Klement, *Dark Lanterns*, p. 137; Nevins, *Ordeal of the Union*, VI, *War for the Union*, II, 396.

53. Thirty-seventh Congress. Session III. (Statute III.) Chap. LXXXI. — An Act relating to Habeas Corpus, and regulating Judicial Proceedings in Certain Cases. Approved, March 3, 1863. 12 *Statutes at Large* 755–58; *Cong. Globe*, XXXIII, pt. 2, Appendix, 217–18; Harold M. Hyman, *A More Perfect Union: The Impact of the Civil War and Reconstruction on the Constitution* (New York: Alfred A. Knopf, 1973), pp. 245–61. For the ambiguities and complexity of the Lincoln administration's position, see Mark E. Neely, Jr., *The Fate of Liberty: Abraham Lincoln and Civil Liberties* (New York, Oxford: Oxford University Press, 1991), pp. 68–74. See also Nevins, *Ordeal of the Union*, VI, *War for the Union*, II, 397; Randall and Donald, *Civil War and Reconstruction*, pp. 306–307; Paludan, *Presidency of Lincoln*, pp. 191–92.

54. E[dwin]. D. Townsend, Assistant Adjutant-General, General Orders, No. 193. War Dept., Adjt. General's Office, Washington, November 22, 1863. O.R., Series Two, IV (serial 117, 1899), 746–47, particularly 746.

55. A. E. Burnside, Major-General, Commanding Department of the Ohio Headquarters Department of the Ohio, Cincinnati, May 18, 1863. To Major Gen. H. W. Halleck, General-in-Chief, Washington, D.C. O.R., Series Two, V (serial 118, 1899), 633, enclosing Proceedings of a military commission convened at Cincinnati, Ohio [trial of

Clement L. Vallandigham], ibid., pp. 633–46, quotation from Twelfth Day, Cincinnati, Ohio, May 6, 1863, Charge, 634. The Vallandigham case is narrated in Neely, *Fate of Liberty*, pp. 65–68; Hyman, *A More Perfect Union*, pp. 261–62; Donald, *Lincoln*, pp. 419–21; Klement, *Dark Lanterns*, pp. 55–56, 74, 103–12; Nevins, *Ordeal of the Union*, VI, *War for the Union*, II, 453–55.

56. Nevins, *Ordeal of the Union*, VI, *War for the Union*, II, 454–55; Randall and Donald, *Civil War and Reconstruction*, p. 304.

57. Klement, *Dark Lanterns*, Chapter II, "The Union Leagues: Patriotic Secret Societies," pp. 34–63. For a scholarly history of one of the most important, see Maxwell Whiteman, *Gentlemen in Crisis: The First Century of the Union League of Philadelphia, 1862–1962* (Philadelphia: The League, 1975).

58. Richard E. Beringer, Herman Hattaway, Archer Jones, William N. Still, Jr., *Why the South Lost the Civil War* (Athens and London: University of Georgia Press, 1986), p. 266, citing Consolidated abstract from returns of the Confederate Army on or about June 30, 1863, O.R., Series Four, II (serial 128, 1900), 615.

59. For the cold water Christmas, Frank E. Vandiver, *Their Tattered Flags: The Epic of the Confederacy* (New York and Evanston: A Harper's Magazine Press Book, Published in Association with Harper & Row, 1970), pp. 165–67; for the loss of territory, ibid., pp. 238–39.

60. Randall and Donald, *Civil War and Reconstruction*, p. 262.

61. Charles P. Roland, *The Confederacy*, Daniel J. Boorstin, ed., *The Chicago History of American Civilization* (Chicago and London: University of Chicago Press, 1960), p. 152; for $11 feeding two people per day, Vandiver, *Their Tattered Flags*, p. 173.

62. For the Richmond riot and the crisis leading to it, Emory M. Thomas, *The Confederate State of Richmond: A Biography of the Capital* (Austin: University of Texas Press, 1971), pp. 111–19; Emory M. Thomas, *The Confederate Nation, 1861–1865* (New York, Hagerstown, San Francisco, London: Harper & Row, Publishers, 1979), pp. 201–205. For riots elsewhere, ibid., p. 204; Beringer et al., *Why the South Lost*, p. 229.

63. Mary Boykin Miller Chesnut, *Mary Chesnut's Civil War*, Comer Vann Woodward, ed. (New Haven and London: Yale University Press, 1981), December 10, 1863, p. 503.

64. Thomas, *Confederate Nation*, p. 193; Archer Jones, *Confederate Strategy from Shiloh to Vicksburg* (Baton Rouge: Louisiana State University Press, 1961), pp. 118–22.

65. A meticulous study of leaders and factions in the Confederate Congress is Thomas B. Alexander and Richard E. Beringer, *The Anatomy of the Confederate Congress: A Study of the Influence of Member Characteristics on Legislative Voting Behavior, 1861–1865* (Nashville: Vanderbilt University Press, 1972); see especially 1, "Profile and Personalities," pp. 13–34, 2, "Political Parties," 35–58, and 3, "Nonpartisan Bases of Factionalism," 58–73. See also Thomas, *Confederate Nation*, pp. 194–95; Vandiver, *Their Tattered Flags*, pp. 175–77; Wilfred Buck Yearns, *The Confederate Congress* (Athens: University of Georgia Press, 1960), especially pp. 37–38.

66. First Congress. Session III. Statute III. Chap. XXXVIII. — An Act to lay Taxes for the common defence, and carry on the Government of the Confederate States. Approved April 24, 1863. Confederate States, Laws, statutes, *The Statutes at Large of the Confederate States of America Passed at the Third Session of the First Congress; 1863*. Carefully collated with the Originals at Richmond, James M. Matthews, ed. (Richmond: R. M. Smith, Printer to Congress, 1863), pp. 115–26; income tax, Sec. 8, pp. 120–21, Sec. 9, pp. 121–22. See also Thomas, *Confederate Nation*, pp. 198–99; Richard Cecil Todd, *Confederate Finance* (Athens: University of Georgia Press, 1954), pp. 141–48.

67. Roland, *The Confederacy*, p. 130, for $40,000,000, 131, for $82,262,350.

68. First Congress. Session III. Statute III. Chap. IX. — An Act to provide for the funding and further issue of Treasury Notes. Matthews, ed., *Statutes at Large . . . Third*

*Session . . . First Congress,* pp. 99–102, Sec. 2, p. 100 for $50,000,000 limit per month. See also Thomas, *Confederate Nation,* p. 197.

69. Roland, *The Confederacy,* pp. 120–21, for statistics; Thomas, *Confederate Nation,* pp. 187–88, for a more detailed financial account; Lynn M. Case and Warren F. Spencer, *The United States and France: Civil War Diplomacy* (Philadelphia: University of Pennsylvania Press, 1970), pp. 403–408, for the diplomatic background.

70. First Congress. Session III. Statute III. Chap. X. — An Act to Regulate Impressments. Approved March 26, 1863. Matthews, ed., *Statutes at Large . . . Third Session . . . First Congress,* pp. 102–104. See also Thomas, *Confederate Nation,* p. 196; Yearns, *Confederate Congress,* pp. 116–20.

71. First Congress. Session III. Statute III. Chap. LXXX. — An Act to repeal certain clauses of An Act entitled "An Act to exempt certain persons from military service," &c., approved October 11, 1862. Approved May 1, 1863. Matthews, ed., *Statutes at Large . . . Third Session . . . First Congress,* pp. 158–59. For the act amended, see First Congress. Session II. Statute II. Chap. XLV. — An Act to exempt certain persons from military duty, and to repeal an Act entitled, "An Act to exempt certain persons from enrollment for service in the army of the Confederate States," approved 21st April, 1862. Approved Oct. 10, 1862. Confederate States, Laws, statutes, *Public Laws of the Confederate States of America, Passed at the Second Session of the First Congress; 1862.* Carefully collated with the Originals at Richmond. James M. Matthews, ed. (Richmond: R. M. Smith, Printer to Congress, 1862), pp. 77–79; and for the latter law, First Congress, Session I. Statute I. Chap. LXXIV. — An Act to exempt certain persons from enrollment for service in the Armies of the Confederate States. Approved April 21, 1862. Confederate States, Laws, statutes, *Public Laws of the Confederate States of America, Passed at the First Session of the First Congress; 1862.* Carefully collated with the Originals at Richmond, James M. Matthews, ed. (Richmond: R. M. Smith, Printer to Congress, 1862), pp. 51–52.

72. For rejection of Presidential power to suspend the privilege of the writ of habeas corpus, see Alexander and Beringer, *Anatomy of the Confederate Congress,* p. 171; Thomas, *Confederate Nation,* pp. 194–95. For the February 27, 1862 suspension, First Congress. Session I. Statute I. Chap. II. — An Act to authorize the suspension of the writ of habeas corpus in certain cases. Approved Feb. 27, 1862. Matthews, ed., *Statutes at Large . . . First Session . . . First Congress,* p. 1. See also Alexander and Beringer, *Anatomy of the Confederate Congress,* pp. 169–70.

73. Roland, *The Confederacy,* p. 77. On Stephens, see also Thomas, *Confederate Nation,* p. 139; James Z. Rabin, "Alexander H. Stephens and Jefferson Davis," *American Historical Review,* 58:2 (April 1953), 290–321. On Joseph E. Brown, see Louise B. Hill, *Joseph E. Brown and the Confederacy* (Chapel Hill: University of North Carolina Press, 1939), and Joseph H. Parks, *Joseph E. Brown of Georgia* (Baton Rouge: Louisiana State University Press, 1977).

74. Lt. Charles C. Jones, Jr., Savannah, Saturday, September 27th, 1862, to the Rev. Charles C. Jones, letter at the University of Georgia, Athens, in Robert Manson Myers, ed., *The Children of Pride: A True Story of Georgia in the Civil War* (New Haven and London: Yale University Press, 1972), pp. 966–68, quotation from 968, Jones's position from biographical sketch, p. 1568.

75. Memoirs Section, 1862–1863, entry of September 18, 1863 [1862], in Woodward, ed., *Mary Chesnut's Civil War,* pp. 455–83, quotation from p. 464. Identification of Dick from index, 852. Mrs. Chesnut's mother was Mary Boykin (Mrs. Stephen Decatur) Miller; ibid., xxx.

76. Ibid., p. 464.

77. Samuel Francis Du Pont, *Samuel Francis Du Pont: A Selection from His Civil War Letters,* John D. Hayes, ed. (3 vols., Ithaca, New York: Published for the Eleutherian Mills Historical Library, Cornell University Press, 1969), I, *The Mission: 1860–1862,* lxxxiii (for statistics), lxxxiv. Hayes, pp. lxxxii–xc, offers the best account of the planning

of the attack, the attack itself, and its aftermath, supplementing Du Pont's own account in III, *The Repulse: 1863–1865*, 5–176. See also Rowena Reed, *Combined Operations in the Civil War* (Annapolis, Maryland: Naval Institute Press, 1978), pp. 282–94. Du Pont was promoted rear-admiral July 30, 1862, to date from July 16; Hayes, ed., *Samuel Francis Du Pont*, I, cxv.

78. Hayes, ed., *Samuel Francis Du Pont*, I, lxxxvii–xc; Du Pont relinquished command of the South Atlantic Blockading Squadron to Rear-Admiral John A. Dahlgren on July 6, 1863; ibid., xc.

79. "I Corps (Longstreet's)," Boatner, *Civil War Dictionary*, pp. 178–79, particularly 178; "II Corps (Jackson's, Ewell's, Early's)," ibid., pp. 179–81, particularly 179; "Longstreet, James ('Pete')," ibid., pp. 490–91, particularly 490; "Jackson, Thomas Jonathan ('Stonewall')," ibid., pp. 432–33, particularly 432; Freeman, *Lee's Lieutenants*, II, 248n for the promotions, 269 for the corps organization; "North Carolina and Southern Virginia, Confederate Dept. of," Boatner, *Civil War Dictionary*, pp. 599–600, particularly 599. For Lee's strength, Livermore, *Numbers and Losses*, p. 99, estimates the total engaged of the Confederates at the forthcoming battle of Chancellorsville as 57,352.

80. For the date of the assumption of command, "Hooker, Joseph," Boatner, *Civil War Dictionary*, pp. 409–10, particularly 409; for Lincoln's famous letter cautioning Hooker, A. Lincoln, Executive Mansion, Washington, January 26, 1863. To Major General Hooker, Autograph Letter Signed, owned by Alfred W. Stern, Chicago, Illinois, in Abraham Lincoln, *The Complete Works of Abraham Lincoln*, Roy P. Basler, ed.; Marion Dolores Pratt and Lloyd A. Dunlop, assoc. eds. (9 vols. inc. index, The Abraham Lincoln Association, Springfield, Illinois; New Brunswick, New Jersey: Rutgers University Press, 1953; index, 1955), VI, 78–79, and *O.R.*, XXV, pt. 2 (serial 40, 1882), 4; see also Williams, *Lincoln Finds a General*, II, Chapter XVII, "Joe Hooker Gets the Army and a Note," 547–70, especially 547–52. Edward J. Stackpole, *Chancellorsville: Lee's Greatest Battle* (Harrisburg, Pennsylvania: The Stackpole Company, 1958), estimates Hooker's army at 134,668 effectives at the beginning of his campaign, p. 32.

81. "Stuart, James Ewell Brown ('Jeb')," Boatner, *Civil War Dictionary*, pp. 812–13 particularly 813. The present account of Chancellorsville is based on the most recent full-length studies, Ernest B. Furgurson, *Chancellorsville 1863: Soul of the Brave* (New York: Alfred A. Knopf, 1992), and Stephen W. Sears, *Chancellorsville* (Boston, New York: Houghton Mifflin Company, 1996); also the classic John Bigelow, Jr., *The Campaign of Chancellorsville: A Strategic and Tactical Study* (New Haven: Yale University Press, 1910); Freeman, *Lee*, II, 505–63; Freeman, *Lee's Lieutenants*, II, 524–635; III, *Gettysburg to Appomattox* (1944), 2–7; Williams, *Lincoln Finds a General*, II, 565–605.

82. There is a highly detailed account of the circumstances of Jackson's wounding in Charles Royster, *The Destructive War: William Tecumseh Sherman, Stonewall Jackson, and the Americans* (New York: Alfred A. Knopf, 1991), pp. 209–21. See also James I. Robertson, Jr., *Stonewall Jackson: The Man, the Soldier, the Legend* (New York: Macmillan Publishing USA, Simon & Schuster Macmillan; London, Mexico City, New Delhi, Singapore, Sydney, Toronto: Prentice Hall International, 1997), pp. 727–36; Freeman, *Lee's Lieutenants*, II, 561–77. For the estimate of Early's strength, Furgurson, *Chancellorsville*, p. 115; for the estimates of Lee's and Jackson's strengths when Jackson undertook his flank march, ibid., p. 142.

83. For the strength of Hooker's main force and that of Sedgwick, Furgurson, *Chancellorsville*, pp. 294, 142, respectively; for Stuart's force, "Chancellorsville Campaign," Boatner, *Civil War Dictionary*, pp. 136–40, particularly 138. For casualties and total strengths, Livermore, *Numbers and Losses*, pp. 98 (Union), 99 (Confederate).

84. Livermore, *Numbers and Losses*, p. 96, gives Confederate strength at Fredericksburg as 78,513 present for duty. His estimate of total Confederates engaged in the Seven Days is 98,481, p. 85; but he credits Lee with only 48,527 engaged at Second Manassas and Chantilly, and 51,844 at Sharpsburg, p. 92.

85. Edwin B. Coddington, *The Gettysburg Campaign: A Study in Command* (New York: Charles Scribner's Sons, 1968), p. 8, citing Memorandum Book, Entry for Feb. 12, 1863, Jedediah Hotchkiss Papers, Library of Congress. On Hotchkiss, see William J. Miller, *Mapping for Stonewall: The Civil War Service of Jed Hotchkiss* (Washington, D.C.: Elliott & Clark Publishing, 1993).

86. Quotation from Freeman, *Lee's Lieutenants*, II, 681, citing Mary Anna Morrison Jackson, *Memoirs of Stonewall Jackson* by His Widow, Mary Anna Jackson, with Introductions by John B. Gordon and Henry M. Fields, and Sketches by Fitzhugh Lee, S[amuel]. G. French and G. F. R. Henderson (Second Edition, Louisville, Ky.: The Prentice Press, Courier-Journal Job Printing Company, 1895), p. 456. For Jackson's last days, death, and burial, see Royster, *Destructive War*, pp. 193–99, 211–31, 229 for date of death, 198 for date of burial; Robertson, *Stonewall Jackson*, pp. 735–62, 750–53 for date of death, 760–61 for date of burial; Freeman, *Lee's Lieutenants*, II, 577–82, 667–89, 678–82 for date of death, 686 for date of burial.

## 8. THREE SEASONS OF BATTLE

1. By command of Major-General McClellan: L[orenzo]. Thomas, Adjutant-General, General Orders, No. 105. Headquarters of the Army, Adjutant-General's Office, Washington, December 3, 1861. The following orders have been received from the Secretary of War. . . . U.S. War Department, *The War of the Rebellion: A Compilation of the Official Records of the Union and Confederate Armies* (four series, 70 vols. in 128, Washington: Government Printing Office, 1880–1901), Series Three, I (serial 122, 1899), 722–23. On December 1, 1861, Cameron reported the total strength of the Army as 660,971; Simon Cameron, Secretary of War, War Department, December 1, 1861. To the President, ibid., 698–708, figure from 699. Hereafter cited as *O.R.*; references are to Series One unless otherwise specified.

2. By order of the Secretary of War: L. Thomas, Adjutant-General. General Orders, No. 33. War Dept., Adjt. General's Office, Washington, April 3, 1862. [Paragraph] III, ibid., Series Three, II (serial 123, 1899), 2–3; see also 3 for Stanton's original, handwritten, unsigned draft.

3. By order of the Secretary of War: L. Thomas, Adjutant-General, General Orders, No. 49. War Dept., Adjt. General's Office, Washington, May 1, 1862, ibid., p. 28; and Edwin M. Stanton, Secretary of War, War Department, Washington, D.C., May 1, 1862, To Major-General Halleck, Pittsburg Landing, ibid., p. 29.

4. By order of the Secretary of War: L. Thomas, Adjutant-General, General Orders, No. 60. War Dept., Adjt. General's Office, Washington, June 6, 1862. [Paragraph] I, ibid., p. 109.

5. Israel Washburn, Jr., Governor of Maine; N[athaniel]. S. Berry, Governor of New Hampshire; Frederick Holbrook, Governor of Vermont; Wm. A. Buckingham, Governor of Connecticut; E[dwin]. D. Morgan, Governor of New York; Charles S. Olden, Governor of New Jersey; A[ndrew]. G. Curtin, Governor of Pennsylvania; A[ugustus]. W. Bradford, Governor of Maryland; F[rancis] H. Peirpont [Pierpont], Governor of Virginia; Austin Blair, Governor of Michigan; J[ohn]. B. Temple, President Military Board of Kentucky; Andrew Johnson, Governor of Tennessee; H[amilton]. R. Gamble, Governor of Missouri; O[liver]. P. Morton, Governor of Indiana; David Tod, Governor of Ohio; Alexander Ramsey, Governor of Minnesota; Richard Yates, Governor of Illinois; Edward Salomon, Governor of Wisconsin, June 28, 1862. To the President. Ibid., p. 180. Abraham Lincoln. Executive Mansion Washington, July 1, 1862. To the Governors of Maine, New Hampshire, Vermont, Connecticut, New York, New Jersey, Pennsylvania, Maryland, Virginia, Michigan, Tennessee, Missouri, Indiana, Ohio, Minnesota, Illinois, and Wisconsin, and the President of the Military Board of Kentucky:

..., ibid., pp. 187–88; reprinted in Abraham Lincoln, *The Collected Works of Abraham Lincoln*, Roy P. Basler, ed., Marion Dolores Pratt and Lloyd A. Dunlop, asst. eds. (9 vols. inc. index, The Abraham Lincoln Association, Springfield, Illinois; New Brunswick: Rutgers University Press, 1953; index, 1955), V, 296–97. Abraham Lincoln. By the President: F[rederick]. W. Seward, Acting Secretary of State. By the President of the United States: A Proclamation [July 1, 1862]. *O.R.*, Series Three, II (serial 123), 185–86. For quotas totaling 334,835 and aggregate of 421,465 men furnished, ibid., p. 188n. For exchanges and negotiations with the governors, William B. Hesseltine, *Lincoln and the War Governors* (New York: Alfred A. Knopf, 1948), pp. 198–200; Governor John A. Andrew of Massachusetts did not sign initially, because as a Radical he distrusted a movement that he perceived as initiated by moderates, but on July 2 he agreed to sign, with his signature postdated to June 28 for release to the press; ibid., p. 199.

6. For the bounty, Edwin M. Stanton, Secretary of War, War Department, July 1, 1862. To Hon. William H. Seward, Astor House, *O.R.*, Series Three, II (serial 123), p. 187. For the slow response, Marvin A. Kreidberg and Merton G. Henry, *History of Military Mobilization in the United States Army 1775–1945* (Department of the Army Pamphlet No. 20–212, Washington: Department of the Army, June 1955), p. 103.

7. Thirty-seventh Congress. Session II. (Statute II.) Chap. CCI. — An Act to Amend the Act for calling forth the Militia to execute the Laws of the Union, suppress Insurrection, and repel Invasion, approved February twenty-eighth, seventeen hundred and ninety-five, and the Acts amendatory thereof, and for other Purposes. Approved, July 17, 1862. U.S., Laws, statutes, *The Statutes at Large of the United States of America, 1789–1873* (17 vols., I–IX, Boston: Charles C. Little and J. Brown, 1845–1854; X–XVII, Boston: Little, Brown, and Company, 1854–1873), 12 (December 5, 1859–March 3, 1863, 1863), 597–600; *The Congressional Globe*, XXXII, part 4, 37th Congress, 2nd Session, *June 23, 1862 to July 17, 1862*, Appendix, 414–15. The legislation specifically referred to is Third Congress. Session I. Statute I. Chap. XXXVI. — An Act to provide for calling forth the Militia to execute the Laws of the Union, suppress insurrections, and repel invasions; and to repeal the act now in force for those purposes. Approved, February 28, 1795. 1 *Statutes at Large* (From the Organization of the Government in 1789, to March 3, 1799, 1845) 424–25; U.S. Congress, [*Annals of the Congress of the United States.*] *The Debates and Proceedings in the Congress of the United States; with an Appendix Containing Important State Papers and Public Documents, and All the Laws of a Public Nature; with a Copious Index* (42 vols., Washington: Printed and Published by Gales and Seaton, 1834–1856), IV, Third Congress: Comprising the Period from December 2, 1793, to March 3, 1795, Inclusive. Compiled from Authentic Materials. (1849). Appendix, 1508–1510.

8. Edwin M. Stanton, Secretary of War. By order of the Secretary of War: E[dwin]. D. Townsend, Assistant Adjutant-General. General Orders, No. 94. War Dept., Adjt. General's Office, Washington, August 4, 1862. *O.R.*, Series Three, II (serial 123), 291–92. The draft machinery was established: By order of the Secretary of War: L[orenzo]. Thomas, Adjutant-General. General Orders, No. 99. War Dept., Adjt. General's Office, Washington, August 9, 1862. Regulations for the Enrollment and Draft of 300,000 Militia. Ibid., pp. 333–35.

9. Thomas M. Vincent, Assistant Adjutant-General. War Department, Adjutant-General's Office, February 2, 1864. Exhibit of the number of soldiers furnished by the several States and Territories for the Volunteer Army of the United States under the calls of 1861 and 1862. Ibid., Series Three, IV (serial 125, 1900), 72–73, totals from 73. See also the quotas and credits for the militia draft of August 4, 1862, ibid., Series Three, II (serial 123), 291n. See also Hesseltine, *Lincoln and the War Governors*, pp. 201–202; Kreidberg and Henry, *History of Military Mobilization*, p. 104.

10. Kenneth P. Williams, *Lincoln Finds a General: A Military Study of the Civil War* (5 vols., New York: The Macmillan Company, 1950–1959), II (1950), 556, citing

Frederick Phisterer, *Statistical Record of the Armies of the United States* (New York: C. Scribner's Sons, 1883), p. 62.

11. Thirty-seventh Congress. Session III. (Statute III.) Chap. LXXV, Approved, March 3, 1863. 12 *Statutes at Large* 731–37; *Cong. Globe*, XXXIII, pt. 2, 37th Congress, 3rd Session, *February 12, 1863 to March 3, 1863; Special Session, March 4–14, 1863*, Appendix, 209–11. On the Enrollment Act and its application, see Eugene C. Murdock, *One Million Men: The Civil War Draft in the North* (Madison: State Historical Society of Wisconsin, 1971), especially on the act itself pp. 6–7; also Kreidberg and Henry, *History of Military Mobilization*, pp. 104–106, 111–12. See also Thirty-eighth Congress, Session I. (Statute I.) Chap. XII. — An Act to amend an Act entitled "An Act for enrolling and calling out the National Forces, and for other purposes," approved March third, eighteen hundred and sixty-three. Approved, February 24, 1864. 13 *Statutes at Large* (December 1863, to December 1864) (Boston: Little, Brown, and Company, 1866), 6–11; *Cong. Globe*, XXXIV, pt. 4, 38th Congress, 1st Session, *June 14, 1864 to July 4, 1864*, Appendix, 140–42, particularly Sec. 17 on conscientious objectors, 13 *Statutes at Large* 9, *Cong. Globe*, p. 141; and Sec. 24, extending the draft to African Americans, 13 *Statutes at Large* 11, *Cong. Globe*, p. 142.

12. Article. I. Section. VIII., paragraph 12, 103rd Congress, 1st Session, Senate Document No. 103–6 (serial 14152). *The Constitution of the United States of America: Analysis and Interpretation: Annotations of Cases Decided in the Supreme Court of the United States to June 29, 1992*. Prepared by the Congressional Research Service, Library of Congress. Johnny H. Killian, George A. Costello, co-editors (Washington: U.S. Government Printing Office, 1996), p. 8.

13. [Opinion on the Draft, September 14?] 1863, Autograph Draft, The Robert Todd Lincoln Collection, Library of Congress, Basler, ed., *Works of Lincoln*, VI, 444–49, quotation from 446.

14. Phillip G. Auchampaugh, "A Great Justice on State and Federal Power. Being the Thoughts of Chief Justice Taney on the Federal Conscription Act," *Tyler's Quarterly Historical and Genealogical Magazine*, 18:2 (October 1936), 72–87; Carl Brent Swisher, *Roger B. Taney* (New York: The Macmillan Company, 1935), pp. 570–71.

15. Selective Draft Law Cases, Argued December 13, 14, 1917. — Decided January 7, 1918. U.S. Supreme Court, *United States Reports* Volume 245, *Cases Adjudged in the Supreme Court at October Term, 1917 from October 1, 1917 to March 4, 1918*, Ernest Knabel, Reporter (New York: The Banks Law Publishing Co., 1918), 366–90, Opinion of the Court, delivered by Mr. Chief Justice [William A.] White, 375–84.

16. 12 *Statutes at Large* 731–37, particularly Secs. 1–3, 731–32; *Cong. Globe*, XXXIII, pt. 2, Appendix, 209–11, Secs. 1–3, 209–10. See also Murdock, *One Million Men*, pp. 6–9; Kreidberg and Henry, *History of Military Mobilization*, pp. 104–106, 111–12.

17. Kreidberg and Henry, *History of Military Mobilization*, p. 106 for 35,883 statistic, citing "Final Report Made to the Secretary of War by the Provost Marshal General of the Operations of the Bureau of the Provost Marshal General of the United States from the Commencement of the Business of the Bureau, March 17, 1863 to March 17, 1866; the Bureau terminating by Law August 28, 1866," III, pt. 1, in U.S. War Department, *Messages and Documents, War Department, 1865–1866* (3 vols., Washington: Government Printing Office, 1866), 175; Kreidberg and Henry, *History of Military Mobilization*, p. 107 for commutation fees.

18. Kreidberg and Henry, *History of Military Mobilization*, p. 108, citing for latter three figures "PMG Report," p. 95.

19. Thomas L. Livermore, *Numbers and Losses in the Civil War in America* (Second Edition, Boston and New York: Houghton, Mifflin and Company, 1901; reprint, Dayton, Ohio: Morningside, 1986), p. 102 for Union, 103 for Confederate.

20. "Seddon, James Alexander," in Mark Mayo Boatner III, *The Civil War Diction-*

*ary* (Revised Edition, New York: Vintage Books, A Division of Random House, Inc., 1991), p. 730.

21. Edwin B. Coddington, *The Gettysburg Campaign: A Study in Command* (New York: Charles Scribner's Sons, 1968), p. 9, citing Charles Marshall, *An Aide-de-Camp of Lee, Being the Papers of Colonel Charles Marshall, Sometime Aide-de-Camp, Military Secretary, and Assistant Adjutant General on the Staff of Robert E. Lee*, Sir Frederick Maurice, ed. (Boston: Little, Brown, and Company, 1927), p. 186. Coddington's is a model campaign history, and the present account of the campaign and battle of Gettysburg is deeply indebted to it. For Lee's conferences and planning, see I, "Lee Prepares for a Summer Campaign," pp. 3–25. See also Douglas Southall Freeman, *R. E. Lee: A Biography* (4 vols., New York: Charles Scribner's Sons; London: Charles Scribner's Sons, Ltd., 1934–1935), III (1934), 18–20 for the initial planning and 20–161 for the campaign and battle. The present account of the Gettysburg campaign also makes much use of Douglas Southall Freeman, *Lee's Lieutenants: A Study in Command* (3 vols., New York: Charles Scribner's Sons, 1942–1944), III, *Gettysburg to Appomattox* (1944), xi–xiii, 2–205; Kenneth P. Williams, *Lincoln Finds a General: A Military Study of the Civil War* (5 vols., New York: The Macmillan Company, 1950–1959), II (1950), Chapters XIX, "Good Marching and Quarrelsome Notes," 606–42, 835–40, XX, "A Courier from Washington at Three A.M.," 643–71, 840–43, XXI, "The First Two Days of Gettysburg," 672–707, 843–47, XXII, "The Battle Ends, the Arguments Begin," 708–29, 847–50, XXIII, "A Feeble Effort at Pursuit," 730–59, 850–56. For a vivid account of the invasion of Pennsylvania by a civilian eyewitness, see Jacob Hoke, *The Great Invasion of 1863; or, General Lee in Pennsylvania. Embracing an Account of The Strength and Organization of the Armies of the Potomac and Northern Virginia; Their Daily Marches with the Routes of Travel, and General Orders Issued; The Three Days of Battle; The Retreat of the Confederates and Pursuit by the Federals; Analytical Index, Maps, Portraits, and a large number of Illustrations of the Battle-field. With an Appendix Containing an Account of the Burning of Chambersburg, Pennsylvania, A Statement of the General Sickles Controversy, and other Valuable Historic Papers* (Dayton, O.: W. J. Shuey, 1887; reprint, New York, London: Thomas Yoseloff, 1959). For a modern account of the preliminaries to the battle, see Wilbur Sturtevant Nye, *Here Come the Rebels!* (Baton Rouge: Louisiana State University Press, 1965). Kent Gramm, *Gettysburg: A Meditation on War and Values* (Bloomington, Indianapolis: Indiana University Press, 1994) is an eloquent fulfillment of its subtitle. Gabor S. Borritt, ed., *The Gettysburg Nobody Knows* (New York, Oxford: Oxford University Press, 1997) presents stimulating essays toward new insights into the battle and campaign.

22. For Ewell's position and command, "Ewell, Richard Stoddert," Boatner, *Civil War Dictionary*, pp. 268–69, particularly 269; "II Corps (Jackson's, Ewell's, Early's)," ibid., pp. 179–81, particularly 180. See also Chapter II, "The Reorganization That Explains Gettysburg," Freeman, *Lee*, III, 8–17, particularly 12, 13–14.

23. For Brandy Station, see Fairfax Downey, *Clash of Cavalry: The Battle of Brandy Station, June 9, 1863* (New York: David McKay Company, Inc., 1959); Coddington, *Gettysburg Campaign*, III, "Brandy Station: A Double Surprise," pp. 47–72, 613–20; Freeman, *Lee's Lieutenants*, III, 5–19; Emory M. Thomas, *Bold Dragoon: The Life of J. E. B. Stuart* (New York, Cambridge, Philadelphia, San Francisco, London, Mexico City, São Paulo, Singapore, Sydney: Harper & Row, Publishers, 1986), pp. 220–30; Mark Nesbitt, *Saber and Scapegoat: J. E. B. Stuart and the Gettysburg Controversy* (Mechanicsburg, Pennsylvania: Stackpole Books, 1994), pp. 38–40; Edward G. Longacre, *The Cavalry at Gettysburg: A Tactical Study of Mounted Operations during the Civil War's Pivotal Campaign 9 June–14 July 1863* (Rutherford, New Jersey: Fairleigh Dickinson University Press, 1986), pp. 39–86; Edward G. Longacre, *General John Buford* (Conshohocken, Pennsylvania: Combined Books, 1995), pp. 159–68.

24. A. Lincoln, Washington, D.C., June 5, 1863. to Major General Hooker, Autograph Letter Signed, Illinois State Historical Library, Springfield, Illinois, Basler, ed., *Works of Lincoln*, VI, 249; *O.R.*, XXVII, pt. 1 (serial 43, 1889), 31.

25. For Hill's promotion and command, "Hill, Ambrose Powell," Boatner, *Civil War Dictionary*, p. 400; "III Corps (A. P. Hill's)," ibid., p. 181. See also Freeman, *Lee*, III, 11, 12, 14, and the authoritative biography, James I. Robertson, Jr., *General A. P. Hill: The Story of a Confederate Warrior* (New York: Random House, 1987), pp. 193–204, particularly 193 for Hill's corps command.

26. A. G. Curtin. By the Governor: [seal] Eli Slifer, Secretary of the Commonwealth. Pennsylvania, ss: In the name and by the authority of the Commonwealth of Pennsylvania. Andrew G. Curtin, Governor of the said Commonwealth. A Proclamation. [June 12, 1863.] *O.R.*, XXVII, pt. 3 (serial 45, 1889), 80–81. On the militia, see Coddington, *Gettysburg Campaign*, Chapter VI, "Pennsylvania Prepares for Invasion," pp. 134–52, 636–43, which appeared essentially, under the same title, in *Pennsylvania History: Quarterly Journal of the Pennsylvania Historical Association*, 31:2 (April 1964), 157–75; also Nye, *Here Come the Rebels!* Chapter 12, "The Minutemen Spring to Arms," pp. 212–21, 380.

27. Abraham Lincoln, By the President: William H. Seward, Secretary of State, June 15, 1863, By the President of the United States of America. A Proclamation. Document Signed, National Archives, Record Group 11, Proclamations, Basler, ed., *Works of Lincoln*, VI, 277–78; *O.R.*, XXVII, pt. 3 (serial 45), 136.

28. A. G. Curtin. By the Governor: [seal] Eli Slifer, Secretary of the Commonwealth. Pennsylvania, ss: In the name and by the authority of the Commonwealth. A Proclamation. [June 26, 1863.] *O.R.*, XXVII, pt. 3 (serial 45), 347–48.

29. Coddington, *Gettysburg Campaign*, pp. 144–45.

30. Chas. W. Sandford, Major-General. Hdqrs 1st Div., New York State National Guards, New York, December 20, 1863. To Brig. Gen. John T. Sprague, Adjutant-General, State of New York. *O.R.*, XXVII, pt. 2 (serial 44, 1889), 227–29, statistic from 227.

31. George W. Fahnestock Diary (7 vols., Jan. 1, 1863–Dec. 31, 1867, Jan. 1, 1869–Dec. 31, 1873), The Historical Society of Pennsylvania, Philadelphia, June 27, 1863.

32. Ibid., June 25, 1863.

33. Quoted in Coddington, *Gettysburg Campaign*, p. 166, citing Early to J. Fraise Richard, May 7, 1866, Jubal A. Early Correspondence, Library of Congress. See in general Coddington's Chapter VII, "The Confederates Plunder Pennsylvania," pp. 153–79, 643–51, which essentially appeared also as "Prelude to Gettysburg: The Confederates Plunder Pennsylvania," *Pennsylvania History*, 30:2 (April 1963), 123–57, quotation from 139.

34. Harrison was not fully identified until the appearance of James O. Hall's article "The Spy Harrison: A Modern Hunt for a Fabled Agent," *Civil War Times Illustrated*, 24:10 (February 1986), 18–25. Harrison reported to Lee through Longstreet; for his information on June 28, see Coddington, *Gettysburg Campaign*, p. 181; Freeman, *Lee's Lieutenants*, III, 48–49. Nesbit, *Saber and Scapegoat* argues with considerable persuasiveness that Stuart is not to be blamed in a major way for the Confederates' cavalry reconnaissance woes, but that the cavalry commander adhered substantially to Lee's (characteristically ambiguous) orders to him. While it is also true that in taking with him the brigades of Brigadier-Generals Wade Hampton, Fitzhugh Lee, and William Henry Fitzhugh Lee (the latter commanded by Colonel John R. Chambliss, Jr., 5th Virginia Cavalry), Stuart left Lee with the cavalry brigades of Brigadier-Generals Beverly H. Robertson, Alfred G. Jenkins, and William E. Jones (along with the independent brigade of Brigadier-General John D. Imboden), and that it is difficult to imagine that the opening of the battle of Gettysburg could have been much different if Stuart had been in contact with Lee, it remains true that Stuart's absence adversely affected Lee's confidence and perhaps his

judgment, and when Stuart rejoined late on July 2 he brought a badly fatigued command unable to contribute all that it might have to the battle of July 3. For Stuart's raid, see also Thomas, *Bold Dragoon*, pp. 239–46; Freeman, *Lee's Lieutenants*, III, 54–72; Longacre, *Cavalry at Gettysburg*, 8, "Stuart's Expedition — Salem to Hanover," pp. 148–60, 295–97, and 11, "Stuart's Expedition — Hanover to Gettysburg," pp. 193–202, 303–304. An especially judicious appraisal is Emory M. Thomas, 5, "Eggs, Aldie, Shepherdstown, and J. E. B. Stuart," in Borrit, ed., *The Gettysburg Nobody Knows*, pp. 101–21, 235–37.

35. The first day at Gettysburg is examined in overwhelming detail in David G. Martin, *Gettysburg July 1* (Completely Revised Edition, Conshohocken, Pennsylvania: Combined Books, 1996). Careful but less minutely detailed coverage appears in Warren W. Hassler, Jr., *Crisis at the Crossroads: The First Day at Gettysburg* (University, Alabama: University of Alabama Press, 1970). The day's principal controversies, especially of leadership, are analyzed in Gary W. Gallagher, ed., *The First Day at Gettysburg: Essays on Confederate and Union Leadership* (Kent, Ohio and London, England: Kent State University Press, 1992). The standard Union and Confederate accounts of the war in the East are again worth consulting: Freeman, *Lee*, III, 65–85; Freeman, *Lee's Lieutenants*, III, 77–109; Williams, *Lincoln Finds a General*, II, 682–91. Coddington, *Gettysburg Campaign*, remains unexcelled; see pp. 263–322, 683–713 for the first day's battle. On Buford's opening of the battle, see Longacre, *Buford*, pp. 180–96, 202–203, and the same author's *Cavalry at Gettysburg*, pp. 180–90.

36. Harry W. Pfanz presents a magisterial assessment of the vexed question whether the Confederates could have taken Cemetery Hill and Culp's Hill on July 1, and whether Ewell is blameworthy for their not doing so, in his *Gettysburg — Culp's Hill and Cemetery Hill* (Gary W. Gallagher, ed., *Civil War America*, Chapel Hill & London: University of North Carolina Press, 1993), pp. 64–152; 416–33. Pfanz gives a briefer appraisal in 3, "'Old Jack' Is Not Here," Borrit, ed., *The Gettysburg Nobody Knows*, pp. 56–74, 232–35. Other acute appraisals are by Alan T. Nolan, "R. E. Lee and July 1 at Gettysburg," in Gallagher, ed., *The First Day at Gettysburg*, pp. 1–29, 144–46, particularly 24–28, and Gary W. Gallagher, "Confederate Corps Leadership on the First Day at Gettysburg: A. P. Hill and Richard S. Ewell in a Difficult Debut," ibid., pp. 30–56, 146–50, particularly 36–40, 47–56. See Coddington, *Gettysburg Campaign*, pp. 301–22; Freeman, *Lee*, III, 70–80, 148–49; Freeman, *Lee's Lieutenants*, III, Chapter VI, significantly and dubiously entitled "Ewell Cannot Reach a Decision," 90–105, and 171–73; Williams, *Lincoln Finds a General*, II, 686–91; Martin, *Gettysburg July 1*, pp. 481–539, 550–67; Hassler, *Crisis at the Crossroads*, pp. 130–38.

37. For more critical views of Lee's decision to fight at Gettysburg, see Alan T. Nolan, *Lee Considered: General Robert E. Lee and Civil War History* (Chapel Hill & London: University of North Carolina Press, 1991), Chapter Four, "General Lee," pp. 59–107, 194–202, particularly 90–101 questioning the whole Gettysburg campaign and 95–96 on staying at Gettysburg after July 1; reprinted in Gary W. Gallagher, ed., *Lee the Soldier* (Lincoln and London: University of Nebraska Press, 1996), pp. 225–74, particularly 250–60, 255–56. A review of the controversy is Gary W. Gallagher, "'If the Enemy Is There, We Must Attack Him': R. E. Lee and the Second Day at Gettysburg," in Gary W. Gallagher, ed., *The Second Day at Gettysburg: Essays on Confederate and Union Leadership* (Kent, Ohio and London, England: Kent State University Press, 1993), pp. 1–32, 173–78. See also Freeman, *Lee*, III, 81–85; Freeman, *Lee's Lieutenants*, III, 106–12; Coddington, *Gettysburg Campaign*, pp. 360–68.

The following account of the second day's battle at Gettysburg draws largely on the meticulously detailed work of Harry W. Pfanz, *Gettysburg: The Second Day* (Chapel Hill and London: University of North Carolina Press, 1987), and for the Cemetery Hill and Culp's Hill phases, the same author's *Gettysburg — Culp's Hill and Cemetery Hill*, pp. 166–283, 434–55; Coddington, *Gettysburg Campaign*, pp. 363–454, 729–74; Gallagher, ed., *Second Day at Gettysburg*; Glenn Tucker, *High Tide at Gettysburg: The Campaign in Pennsylvania* (Indianapolis, New York: The Bobbs-Merrill Company, Inc. Publishers, 1958), pp. 197–306; Freeman, *Lee*, III, 86–105; Freeman, *Lee's Lieutenants*, III, 109–40; Williams, *Lincoln Finds a General*, II, 693–706.

For an admirably objective discussion of the reasons for the lateness of Longstreet's attack on July 2, see Chapter 6, "Confederate Preparations, 2 July," in Pfanz, *Gettysburg: The Second Day*, pp. 104–23, 487–91. This analysis, though not uncritical of Longstreet, offsets the excessively harsh treatment of him by Freeman in *Lee*, III, 82–99, 149–50 and, to a lesser extent, in *Lee's Lieutenants*, III, 110–20, 173–76; although Freeman himself concluded that the Federal left was held strongly enough early enough that no Confederate assault upon it on July 2 was likely to succeed, ibid., Appendix II, "Organization of the Federal Left at Gettysburg, July 1–2, 1863," 757–60. Tucker, *High Tide at Gettysburg*, pp. 231–36, 245–48, is sympathetic to Longstreet, as is William Garrett Piston, *Lee's Tarnished Lieutenant: James Longstreet and His Place in Southern History* (Athens and London: University of Georgia Press, 1987), pp. 50–58; the latter book is primarily a study of how Longstreet's willingness to criticize Lee and his postwar Republicanism became the foundations for making him a scapegoat for Confederate defeat. The standard modern biography is remarkably objective and is indeed more critical of Longstreet on July 2 than the present writer is inclined to be: Jeffry D. Wert, *General James Longstreet: The Confederacy's Most Controversial Soldier—A Biography* (New York, London, Toronto, Sydney, Tokyo, Singapore: Simon & Schuster, 1993), pp. 257–79.

For Sickles's advance to the Peach Orchard salient, see Coddington, *Gettysburg Campaign*, pp. 343–57, 385–86; Pfanz, *Gettysburg: The Second Day*, pp. 93–103, and Chapter 7, "Sickles Takes Up the Forward Line," pp. 124–48, 491–96; and William Glenn Robertson, "The Peach Orchard Revisited: Daniel E. Sickles and the Third Corps on July 2, 1863," Gallagher, ed., *Second Day at Gettysburg*, pp. 33–56, 178–82. Kent Gramm, 4, "The Chances of War: Lee, Longstreet, Sickles, and the First Minnesota Volunteers," Boritt, ed., *The Gettysburg Nobody Knows*, pp. 75–100, 234–35 ponders the effects of contingency upon the events of the battle on the Union left on July 2.

Glenn LaFantasie, 2, "Joshua Chamberlain and the American Dream," ibid., pp. 31–55, 254–56, discusses the recent rise of Chamberlain to the most prominent role in histories of the defense of Little Round Top. Oliver Willcox Norton, a participant, presents much evidence regarding conflicting claims to prominence in that defense in *The Attack and Defense of Little Round Top, Gettysburg, July 2, 1863* (New York: The Neale Publishing Company, 1913; reprint, Gettysburg, Pennsylvania: Stan Clark Military Books, 1992). On the battle for Little Round Top, see also Pfanz, *Gettysburg: The Second Day*, Chapter 10, "Little Round Top," pp. 201–40, 505–13; Coddington, *Gettysburg Campaign*, pp. 388–96, 739–45.

The numbers—13,000 Confederates in the battle on the Union left below the Round Tops, 10,000 Federals, 15,000 in the Sixth Corps—are based, respectively, on calculations from Coddington's estimates of the total size of the Army of Northern Virginia, *Gettysburg Campaign*, pp. 248–49; the estimates of those present from the Union Third Corps in Freeman, *Lee's Lieutenants*, Appendix II, 759; and Coddington's estimate that the Sixth Corps "represented about a fifth of his [Meade's] infantry strength balanced against his estimate of the size of Meade's army," pp. 356, 249–50.

38. For the climactic Confederate attack on July 3 known as Pickett's Charge, and for the historical controversies surrounding it, see Carol Reardon, *Pickett's Charge in History and Memory*, Gary W. Gallagher, ed., *Civil War America* (Chapel Hill and London: University of North Carolina Press, 1998). See also George R. Stewart, *Pickett's Charge: A Microhistory of the Final Attack at Gettysburg, July 3, 1863* (Boston: Houghton Mifflin Company, 1959). Salient points are made by Carol Reardon also in 6, "'I Think the Union Army Had Something to Do with It': The Pickett's Charge Nobody Knows,"

Boritt, ed., *The Gettysburg Nobody Knows*, pp. 122–43, 237–42, and in Carol Reardon, "Pickett's Charge: The Convergence of History and Myth in the Southern Past," Gary W. Gallagher, ed., *The Third Day at Gettysburg & Beyond* (Chapel Hill & London: University of North Carolina Press, 1994), pp. 56–92. In the latter book, see also William Garrett Piston, "Cross Purposes: Longstreet, Lee, and Confederate Attack Plans for July 3 at Gettysburg," pp. 31–55. See also Coddington, *Gettysburg Campaign*, pp. 454–64, 483–520, 526–34; Freeman, *Lee*, III, 103–35; Freeman, *Lee's Lieutenants*, III, 144–64; Tucker, *High Tide at Gettysburg*, pp. 331–79; Williams, *Lincoln Finds a General*, II, 709–19, 722–24.

For the morning action on Culp's Hill, see especially Pfanz, *Gettysburg — Culp's Hill and Cemetery Hill*, pp. 284–335, 435–59; Coddington, *Gettysburg Campaign*, pp. 468–76, 778–82.

Coddington, *Gettysburg Campaign*, p. 777 n114 estimates Pickett's Division at 5,000 men, and p. 462 offers the estimate of 13,500 as the total strength of the assault. Ibid., p. 462 gives the strength of the supporting artillery as 159 guns, p. 477 the number of Union guns from Ziegler's Grove just west of Cemetery Hill to Little Round Top as seventy-seven.

39. For the cavalry battle, see Longacre, *Cavalry at Gettysburg*, pp. 220–25, 226–31, 237–39, 244; Thomas, *Bold Dragoon*, pp. 247–49; Coddington, *Gettysburg Campaign*, pp. 520–21. For Gregg's statement that Confederate sources said Stuart had from 6,000 to 7,000 men, ibid., p. 801 n153, citing Gregg to J. E. Carpenter, Dec. 27, 1877, Copy, William Brooke Rawle Papers, The Historical Society of Pennsylvania. The present estimates of strength are based on units engaged and Coddington's figures ibid., pp. 801–802 n153. Longacre, *Cavalry at Gettysburg*, p. 220 estimates Stuart's total force at 6,000. Losses were relatively small; Longacre, ibid., p. 244, accepts the figures of 254 total Federal casualties and almost 200 Confederate. For Custer's promotion, "Custer, George Armstrong," in Francis B. Heitman, *Historical Register and Dictionary of the United States Army, From Its Organization, September 29, 1789, to March 2, 1903. Published under act of Congress approved March 2, 1903. 57th Congress, Second Session, House Document 446 (serial 4536).* (2 vols., Washington: Government Printing Office, 1903), I, 348.

40. For Confederate losses, Livermore, *Numbers and Losses*, p. 103; for Union, ibid., p. 102. For Lincoln's displeasure with Meade, see particularly his unsent letter of rebuke, Executive Mansion, Washington, July 14, 1863. Major General Meade, Autograph Letter, Robert Todd Lincoln Collection, Library of Congress, Basler, ed., *Works of Lincoln*, VI, 327–28; also A. Lincoln, Soldiers' Home, [Washington,] July 6, 1863 — 7 p.m. Major-General Halleck, ibid., 318, from O.R. XXVII, pt. 3 (serial 45), 567. For a highly critical account of Meade's conduct of the pursuit, see Williams, *Lincoln Finds a General*, II, 730–56; for a judicious and more sympathetic view, Coddington, *Gettysburg Campaign*, pp. 536–73, 807–20. Also supportive of Meade is A. Wilson Greene, "From Gettysburg to Falling Waters: Meade's Pursuit of Lee," Gallagher, ed., *Third Day at Gettysburg & Beyond*, pp. 161–201. The standard biography of Meade remains Freeman Cleaves, *Meade of Gettysburg* (Norman: University of Oklahoma Press, 1960); for the Gettysburg campaign, see pp. 120–88, particularly pp. 172–88 for the pursuit.

41. Livermore, *Numbers and Losses*, pp. 86 for Seven Days casualties, 89 for Second Manassas and Chantilly casualties and strength, 92 for Antietam casualties and strength, 99 for Chancellorsville casualties and strength. The figure of 85,500 at the Seven Days is Freeman's, *Lee*, II, 230; it seems more likely than the 95,481 accepted by Livermore, *Numbers and Losses*, p. 86.

42. Freeman, *Lee's Lieutenants*, I, *Manassas to Malvern Hill* (1942), xviii.

43. Craig L. Symonds, *Joseph E. Johnston: A Civil War Biography* (New York, London: W. W. Norton & Company, 1992), p. 183, for Davis, Holmes, and Randolph; "Ran-

dolph, George Wythe," Boatner, *Civil War Dictionary*, pp. 678–79, particularly 679 for the date of Randolph's resignation.

44. Roy W. Curry, "James A. Seddon, a Southern Prototype," *Virginia Magazine of History and Biography*, 63:2 (April 1955), 123–50.

45. "Division of the West, Confed.," Boatner, *Civil War Dictionary*, p. 241.

46. Symonds, *Johnston*, pp. 187–92; Thomas Lawrence Connelly, *Autumn of Glory: The Army of Tennessee, 1862–1865* (Baton Rouge: Louisiana State University Press, 1971), pp. 33–41; Archer Jones, *Confederate Strategy from Shiloh to Vicksburg* (Baton Rouge: Louisiana State University Press, 1961), pp. 111–26.

47. Quoted in Frank E. Vandiver, *Their Tattered Flags: The Epic of the Confederacy* (New York and Evanston: A Harper's Magazine Book, Published in Association with Harper & Row, 1970), p. 185, citing Johnston to Louis T. Wigfall, March 8, 1863, Wigfall Family Papers, typescripts, Archives Collection, The University of Texas at Austin.

48. Symonds, *Johnston*, pp. 193–96; Connelly, *Autumn of Glory*, pp. 40–41; Archer Jones, *Confederate Strategy*, pp. 127–30.

49. "Banks, Nathaniel Prentiss," Boatner, *Civil War Dictionary*, p. 42. For the campaign, see Edward Cunningham, *The Port Hudson Campaign 1862–1863* (Baton Rouge: Louisiana State University Press, 1963).

50. This account of the Vicksburg campaign is influenced largely by Williams, *Lincoln Finds a General*, IV, *Iuka to Vicksburg*, Chapters X, "Memphis Interlude," 286–305, 541–46, XI, "Winter in the Bayous," 306–45, 546–57, XII, "The Battle-Studded Weeks," 346–87, 557–65, and XIII, "Unrelenting Siege and Final Victory," 388–425, 565–73; Bruce Catton, *Grant Moves South* (Boston, Toronto: Little, Brown and Company, 1960), Chapters Eighteen, "Winter of Discontent," pp. 366–87, 526–28, Nineteen, "The Man on the River," pp. 388–406, 528–29, Twenty, "An End to Worry," pp. 407–25, 529–31, Twenty-one, "'Hardtack! Hardtack!'" pp. 426–49, 531–34; John F. Marszalek, *Sherman: A Soldier's Passion for Order* (New York: The Free Press, A Division of Macmillan, Inc.; Toronto: Maxwell Macmillan Canada; New York, Oxford, Singapore, Sydney: Maxwell Macmillan International, 1991), Chapter 10, "Battling the Bayous to Reach the Vicksburg Fortress," pp. 202–31, 536–41; James R. Arnold, *Grant Wins the War: Decision at Vicksburg* (New York, Chichester, Weinheim, Brisbane, Singapore, Toronto: John Wiley & Sons, Inc., 1997).

51. Edwin M. Stanton, Secretary of War. Confidential. War Department, Washington City, October 21, 1862. O.R., XVII, pt. 2 (serial 25, 1887), 282.

52. U. S. Grant, Major-General, Headquarters La Grange, Tenn., November 1, 1862 — 7.45 p.m. To Maj. Gen. H. W. Halleck, General-in-Chief. Ibid., XVII, pt. 1 (serial 24, 1886), 469.

53. H. W. Halleck, General-in-Chief. War Department, Washington November 11, 1862. To Major-General Grant, La Grange, Tenn. Ibid.

54. H. W. Halleck, General-in-Chief. Washington, December 18, 1862 — 10.30 a.m. To Maj. Gen. U. S. Grant, ibid., 476.

55. "Mississippi, McClernand's Union Army of the," Boatner, *Civil War Dictionary*, p. 554; "Morgan, George Washington," ibid., pp. 565–66, particularly 566.

56. U. S. Grant, Major-General, Commanding, Memphis, Tenn., January 11, 1863 — 3:30 p.m. To Maj. Gen. H. W. Halleck, General-in-Chief. O.R., XVII, pt. 2 (serial 25), 553. Porter became acting rear admiral October 1, 1862; Chester G. Hearn, *Admiral David Dixon Porter: The Civil War Years* (Annapolis, Maryland: Naval Institute Press, 1996), pp. 141–42 and 336n. On July 16 Porter was promoted to permanent rear admiral, ranking from July 4; ibid., pp. 237 and 345n.

57. H. W. Halleck, General-in-Chief, War Department, Washington, January 12, 1863. To Major-General Grant, Memphis, Tenn. Ibid., p. 555.

58. "McClernand, John Alexander," Boatner, *Civil War Dictionary*, p. 525; "XIII Corps (Tenn., Gulf)," ibid., p. 194.

59. Dee Alexander Brown, *Grierson's Raid: A Cavalry Adventure of the Civil War* (Urbana: University of Illinois Press, 1954); William H. Leckie and Shirley A. Leckie, *Unlikely Warriors: General Benjamin H. Grierson and His Family* (Norman: University of Oklahoma Press, 1984), pp. 84–89; "Grierson's Raid," Boatner, *Civil War Dictionary*, pp. 359–60, 359 for numbers, 360 for losses.

60. "McPherson, James Birdseye," Heitman, *Historical Register and Dictionary*, I, 681.

61. Ulysses S. Grant, *Personal Memoirs of U. S. Grant* (2 vols., New York: C. L. Webster & Co., 1885–1886), I, 480–81.

62. "Pemberton, John Clifford," Boatner, *Civil War Dictionary*, p. 631.

63. Earl Schenck Miers, *The Web of Victory: Grant at Vicksburg* (New York: Alfred A. Knopf, 1955), p. 60.

64. J. E. Johnston. Tullahoma, May 1, 1863. To Lieutenant-General Pemberton, *O.R.*, XXIV, pt. 3 (serial 38, 1889), 808. Jeffrey N. Lash, *Destroyer of the Iron Horse. General Joseph E. Johnston and Confederate Rail Transport* (Kent, Ohio and London: Kent State University Press, 1991) argues harshly that in the Vicksburg campaign and elsewhere Johnston failed largely because he did not make proper use of the railroads to move troops and supplies.

65. J. C. Pemberton. Lieutenant-General. Headquarters. Gainesville, Ala., August 25, 1863. To S. Cooper, Adjutant and Inspector General, Richmond, Va. [reports of operations April 4–July 4, 1863], ibid., pt. 1 (serial 36, 1889), 249–95, quoting telegram to Major-General [Carter L.] Stevenson, April 23, and telegram to Brigadier-General [John S.] Bowen, April 28, p. 256.

66. William C. Everhart, *Vicksburg National Military Park, Mississippi* (National Park Service Historical Handbook Series No. 21, Washington, D.C.: United States Government Printing Office, 1954), p. 22.

67. Ibid., p. 21.

68. Grant, *Memoirs*, I, 488.

69. J. E. Johnston, General. Jackson, Miss., May 13, 1863. To James A. Seddon, *O.R.*, XXIV, pt. 1 (serial 36), 215.

70. Everhart, *Vicksburg National Military Park*, p. 25.

71. J. E. Johnston. Camp, Between Livingston and Brownsville, May 17, 1863. (Received, May 18, in Vicksburg.) To Lieutenant-General Pemberton. *O.R.*, XXIV, pt. 3 (serial 38), 888.

72. Everhart, *Vicksburg National Military Park*, p. 40, for number of guns; "Vicksburg Campaign," Boatner, *Civil War Dictionary*, pp. 871–77, specifically 877 for number of troops.

73. Williams, *Lincoln Finds a General*, IV, 420.

74. Ibid.

75. Ibid.

76. "Port Hudson, La.," Boatner, *Civil War Dictionary*, p. 663 for the figure of 5,500; Cunningham, *Port Hudson Campaign*, particularly pp. 53–56 for a somewhat negative appraisal of the role of the African Americans; Joseph T. Glatthaar, *Forged in Battle: The Civil War Alliance of Black Soldiers and White Officers* (New York: The Free Press, A Division of Macmillan, Inc.; London: Collier Macmillan Publishers, 1990), pp. 123–29.

77. A. Lincoln, Executive Mansion, Washington, August 26, 1863. To Hon. James C. Conkling, Letter Signed, Illinois State Historical Library, Springfield, Illinois, and Autograph Draft and Autograph Draft Signed, Robert Todd Lincoln Collection, LC, in Basler, ed., *Collected Works of Lincoln*, VI, 406–10, quotation from 409.

78. "Helena, Ark.," Boatner, *Civil War Dictionary*, pp. 392–93, particularly 393; "Taylor, Richard ('Dick')," ibid., pp. 827–28, particularly 828 for the District of Western Louisiana; "Trans-Mississippi, Confederate District, Department, and Army," ibid., pp. 845–46, particularly 845 for Smith's appointment to command; "Smith, Edmund Kirby,"

ibid., pp. 769–71. The overall account here of Smith's command in the Trans-Mississippi is based mainly on Robert L. Kerby, *Kirby Smith's Confederacy: The Trans-Mississippi South* (New York: Columbia University Press, 1972).

79. Michael Fellman, *Inside War: The Guerrilla Conflict in Missouri During the American Civil War* (New York, Oxford: Oxford University Press, 1989); Richard S. Brownlee, *Gray Ghosts of the Confederacy: Guerrilla Warfare in the West* (Baton Rouge: Louisiana State University Press, 1958); William E. Connelly, *Quantrill and the Border Wars* (Cedar Rapids, Iowa: The Torch Press, 1910).

80. "Cumberland, Union Department and Army of the," Boatner, *Civil War Dictionary*, pp. 212–13, particularly 212.

81. W. S. Rosecrans, Major-General, Murfreesborough, Tenn., June 11, 1863. To Maj. Gen. H. W. Halleck, General-in-Chief. O.R., XXIII, pt. 1 (serial 34, 1889), 8. For Rosecrans's campaign from after Stones River to the capture of Chattanooga, see Peter Cozzens, *This Terrible Sound: The Battle of Chickamauga* (Urbana and Chicago: University of Illinois Press, 1992), pp. 21–62; Williams, *Lincoln Finds a General*, V, *Prelude to Chattanooga* (1959), 209–47; William M. Lamers, *The Edge of Glory: A Biography of General William S. Rosecrans, U.S.A.* (New York: Harcourt, Brace & World, Inc., 1961), pp. 245–308; Connelly, *Autumn of Glory*, pp. 70–173.

82. H. W. Halleck, General-in-Chief, War Department, Washington, June 11, 1863 — 3 p.m. To Major-General Rosecrans, Murfreesborough, Tenn.; H. W. Halleck, General-in-Chief, War Department, Washington, June 16, 1863 — 2 p.m. To Major-General Rosecrans, Murfreesborough, Tenn. Ibid., p. 10.

83. W. S. Rosecrans, Headquarters Army of the Cumberland, June 24, 1863 — 2.10 a.m. To Major-General Halleck, General-in-Chief. Ibid.

84. Cozzens, *This Terrible Sound*, pp. 62–90; Williams, *Lincoln Finds a General*, V, 247–55; Lamers, *Edge of Glory*, pp. 307–18; Connelly, *Autumn of Glory*, pp. 173–95.

85. Cozzens, *This Terrible Sound*, pp. 49, 56 for Buckner, 37–38 for Breckinridge and Walker, 59–60 for Longstreet's departure from Virginia, 95 for Hood's arrival, 299 for Longstreet's own arrival; Connelly, *Autumn of Glory*, pp. 149–50 for Buckner, 149 for Breckinridge and Walker, 151–52, 159–62 for Longstreet; Freeman, *Lee's Lieutenants*, III, 224–29 for Longstreet's movement; George Edgar Turner, *Victory Rode the Rails: The Strategic Place of the Railroads in the Civil War* (Indianapolis, New York: The Bobbs-Merrill Company, Inc. Publishers, 1953), pp. 282–86 for Longstreet's movement; Livermore, *Numbers and Losses*, p. 106 for Longstreet's strength. Buckner had been promoted to major-general August 16, 1862; "Buckner, Simon Bolivar," Boatner, *Civil War Dictionary*, pp. 95–96, particularly 96.

86. This account of Chickamauga is based largely on Cozzens's excellent *This Terrible Sound*, pp. 90–528; Williams, *Lincoln Finds a General*, V, Chapter IX, "Chickamauga," 239–69; Lamers, *Edge of Glory*, pp. 308–365; Connelly, *Autumn of Glory*, pp. 173–234. For date of Polk's promotion to lieutenant-general, "Polk, Leonidas," Boatner, *Civil War Dictionary*, pp. 657–58, particularly 658. Livermore, *Numbers and Losses*, p. 105 for Union casualties, pp. 105–106 and particularly 106 for Confederate casualties. See "Hill, Daniel Harvey," Boatner, *Civil War Dictionary*, p. 401, and "Polk, Leonidas," ibid., pp. 657–58, particularly 658, for their respective promotions.

87. Bruce Catton, *Grant Takes Command* (Boston, Toronto: Little, Brown and Company, 1969), pp. 31–44; Peter Cozzens, *The Shipwreck of Their Hopes: The Battles for Chattanooga* (Urbana and Chicago: University of Illinois Press, 1994), pp. 11–22; Lamers, *Edge of Glory*, pp. 370–73; Connelly, *Autumn of Glory*, pp. 255–60.

88. "Osterhaus, Peter Joseph," Heitman, *Historical Register and Dictionary*, I, 761.

89. Catton, *Grant Takes Command*, pp. 30, 32; Cozzens, *Shipwreck*, pp. 2, 108–10; Marszalek, *Sherman*, pp. 237–41.

90. "Grant, Ulysses Simpson," Heitman, *Historical Register and Dictionary*, I, 470,

for promotion; "Mississippi, Union Military Division of the," Boatner, *Civil War Dictionary*, p. 555; Catton, *Grant Takes Command*, pp. 33–34 for meeting with Stanton.

91. Turner, *Victory Rode the Rails*, pp. 287–94; Benjamin P. Thomas and Harold M. Hyman, *Stanton: The Life and Times of Lincoln's Secretary of War* (New York: Alfred A. Knopf, 1962), pp. 286–89.

92. "Hazen, William Babcock," Boatner, *Civil War Dictionary*, pp. 390–91, particularly 390. For the opening of the supply line, Cozzens, *Shipwreck*, pp. 51–65; Catton, *Grant Takes Command*, pp. 44–56.

93. "Turchin, John Basil," Boatner, *Civil War Dictionary*, p. 853.

94. Connelly, *Autumn of Glory*, pp. 260–61; Cozzens, *Shipwreck*, Chapter Seven, "The Chance of Success May be Calculated at Zero," pp. 78–100.

95. "Thomas, George Henry," Boatner, *Civil War Dictionary*, p. 836.

96. For the quotation from Dana, [C. A. Dana,] Chattanooga, November 26, 1863 — 10 a.m. To Hon. E. M. Stanton, Secretary of War, *O.R.*, XXXI, pt. 2 (serial 55, 1890), p. 69. This account of the battle of Chattanooga synthesizes material from Catton, *Grant Takes Command*, pp. 64–85; Connelly, *Autumn of Glory*, pp. 270–76; Cozzens, *Shipwreck*, pp. 115–391; James Lee McDonough, *Chattanooga — A Death Grip on the Confederacy* (Knoxville: University of Tennessee Press, 1984), pp. 102–219.

97. M. C. Meigs, Journal of the Battle of Chattanooga, M. C. Meigs Papers, Library of Congress.

98. Livermore, *Numbers and Losses*, p. 107 for Union losses, pp. 107–108, particularly 108 for Confederate.

99. For a superb modern history and interpretation of the Gettysburg Address, see Garry Wills, *Lincoln at Gettysburg: The Words That Remade America* (New York, London, Toronto, Sydney, Tokyo, Singapore: A Touchstone Book, Published by Simon & Schuster, 1992). For various drafts and reports of the address, Basler, ed., *Works of Lincoln*, VII, 17–23.

## 9. ON THE HORIZON: THE POSTWAR WORLD

1. Sumner to John Bright, July 21, 1863, quoted in James M. McPherson, *The Struggle for Equality: Abolitionists and the Negro in the Civil War and Reconstruction* (Princeton, New Jersey: Princeton University Press, 1964), p. 124, citing Edward L. Pierce, *Memoir and Letters of Charles Sumner* (4 vols., Boston: Roberts Brothers, 1877–1893), IV, 143.

2. Abraham Lincoln, December 1, 1862. To Fellow-citizens of the Senate and House of Representatives: Document Signed, National Archives, Record Group 46, Senate 37A F1, Abraham Lincoln, *The Collected Works of Abraham Lincoln*, Roy P. Basler, ed.; Marion Dolores Pratt and Lloyd A. Dunlop, asst. eds. (9 vols. inc. index, The Abraham Lincoln Association, Springfield, Illinois; New Brunswick: Rutgers University Press, 1953; index, 1955), V, 518–37, particularly pp. 520–21, 529–37, quotation from 534.

3. McPherson, *Struggle for Equality*, pp. 125–26; Eleanor Flexner, *Century of Struggle: The Women's Rights Movement in the United States* (Cambridge, Massachusetts: The Belknap Press of Harvard University Press, 1975), pp. 109–11, particularly 111 for number of signatures.

4. McPherson, *Struggle for Equality*, pp. 180–83.

5. Ibid., pp. 183–86; Robert Dale Owen, J. McKaye, Saml. G. Howe, Commissioners. Office of the American Freedmen's Inquiry Commission, New York City, May 15, 1864. To the Hon. Edwin M. Stanton, Secretary of War, U.S. War Department, *The War of the Rebellion: A Compilation of the Official Records of the Union and Confederate Armies* (four series, 70 vols. in 128, Washington: Government Printing Office, 1880–

1901), Series Three, IV (serial 125, 1900), 289–382, quotation from 381. Hereafter cited as O.R.; references are to Series One unless otherwise specified.

6. McPherson, *Struggle for Equality*, pp. 188–89; Abraham Lincoln, Dec. 17, 1863. To the Senate and House of Representatives, Autograph Document Signed, Pierpont Morgan Library, New York City; Document Signed, National Archives, Record Group 46, Senate 38A F2, in Basler, ed., *Works of Lincoln*, VII, 76–77, quotation from 77.

7. McPherson, *Struggle for Equality*, pp. 189–90; Allan Nevins, *Ordeal of the Union* (8 vols., *Ordeal of the Union*, I, *Fruits of Manifest Destiny 1847–1852; Ordeal of the Union*, II, *A House Dividing 1852–1857* [New York, London: Charles Scribner's Sons, 1947]; III, *The Emergence of Lincoln*, I, *Douglas, Buchanan, and Party Chaos 1857–1859; IV, The Emergence of Lincoln*, II, *Prologue to Civil War 1859–1860* [New York: Charles Scribner's Sons, 1950]; V, *The War for the Union*, I, *The Improvised War 1861–1862* [New York: Charles Scribner's Sons, 1959]; VI, *The War for the Union*, II, *War Becomes Revolution* [New York: Charles Scribner's Sons, 1960]; VII, *The War for the Union*, III, *The Organized War 1863–1864; VIII, The War for the Union*, IV, *The Organized War to Victory 1864–1865* [New York: Charles Scribner's Sons, 1971]), VII, *War for the Union*, III, 644.

8. Quoted in George M. Fredrickson, *The Black Image in the White Mind: The Debate on Afro-American Character and Destiny, 1817–1914* (New York, Evanston, San Francisco, London: Harper & Row, Publishers, 1971), pp. 39–40, citing *The American Freedman*, II (December 1867), 325.

9. These themes, carried by Fredrickson through the Civil War and beyond, are established in Winthrop D. Jordan, *White over Black: American Attitudes Toward the Negro, 1550–1812* (Published for the Institute of Early American History and Culture at Williamsburg, Virginia, Chapel Hill: University of North Carolina Press, 1968); see especially pp. 4–11 on the meaning of blackness to the English and their reaction to Africans' blackness.

10. [c. August 26, 1863?], Autograph Document, The Robert Todd Lincoln Collection of the Papers of Abraham Lincoln, Library of Congress, Basler, ed., *Works of Lincoln*, VI, 410–11, first quotation from 410, others from 411.

11. A. Lincoln, Executive Mansion, Washington, August 26, 1863. To Hon. James C. Conkling, Letter Signed, Illinois State Historical Library, Springfield, Illinois; Autograph Draft and Autograph Draft Signed, Robert Todd Lincoln Collection, LC, ibid., pp. 406–10.

12. Abraham Lincoln, Washington, December 8, 1863. To Fellow citizens of the Senate and House of Representatives: Document Signed, National Archives, Record Group 233, Thirty-eighth Congress, First Session, House of Representatives, Executive Document No. 1; Autograph Draft (partial), Robert Todd Lincoln Collection, LC, ibid., VII, 36–53, quotation from 49–50.

13. "Gillmore, Quincy Adams," Mark Mayo Boatner III, *The Civil War Dictionary* (Revised Edition, New York: Vintage Books, A Division of Random House, Inc., 1991), p. 343.

14. For Strong and his brigade, "Strong, George Crockett," ibid., pp. 811–12, particularly 812; Strong was promoted major-general, U.S.V., to rank from July 18, 811; he died July 30, 812. For Strong's request for the 54th Massachusetts, Joseph T. Glatthaar, *Forged in Battle: The Civil War Alliance of Black Soldiers and White Officers* (New York: The Free Press, A Division of Macmillan, Inc.; London: Collier Macmillan Publishers, 1990), p. 137, and for the assault on Fort Wagner, 136–41. For Putnam and the assault, "Fort Wagner, S.C.," Boatner, *Civil War Dictionary*, p. 301, and for Putnam, "Putnam, Haldimand Sumner," Francis B. Heitman, *Historical Register and Dictionary of the United States Army, From Its Organization, September 29, 1789, to March 2, 1903*. Published under act of Congress approved March 2, 1903. 57th Congress, Second Session, House Document 446 (serial 4536). (2 vols., Washington: Government Printing Office,

1903) I, 810. See also Bernard C. Nalty, *Strength for the Fight: A History of Black Americans in the Military* (New York: The Free Press, A Division of Macmillan, Inc.; London: Collier Macmillan Publishers, 1986), pp. 38–39. Nalty's is the best history of blacks in the military generally, Glatthaar's the best of blacks in the Union Army during the Civil War. Also still useful is Dudley Taylor Cornish, *The Sable Arm: Negro Troops in the Union Army, 1861–1865* (New York: Longmans, Green, 1956). The standard history of the 54th Massachusetts is Peter Burchard, *One Gallant Rush: Robert Gould Shaw and His Brave Black Regiment* (New York: St Martin's Press, 1865). The casualty figures are from Thomas L. Livermore, *Numbers and Losses in the Civil War in America* (Second Edition, Boston and New York: Houghton, Mifflin and Company, 1901; reprint, Dayton, Ohio: Morningside, 1986), p. 104 for the Union and Confederates engaged, 105 for Confederate losses.

15. To James C. Conkling, August 26, 1863, Basler, ed., *Works of Lincoln*, VI, 409 (first two paragraphs), 410.

16. Nalty, *Strength for the Fight*, pp. 39–41; Glatthaar, *Forged in Battle*, pp. 169–76.

17. McPherson, *Struggle for Equality*, pp. 126, 127.

18. Nevins, *Ordeal of the Union*, VII, *War for the Union*, III, 155–57.

19. Iver Bernstein, *The New York City Draft Riots: Their Significance for American Society and Politics in the Age of the Civil War* (New York: Oxford University Press, 1990) deals succinctly with the riots and emphasizes their background and consequences. Adrian Cook, *The Armies in the Streets: The New York City Draft Riots of 1863* (Lexington: University Press of Kentucky, 1974) emphasizes the riots more directly.

20. "Morgan's Ohio Raid," Boatner, *Civil War Dictionary*, pp. 568–69; 7, "A Month of Hopes and Despairs: Morgan's Indiana and Ohio Raid (July 1–26, 1863)," Edward G. Longacre, *Mounted Raids of the Civil War* (South Brunswick and New York: A. S. Barnes and Company; London: Thomas Yoseloff Ltd, 1975), pp. 175–201, 178 for Morgan's initial strength, 200 for those still with him on July 26.

21. Nevins, *Ordeal of the Union*, VII, *War for the Union*, III, 168–70, 171–72, 177; James G. Randall, *Lincoln the President* (4 vols., New York: Dodd, Mead & Company, 1946–1955, IV, *Last Full Measure*, coauthored with Richard N. Current), III, *Midstream* (1952), 219–20, 263–74, particularly 274 for Brough's margin.

22. Nevins, *Ordeal of the Union*, VII, *War for the Union*, III, 171–72, 178; Randall, *Lincoln the President*, III, 274–75, 275 for election statistics.

23. Randall, *Lincoln the President*, III, 278–79, the latter for statistics.

24. Ibid., p. 279 and n.

25. Ibid., pp. 280–88.

26. Ibid., pp. 245–47.

27. Lincoln to Congress, December 8, 1863, Basler, ed., *Works of Lincoln*, VII, 36.

28. Ibid., p. 50.

29. Abraham Lincoln, By the President: William H. Seward, Secretary of State. December 8, 1863, By the President of the United States: A Proclamation, Document Signed, National Archives, FS Record Group 11, Proclamations, ibid., pp. 53–57, particularly 54 for pardon and oath, 55 for exceptions and 10-percent plan. The presidential "Power to grant Reprieves and Pardons for Offenses against the United States, except in cases of Impeachment," is found in Article. II. Section. II., paragraph 1, U.S. Constitution, 103rd Congress, 1st Session, Senate Document No. 103–6 (serial 14152), *The Constitution of the United States of America: Analysis and Interpretation: Annotations of Cases Decided by the Supreme Court of the United States to June 29, 1992*, Prepared by the Congressional Research Service, Library of Congress, Johnny H. Killian, George A. Costello, co-editors (Washington: U.S. Government Printing Office, 1996), p. 13.

30. Lincoln to Congress, December 8, 1863, Basler, ed., *Works of Lincoln*, VII, 52.

31. Ibid.

32. Proclamation of December 8, 1863, ibid., p. 56.

33. For Johnson's military rank, "Johnson, Andrew," Heitman, *Historical Register and Dictionary*, I, 574.

34. William B. Hesseltine, *Lincoln's Plan of Reconstruction*, Introduction by Richard N. Current (Chicago: Quadrangle Paperbacks, Quadrangle Books, 1967), pp. 48–65, 101–103, 127–30, particularly 56 for Johnson's appointment as military governor; Randall and Current, *Lincoln the President*, IV, 20–21 and 21n for Brownlow.

35. LaWanda Cox, *Lincoln and Black Freedom: A Study in Presidential Leadership* (Columbia: University of South Carolina Press, 1981), p. 46; Randall and Current, *Lincoln the President*, IV, 11–14, particularly 13 for date of election, 14 for date of House vote; Hesseltine, *Lincoln's Plan*, pp. 66–67; Nevins, *Ordeal of the Union*, VII, *War for the Union*, III, 459.

36. Hesseltine, *Lincoln's Plan*, pp. 65–66; Randall and Current, *Lincoln the President*, IV, 11–12.

37. Robert S. Holzman, *Stormy Ben Butler* (New York: The Macmillan Company, 1954), p. 104 for delivery of order, p. 103 for date of order.

38. Randall and Current, *Lincoln the President*, IV, 14–17, particularly 17 for voting statistics; Cox, *Lincoln and Black Freedom*, pp. 49–72.

39. Randall and Current, *Lincoln the President*, IV, 17–18, particularly 18 for voting statistics; Cox, *Lincoln and Black Freedom*, pp. 73–103; Hesseltine, *Lincoln's Plan*, pp. 126–27, particularly 127 for voting results.

40. Kenneth P. Williams, *Lincoln Finds a General: A Military Study of the Civil War* (5 vols., New York: The Macmillan Company, 1950–1959), V, *Prelude to Chattanooga*, 108–17; Randall and Current, *Lincoln the President*, IV, 22–23.

41. Randall and Current, *Lincoln the President*, IV, 22–24, particularly 23 for voting results; Hesseltine, *Lincoln's Plan*, pp. 106–108.

42. Randall and Current, *Lincoln the President*, IV, 24–27; Hesseltine, *Lincoln's Plan*, pp. 108–109; "Olustee (Ocean Pond)," Boatner, *Civil War Dictionary*, p. 608.

43. Thomas C. Cochran, "Did the Civil War Retard Industrialization?" *Mississippi Valley Historical Review*, 48:2 (September 1961), 197–210, precipitated rethinking of the conventional wisdom that held that the Civil War must have stimulated economic growth. It is reprinted in Ralph L. Andreano, ed., *The Economic Impact of the American Civil War* (Cambridge, Massachusetts: Schenckman Publishing Co., 1967), pp. 148–60. The statistical series promoting Cochran's thinking appear in Robert E. Gallman, "Commodity Output, 1839–1899," Conference on Research in Income and Wealth, National Bureau of Economic Research, *Trends in the American Economy in the Nineteenth Century* (Studies in Income and Wealth Volume Twenty-four by the Conference on Research in Income and Wealth, A Report of the National Bureau of Economic Research, New York; Princeton: Princeton University Press, 1960), pp. 13–67. See particularly Table 1. "Commodity Output, Population, and Gainful Workers in Commodity Production, Quinquennial, 1839–1859 and 1869–1899," p. 16, and pp. 15, 17, especially 15 for total commodity output. For value added by manufacture, Cochran, "Industrialization," p. 199 (*MVHR*) and p. 150 (Andreano); Gallman, "Commodity Output," Table 3. "Decennial Rates of Change of Value Added in 1879 Prices, by Sector, Quinquennial, 1839–1859 and 1869–1899," p. 24; Table 5. "Price Indexes of Value Added, Commodity Producing Sectors, Quinquennial, 1839–1859 and 1869–1899," p. 28; Appendix, pp. 42–67, particularly Table A-1. "Value Added by Agriculture, Mining, Manufacturing, and Construction, Quinquennial, 1839–1859 and 1869–1899," p. 43. For pig iron production in tons, Cochran, "Industrialization," p. 200 (*MVHR*) and p. 150 (Andreano), citing U.S. Bureau of the Census with the Cooperation of the Social Science Research Council, *Historical Statistics of the United States: Colonial Times to 1957, A Statistical Abstract*

*Supplement* (U.S. Department of Commerce, Frederick H. Mueller, Secretary; Bureau of the Census, Robert W. Burgess, Director; Washington, D.C.: U.S. Government Printing Office, 1960), Series M 195–210, "Iron Ore and Pig Iron: 1799 to 1956," particularly M 207, Pig Iron Shipments, p. 365; see also Gallman, "Commodity Output," Table A-4, "Value Added by Mining, Current and 1879 Prices, Quinquennial, 1839–1859 and 1869–1899," p. 54 and notes, p. 55, *Iron*. For bituminous coal, Cochran, "Industrialization," p. 200 (*MVHR*) and p. 150 (Andreano), citing *Historical Statistics*, Series M 88–101, "Bituminous Coal — Production, Average Value, Freight Charges, Foreign Trade, Stocks, Number of Mines, and Modernization: 1800 to 1956," particularly M 88, Production, pp. 356–357 and specifically 357. For woolen production, Cochran, "Industrialization," p. 201 (*MVHR*) and p. 151 (Andreano), citing *Historical Statistics*, Series K 240–41, "Shorn Wool Production and Price: 1869 to 1957," particularly K 240, Production, p. 294. For mechanization of agriculture, Cochran, "Industrialization," pp. 202–203 (*MVHR*) and 151–52 (Andreano), citing *Historical Statistics*, Series K 150–58, "Farm Machinery and Equipment: 1850 to 1857," K 158, Value of farm implements and machinery ($1,000,000), pp. 284–85, particularly 285. Early critiques of the Cochran thesis are Stephen Salsbury, "The Effects of the Civil War on American Industrial Development," Andreano, ed., *Economic Impact*, pp. 180–89, which contends that Cochran overrelied on statistics, and Pershing Vartanian, "The Cochran Thesis: A Critique in Statistical Analysis," *Journal of American History*, 51:1 (June 1964), 77–89, which questions the ways in which Cochran used statistics. Nevertheless, Stanley L. Engerman, in "The Economic Impact of the Civil War," Andreano, ed., *Economic Impact*, pp. 179–90, generally vindicates Cochran, as on the whole do the essays in Conference on American Economic Industrial Change, 1850–1873, and the Impact of the Civil War, Greenville, Delaware, 1964, *Economic Change in the Civil War Era*, David T. Gilchrist and W. David Lewis, eds. (Greenville, Delaware: Eleutherian Mills–Hagley Foundation, 1965). Harry N. Scheiber, "Economic Change in the Civil War Era: An Analysis of Recent Studies," *Civil War History: A Journal of the Middle Period*, 11:4 (Dec. 1965), 396–411, reviews the literature, especially the two anthologies. James Matthew Gallman finds support for the thesis in his history of a single city at war, *Mastering Wartime: A Social History of Philadelphia during the Civil War* (Cambridge, New York, Port Chester, Melbourne, Sydney: Cambridge University Press, 1990), pp. 253–65. Banking and finance may fit less comfortably than other sectors of the economy into the Cochran thesis; Jeffrey Williamson argues persuasively that Civil War finance encouraged postwar growth in "Watersheds and Turning Points: Conjectures on the Long-Term Impact of Civil War Financing," *Journal of Economic History*, 34:4 (September 1974), 636–61. For Walt W. Rostow's stages of economic growth, see his *The Process of Economic Growth* (Second Edition, New York and Oxford: Oxford University Press, 1960), particularly p. 95 for the takeoff stage.

44. Cochran, "Industrialization," p. 201 (*MVHR*) and p. 152 (Andreano), citing *Historical Statistics*, Series Q 43, "Miles of Railroad Built: 1830 to 1925," p. 428 for railroad track mileage; Cochran, "Industrialization," pp. 203–204 (*MVHR*) and pp. 152–53 (Andreano), citing *Historical Statistics*, Series X 20–46, "All Banks — Number of Banks and Principal Assets and Liabilities: 1834 to 1957," M 22, Loans, pp. 623–25, particularly 624–25, for bank loans.

45. Nevins, *Ordeal of the Union*, VI, *War for the Union*, II, 492–94.

46. Ibid., pp. 485–86.

47. Ibid., pp. 487–88.

48. Ibid., p. 488.

49. Ibid., pp. 505–11; for Meigs, 471–78; for Stanton, Benjamin P. Thomas and Harold M. Hyman, *Stanton: The Life and Times of Lincoln's Secretary of War* (New York: Alfred A. Knopf, 1962), pp. 362–64; for Chase and Sprague, Thomas Graham Belden

and Marva Robins Belden, *So Fell the Angels* (Boston, Toronto: Little, Brown and Company, 1956), especially pp. 43, 51–52, 90–94, 123 (95 for Sprague's wedding date, 82 for his entry into the Senate).

50. Fawn M. Brodie, *Thaddeus Stevens: Scourge of the South* (New York: W. W. Norton & Company, Inc., 1959), Chapter Fourteen, "Economic Heretic," pp. 169–86, particularly 175, 178.

51. Ibid., p. 179.

52. Robert P. Sharkey, *Money, Class, and Party: An Economic Study of the Civil War and Reconstruction* (Baltimore: The Johns Hopkins Press, 1959), Chapter VII, "Conclusion," pp. 276–311, judiciously discusses these issues.

53. Nevins, *Ordeal of the Union*, V, *War for the Union*, I, v.

54. Ibid., VIII, *War for the Union*, IV, 395.

55. Robert H. Wiebe, *The Search for Order, 1877–1920* (David Donald, gen. ed., *The Making of America*, New York: Hill and Wang, 1967), Chapter Two, "The Distended Society," pp. 11–43.

56. Nevins, *Ordeal of the Union*, VIII, *War for the Union*, IV, 395.

57. Ibid., VII, *War for the Union*, III, 25.

58. F[rederick]. W. Sims, Major and Quartermaster. Railroad Bureau, C.S.A., Richmond, October 23, 1863. To Brig. Gen. A. R. Lawton, Quartermaster-General, Richmond, *O.R.*, Series Four, I (serial 127, 1900), 881–83, particularly 881–882.

59. Nevins, *Ordeal of the Union*, VII, *War for the Union*, III, 19–23; Emory M. Thomas, *The Confederate Nation 1861–1865* (New York, Hagerstown, San Francisco, London: Harper & Row, Publishers, 1979), pp. 204–205.

60. Nevins, *Ordeal of the Union*, VII, *War for the Union*, III, 19–21; Frank E. Vandiver, *Their Tattered Flags: The Epic of the Confederacy* (New York and Evanston: A Harper's Magazine Press Book, Published in Association with Harper & Row, 1970), pp. 238–39, 270, 295, 298 on Northrop, 54, 93, 270 on Myers (Thomas, *Confederate Nation*, pp. 134–35, takes a more jaundiced view of Myers than does Nevins); "Myers, Abraham C.," Boatner, *Civil War Dictionary*, p. 577 for date of his resignation; "Lawton, Alexander Robert," ibid., p. 479 for date of his appointment.

61. Lynn M. Case and Warren F. Spencer, *The United States and France: Civil War Diplomacy* (Philadelphia: University of Pennsylvania Press, 1970), pp. 356, 357, 389, 408, 420.

62. Nevins, *Ordeal of the Union*, VI, *War for the Union*, II, 266–67, for *Alabama*; ibid., VII, *War for the Union*, III, 483–87, for *Alabama* and other raiders, 494–96, for *Alexandra*; Thomas, *Confederate Nation*, pp. 182–83; Frank J. Merli, "Crown versus Cruiser: The Curious Case of the *Alexandra*," *Civil War History: A Journal of the Middle Period*, 9:2 (June 1963), 167–77, and his essentially identical revisiting of the issues in Frank J. Merli, *Great Britain and the Confederate Navy 1861–1865* (Bloomington, London: Indiana University Press, 1970), Eight, "A Curious Case," pp. 161–77; Martin B. Duberman, *Charles Francis Adams 1807–1886* (Boston: Houghton Mifflin Company, The Riverside Press, Cambridge, 1966), pp. 293–94, 300–304, for *Alabama*, 304, 309, for *Alexandra*.

63. Nevins, *Ordeal of the Union*, VII, *War for the Union*, III, 367, 506; Thomas, *Confederate Nation*, p. 184; Duberman, *Charles Francis Adams*, p. 304. For a detailed consideration of the legal issues, Stuart L. Bernath, *Squall Across the Atlantic: American Civil War Prize Cases and Diplomacy* (Berkeley and Los Angeles: University of California Press, 1970).

64. David Paul Crook, *The North, the South, and the Powers, 1861–1865* (New York: John Wiley & Sons, 1974), pp. 309–314, 332–39; Case and Spencer, *United States and France*, pp. 398–425, particularly 413 for Roebuck's withdrawal of his resolution; Nevins, *Ordeal of the Union*, VII, *War for the Union*, III, 491–92, particularly 492 for Bright.

65. Merli, *Great Britain and the Confederate Navy*, Nine, "Laird Rams: Part One," pp. 178–94, Ten, "Laird Rams: Part Two," pp. 195–217; Duberman, *Charles Francis Adams*, pp. 308–14; Nevins, *Ordeal of the Union*, VII, *War for the Union*, III, 496–504.

66. J. P. Benjamin, Secretary of State, Department of State, Richmond, August 4, 1863. To Hon. James M. Mason, London. U.S. Naval War Records Office, *Official Records of the Union and Confederate Navies in the War of the Rebellion* (two series, 30 vols., Washington: Government Printing Office, 1894–1922), Series Two, III (1922), 852; J. M. Mason, London, October 19, 1863. To the President. Ibid., pp. 934–35; Frank Lawrence Owsley, *King Cotton Diplomacy: Foreign Relations of the Confederate States of America* (Second Edition, Revised by Harriet Chappell Owsley, Chicago: University of Chicago Press, 1959), pp. 491–92.

67. J. P. Benjamin, Department of State, Richmond, October 8, 1863. To the President. *Official Records of the Navies*, Series Two, III, 928–29, with Enclosure, J. P. Benjamin, Secretary of State. Department of State, Richmond, October 8, 1863. To A. Fullerton, Esq, Savannah, Ga., ibid., 929–30.

68. Owsley, *King Cotton Diplomacy*, pp. 367, 375–76 for McRae and the Erlanger loans, 387–88 for McRae and blockade running and action of February 6, 1864, 389–91 for Bayne. For the actions of Congress, First Congress. Session IV. Statute IV. Chap. XXIII. — An Act to prohibit the importation of luxuries, or of articles not necessaries or of common use. Approved February 6, 1864. Confederate States, Laws, statutes, *Public Laws of the Confederate States of America, Passed at the Fourth Session of the First Congress; 1863–4.* Carefully collated with the Originals at Richmond, James M. Matthews, ed. (Richmond: R. M. Smith, Printer to Congress, 1864), 178–81; Chap. XXIV. — A bill to impose regulations upon the foreign commerce of the Confederate States to provide for the common defence. Approved February 6, 1864. Ibid., pp. 181–83. The same act and bill appear without chapter headings and otherwise in slightly different form in O.R., Series Four, III (serial 129, 1900), 78–80, 80–82.

69. Owsley, *King Cotton Diplomacy*, p. 261.

70. "Johnston, Joseph Eggleston," Boatner, *Civil War Dictionary*, p. 441; "Tennessee, Confederate Army of," ibid., pp. 828–29, particularly 829.

71. "Bristoe Station," ibid., pp. 87, 88 for casualties; Williams, *Lincoln Finds a General*, II, 767; Douglas Southall Freeman, *Lee's Lieutenants: A Study in Command* (3 vols., New York: Charles Scribner's Sons, 1942–1944), III, *Gettysburg to Appomattox*, 238–47; Douglas Southall Freeman, *R. E. Lee: A Biography* (4 vols., New York: Charles Scribner's Sons; London: Charles Scribner's Sons, Ltd., 1934–1935), III (1934), 174–85.

72. "Rappahannock Bridge and Kelly's Ford," Boatner, *Civil War Dictionary*, pp. 680–81, particularly 681 for casualties; Freeman, *Lee's Lieutenants*, III, 264–69; Freeman, *Lee*, III, 5–29.

73. See particularly Freeman, *Lee's Lieutenants*, I, *Manassas to Malvern Hill*, xvii.

74. Ibid., III, 269–79; Freeman, *Lee*, III, 194–205; Williams, *Lincoln Finds a General*, II, 771–73.

75. Thomas B. Alexander and Richard E. Beringer, *The Anatomy of the Confederate Congress: A Study of the Influences of Member Characteristics on Legislative Voting Behavior, 1861–1865* (Nashville: Vanderbilt University Press, 1972), pp. 44–45, 47 and n; Table 2-2, "Comparison of Roll-Call Voting by Indicative Pairs of Groups in the Confederate Congress," pp. 48–49; also pp. 39–44.

76. Ibid., pp. 38, 44, 45, 46; for Vance, Nevins, *Ordeal of the Union*, VII, *War for the Union*, III, 377–78, 467; Glenn Tucker, *Zeb Vance: Champion of Personal Freedom* (Indianapolis: The Bobbs-Merrill Company, Inc., 1966); Richard E. Yates, *The Confederacy and Zeb Vance* (Tuscaloosa: University of Alabama Press, 1958).

77. Alexander and Beringer, *Anatomy of the Confederate Congress*, p. 45.

78. First Congress. Session IV. Statute IV. Chap. III. — An Act to prevent the en-

listment or enrollment of substitutes in the military service of the Confederate States. Approved December 28, 1863. Matthews, ed., *Laws of the Confederate States, Fourth Session, First Congress*, p. 172. See also Chap. IV. — An Act to put an end to the exemption from military service of those who have heretofore furnished substitutes. Approved January 5, 1864. Ibid.

79. A bill to impose regulations upon foreign commerce, ibid., pp. 181–83, exportation of cotton prohibited, 181, except the Confederate States government may export it and similar items (particularly tobacco), 182 (in slightly different form in O.R., Series Four, III [serial 129, 1900], 80–82, particularly 80, 81 for those specific items); Chap. XXIII. — An Act to prohibit the importation of luxuries, Matthews, ed., *Public Laws of the Confederate States, First Congress, Fourth Session*, pp. 179–81 (in slightly different form, O.R., Series Four, III [serial 129], 78–80); First Congress. Session IV. Chap. XXXVII. — An Act to suspend the privilege of the writ of habeas corpus in certain areas. Approved February 15, 1864. Matthews, ed., *Public Laws of the Confederate States, First Congress, Fourth Session*, pp. 187–89; Chap. LXV. — An Act to organize forces to serve during the war. Approved February 17, 1864. Ibid., pp. 211–15; draft extended to all white men between seventeen and fifty, Sec. 2, p. 211; other details, Sec. 5, p. 211.

80. Thomas, *Confederate Nation*, pp. 194–99; Emory M. Thomas, *The Confederacy as a Revolutionary Experience* (Englewood Cliffs, New Jersey: Prentice-Hall, Inc., 1971), pp. 73–78.

81. P. R. Cleburne, major-general commanding division; D[aniel]. C. Govan, brigadier-general; John E. Murray, colonel Fifth Arkansas; G. F. Baucum, colonel Eighth Arkansas; Peter Snyder, lieutenant-colonel, commanding Sixth and Seventh Arkansas; E. Warfield, lieutenant-colonel, Second Arkansas; M[ark]. P. Lowrey, brigadier-general; A. B. Hardcastle, colonel, Thirty-second and Forty-fifth Mississippi; F. A. Ashford, major Sixteenth Alabama; John W. Colquitt, colonel First Arkansas; Rich. J. Person, major Arty and Fifth Confederate; G. S. Deckers, major Thirty-fifth and Eighth Tennessee; J. H. Collett, captain, commanding Seventh Texas; J[ohn]. H. Kelly, brigadier-general, commanding Cavalry Division. [January 2, 1864.] To Commanding General, the Corps, Division, Brigade, and Regimental Commanders of the Army of Tennessee. O.R., LII, pt. 2 (serial 110, 1898), 586–92; Jefferson Davis. Richmond, Va., January 13, 1864. To General W. H. T. Walker, Army of Tennessee, Dalton, Ga., ibid., p. 596; J. E. Johnston, General. Dalton, February 2, 1864. To Hon. James A. Seddon, Secretary of War, ibid., pp. 608–609; Craig L. Symonds, *Joseph E. Johnston: A Civil War Biography* (New York, London: W. W. Norton & Company, 1992), pp. 260–61; Thomas Lawrence Connelly, *Autumn of Glory: The Army of Tennessee, 1862–1865* (Baton Rouge: Louisiana State University Press, 1971), pp. 318–21.

82. Nevins, *Ordeal of the Union*, VII, *War for the Union*, III, 407–11; Vandiver, *Their Tattered Flags*, p. 282.

83. Nevins, *Ordeal of the Union*, VII, *War for the Union*, III, 411; Emory Thomas, *Confederacy as a Revolutionary Experience*, p. 204.

84. Alexander and Beringer, *Anatomy of the Confederate Congress*, p. 204.

85. Thirty-eighth Congress. Session I. (Statute I.) Chap. XIV. — An Act reviving the Grade of Lieutenant-General in the United States Army. Approved, February 29, 1864. U.S., Laws, statutes, *The Statutes at Large of the United States of America* (17 vols., I–IX, Boston: Charles C. Little and J. Brown, 1845–1854; X–XVII, Boston: Little, Brown, and Company, 1855–1873), 13 (December 1863, to December 1865) (1866), 11–12; *The Congressional Globe, July 4, 1864*, Appendix, p. 142. For the House: *Cong. Globe*, XXXIV, pt. 1, 38th Congress, 1st Session, *December 7, 1863 to March 7, 1864*, New Series, No. 27, Tuesday, February 2, 1864, pp. 427–31 (427 for text of resolution, 431 for its acceptance); for the Senate, ibid., New Series, No. 50, Thursday, February 25, 1864, pp. 789–98 (798 for resolution and its passage). [speech to General Grant]: to General Grant [March 9,

1864]. Autograph Draft, owned by Ulysses S. Grant, III, Washington, D.C., Basler, ed., *Works of Lincoln*, VII, 234.

86. "Bragg, Braxton," Boatner, *Civil War Dictionary*, pp. 78–79, particularly 78.

## 10. TRADITIONAL POLITICS AND MODERN WAR

1. Thomas Graham Belden and Marva Robins Belden, *So Fell the Angels* (Boston, Toronto: Little, Brown and Company, 1956), pp. 103–104, 112–13; Allan Nevins, *Ordeal of the Union* (8 vols., *Ordeal of the Union*, I, *Fruits of Manifest Destiny 1847–1852*; *Ordeal of the Union*, II, *A House Dividing 1852–1857* [New York, London: Charles Scribner's Sons, 1947]; III, *The Emergence of Lincoln*, I, *Douglas, Buchanan, and Party Chaos 1857–1859*; IV, *The Emergence of Lincoln*, II, *Prologue to Civil War 1859–1860* [New York: Charles Scribner's Sons, 1950]; V, *The War for the Union*, I, *The Improvised War 1861–1862* [New York: Charles Scribner's Sons, 1959]; VI, *The War for the Union*, II, *War Becomes Revolution* [New York: Charles Scribner's Sons, 1960]; VII, *The War for the Union*, III, *The Organized War 1863–1864*; VIII, *The War for the Union*, IV, *The Organized War to Victory 1864–1865* [New York: Charles Scribner's Sons, 1971]), *Ordeal of the Union*, VIII, *War for the Union*, IV, 66–67; James G. Randall, *Lincoln the President* (4 vols., New York: Dodd, Mead & Company, 1946–1955, IV, *Last Full Measure*, coauthored with Richard N. Current), IV, 90–98, 104–107.

2. Randall and Current, *Lincoln the President*, IV, 96; James G. Randall and David Donald, *The Civil War and Reconstruction* (Second Edition, Revised with Enlarged Bibliography, Lexington, Massachusetts: D.C. Heath and Company, A Division of Raytheon Education Company, 1969), p. 465n.

3. Quoted passages from Randall and Current, *Lincoln the President*, IV, 99, citing ms. copies of the circular as enclosed in letter from Jesse Dubois, Springfield, Illinois, to Lincoln, February 25, 1864, The Robert Todd Lincoln Collection of the Papers of Abraham Lincoln, Library of Congress, 30936; copy sent to Lincoln by Philip Speed, U.S. Internal Revenue Collector's Office, Louisville, Kentucky; copy bearing the frank of Republican Representative Henry T. Blow of Missouri, both in the same collection; copies in Anna E. Dickinson MSS. and Simon Cameron MSS., LC; Nevins, *Ordeal of the Union*, VIII, *War for the Union*, IV, 67; Belden and Belden, *So Fell the Angels*, pp. 113–14.

4. Belden and Belden, *So Fell the Angels*, pp. 114–20; Randall and Current, *Lincoln the President*, IV, 102–104.

5. Belden and Belden, *So Fell the Angels*, p. 116; for date, Randall and Current, *Lincoln the President*, IV, 107.

6. Randall and Current, *Lincoln the President*, IV, 113–17; Nevins, *Ordeal of the Union*, VIII, *War for the Union*, IV, 72–74.

7. This is the overall thesis of William B. Hesseltine, *Lincoln and the War Governors* (New York: Alfred A. Knopf, 1948); see especially pp. vi, 390–93. On the National Union Convention, Randall and Current, *Lincoln the President*, IV, 117–37; Nevins, *Ordeal of the Union*, VIII, *War for the Union*, IV, 70–72, 74–78.

8. Phillip Shaw Paludan, *The Presidency of Abraham Lincoln* (Lawrence: University Press of Kansas, 1994), pp. 271–74 for further discussion of the convention, 274 for balloting; David Herbert Donald, *Lincoln* (New York, London, Toronto, Sydney, Tokyo, Singapore: Simon & Schuster, 1995), pp. 504–507, 505 for balloting.

9. Randall and Current, *Lincoln the President*, IV, 126 on Missouri, 127–28 on Raymond; Nevins, *Ordeal of the Union*, VIII, *War for the Union*, IV, 77 on Missouri; Donald, *Lincoln*, p. 505 for Missouri and Raymond.

10. The platform is printed in Abraham Lincoln, *The Collected Works of Abraham Lincoln*, Roy P. Basler, ed.; Marion Dolores Pratt and Lloyd A. Dunlop, asst. eds. (9 vols.

inc. index, The Abraham Lincoln Association, Springfield, Illinois; New Brunswick: Rutgers University Press, 1953; index, 1955), from the *New York Tribune*, June 10, 1864, p. 1, VII, 381–82, quotation from 382.

11. Ibid., p. 382.

12. Paludan, *Presidency of Lincoln*. pp. 273–74; Donald, *Lincoln*, pp. 505–506; Randall and Current, *Lincoln the President*, IV, 130–36; Nevins, *Ordeal of the Union*, VIII, *War for the Union*, IV, 75–78.

13. Abraham Lincoln, Executive Mansion. Washington. June 27, 1864. to Hon. William Dennison & others, a Committee of the National Union Convention, Autograph Draft Signed, Illinois State Historical Library, Springfield, Illinois; Letter Signed, owned by W. Easton Louttit, Jr., Providence, Rhode Island, Basler, ed., *Works of Lincoln*, VII, 411.

14. [Reply to Committee Notifying Lincoln of His Renomination,] June 9, 1864, ms. copy in The Robert Todd Lincoln Collection of the Papers of Abraham Lincoln, Library of Congress; *New York Tribune*, June 10, 1864, p. 1, Basler, ed., *Works of Lincoln*, VII, 380, with 381–84n citing sources and indicating, 382–83n, slight variations in *Tribune* text.

15. William T. Sherman, *Memoirs of General William T. Sherman by Himself* (2 vols., New York: D. Appleton & Company, 1884), II, 15, and muster rolls, 16–21.

16. Abraham Lincoln, Executive Mansion February 1st, 1864, Ordered:, Document Signed, owned by Harry MacNeill Bland, New York City, Basler, ed., *Works of Lincoln*, VII, 164.

17. Thirty-eighth Congress. Session I. (Statute I.) Chap. XIII. — An Act to amend an Act entitled "An Act for enrolling and calling out the National Forces, and for other Purposes," approved March third, eighteen hundred and sixty-three. Approved, February 24, 1864. U.S., Laws, statutes, *The Statutes at Large of the United States of America* (17 vols., I–IX, Boston: Charles C. Little and J. Brown, 1845–1854; X–XVII, Boston: Little, Brown and Company, 1855–1863), 13 (December 1863, to December 1865) (1866), 6–11; for substitutes, Secs. 4–5, pp. 6–7; for commutation, Sec. 5, pp. 6–7, particularly 7, for abolition of the distinction between classes, Sec. 11, p. 9; *The Congressional Globe*, XXXIV, pt. 4, 38th Congress, 1st Session, *June 14, 1864 to July 4, 1864*, Appendix, pp. 140–42, Secs. 4–5, 11, p. 141.

18. Geo. D. Ruggles, Assistant Adjutant-General. War Dept., Provost-Marshal-General's Office, Washington, D.C., December 15, 1863. To Maj. J. W. T. Gardiner, U.S. Army, Actg. Asst. Prov. Mar. Gen. for Maine, Augusta, Me, (Similar letters sent to other Northern states.) U.S. War Department, *The War of the Rebellion: A Compilation of the Official Records of the Union and Confederate Armies* (four series, 70 vols. in 128, Washington: Government Printing Office, 1880–1901), Series Three, III (serial 124, 1899), 1173. Hereafter cited as *O.R.*; references are to Series One unless otherwise specified. For conscientious objectors in the law of Feb. 24, 1864, Sec. 17, 13 *Statutes at Large* 9; *Cong. Globe*, XXXIV, pt. 4, Appendix, p. 141. See Peter Brock, *Pacifism in the United States: From the Colonial Era to the First World War* (Princeton, New Jersey: Princeton University Press, 1968), pp. 713, 735–55, 768–78, 924; Edward Needles Wright, *Conscientious Objectors in the Civil War* (Philadelphia: University of Pennsylvania Press; London: Humphrey Milford, Oxford University Press, 1931); Randall and Current, *Lincoln the President*, IV, 172–75; Randall and Donald, *Civil War and Reconstruction*, pp. 318–19.

19. Eugene C. Murdock, *One Million Men: The Civil War Draft in the North* (Madison: The State Historical Society of Wisconsin, 1971), 6, "Filling Quotas," pp. 154–78; 7, "Substitution," pp. 178–96; 8, "Commutation," pp. 197–217; 9, "The Jumpers: Operations," pp. 218–36; 10, "The Jumpers: Punishment," pp. 237–54; 11, "The Brokers: 'Necessary . . . ,'" pp. 255–75; 12, "The Brokers: . . . 'Evils,'" pp. 276–304; 13, "The Aliens,"

pp. 305–32; particularly p. 197 for commutation fee; Ella Lonn, *Desertion during the Civil War* (New York, London: The Century Company, 1928), p. 104 for bounties in 1864.

20. Abraham Lincoln, Executive Mansion. Washington, March 14th, 1864, Document Signed, Illinois State Historical Library, Springfield, Illinois, Basler, ed., *Works of Lincoln*, VII, 245.

21. James M. McPherson, *Battle Cry of Freedom: The Civil War Era* (New York, Oxford: Oxford University Press, 1988), pp. 719–20, particularly 720 for 136,000 estimate; Abstract from return of the Army of the Potomac, Maj. Gen. George G. Meade, U.S. Army, commanding, for the month of March, 1864, O.R., XXXIII (serial 60, 1891), 776 for Army of the Potomac figure; Bruce Catton, *A Stillness at Appomattox* (Garden City, New York: Doubleday & Company, Inc., 1953), pp. 33–36.

22. "Meade, George Gordon," Francis B. Heitman, *Historical Register and Dictionary of the United States Army, From Its Organization September 29, 1789, to March 2, 1903*. Published under act of Congress approved March 2, 1903. 57th Congress, Second Session, House Document 446 (serial 4536). (2 vols., Washington: Government Printing Office, 1903), I, 700.

23. "Halleck, Henry Wager," Boatner, *Civil War Dictionary*, p. 367.

24. "Mississippi, Union Military Division of the," ibid., p. 355, for command change; "Sherman, William Tecumseh," Heitman, *Historical Register and Dictionary*, I, 882 for rank.

25. "Tennessee, Union Department and Army of the," Boatner, *Civil War Dictionary*, p. 830; "McPherson, James Birdseye," ibid., p. 538.

26. "Cumberland, Union Department and Army of the," ibid., p. 212; "Ohio, Union Department and Army of the," ibid., pp. 606–607, particularly 606; "Schofield, John McAllister," ibid., pp. 726–27, particularly 727.

27. Bruce Catton, *Grant Takes Command* (Boston, Toronto: Little, Brown and Company, 1969), pp. 132, 137–40; John F. Marszalek, *Sherman: A Soldier's Passion for Order* (New York: The Free Press, A Division of Macmillan, Inc.; Toronto: Maxwell Macmillan Canada; New York, Oxford, Singapore, Sydney: Maxwell Macmillan International, 1993), pp. 257–59.

28. A. Lincoln, Copy — one also sent to Gen. Halleck, Executive Mansion, Washington, Jan. 13, 1862. To Brig. Genl. Buell, Autograph Letter Signed, Edwin M. Stanton Papers, LC, Basler, ed., *Works of Lincoln*, V, 98–99.

29. H. W. Halleck, Major-General, Saint Louis, January 16, 1862. To Brig. Gen. D.C. Buell, Louisville, Ky. O.R., VII (serial 7, 1882), 533.

30. "Virginia and North Carolina, Union Department of," Boatner, *Civil War Dictionary*, p. 849; "James, Union Army of the," ibid., p. 434; Edward G. Longacre, *Army of Amateurs: General Benjamin F. Butler and the Army of the James* (Mechanicsburg, PA: Stackpole Books, 1997), pp. 9–43.

31. "West Virginia, Union Department and Army of," Boatner, *Civil War Dictionary*, p. 907; "Sigel, Franz," ibid., p. 761.

32. "Banks, Nathaniel Prentiss," ibid., p. 42 for his command of the Department of the Gulf; Catton, *Grant Takes Command*, pp. 93–95, 98–99, 101–103; Herman Hattaway and Archer Jones, *How the North Won: A Military History of the Civil War* (Urbana, Chicago, London: University of Illinois Press, 1983), pp. 518–19 for the plan against Mobile.

33. U. S. Grant, Lieutenant-General. Culpeper Court-House, Va., April 9, 1864. To Maj. Gen. G. G. Meade, Commanding Army of the Potomac. O.R., XXXIII (serial 60), 827–29, quotation from 828; quoted passage also in Ulysses S. Grant, *Personal Memoirs of U. S. Grant* (2 vols., New York: C. L. Webster & Co., 1885–1886), II, 135n.

34. U. S. Grant, Lieutenant-General. Private and Confidential. Headquarters Ar-

mies of the United States, Washington, D.C., April 4, 1864. To Maj. Gen. W. T. Sherman, Commanding Military Division of the Mississippi, *O.R.*, XXXII, pt. 3 (serial 59, 1891), 245–46, quotation from 246; quoted passage also in Grant, *Memoirs*, II, 131n.

35. Douglas Southall Freeman, *R. E. Lee: A Biography* (4 vols., New York: Charles Scribner's Sons; London: Charles Scribner's Sons, Ltd., 1934–1935), III (1934), 398, citing John William Jones, *Personal Reminiscences, Anecdotes and Letters of Gen. Robert E. Lee* (Published by Authority of the Lee Family, and of the Faculty of Washington and Lee University, New-York: D. Appleton and Company, 1874), p. 40.

36. U. S. Grant, Lieutenant-General, Headquarters Armies of the United States, Near Spotsylvania Court-House, May 11, 1864 — 8.30 a.m. To Maj. Gen. H. W. Halleck, Chief of Staff, *O.R.*, XXXVI, pt. 2 (serial 68, 1891), 627–28, quotation from 627; quotation also in Grant, *Memoirs*, II, 226.

37. The maneuvers of the campaign confirm that the design was to outmaneuver and thereby to trap Lee's army. Planning the campaign, Grant spoke not of destroying but implied capturing that army. E. g., "I will move against Lee's army, attempting to turn him by one flank or the other." U. S. Grant, Lieutenant-General. Confidential. Hdqrs. Armies of the United States, Culpeper Court-House, Va., April 29, 1864. To Major-General Halleck, Chief of Staff of the Army, *O.R.*, XXX, 1017–18, quotation from 1017.

38. Joseph P. Cullen, *The Battles of Fredericksburg, Chancellorsville, the Wilderness, and Spotsylvania Court House: Where a Hundred Thousand Fell* (National Park Service Historical Handbook Series No. 39, Washington, D.C.: United States Government Printing Office, 1966), p. 45. On the battle of the Wilderness see Gary W. Gallagher, ed., *The Wilderness Campaign* (Military Campaigns of the Civil War, Chapel Hill & London: University of North Carolina Press, 1997); Robert Garth Scott, *Into the Wilderness with the Army of the Potomac* (Bloomington: Indiana University Press, 1985); Noah Andre Trudeau, *Bloody Roads South: The Wilderness to Cold Harbor May–June 1864* (Boston, Toronto, London: Little, Brown and Company, 1989), pp. 26–116; Catton, *Stillness at Appomattox*, pp. 55–91; Catton, *Grant Takes Command*, Chapter Ten, "In the Wilderness," pp. 179–201; Freeman, *Lee*, III, 266–84; Douglas Southall Freeman, *Lee's Lieutenants: A Study in Command* (3 vols., New York: Charles Scribner's Sons, 1942–1944), III, *Gettysburg to Appomattox*, 343–72; and especially the most recent comprehensive study, Gordon C. Rhea, *The Battle of the Wilderness May 5–6, 1864* (Baton Rouge and London: Louisiana State University Press, 1994).

39. "Wilderness," Boatner, *Civil War Dictionary*, pp. 919–25, particularly 925.

40. The moment of Grant's directing the army southward is depicted dramatically in Catton, *Stillness at Appomattox*, pp. 91–92, and Catton, *Grant Takes Command*, pp. 207–209.

41. For Spotsylvania, see Gordon C. Rhea, *The Battles for Spotsylvania Court House and the Road to Yellow Tavern May 7–12, 1864* (Baton Rouge and London: Louisiana State University Press, 1997), William D. Matter, *If It Takes All Summer: The Battle of Spotsylvania* (Chapel Hill & London: University of North Carolina Press, 1988); Trudeau, *Bloody Roads South*, pp. 121–213; Catton, *Stillness at Appomattox*, pp. 93–99, 105–32; Catton, *Grant Takes Command*, pp. 210–43; Freeman, *Lee*, III, 297–340; Freeman, *Lee's Lieutenants*, III, 375–410, 434–41.

42. Grant, *Memoirs*, II, 177–78.

43. "Spotsylvania Campaign," Boatner, *Civil War Dictionary*, pp. 783–89, specifically 788 for numbers and losses on May 10 and 12; Cullen, *Battles*, p. 53 for total Union loss; Trudeau, *Bloody Roads South*, p. 213 for total Confederate loss. "Warren, Gouverneur Kemble," Boatner, *Civil War Dictionary*, p. 891, for Warren's promotion and command of the Fifth Corps. For the shuffling of Confederate commanders, Freeman, *Lee's Lieutenants*, III, 390–91. David A. Russell was promoted from colonel, 7th Massachu-

setts, to brigadier-general, U.S.V., November 29, 1862; he was brevetted brigadier-general, U.S.A., to date from May 6, 1864, major-general, U.S.A., and promoted to full major-general, U.S.A., as of September 19, 1864; "Russell, David Allen," Heitman, *Historical Register*, I, 852.

44. Trudeau, *Bloody Roads South*, pp. 220–59; Catton, *Stillness at Appomattox*, pp. 133–49; Catton, *Grant Takes Command*, pp. 251–57; Freeman, *Lee*, III, 346–374; Freeman, *Lee's Lieutenants*, III, 496–504. Wright had just taken over the Sixth Corps in succession to Sedgwick, who was killed by a sharpshooter on May 9; "Sedgwick, John," Boatner, *Civil War Dictionary*, pp. 730–31, particularly 730.

45. For losses, "Cold Harbor," Boatner, *Civil War Dictionary*, pp. 162–64, particularly 163. For the battle, see also Trudeau, *Bloody Roads South*, pp. 259–306; Catton, *Stillness at Appomattox*, pp. 156–69; Catton, *Grant Takes Command*, pp. 257–68; Freeman, *Lee*, III, 373–95; Freeman, *Lee's Lieutenants*, III, 504–508.

46. Grant, *Memoirs*, II, 140–41.

47. Nevins, *Ordeal of the Union*, VIII, *War for the Union*, IV, 45 and, for Confederate casualties, 45n. See again Cullen, *Battles*, p. 45, for the numbers of the rival armies at the beginning of the campaign.

48. "Smith, William Farrar," Boatner, *Civil War Dictionary*, pp. 775–76, particularly 775.

49. "Petersburg Assaults of 15–18 June '64," ibid., pp. 644–46, particularly 644 for Beauregard's and Smith's initial numbers; Thomas L. Livermore, *Numbers and Losses in the Civil War in America* (Second Edition, Boston and New York: Houghton, Mifflin and Company; reprint, Dayton, Ohio: Morningside, 1986), p. 141 for final numbers. For the opening of the Petersburg campaign, see also Noah Andre Trudeau, *The Last Citadel: Petersburg, Virginia June 1864–April 1865* (Baton Rouge: Louisiana State University Press, 1991), pp. 33–55; Longacre, *Army of Amateurs*, Chapter Eight, "Four Days of Frustration," pp. 143–62; Catton, *Stillness at Appomattox*, pp. 185–99; Catton, *Grant Takes Command*, pp. 280–94; Freeman, *Lee*, III, 396–425; Freeman, *Lee's Lieutenants*, III, 528–38.

50. "Hancock, Winfield Scott," Boatner, *Civil War Dictionary*, pp. 372–73, particularly 372; for Birney, Catton, *Stillness at Appomattox*, p. 195.

51. Catton, *Stillness at Appomattox*, p. 212, for loss of prisoners; John Gibbon, *Personal Recollections of the Civil War* (New York, London: G. P. Putnam's Sons, 1928), pp. 227–28 for the division's losses in the campaign; "Hill, Ambrose Powell," Boatner, *Civil War Dictionary*, p. 400, for the return of Hill. Trudeau, *Last Citadel*, pp. 60–79; James I. Robertson, Jr., *General A. P. Hill: The Story of a Confederate Warrior* (New York: Random House, 1987), pp. 284–89.

52. Theodore Lyman, *Meade's Headquarters, 1863–1865: Letters of Colonel Theodore Lyman from the Wilderness to Appomattox*, Selected and Edited by George R. Agassiz (Boston: The Atlantic Monthly Press, 1922), pp. 181–82. Lyman was a volunteer aide-de-camp to Meade: "Lyman, Theodore," Boatner, *Civil War Dictionary*, pp. 496–97. For the Petersburg mine, Trudeau, *Last Citadel*, pp. 99–127; Catton, *Stillness at Appomattox*, pp. 218–27, 235–53; Freeman, *Lee's Lieutenants*, III, 541–44; Freeman, *Lee*, III, Chapter XXVI, "Lee Encounters a New Type of Warfare ('The Crater,' July 30, 1864)," pp. 463–78.

53. "IX Corps," Boatner, *Civil War Dictionary*, p. 192.

54. Livermore, *Numbers and Losses*, p. 116. Statistics of Confederate losses are incomplete; ibid., p. 117.

55. Thirty-eighth Congress. Session I. (Statute I.) — Chap. CCXXXVII. — An Act further to regulate and provide for the enrolling and calling out of the National Forces, and for other purposes. Approved, July 4, 1864. 13 *Statutes at Large* 379–90; *Cong. Globe*, XXXIV, pt. 4, Appendix, 257.

56. Martin B. Duberman, *Charles Francis Adams 1807–1886* (Boston: Houghton Mifflin Company, The Riverside Press Cambridge, 1961), pp. 293–94 on the background of vessel "290," or hull No. 290. For the career of the *Alabama*, Charles M. Robinson III, *Shark of the Confederacy: The Story of the CSS* Alabama (Annapolis, Maryland: Naval Institute Press, 1996); Raimondo Luraghi, *A History of the Confederate Navy*, tr. Paolo E. Coletta (Annapolis, Maryland: Naval Institute Press, 1996), pp. 77, 202 (for date of launching), 224–32, 272, 287, 315–20.

57. Nevins, *Ordeal of the Union*, VIII, *War for the Union*, IV, 90.

58. Ibid., pp. 89–90; Luraghi, *Confederate Navy*, pp. 315–20.

59. "Red River Campaign," Boatner, *Civil War Dictionary*, pp. 685–89; "Gulf, Union Department of the," ibid., p. 364; "XVI Corps," ibid., pp. 195–96, particularly 196; "XVII Corps," ibid., pp. 196–97, "Detachment, Army of the Tennessee," ibid., p. 237; "Red River Division, XVII Corps," ibid., p. 689.

60. For Butler's Bermuda Hundred campaign see Longacre, *Army of Amateurs*, pp. 84–113 (and pp. 113–23 for the detachment of the Eighteenth Corps and its role at Cold Harbor); Catton, *Grant Takes Command*, pp. 244–47, 280–283; Freeman, *Lee's Lieutenants*, III, 456–95.

61. William C. Davis, *The Battle of New Market* (Garden City, New York: Doubleday & Company, Inc., 1975); Catton, *Grant Takes Command*, p. 248; Freeman, *Lee's Lieutenants*, III, 515–16.

62. "II Corps (Jackson's, Ewell's, Early's), Confed. Army of Northern Va.," Boatner, *Civil War Dictionary*, pp. 179–81, particularly 180 for date of Early's command; Freeman, *Lee's Lieutenants*, III, 510, for Early's rank as temporary lieutenant-general, citing Marcus J. Wright, compiler, *General Officers of the Confederate Army, Officers of the Executive Departments of the Confederate States, Members of the Confederate Congress by States* (New York: The Neale Publishing Company, 1911), p. 19. For Early's campaign in the Shenandoah through the Washington raid, see Gary W. Gallagher, ed., *Struggle for the Shenandoah: Essays on the 1864 Valley Campaign* (Kent, Ohio, and London, England: Kent State University Press, 1991), especially Gary W. Gallagher, "The Shenandoah Valley in 1864," pp. 1–18, particularly 6–12; Jeffry D. Wert, "Jubal A. Early and Confederate Leadership," pp. 19–40, particularly 19–24; also Freeman, *Lee's Lieutenants*, III, 557–68; Catton, *Stillness at Appomattox*, pp. 259–67; Randall and Current, *Lincoln the President*, IV, 198–202. For the raid on Washington in particular, see Benjamin Franklin Cooling, *Symbol, Sword, and Shield: Defending Washington during the Civil War* (Hamden, Connecticut: Archon Books, 1975; Shippensburg, PA: White Mane Publishing Company, Inc., 1991), 7, "Attack on the Capital," pp. 173–210; the same author's *Jubal Early's Raid on Washington, 1864* (Baltimore, Maryland: Nautical & Aviation Publishing Company of America, 1989); Frank E. Vandiver, *Jubal's Raid: General Jubal Early's Famous Attack on Washington* (New York: The McGraw-Hill Book Company, 1960). See also Benjamin Franklin Cooling's book on the most important battle of Early's campaign, *Monocacy: The Battle That Saved Washington* (Shippensburg, PA: White Mane Publishing Company, Inc., 1997).

63. Henry Kyd Douglas, *I Rode with Stonewall: Being chiefly the war experiences of the youngest member of Jackson's staff from the John Brown Raid to the hanging of Mrs.* [Mary E. Jenkins] *Surratt* (Chapel Hill: University of North Carolina Press, 1940), p. 296.

64. Abraham Lincoln, By the President: William H. Seward, Secretary of State, July 18, 1864, By the President of the United States of America: A Proclamation. Document Signed, National Archives, Record Group 11, Proclamations, Basler, ed., *Works of Lincoln*, VII, 448–49.

65. Horace Greeley, New York, July 7, 1864, Hon. Abraham Lincoln, Robert Todd Lincoln Collection, LC, ibid., p. 435n. On Greeley and the election of 1864, see Nevins,

*Ordeal of the Union*, VIII, *War for the Union*, IV, 91, 95–96; Randall and Current, *Lincoln the President*, IV, 90, 106, 115, 118, 156–57.

66. A. Lincoln, Washington, D.C., July 9, 1864, Hon. Horace Greely [sic]. Autograph Draft Signed, Robert Todd Lincoln Collection, LC; Letter Signed, owned by Mrs. James Wadsworth Geneseo, New York, Basler, ed., *Works of Lincoln*, VII, 435.

67. A. Lincoln, Executive Mansion, Washington, July 18, 1864. To Whom it may concern, Autograph Letter Signed—Photostat, The Abraham Lincoln Association, Springfield, Illinois; Autograph Draft Signed, Robert Todd Lincoln Collection, LC, ibid., p. 451.

68. On Greeley's mission to the Confederate emissaries, see Randall and Current, *Lincoln the President*, IV, 156–64; Donald, *Lincoln*, pp. 521–23; Edward Chase Kirkland, *The Peacemakers of 1864* (New York: The Macmillan Company, 1927), pp. 85–92.

69. Quoted in James M. McPherson, *The Struggle for Equality: Abolitionists and the Negro in the Civil War and Reconstruction* (Princeton, New Jersey: Princeton University Press, 1964), p. 276, citing *The Independent*, June 30, 1864, p. 1. For the Frémont campaign, ibid., pp. 269–80; Donald, *Lincoln*, pp. 503, 525, 534–35; Nevins, *Ordeal of the Union*, VIII, *War for the Union*, IV, 17, 70–74, 103–107; Randall and Current, *Lincoln the President*, IV, 90–92, 111–17.

70. For Tennessee, LaWanda Cox, *Lincoln and Black Freedom: A Study in Presidential Leadership* (Columbia: University of South Carolina Press, 1981), pp. 148–50; William B. Hesseltine, *Lincoln's Plan of Reconstruction*, Introduction by Richard N. Current (Chicago: Quadrangle Paperbacks, Quadrangle Books, 1967), pp. 101–103. For Arkansas, ibid., pp. 106–108; Nevins, *Ordeal of the Union*, VIII, *War for the Union*, IV, 83–84.

71. Cox, *Lincoln and Black Freedom*, pp. 97–115; Donald, *Lincoln*, pp. 484–88, 509; Hesseltine, *Lincoln's Plan of Reconstruction*, pp. 126–27; Paludan, *Presidency of Lincoln*, pp. 161, 238–55, 263–64; Randall and Current, *Lincoln the President*, IV, 16–19.

72. Eric L. McKitrick, *Andrew Johnson and Reconstruction* (Chicago: University of Chicago Press, 1960), pp. 103–108; Cox, *Lincoln and Black Freedom*, pp. 6–7, 11–16, 150–51.

73. McKitrick, *Johnson and Reconstruction*, pp. 99–101 for Stevens's thesis and 110–12 for Sumner's; Fawn M. Brodie, *Thaddeus Stevens: Scourge of the South* (New York: W. W. Norton & Company, Inc., 1959), pp. 207–209; David Donald, *Charles Sumner and the Rights of Man* (New York: Alfred A. Knopf, 1970), pp. 52–57, 65–69, 121–22, 137–41, 220–21, 228, 238–44.

74. McKitrick, *Johnson and Reconstruction*, pp. 113–15; John W. Burgess, *Reconstruction and the Constitution, 1866–1876* (New York: Charles Scribner's Sons, 1902), pp. 59–60. Article. IV. Section. IV. "The United States shall guarantee to every State in the Union a Republican Form of Government . . ."; 103rd Congress, 1st Session, Senate Document No. 103–6 (Serial 14152), *The Constitution of the United States of America: Analysis and Interpretation: Annotations of Cases Decided by the Supreme Court of the United States to June 29, 1992*, Prepared by the Congressional Research Service, Library of Congress, Johnny H. Killian, George A. Costello, co-editors (Washington: U.S. Government Printing Office, 1996), p. 17.

75. *Cong. Globe*, XXXIV, pt. 4, New Series, No. 216, Saturday, July 2, 1864, 3448–49. For the evolution of Lincoln's relations with Congress from the 10-percent plan through the Wade-Davis Bill, see Donald, *Lincoln*, pp. 471–73, 477, 484, 487–88, 496, 507, 509–10; Hesseltine, *Lincoln's Plan of Reconstruction*, pp. 75–81, 95–101, 109–17; Paludan, *Presidency of Lincoln*, pp. 250–51, 264–66; Randall and Current, *Lincoln the President*, IV, 75–81, 95–101, 109–14.

76. For May 4, 1864 passage in the House, *Cong. Globe*, XXXIV, pt. 3, 38th Con-

gress, 1st Session, *April 29, 1864 to June 14, 1864*, New Series, No. 131, Thursday, May 5, 1864, 2095–96; New Series, No. 132, Thursday, May 5, 1864, 2097, 2108, particularly 2108 for passage; for Senate passage on July 2, ibid., XXXIV, pt. 4, New Series, No. 219, Thursday, July 4, 1864, 3491; for the bill, H. R. No. 244, ibid., New Series, No. 216, Saturday, July 2, 1864, 3448–49. For the background, see Donald, *Lincoln*, p. 510; Hesseltine, *Lincoln's Plan of Reconstruction*, pp. 110–19; Paludan, *Presidency of Lincoln*, pp. 266, 280–81; Randall and Current, *Lincoln the President*, IV, 188–91.

77. Donald, *Lincoln*, pp. 510–11; Hesseltine, *Lincoln's Plan of Reconstruction*, p. 119; Randall and Current, *Lincoln the President*, IV, 119.

78. Abraham Lincoln. By the President, William H. Seward, Secretary of State. July 8, 1864, By the President of the United States. A Proclamation. Document Signed, National Archives, RG11, Proclamations; Autograph Draft, Fred L. Emerson Foundation, Auburn, New York, Basler, ed., *Works of Lincoln*, VII, 434–35, quotation from 434. Article. I. Section. II. Paragraph 2 of the Constitution provides: "... If any Bill shall not be returned by the President within ten Days (Sundays excepted) after it shall have been presented to him, the Same shall be a Law, in like Manner as if he had signed it, unless the Congress by their Adjournment prevent its Return, in which Case it shall not be a Law." U.S. Constitution, 103rd Congress, 1st Session, Senate Document No. 103–6 (Serial 14152), *Constitution of the United States*, pp. 7–8.

79. The manifesto was published August 5, 1864 in the *New York Tribune*, p. 1. The quotations here are from extracts as printed in Edward McPherson, *The Political and Social History of the United States of America During the Great Rebellion, Including A Classified Summary of the Legislation of the Second Session of the Thirty-sixth Congress, the Three Sessions of the Thirty-Seventh Congress, the First Session of the Thirty-eighth Congress, with the Votes Thereon, and the Important Executive, Judicial, and Politico-Military Facts of That Eventful Period; Together with the Organization, Legislation, and General Proceedings of the Rebel Administration; and an Appendix Containing the Principal Political Facts of the Campaign of 1864, a Chapter on the Church and the Rebellion, and the Proceedings of the Second Session of the Thirty-eighth Congress* (Second Edition, Washington: Philip & Solomons, 1865), p. 332. For the Democratic National Convention, Donald, *Lincoln*, p. 530; Nevins, *Ordeal of the Union*, VIII, *War for the Union*, IV, 98–103; Paludan, *Presidency of Lincoln*, pp. 283–84; Randall and Current, *Lincoln the President*, IV, 216–18, 220–22.

80. Belden and Belden, *So Fell the Angels*, pp. 123–25; Nevins, *Ordeal of the Union*, VIII, *War for the Union*, IV, 78–80; Randall and Current, *Lincoln the President*, IV, 181–83.

81. Quoted in Randall and Current, *Lincoln the President*, IV, 183, citing ms. transcription of shorthand record, dictated by Governor John Brough of Ohio and dated July 12, 1864, Vol. 20, Letters and Papers of William Henry Smith, Ohio State Archaeological and Historical Society, Columbus, Ohio.

82. Donald, *Lincoln*, pp. 508–509; Paludan, *Presidency of Lincoln*, p. 287; Randall and Current, *Lincoln the President*, IV, 184–85.

83. Donald, *Lincoln*, p. 525; Nevins, *Ordeal of the Union*, VIII, *War for the Union*, IV, 104–108; Randall and Current, *Lincoln the President*, IV, 113, 181, 188, 215, 224–27.

84. McPherson, *Political History*, pp. 419–20 for the platform, quotations from 419.

85. Ibid., p. 419.

86. Nevins, *Ordeal of the Union*, VIII, *War for the Union*, IV, 95, 99–100.

87. Orange New Jersey Sept 8 1864, Geo B McClellan, to Hon Horatio Seymour and others, Committee etc. Autograph Letter Signed, Samuel L. M. Barlow Papers, Henry E. Huntington Library, Art Gallery, and Botanical Gardens, San Marino, California, George B. McClellan, *The Civil War Papers of George B. McClellan, 1860–1865*, Stephen W. Sears, ed. (New York: Ticknor & Fields, 1989), pp. 595–97, quotation from

595–96. For McClellan and the nomination, see Stephen W. Sears, *George B. McClellan: The Young Napoleon* (New York: Ticknor & Fields, 1988), pp. 371–76.

88. Autograph Document Signed, LC; Document Signed — Facsimile, Stan. V. Henkels Catalog 114, No. 41, January 4, 1924, Basler, ed., Works of Lincoln, VII, 514. Ibid., 514n, for subsequent statement from diary of John Hay, LC, November 11, 1864.

## 11. SUSPENSE AND RESOLUTION

1. First quotation, U. S. Grant, Lieutenant-General. Culpeper Court-House, Va., April 9, 1864. To Maj. Gen. G. G. Meade, Commanding Army of the Potomac. U.S. War Department, *The War of the Rebellion: A Compilation of the Official Records of the Union and Confederate Armies* (four series, 70 vols. in 128, Washington: Government Printing Office, 1880–1901), Series One, XXXIII (serial 60, 1891), 827–29, quotation from 829. Hereafter cited as O.R.; references are to Series One unless otherwise specified. Quoted passage also in Ulysses S. Grant, *Personal Memoirs of U. S. Grant* (2 vols., New York: C. L. Webster & Co., 1885–1886), II, 135n. Second and third quotations, U. S. Grant, Lieutenant-General. Private and Confidential. Headquarters Armies of the United States, Washington, D.C., April 4, 1864. To Maj. Gen. W. T. Sherman, Commanding Military Division of the Mississippi, O.R., XXXII, pt. 3 (serial 59, 1891), 245–46, quotations from 246; quotations also in Grant, *Memoirs*, II, 131n. For conference between Grant and Sherman in which Sherman helped shape his orders, see Bruce Catton, *Grant Takes Command* (Boston, Toronto: Little, Brown and Company, 1969), p. 137; John F. Marszalek, *Sherman: A Soldier's Passion for Order* (New York: The Free Press, A Division of Macmillan, Inc.; Toronto: Maxwell Macmillan Canada; New York, Oxford, Singapore, Sydney: Maxwell Macmillan International, 1993), pp. 257–58.

2. William T. Sherman, *Memoirs of General William T. Sherman by Himself* (2 vols., New York: D. Appleton & Company, 1875), II, 99.

3. Grant, *Memoirs*, II, 344, 345. For the duel for Atlanta, see Albert Castel, *Decision in the West: The Atlanta Campaign of 1864* (Lawrence: University Press of Kansas, 1992); Marszalek, *Sherman*, Chapter 12, "Atlanta Falls," pp. 259–87; Craig L. Symonds, *Joseph E. Johnston: A Civil War Biography* (New York, London: W. W. Norton & Company, 1992), pp. 249–331; Thomas Lawrence Connelly, *Autumn of Glory: The Army of Tennessee, 1862–1865* (Baton Rouge: Louisiana State University Press, 1971), pp. 281–471.

4. "Atlanta Campaign," Mark Mayo Boatner III, *The Civil War Dictionary* (Revised Edition, New York: Vintage Books, A Division of Random House, Inc., 1991), pp. 30–34, particularly 30. See also Sherman, *Memoirs*, II, 19–21, 23 for the aggregate and field strength of Sherman's forces.

5. Thomas L. Livermore, *Numbers and Losses in the Civil War in America* (Second Edition, Boston and New York: Houghton, Mifflin and Company, 1901; reprint, Dayton, Ohio: Morningside, 1986), pp. 120–21, particularly 121.

6. W. T. Sherman, Major-General. Hdqrs. Military Division of the Mississippi, In the Field, Chattanooga, May 5, 1864 — 9 a.m. (Received 11:15 a.m.) to A. Lincoln, President of the United States, Washington, D.C., O.R., XXXVIII, pt. 4 (serial 75, 1891), 33–34, quotation from 33; spelling and punctuation of the text herein is from ms. in The Robert Todd Lincoln Collection of the Papers of Abraham Lincoln, Library of Congress, as printed in Abraham Lincoln, *The Collected Works of Abraham Lincoln*, Roy P. Basler, ed.; Marion Dolores Pratt and Lloyd A. Dunlop, asst. eds. (9 vols. inc. index, The Abraham Lincoln Association, Springfield, Illinois; New Brunswick: Rutgers University Press, 1953; index, 1955), VII, 330–31n, quotation from 330. For the armies' paring their transport to bare essentials, see Sherman, *Memoirs*, II, 7–12, 31; Castel, *Decision in the West*, pp. 117, 124–25. For the number of animals, ibid., p. 117. On the rail lines, ibid., pp. 91–93, 116; Marszalek, *Sherman*, pp. 260–61.

7. Thirty-seventh Congress. Session II. (Statute II.) Chap. XV. — An Act to authorize the President of the United States in certain Cases to take Possession of Railroad and Telegraph Lines, and for other Purposes. Approved, January 31, 1862. U.S. Laws, statutes, *The Statutes at Large of the United States of America, 1789–1873* (17 vols., I–IX, Boston: Charles C. Little and J. Brown, 1845–1854; X–XVII, Boston: Little, Brown, and Company, 1855–1873), 12 (December 5, 1859–March 3, 1863) (1863), 334–35; *The Congressional Globe*, XXXII, pt. 4, 37th Congress, 2nd Session, *June 23, 1862 to July 17, 1862,* Appendix, 334–35; with slight variations, O.R., Series Three, I (serial 122, 1899), 879.

8. "McCallum, Daniel Craig," Francis B. Heitman, *Historical Register and Dictionary of the United States Army, From Its Organization September 29, 1789, to March 2, 1903.* Published under act of Congress approved March 2, 1903. 57th Congress, Second Session, House Document 446 (serial 4536). 2 vols., Washington: Government Printing Office, 1903), I, 653; George Edgar Turner, *Victory Rode the Rails: The Strategic Place of the Railroads in the Civil War* (Indianapolis, New York: The Bobbs-Merrill Company, Inc., Publishers, 1953), pp. 155–58.

9. "Haupt, Herman," Heitman, *Historical Register*, I, 512; Turner, *Victory Rode the Rails*, pp. 150–61; Francis A. Lord, *Lincoln's Railroad Man: Herman Haupt* (Rutherford, Madison, Teaneck, New Jersey: Fairleigh Dickinson University Press, 1969), especially pp. 43–279.

10. Ora Elmer Hunt, "Federal Military Railroads," Francis Trevelyan Miller, ed. in chief, Robert S. Lanier, managing ed., *The Photographic History of the Civil War* (10 vols., New York: The Review of Reviews Co., 1911–1912), V, O. E. Hunt, ed., O. E. Hunt, J. W. Mallet, David Gregg McIntosh, T. M. R. Talcott, Frederick M. Colston, contributors, *Forts and Artillery*, 274–302, quotation from 280.

11. "Haupt, Herman," Heitman, *Historical Register*, I, 512. See Lord, *Lincoln's Railroad Man*, pp. 243–54, and for Haupt in the Gettysburg campaign, ibid., 11, "Old Classmates Meet at Gettysburg," pp. 215–42, and Turner, *Victory Rode the Rails*, pp. 275–81.

12. Thomas Weber, *The Northern Railroads in the Civil War* (New York: King's Crown Press, 1952), p. 201; Turner, *Victory Rode the Rails*, Chapter XXIV, "Supplying Sherman in the Atlanta Campaign," pp. 319–36.

13. "Forrest, Nathan Bedford," Boatner, *Civil War Dictionary*, pp. 288–89, particularly 289.

14. "Brice's Cross Roads," ibid., p. 85.

15. On Forrest, see John Allan Wyeth, *Life of General Nathan Bedford Forrest* (New York and London: Harper & Brothers, 1899), republished as *That Devil Forrest: Life of General Nathan Bedford Forrest*, Foreword by Henry Steele Commager (New York: Harper & Brothers, Publishers, 1959), and Brian Steel Wills, *A Battle from the Start: The Life of Nathan Bedford Forrest* (New York: HarperCollins, 1992).

16. "Tennessee, Confederate Army of," Boatner, *Civil War Dictionary*, pp. 828–29, specifically 829 for the date of Hood's command. Hood had been promoted to lieutenant-general July 17; he was advanced to temporary full general on the date he received the army command and retained that rank until January 23, 1865; "Hood, John Bell," ibid., pp. 407–408, particularly 408.

17. Livermore, *Numbers and Losses*, 122.

18. "Atlanta, Battle of," Boatner, *Civil War Dictionary*, pp. 28–30, particularly 29 for the Georgia militia and 30 for figures of totals engaged and casualties, the latter drawn from Livermore, *Numbers and Losses*, pp. 122–23, particularly 123.

19. Livermore, *Numbers and Losses*, p. 124.

20. "Stoneman's and McCook's Raids to Macon and Lovejoy, 26–31 July '64," Boatner, *Civil War Dictionary*, pp. 801–802, particularly 802 for casualties.

21. J. B. Hood, General. Atlanta, Ga., August 26, 1864. To Hon. James A. Seddon,

Richmond. J. B. Hood, Atlanta, August 27, 1864. To Hon. J. A. Seddon, Secretary of War. *O.R.*, XXXVIII, pt. 5 (serial 76, 1891), 990, 993.

22. "XI Corps," "XII Corps," "XX Corps," Boatner, *Civil War Dictionary*, pp. 193–94 (particularly 194), 194, 195.

23. [Brigadier-General] F[rancis]. A. Shoup, Chief of Staff. Atlanta, August 28, 1864 — 6 p.m. (Via East Point.) To Brigadier-General [Frank C.] Armstrong. *O.R.*, XXXVIII, pt. 5, 998.

24. W. T. Sherman, Major-General. Near Lovejoy's Station, Twenty-six miles south of Atlanta, Ga., September 3, 1864 — 6 a.m. (Received 5.30 p.m. 4th.) Ibid., p. 777.

25. "Sherman, William Tecumseh," Heitman, *Historical Register*, I, 882.

26. Farragut had been promoted rear-admiral on July 16, 1862; "Farragut, David Glasgow," Boatner, *Civil War Dictionary*, pp. 275–76, particularly 276. For the battle, see William N. Still, Jr., *Iron Afloat: The Story of the Confederate Ironclads* (Nashville: Vanderbilt University Press, 1971), pp. 200–11; Raimondo Luraghi, *A History of the Confederate Navy*, tr. Paolo E. Coletta (Annapolis, Maryland: Naval Institute Press, 1996), pp. 320–28. Luraghi states the consensus when he writes: "That Farragut had cried: 'Damn the torpedoes, full speed ahead!' [or 'Damn the torpedoes, four bells!'] is probably a legend, made up much later, yet this in no way detracts from his gallantry and daring"; ibid., p. 453 n68. The "torpedoes" would today be called mines, for which see Milton F. Perry, *Infernal Machines: The Story of Confederate Submarine and Mine Warfare* (Baton Rouge: Louisiana State University Press, 1965), particularly Chapter XV, "'Damn the Torpedoes!'" pp. 158–63 for Mobile Bay.

27. Bruce Catton, *Grant Takes Command*, pp. 313–16; Bruce Catton, *A Stillness at Appomattox* (Garden City, New York: Doubleday & Company, Inc., 1953), pp. 266–67; "XIX Corps," Boatner, *Civil War Dictionary*, p. 198.

28. Douglas Southall Freeman, *Lee's Lieutenants: A Study in Command* (3 vols., New York Charles Scribner's Sons, 1942–1944), III, *Gettysburg to Appomattox*, 571–74; "Chambersburg," Boatner, *Civil War Dictionary*, p. 136; "Jones, William Edmonson," Boatner, *Civil War Dictionary*, p. 444; "Johnson, Bradley Tyler," ibid., p. 437.

29. Freeman, *Lee's Lieutenants*, III, 572–73; "Moorefield," Boatner, *Civil War Dictionary*, p. 564.

30. U. S. Grant, Lieutenant-General. City Point, Va., July 15, 1864. To Major-General Halleck, Washington, D.C., *O.R.*, XXXVII, pt. 2 (serial 71, 1891), 328–29, quotation from 329. For the Shenandoah Valley Campaign of 1864, see Gary W. Gallagher, ed., *Struggle for the Shenandoah: Essays on the 1864 Valley Campaign* (Kent, Ohio, and London, England: The Kent State University Press, 1991); Catton, *Grant Takes Command*, pp. 313–17, 342–49 (especially for the command arrangements), 362–64, 377–81; Catton, *Stillness at Appomattox*, pp. 268–317; Freeman, *Lee's Lieutenants*, III, 574–87, 595–612, 617, 635–36; Roy Morris, Jr., *Sheridan: The Life and Wars of General Phil Sheridan* (New York: Crown Publishers, Inc., 1992), pp. 179–239.

31. For Sheridan's earlier Civil War career, see Morris, *Sheridan*, pp. 41–153; Richard O'Connor, *Sheridan the Inevitable* (Indianapolis, New York: The Bobbs-Merrill Company, 1953), pp. 52–144. For the Franklin idea, Morris, *Sheridan*, p. 153; O'Connor, *Sheridan*, p. 148. On command of the Cavalry Corps, Pleasonton led the corps May 22, 1863–January 22, 1864 and, after a leave of absence, February 12–March 25, 1864; "Pleasonton, Alfred," Boatner, *Civil War Dictionary*, pp. 655–56, particularly 656. (Brigadier-General David McMurtrie Gregg commanded the corps during Pleasonton's leave of absence; "Gregg, David McMurtrie," ibid., p. 357.) Pleasonton had been promoted from brigadier to major-general, U.S.V., on June 22, 1863; ibid., p. 656; "Pleasonton, Alfred," Heitman, *Historical Register*, I, 795. For Buford, "Buford, John," ibid., p. 97; he received on his deathbed his commission as major-general, U.S.V., dated July 1, 1863; ibid., from

"Buford, John," Ezra J. Warner, *Generals in Blue: Lives of the Union Commanders* (Baton Rouge: Louisiana State University Press, 1964), p. 53; for the commission, see also "Buford, John," Heitman, *Historical Register*, I, 260; the standard biography is now Edward G. Longacre, *General John Buford* (Conshohocken, PA: Combined Books, 1995), p. 245 for the delivery of his promotion on December 16, 1863, 246 for his death later in the day. Sheridan commanded the Cavalry Corps from April 4, 1864; "Cavalry Corps, Union Army of the Potomac," Boatner, *Civil War Dictionary*, pp. 201–202, particularly 201.

32. Philip H. Sheridan, *Personal Memoirs of P. H. Sheridan, General United States Army* (2 vols., New York: Charles L. Webster & Company, 1888), II, 355. For Sheridan's command of the Cavalry Corps before he moved to the Valley, see Morris, *Sheridan*, pp. 153–81; O'Connor, *Sheridan*, pp. 126–85; Catton, *Stillness at Appomattox*, pp. 95–96, 99–101, 149–51; Gordon C. Rhea, *The Battle of the Wilderness May 5–6, 1864* (Baton Rouge and London: Louisiana State University Press, 1994), pp. 40–41, 91–92, 253–61, 270, 339–41, 344–45, 349, 378–79, 433–34; Gordon C. Rhea, *The Battles for Spotsylvania Court House and the Road to Yellow Tavern May 7–12, 1864* (Baton Rouge and London: Louisiana State University Press, 1997), pp. 9–10, 22, 30–37, 40–42, 47, 49, 66–69, 76, 87, 96–100, 103, 114–21, 189–212, 314–15, 318, 372–73 n94.

33. Sheridan, *Memoirs*, II, 368–69. For this incident, see also Horace Porter, *Campaigning with Grant* (New York: The Century Co., 1897), pp. 83–84; Rhea, *Spotsylvania Court House*, pp. 9–10, 67–69.

34. Sheridan, *Memoirs*, II, 369. See also Porter, *Campaigning with Grant*, p. 84.

35. Freeman, *Lee's Lieutenants*, III, 419–31; Morris, *Sheridan*, pp. 165–69; O'Connor, *Sheridan*, 9, "A Charge at Yellow Tavern," pp. 163–72; Rhea, *Spotsylvania Court House*, pp. 189–212; Emory M. Thomas, *Bold Dragoon: The Life of J. E. B. Stuart* (New York, Cambridge, Philadelphia, San Francisco, London, Mexico City, São Paulo, Singapore, Sydney: Harper & Row, Publishers, 1986), pp. 288–97.

36. For the appointment of Sheridan to field command against Early and to command the Middle Military District, see By order of the Secretary of War: E[dward]. D. Townsend, Assistant Adjutant-General. General Orders, No. 240. War Dept., Adjt. General's Office, Washington, August 7, 1864, *O.R.*, XLIII, pt. 1 (serial 90, 1893), 719. See also Grant, *Memoirs*, II, 319–21; Sheridan, *Memoirs*, I, 464–65; "Middle Military Division, Department and Army of the Shenandoah," Boatner, *Civil War Dictionary*, p. 549; "VI Corps," ibid., p. 191; "VIII Corps," ibid., pp. 191–92; "West Virginia, Union Department and Army of the," for the designation of the Eighth Corps, ibid., p. 907; "XIX Corps," ibid., p. 198; "Cavalry Corps, Army of the Potomac," ibid., pp. 201–202, particularly 202. For numbers, [Captain] E[nos]. B. Parsons, Late Provost-Marshal-General, Middle Military District. Headquarters Military Division of the Gulf, Office of the Chief Signal Officer, New Orleans, La., November 18, 1865. To Maj. Gen. P. H. Sheridan. With Addenda, P. H. Sheridan, Major-General. Headquarters Middle Military Division, September 13, 1864. To Brig. Gen. L. Thomas, Adjutant-General, U.S. Army, *O.R.*, XLIII, pt. 1, 60, and Field return of troops in the field belonging to the Middle Military Division, September 10, 1864. Ibid., p. 61.

37. U. S. Grant, Lieutenant-General. City Point, Va., August 1, 1864 — 11.30 a.m. (Received 10.20 p.m.) To Major-General Halleck, Washington. *O.R.*, XXXVII, pt. 2, 588.

38. U. S. Grant, Lieutenant-General. Headquarters, In the Field, Monocacy Bridge, Md. August 5, 1864 — 8 p.m. To Major-General Hunter, Commanding Department of West Virginia, ibid., pp. 697–98, quotation from 698.

39. U. S. Grant, Lieutenant-General, City Point, Va., August 26, 1864 — 2.30 p.m. (Received 12.10 a.m. 27th.) To Major-General Sheridan, Halltown, Va., ibid., pp. 916–17, quotation from 917.

40. H. W. Halleck, Major-General and Chief of Staff. Washington, August 3,

1864. — 2.30 p.m. To Lieutenant-General Grant, City Point, Va. Ibid., XXXVII, pt. 2, 582–83, quotation from 583.

41. Freeman, *Lee's Lieutenants*, III, 574; ibid., p. 299 for McLaws's removal from command; for numbers, "Shenandoah Valley Campaign of Sheridan," Boatner, *Civil War Dictionary*, pp. 743–46, particularly 743.

42. Halleck to Grant, Aug. 3, 1864, O.R., XXXVII, pt. 2, 582.

43. U. S. Grant, Lieutenant-General. City Point, Va., August 12, 1864 — 9 a.m. (Received 7 p.m.) To Major-General Halleck, Washington, D.C., ibid., XLIII, pt. 1, 775.

44. U. S. Grant, Lieutenant-General. Strawberry Plains, Va., August 14, 1864 — 10 a.m. (Received 9 a.m. 15th.) To Maj. Gen. H. W. Halleck, Washington, D.C. Ibid., p. 791.

45. Sheridan, *Memoirs*, I, 488.

46. A. Lincoln, Office U.S. Military Telegraph, War Department, Washington, D.C., August 3, 1864. To Lieut.-Genl. Grant City-Point, Va., Autograph Letter Signed, National Archives, RG107, Presidential Telegrams, I, 121, Basler, ed., *Works of Lincoln*, VII, 476. Lincoln referred to U. S. Grant, Lieutenant-General. City Point, Va., August 1, 1864 — 11.30 a.m. (Received 10.20 p.m.) To Major-General Halleck, Washington, O.R., XXXVII, pt. 2, 558, particularly a passage reading: "Unless General Hunter is in the field in person, I want Sheridan put in command of all the troops in the field, with instructions to put himself south of the enemy and follow him to the death. Wherever the enemy goes let our troops go also."

47. Sheridan, *Memoirs*, II, 9 for quotation; Grant, *Memoirs*, II, 329.

48. For the strength of both sides, "Winchester, Va., (Third Battle of . . . , or Opequon)," Boatner, *Civil War Dictionary*, pp. 937–40, particularly 940, citing for the Confederates Freeman, *Lee's Lieutenants*, III, 577, 581. For losses, Livermore, *Numbers and Losses*, p. 127. "Gordon, John Brown," Boatner, *Civil War Dictionary*, pp. 348–49, particularly 348, for Gordon's promotion to major-general May 14, 1864.

49. "Fisher's Hill," Boatner, *Civil War Dictionary*, pp. 280–81, particularly 281, citing for Federal casualties O'Connor, *Sheridan*, p. 210.

50. Sheridan, *Memoirs*, II, 81.

51. Ibid.

52. "Cedar Creek," Boatner, *Civil War Dictionary*, pp. 132–34, particularly 134. In addition to the general sources on the 1864 Valley Campaign, see Thomas A. Lewis, *The Guns of Cedar Creek* (New York, Cambridge, Philadelphia, San Francisco, London, Mexico City, São Paulo, Singapore, Sydney: Harper & Row, Publishers, 1988).

53. "Sherman, William Tecumseh," "Meade, George Gordon," "Sheridan, Philip Henry," Heitman, *Historical Register*, I, 882, 700, 881.

54. Allan Nevins, *Ordeal of the Union* (8 vols., *Ordeal of the Union*, I, *Fruits of Manifest Destiny 1847–1852*; *Ordeal of the Union*, II, *A House Dividing 1852–1857* [New York, London: Charles Scribner's Sons, 1947]; III, *The Emergence of Lincoln*, I, *Douglas, Buchanan, and Party Chaos 1857–1859*; IV, *The Emergence of Lincoln*, II, *Prologue to Civil War 1859–1860* [New York: Charles Scribner's Sons, 1950]; V, *The War for the Union*, I, *The Improvised War 1861–1862* [New York: Charles Scribner's Sons, 1959]; VI, *The War for the Union*, II, *War Becomes Revolution* [New York: Charles Scribner's Sons, 1960], VII, *The War for the Union*, III, *The Organized War 1863–1864*; VIII, *The War for the Union*, IV, *The Organized War to Victory 1864–1865* [New York: Charles Scribner's Sons, 1971]), *Ordeal of the Union*, VIII, *War for the Union*, IV, 104, citing Garfield from Cincinnati to Lucretia Rudolph Garfield, September 13, 1864, James A. Garfield Papers, LC.

55. [Unsigned,] [Orange, New Jersey, c. September 4, 1864] Gentlemen: [To the Democratic Nomination Committee], Autograph Letter, George B. McClellan Papers, LC, George B. McClellan, *The Civil War Papers of George B. McClellan: Selected Corre-*

*spondence, 1860–1865,* Stephen W. Sears, ed. (New York: Ticknor & Fields, 1989), pp. 590–92, quotation from 591.

56. Frank L. Klement, *Dark Lanterns: Secret Political Societies, Conspiracies, and Treason Trials in the Civil War* (Baton Rouge and London: Louisiana State University Press, 1984), pp. 193–201; Nevins, *Ordeal of the Union,* VIII, *War for the Union,* IV, 132–34.

57. Nevins, *Ordeal of the Union,* VIII, *War for the Union,* IV, 105, citing (106n) *The New York Herald, New York Tribune, The New-York Times,* all Sept. 23, 1864, p. 1.

58. James G. Randall, *Lincoln the President* (4 vols., New York: Dodd, Mead & Company, 1946–1955, IV, *Last Full Measure,* coauthored with Richard N. Current), IV, 237–41, particularly 241. See also David Herbert Donald, *Lincoln* (New York, London, Toronto, Sydney, Tokyo, Singapore: Simon & Schuster, 1995), pp. 530–45; Nevins, *Ordeal of the Union,* VIII, *War for the Union,* IV, 103, 110–13.

59. Randall and Current, *Lincoln the President,* IV, 227–32, 249–53, particularly 252 for assessments; Nevins, *Ordeal of the Union,* VIII, *War for the Union,* IV, 103–107, 110–11; Allan Nevins, *Frémont: Pathmarker of the West* (New York, London, Toronto: Longmans, Green and Co., 1955), pp. 577–82; Donald, *Lincoln,* pp. 533–35; Phillip Shaw Paludan, *The Presidency of Abraham Lincoln* (Lawrence: University Press of Kansas, 1994), pp. 288–89.

60. Richard Yates, November 1, 1864 — 5.02 p.m. (Received 8.30 p.m.) To His Excellency Abraham Lincoln, President of the United States, Washington, D.C., *O.R.,* Series Three, IV (serial 125, 1899), 871–72, quotation from 872. For the soldier vote, see Nevins, *Ordeal of the Union,* VIII, *War for the Union,* IV, 135–36, 137–38; Paludan, *Presidency of Lincoln,* pp. 289–90; Randall and Current, *Lincoln the President,* IV, 253–58; Catton, *Stillness at Appomattox,* pp. 322–24.

61. Noah Brooks, *Washington in Lincoln's Time* (New York: The Century Co., 1895), pp. 216–17.

62. Randall and Current, *Lincoln the President,* IV, 226, citing *The New York Herald,* Sept. 15, 1864, p. 4, c. 2.

63. Nevins, *Ordeal of the Union,* VIII, *War for the Union,* IV, 136–37; Randall and Current, *Lincoln the President,* IV, 234–35.

64. Everette B. Long with Barbara Long, *The Civil War Day by Day: An Almanac 1861–1865,* Foreword by Bruce Catton (Garden City, New York: Doubleday & Company, Inc., 1971), October 13, Thursday, 1864, p. 583 for statistics; William B. Hesseltine, *Lincoln's Plan of Reconstruction,* Introduction by Richard N. Current (Chicago: Quadrangle Paperbacks, Quadrangle Books, 1967), pp. 130–31.

65. Office U.S. Military Telegraph, War Department, Washington, D.C., October 13th. 1864. Autograph Document, Henry E. Huntington Library, Art Gallery, and Botanical Gardens, San Marino, California, Basler, ed., *Works of Lincoln,* VIII, 46. The addition of Nevada's vote is not in Lincoln's autograph; ibid., n; See also for Nevada, Randall and Current, *Lincoln the President,* IV, 236–37.

66. Eugene H. Roseboom, *A History of Presidential Elections* (New York: The Macmillan Company, 1957), p. 202.

67. Paludan, *Presidency of Lincoln,* p. 289; Randall and Current, *Lincoln the President,* IV, 261.

68. For a detailed analysis of the attitudes of the Republican majority produced by the election on Reconstruction issues, see David Donald, *The Politics of Reconstruction 1863–1867* (Baton Rouge: Louisiana State University Press, 1965), pp. 34–36, 42–44.

69. Nevins, *Ordeal of the Union,* VIII, *War for the Union,* IV, 139.

70. Sears, *McClellan,* p. 385 for the resignation and p. 386 for the statement; Geo B McClellan, Orange Nov 10/64 to S.L.M.B. [Samuel L. M. Barlow], Autograph Letter

Signed, Samuel L. M. Barlow Papers, Huntington Library, Sears, ed., *Papers of McClellan*, pp. 618–19, quotation from 618.

71. November 10, 1864, Autograph Document, Southworth Library, Dryden, New York, Basler, ed., *Works of Lincoln*, VIII, 100–101, quotation from 101.

72. August 19, 1864, Diary of Joseph T. Mills, Manuscript, Wisconsin Historical Society, Madison, Wisconsin, ibid., VII, 506–508, quotations from 506, 507.

### 12. THE RELENTLESS WAR

1. U. S. Grant, Lieutenant-General. City Point, Va., October 3, 1864 — 7 p.m. To Maj. Gen. P. H. Sheridan, Harrisonburg, Va., U.S. War Department, *The War of the Rebellion: A Compilation of the Official Records of the Union and Confederate Armies* (four series, 70 vols. in 128, Washington: Government Printing Office, 1880–1901), Series One, XLIII, pt. 2 (serial 91, 1893), 266. Hereafter cited as O.R.; references are to Series One unless otherwise specified.

2. P. H. Sheridan, Major-General. Woodstock, Va., October 7, 1864 — 9 p.m. (Received 9th.) To Lieut. Gen. U. S. Grant, Commanding Armies of the United States. Ibid., pp. 308–309.

3. Ibid., p. 309.

4. M. C. Meigs Diary, October 12–13, 1865, M. C. Meigs Papers, Library of Congress, Washington.

5. P. H. Sheridan, Major-General, Commanding. Headquarters Middle Military Division, November 24, 1864. To Maj. Gen. H. W. Halleck, U.S. Army Chief of Staff, Washington, D.C., O.R., XLIII, pt. 1 (serial 90, 1893), 37–38, figures from 37.

6. By command of Maj. Gen. P. H. Sheridan: James W. Forsyth, Lieutenant-Colonel [U.S.A., assistant inspector general] and Chief of Staff. Headquarters Middle Military Division, November 27, 1864. To Bvt. Maj. Gen. Wesley Merritt, Commanding First Cavalry Division. Ibid., pp. 55–56.

7. U. S. Grant, Lieutenant-General. City Point, Va., July 15, 1864. To Major-General Halleck, Washington, D.C., ibid., XXXVII, pt. 2 (serial 71, 1891), 328–29, quotation from 329.

8. By order of Maj. Gen. W. T. Sherman: [Major, U.S.V.] J[ohn]. H. Hammond, Assistant Adjutant-General. Special Orders, No. 254. Headquarters Fifth Division, Memphis, September 27, 1862. O.R., XVII, pt. 2 (serial 25, 1886), 240.

9. Ibid.

10. W. T. Sherman, Major-General, Hdqrs. First Division, Dist. of West Tennessee, Memphis, October 4, 1862. To Maj. Gen. U. S. Grant, Commanding District of West Tennessee, Jackson. Ibid., pp. 261–62, quotation from 261.

11. W. T. Sherman, Major-General, Commanding. Memphis, October 22, 1862. To Miss P. A. Fraser, Memphis. Ibid., pp. 287–88, quotation from 288.

12. Lloyd Lewis, *Sherman: Fighting Prophet* (New York: Harcourt, Brace and Company, 1932), p. 250; John F. Marszalek, *Sherman: A Soldier's Passion for Order* (New York: The Free Press, A Division of Macmillan, Inc.; Toronto: Maxwell Macmillan Canada; New York, Oxford, Singapore, Sydney: Maxwell Macmillan International, 1993), pp. 194–95; James M. Merrill, *William Tecumseh Sherman* (Chicago, New York, San Francisco: Rand McNally & Company, 1971), pp. 207–208.

13. U. S. Grant, Lieutenant-General, City Point, Virginia. September 12, 1864. To Major-General W. T. Sherman, Commanding Military Division of the Mississippi. O.R., XXXIX, pt. 2 (serial 79, 1892), 364–65, quotation from 365. Also with slight variations in William T. Sherman, *Memoirs of General William T. Sherman by Himself* (2 vols., New York: D. Appleton and Company, 1875), II, 112–13, quotation from 113.

14. John M. Corse, Brigadier-General, Allatoona, Georgia, October 6, 1864 — 2 p.m. (Received 3.15 p.m.) To Captain [U.S.V.] L[ewis]. M. Dayton, Aide-de-Camp. O.R., XXXIX, pt. 3 (serial 80, 1892), 113; Sherman, *Memoirs*, II, 147–48. See Marszalek, *Sherman*, pp. 290–93; Thomas Lawrence Connelly, *Autumn of Glory: The Army of Tennessee, 1862–1865* (Baton Rouge: Louisiana State University Press, 1971), pp. 477–86.

15. Quotation from Sherman, *Memoirs*, II, 151.

16. Marszalek, *Sherman*, p. 296, particularly for September 28 date; Lewis, *Sherman: Fighting Prophet*, pp. 425–26, 430–31; "Franklin and Nashville Campaign," Mark Mayo Boatner III, *The Civil War Dictionary* (Revised Edition, New York: Vintage Books, A Division of Random House, Inc., 1991), pp. 305–309, particularly 307 for the Fourth and Twenty-third Corps. For the evolution of the plan, indication of the troops involved, and the October 30 date, Sherman, *Memoirs*, II, 151–63, particularly 162–63 for the date.

17. Sherman, *Memoirs*, II, 111.

18. Ibid., pp. 111–12.

19. By order of Maj. Gen. W. T. Sherman: L. M. Dayton, Aide-de-Camp, Special Field Orders, No. 67. Hdqrs., Military Division of the Mississippi, In the Field, Atlanta, Ga., September 8, 1864, O.R., XXXVIII, pt. 5 (serial 77, 1891), 837–38; for the statistics, Marszalek, *Sherman*, p. 285.

20. U. S. Grant, Lieutenant-General, City Point, Va., November 1, 1864 — 6 p.m. To Major-General Sherman, Atlanta, Ga. O.R., XXXIX, pt. 3 (serial 80), 576; Sherman, *Memoirs*, II, 164; for the background, Bruce Catton, *Grant Takes Command* (Boston, Toronto: Little, Brown and Company, 1969), pp. 385–89; Marszalek, *Sherman*, pp. 288–90, 293–96.

21. W. T. Sherman, Major-General, Commanding. Hdqrs. Military Division of the Mississippi, In the Field, Rome, Georgia, November 2, 1864. To Lieutenant-General U. S. Grant, City Point, Virginia. O.R., XXXIX, pt. 3 (serial 80), 594–95; Sherman, *Memoirs*, II, 165.

22. W. T. Sherman, Major-General, Commanding. October 19, 1864. To Col. [U.S.A., assistant aide-de-camp] A[mos]. Beckwith [Chief-Commissary and Acting Chief-Quartermaster,] Atlanta, Georgia. O.R., XXXIX, pt. 3 (serial 80), 358–59; Sherman, *Memoirs*, II, 159.

23. W. T. Sherman, Major-General, Hdqrs. Military Division of the Mississippi, Atlanta, Ga., September 20, 1864. To Lieut. Gen. U. S. Grant, City Point, Virginia O.R., XXXIX, pt. 2 (serial 79), 411–13, quotation from 412; Sherman, *Memoirs*, II, 113–16, quotation from 115.

24. Same document, quotation from O.R., XXXIX, pt. 2 (serial 79), 412; Sherman, *Memoirs*, II, 115.

25. W. T. Sherman, Major-General, Commanding. Hdqrs. Military Division of the Mississippi, In the Field, Allatoona, Ga. October 9, 1864 — 7.30 pm. (Received 11 a.m. 10th) To Lieutenant-General Grant, City Point, Va. O.R., XXXIX, pt. 3 (serial 80), 162; Sherman, *Memoirs*, II, 152.

26. U. S. Grant, Lieutenant-General. City Point, Virginia, November 2, 1864 — 11.30 a.m. To Major-General Sherman, Rome, Ga. O.R., XXXIX, pt. 3 (serial 80), 594; Sherman, *Memoirs*, II, 152.

27. Sherman, *Memoirs*, II, 168.

28. "March to the Sea," Boatner, *Civil War Dictionary*, pp. 509–12, particularly 509; "Kilpatrick, Hugh Judson," ibid., pp. 459–69; Sherman, *Memoirs*, II, 171 (ibid., 176 states there were sixty-five guns); Lewis, *Sherman: Fighting Prophet*, p. 433 for destruction of the telegraph.

29. By order of Major-General W. T. Sherman: L. M. Dayton, Aide-de-Camp, Special Field Orders, No. 120, Hdqrs. Mil. Div. of the Miss., In the Field, Kingston, Ga., November 9, 1864. O.R., XXXIX, pt. 3 (serial 80), 713–14, quotation from 713; Sherman,

*Memoirs*, II, 174–76, quotation from 175. Ibid., p. 176 for the numbers of wagons and ambulances.

30. Special Field Orders, No. 120, *O.R.*, XXXIX, pt. 3 (serial 80), 713–14; Sherman, *Memoirs*, II, 175.

31. Special Field Orders, No. 120, *O.R.*, XXXIX, pt. 3 (serial 80), 714; Sherman, *Memoirs*, II, 175.

32. Sherman, *Memoirs*, II, 178–79.

33. "March to the Sea," Boatner, *Civil War Dictionary*, p. 509 for the troops; "South Carolina, Georgia, and Florida, Confederate Department of," ibid., pp. 779–80, particularly 780; "Division of the West, Confed.," ibid., p. 241.

34. Lewis, *Sherman: Fighting Prophet*, pp. 449–50 for the appeals; Sherman, *Memoirs*, II, 188 for his entry into Milledgeville, 188 and 190 for the real and mock Georgia legislature, 188–90 for the appeals.

35. Lewis, *Sherman: Fighting Prophet*, p. 460 for Millen, 431 for Andersonville; Marszalek, *Sherman*, p. 305 for Millen.

36. "Andersonville Prison," Boatner, *Civil War Dictionary*, p. 15. See Ovid L. Futch, *History of Andersonville Prison* (Gainesville: University of Florida Press, 1968). William Marvel, *Andersonville: The Last Depot* (Chapel Hill and London: University of North Carolina Press, 1994) attempts to make the case that the Confederacy and Henry Wirz administered the prison about as humanely as straitened circumstances permitted, thus Marvel applies scholarly methods to a cause that has become one of the more dubious enthusiasms of latter-day Confederate sympathizers.

37. William B. Hesseltine, *Civil War Prisons: A Study in War Psychology* (Columbus: Ohio State University Press, 1930); William B. Hesseltine, ed., *Civil War Prisons* (Kent, Ohio: Kent State University Press, 1972), reprint of a special issue of *Civil War History: A Journal of the Middle Period*, 8:2 (June 1962), 117–232.

38. W. T. Sherman, Major-General. Hdqrs. Military Division of the Mississippi, In the Field, Savannah, Ga., January 1, 1865. To Maj. Gen. H. W. Halleck, Chief of Staff, Washington City, D.C. *O.R.*, XLIV (serial 93, 1893), 7–14, quotation from 9.

39. Ibid., p. 13.

40. W. T. Sherman, Major-General. Headquarters Military Division of the Mississippi, In the Field, Savannah, Ga., December 24, 1864. To Major-General H. W. Halleck, Chief of Staff, Washington City, D.C., ibid., pp. 798–800, quotation from 799; Sherman, *Memoirs*, II, 226–28, quotation from 227.

41. W. T. Sherman, Major-General. Near Lovejoy's, Ga., September 4, 1864 — 9 a.m. To Maj. Gen. H. W. Halleck, Washington, D.C., *O.R.*, XXXVIII, pt. 5 (serial 77, 1891), 794; Sherman, *Memoirs*, II, 111.

42. W. T. Sherman, Major-General Commanding. Headquarters Military Division of the Mississippi, In the Field, Atlanta, Georgia, September 12, 1864. To James M. Calhoun, Mayor, E. E. Rawson, and S. C. Welles, Representing City Council of Atlanta. *O.R.*, XXXIX, pt. 2 (serial 79, 1892), 418–19, quotation from 419; Sherman, *Memoirs*, II, 125–27, quotation from 126.

43. Sherman, *Memoirs*, II, 197. The attack on Fort McAllister is described ibid., pp. 195–200; Marszalek, *Sherman*, pp. 307–309; Lewis, *Sherman: Fighting Prophet*, pp. 463–64.

44. W. T. Sherman, Major-General: Headquarters Military Division of the Mississippi, In the Field, near Savannah, Ga., December 17, 1864. To General William J. Hardee Commanding Confederate Forces in Savannah. *O.R.*, XLIV (serial 80), 737.

45. Inclosure to preceding letter. J. B. Hood, General. Headquarters Army of Tennessee, In the Field, October 12, 1864. To the Officer Commanding U.S. Forces at Resaca, Ga. [James Baird Weaver. Colonel, 2nd Iowa Infantry], ibid.; Sherman, *Memoirs*, II, 155.

46. W. T. Sherman, Major-General. Savannah, Ga., December 22, 1864. (Via Fort Monroe 6.45 p.m. 25th.) *O.R.*, XLIV (serial 80), 783. For Hardee's escape, Lewis, *Sherman: Fighting Prophet*, p. 469; Marszalek, *Sherman*, p. 308.

47. W. T. Sherman, Major-General. Headquarters Military Division of the Mississippi, In the Field, Savannah, Ga., December 24, 1864. To Major-General H. W. Halleck, Chief-of-staff, Washington City, D.C., *O.R.*, XLIV (serial 80), 798–800, quotation from 799; Sherman, *Memoirs*, II, 226–28, quotation from 227–28.

48. Mary Boykin Miller Chesnut, *Mary Chesnut's Civil War*, ed. Comer Vann Woodward (New Haven and London: Yale University Press, 1981), p. 642 (September 1, 1864).

49. [Second Congress. Second Session. Chap.] No. 195. "An Act to amend the law relating to Impressments. Approved, March 18, 1865. Endorsed: "A true copy. James M. Matthews, Law Clerk." Text from certified copy in Duke University Library, Confederate States, Laws, statutes, *Laws and Joint Resolutions of the Last Session of the Confederate Congress, Together with the Secret Acts of Previous Congresses*, With an Introduction and a Bibliographical Note by Charles W. Ramsdell, ed. (Durham, N.C.: Duke University Press, 1941), pp. 151–53. Also in *O.R.*, Series Four, III (serial 129, 1900), 1170, with slight changes and without session and chapter numbers. On habeas corpus, James G. Randall and David Donald, *The Civil War and Reconstruction* (Second Edition, Revised with Enlarged Bibliography, Lexington, Massachusetts: D.C. Heath and Company, A Division of Raytheon Education Company, 1969), p. 521.

50. Quoted in Henry G. Connor, *John Archibald Campbell, Associate Justice of the United States Supreme Court, 1851–1861* (Boston and New York: Houghton Mifflin Company, 1920), pp. 175–76.

51. Consolidated abstract from returns of the Confederate Army on or about December 31, 1864. [Compiled from such returns as are on file in the War Department.] *O.R.*, Series Four, III (serial 129, 1900), 989.

52. Emory M. Thomas, *The Confederate Nation 1861–1865* (New York, Hagerstown, San Francisco, London: Harper & Row, Publishers, 1979), p. 287; Randall and Donald, *Civil War and Reconstruction*, pp. 516–17.

53. Charles P. Roland, *The Confederacy* (Daniel J. Boorstin, ed., *The Chicago History of American Civilization*, Chicago and London: University of Chicago Press, 1960), p. 143. See also Randall and Donald, *Civil War and Reconstruction*, pp. 267–68, 426, 521; for Sherman and Brown, see Marszalek, *Sherman*, p. 289.

54. Richard E. Beringer, Herman Hattaway, Archer Jones, William N. Still, Jr., *Why the South Lost the Civil War* (Athens and London: University of Georgia Press, 1986), pp. 231–34, particularly 233 for troops withheld from Confederate service.

55. Jefferson Davis, Richmond, Va., November 7, 1864. To the Senate and House of Representatives of the Confederate States of America. Confederate States, President, *A Compilation of the Messages and Papers of the Confederacy Including the Diplomatic Correspondence 1861–1865*, James D. Richardson, ed. (Published by Permission of Congress, 2 vols., Nashville: United States Publishing Company, 1905), I, 482–500, discussion of "Employment of Slaves," 493–96, quotation from 495. Davis's discussion of employing slaves is reprinted, along with numerous related documents, in Robert F. Durden, *The Gray and the Black: The Confederate Debate on Emancipation* (Baton Rouge: Louisiana State University Press, 1972), pp. 104–106, quotation from 105.

56. Howell Cobb, Major-General. Hdqrs. Georgia Reserves and Mil. Dist. of Georgia. To Hon. James A. Seddon, Secretary of War, Richmond, Va. *O.R.*, Series Four, III (serial 129, 1900), 1009–1010, quotation from 1009; Durden, *Gray and Black*, p. 208.

57. R. E. Lee, General. Headquarters Army of Northern Virginia, January 11, 1865. To Hon. Andrew Hunter, Richmond, Va. *O.R.*, Series Four, III (serial 129), 1012–13, quotation from 1013.

58. By order: S. Cooper, Adjutant and Inspector General, General Orders, No. 14. Adjt. and Insp. General's Office, Richmond, Va, March 23, 1865. [Paragraph] I. The following act of Congress . . . published for the information and direction of all concerned: An Act to increase the military force of the Confederate States of America. Approved, March 13, 1865. O.R., Series Four, III (serial 129), 1161; Confederate States, Laws, statutes, *Laws of the Last Confederate Congress*, identifying [Second Congress. Second Session. Chap.] No. 148, pp. 118–19, particularly 118 for relevant section, 1, text of this section from O.R.; Durden, *Gray and Black*, p. 202.

59. Thomas, *Confederate Nation*, pp. 296–97; Frank Lawrence Owsley, *King Cotton Diplomacy: Foreign Relations of the Confederate States of America* (Second Edition, Revised by Harriet Chappell Owsley, Chicago: University of Chicago Press, 1959), pp. 532–41.

60. "Bragg, Braxton," Boatner, *Civil War Dictionary*, pp. 78–79, particularly 79.

61. An Act to provide for the appointment of a General-in-chief of the Armies of the Confederate States. Approved, January 23, 1865. Included in I. By order: S. Cooper, Adjutant and Inspector General. General Orders, No. 3. Adjt. and Insp. General's Office. Richmond, Va., February 6, 1865. Announcing II., appointment of General Robert E. Lee. O.R., XLVI, pt. 2 (serial 97, 1895), 1205; act also in Confederate States, Laws, statutes, *Laws of the Last Confederate Congress*, pp. 22–23, text from O.R., Series III, V (serial 126, 1900) 688, but identifying the act as [Second Congress. Second Session. Chap.] No. 35.

62. Roland, *The Confederacy*, p. 180.

63. Jefferson Davis, *The Rise and Fall of the Confederate Government* (2 vols., New York: D. Appleton and Company, 1881), I, 518.

64. John D. Nicolay and John Hay, *Abraham Lincoln: A History* (10 vols., New York: The Century Co., 1890), X, 93–112, quotation from 94–95; James G. Randall, *Lincoln the President* (4 vols., New York: Dodd, Mead & Company, 1946–1955, IV, *Last Full Measure*, coauthored with Richard N. Current), IV, 326–30, for Greeley's and Blair's peace efforts.

65. Jefferson Davis, Richmond, Va., January 12, 1865. To F. P. Blair, Esq. Richardson, ed., *Messages and Papers of the Confederacy*, I, 521.

66. A. Lincoln, Washington, Jan. 18, 1865, to F. P. Blair, Esq. Autograph Letter Signed, Illinois Historical Society, Springfield, Illinois; Autograph Draft Signed, The Robert Todd Lincoln Collection of the Papers of Abraham Lincoln, Library of Congress; Autograph Letter Signed, Henry E. Huntington Library, Art Gallery, and Botanical Gardens, San Marino, California; Autograph Letter Signed copy, Fred L. Emerson Foundation, Auburn, New York, Abraham Lincoln, *The Collected Works of Abraham Lincoln*, Roy P. Basler, ed.; Marion Dolores Pratt and Lloyd A. Dunlop, asst. eds. (9 vols. inc. index, The Abraham Lincoln Association, Springfield, Illinois; New Brunswick: Rutgers University Press, 1953; index, 1955), VIII, 220–21, quotation from 221.

67. Jefferson Davis, Richmond, January 28, 1865. To Alex H. Stephens, Robert M. T. Hunter, John A. Campbell, Richardson, ed., *Messages and Papers of the Confederacy*, I, 529. For the Stephens-Hunter-Campbell peace effort and the subsequent Hampton Roads conference, see Randall and Current, *Lincoln the President*, IV, 329–30; Catton, *Grant Takes Command*, pp. 419–22; Thomas, *Confederate Nation*, pp. 294–95. For Campbell's resignation from the Supreme Court, Charles Warren, *The Supreme Court in United States History* (Revised Edition, 2 vols., Boston, Toronto: Little, Brown and Company, 1926), II, 1836–1918, 375; for his appointment as Assistant Secretary of War, Chesnut, *Mary Chesnut's Civil War*, ed. Woodward, p. 479n. For Benjamin as Secretary of War, Thomas, *Confederate Nation*, p. 149.

68. U. S. Grant Lt Genl, from City Point Va. Feby 1st. 10.30 P. M. 1865, to Hon. Edwin M. Stanton, Secy of War, copy with Autograph Document, Robert Todd Lincoln

Collection, LC; Document Signed, National Archives, RG233, Abraham Lincoln, Executive Mansion, February 10th, 1865. To the Honorable, the House of Representatives, Basler, ed., *Works of Lincoln*, VIII, 274–85, Grant's letter on 282. Lincoln told the House, same page: "This despatch of Gen. Grant changed my purpose. . . ." Grant's letter also appears, with slight variations, in O.R., XLVI, pt. 2 (serial 97, 1895), 342–43.

69. Roland, *The Confederacy*, pp. 282–83; Frank E. Vandiver, *Their Tattered Flags: The Epic of the Confederacy* (New York and Evanston: A Harper's Magazine Press Book, Published in Association with Harper & Row, 1970), p. 293, the latter especially for the second meeting with Hunter.

70. Abraham Lincoln, December 6, 1864. To Fellow-citizens of the Senate and House of Representatives. Document Signed, National Archives, RG46A, Senate 38A fl; Document Signed, The Rosenbach Company, Philadelphia and New York, Basler, ed., *Works of Lincoln*, VIII, 136–53, quotation from 149.

71. *The Congressional Globe*, XXXIV, pt. 2, 38th Congress, 1st Session, *March 7, 1864 to April 29, 1864*, New Series No. 99, Saturday, April 9, 1864, proceedings of April 18, 1864, 1490; ibid., XXXIV, pt. 4, *June 14 to July 14, 1864*, New Series, No. 187, Thursday, June 16, 1864, proceedings of June 15, 2977 for amendment, 2977–92 and No. 188, Friday, June 17, 1864, 2993–95 for debate, 2995 for vote.

72. In his annual message to Congress of December 6, 1864, Lincoln said (Basler, ed., *Works of Lincoln*, VIII, 149): "In this case the common end is the maintenance of the Union; and, among the means to secure that end, such will, through the election, is most clearly declared in favor of such constitutional amendment [to abolish slavery]."

73. Randall and Current, *Lincoln the President*, IV, 303; Nicolay and Hay, *Lincoln*, X, 77–78.

74. Randall and Current, *Lincoln the President*, IV, 309–10, 311–12; David Herbert Donald, *Lincoln* (New York, London, Toronto, Sydney, Tokyo, Singapore, 1995), p. 554; Phillip Shaw Paludan, *The Presidency of Abraham Lincoln* (Lawrence: University Press of Kansas, 1994), pp. 301–302; Isaac N. Arnold, *The Life of Abraham Lincoln* (Chicago: Jensen, McClurg & Co., 1885), pp. 358–59.

75. Randall and Current, *Lincoln the President*, IV, 310–13. Amendment [X.] provides: "The powers not delegated to the United States by the Constitution, nor prohibited by it to the States, are reserved to the States respectively, or to the people." U.S. Constitution, 103rd Congress, 1st Session, Senate Document No. 103–6 (serial 14152), *The Constitution of the United States of America: Analysis and Interpretation: Annotations of Cases Decided in the Supreme Court of the United States to June 29, 1992*. Prepared by the Congressional Research Service, Library of Congress, Johnny H. Killian, George A. Costello, co-editors (Washington: U.S. Government Printing Office, 1996), p. 27.

76. *Cong. Globe*, XXXV, pt. 1, 38th Congress, 2nd Session, and Special Session of the Senate, *December 5, 1864 to March 3, 1865*, New Series, No. 34, Thursday, February 2, 1865, proceedings of January 31, 1865, 531; Randall and Current, *Lincoln the President*, IV, 313. The text reads:

Amendment XIII.
1. Neither slavery nor involuntary servitude, except as a punishment for crime whereof the party shall have been duly convicted, shall exist within the United States, or any place subject to their jurisdiction.
2. Congress shall have power to enforce this article by appropriate legislation. (U.S. Constitution, 103rd Congress, 1st Session, Senate Document No. 103–6 (serial 14152) *Constitution of the United States*, p. 30.)

77. Randall and Current, *Lincoln the President*, IV, 313–14; Donald, *Lincoln*, p. 554.

78. Response to a Serenade, February 1, 1865, from *New York Tribune*, Feb. 3, 1865, p. 5, col. 3, Basler, ed., *Works of Lincoln*, VIII, 254–55.

79. Ibid., p. 254.

80. Randall and Current, *Lincoln the President*, IV, 315; Randall and Donald, *Civil War and Reconstruction*, pp. 346, 397.

81. Thirty-seventh Congress. Session II. (Statute II.) Chap. CXCV. — An Act to suppress Insurrection, to punish Treason and Rebellion, to seize and confiscate the Property of Rebels, and for other Purposes. Approved, July 17, 1862. U.S., Laws, statutes, *The Statutes at Large of the United States of America*, 1789–1873 (17 vols., I–IX, Boston: Charles C. Little and J. Brown, 1845–1854; X–XVII, Boston: Little, Brown, and Company, 1855–1873), 12 (December 5, 1859–March 3, 1863) (1863), 589–92; *Cong. Globe*, XXXII, pt. 4, 37th Congress, 2nd Session, *June 22, 1862 to July 17, 1862*, Appendix, 412–13. For Lincoln's rejection, [Abraham Lincoln] July 17, 1862, to Fellow-Citizens of the Senate and House of Representatives, and to Fellow Citizens of the House of Representatives, Autograph Draft, Robert Todd Lincoln Collection, LC, Basler, ed., *Works of Lincoln*, V, 328, 328–31. The reader should recall that Article. III. Section 3. of the Constitution states: "The Congress shall have power to declare the punishment of treason, but no attainder of treason shall work corruption of blood, or forfeiture except during the life of the person attainted." U.S. Constitution, 103rd Congress, 1st Session, Senate Document No. 103–6 (serial 14152), *Constitution of the United States*, p. 16.

82. Thirty-seventh Congress. Session II. (Statute II.) Chap. XCVIII. — An Act for the Collection of direct taxes in Insurrectionary Districts within the United States, and for other Purposes. Approved, June 7, 1861. 12 *Statutes at Large*, 422–26; *Cong. Globe*, XXXII, pt. 4, Appendix, 361–62.

83. Willie Lee Rose, *Rehearsal for Reconstruction: The Port Royal Experiment*, Introduction by Comer Vann Woodward (Indianapolis and New York: A Brown Thrasher Book, The Bobbs-Merrill Company, Inc., Publishers, 1964), pp. 201–202; Thirty-seventh Congress. Session III. (Statute III.) Chap. XXI. — An Act to amend an Act entitled "An Act for the Collection of Direct Taxes in Insurrectionary Districts within the United States and for other Purposes," approved June seven eighteen hundred and sixty-two. Approved, February 6, 1863. 12 *Statutes at Large* 640–641; *Cong. Globe*, XXXIII, pt. 2, 37th Congress, 3rd Session, *February 12, 1863 to March 14, 1863*, Appendix, 182.

84. Rose, *Rehearsal for Reconstruction*, pp. 214–15.

85. Abraham Lincoln, September 16, 1863, To the Hon: Abraham D. Smith, Hon: William E. Wording, and Hon: William Henry Brisbane, Tax Commissioners for the District of South Carolina: Document Signed, National Archives, FI RG 58, Direct Tax Commission of South Carolina, Basler, ed., *Works of Lincoln*, VI, 453–59, particularly 456–57; Rose, *Rehearsal for Reconstruction*, pp. 275–81, particularly 275 for statistics and 275n for acreage involved in Lincoln's plan; James M. McPherson, *The Struggle for Equality: Abolitionists and the Negro in the Civil War and Reconstruction* (Princeton, New Jersey: Princeton University Press, 1964), pp. 249–55, particular 253 for February 18, 1864 auction.

86. By command of Major-General Banks. Rich'd. B. Irwin, Lieutenant-Colonel [U.S.A.], Assistant Adjutant-General. General Orders, No. 12. Hdqrs. Department of the Gulf, New Orleans, January 29, 1963. O.R., XV (serial 21, 1886), 666–67; By command of Major-General Banks, George B. Drake [Lieutenant-Colonel, U.S.A.], Assistant Adjutant-General, General Orders, No. 23. Hdqrs. Department of the Gulf, February 3, 1864. Ibid., XXXIV, pt. 2 (serial 62, 1891), 227–31.

87. McPherson, *Struggle for Equality*, pp. 289–93; LaWanda Cox, *Lincoln and Black Freedom: A Study in Presidential Leadership* (Columbia: University of South Carolina Press, 1981), pp. 75, 111, 122, 131–33.

88. Article. III. Section. 3, 103rd Congress, 1st Session, Senate Document No. 103–6 (serial 14152) *Constitution of the United States*, p. 16.

89. McPherson, *Struggle for Equality*, pp. 249, 253–57, 259.

90. By order of Maj. Gen. W. T. Sherman: L. M. Dayton, Assistant Adjutant-General. Special Field Orders, No. 15. Hdqrs. Mil. Div. of the Mississippi, In the Field, Savannah, Ga., January 16, 1865. *O.R.*, XLVII, pt. 2 (serial 99, 1895), 60–62, quotation from [Paragraph] I., 60.

91. Ibid., I., p. 60 for "abandoned," III., p. 61 for other quotations.

92. Ibid., VI., p. 62.

93. Ibid., II., p. 61, V., pp. 61–62.

94. McPherson, *Struggle for Equality*, p. 258.

95. Rose, *Rehearsal for Reconstruction*, pp. 328–30; for Saxton's rank, "Saxton, Rufus," Francis B. Heitman, *Historical Register and Dictionary of the United States Army, From Its Organization September 23, 1789, to March 2, 1903*. Published under act of Congress approved March 2, 1903. 57th Congress, Second Session, House Document 446 (serial 4536). (2 vols., Washington: Government Printing Office, 1903), I, 862.

96. For 40,000 figure, McPherson, *Struggle for Equality*, p. 259, Rose, *Rehearsal for Reconstruction*, p. 330, and p. 331 for 5,000 figure; Thirty-eighth Congress. Session II. Statute II. Chap. XC. — An Act to establish a Bureau for the Relief of Freedmen and Refugees. Approved, March 3, 1865. 13 *Statutes at Large* (December 1863, to December, 1865) (1866) 507–509, for abandoned lands, Sec. 4, 508–509, quotations from 508; *Cong. Globe*, XXXV, pt. 2, 38th Congress, 2nd Session, *February 17, 1865 to March 11, 1865*, Appendix, 141.

97. Andrew Johnson. By the President: William H. Seward, Secretary of State. [May 29, 1865] By the President of the United States of America. A Proclamation. U.S. President, *A Compilation of the Messages and Papers of the Presidents, 1789–1908* (With Revisions.) James D. Richardson, ed. (11 vols., Washington: Bureau of National Literature and Art, 1911), VI, 310–12, 310 for grant of amnesty, 310–11 for oath, 311–12 for exemptions, quotation from 310; Eric L. McKitrick, *Andrew Johnson and Reconstruction* (Chicago: University of Chicago Press, 1960), p. 49; McPherson, *Struggle for Equality*, p. 320.

98. For Johnson's land policy, Rose, *Rehearsal for Reconstruction*, pp. 351–52; for his order to Howard, ibid., pp. 352–53; for Howard's visit to sea islands, ibid., pp. 353–56, McPherson, *Struggle for Equality*, pp. 408–409; for removal of Saxton, Rose, *Rehearsal for Reconstruction*, pp. 356–57, McPherson, *Struggle for Equality*, p. 409 including date; for Howard's appointment, Rose, *Rehearsal for Reconstruction*, p. 339, "Howard, Oliver Otis," Boatner, *Civil War Dictionary*, pp. 413–14, particularly 413 including date.

99. Thirty-ninth Congress. Session I. (Statute I.) Chap. CC. — An Act to continue in force and to amend "An Act to establish a Bureau for the Relief of Freedmen and Refugees," and for other Purposes. 14 *Statutes at Large* (December, 1865, to March, 1867) (1868), 173–77, overriding of veto, 177, Sec. 11 on restoration of lands, 176; *Cong. Globe*, XXXVI, pt. 5, 39th Congress, 1st Session, *July 16, 1866 to July 28, 1866*, Appendix, 366–67, overriding of veto, 367, Sec. 11, 367; McPherson, *Struggle for Equality*, pp. 347–49, 409; George R. Bentley, *A History of the Freedmen's Bureau* (Philadelphia: University of Pennsylvania Press, 1955), p. 134.

100. McPherson, *Struggle for Equality*, pp. 308–309.

## 13. The Fires Die

1. For Liddell Hart on Sherman, see Basil Henry Liddell Hart, *Sherman: Soldier, Realist, American* (New York: Frederick A. Praeger, Publisher, 1958), especially pp. vii–viii, and the same author's *Strategy* (Second Revised Edition, New York: Frederick A. Praeger, Publisher, 1967), especially p. 153. For the interpretation of Sherman and of campaigns aimed at the enemy's economy and population in the textbook of the later-nineteenth-century American military critic Captain John Bigelow, 10th Cavalry, see Bigelow's *The Principles of Strategy Illustrated Mainly from American Campaigns*

(Thomas E. Griess and Jay Luvaas, eds., *The West Point Military Library*, New York: Greenwood, 1968, reprint of Second Edition, Revised and Enlarged, Philadelphia: J. B. Lippincott Company, 1894), pp. 144–47, 224–26, 229, 263.

2. For Schofield's criticisms, see his notes on various campaigns, John M. Schofield Papers, Box 93, Library of Congress.

3. For numbers, "Franklin and Nashville Campaign," Mark Mayo Boatner III, *The Civil War Dictionary* (Revised Edition, New York: Vintage Books, A Division of Random House, Inc., 1991), pp. 305–309, particularly 307. See also Albert Castel, *Decision in the West: The Atlanta Campaign of 1864* (Lawrence: University Press of Kansas, 1992), p. 555; Thomas Lawrence Connelly, *Autumn of Glory: The Army of Tennessee, 1862–1865* (Baton Rouge: Louisiana State University Press, 1971), pp. 489–91.

4. "Division of the West, Confed.," Boatner, *Civil War Dictionary*, p. 241, including date; Connelly, *Autumn of Glory*, p. 472.

5. Thomas L. Livermore, *Numbers and Losses in the Civil War in America* (Second Edition, Boston and New York: Houghton, Mifflin and Company, 1901; reprint, Dayton, Ohio: Morningside, 1986), pp. 131 (Union), 132 (Confederate) for total casualties; "Franklin," Boatner, *Civil War Dictionary*, pp. 304–305, particularly 305 for Confederate generals killed; Castel, *Decision in the West*, pp. 556–57, 556 for the numbers attacking, 557 for the Confederate generals; Connelly, *Autumn of Glory*, pp. 503–506. The best overview of the battle and of the campaign of which it was a part is Wiley Sword, *Embrace an Angry Wind: The Confederacy's Last Hurrah: Spring Hill, Franklin, and Nashville* (New York: HarperCollins, 1991).

6. Schofield's notes on a paper by J. H. Chalmers, "Forrest and His Campaigns," Schofield Papers, Box 93, LC.

7. For Smith's numbers, Shelby Foote, *The Civil War: A Narrative* (3 vols., New York: Random House, 1958–1974), III, *Red River to Appomattox*, 681; for the status of his troops, "XVI Corps," Boatner, *Civil War Dictionary*, pp. 195–96, particularly 196.

8. Livermore, *Numbers and Losses*, p. 132 for Union strength, p. 133 for Union losses and Confederate statistics. For the battle, in addition to the sources already cited for the campaign, "Nashville," Boatner, *Civil War Dictionary*, pp. 579–82; Connelly, *Autumn of Glory*, pp. 507–13. On Thomas's relations with his superiors, it is worth noting Sherman's unfair, even prevaricating descriptions of his efforts in the Atlanta campaign, as reported in Castel, *Decision in the West*, pp. 284–85, 539, 571. Logan commanded the Fifteenth Corps December 11, 1863 to July 22, 1864 (when he took temporary command of the Army of the Tennessee in place of McPherson), July 27–September 23, 1864 and again January 8–May 23, 1865; "Logan, John Alexander," Boatner, *Civil War Dictionary*, pp. 486–87, particularly 487.

9. Allan Nevins, *Ordeal of the Union* (8 vols., *Ordeal of the Union*, I, *Fruits of Manifest Destiny 1847–1852; Ordeal of the Union*, II, *A House Dividing 1852–1857* [New York, London: Charles Scribner's Sons, 1947]; III, *The Emergence of Lincoln*, I, *Douglas, Buchanan, and Party Chaos 1857–1859;* IV, *The Emergence of Lincoln*, II, *Prologue to Civil War 1859–1860* [New York: Charles Scribner's Sons, 1950]; V, *The War for the Union*, I, *The Improvised War 1861–1862* [New York: Charles Scribner's Sons, 1959]; VI, *The War for the Union*, II, *War Becomes Revolution* [New York: Charles Scribner's Sons, 1960]; VII, *The War for the Union*, III, *The Organized War 1863–1864;* VIII, *The War for the Union*, IV, *The Organized War to Victory 1864–1865* [New York: Charles Scribner's Sons, 1971]), *Ordeal of the Union*, VIII, *War for the Union*, IV, 188, quoting Thomas R. Hay, *Hood's Tennessee Campaign* (New York: W. Neale, 1929), p. 181.

10. William T. Sherman, *Memoirs of General William T. Sherman by Himself* (2 vols., New York: D. Appleton & Company, 1875), II, 249.

11. Lloyd Lewis, *Sherman: Fighting Prophet* (New York: Harcourt, Brace and Company, 1932), p. 467; see pp. 467–88 for a discussion of Sherman's stay in Savannah.

12. W. T. Sherman, Major-General, Headquarters Military Division of the Missis-

sippi, In the Field, Savannah, Georgia, December 24, 1864. To Maj. Gen. H. W. Halleck, Chief of Staff, Washington City, D.C., U.S. War Department, *The War of the Rebellion: A Compilation of the Official Records of the Union and Confederate Armies* (four series, 70 vols. in 128, Washington: Government Printing Office, 1880–1901), Series One, XLIV (serial 92, 1893), 798–800, quotation from 799. Hereafter cited as *O.R.*; references are to Series One unless otherwise specified. Quoted passage also in Sherman, *Memoirs*, II, 226–28, quotation from 228. For Grant's acceding to Sherman's views, U. S. Grant, Lieutenant-General. Headquarters Armies of the United States. City Point, Va. December 27, 1864. To Maj. Gen. W. T. Sherman, Commanding Military Division of the Mississippi. *O.R.*, XLIV (serial 92), 820–22.

13. H. W. Halleck, Major-General and Chief of Staff. Headquarters of the Army, Washington, January 1, 1865. (Received 12th.) To Maj. Gen. W. T. Sherman, Savannah, Ga. *O.R.*, XLVII, pt. 2 (serial 99, 1895), 3–4, quotation from 3. For Butler's strength, "Fort Fisher, N. C., 7–27 Dec. '64," Boatner, *Civil War Dictionary*, pp. 292–93, particularly 293. The history of the defense of Fort Fisher against Butler is told in detail in Rod Gragg, *Confederate Goliath: The Battle of Fort Fisher* (New York: HarperCollins Publishers, 1991), pp. 30–78. See also Edward G. Longacre, *Army of Amateurs: General Benjamin F. Butler and the Army of the James, 1863–1865* (Mechanicsburg, PA: Stackpole Books, 1997), pp. 231–37, 245–59.

14. "Terry, Alfred Howe," Boatner, *Civil War Dictionary*, p. 831; "Fort Fisher, N. C., 6–15 '65," ibid., pp. 293–95, particularly 293 for the Provisional Corps and its commanding general; Gragg, *Confederate Goliath*, pp. 101–236 for the campaign.

15. "Fort Fisher, N. C., 6–15 Jan. '65," Boatner, *Civil War Dictionary*, p. 294.

16. Gragg, *Confederate Goliath*, pp. 245–47.

17. "Terry, Alfred Howe," Boatner, *Civil War Dictionary*, p. 831; "XXIII Corps," ibid., pp. 199–200, particularly 200. On January 31, 1865, Schofield became commanding general of a reestablished Department of North Carolina (earlier abolished July 15, 1863); ibid., p. 200, and for abolition and re-creation, "North Carolina, Union Department of," ibid., pp. 598–99, particularly 599.

18. "Carolinas Campaign," ibid., pp. 123–27, particularly 125; "Hampton, Wade," ibid., pp. 370–71, particularly 371 for Hampton's promotion; Lewis, *Sherman: Fighting Prophet*, pp. 488–89; John F. Marszalek, *Sherman: A Soldier's Passion for Order* (New York: The Free Press, A Division of Macmillan, Inc.; Toronto: Maxwell Macmillan Canada; New York, Oxford, Singapore, Sydney: Maxwell Macmillan International, 1993), pp. 317–18.

19. For Confederate numbers, "Carolinas Campaign," Boatner, *Civil War Dictionary*, p. 125.

20. Lewis, *Sherman: Fighting Prophet*, pp. 488–92, particularly 490 for Hardee's hope, 491 for the days of rain; Marszalek, *Sherman*, pp. 317–18.

21. Lewis, *Sherman: Fighting Prophet*, p. 490.

22. Ibid., p. 489.

23. Sherman, *Memoirs*, II, 254.

24. Ibid.

25. Lewis, *Sherman: Fighting Prophet*, p. 496.

26. The burning of Charleston is carefully dissected in Charles Royster, *The Destructive War: William Tecumseh Sherman, Stonewall Jackson, and the Americans* (New York: Alfred A. Knopf, 1991), Chapter 1, "The Destruction of Columbia," pp. 3–33; see also Lewis, *Sherman: Fighting Prophet*, pp. 500–508; Marszalek, *Sherman*, pp. 322–25. On the destructiveness of the march through South Carolina generally, see Mark Grimsley, *The Hard Hand of War: Union Military Policy toward Southern Civilians, 1861–1865* (Cambridge; New York; Oakleigh, Melbourne, Australia: Cambridge University Press, 1995), pp. 201–204, 202 for Columbia.

27. Samuel Francis Du Pont, *Samuel Francis Du Pont: A Selection from His Civil War Letters*, John D. Hayes, ed. (3 vols., Ithaca, New York: Published for the Eleutherian Mills Historical Library, Cornell University Press, 1969), I, *The Mission: 1860–1862*, Introduction, xc, for Dahlgren's succession; Albert Gleaves, *Life and Letters of Rear Admiral Stephen B. Luce, U.S. Navy, Founder of the Naval War College* (New York & London: G. P. Putnam's Sons. The Knickerbocker Press, 1925), p. 102 for Charleston and the conception of the Naval War College.

28. "Tennessee, Confederate Army of," Boatner, *Civil War Dictionary*, pp. 828–29, particularly 829.

29. For Johnston's 1865 campaign against Sherman, see Craig L. Symonds, *Joseph E. Johnston: A Civil War Biography* (New York, London: W. W. Norton & Company, 1992), pp. 344–53; Lewis, *Sherman: Fighting Prophet*, pp. 508–17, 527–30; Marszalek, *Sherman*, pp. 325–30; Connelly, *Autumn of Glory*, pp. 520–31. The three full generals were Johnston, Beauregard, and Bragg; "Tennessee, Confederate Army of," Boatner, *Civil War Dictionary*, p. 829.

30. Liddell Hart, *Sherman*, pp. 389–90, and also for Howard's views, Lewis, *Sherman: Fighting Prophet*, p. 516; Sherman, *Memoirs*, II, 304. For the battle of Bentonville, Symonds, *Johnston*, pp. 348–51; Lewis, *Sherman: Fighting Prophet*, pp. 515–16; Connelly, *Autumn of Glory*, pp. 526–29.

31. W. T. Sherman, Major-General Commanding. Hdqrs. Military Division of the Mississippi, In the Field, Atlanta, Ga., September 12, 1864. To James M. Calhoun, Mayor, E. E. Rawson, and S. C. Wells, Representing City Council of Atlanta. O.R., XXXIX, pt. 2 (serial 77, 1892), 418–19, quotation from 419; Sherman, *Memoirs*, II, 125–27, quotation from 127.

32. "Carolinas Campaign," Boatner, *Civil War Dictionary*, p. 126 for Confederate strength, p. 127 for Union strength.

33. Lewis, *Sherman: Fighting Prophet*, p. 521 for Sherman's departure; Walter Birkbeck Wood and James E. Edmonds, *A History of the Civil War in the United States, 1861–5* (New York: G. P. Putnam's Sons; London: Methuen & Co., 1905), pp. 465–66 for the length of marches.

34. Douglas Southall Freeman, *R. E. Lee: A Biography* (4 vols., New York: Charles Scribner's Sons; London: Charles Scribner's Sons, Ltd., 1934–1935), IV, 503, citing John William Jones, *Life and Letters of Robert E. Lee, Soldier and Man* (New York and Washington: The Neale Publishing Company, 1906), p. 145.

35. Freeman, *Lee*, III (1934), 497, 499, 516–17, 541–42; IV, 5–6, 25; Douglas Southall Freeman, *Lee's Lieutenants: A Study in Command* (3 vols., New York: Charles Scribner's Sons, 1942–1944), III, *Gettysburg to Appomattox*, 623–24.

36. Noah Andre Trudeau, *The Last Citadel: Petersburg, Virginia June 1864–April 1865* (Baton Rouge: Louisiana State University Press, 1991), pp. 158–74, which begins with Warren in position on August 17; Bruce Catton, *Grant Takes Command* (Boston, Toronto: Little, Brown and Company, 1969), pp. 350–51; "Globe Tavern," Boatner, *Civil War Dictionary*, pp. 345–46; Freeman, *Lee*, III, 485–88; Freeman, *Lee's Lieutenants*, III, 588–89; James I. Robertson, Jr., *A. P. Hill: The Story of a Confederate Warrior* (New York: Random House, 1987), pp. 296–98.

37. "Reams's Station," Boatner, *Civil War Dictionary*, p. 683 for losses; Trudeau, *Last Citadel*, pp. 177–91; Bruce Catton, *A Stillness at Appomattox* (Garden City, New York: Doubleday & Company, Inc., 1953), p. 320; Catton, *Grant Takes Command*, p. 352; Freeman, *Lee's Lieutenants*, III, 589–90; Robertson, *A. P. Hill*, pp. 298–301. Gibbon had been promoted on June 7, "Gibbon, John," Boatner, *Civil War Dictionary*, pp. 340–41, particularly 340.

38. Livermore, *Numbers and Losses*, p. 128 for Federal numbers and losses and Confederate losses, p. 129 for Confederates engaged. An account of this action and the

immediately following late September and early October battles south of the James is Richard J. Sommers, *Richmond Redeemed: The Siege at Petersburg*, Foreword by Frank E. Vandiver (Garden City, New York: Doubleday & Company, Inc., 1981), pp. 1–176 for north of the James. See also Trudeau, *Last Citadel*, pp. 209–17; Catton, *Grant Takes Command*, pp. 366–67; Freeman, *Lee*, III, 499–504; Freeman, *Lee's Lieutenants*, III, 590–94: Longacre, *Army of Amateurs*, pp. 211–20. For Ewell's assignment to the Department of Richmond, "Richmond, Va., Confederate Department and Defenses of," Boatner, *Civil War Dictionary*, p. 698. "Anderson, Richard Heron ('Dick')," ibid., p. 14, gives his promotion to lieutenant-general May 31, 1864.

39. For losses, "Poplar Springs Church, Va. (Peeble's Farm, Pegram's Farm)," Boatner, *Civil War Dictionary*, p. 367. For the most authoritative account, Sommers, *Richmond Redeemed*, pp. 177–418. See also Trudeau, *Last Citadel*, pp. 212–17; Catton, *Grant Takes Command*, p. 367; Robertson, *A. P. Hill*, pp. 303–304.

40. Trudeau, *Last Citadel*, pp. 224–25, 228–30, 237–41, 247–48, particularly 248 for casualties; Longacre, *Army of Amateurs*, pp. 229–31. For Weitzel's command, "XVIII Corps," Boatner, *Civil War Dictionary*, pp. 197–98, particularly 198; for Longstreet's return, "Longstreet, James," ibid., pp. 490–91, particularly 491.

41. Livermore, *Numbers and Losses*, p. 131 for casualties; Trudeau, *Last Citadel*, pp. 225–28, 230–37, 241–47, 248–53; Catton, *Grant Takes Command*, p. 381; Freeman, *Lee*, III, 513–14; Freeman, *Lee's Lieutenants*, III, 615–16; Robertson, *A. P. Hill*, pp. 306–307.

42. Trudeau, *Last Citadel*, pp. 263–85; Freeman, *Lee*, 521; Robertson, *A. P. Hill*, pp. 308–309.

43. Freeman, *Lee*, III, 518 for Confederate numbers; for Union, Richard Wayne Lykes, *Campaign for Petersburg* (National Park Service History Series, Washington, D.C.: National Park Service, U.S. Department of the Interior, 1970), p. 44.

44. For City Point, Catton, *Stillness at Appomattox*, pp. 321–22; for Confederate hunger, Freeman, *Lee's Lieutenants*, III, 619–20, particularly 620 for short rations in January.

45. Trudeau, *Last Citadel*, pp. 312–22, particularly 322 for casualties; "Dabney's Mills, Va. (Hatcher's Run; Boydton Road; Armstrong's Mill; Rowanty Creek; Vaughan Road), 5–7 February '65," Boatner, *Civil War Dictionary*, p. 217.

46. Lykes, *Campaign for Petersburg*, p. 63.

47. Robertson, *A. P. Hill*, pp. 3–4, 11–12, 22–23, 25–26, 28, 134, 206, 249–50, 260–62, 268, 272, 299, 310, 313.

48. Trudeau, *Last Citadel*, pp. 334–36; Freeman, *Lee*, IV, 14–17; Freeman, *Lee's Lieutenants*, III, 645–47. For Gordon's promotion to major-general, "Gordon, John Brown," Boatner, *Civil War Dictionary*, pp. 348–49, particularly 348.

49. For lower Confederate casualty estimates, Trudeau, *Last Citadel*, p. 354, for higher, Freeman, *Lee's Lieutenants*, III, 651, Foote, *Civil War*, III, 843; for Federal losses, Trudeau, *Last Citadel*, p. 353. For accounts of the battle, Trudeau, *Last Citadel*, pp. 335–54; Freeman, *Lee*, IV, 17–21; Freeman, *Lee's Lieutenants*, III, 647–54; Catton, *Grant Takes Command*, pp. 434–35; Catton, *Stillness at Appomattox*, pp. 335–38.

50. "Waynesboro," Boatner, *Civil War Dictionary*, pp. 897–98; Freeman, *Lee's Lieutenants*, III, 635–36; Catton, *Stillness at Appomattox*, pp. 341–42.

51. "Cavalry Corps, Union Army of the Potomac," Boatner, *Civil War Dictionary*, pp. 201–202, particularly 202 for the corps organization; "Gregg, David McMurtrie," "Crook, George," ibid., pp. 357, 209 for Crook's succeeding Gregg in command of the 2nd Division.

52. P. H. Sheridan, *Personal Memoirs of P. H. Sheridan, General United States Army* (2 vols., New York: Charles L. Webster & Company, 1888), II, 128; Roy Morris, Jr.,

*Sheridan: The Life and Wars of General Phil Sheridan* (New York: Crown Publishers, Inc., 1992), p. 241; for Sheridan's authority to remove Warren, Catton, *Grant Takes Command*, p. 444.

53. "Lee, Fitzhugh," Boatner, *Civil War Dictionary*, p. 475.

54. For Five Forks, Trudeau, *Last Citadel*, pp. 390–96; Noah Andre Trudeau, *Out of the Storm: The End of the Civil War, April–June 1865* (Boston, New York, Toronto, London: Little, Brown and Company, 1994), pp. 19–47; Freeman, *Lee's Lieutenants*, III, 657–80; Freeman, *Lee*, IV, 22–49; Catton, *Stillness at Appomattox*, pp. 346–47, 351–63; Catton, *Grant Takes Command*, pp. 442–45; Morris, *Sheridan*, pp. 245–51.

55. R. E. Lee, General. Headquarters Army of Northern Virginia, April 2, 1865. To Hon. Secretary of War, Richmond, Va. O.R., XLVI, pt. 3 (serial 97, 1894), 1195. For Breckinridge's appointment, "Breckinridge, John Cabell," Boatner, *Civil War Dictionary*, pp. 82–83, particularly 83. He had been promoted to major-general April 14, 1862; ibid., p. 83.

56. Freeman, *Lee*, IV, 49–50 for Davis and the message from Lee; Alfred Hoyt Bill, *The Beleaguered City: Richmond, 1861–1865* (New York: Alfred A. Knopf, 1946), pp. 269–75 for the evacuation (including 270 for Davis's receipt of Lee's message); Emory M. Thomas, *The Confederate Nation 1861–1865* (New York, Hagerstown, San Francisco, London: Harper & Row, Publishers, 1979), p. 300 for the evacuation, pp. 300–301 for Davis's trip to Danville.

57. For the Appomattox campaign, see Trudeau, *Out of the Storm*, Chapter Four, "The Death of an Army," pp. 89–116 and 117–32; Freeman, *Lee*, IV, 50–121; Freeman, *Lee's Lieutenants*, III, 679–729; Catton, *Grant Takes Command*, pp. 448–56; Catton, *Stillness at Appomattox*, pp. 365–80.

58. Trudeau, *Out of the Storm*, pp. 27–28, 30, 32, 44–45, 398–418; Morris, *Sheridan*, pp. 245, 247–51, 376–77; Catton, *Grant Takes Command*, pp. 442–45.

59. Freeman, *Lee's Lieutenants*, III, 703–11, particularly 711 for total casualties.

60. John B. Gordon, *Reminiscences of the Civil War* (New York: Charles Scribner's Sons, 1903), p. 438. Freeman, *Lee's Lieutenants*, III, 729n, without citing a source, gives a later, more grandiloquent version.

61. James Longstreet, *From Manassas to Appomattox: Memoirs of the Civil War in America* (Philadelphia: J. B. Lippincott Company, 1896), p. 625.

62. U. S. Grant, Lieutenant-General, Commanding Armies of the United States, Headquarters Armies of the United States, April 7, 1865 — 5 p.m. To General R. E. Lee, Commanding C. S. Army. O.R., XLVI, pt. 3 (serial 97), 619. This account of the surrender negotiations is based largely on Freeman, *Lee*, IV, 120–48; Freeman, *Lee's Lieutenants*, III, 729–43; Catton, *Grant Takes Command*, pp. 456–68; Trudeau, *Out of the Storm*, pp. 133–49.

63. R. E. Lee, General, April 7, 1865. To Lieut. Gen. U. S. Grant, Commanding Armies of the United States. O.R., XLVI, pt. 3 (serial 97), 619.

64. R. E. Lee, General. April 9, 1865. To Lieut. Gen. U. S. Grant, Commanding U.S. Armies: Ibid., p. 664.

65. For the number surrendered, Tabular statement of officers and men of the Confederate Army paroled at Appomattox Courthouse. [Compiled from parole lists.] Ibid., pt. 1 (serial 95, 1894), 1277–79, recapitulation 1279. For the ceremonies, Joshua Lawrence Chamberlain, *The Passing of the Armies: An Account of the Final Campaign of the Army of the Potomac, Based upon Personal Reminiscences of the Fifth Army Corps* (New York, and London: G. P. Putnam's Sons, 1915), pp. 257–66; Freeman, *Lee's Lieutenants*, III, 744–52; Trudeau, *Out of the Storm*, pp. 149–50.

66. Nevins, *Ordeal of the Union*, VIII, *War for the Union*, IV, 297, for the flags; Trudeau, *Out of the Storm*, p. 80 giving the specific companies; "Richmond, Va., Surren-

der," Boatner, *Civil War Dictionary*, p. 699, for the formal ceremony; Nevins, *Ordeal of the Union*, VIII, *War for the Union*, IV, 296–300, and Bill, *Beleaguered City*, pp. 276–79, for the Union army's entry into the city more generally.

67. James G. Randall, *Lincoln the President* (4 vols., New York: Dodd, Mead & Company, 1946–1955), IV, *Last Full Measure*, coauthored with Richard N. Current), IV, 344–47; Bill, *Beleaguered City*, pp. 279–80.

68. A. Lincoln. Head Quarters Armies of the United States, City-Point, April 6, 1865. To Major General Weitzel Richmond, Va. Autograph Letter Signed, Library of Congress, Abraham Lincoln, *The Collected Works of Abraham Lincoln*, Roy P. Basler, ed., Marion Dolores Pratt and Lloyd A. Dunlop, asst. eds. (9 vols. inc. index, The Abraham Lincoln Association, Springfield, Illinois; New Brunswick: Rutgers University Press, 1953; index, 1955), VIII, 389; also, with slight variations, in *O.R.*, XLVI, pt. 3 (serial 97), 640; *New York Tribune*, April 8, 1865, p. 1. On Lincoln's discussion with Campbell and the latter's response, Nevins, *Ordeal of the Union*, VIII, *War for the Union*, IV, 302–306; William B. Hesseltine, *Lincoln's Plan of Reconstruction*, Introduction by Richard N. Current (Chicago: Quadrangle Paperbacks, Quadrangle Books, 1967), pp. 137–39; Randall and Current, *Lincoln the President*, IV, 353–56, 358–59.

69. Randall and Current, *Lincoln the President*, IV, 355, citing Dana to Stanton, April 7, 1865, Stanton MSS., LC.

70. Gideon Welles, *Diary of Gideon Welles, Secretary of the Navy Under Lincoln and Johnson*, Ed. Howard K. Beale, Assisted by Alan W. Brownsword, With an Introduction by Howard K. Beale and appendices drawn from Welles's correspondence (3 vols., New York: W. W. Norton & Company, Inc., 1960), II, *April 1, 1864–December 31, 1866*, Thursday, April [*sic*] 13, [1865], 279–80. On the Cabinet discussions, see Randall and Current, *Lincoln the President*, IV, 357–58; Hesseltine, *Lincoln's Plan of Reconstruction*, p. 138.

71. A. Lincoln, Office U.S. Military Telegraph, War Department, Washington, D.C., April 12, 1865, "Cypher," to Major General Weitzel, Richmond, Va. Autograph Letter Signed, National Archives, Record Group 107, Presidential Telegrams, I, 386–87, Basler, ed., *Works of Lincoln*, VIII, 406–407, quotation from 406.

72. March 4, 1865, endorsed "Original manuscript of second Inaugural presented to Major John Hay. A. Lincoln. April 10, 1865," Autograph Document, LC, Basler, ed., *Works of Lincoln*, VIII, 332–33, quotation from 333. On January 12, 1864, Hay had been commissioned major, assistant adjutant-general, U.S.V., and he was to be brevetted lieutenant-colonel, U.S.V., and colonel, U.S.V., May 31, 1865; "Hay, John," Francis B. Heitman, *Historical Register and Dictionary of the United States Army, From Its Organization, September 29, 1789, to March 2, 1903*, Published under act of Congress approved March 2, 1903. 57th Congress, 2nd Session, House Document 446 (serial 4536). (2 vols., Washington: Government Printing Office, 1903), I, 514.

73. Last Public Address, April 11, 1865, Autograph Document—Photostat, The Abraham Lincoln Association, Springfield, Illinois, Basler, ed., *Works of Lincoln*, VIII, 399–405, quotation from 399, comments on Louisiana, 401–405.

74. Frederick W. Seward, *Reminiscences of a War-Time Statesman and Diplomat, 1830–1915, by Frederick W. Seward, Assistant Secretary of State during the Administrations of Lincoln, Johnson, and Hayes* (New York: G. P. Putnam's Sons, 1916), p. 256. For the Cabinet meeting, Randall and Current, *Lincoln the President*, IV, 362–63; Nevins, *Ordeal of the Union*, VIII, *War for the Union*, IV, 332–35; Benjamin P. Thomas and Harold M. Hyman, *Stanton: The Life and Times of Lincoln's Secretary of War* (New York: Alfred A. Knopf, 1963), pp. 357–58.

75. Quoted in Frank Abiel Flower, *Edwin McMasters Stanton: The Autocrat of Rebellion, Emancipation, and Reconstruction* (Akron, Ohio: Saalfield Publishing Co., 1905), pp. 301–302.

76. Salmon P. Chase, *Inside Lincoln's Cabinet: The Civil War Diaries of Salmon P. Chase*, ed. David Donald (New York: Longmans, Green and Co., 1954), April [?], 1865, p. 268.

77. Welles, *Diaries*, Friday [April] 14, [1865,] II, 280–87, particularly 281; Randall and Current, *Lincoln the President*, IV, 362, 363.

78. Sherman, *Memoirs*, II, 326. For the conference, Randall and Current, *Lincoln the President*, IV, 351; Nevins, *Ordeal of the Union*, VIII, *War for the Union*, IV, 289–91; Catton, *Grant Takes Command*, pp. 437–39; Marszalek, *Sherman*, pp. 336–38; Lewis, *Sherman: Fighting Prophet*, pp. 521–25.

79. Sherman, *Memoirs*, II, 327.

80. David D. Porter, *The Naval History of the Civil War* (New York: The Sherman Publishing Company, 1886), pp. 794–96; Sherman, *Memoirs*, II, 328–31.

81. Lewis, *Sherman: Fighting Prophet*, pp. 544–45; Thomas and Hyman, *Stanton*, pp. 348, 413 for the failure to send the directive to Sherman. For the negotiations with Johnston, Lewis, *Sherman: Fighting Prophet*, pp. 527–44, 554–56; Marszalek, *Sherman*, pp. 338–49; Symonds, *Johnston*, pp. 353–57; Thomas and Hyman, *Stanton*, pp. 405–14.

82. Lewis, *Sherman: Fighting Prophet*, p. 539, citing a letter to Brigadier-General, U.S.V., John A. Rawlins.

83. For Johnston's numbers, Foote, *Civil War*, III, 996.

84. Nevins, *Ordeal of the Union*, VIII, *War for the Union*, IV, 305.

85. Sherman, *Memoirs*, II, 327.

86. Everette B. Long, with Barbara Long, *The Civil War Day by Day: An Almanac 1861–1865*, Foreword by Bruce Catton (Garden City, New York: Doubleday & Company, Inc., 1971), pp. 710–11 for Union Army and total casualties, 711 for Federal Navy casualties, 712 for World War II casualties. See also Introduction, n7, p. 815 above. The total population of the United States in 1940 was 150,622,754; in the Continental United States, 131,669,275; U.S. Bureau of the Census, Vincent P. Barabba, Director; U.S. Department of Commerce, Rogers C. B. Morton, Secretary; James L. Pate, Assistant Secretary for Economic Affairs, *Historical Statistics of the United States: Colonial Times to 1970* (2 parts [vols.], Washington, D.C.: U.S. Government Printing Office, 1975), Part I, Series A9, p. 9, and A1, p. 8.

87. Edward G. Longacre, *From Union Stars to Top Hat: a biography of the extraordinary General James Harrison Wilson* (Harrisburg, Pennsylvania: Stackpole Books, 1972), p. 215. For the campaign, see ibid., pp. 198–216; James Pickett Jones, *Yankee Blitzkrieg: Wilson's Raid through Alabama and Georgia* (Athens: University of Georgia Press, 1976); Trudeau, *Out of the Storm*, pp. 154–58, 159–68, 170, 172–73, 179–80, 186–87. For Forrest's promotion, "Forrest, Nathan Bedford," Boatner, *Civil War Dictionary*, pp. 288–89, particularly 289.

88. Trudeau, *Out of the Storm*, pp. 152–54, 158–59, 167, 168–69, 171–72, 174–79, 180–86, 259–60; "Alabama, Mississippi, and East Louisiana, Confed. Dept. of," Boatner, *Civil War Dictionary*, p. 5. "Canby, Edward Richard Sprigg," Heitman, *Historical Register*, I, 279, for his promotion to brigadier-general, U.S.V., March 31, 1862 and major-general, U.S.V., May 7, 1864. "Taylor, Richard ('Dick')," Boatner, *Civil War Dictionary*, pp. 827–28, particularly 827, for his promotion to lieutenant-general May 16, 1864.

89. Osterhaus was major-general, U.S.V., since July 23, 1864, and since January 8 Canby's chief of staff; "Osterhaus, Peter Joseph," Boatner, *Civil War Dictionary*, p. 613, and for confirmation of promotion, Heitman, *Historical Register*, I, 761. Trudeau, *Out of the Storm*, Chapter Nineteen, "The Trans-Mississippi," pp. 335–41, particularly 340–41 for date of the surrender; Nevins, *Ordeal of the Union*, VIII, *War for the Union*, IV, 360, for Buckner's part in the surrender. Buckner had been promoted to lieutenant-general September 20, 1864, confirmed January 17, 1865; "Buckner, Simon Bolivar," Boatner, *Civil War Dictionary*, pp. 95–96, particularly 96.

90. Trudeau, *Out of the Storm*, p. 373; "Shelby, Joseph O. ('Jo')," Boatner, *Civil War Dictionary*, p. 737.

91. Trudeau, *Out of the Storm*, p. 292–93, 297 for Davis's capture, pp. 385–86 for subsequent events; Clement Eaton, *Jefferson Davis* (New York: The Free Press, A Division of Macmillan Publishing Co., Inc.; London: Collier Macmillan Publishers, 1977), pp. 260–61 for the capture, pp. 262–67 for subsequent events, particularly 263 for the date of release.

92. Nevins, *Ordeal of the Union*, VIII, *War for the Union*, IV, 362; Eric L. McKitrick, *Andrew Johnson and Reconstruction* (Chicago: University of Chicago Press, 1960), pp. 48–49 for the beginnings of amnesty.

93. Trudeau, *Out of the Storm*, pp. 262, 375–77, particularly 375 for the date of execution; "Wirz, Henry," Boatner, *Civil War Dictionary*, pp. 941–42.

94. Frank Lawrence Owsley, Jr., *The C.S.S. Florida: Her Building and Operations* (Philadelphia: University of Pennsylvania Press, 1965), Chapter Seven, "The Capture of the *Florida*," pp. 137–55, particularly 141 for the capture, 153 for Seward, 147 for the "accident," 148 for the sinking, and 148–51 for the circumstances of the sinking.

95. Trudeau, *Out of the Storm*, pp. 366–79, particularly 368 for the whalers, 370 for the lowering of the *Shenandoah's* flag; Raimondo Luraghi, *A History of the Confederate Navy*, tr. Paolo E. Coletta (Annapolis, Maryland: Naval Institute Press, 1996), pp. 341, 344.

96. Andrew Johnson. By the President: W[illiam]. Hunter, Acting Secretary of State. [May 10, 1865] By the President of the United States of America. A Proclamation. U.S. President, *A Compilation of the Messages and Papers of the Presidents 1789–1908 (With Revisions)*, James D. Richardson, ed. (11 vols., Washington: Bureau of National Literature and Art, 1911), VI, 308–309.

97. Edward Porter Alexander, *Military Memoirs of a Confederate: A Critical Narrative* (New York: Charles Scribner's Sons, 1907), pp. 604–605, quotations from 605. For Alexander's position and promotion, "Alexander, Edward Porter," Boatner, *Civil War Dictionary*, p. 7.

98. Charles H. Weigley of Richland, Lebanon County, Pennsylvania has shared with me his extensive research into the family's genealogy, which I have drawn on to prevent myself from confusing relationships across the generations. According to Samuel P. Bates, *History of Pennsylvania Volunteers, 1861–5, Prepared in Compliance with Acts of the Legislature* (5 vols., Harrisburg: B. Singerly, State Printer, 1869–1871), II (1869), 1126, Francis Weigley died in the Confederate prison at Florence, South Carolina, but family tradition makes this conclusion doubtful.

## NOTES ON MAPS

THE UNITED STATES DURING THE CIVIL WAR. For dates of territorial reorganizations, Everette B. Long with Barbara Long, *The Civil War Day by Day: An Almanac 1861–1865*, Foreword by Bruce Catton (Garden City, New York: Doubleday & Company, Inc., 1971): Arizona Terr., 1863, "February 24, Tuesday," pp. 322–323, particularly 323; Colorado Terr., 1861, "February 24, Thursday," p. 42; Dakota Terr. and, with boundary as shown, Nebraska Terr., 1861, "March 2, Saturday," p. 44; Idaho Terr., 1863, "March 3, Tuesday," pp. 325–326, particularly 325; Montana Terr., 1864, "May 26, Thursday," p. 509. For Kansas statehood, 1861, "January 29, Tuesday," p. 30. For Nevada statehood, 1864, "October 31, Monday," p. 591.

THE PRINCIPAL THEATER OF WAR and AREA OF THE WESTERN CAMPAIGNS. For the date of the completion of the Alabama and Mississippi Railroad between Selma, Alabama and Meridian, Mississippi, George Edgar Turner, *Victory Rode the Rails: The Strategic Place of the Railroads in the Civil War* (Indianapolis, New York: The Bobbs-Merrill Company, Inc., Publishers, 1953), p. 237.

Sources for officers' grades and brevets that because of timing differ on the maps from the text follow; note that promotions and brevets were sometimes awarded retroactively, especially at the end of the war, so that they may not have been in effect at the time of a particular map.

ANTIETAM. "Doubleday, Abner," BG, USV, Feb. 3, 1862, MG, USV, Nov. 29, 1862, Francis B. Heitman, *Historical Register and Dictionary of the United States Army, From Its Organization, September 20, 1789, to March 2, 1903* (Published under act of Congress approved March 2, 1903, 57th Congress, 2nd Session, House Document 445 [serial 4536], 2 vols., Washington: Government Printing Office, 1903) I, 380, Mark Mayo Boatner III, *The Civil War Dictionary* (Revised Edition, New York: Vintage Books, A Division of Random House, Inc., 1991), p. 244; "Meade, George Gordon," BG, USV, Aug. 31, 1861, MG, USV, Nov. 29, 1862, BG, USA, July 3, 1863, MG, USA, Aug. 18, 1864, Heitman, I, 700; "Pleasonton, Alfred," BG, USV, July 16, 1862, MG, USV, June 22, 1863, Heitman, I, 795, Boatner, pp. 655–656, particularly 656; "Sturgis, Samuel Davis," BG, USV, Aug. 10, 1861, MG, USV, July 4, 1862, Bvt. BG and MG, USA, March 13, 1865, Heitman, I, 934, Boatner, pp. 816–817, particularly 816, but for specific date of BG, USV "Sykes, George," BG, USV, Sept. 28, 1861, MG, USV, Nov. 29, 1862, Bvt. BG and MG, USA, March 13, 1865, Heitman, I, 941–942, particularly 942, Boatner, p. 825, with specific dates for USV grades only; "Anderson, Richard Heron," BG, July 18, 1861, MG, July 14, 1862, Boatner, p. 19, temporary LTG, May 31, 1864, Douglas Southall Freeman, *Lee's Lieutenants: A Study in Command* (3 vols., New York: Charles Scribner's Sons, 1942–1944), III, *Gettysburg to Appomattox*, 510n; "Early, Jubal Anderson," BG, July 21, 1861, MG, April 23, 1863, Boatner, pp. 254, 255, temporary LTG, May 31, 1864, Freeman, III, 510 and n; "Hood, John Bell," BG March 3, 1862, MG Oct. 10, 1862, LTG Sept. 20, 1863, temporary Gen July 18, 1864–Jan. 232, 1865, Boatner, pp. 407–408, particularly 408; "Walker, John G.," BG, Jan. 9, 1862, MG, Nov. 8, 1865, Boatner, p. 885.

GETTYSBURG. THE SECOND DAY. "Gibbon, John," BG, USV, May 2, 1862, MG, USV, June 7, 1864, Bvt. BG and MG, USA, March 13, 1865, I, 452, Boatner, pp. 340–341, particularly 349, with specific dates for USV grades only; "Humphreys, Andrew Atkinson," BG, USV, April 21, 1862, MG, USV, July 8, 1863, Bvt. BG and MG, USA, March 13, 1865, Heitman, I, 554–555, Boatner, p. 417, with specific dates for USV grades only. BG William Smith's Confederate Brigade of Rodes's Division, Ewell's Corps, had been detached to guard the York Pike, off the map; Freeman, *Lee's Lieutenants*, III, 129.

# Bibliography

## GENERAL WORKS

A number of general histories of the war have influenced this history without occasioning their specific citation in the endnotes. Such works are listed here, along with general histories that do appear in the endnotes but that merit attention again so that they will not be overlooked; the latter are indicated here by an asterisk (*).

Adams, Michael C. C. *Our Masters the Rebels: A Speculation on Union Military Failure in the East.* Cambridge, Massachusetts and London, England: Harvard University Press, 1978. Reprinted as *Fighting for Defeat: Union Military Failure in the East.* Lincoln and London: University of Nebraska Press, 1992. A sophisticated study of a psychological dimension of the war: the psychological ascendancy of Confederate leaders over their Union opponents because Northerners as well as Southerners believed the myth of the intrinsic military superiority of an agrarian, aristocratic society over an urban, industrial one. The title notwithstanding, the book also considers the West — where Union leaders were not so susceptible to the myth.

Belz, Herman. *Reconstructing the Union: Theory and Policy during the Civil War.* Ithaca, New York: Published for the American Historical Association, Cornell University Press, 1969. Still the best history of the wartime beginnings of Reconstruction policy.

*Beringer, Richard E.; Herman Hattaway; Archer Jones; and William N. Still, Jr. *Why the South Lost the Civil War.* Athens and London: The University of Georgia Press, 1986. While including political and military history, this work emphasizes the social and cultural experiences of the South at war, particularly emphasizing why the outcome can be regarded as the product of a Southern failure of will.

*Boatner, Mark Mayo, III. *The Civil War Dictionary.* Revised Edition. New York: Vintage Books, A Division of Random House, Inc., 1991. The present work relies primarily on Boatner for specifics of military organizations and individuals' promotions and assignments; where any doubt about accuracy arose, other reference works have been used to check against Boatner.

Catton, Bruce. *The Centennial History of the Civil War.* Everette B. Long, director of research. 3 vols. Garden City, New York: Doubleday & Company, Inc., 1961–1965.
I. *The Coming Fury.* 1961.
II. *Terrible Swift Sword.* 1963.
III. *Never Call Retreat.* 1965.
To be read along with Shelby Foote, *The Civil War: A Narrative,* cited below; an eloquent narrative history written primarily from a Union perspective.

Cullen, Tim. *The Civil War in Popular Culture: A Reusable Past.* Washington and London: Smithsonian Institution Press, 1995. An insightful and amusing guide to the revival of the national fascination with the war.

Dyer, Frederick N. *A Compendium of the War of the Rebellion: From Official Records of the Union and Confederate Armies, Reports of the Adjutant Generals of the Several States, the Army Registers, and Other Reliable Documents and Sources.* Des

Moines, Iowa: Dyer Publishing Co., 1904. Reprinted with an Introduction, Dayton, Ohio: Morningside, 1978. The most complete and reliable collection of details and statistics of Union Army organization, including unit casualties, actions and battles, and Union regiments. In spite of the subtitle, the coverage is almost entirely of the Union Army.

Eicher, David. *The Civil War in Books: An Analytical Bibliography.* Foreword by Gary W. Gallagher. Urbana and Chicago: University of Illinois Press, 1997. An admirably comprehensive listing with useful comments.

Faust, Patricia L., ed.; Norman C. Delaney, Edward G. Longacre, John E. Stancheck. Jeffry D. Wert, assoc. eds.; Marsha L. Larsen, editorial asst. *The Historical Times Illustrated Encyclopedia of the Civil War.* New York, Cambridge, Philadelphia, San Francisco, Washington, London, Mexico City, São Paulo, Sydney: Harper & Row, Publishers, 1986. A reliable reference work whose entries are generally more interpretative than those in Mark Mayo Boatner III, *The Civil War Dictionary.*

*Foote, Shelby. *The Civil War: A Narrative.* 3 vols. New York: Random House, 1958–1974.
I. *Fort Sumter to Perryville.* 1958.
II. *Fredericksburg to Meridian.* 1963.
III. *Red River to Appomattox.* 1974.
Along with Bruce Catton, *The Centennial History of the Civil War*, Shelby Foote's work is one of the two outstanding modern literary treatments of the war. Foote's is written from a Confederate perspective, sometimes idiosyncratically so. As the volume titles suggest, it also emphasizes the Western theater more than does Catton's work.

Fredrickson, George M. *The Inner Civil War: Northern Intellectuals and the Civil War.* Urbana: University of Illinois Press, 1965. A perceptive analysis of the Northern intellectuals' difficult progress toward acceptance of the new nation of consolidated power.

Freeman, Frank R. *Microbes and Minie Balls: An Annotated Bibliography of Civil War Medicine.* Rutherford, Madison, and Teaneck: Fairleigh Dickinson University Press; London and Toronto: Associated University Presses, 1993. The standard medical bibliography.

Glatthaar, Joseph T. *Partners in Command: The Relationships Between Leaders in the Civil War.* New York: The Free Press, A Division of Macmillan, Inc.; Toronto: Maxwell Macmillan Canada; New York, Oxford, Singapore, Sydney: Maxwell Macmillan International, 1994. A judicious analysis of the influence of personalities and personal relationships on the military conduct of the war.

Hattaway, Herman. *Shades of Blue and Gray: An Introductory Military History of the Civil War.* Columbia and London: University of Missouri Press, 1997. The best brief military history.

*Hattaway, Herman, and Archer Jones. *How the North Won: A Military History of the Civil War.* Urbana, Chicago, London: University of Illinois Press, 1983. Although the present writer disagrees with much in this book, particularly its argument for the utility of a raiding strategy against the enemy's economy rather than a strategy aimed at the destruction of the enemy's armies, for comprehensive coverage grounded in a superb knowledge of the history of warfare it is the best one-volume military history of the war.

Johnson, Robert Underwood, and Clarence Clough Buel, eds. *Battles and Leaders of the Civil War: Being for the Most Part Contributions by Union and Confederate Officers: Based upon "The Century" War Series.* 4 vols. New York: The Century Company, 1887–1888.

Jones, Archer. *Civil War Command and Strategy: The Process of Victory and Defeat.* New York: The Free Press, A Division of Macmillan, Inc.; Toronto: Maxwell Macmillan Canada; New York, Oxford, Singapore, Sydney: Maxwell Macmillan International, 1992. Jones's knowledge of the military conduct of the Civil War in relation to military history at large is unexcelled, and he puts that knowledge to good use here.

*Long, Everette B., with Barbara Long. *The Civil War Day by Day: An Almanac 1861–1865.* Foreword by Bruce Catton. Garden City, New York: Doubleday & Company, Inc., 1971. Invaluable not only for its daily chronicle of events but for a wealth of statistical data.

*McPherson, James M. *Battle Cry of Freedom: The Civil War Era.* New York, Oxford: Oxford University Press, 1988. The best comprehensive one-volume history, notable for emphasis upon the contingency of events one upon another and its rejection of theories of inevitability. An eminently readable book as well.

McPherson, James M. *Drawn with the Sword: Reflections on the American Civil War.* New York, Oxford: Oxford University Press, 1996. Interpretative essays by today's leading academic authority on the war.

McPherson, James M. *Ordeal by Fire: The Civil War and Reconstruction.* New York: Alfred A. Knopf, 1982. A more brief overview than the same author's *Battle Cry of Freedom.*

Nevins, Allen. *Ordeal of the Union.* 8 vols., 1947–1971.

    I–II. *Ordeal of the Union.* I. *Fruits of Manifest Destiny 1847–1852.* II. *A House Divided 1852–1857.* New York, London: Charles Scribner's Sons, 1947.

    III–IV. *The Emergence of Lincoln.* I. *Douglas, Buchanan, and Party Chaos 1857–1859.* II. *Prologue to Civil War 1859–1861.* New York, London: Charles Scribner's Sons, 1950.

    V–VIII. *The War for the Union.* I. *The Improvised War 1861–1862.* New York: Charles Scribner's Sons, 1959. II. *War Becomes Revolution.* New York: Charles Scribner's Sons, 1960. III. *The Organized War 1863–1864.* IV. *The Organized War to Victory 1864–1865.* New York: Charles Scribner's Sons, 1971.

A magisterial work in the grand style of the nineteenth-century age of history as literature.

Paludan, Phillip S. *A Covenant with Death: The Constitution, Law, and Equality in the Civil War Era.* Urbana and London: University of Illinois Press, 1975. A history of ideas focusing on constitutional issues and their implications for succeeding generations.

*Randall, James G., and David Donald. *The Civil War and Reconstruction.* Second Edition, Revised with Enlarged Bibliography. Lexington, Massachusetts: D.C. Heath and Company, A Division of Raytheon Education Company, 1969. This older survey remains valuable because of its unusual wealth of detail.

Roland, Charles P. *An American Iliad: The Story of the Civil War.* Lexington: The University Press of Kentucky, 1991. A reliable brief survey.

Shattuck, Gardiner H. *A Shield and a Hiding Place: The Religious Life of the Civil War Armies.* Macon, Georgia: Mercer University Press, 1982. It would be difficult to exaggerate the centrality of religion in the lives of Americans of the Civil War era, including the soldiers. This book introduces the religious life of the armies.

*Warner, Ezra J. *Generals in Blue: Lives of the Union Commanders.* Baton Rouge: Louisiana State University Press, 1964.

*Warner, Ezra J. *Generals in Gray: Lives of the Confederate Commanders.* Baton Rouge: Louisiana State University Press, 1959.

The standard biographical reference works on general officers.

Welcher, Frank J. *The Union Army, 1861–1865: Organization and Operations*. 2 vols. Bloomington and Indianapolis: Indiana University Press, 1989–1992.
I. *The Eastern Theater*.
II. *The Western Theater*.
Basic information on major formations and sketches of engagements.

Wilson, Edmund. *Patriotic Gore: Studies in the Literature of the American Civil War*. New York: Oxford University Press, 1962. Reprint, New York: W. W. Norton and Company, Inc., 1994. A frequently wrongheaded but challenging appraisal of the literary side of the war.

## OTHER WORKS CITED

Adams, Charles Francis. "The *Trent* Affair." *American Historical Review*. 17:4 (July 1912), 540–62.

Adams, George Worthington. *Doctors in Blue: The Medical History of the Union Army in the Civil War*. New York: H. Schuman, 1952; Baton Rouge and London: Louisiana State University Press, 1980.

Alexander, De Alva S. *A Political History of the State of New York*. 4 vols. New York: H. Holt and Company, 1906–1923.

Alexander, Edward Porter. *Military Memoirs of a Confederate: A Critical Narrative*. New York: Charles Scribner's Sons, 1907.

Alexander, Thomas B., and Richard E. Beringer. *The Anatomy of the Confederate Congress: A Study of the Influence of Member Characteristics on Legislative Voting Behavior, 1861–1865*. Nashville: Vanderbilt University Press, 1972.

Andreano, Ralph L., ed. *The Economic Impact of the American Civil War*. Cambridge, Massachusetts: Schenckman Publishing Company, 1967.

Arnold, Isaac N. *The Life of Abraham Lincoln*. Chicago: Jensen, McClurg & Co., 1885.

Arnold, James R. *Grant Wins the War: Decision at Vicksburg*. New York, Chichester, Weinheim, Brisbane, Singapore, Toronto: John Wiley & Sons, Inc., 1997.

Auchampaugh, Phillip G. "A Great Justice on State and Federal Power. Being the Thoughts of Chief Justice Taney on the Federal Conscription Act." *Tyler's Quarterly Historical and Genealogical Magazine*. 18:2 (Oct. 1936), 72–87.

Bates, David Homer. *Lincoln in the Telegraph Office: Recollections of the United States Military Telegraph Corps during the Civil War*. New York: The Century Company, 1907.

Bates, Samuel P. *History of Pennsylvania Volunteers, 1861–5*. Prepared in Compliance with Acts of the Legislature. 5 vols. Harrisburg: B. Singerly, State Printer, 1869–1871.

Baxter, James Phinney, 3rd. *The Introduction of the Ironclad Warship*. Cambridge, Massachusetts: Harvard University Press, 1933.

Belden, Thomas Graham and Marva Robins. *So Fell the Angels*. Boston, Toronto: Little, Brown and Company, 1956.

Bentley, George R. *A History of the Freedmen's Bureau*. Philadelphia: University of Pennsylvania Press, 1955.

Bernath, Stuart L. *Squall Across the Atlantic: American Civil War Prize Cases and Diplomacy*. Berkeley and Los Angeles: University of California Press, 1970.

Bernstein, Iver. *The New York City Draft Riots: Their Significance for American Society and Politics in the Age of the Civil War*. New York, Oxford: Oxford University Press, 1990.

Bigelow, John. *The Principles of Strategy Illustrated Mainly from American Campaigns*. Second Edition, Revised and Enlarged. Philadelphia: J. B. Lippincott Company,

1894. Reprint, Thomas E. Griess and Jay Luvaas, eds. *The West Point Military Library.* New York: Greenwood, 1968.

Bigelow, John, Jr. *The Campaign of Chancellorsville: A Strategic and Tactical Study.* New Haven: Yale University Press, 1910.

Bill, Alfred Hoyt. *The Beleaguered City: Richmond, 1861–1865.* New York: Alfred A. Knopf, 1946.

Black, Robert C. *The Railroads of the Confederacy.* Chapel Hill: University of North Carolina Press, 1952.

Bogue, Allan G. "Bloc and Party in the United States Senate: 1861–1865." *Civil War History: A Journal of the Middle Period.* 13:3 (Sept. 1967), 221–241.

Bogue, Allan G. *The Earnest Men: The Republicans of the Civil War Senate.* Ithaca, New York: Cornell University Press, 1981.

Bogue, Allan G. "The Radical Voting Dimension in the U.S. Senate during the Civil War." *Journal of Interdisciplinary History.* 3:4 (Winter 1973), 449–74.

Boritt, Gabor S., ed. *The Gettysburg Nobody Knows.* New York, Oxford: Oxford University Press, 1997.

Brock, Peter. *Pacifism in the United States: From the Colonial Era to the First World War.* Princeton, New Jersey: Princeton University Press, 1968.

Brodie, Barnard and Fawn M. *From Crossbow to H-Bomb.* Revised and Enlarged Edition. Bloomington & London: Indiana University Press, 1973.

Brodie, Fawn M. *Thaddeus Stevens: Scourge of the South.* New York: W. W. Norton & Company, Inc., 1959.

Brooks, Noah. *Washington in Lincoln's Time.* New York: The Century Company, 1895.

Brown, Dee Alexander. *Grierson's Raid: A Cavalry Adventure of the Civil War.* Urbana: University of Illinois Press, 1954.

Brown, George William. *Baltimore and the Nineteenth of April 1861: A Study of the War.* Johns Hopkins University Studies in Historical and Political Science, Extra Volume 3. Baltimore, Maryland: N. Murray, 1887.

Browning, Robert S. *Two If By Sea: The Development of American Coastal Defense Policy.* Contributions in Military History, Number 33. Westport, Connecticut; London, England: Greenwood Press, 1983.

Brownlee, Richard S. *Gray Ghosts of the Confederacy: Guerrilla Warfare in the West.* Baton Rouge: Louisiana State University Press, 1958.

Burchard, Peter. *One Gallant Rush: Robert Gould Shaw and His Brave Black Regiment.* New York: St. Martin's Press, 1965.

Case, Lynn M., and Warren F. Spencer. *The United States and France: Civil War Diplomacy.* Philadelphia: University of Pennsylvania Press, 1957.

Castel, Albert. *Decision in the West: The Atlanta Campaign of 1864.* Lawrence: University Press of Kansas, 1992.

Castel, Albert. "The Fort Pillow Massacre: A Fresh Evaluation of the Evidence." *Civil War History: A Journal of the Middle Period.* 41:1 (March 1958), 37–50.

Castel, Albert. *General Sterling Price and the Civil War in the West.* Baton Rouge: Louisiana State University Press, 1968.

Catton, Bruce. *Glory Road: The Bloody Route from Fredericksburg to Gettysburg.* Garden City, N.Y.: Doubleday & Company, Inc., 1952.

Catton, Bruce. *Grant Moves South.* Boston, Toronto: Little, Brown and Company, 1960.

Catton, Bruce. *Grant Takes Command.* Boston, Toronto: Little, Brown and Company, 1969.

Catton, Bruce. *Mr. Lincoln's Army.* Garden City, N.Y.: Doubleday & Company, Inc., 1951.

Catton, Bruce. *A Stillness at Appomattox.* Garden City, New York: Doubleday & Company, Inc., 1953.

Chamberlain, Joshua Lawrence. *The Passing of the Armies: An Account of the Final Campaign of the Army of the Potomac, Based upon Personal Reminiscences of the Fifth Army Corps*. New York, and London: G. P. Putnam's Sons, 1915.

Chandler, David G. *The Campaigns of Napoleon*. New York: The Macmillan Company, 1966.

Chase, Salmon P. *Diary and Correspondence of Salmon P. Chase*. Annual Report of the American Historical Association, 1902. 2 vols. In II, *Sixth Report* of Historical Manuscripts Commission; With *Diary and Correspondence of Salmon P. Chase*.

Chase, Salmon P. *Inside Lincoln's Cabinet: The Civil War Diaries of Salmon P. Chase*. David Donald, ed. New York: Longmans, Green and Co., 1954.

Chesnut, Mary Boykin Miller. *Mary Chesnut's Civil War*. Comer Vann Woodward, ed. New Haven and London: Yale University Press, 1981.

Cimprich, John, and Robert C. Mainfort, Jr. "Fort Pillow Revisited: New Evidence about an Old Controversy." *Civil War History: A Journal of the Middle Period*. 28:4 (Dec. 1982), 293–306.

Clary, David A. *Fortress America: The Corps of Engineers, Hampton Roads, and United States Coastal Defense*. Charlottesville: University Press of Virginia, 1990.

Cleaves, Freeman. *Meade of Gettysburg*. Norman: University of Oklahoma Press, 1960.

Cochran, Thomas. "Did the Civil War Retard Industrialization?" *The Mississippi Valley Historical Review*. 48:2 (Sept. 1961), 197–210. Also in Ralph L. Andreano, ed. *The Economic Impact of the American Civil War*. Cambridge, Massachusetts: Schenckman Publishing Co., 1967. Pp. 148–160.

Coddington, Edwin B. *The Gettysburg Campaign: A Study in Command*. New York: Charles Scribner's Sons, 1968.

Coddington, Edwin B. "Pennsylvania Prepares for Invasion." *Pennsylvania History: Quarterly Journal of the Pennsylvania Historical Association*. 31:2 (April 1964), 157–175.

Coddington, Edwin B. "Prelude to Gettysburg: The Confederates Plunder Pennsylvania." *Pennsylvania History: Quarterly Journal of the Pennsylvania Historical Association*. 30:2 (April 1963), 123–137.

Colton, Ray C. *The Civil War in the Western Territories: Arizona, Colorado, New Mexico, and Utah*. Norman and London: University of Oklahoma Press, 1959.

Confederate States. President. *A Compilation of the Messages and Papers of the Confederacy, Including the Diplomatic Correspondence, 1861–1865*. Published by Permission of Congress. James D. Richardson, ed. 2 vols. Nashville, Tennessee: United States Publishing Company, 1905.

Confederate States. Laws, statutes. *Laws and Joint Resolutions of the Last Session of the Confederate Congress, Together with the Secret Acts of Previous Congresses*. With an Introduction and a Bibliographical Essay by Charles W. Ramsdell, ed. Durham, N.C.: Duke University Press, 1941.

Confederate States. Laws, statutes. *Public Laws of the Confederate States of America, Passed at the First Session of the First Congress; 1862*. Carefully collated with the Originals at Richmond. James M. Matthews, ed. Richmond: R. M. Smith, Printer to Congress, 1862.

Confederate States. Laws, statutes. *Public Laws of the Confederate States of America, Passed at the Second Session of the First Congress; 1862*. Carefully collated with the Originals at Richmond. James M. Matthews, ed. Richmond: R. M. Smith, Printer to Congress, 1862.

Confederate States. Laws, statutes. *The Statutes at Large of the Confederate States of America Passed at the Third Session of the First Congress; 1863*. Carefully collated with the Originals at Richmond. James M. Matthews, ed. Richmond: R. M. Smith, Printer to Congress, 1863.

Confederate States. Laws, statutes. *The Statutes at Large of the Confederate States of America, Passed at the Fourth Session of the First Congress; 1863–4.* Carefully collated with the Originals at Richmond. James M. Matthews, ed. Richmond: R. M. Smith, Printer to Congress, 1864.

Confederate States. Laws, statutes. *The Statutes at Large of the Provisional Government of the Confederate States of America, from the Institution of the Government, February 8, 1861, to Its Termination, February 18, 1862, Inclusive. Arranged in Chronological Order. Together with the Constitution for the Provisional Government, and the Permanent Constitution of the Confederate States, and the Treaties Concluded by the Confederate States with the Indian Tribes.* James M. Matthews, ed. By Authority of Congress. Richmond: R. M. Smith, Printer to Congress, 1864.

Conference on American Economic Institutional Change, 1850–1873, and the Impact of the Civil War, Greenville, Delaware, 1964. *Economic Change in the Civil War Era.* David T. Gilchrist and W. David Lewis, eds. Greenville, Delaware: Eleutherian Mills-Hagley Foundation, 1965.

Connelly, Thomas Lawrence. *Army of the Heartland: The Army of Tennessee, 1861–1862.* Baton Rouge: Louisiana State University Press, 1967.

Connelly, Thomas Lawrence. *Autumn of Glory: The Army of Tennessee, 1862–1865.* Baton Rouge: Louisiana State University Press, 1971.

Connelly, Thomas Lawrence, and Archer Jones. *The Politics of Command: Factions and Ideas in Confederate Strategy.* Baton Rouge: Louisiana State University Press, 1973.

Connelly, William E. *Quantrill and the Border Wars.* Cedar Rapids, Iowa: The Torch Press, 1910.

Connor, Henry G. *John Archibald Campbell, Associate Justice of the United States Supreme Court, 1851–1861.* Boston and New York: Houghton Mifflin Company, 1920.

Cook, Adrian. *The Armies in the Streets: The New York City Draft Riots of 1863.* Lexington: University Press of Kentucky, 1974.

Cooke, John Esten. *A Life of Gen. Robert E. Lee.* New York: D. Appleton and Company, 1871.

Cooling, Benjamin Franklin. *Forts Henry and Donelson: The Key to the Confederate Heartland.* Knoxville: University of Tennessee Press, 1987.

Cooling, Benjamin Franklin. *Jubal Early's Raid on Washington, 1864.* Baltimore, Maryland: Nautical & Aviation Publishing Company of America, 1989.

Cooling, Benjamin Franklin. *Monocacy: The Battle That Saved Washington.* Shippensburg, PA: White Mane Publishing Company, Inc., 1991.

Cooling, Benjamin Franklin. *Symbol, Sword, and Shield: Defending Washington during the Civil War.* Hamden, Connecticut: Archon Books, 1975; Shippensburg, PA: White Mane Publishing Company, Inc., 1991.

Cooper, Samuel. "Confederate Losses During the Civil War — Correspondence Between Dr. Joseph Jones and General Samuel Cooper." *Southern Historical Society Papers.* 7:6 (June 1879), 287–90.

Cornish, Dudley Taylor. *The Sable Arm: Negro Troops in the Union Army, 1861–1865.* New York: Longmans, Green and Co., 1956.

Cottom, Robert I., Jr., & Mary Ellen Hayward. *Maryland in the Civil War: A House Divided.* Baltimore: Published by The Maryland Historical Society, Distributed by the Johns Hopkins University Press, 1989.

Coulter, Ellis Merton. *The Civil War and Readjustment in Kentucky.* Chapel Hill: University of North Carolina Press, 1926.

Cox, LaWanda. *Lincoln and Black Freedom: A Study in Presidential Leadership.* Columbia: University of South Carolina Press, 1981.

Cozzens, Peter. *No Better Place to Die: The Battle of Stones River.* Urbana and Chicago: University of Illinois Press, 1990.

Cozzens, Peter. *The Shipwreck of Their Hopes: The Battles for Chattanooga*. Urbana and Chicago: University of Illinois Press, 1994.

Cozzens, Peter. *This Terrible Sound: The Battle of Chickamauga*. Urbana and Chicago: University of Illinois Press, 1992.

Craig, Gordon A. *The Politics of the Prussian Army 1640–1945*. New York and Oxford: Oxford University Press, 1956.

Crawford, Samuel Wylie. *The Genesis of the Civil War: The Story of Sumter, 1860–1861*. New York: C. L. Webster & Company, 1887.

Crook, David Paul. *The North, the South, and the Powers, 1861–1865*. New York: John Wiley & Sons, 1974.

Cullen, Joseph P. *The Battles of Fredericksburg, Chancellorsville, the Wilderness, and Spotsylvania Court House: Where a Hundred Thousand Fell*. National Park Service Historical Handbook Series No. 39. Washington, D.C.: United States Government Printing Office, 1966.

Cunliffe, Marcus. *Soldiers & Civilians: The Martial Spirit in America 1775–1865*. Boston, Toronto: Little, Brown and Company, 1973.

Cunningham, Edward. *The Port Hudson Campaign, 1862–1863*. Baton Rouge: Louisiana State University Press, 1963.

Cunningham, Horace H. *Doctors in Gray: The Confederate Medical Service*. Baton Rouge: Louisiana State University Press, 1958; Baton Rouge and London: Louisiana State University Press, 1986.

Cunningham, Horace H. *Field Medical Services at the Battle of Manassas (Bull Run)*. Athens: University of Georgia Press, 1968.

Current, Richard N., ed. in chief. Paul D. Escott, Lawrence N. Powell, James I. Robertson, Jr., Emory M. Thomas, editorial board. *Encyclopedia of the Confederacy*. 4 vols. New York, London, Toronto, Sydney, Tokyo, Singapore: Simon & Schuster, A Paramount Communications Company, 1993. Also, with same eds. *The Confederacy: Macmillan Information Now Encyclopedia*. Selections from the Four-Volume Simon & Schuster *Encyclopedia of the Confederacy*. New York: Simon & Schuster Macmillan; London, Mexico City, New Delhi, Singapore, Sydney, Toronto: Prentice Hall International, 1997.

Curry, Leonard P. *Blueprint for Modern America: Nonmilitary Legislation of the First Civil War Congress*. Nashville: Vanderbilt University Press, 1968.

Curry, Richard Orr. "Copperheadism and Continuity: The Anatomy of a Stereotype." *The Journal of Negro History*. 57:1 (Jan. 1972), 29–36.

Curry, Richard Orr. *House Divided: A Study of Statehood Politics and the Copperhead Movement in West Virginia*. Pittsburgh: University of Pittsburgh Press, 1964.

Curry, Roy W. "James A. Seddon, a Southern Prototype." *The Virginia Magazine of History and Biography*. 63:2 (April 1955), 123–150.

Daly, Robert W. *How the Mer[sic]imac Won: The Strategic Story of the CSS Virginia*. New York: Thomas Y. Crowell Co., 1957.

Davis, Jefferson. *The Rise and Fall of the Confederate Government*. 2 vols. New York: D. Appleton and Company, 1881.

Davis, William C. *Battle at Bull Run: A History of the First Major Campaign of the American Civil War*. Garden City, New York: Doubleday & Company, Inc., 1977.

Davis, William C. *The Battle of New Market*. Garden City, New York: Doubleday & Company, Inc., 1975.

Davis, William C. *Duel between the First Ironclads*. Garden City, New York: Doubleday & Company, Inc., 1975.

Democratic Party. Pennsylvania. State Central Committee. *Address of the Democratic State Convention Held at Harrisburg, July 4, 1862, and the Proceedings of the Democratic State Central Committee held at Philadelphia, July 29, 1862*. Philadelphia: T. B. Florence & Co., 1862.

DeRosa, Marshall L. *The Confederate Constitution of 1861: An Inquiry into American Constitutionalism.* Columbia: University of Missouri Press, 1996.

Dew, Charles B. *Ironmaker to the Confederacy: Joseph R. Anderson and the Tredegar Iron Works.* New Haven and London: Yale University Press, 1966.

Donald, David. *Charles Sumner and the Coming of the Civil War.* New York: Alfred A. Knopf, 1961.

Donald, David. *Charles Sumner and the Rights of Man.* New York: Alfred A. Knopf, 1970.

Donald, David Herbert. *Lincoln.* New York, London, Toronto, Sydney, Tokyo, Singapore: Simon & Schuster, 1995.

Donald, David. *The Politics of Reconstruction, 1863–1867.* Baton Rouge: Louisiana State University Press, 1965.

Douglas, Henry Kyd. *I Rode with Stonewall: Being chiefly the war experiences of the youngest member of Jackson's staff from the John Brown raid to the hanging of Mrs. [Mary E. Jenkins] Surratt.* Chapel Hill: University of North Carolina Press, 1940.

Downey, Fairfax. *Clash of Cavalry: The Battle of Brandy Station, June 9, 1863.* New York: David McKay Company, Inc., 1959.

Duberman, Martin B. *Charles Francis Adams 1807–1886.* Boston: Houghton Mifflin Company, The Riverside Press, Cambridge, 1961.

Du Pont, Samuel Francis. *Samuel Francis Du Pont: A Selection from His Civil War Letters.* John D. Hayes, ed. 3 vols. Ithaca, New York: Published for the Eleutherian Mills Historical Library, Cornell University Press, 1969.

Dupuy, Richard Ernest. *The Compact History of the United States Army.* New York: Hawthorn Books, 1956.

Durden, Robert F. *The Gray and the Black: The Confederate Debate on Emancipation.* Baton Rouge: Louisiana State University Press, 1972.

Eaton, Clement. *Jefferson Davis.* New York: The Free Press, A Division of Macmillan Publishing Co.; London: Collier Macmillan Publishers, 1977.

Eisenhower, John S. D. *Agent of Destiny: The Life and Times of General Winfield Scott.* New York, London, Toronto, Singapore, Sydney: The Free Press, 1997.

Elliott, Charles Winslow. *Winfield Scott: The Soldier and the Man.* New York: The Macmillan Company, 1937.

Emilio, Luis F. *History of the Fifty-fourth Regiment of Massachusetts Volunteer Infantry.* Second Edition. Revised and Corrected, with Appendix upon Treatment of Colored Prisoners of War. Boston: Boston Book Company, 1894.

Ergang, Robert R. *The Potsdam Führer: Frederick William I, Father of Prussian Militarism.* New York: Columbia University Press, 1941.

Everhart, William C. *Vicksburg National Military Park, Mississippi.* National Park Service Historical Handbook Series No. 21. Washington, D.C.: United States Government Printing Office, 1954.

Fahnestock, George W. Diary. 7 vols., Jan. 1, 1863–Dec. 31, 1867, Jan. 1, 1869–Dec. 31, 1873. The Historical Society of Pennsylvania, Philadelphia.

*The Federal Cases: Comprising Cases Argued and Determined in the Circuit and District Courts of the United States from the Earliest Times to the Beginning of the Federal Reporter* [1789–1880]. Arranged Alphabetically by the Titles of the Cases and Numbered Consecutively. 30 vols. St. Paul: West Publishing Co., 1894–1897.

*The Federal Reporter, with Key-Number Annotations.* Permanent Edition. March 1880–November 1924. 300 vols. St. Paul: West Publishing Co., 1880–1925.

Fehrenbacher, Don E. *The Dred Scott Case: Its Significance in American Law and Politics.* New York: Oxford University Press, 1978.

Fellman, Michael. *Inside War: The Guerrilla Conflict in Missouri During the American Civil War.* New York, Oxford: Oxford University Press, 1989.

Ferris, Norman B. *The* Trent *Affair: A Diplomatic Crisis.* Knoxville: The University of Tennessee Press, 1977.

Fessenden, Francis. *Life and Public Services of William Pitt Fessenden, United States Senator from Maine 1854–1864; Secretary of the Treasury 1864–1865; United States Senator from Maine 1865–1869, by his Son Francis Fessenden.* 2 vols. Boston and New York: Houghton, Mifflin and Company, 1907.

Flexner, Eleanor. *Century of Struggle: The Women's Rights Movement in the United States.* Cambridge, Massachusetts and London, England: The Belknap Press of Harvard University Press, 1975.

Flower, Frank Abiel. *Edwin McMasters Stanton: The Autocrat of Rebellion, Emancipation, and Reconstruction.* Akron, Ohio: Saalfield Publishing Co., 1889.

Foner, Eric. *Free Soil, Free Labor, Free Men: The Ideology of the Republican Party before the Civil War.* London, Oxford, New York: Oxford University Press, 1970.

Fox, William Freeman. *Regimental Losses in the American Civil War, 1861–1865: A Treatise on the Extent and Nature of the Military Losses in the Union Regiments, with Full and Exhaustive Statistics Compiled from the Official Records on File in the State Military Bureaus and at Washington.* Albany, New York: Albany Publishing Company, 1889.

Franklin, John Hope. *The Militant South, 1800–1861.* Cambridge, Massachusetts: Harvard University Press, 1956.

Frassanito, William A. *Antietam: The Photographic Legacy of America's Bloodiest Day.* New York: Charles Scribner's Sons, 1978.

Frassanito, William A. *Early Photography at Gettysburg.* Gettysburg, PA 17325: Thomas Publications, 1995.

Frassanito, William A. *Gettysburg: A Journey in Time.* New York: Charles Scribner's Sons, 1975.

Frederickson, George M. *The Black Image in the White Mind: The Debate on Afro-American Character and Destiny, 1817–1914.* New York, Evanston, San Francisco, London: Harper & Row, 1971.

Freeman, Douglas Southall. *Lee's Lieutenants: A Study in Command.* 3 vols. New York: Charles Scribner's Sons, 1942–1944. See also Douglas Southall Freeman, *Lee's Lieutenants: A Study in Command.* Abridged in one volume by Stephen W. Sears. Introduction by James M. McPherson. New York: Scribner, 1998.

Freeman, Douglas Southall. *R. E. Lee: A Biography.* 4 vols. New York: Charles Scribner's Sons; London: Charles Scribner's Sons Ltd., 1934–1935. See also Douglas Southall Freeman, *Lee: An Abridgment on One Volume of the Four-Volume R. E. Lee.* Richard Harwell, ed. New York: Charles Scribner's Sons, 1964.

Freidel, Frank B. *Francis Lieber: Nineteenth-Century Liberal.* Baton Rouge: Louisiana State University Press, 1948.

Friedman, Leon, comp. *The Law of War: A Documentary History.* With a Foreword by Telford Taylor. 2 vols. New York: Random House, 1972.

Furgurson, Ernest B. *Chancellorsville 1863: Soul of the Brave.* New York: Alfred A. Knopf, 1992.

Gallagher, Gary W., ed. *Antietam: Essays on the 1862 Maryland Campaign.* Kent, Ohio and London, England: Kent State University Press, 1989.

Gallagher, Gary W., ed. *The First Day at Gettysburg: Essays on Confederate and Union Leadership.* Kent, Ohio and London, England: Kent State University Press, 1992.

Gallagher, Gary W., ed. *The Fredericksburg Campaign: Decision on the Rappahannock.* Chapel Hill & London: University of North Carolina Press, 1995.

Gallagher, Gary W., ed. *Lee the Soldier.* Lincoln and London: University of Nebraska Press, 1996.

Gallagher, Gary W., ed. *The Second Day at Gettysburg: Essays on Confederate and Union Leadership*. Kent, Ohio and London, England: Kent State University Press, 1993.

Gallagher, Gary W., ed. *Struggle for the Shenandoah: Essays on the 1864 Valley Campaign*. Kent, Ohio and London, England: Kent State University Press, 1991.

Gallagher, Gary W., ed. *The Third Day at Gettysburg & Beyond*. Chapel Hill & London: University of North Carolina Press, 1994.

Gallagher, Gary W., ed. *The Wilderness Campaign (Military Campaigns of the Civil War)*. Chapel Hill & London: University of North Carolina Press, 1997.

Gallman, James Matthew. *Mastering Wartime: A Social History of Philadelphia during the Civil War*. Cambridge, New York, Port Chester, Melbourne, Sydney: Cambridge University Press, 1990.

Gallman, Robert E. "Commodity Output, 1839–1899." Conference on Research in Income and Wealth, National Bureau of Economic Research. *Trends in the American Economy in the Nineteenth Century*. Studies in Income and Wealth Volume Twenty-four by the Conference on Research in Income and Wealth. A Report of the National Bureau of Economic Research. Princeton: Princeton University Press, 1960. Pp. 13–67.

Gibbon, John. *Personal Recollections of the Civil War*. New York, London: G. P. Putnam's Sons, 1928.

Gillett, Mary C. *The Army Medical Department, 1818–1865*. Army Historical Series. Washington, D.C.: Center of Military History United States Army, 1987.

Glatthaar, Joseph T. *Forged in Battle: The Civil War Alliance of Black Soldiers and White Officers*. New York: The Free Press, A Division of Macmillan, Inc.; London: Collier Macmillan Publishers, 1990.

Gleaves, Albert. *Life and Letters of Rear Admiral Stephen B. Luce, U.S. Navy, Founder of the Naval War College*. New York & London: G. P. Putnam's Sons, The Knickerbocker Press, 1925.

Goff, Richard D. *Confederate Supply*. Durham, North Carolina: Duke University Press, 1969.

Gordon, John B. *Reminiscences of the Civil War*. New York: Charles Scribner's Sons, 1903.

Gragg, Rod. *Confederate Goliath: The Battle of Fort Fisher*. New York: HarperCollins Publishers, 1991.

Gramm, Kent. *Gettysburg: A Meditation on War and Values*. Bloomington, Indianapolis: Indiana University Press, 1994.

Grant, Ulysses S. *Personal Memoirs of Ulysses S. Grant*. 2 vols. New York: Charles H. Webster & Co., 1885–1886.

Griffith, Paddy. *Battle Tactics of the Civil War*. New Haven and London: Yale University Press, 1989.

Grimsley, Mark. *The hard hand of war: Union military policy toward Southern civilians*. Cambridge; New York; Oakleigh, Melbourne, Australia: Cambridge University Press, 1995.

Hagerman, Edward. *The American Civil War and the Origins of Modern Warfare: Ideas, Organization, and Field Command*. Bloomington & Indianapolis: Indiana University Press, 1988.

Hall, James O. "The Spy Harrison: A Modern Hunt for a Fabled Agent." *Civil War Times Illustrated*. 24:10 (Feb. 1986), 18–25.

Halleck, Henry Wager. *Elements of Military Art and Science, or, Course of Instruction in Strategy, Fortification, Tactics of Battle &c Embracing the Duties of Staff, Infantry, Cavalry, Artillery, and Engineers. Adapted to the Use of Volunteers and Militia*. 443 & 445 Broadway, New York: D. Appleton, 1846. Third Edition, with Critical

Notes on the Mexican and Crimean Wars. 443 & 445 Broadway, New York; 16 Little Britain, London: D. Appleton & Company, 1862.

Hammond, Bray. *Banks and Politics in America from the Revolution to the Civil War.* Princeton, New Jersey: Princeton University Press, 1957.

Hammond, Bray. "The North's Empty Purse, 1861–1862." *American Historical Review.* 67:1 (Oct. 1961), 1–18.

Hammond, Bray. *Sovereignty and an Empty Purse: Banks and Politics in the Civil War.* Princeton, New Jersey: Princeton University Press, 1970.

Harris, William A. *The Record of Fort Sumter from Its Occupation by Major Anderson to Its Reduction by Confederate Troops.* Pamphlet, Columbia, South Carolina, 1862.

Hassler, Warren W., Jr. *Crisis at the Crossroads: The First Day at Gettysburg.* University, Alabama: University of Alabama Press, 1970.

Hassler, Warren W., Jr. *General George B. McClellan: Shield of the Union.* Baton Rouge: Louisiana State University Press, 1957.

Hay, John Milton. *Lincoln and the Civil War in the Diaries of John Hay.* Selected and With an Introduction by Tyler Dennett. New York: Dodd, Mead & Company, 1939.

Hay, Thomas R. *Hood's Tennessee Campaign.* New York: W. Neale, 1929.

Hearn, Chester G. *Admiral David Dixon Porter: The Civil War Years.* Annapolis, Maryland: Naval Institute Press, 1994.

Heitman, Francis B. *Historical Register and Dictionary of the United States Army, From Its Organization, September 29, 1789, to March 2, 1903.* Published under act of Congress approved March 2, 1903. 57th Congress, 2nd Session, House Document 446 (serial 4536). 2 vols. Washington: Government Printing Office, 1903.

Henderson, George Francis Robert. *The Campaign of Fredericksburg, Nov.–Dec., 1862: A Tactical Study for Officers.* Third Edition. London, Chatham: Gage & Polden, 1891. Appears as pt. II, pp. 9–119 in next entry.

Henderson, George Francis Robert. *The Civil War: A Soldier's View: A Collection of Civil War Writings by Col. G. F. R. Henderson.* Jay Luvaas, ed. Chicago: University of Chicago Press, 1958.

Henderson, George Francis Robert. *Stonewall Jackson and the American Civil War.* With an Introduction by Garnet first Viscount Wolseley. New Impression. 2 vols. London, New York: Longmans, Green and Company, 1900.

Hennessy, John J. *Return to Bull Run: The Campaign and Battle of Second Manassas.* New York, London, Toronto, Sydney, Tokyo, Singapore: Simon & Schuster, A Paramount Communications Company, 1993.

Henry, John Milton. "The Revolution in Tennessee, February, 1861, to June, 1861." *Tennessee Historical Quarterly.* 18:2 (July 1959), 99–119.

Hesseltine, William B. *Civil War Prisons: A Study in War Psychology.* Columbus: Ohio State University Press, 1930.

Hesseltine, William B. *Lincoln and the War Governors.* New York: Alfred A. Knopf, 1948.

Hesseltine, William B. *Lincoln's Plan of Reconstruction.* Introduction by Richard N. Current. Chicago: Quadrangle Paperbacks, Quadrangle Books, 1967.

Hesseltine, William B., ed. *Civil War Prisons.* Kent, Ohio: Kent State University Press, 1972. Reprint of a special issue of *Civil War History: A Journal of the Middle Period.* 8:2 (June 1962), 117–232.

Hill, Louise B. *Joseph E. Brown and the Confederacy.* Chapel Hill: University of North Carolina Press, 1939.

Hoke, Jacob. *The Great Invasion of 1863; or, General Lee in Pennsylvania, Embracing an Account of the Strength and Organization of the Armies of the Potomac and Northern Virginia; Their Daily Marches with the Routes of Travel, and General Orders*

*Issued; The Three Days of Battle; The Retreat of the Confederates and Pursuit by the Federals; Analytical Index, Maps, Portraits, and a Large Number of Illustrations of the Battle-field, With an Appendix Containing an Account of the Burning of Chambersburg, Pennsylvania, A Statement of the General Sickles Controversy, and other Valuable Historic Papers.* Dayton, O.: W. J. Shuey, 1887; reprint, New York, London: Thomas Yoseloff, 1989.

Holzman, Robert S. *Stormy Ben Butler.* New York: The Macmillan Company, 1954.

Hyman, Harold M. *A More Perfect Union: The Impact of the Civil War and Reconstruction on the Constitution.* New York: Alfred A. Knopf, 1973.

Isely, Jeter A., and Philip A. Crowl. *The U.S. Marines and Amphibious War: Its Theory, and Its Practice in the Pacific.* Princeton, New Jersey: Princeton University Press, 1951.

Jackson, Mary Anna Morrison. *Memoirs of Stonewall Jackson by His Widow, Mary Anna Jackson,* with Introductions by John B. Gordon and Henry M. Fields, and Sketches by Fitzhugh Lee, Samuel G. French, and George F. R. Henderson. Second Edition. Louisville, Ky.: The Prentice Press, Courier-Journal Job Printing Company, 1895.

Jamieson, Perry D. *Crossing the Deadly Ground: United States Army Tactics, 1865–1899.* Tuscaloosa & London: University of Alabama Press, 1994.

Johnston, Angus James. *Virginia Railroads in the Civil War.* Chapel Hill: Published for the Virginia Historical Society by the University of North Carolina Press, 1961.

Jones, Archer. *Confederate Strategy from Shiloh to Vicksburg.* Baton Rouge: Louisiana State University Press, 1961.

Jones, James Pickett. *Yankee Blitzkrieg: Wilson's Raid through Alabama and Georgia.* Athens: University of Georgia Press, 1976.

Jones, John B. *A Rebel War Clerk's Diary at the Confederate Capital.* 2 vols. Philadelphia: J. B. Lippincott Company, 1866. Also published as *A Rebel War Clerk's Diary.* Condensed, edited, and annotated by Earl Schenck Miers. Complete in one volume. New York: Sagamore Press, Inc., Publishers, 1958.

Jones, John William. *Life and Letters of Robert E. Lee, Soldier and Man.* New York and Washington: The Neale Publishing Company, 1906.

Jones, John William. *Personal Reminiscences, Anecdotes and Letters of Gen. Robert E. Lee.* Published by Authority of the Lee Family and of the Faculty of Washington and Lee University. New York: D. Appleton and Company, 1874.

Jones, Joseph. "Confederate Losses During the Civil War—Correspondence Between Dr. Joseph Jones and General Samuel Cooper." *Southern Historical Society Papers.* 7:6 (June 1879), 287–290.

Jordan, Winthrop D. *White over Black: American Attitudes Toward the Negro, 1550–1812.* Published for the Institute of Early American History and Culture at Williamsburg, Virginia, Chapel Hill: University of North Carolina Press, 1968.

Kerby, Robert L. *Kirby Smith's Confederacy: The Trans-Mississippi South.* New York: Columbia University Press, 1972.

Kirkland, Edward Chase. *The Peacemakers of 1864.* New York: The Macmillan Company, 1927.

Kleber, John E., editor in chief; Thomas D. Clark, Lowell H. Harrison, James C. Klotter, assoc. eds. *The Kentucky Encyclopedia.* Lexington: University Press of Kentucky, 1992.

Klein, Philip Shriver. *President James Buchanan: A Biography.* University Park, Pennsylvania: Pennsylvania State University Press, 1962.

Klement, Frank L. *The Copperheads in the Middle West.* Chicago: University of Chicago Press, 1960.

Klement, Frank L. *Dark Lanterns: Secret Political Societies, Conspiracies, and Treason Trials in the Civil War.* Baton Rouge and London: Louisiana State University Press, 1984.

Klement, Frank L. *The Limits of Dissent: Clement L. Vallandigham & the Civil War.* Lexington: University Press of Kentucky, 1970.

Kreidberg, Marvin A., and Merton G. Henry. *History of Military Mobilization in the United States Army 1775–1945.* Department of the Army Pamphlet 20–212. Washington: Department of the Army, June 1955.

Krick, Robert K. *Conquering the Valley: Stonewall Jackson at Port Republic.* New York: William Morrow and Company, Inc., 1996.

Krick, Robert K. *Stonewall Jackson at Cedar Mountain.* Chapel Hill and London: University of North Carolina Press, 1990.

Lamers, William M. *The Edge of Glory: A Biography of General William S. Rosecrans, U.S.A.* New York: Harcourt, Brace, & World, Inc., 1961.

Lash, Jeffrey. *Destroyer of the Iron Horse: General Joseph E. Johnston and Confederate Rail Transport.* Kent, Ohio and London, England: Kent State University Press, 1991.

Leckie, William H., and Shirley A. Leckie. *Unlikely Warriors: General Benjamin H. Grierson and His Family.* Norman: University of Oklahoma Press, 1984.

Leech, Margaret. *Reveille in Washington.* New York and London: Harper & Brothers, Publishers, 1941.

Lewis, Emanuel Raymond. *Seacoast Fortifications of the United States: An Introductory History.* City of Washington: Smithsonian Institution Press, 1970.

Lewis, Lloyd. *Captain Sam Grant.* Boston: Little, Brown and Company, 1950.

Lewis, Lloyd. *Sherman: Fighting Prophet.* New York: Harcourt, Brace and Company, 1932.

Lewis, Virgil A., ed. *How West Virginia Was Made: Proceedings of the First Convention of the People of Northwestern Virginia at Wheeling, May 13, 14 and 15, 1861, and the Journal of the Second Convention of the People of Northwestern Virginia at Wheeling, Which Assembled June 11th 1861.* With Appendices and an Introduction, Annotations and Addenda. Charleston, West Virginia: News-Mail Company, Public Printer, 1909.

Liddell Hart, Basil Henry. *Sherman: Soldier, Realist, American.* New York: Frederick A. Praeger, Publisher, 1958.

Liddell Hart, Basil Henry. *Strategy.* Second Revised Edition. New York: Frederick A. Praeger, Publisher, 1967.

Lincoln, Abraham. *The Collected Works of Abraham Lincoln.* Roy P. Basler, ed. Marion Dolores Pratt and Lloyd A. Dunlop, assoc. eds. 9 vols. inc. index. The Abraham Lincoln Association, Springfield, Illinois. New Brunswick, New Jersey: Rutgers University Press, 1953; index, 1955. *Supplement 1832–1865.* Roy P. Basler, ed. Contributions in American Studies, Number 7. Westport, Connecticut; London, England: Greenwood Press, 1974.

Lincoln, Abraham. *Complete Works of Abraham Lincoln.* John G. Nicolay and John Milton Hay, eds. With a General Introduction by Richard Watson Gilder and Special Articles by Other Eminent Persons. New and Enlarged Edition. 12 vols. New York: Francis D. Tandy Co., 1905.

Livermore, Thomas L. *Numbers and Losses in the Civil War in America 1861–65.* Second Edition. Boston and New York: Houghton, Mifflin and Company, 1901. Reprint, Dayton, Ohio: Morningside, 1986.

Long, David E. *The Jewel of Liberty: Abraham Lincoln's Re-election and the End of Slavery.* Mechanicsburg, Pennsylvania: Stackpole Books, 1994.

Longacre, Edward G. *Army of Amateurs: General Benjamin F. Butler and the Army of the James.* Mechanicsburg, PA: Stackpole Books, 1997.

Longacre, Edward G. *The Cavalry at Gettysburg: A Tactical Study of Mounted Operations during the Civil War's Pivotal Campaign 9 June–14 July 1863.* Rutherford, New Jersey: Fairleigh Dickinson University Press, 1989.

Longacre, Edward G. *Combined Raids of the Civil War.* South Brunswick and New York: A. S. Barnes and Company; London: Thomas Yoseloff Ltd, 1975.

Longacre, Edward G. *From Union Stars to Top Hat: A biography of the extraordinary General James Harrison Wilson.* Harrisburg, Pennsylvania: Stackpole Books, 1972.

Longacre, Edward G. *General John Buford.* Conshohocken, Pennsylvania: Combined Books, 1995.

Longstreet, James. *From Manassas to Appomattox: Memoirs of the Civil War.* Philadelphia: J. B. Lippincott Company, 1896.

Lonn, Ella. *Desertion during the Civil War.* New York, London: The Century Company, 1928.

Lord, Francis A. *Lincoln's Railroad Man: Herman Haupt.* Rutherford, Madison, Teaneck, New Jersey: Fairleigh Dickinson University Press, 1969.

Luraghi, Raimondo. *A History of the Confederate Navy.* Tr. Paolo Coletta. Annapolis, Maryland: Naval Institute Press, 1996.

Lykes, Richard Wayne. *Campaign for Petersburg.* National Park Service History Series. Washington, D.C.: National Park Service, U.S. Department of the Interior, 1970.

Lyman, Theodore. *Meade's Headquarters, 1863–1865, Letters of Colonel Theodore Lyman from the Wilderness to Appomattox.* Selected and Edited by George R. Agassiz. Boston: The Atlantic Monthly Press, 1922.

McClellan, George B. *The Civil War Papers of George B. McClellan: Selected Correspondence, 1860–1865.* Stephen W. Sears, ed. New York: Ticknor & Fields, 1989.

McClellan, George B. *McClellan's Own Story: The War for the Union, The Soldiers Who Fought It, The Civilians Who Directed It and His Relations to It and to Them.* New York: Charles L. Webster & Company, 1887.

McDonough, James Lee. *Chattanooga — A Death Grip on the Confederacy.* Knoxville: University of Tennessee Press, 1984.

McDonough, James Lee. *Shiloh — in Hell before Night.* Knoxville: University of Tennessee Press, 1977.

McDonough, James Lee. *Stones River — Bloody Winter in Tennessee.* Knoxville: University of Tennessee Press, 1980.

McKitrick, Eric L. *Andrew Johnson and Reconstruction.* Chicago: University of Chicago Press, 1960.

McMurry, Richard M. *Two Great Rebel Armies: An Essay in Confederate Military History.* Chapel Hill & London: University of North Carolina Press, 1989.

McPherson, Edward. *The Political History of the United States of America, During the Great Rebellion, from November 6, 1860, to July 4, 1864; Including a Classified Summary of the Legislation of the Thirty-sixth Congress, the Three Sessions of the Thirty-seventh Congress, the First Session of the Thirty-eighth Congress, with the Votes Therein, and the Important Executive, Judicial and Politico-Military Facts of that Eventful Period; Together with the Organization, Legislation, and General Proceedings of the Rebel Administration.* Washington, D.C.: Philip & Solomons, 1864.

McPherson, James M. *For Cause and Comrades: Why Men Fought in the Civil War.* New York, Oxford: Oxford University Press, 1997.

McPherson, James M. *The Struggle for Equality: Abolitionists and the Negro in the Civil War and Reconstruction.* Princeton, New Jersey: Princeton University Press, 1964.

McPherson, James M. *What They Fought For 1861–1865.* Baton Rouge: Louisiana State University Press, 1994.

McWhiney, Grady, and Perry D. Jamieson. *Attack and Die: Civil War Tactics and the Southern Heritage.* University, Alabama: University of Alabama Press, 1962.

Mahan, Dennis Hart. *An Elementary Treatise on Advanced Guard, Out-Post, and Detachment Service of Troops, and the Manner of Posting and Handling Them.* Revised Edition. New York: John Wiley, 1864.

Marshall, Charles. *An Aide-de-Camp of Lee, Being the Papers of Colonel Charles Marshall, Sometime Aide-de-Camp, Military Secretary, and Assistant Adjutant-General on the Staff of Robert E. Lee.* Sir Frederick Maurice, ed. Boston: Little, Brown, and Company, 1927.

Marszalek, John F. *Sherman: A Soldier's Passion for Order.* New York: The Free Press, A Division of Macmillan, Inc.; Toronto: Maxwell Macmillan Canada; New York, Oxford, Singapore, Sydney: Maxwell Macmillan International, 1993.

Martin, David G. *Gettysburg July 1.* Completely Revised Edition. Conshohocken, Pennsylvania: Combined Books, 1996.

Marvel, William. *Andersonville: The Last Depot.* Chapel Hill and London: University of North Carolina Press, 1994.

Marvel, William. *Burnside.* Chapel Hill & London: University of North Carolina Press, 1991.

Massachusetts, Adjutant-General. *Massachusetts Adjutant-General's Report for 1857.* Boston: Commonwealth of Massachusetts, 1858.

Matter, William D. *If It Takes All Summer: The Battle of Spotsylvania.* Chapel Hill & London: University of North Carolina Press, 1988.

Maxwell, William Quentin. *Lincoln's Fifth Wheel: The Political History of the United States Sanitary Commission.* New York, London, Toronto: Longmans, Green & Co., 1956.

Meigs, Montgomery Cunningham. Papers. Library of Congress.

Meigs, Montgomery Cunningham. "The Relations of President Lincoln and Secretary Stanton to the Military Commanders of the Civil War." *American Historical Review.* 26:2 (Jan. 1921), 285–303.

Meredith, Roy. *Storm over Sumter: The Opening Engagement of the Civil War.* New York: Simon and Schuster, 1957.

Merli, Frank J. "Crown versus Cruiser: The Curious Case of the *Alexandra.*" *Civil War History: A Journal of the Middle Period.* 9:2 (June 1963), 167–77.

Merli, Frank J. *Great Britain and the Confederate Navy 1861–1865.* Bloomington, London: Indiana University Press, 1970.

Merrill, James M. *Battle Flags South: The Story of the Civil War Navies on Western Waters.* Rutherford, Madison, Teaneck: Fairleigh Dickinson University Press, 1970.

Merrill, James M. *William Tecumseh Sherman.* Chicago, New York, San Francisco: Rand McNally & Company, 1971.

Miers, Earl Schenck. *The Web of Victory: Grant at Vicksburg.* New York: Alfred A. Knopf, 1955.

Miller, Francis Trevelyan, ed. Robert S. Lanier, managing ed. *The Photographic History of the Civil War.* 10 vols. New York: The Review of Reviews Co., 1911–1912.

Miller, William J. *Mapping for Stonewall: The Civil War Service of Jed Hotchkiss.* Washington, D.C.: Elliott & Clark Publishing, 1993.

Mink, Charles R. "General Orders, No. 11: The Forced Evacuation of Civilians during the Civil War." *Military Affairs, the journal of military history, including theory and technology.* 27:4 (Dec. 1980), 132–36.

Mitchell, Reid. *Civil War Soldiers.* New York: Viking, 1988.

Mitchell, Reid. *The Vacant Chair: The Northern Soldier Leaves Home*. New York, Oxford: Oxford University Press, 1993.

Mitchell, Stewart. *Horatio Seymour of New York*. Cambridge, Massachusetts: Harvard University Press, 1938.

Morris, Roy, Jr. *Sheridan: The Life and Wars of General Phil Sheridan*. New York: Crown Publishers, Inc., 1992.

Morrison, James L., Jr. *"The Best School in the World": West Point, the Pre–Civil War Years, 1833–1866*. Kent, Ohio: Kent State University Press, 1986.

Murdock, Eugene C. *One Million Men: The Civil War Draft in the North*. Madison: State Historical Society of Wisconsin, 1971.

Murfin, James V. *The Gleam of Bayonets: The Battle of Antietam and the Maryland Campaign of 1862*. South Brunswick, New Jersey: A. S. Barnes & Co., Inc., 1965.

Myers, Robert Manson, ed. *The Children of Pride: A True Story of Georgia in the Civil War*. New Haven and London: Yale University Press, 1972.

Nalty, Bernard C. *Strength for the Fight: A History of Black Americans in the Military*. New York: The Free Press, A Division of Macmillan, Inc.; London: Collier Macmillan Publishers, 1986.

*The National Almanac and Annual Record for the Year 1863*. Philadelphia: George W. Childs, 1863.

Neely, Mark E., Jr. *The Fate of Liberty: Abraham Lincoln and Civil Liberties*. New York, Oxford: Oxford University Press, 1991.

Nesbitt, Mark. *Saber and Scapegoat: J. E. B. Stuart and the Gettysburg Controversy*. Mechanicsburg, Pennsylvania: Stackpole Books, 1994.

Nevins, Allan. *Frémont: Pathmarker of the West*. New York, London, Toronto: Longmans, Green and Co., 1955.

*New York Tribune Almanac 1864*. New York: New York Tribune, 1864.

Nichols, Roy Franklin. *The Disruption of American Democracy*. New York: The Macmillan Company, 1948.

Nicolay, John G. *The Outbreak of Rebellion*. New York: C. Scribner's Sons, 1881.

Nicolay, John G., and John Milton Hay. *Abraham Lincoln: A History*. 10 vols. New York: The Century Co., 1890.

Niven, John. *Gideon Welles: Lincoln's Secretary of the Navy*. New York: Oxford University Press, 1973.

Nolan, Alan T. *Lee Considered: General Robert E. Lee & Civil War History*. Chapel Hill & London: University of North Carolina Press, 1991.

Norton, Oliver Willcox. *The Attack and Defense of Little Round Top, Gettysburg, July 2, 1863*. New York: The Neale Publishing Company, 1913. Reprint, Gettysburg, Pennsylvania: Stan Clark Military Books, 1992.

Nye, Wilbur Sturtevant. *Here Come the Rebels!* Baton Rouge: Louisiana State University Press, 1965.

Oberholtzer, Ellis Paxson. *Jay Cooke: Financier of the Civil War*. 2 vols. Philadelphia: G. W. Jacobs & Co., 1907.

O'Connor, Richard. *Sheridan the Inevitable*. Indianapolis, New York: The Bobbs-Merrill Company, 1953.

Owsley, Frank Lawrence. *King Cotton Diplomacy: Foreign Relations of the Confederate States of America*. Second Edition, revised by Harriet Chappell Owsley. Chicago: The University of Chicago Press, 1959.

Owsley, Frank Lawrence, Jr. *The C.S.S. Florida: Her Building and Operations*. Philadelphia: University of Pennsylvania Press, 1965.

Paludan, Phillip Shaw. *The Presidency of Abraham Lincoln*. Lawrence: University Press of Kansas, 1994.

Paris, Louis Philippe Albert d'Orléans; comte de. *History of the Civil War in America.* 4 vols. Philadelphia: Porter & Coates, 1875–1888.

Parks, Joseph H. *Joseph E. Brown of Georgia.* Baton Rouge: Louisiana State University Press, 1977.

Patrick, Rembert W. *Jefferson Davis and His Cabinet.* Baton Rouge: Louisiana State University Press, 1959.

Pearson, Henry Greenleaf. *The Life of John A. Andrew, Governor of Massachusetts, 1861–1865.* 2 vols. Boston and New York: Houghton, Mifflin and Company, 1904.

Perry, Milton F. *Infernal Machines: The Story of Confederate Submarine and Mine Warfare.* Baton Rouge: Louisiana State University Press, 1965.

Pfanz, Harry W. *Gettysburg — Culp's Hill and Cemetery Hill.* Gary W. Gallagher, ed. *Civil War America.* Chapel Hill & London: University of North Carolina Press, 1993.

Pfanz, Harry W. *Gettysburg: The Second Day.* Chapel Hill and London: University of North Carolina Press, 1987.

Phillips, Ulrich Bonnell. *The Life of Robert Toombs.* New York: The Macmillan Company, 1913.

Phisterer, Frederick. *Statistical Record of the Armies of the United States.* New York: C. Scribner's Sons, 1883.

[Pierce, Edward L.] "The Contrabands at Fortress Monroe." *The Atlantic Monthly, A Magazine of Literature, Science, Art, and Politics.* 8:11 (Nov. 1861), 626–40.

Piston, William Garrett. *Lee's Tarnished Lieutenant: James Longstreet and His Place in Southern History.* Athens and London: University of Georgia Press, 1987.

Porter, David D. *The Naval History of the Civil War.* New York: The Sherman Publishing Company, 1886.

Porter, Horace. *Campaigning with Grant.* New York: The Century Co., 1897.

Potter, David M. *The Impending Crisis 1848–1861.* Completed and Edited by Don E. Fehrenbacher. New York, Evanston, San Francisco, London: Harper & Row, Publishers, 1976.

Potter, David M. *Lincoln and His Party in the Secession Crisis.* New Haven: Yale University Press; London: Humphrey Milford, Oxford University Press, 1942.

Pratt, Fletcher. *The Navy: A History.* Garden City, New York: Garden City Publishing Co., Inc., 1941.

Priest, John Michael. *Antietam: The Soldiers' Battle.* Shippensburg, Pennsylvania: White Mane Publishing Company, 1989.

Priest, John Michael. *Before Antietam: The Battle for South Mountain.* Foreword by Edwin C. Bearss. Shippensburg, Pennsylvania: White Mane Publishing Company, 1992.

Rabin, James Z. "Alexander H. Stephens and Jefferson Davis." *American Historical Review.* 58:2 (April 1953), 290–321.

Rable, George C. *The Confederate Republic: A Revolution against Politics.* Chapel Hill and London: University of North Carolina Press, 1994.

Randall, James G. *Lincoln the President.* 4 vols. IV, *Last Full Measure,* coauthored with Richard N. Current. New York: Dodd, Mead & Company, 1946–1955.

Randall, Ruth Painter. *Colonel Elmer Ellsworth: A Biography of Lincoln's Friend and First Hero of the Civil War.* Boston: Little, Brown and Company, 1960.

Reed, Rowena. *Combined Operations in the Civil War.* Annapolis, Maryland: Naval Institute Press, 1976.

Rhea, Gordon C. *The Battle of the Wilderness May 5–6, 1864.* Baton Rouge and London: Louisiana State University Press, 1994.

Rhea, Gordon C. *The Battles for Spotsylvania Court House and the Road to Yellow Tavern.* Baton Rouge and London: Louisiana State University Press, 1997.

Robertson, James I., Jr. *General A. P. Hill: The Story of a Confederate Warrior*. New York: Random House, 1987.

Robertson, James I., Jr. *Stonewall Jackson: The Man, the Soldier, the Legend*. New York: Macmillan USA, Simon & Schuster; London, Mexico City, New Delhi, Singapore, Sydney, Toronto: Prentice Hall International, 1997.

Robinson, Charles M., III. *Shark of the Confederacy: The Story of the CSS* Alabama. Annapolis, Maryland: Naval Institute Press, 1996.

Robinson, William Morrison. *The Confederate Privateers*. New Haven: Yale University Press; London: Humphrey Milford, Oxford University Press, 1928.

Roland, Charles P. *Albert Sidney Johnston: Soldier of Three Republics*. Austin: The University of Texas Press, 1964.

Roland, Charles P. *The Confederacy*. Daniel J. Boorstin, ed. *The Chicago History of American Civilization*. Chicago and London: University of Chicago Press, 1960.

Rose, Willie Lee. *Rehearsal for Reconstruction: The Port Royal Experiment*. With an Introduction by Comer Vann Woodward. Indianapolis and New York: A Brown Thrasher Book, The Bobbs-Merrill Company, Inc., Publishers, 1964.

Roseboom, Eugene H. A *History of Presidential Elections*. New York: The Macmillan Company, 1957.

Rosinski, Herbert. *The German Army*. Second Edition. Washington: The Infantry Journal, 1944.

Rostow, Walt W. *The Process of Economic Growth*. Second Edition. New York and Oxford: Oxford University Press, 1960.

Rothenberg, Gunther E. *The Art of Warfare in the Age of Napoleon*. Bloomington and London: Indiana University Press, 1978.

Royster, Charles. *The Destructive War: William Tecumseh Sherman, Stonewall Jackson, and the Americans*. New York: Alfred A. Knopf, 1991.

Rutland, Robert. "The Copperheads of Iowa: A Re-examination." *Iowa Journal of History*. 52:1 (Jan. 1954), 1–54.

Scheiber, Harry N. "Economic Change in the Civil War Era: An Analysis of Recent Studies." *Civil War History: A Journal of the Middle Period*. 11:4 (Dec. 1965), 336–411.

Schofield, John McAllister. Papers. Library of Congress.

Schroeder-Lein, Glenna R. *Confederate Hospitals on the Move: Samuel H. Stout and the Army of Tennessee*. Columbia: University of South Carolina Press, 1994.

Scott, Robert Garth. *Into the Wilderness with the Army of the Potomac*. Bloomington: Indiana University Press, 1985.

Scruggs, Jack. "Arkansas in the Secession Crisis." *Arkansas Historical Quarterly*. 12:2 (July 1953), 179–192.

Sears, Stephen W. *Chancellorsville*. Boston, New York: Houghton Mifflin Company, 1996.

Sears, Stephen W. *George B. McClellan: The Young Napoleon*. New York: Ticknor & Fields, 1989.

Sears, Stephen W. *Landscape Turned Red: The Battle of Antietam*. New York: Ticknor & Fields, 1983.

Sears, Stephen W. *To the Gates of Richmond: The Peninsula Campaign*. New York: Ticknor & Fields, 1992.

Seward, Frederick W. *Reminiscences of a War-Time Statesman and Diplomat, 1830–1915, by Frederick W. Seward, Assistant Secretary of State during the Administrations of Lincoln, Johnson, and Hayes*. New York and London: G. P. Putnam's Sons, 1915.

Shanks, Henry. *The Secession Movement in Virginia, 1847–1861*. Richmond, Virginia: Garrett and Massie, 1934.

Shannon, Fred Albert. *The Organization and Administration of the Union Army.* 2 vols. Cleveland: The Arthur H. Clark Company, 1928.

Sharkey, Robert P. *Money, Class, and Party: An Economic Study of Civil War and Reconstruction.* Baltimore: Johns Hopkins Press, 1959.

Shea, William L., and Earl J. Hess. *Pea Ridge: Civil War Campaign in the West.* Chapel Hill & London: University of North Carolina Press, 1992.

Sheridan, Philip H. *Personal Memoirs of P. H. Sheridan, General United States Army.* 2 vols. New York: Charles L. Webster & Company, 1888.

Sherman, William T. *Memoirs of General William T. Sherman by Himself.* 2 vols. New York: D. Appleton & Company, 1875.

Silbey, Joel N. *A Respectable Minority: The Democratic Party in the Civil War Era, 1860–1868.* New York: W. W. Norton & Co., 1977.

Sitterson, Joseph Carlyle. *The Secession Movement in North Carolina.* Chapel Hill: University of North Carolina Press, 1939.

Slotkin, Richard. *The Fatal Environment: The Myth of the Frontier in the Age of Industrialization, 1800–1900.* Middletown, Connecticut: Wesleyan University Press, 1985.

Slotkin, Richard. *Gunfighter Nation: The Myth of the Frontier in Twentieth-Century America.* New York: Atheneum; Toronto: Maxwell Macmillan Canada; New York, Oxford, Singapore, Sydney: Maxwell Macmillan International, 1992.

Slotkin, Richard. *Regeneration Through Violence: The Mythology of the American Frontier, 1600–1800.* Middletown, Connecticut: Wesleyan University Press, 1973.

Sommers, Richard J. *Richmond Redeemed: The Siege at Petersburg.* Foreword by Frank E. Vandiver. Garden City, New York: Doubleday & Company, Inc., 1981.

Stackpole, Edward J. *Chancellorsville: Lee's Greatest Battle.* Harrisburg, Pennsylvania: The Stackpole Company, 1958.

Stackpole, Edward J. *Drama on the Rappahannock: The Fredericksburg Campaign.* Harrisburg, Pennsylvania: Military Service Publishing Company, 1957.

Stampp, Kenneth M. *And the War Came: The North and the Secession Crisis, 1860–61.* Chicago and London: Phoenix Books, The University of Chicago Press, 1964.

Steiner, Paul E. *Disease in the Civil War: Natural Biological Warfare in 1861–1865.* Philadelphia: Whitman Publishing Company, 1968.

Stewart, George R. *Pickett's Charge: A Microhistory of the Final Attack at Gettysburg, July 3, 1863.* Boston: Houghton Mifflin Company, 1959.

Still, William N., Jr. *Iron Afloat: The Story of the Confederate Armorclads.* Nashville: Vanderbilt University Press, 1971.

Strode, Hudson. *Jefferson Davis.* 2 vols. New York: Harcourt, Brace and Company, 1955–1964.

Svenson, Peter. *Battlefield: Farming a Civil War Battleground.* Boston, London: Faber and Faber, 1992.

Swanberg, William A. *First Blood: The Story of Fort Sumter.* New York: Charles Scribner's Sons, 1957.

Swisher, Carl Brent. *American Constitutional Development.* Second Edition. Boston, New York, Chicago, Dallas, Atlanta, San Francisco: Houghton Mifflin Company, The Riverside Press Cambridge, 1954.

Swisher, Carl Brent. *Roger B. Taney.* New York: The Macmillan Company, 1935.

Sword, Wiley. *Embrace an Angry Wind: The Confederacy's Last Hurrah: Spring Hill, Franklin, and Nashville.* New York: HarperCollins, 1991.

Sword, Wiley. *Shiloh: Bloody April.* Dayton, Ohio: Press of Morningside Bookshop, 1988.

Symonds, Craig L. *Joseph E. Johnston: A Civil War Biography.* New York, London: W. W. Norton & Company, 1992.

Tanner, Robert G. *Stonewall in the Valley: Thomas "Stonewall" Jackson's Shenandoah Valley Campaign Spring 1862*. Updated and revised. Mechanicsburg, PA: Stackpole Books, 1996.

Thomas, Benjamin P., and Harold Hyman. *Stanton: The Life and Times of Lincoln's Secretary of War*. New York: Alfred A. Knopf, 1962.

Thomas, Emory M. *Bold Dragoon: The Life of J. E. B. Stuart*. New York, Cambridge, Philadelphia, San Francisco, Singapore, Sydney: Harper & Row, Publishers, 1986.

Thomas, Emory M. *The Confederacy as a Revolutionary Experience*. Englewood Cliffs, New Jersey: Prentice-Hall, Inc., 1971.

Thomas, Emory M. *The Confederate Nation 1861–1865*. New York, Hagerstown, San Francisco, London: Harper & Row, Publishers, 1979.

Thomas, Emory M. *The Confederate State of Richmond: A Biography of the Capital*. Austin: University of Texas Press, 1971.

Thomas, Emory M. *Robert E. Lee: A Biography*. New York, London: W. W. Norton & Company, 1995.

Todd, Robert Cecil. *Confederate Finance*. Athens: The University of Georgia Press, 1954.

Trefousse, Hans L. *Ben Butler: The South Called Him BEAST!* New York: Twayne Publishers, 1957.

Trefousse, Hans L. *The Radical Republicans: Lincoln's Vanguard for Racial Justice*. New York: Alfred A. Knopf, 1969.

Trudeau, Noah Andre. *Bloody Roads South: The Wilderness to Cold Harbor May–June 1864*. Boston, Toronto, London: Little, Brown and Company, 1989.

Trudeau, Noah Andre. *The Last Citadel: Petersburg, Virginia June 1864–April 1865*. Baton Rouge: Louisiana State University Press, 1991.

Trudeau, Noah Andre. *Out of the Storm: The End of the Civil War, April–June 1865*. Boston, New York, Toronto, London: Little, Brown and Company, 1994.

Tucker, Glenn. *High Tide at Gettysburg: The Campaign in Pennsylvania*. Indianapolis, New York: The Bobbs-Merrill Company, Inc., Publishers, 1958.

Tucker, Glenn. *Zeb Vance: Champion of Personal Freedom*. Indianapolis: The Bobbs-Merrill Company, Inc., 1966.

Turner, George Edgar. *Victory Rode the Rails: The Strategic Place of the Railroads in the Civil War*. Indianapolis, New York: The Bobbs-Merrill Company, Inc., Publishers, 1953.

U.S. Bureau of the Census. *Historical Statistics of the United States: Colonial Times to 1970*. U.S. Bureau of the Census, Vincent P. Barabba, Director. U.S. Department of Commerce, Rogers C. B. Morton, Secretary. James L. Pate, Assistant Secretary for Economic Affairs. Bicentennial Edition. 2 parts [vols.]. Washington, D.C.: U.S. Government Printing Office, 1975.

U.S. Bureau of the Census with the Cooperation of the Social Science Research Council. *Historical Statistics of the United States, Colonial Times to 1957, A Statistical Abstract Supplement*. U.S. Department of Commerce, Frederick H. Mueller, Secretary. Bureau of the Census, Robert W. Burgess, Director. Washington, D.C.: U.S. Government Printing Office, 1960.

U.S. Congress. [*Annals of the Congress of the United States.*] *The Debates and Proceedings in the Congress of the United States; with an Appendix Containing Important State Papers and Public Documents, and All the Laws of a Public Nature; with a Copious Index*. 42 vols. Washington: Printed and Published by Gales and Seaton, 1834–1856.

U.S. Congress. *The Congressional Globe*. [23rd Congress to 42nd Congress, Dec. 2, 1833 to March 3, 1873.] 109 vols. Washington: Printed at the *Globe* Office for the Editors, 1834–1873.

U.S. Congress. Thirty-seventh Congress, Third Session, House of Representatives. Rep[ort] of Com[mittee]. *Report of the Joint Committee on the Conduct of the War.* 3 vols. Washington: Government Printing Office, 1863.

U.S. Constitution. 103rd Congress, 1st Session, Senate Document No. 103–6 (serial 14152). *The Constitution of the United States of America: Analysis and Interpretation: Annotations of Cases Decided in the Supreme Court of the United States to June 29, 1992.* Prepared by the Congressional Research Service, Library of Congress. Johnny H. Killian, George A. Costello, co-editors. Washington: U.S. Government Printing Office, 1996.

U.S. Laws, statutes. *The Statutes at Large of the United States of America.* 17 vols. I–IX, Boston: Charles C. Little and J. Brown, 1845–1854; X–XVII, Boston: Little, Brown, and Company, 1855–1873.

U.S. Naval War Records Office. *Official Records of the Union and Confederate Navies in the War of the Rebellion.* Two series, 30 vols. Washington: Government Printing Office, 1894–1922.

U.S. President. *A Compilation of the Messages and Papers of the Presidents, 1789–1908* (With Revisions.) James D. Richardson, ed. 11 vols. Washington: Bureau of National Literature and Art, 1911.

U.S. Supreme Court. Jeremiah S. Black [ed.] *Reports of Cases Argued and Determined in the Supreme Court of the United States.* 2 vols. Washington, D.C.: W. H. & O. H. Morrison, Law Publishers and Booksellers, 1861–1862.

U.S. Supreme Court. Benjamin C. Howard, ed. *Reports of Cases Argued and Adjudged in the Supreme Court of the United States.* 24 vols. I–III, Philadelphia: T. & J. W. Johnson, Law Booksellers, 1843–1845; IV–XII, Boston: Charles C. Little and James Brown, Law Publishers and Booksellers, 1846–1851; XIII–XVIII, Boston: Little, Brown and Company, Law Publishers and Booksellers, 1852–1856; XIX–XXIV, Washington, D.C.: William H. Morrison, Law Publishers and Booksellers, 1857–1861.

U.S. Supreme Court. John William Wallace, reporter. *Cases Argued and Adjudged in the Supreme Court of the United States.* 23 vols. Washington, D.C.: W. H. and D. H. Morrison, Law Publishers and Booksellers, 1867–1875.

U.S. Treasury, Department of the. *Report of the Secretary of the Treasury on the State of the Finances for the Year 1865.* Thirty-ninth Congress, First Session, House Executive Document No. 3 (serial 1254). Washington: Government Printing Office, 1865.

U.S. War Department. *Messages and Documents, War Department, 1865–1866.* 3 vols. Washington: Government Printing Office, 1866.

U.S. War Department. *The War of the Rebellion: A Compilation of the Official Records of the Union and Confederate Armies.* Four series, 70 vols. in 128 vols. Washington: Government Printing Office, 1880–1901.

After the publication of Series One, XXI, the editors initiated a continuous sequence of Arabic-numeral serial numbers running throughout all four series. The present work uses the serial numbers along with volume and part numbers, supplying the missing serial numbers for those volumes that preceded adoption of such numbers.

Vandiver, Frank E. *Jubal's Raid: General Early's Famous Attack on Washington.* New York: McGraw-Hill Book Company, 1960.

Vandiver, Frank E. *Ploughshares into Swords: Josiah Gorgas and Confederate Ordnance.* Austin: University of Texas Press, 1952.

Vandiver, Frank E. *Their Tattered Flags: The Epic of the Confederacy.* New York and Evanston: A Harper's Magazine Press Book, Published in Association with Harper & Row, 1970.

Vartanian, Pershing. "The Cochran Thesis: A Critique in Statistical Analysis." *Journal of American History.* 51:1 (June 1964), 77–89.

Voegeli, Victor Jacques. *Free But Not Equal: The Midwest and the Negro during the Civil War.* Chicago & London: University of Chicago Press, 1967.

Von Abele, Rudolph R. *Alexander H. Stephens: A Biography.* New York: Alfred A. Knopf, 1946.

Wainwright, Nicholas B. "The Loyal Opposition in Civil War Philadelphia." *Pennsylvania Magazine of History and Biography.* 88:3 (July 1964), 294–315.

Walker, Alyce Billings, ed. *Alabama: A Guide to the Deep South.* New Revised Edition, Originally Compiled by the Federal Writers Project of the Works Progress Administration in the State of Alabama, later called the Writers Program. *American Guide Series.* Harry Hanson, gen. ed. New York: Hastings House, Publishers, 1975.

Warren, Charles. *The Supreme Court in United States History.* 2 vols. Boston, Toronto: Little, Brown and Company, 1926.

Weber, Thomas. *The Northern Railroads in the Civil War, 1861–1865.* New York: King's Crown Press, 1952.

Weinberg, Gerhard L. *A World at Arms: A Global History of World War II.* Cambridge; New York; Oakleigh, Victoria, Australia: Cambridge University Press, 1994.

Welles, Gideon. *Diary of Gideon Welles, Secretary of the Navy under Lincoln and Johnson.* Howard K. Beale, ed. Assisted by Alan W. Brownsword. With an Introduction by Howard K. Beale and appendices drawn from Welles's correspondence 3 vols. New York: W. W. Norton & Company, Inc., 1960.

Wert, Jeffry D. *General James Longstreet: The Confederacy's Most Controversial Soldier — A Biography.* New York, London, Toronto, Sydney, Tokyo, Singapore: Simon & Schuster, 1993.

West Virginia. Constitutional Convention. 1861–1863. *Debates and Proceedings of the First Constitutional Convention of West Virginia, 1861–1863.* Charles H. Ambler, Francis H. Atwood, and William B. Mathews, eds. 1 vol. in 3. Huntington, West Virginia: Gentry Brothers, Printers, 1939.

Whiteman, Maxwell. *Gentlemen in Crisis, 1862–1962: The First Century of the Union League of Philadelphia.* Philadelphia: The League, 1975.

Wiebe, Robert H. *The Search for Order, 1877–1820.* David Donald, gen. ed. *The Making of America.* New York: Hill and Wang, 1967.

Wiley, Bell Irvin. *The Life of Billy Yank: The Common Soldier of the Union.* Indianapolis, New York: The Bobbs-Merrill Company Publishers, 1952.

Wiley, Bell Irvin. *The Life of Johnny Reb: The Common Soldier of the Confederacy.* Indianapolis, New York: The Bobbs-Merrill Company Publishers, 1943.

Wilkes, Charles. *Autobiography of Rear Admiral Charles Wilkes, U.S. Navy, 1798–1877.* William James Morgan, David B. Tyler, Joye L. Lockhart, Mary F. Loughlin, eds. With an Introduction by John D. H. Kane, Jr. Washington: Naval History Division Department of the Navy, 1978.

Williams, Kenneth P. *Lincoln Finds a General: A Military Study of the Civil War.* 5 vols. New York: The Macmillan Company, 1950–1959.

Williams, Thomas Harry. "Investigation: 1862." *American Heritage.* 6:6 (Dec. 1954), 16–21.

Williams, Thomas Harry. *Lincoln and the Radicals.* Madison: University of Wisconsin Press, 1941.

Williams, Thomas Harry. *P. G. T. Beauregard: Napoleon in Gray.* Baton Rouge: Louisiana State University Press, 1956.

Williamson, Jeffrey. "Watersheds and Turning Points: Conjectures on the Long-Term Impact of Civil War Financing." *Journal of Economic History.* 34:4 (Sept. 1974), 636–61.

Wills, Brian Steel. *A Battle from the Start: The Life of Nathan Bedford Forrest.* New York: HarperCollins, 1992.

Wills, Garry. *Inventing America: Jefferson's Declaration of Independence*. Garden City, New York: Doubleday & Company, Inc., 1978.

Wills, Garry. *Lincoln at Gettysburg: The Words That Remade America*. New York, London, Toronto, Sydney, Tokyo, Singapore: Simon & Schuster, 1992.

Woodworth, Steven E. *Davis and Lee at War*. Lawrence: University Press of Kansas, 1995.

Wooster, Ralph A. *The Secession Conventions of the South*. Princeton, New Jersey: Princeton University Press, 1962.

Wright, Edward Needles. *Conscientious Objectors in the Civil War*. Philadelphia: University of Pennsylvania Press; London: Humphrey Milford, Oxford University Press, 1931.

Wright, Marcus J., comp. and preparer. *General Officers of the Confederate Army, Officers of the Executive Departments of the Confederate States, Members of the Confederate Congress by States*. New York: The Neale Publishing Company, 1911.

Writers' Program, Pennsylvania. *Pennsylvania: A Guide to the Keystone State*. Compiled by workers of the Writers' Program of the Works Projects Administration in the State of Pennsylvania. *American Guide Series*. Co-sponsored by the Pennsylvania Historical Commission and the University of Pennsylvania. New York: Oxford University Press, 1940.

Wyeth, John Allan. *Life of General Nathan Bedford Forrest*. New York and London: Harper & Brothers, 1899. Republished as *That Devil Forrest: Life of General Nathan Bedford Forrest*. Foreword by Henry Steele Commager. New York: Harper & Brothers, Publishers, 1959.

Yates, Richard E. *The Confederacy and Zeb Vance*. Tuscaloosa: University of Alabama Press, 1958.

Yearns, Wilfred Buck. *The Confederate Congress*. Athens: University of Georgia Press, 1960.

# Index

Page references in *italics* indicate maps

**Russell F. Weigley** is Distinguished University Professor of History Emeritus at Temple University. He is the author of numerous books, including *The American Way of War: A History of United States Military Strategy and Policy*; *Eisenhower's Lieutenants: The Campaign of France and Germany, 1944–45*; and *The Age of Battles: The Quest for Decisive Warfare from Breitenfeld to Waterloo*, all available from Indiana University Press.